W9-BDB-709

EIFFEL: THE LANGUAGE

PRENTICE HALL
OBJECT-ORIENTED
SERIES

D. MANDRIOLI AND B. MEYER (EDS)
Advances in Object-Oriented Software Engineering

EIFFEL
THE LANGUAGE

Bertrand Meyer

INTERACTIVE SOFTWARE ENGINEERING, SANTA BARBARA
AND SOCIÉTÉ DES OUTILS DU LOGICIEL, PARIS

PRENTICE HALL

New York · London · Toronto · Sydney · Tokyo · Singapore

First published 1992 by
Prentice Hall Europe
Campus 400, Maylands Avenue,
Hemel Hempstead, Herts HP2 7EZ
A division of Simon and Schuster
International Group

© Bertrand Meyer, 1992

All rights reserved.
No part of this publication may be reproduced, stored
in a retrieval system, or transmitted, in any form, or
by any means, electronic, mechanical, photocopying,
recording or otherwise, without prior permission, in
writing, from the publisher.

Reprinted with corrections, 1992

LIBRARY OF CONGRESS CATALOGING-IN-PUBLICATION DATA

A CIP catalogue record for this book is available from
the Library of Congress

BRITISH LIBRARY CATALOGUING IN PUBLICATION DATA

Meyer, Bertrand
  Eiffel: the language.
  I. Title
  005.362

  ISBN 0–13–247925–7

5 6 7 8 9   02 01 00 99 98

Must it be assumed that because we are engineers beauty is not our concern, and that while we make our constructions robust and durable we do not also strive to make them elegant?

Is it not true that the genuine conditions of strength always comply with the secret conditions of harmony?

The first principle of architectural esthetics is that the essential lines of a monument must be determined by a perfect adaptation to its purpose.

Gustave Eiffel
1887

From his response in the newspaper Le Temps *to a petition by members of the literary and artistic Establishment protesting his project of elevating a tower of iron in Paris.*

Abridged table

The full table of contents starts on page xxiii.

Preface

Meeting the challenge of software quality

Eiffel embodies a "certain idea" of software construction: the belief that it is possible to treat this task as a serious engineering enterprise, whose goal is to yield quality software through the careful production and continuous enhancement of parameterizable, scientifically specified reusable components, communicating on the basis of clearly defined contracts and organized in systematic multi-criteria classifications.

Such aims lead to a *new culture* of software development, focusing on the reuse of industrial-grade components, on the development of complete systems rather than just programs, and on the long-term investment in tools and libraries, capturing the software know-how of an organization. Even more importantly, they mean accepting the challenge of quality in software.

Eiffel is nothing else than these principles taken to their full consequences. In particular, the engineering of quality software components requires an appropriate notation; this book describes such a notation – Eiffel as a language for analysis, design and implementation.

A language, of course, is not enough. To achieve quality and move to the new culture, we must understand the methodological background; we must have access to a large body of good pre-built reusable components; and we need the appropriate development tools. For several years, the work on Eiffel has been proceeding in all of these directions, resulting in a method, a language, a set of libraries, and a CASE (Computer-Aided Software Engineering) environment.

What you will find below is a description of the language part of Eiffel. Other books cover the complementary aspects: *Object-Oriented Software Construction* presents the method in detail; *Eiffel: The Libraries* and *Eiffel: The Environment* describe the required library and tool support.

For the precise reference to the books mentioned here, see appendix C, "An Eiffel Bibliography", page 509.

Thought and expression

Inaccurate as it would be to consider language issues only, the reverse mistake is just as damaging.

A strange idea has become prevalent in some software circles: the claim that languages, after all, are not that important. Requests are even heard here and there for a bizarre animal, the "language-independent methodology" – about as useful as a bird without wings, and just as likely.

In software perhaps more than anywhere else, thought is inseparable from its expression. To obtain good software, a good notation is not sufficient; but it is certainly necessary.

Old, new and out

The language concepts in Eiffel are not, of course, entirely new. Some key ideas came from earlier designs, most notably Simula 67, Algol variants (especially Algol W), Alphard, CLU, Ada, and an early version of the Z specification language. Among the novel aspects are a number of language constructs – in the areas of inheritance, typing, exceptions and assertions among others – as well as the choice of concepts from various sources and their combination into a coherent edifice. In particular, Eiffel is original in its association of an assertion facility (coming from work on program verification and formal specification) with a full object-oriented approach emphasizing multiple and repeated inheritance and information hiding.

Also notable is the set of ideas that have *not* been retained. To design is to renounce. Although designers rarely speak about this aspect, an engineering product is defined by what it has excluded as much as by what it has retained. In Eiffel, where so much attention was devoted to keeping the language small and trying to make it elegant, readers will be surprised, perhaps shocked in some cases, not to find some broadly accepted concepts such as global variables, enumeration types, subrange types, goto instructions (as well as the many disguises that have been invented for them over the years, such as "exit", "break", "continue" and the like), variables and arguments denoting routines or routine pointers, undisciplined type conversions ("casts"), pointer arithmetic, language-defined input and output, main programs, routine pointers, and quite a few others.

The exclusion of these concepts does not mean that all of them are intrinsically bad, although some obviously are; others are simply redundant or incompatible with mechanisms that were more important for the Eiffel software development method.

The signal and the noise

Simple does not mean simplistic. The language definition, as it appears in this book, includes a few notions that are definitely non-trivial, particularly the full feature adaptation mechanism, repeated inheritance, and the details of type checking. Several reasons justify the presence of these more advanced elements: only a small number of constructs are involved; the basic ideas are straightforward, and the more difficult aspects simply result from pushing the basic ideas to their full consequences; simple uses will yield the expected

On the mechanisms mentioned here, see chapters 10, 11 and 22.

results, according to the "principle of least surprise"; there is no need to understand all the details for ordinary use (and you will indeed find SHORTCUT signs inviting you to skip the more specialized sections); and the extra power granted by the language's most sophisticated facilities, far from being mere gadgetry, addresses some of the most difficult issues of large-scale software development.

In other words, what the language design has sought is the highest possible *signal-to-noise* ratio, allowing users of the language to make the most out of their intellectual energy. This means getting rid of the noise (features which make the language bigger without contributing any really new concept): who needs three forms of loop when a general enough one will do, or special syntax for array access when we can simply view arrays as "container" structures described by a library class? But it also means reaching for the highest possible level of signal: including the appropriate constructs to deal with the truly difficult cases of software development, especially those which arise in the construction of large and ambitious systems.

When the time comes to decide what is essential and what is superfluous, there is no substitute for experience with the language in many projects and application areas. Interactive Software Engineering has been an extensive user of Eiffel for several years, and except for a few interfaces to other tools (viewed by the Eiffel side as "external software" according to the techniques of chapter 24) all our developments today, including ISE's Eiffel compiler-interpreter and the supporting environment, are done in Eiffel. In addition to our own practice, we have observed users of our tools in their development of systems ranging over most application areas of computers.

Appendix B draws on the Eiffel experience to discuss the issues of language design and evolution.

Such experience, although not a guarantee against mistakes, provides crucial background for the choices that await language designers.

Language level

If you have read previous publications about Eiffel, including *Object-Oriented Software Construction*, you will notice some differences with the language described here. This book indeed presents Eiffel version 3, which benefits from the accumulated experience mentioned above. The differences with previous versions do not affect the fundamental semantics of Eiffel; rather, they bring in simplifications in some areas and a few extensions in others. Although long-time Eiffel users and enthusiasts may at first be surprised by some of these changes, I hope they will soon realize that this update brings local but significant improvements to the language, without impairing the consistency and simplicity of its basic design.

A list of changes may be found in two appendices, one giving the old-to-new dictionary, the other the new-to-old correspondence. The second of these, meant for readers using a compiler which has not yet been brought up to level 3, should be of temporary value only.

→ Old-to-new is in appendix E and new-to-old in appendix F.

Language evolution is a delicate issue; one must walk a fine line between unjustified upheaval and undue conservatism. An appendix discusses this question.

→ See appendix B.

The future of Eiffel

The publication of this book marks a turning point in the evolution of Eiffel: the passage from single to multiple sources and from individual control to collective oversight.

Until recently, one company (Interactive Software Engineering) was the sole supplier of Eiffel compilers, and one person (me) was in charge of the language definition. The situation has changed radically: competing implementations are now available, a development that we not only accept but welcome; and control over the future of the language is being handed over to an organization representing the users and implementors of Eiffel worldwide, the Nonprofit International Consortium for Eiffel.

About the Consortium, see the note entitled "On the status of Eiffel" which follows this preface.

The Consortium will be the appropriate vector for the evolution of Eiffel. This may appear to violate the precept set forth by D.W. Barron:

> *As a working hypothesis we can suggest that the probability of achieving clearly seen and sensible objectives in language design is in inverse proportion to the number of people involved in the design process. Thus the best languages are those designed by a single [...] individual or a small coherent group. [...] The worst languages are those "designed" by large committees.*

D.W. Barron, "An Introduction to the Study of Programming Languages", Cambridge University Press, 1977, page 144.

These observations are undeniably accurate for the initial design of a language. After the individual or small group have done their best, however, there does come a time for committees. This time has been reached for Eiffel. The design is in place; it has been tested by thousands of software developers in many different countries. Work certainly remains to be done, but it does not affect the essential concepts, and much of it is probably beyond the grasp of any single person anyway.

Some Eiffel enthusiasts have voiced fears about the dangers of committee-controlled evolution, particularly the propensity of committees to indulge in what was called gadgetry above and is also known as "featurism": repeated addition of special-purpose facilities, which may individually please specific constituencies, but will collectively destroy the consistency of the design. The risk exists, but perhaps less than with some other language, as the Eiffel community may be trusted to understand the virtues of design simplicity. Besides, the original designer should still be around for some time, as a kind of Commendatore's *statua gentilissima* ready to intervene at the earliest sign of debauchery.

Missing elements

There are two areas in which I would have liked this book to go further.

One is the old but still thorny problem of numerical precision in floating-point computation, for which Eiffel relies on quite traditional solutions, with imprecisely defined semantics. A rigorous approach to this problem, in line with the systematic treatment of other aspects in Eiffel, should be possible, but will require the collaboration of experts in numerical analysis as well as software engineering.

The other missing part is concurrency. There is in fact a language design for concurrency in Eiffel, based on a simple extension (one keyword) and consistent with the theory underlying Eiffel ("Design by Contract"). Yet I stopped short of including the description of this mechanism here because as of this writing it has not yet been implemented. No official programming language document should ever be published unless all major components of the language have been successfully implemented – a principle applied applied throughout the evolution of Eiffel and, before it, to just about every successful language. (The counter-examples, languages that attracted considerable interest upon publication but then failed because they proved too hard to implement, are all too familiar.)

On the concurrency mechanism for Eiffel, see "Sequential and Concurrent Object-Oriented Programming", in "An Eiffel Collection". Appendix C gives the exact reference.

Acknowledgments

I am responsible for the deficiencies of Eiffel and of this book. Both would be much worse, however, had I not benefited from the enlightening, reasoned, educated, patient and stubborn suggestions of many people – too many, in fact, to allow a fair acknowledgment. Let me cite a few, with apologies to the others.

A prominent role was played by Jean-Marc Nerson, who has been associated with the design of Eiffel right from the start, and to whom many of its best features are directly traceable.

Under the leadership of Philippe Stephan, the development team for ISE's version 3 implementation, especially Frédéric Dernbach and Raphael Manfredi, devised elegant and efficient implementation techniques, and in the process provided essential in-depth suggestions and criticism on both the language and the book.

I am particularly grateful to three colleagues who contributed key input on both the text and the language: Michael Schweitzer, author of the Eiffel/S compiler for MS-DOS, who provided the invaluable perspective of an independent implementor; Kim Waldén, whose deep and detailed comments on all aspects of this work were especially influential, and who generously provided decisive help at various stages; and John Potter, who contributed fundamental insights on the inheritance mechanism.

Others who provided important ideas were Roger Rousseau, Steve Tynor, Jim Gish, Norman Shelley, Erland Sommarskog, Rick Jones, Robert Switzer, Frieder Monninger, Paul Tarvydas, Peter Lohr, David Yost, Bob Weiner, Gerardo Horvilleur, Paul Dubois, David Butler, John Anderson, Stavros Macrakis, John Sarkela, Serge Granik, Jean-Claude Boussard, Frédérique Sada, Cyrille Gindre, Andreas Schramm, Dave Berry, Tal Lancaster. The criticism of Pierre America and William Cook on some aspects of the language was also much appreciated.

The help of my colleagues at ISE and SOL was essential, especially as part of the sobering process of implementing the language. I cannot mention all, but have a special debt to Annie Meyer, Tom McCarthy, Darcy Harrison, Jean-Pierre Sarkis, Frédéric Deramat, Gurvan-Yves Lullien, Olivier Mallet, Reynald Bouy, Deniz Yuksel, Frédéric Lalanne, Philippe Lahire, Vincent Kraemer, Kim Rochat, Philip Hucklesby and Philippe Elinck.

Bruce Anderson (acting as a reviewer for Prentice-Hall), Bob Weiner, Kim Rochat, Roxanne Rochat, Vincent Kraemer, Stefan Ludwig, Keith Robertson, Christian Tanzer and Irina Piens read earlier versions of this book and came up with many constructive comments.

Started through the efforts of David Yost, the Usenet newsgroup *comp.lang.eiffel*, an international electronic bulletin board devoted to the discussion of Eiffel-related issues, has been in operation since 1988. The debates there have been of excellent quality, reflecting the maturity of the Eiffel community and serving as a model of what the electronic medium can achieve. (The only regret is the limited availability of past postings, a number of which would deserve republication in a more traditional format.) The plans for many of the Eiffel 3 changes were initially posted on *comp.lang.eiffel*, eliciting feedback and criticism which led to improvements and avoided some potential mistakes. Many thanks to all contributors.

Eiffel would not exist today without the support and enthusiasm of its users. My biggest debt is to all the software developers the world over who have chosen to rely on Eiffel for their projects. I thank them for their trust and hope that this book will be up to their exacting standards of quality.

Santa Barbara   B.M.
July 1991
March 1992 (second printing, with corrections)

About the status of Eiffel

The design of the Eiffel language is in the public domain. Any individual or organization is welcome to build on the ideas developed in this book and to produce compilers, interpreters, tools and libraries for Eiffel.

The evolution of Eiffel is controlled by the Nonprofit International Consortium for Eiffel (NICE), incorporated in California as a non-profit organization. Membership in NICE is open to any interested party worldwide. Members can participate in technical committees devoted to the language, libraries and other aspects of the evolution of Eiffel. NICE is also the primary interface to standards organizations and other industry bodies.

NICE is also the holder of the Eiffel trademark and is entitled to grant the use of this name in connection with products or tools. Only technical criteria (as opposed to commercial considerations) will be used in granting such permissions; they may include such requirements as passing a validation suite.

For information on membership in NICE please write to

Nonprofit International Consortium for Eiffel
P.O. Box 6884
Santa Barbara, CA 93160
USA

One specific implementation of Eiffel was developed by Interactive Software Engineering (ISE). For information on this implementation and distributors in various countries, please contact:

Interactive Software Engineering Inc.
Attn: Eiffel products
270 Storke Road Suite 7
Goleta, CA 93117 USA
Telephone 805-685-1006, Fax 805-685-6869, E-mail queries@eiffel.com

About the language description

In a book describing the language support for a radically new approach to software construction, it was natural to take a fresh look not only at the subject matter but also at the techniques used to present it.

To help you enjoy the discussion of Eiffel, here are a few notes about the description method, and about the reasons that led to it.

Types of description, levels of discourse

The describer of a programming, design or analysis language faces an interesting task. He must address several constituencies: interested bystanders, novices starting to use the language, experienced users, authors of compilers and interpreters. He must satisfy several requirements: explaining the concepts in a clear way; teaching the use of the language; giving examples; providing a precise reference to answer questions of details and remove possible ambiguities or contradictions.

The almost universal response to these conflicting goals is to write at least two documents: a *user's manual* and a *reference manual*, the latter also called "report". The user's manual is supposed to be readable by ordinary human beings; the reference manual must be precise, accurate and, as the accepted consequence, hard to read and boring. The reference manual is indispensable, however, for implementors, and users may also need it when they run into tricky questions or apparent ambiguities. Often, there is a third document, a tutorial.

Having experienced this division, on the reader's side of the fence, when using programming languages as well as software tools (for which the same problems arise, usually with the same solutions), I have come to dislike it profoundly. In spite of all the good intentions that justify the multi-document structure, the net result is that, in any serious use of the language or tools, you keep shuffling between the documents involved when seeking information about the available features and their properties. Sometimes you will look at the user's manual and fail to find the detailed information that you need; but when you look at the reference manual you miss the necessary informal explanations, comments and examples. If, as is too often the case, you end up looking in both places, you find repetitions, which waste your time, or even apparent contradictions.

This book innovates by being both a reference and a user's manual, and by addressing the needs of both users (beginning or advanced) and implementors (authors of compilers or interpreters). It also includes a tutorial overview.

The overview is chapter 1, "Invitation to Eiffel".

Of course, by trying to cater to several audiences, it may fail to satisfy any of them. This will be for the reader to judge.

Formality

To compound the difficulty, the "reference" parts of the presentation, intended to serve as official answer to questions about the syntax, validity rules and semantics of language constructs, are more formalized than in most existing language references. These official elements have to coexist with much more informal explanations, comments, examples and advice.

Not that this work can claim to offer a truly *formal* description of Eiffel; this would have required a mathematical specification based on the methods of axiomatic or denotational semantics (which I have tried to summarize, at an introductory level, in another book). The aims here are more modest, but every effort has been devoted to specifying Eiffel with as much precision as can be afforded without resorting to mathematics. An earlier article argued that one of the important byproducts of writing formal specifications may be informal descriptions of a new and better kind, *derived from* the formal ones, which they serve as accompaniment and running commentary. Although no such derivation was used here, readers familiar with formal methods will recognize their influence and a style which resembles what one could find in a non-formal specification resulting from a detour through mathematical formality.

See the book "Introduction to the Theory of Programming Languages", Prentice-Hall International, 1990.

The article mentioned is "On Formalism in Specifications", IEEE Software, 2, 1, January 1985, pages 6-26, especially page 24 and figure 5.

As an example of the effort made to achieve more precision than is customary, most of the validity constraints (rules governing such aspects as type compatibility or the number of actual arguments to a routine) are expressed as necessary and **sufficient** conditions. As a user of programming languages manuals, I have long been puzzled by their focus on **necessary** conditions: the source of the assignment *must* be of the same type as the target, the number of actual arguments *must* be the same as the number of formal arguments, and so on. All this is fine, but how do I know that I have considered all the relevant "musts" and that now I *may* submit my result as a valid piece of software?

For an example of a language specified in a formal way, see R. C. Holt et al., "The Turing Programming Language", Prentice-Hall International, 1988.

To address this question in a systematic way, the description of almost every construct (such as Class, Instruction or Expression) includes a validity constraint of the form "this will be valid *if and only if* the following conditions are satisfied...". The first *if* indicates that the conditions given are sufficient.

This style may contribute to making the presentation appear somewhat pedantic at times. It also carries some dangers: if you forget a condition, you give users a misplaced sense of security, whereas with the "must" style, since you never claim exhaustivity, they learn to be wary. But I felt that the sometimes painstaking task of producing the complete list of validity requirements should be the responsibility of the language specifier, not a job left for each language user to handle individually.

Others, it is hoped, will capitalize on this book's attempt at precision and rigor to produce formal specifications of Eiffel.

Order of presentation

As if all this was not already making the task impossible, two of the major goals for this book were to make it, against all odds, not *too* boring, and to encourage readers to study it in the way one should approach any decent book save for dictionaries and railway timetables: sequentially, from cover to cover.

This has meant another change from the common practice in language books, affecting the order of introduction of the various concepts.

The traditional order is bottom-up: first the lexical constituents (character set, constants, identifiers), then on to expressions, instructions and higher-level structuring mechanisms.

Here, in contrast, the presentation is top-down; once you have read the initial overview chapter and a short chapter introducing basic conventions, you will learn about the overall architecture of software systems written in Eiffel, then about the structure of their individual modules (classes), then about the routines, the attributes, the run-time model, and the lower-level constituents of Eiffel software.

The reason for this departure from the conventional order is to make sure that the key concepts and constructs are introduced first, enabling you to keep in mind the "big picture" throughout the presentation. After all, the details of bit constants and the representation of special characters in strings, although useful in some cases, are not what makes Eiffel exciting; it is more rewarding to understand right away how to build and read software systems at the highest level.

→ *"Construct" is defined more precisely below.*

The presentation is divided into five parts:

- Part A, Introduction, includes an overview of the language and a presentation of the conventions used for syntactic and semantic construct descriptions.

- Part B, Structure, describes how Eiffel software is organized, explaining the architectural notions of system, cluster, class and feature, the inheritance and client relations between classes, routines, assertions, the feature adaptation mechanism based on inheritance, and the type system with the associated notion of conformance.

- Part C, Contents, covers the inner parts of classes and features and their effect on software execution: control structures, instructions, exceptions, attributes, objects, values, expressions, entities, calls, interface with other languages, and the lexical structure of software texts.

- Part D, Kernel Library elements, introduces some basic library facilities, covering universal features (available to all classes), persistence, arrays, strings, arithmetic classes, input and output.

- Part E, Appendices, includes a presentation of recommended style standards, a discussion of the issues of language design and evolution, a bibliography on Eiffel, a description of Lace (the Language for Assembling Classes in Eiffel, used to combine classes into executable systems), two summaries of the differences between Eiffel 3 and previous versions (in both the old-to-new and new-to-old directions), and reference information: reserved words, precedence, syntax reference in three different forms (textual order, alphabetical order, diagrams), index.

Paragraph types and road signs

For the reader of this book, the language description strategy described above has two significant consequences.

First, the top-down order of presentation implies that once in a while, as you read the presentation, you will be requested to perform an "act of faith" when seeing a reference to a concept that will only be defined precisely in a later part of the discussion. Such *forward references* are inevitable regardless of the style of presentation, since any useful programming language, even one such as Eiffel for which simplicity was a constant design obsession, includes concepts so intricately related as to make a linear presentation next to impossible; but the top-down style causes even more of them.

Next, the other key decisions – merging the reference manual and user manual into a single book, attempting to satisfy at once the needs of diverse audiences – mean that several types of discourse are interwoven in the discussion, belonging to various levels of formality and not all enjoying the same official status.

This book uses a number of devices to guide you through these different components of the presentation. In particular, it relies on a system of *road signs*, printed in the left margin, and notes, printed in the right margin, to help you grasp right away the type and level of individual components.

The whole set of road signs appears on the next page.

A road sign indicates the nature of some part of the text: comment, preview, reminder, shortcut, syntax, validity, semantics, examples, caveat. Usually the sign applies to the marked paragraph, although it sometimes covers the following few paragraphs as well; if it is attached to the first paragraph of a section, it applies to the entire section.

Let us take a look at the various road signs; this will also serve to explain the presentation style.

Cross-references and shortcuts

Forward references are much less confusing if they are explicitly signaled. All forward references are marked by a note in the right margin, preceded by the symbol → and indicating where to look for the final word on a concept being used ahead of its full definition.

← The above use of "construct" was a forward reference.

In many cases, it will be necessary to include a partial explanation of the concept at the point of forward reference. The PREVIEW road sign indicates that this explanation is only temporary, although it suffices for the needs of the discussion at this point.

Because this book is meant to be read by human beings with less than unbounded memory, it also includes *backward references*: pointers to the place where a certain concept was originally introduced. Backward references are given as right-margin notes preceded by ←.

Sometimes, a summary review of the concept is given at the point of backward reference; the corresponding paragraph is then labeled by the REMINDER road sign, indicating that the new explanation is only there to refresh the reader's memory, and that the official definition is the earlier one.

Road Signs

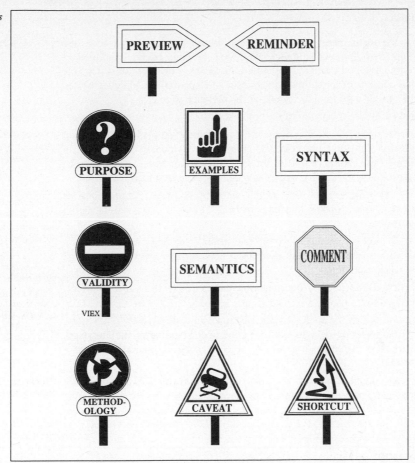

The use of cross-references, backward and forward, is particularly generous. To facilitate quick retrieval, most of these references include page numbers, often in addition to section numbers. To avoid bothering readers who follow the presentation sequentially, they are almost entirely confined to the right margin; but they should prove invaluable to anyone seeking to gain a thorough understanding of the concepts involved, with all their intertwining.

Besides cross references, other notes will also appear occasionally in the right margin; they are not part of the language definition, but give auxiliary information, such as bibliographic references, usually pointing to the detailed Eiffel bibliography of appendix C.

Another "directional" road sign is the SHORTCUT warning, which accompanies a note indicating that some part of the discussion (usually an entire section, or the remainder of a chapter) may be skipped at first reading. This applies to finer aspects of the presentation, which will be of interest to readers wishing to become acquainted with the details of Eiffel, but are not essential to an overall understanding. Typically, such aspects would have appeared in a reference manual but not in a user's manual.

The desire to make fast back and forth searches easier also explains why the page number appears (in small print) even on the first page of a chapter – favoring reader's convenience over typographical tradition.

Describing a construct

The most important parts of the language description are of course the specifications of individual language structures, or **constructs**. Examples of constructs are Class, Instruction, Expression, Identifier. For most constructs, the presentation consists of the following sequence of elements, each labeled by the corresponding road sign from the figure on the previous page.

- PURPOSE: a brief explanation of the construct's role.

- EXAMPLES: one or more typical uses. Some of the examples were designed specifically for this presentation; many others come, sometimes in simplified form, from the text of the Basic Eiffel Libraries, which form an important body of carefully written and heavily exercised Eiffel software.

  The EXAMPLES sign is the "interesting detail" pictogram of the Swedish Recreation Standard.

- SYNTAX: Specification of the textual form of software components, or **specimens**, corresponding to each construct. Syntax is described through a simple formalism.

  → 2.2, starting on page 23, explains the syntax notation. "Specimen" is also defined on page 23.

- VALIDITY: Rules such as typing constraints, stating restrictions on permissible specimens of the construct, not captured by the syntactical specification alone.

  → The notion of validity is discussed in 2.6 and 2.7, starting on page 26; the role of validity codes, such as VIEX next to the road sign on the figure, is explained on page 27.

- SEMANTICS: Description of the meaning (that is to say, the run-time effect) of the construct.

For users as well as for implementors, distinguishing clearly between syntax, constraints and semantics is essential to a good understanding of the language. Every construct has a certain structure, is subject to some limitations, and has a certain effect.

The SYNTAX, VALIDITY and SEMANTICS paragraphs constitute the core of the official language definition. They are complemented in this role by paragraphs labeled DEFINITION, which introduce terms to be used thereafter with a precise meaning.

There is no road sign for DEFINITION.

Comments, warnings and advice

Additional paragraphs, liberally interspersed in the rest of the discussion, serve explanatory purposes and are outside of the language definition proper:

- COMMENT: Time to stop for some explanations, discussions and informal addenda.

- METHODOLOGY: Advice on how to use individual constructs in the Eiffel software development method.

- CAVEAT: Remarks alerting you to slippery road segments – possible misunderstandings which could lead to mistakes or improper use of the language.

  The road sign for METHODOLOGY suggests the proper way to go around an intersection – with apologies to readers from the British Isles, Australia, Japan, Singapore etc. who might think of it as the wrong way.

- PREVIEW, REMINDER: As discussed above.

Of course, not every paragraph is labeled. Unlabeled paragraphs generally fall under the "comment" category.

Graphical representations

For analysis and design discussions, for explaining software structures to others, for exploring classes and systems with "browsers" and other interactive tools, it is often useful to display information graphically.

The presentation of the most important language constructs includes a description of associated graphical conventions, based on some results of an effort directed by Jean-Marc Nerson to develop standardized pictorial representations of Eiffel software components – classes with their client and inheritance relations, features, assertions, indexing information etc. – in a simple and immediately understandable visual form.

The notation is known as BON – Better Object Notation – and is described in "Extending Eiffel Toward O-O Analysis and Design". See the reference in appendix C.

These conventions are obviously not part of the language; they merely assist software construction and understanding. The form presented here is neither final nor complete; other publications will describe the notation in detail.

The cake and its icing

A more general question arises from the last observation: what then, among the elements explained in this book, *is* officially part of the Eiffel language?

From the preceding discussion, it is clear that some parts, such as the paragraphs labeled SYNTAX, VALIDITY and SEMANTICS, definitely belong to the cake – the actual definition of Eiffel as a language. In contrast, the introductory overview of chapter 1 is only part of the icing, and so is anything labeled COMMENT, CAVEAT or METHODOLOGY in the subsequent chapters.

This leaves some areas of uncertainty, especially around the Eiffel libraries, which are looted regularly in parts B and C for illustrations of language constructs, and provide most of the facilities described in part D: universal features, arrays, strings, persistence, basic arithmetic, input and output. (The classes of part D belong to the Kernel Library, containing fundamental facilities; the classes providing construct examples, sometimes in adapted or simplified form, are mostly from the Data Structure, Graphics and Parsing libraries.)

Chapter 26 discusses the status of libraries. When reading about the Kernel Library classes of part D, you may consider their interfaces – what in Eiffel is called their **short form**, excluding implementation aspects – to be part of the official description of Eiffel, although separate from the language proper. This does not apply to the other libraries, whose class extracts are used merely as examples.

→ See 7.14, starting on page 103, about the short form.

The decision to give an official status to the specification of some Kernel Library classes is subject to discussion. An argument against it is that these classes are not the only possible ones, and that their inclusion here might be unfairly preventing others from coming up with a better notion of (say) arrays. On closer look, however, several reasons suggest that one should not be too shy about enforcing a standard here:

• One of the major attractions of Eiffel is precisely the presence of a standardized set of carefully designed libraries. It would be regrettable to forsake such a benefit simply out of a concern for fairness to other potential but as yet unproven solutions.

• Most applications will need some of the Kernel Library classes selected for this book.

- Only the interface is specified. This leaves room for multiple, competing implementations.

- Encouraging the use of a standard set of library classes is not the same as claiming they are the last word. Improvements may be expected in the future. Eiffel's design makes it possible to cushion the effect of such changes on systems using the classes affected, thanks to mechanisms such as "obsolete" features and classes and, more generally, to the client-supplier independence enforced by the language and the method.

→ See 5.17, beginning on page 73, on obsolete features.

As with the rest of the language, future decisions on these issues will rest with the Consortium. As with the rest of the language, I have tried to lay the ground for the Consortium's work and to proceed as far as a single person could go.

Contents

Part A

Introduction

1

Invitation to Eiffel

1.1 Overview

The following chapters provide a detailed description of the various constructs of Eiffel. To understand the details, however, you will need to keep in mind the overall perspective.

To help in this effort, this chapter offers a short guided tour of the language.

1.2 Design principles

The aim of Eiffel is to help specify, design, implement and change quality software. This goal of quality in software is a combination of many factors; the language design concentrated on the factors which, in the the current state of the industry, are in direst need of improvements.

A major one is **reusability**, or the ability to produce components that may be used in many different applications. Another is **extendibility**: "soft" as software is supposed to be, it is notoriously hard to modify software systems, especially large ones.

A more detailed discussion of some of the design goals behind Eiffel may be found in "From Structured Programming to Object-Oriented Design: The Road to Eiffel", in "An Eiffel Collection". See the bibliography of appendix C.

Among quality factors, reusability and extendibility play a special role: satisfying them means having *less* software to write – and hence more time to devote to other important goals such as efficiency, ease of use or integrity.

The third fundamental factor is **reliability**. Techniques such as assertions, disciplined exception handling and static typing, enabling developers to produce software with dramatically fewer bugs, are part of Eiffel's approach to the engineering of quality software.

Great attention was also paid to three essential aspect:

• Enabling implementors to produce language processing tools (especially compilers) of high **efficiency**, so that systems developed in Eiffel may run under speed and space conditions comparable to those of programs written in lower-level traditional languages.

- Ensuring **openness**, so that Eiffel software may cooperate with programs written in other languages.
- Guaranteeing **portability** by a platform-independent language definition, so that the same semantics may be supported on many different platforms.

1.3 Object-oriented design

METHOD-OLOGY

To achieve reusability, extendibility and reliability, the principles of object-oriented design provide the best known technical answer.

An in-depth discussion of these principles would fall beyond the scope of this book, but we need to recall the basic ideas. The following will serve as a working definition:

See the book "Object-Oriented Software Construction" for a discussion of the principles and techniques of object-oriented design.

DEFINITION:
Object-Oriented Design

> Object-oriented design is the construction of software systems as structured collections of **classes**, or abstract data type implementations.

COMMENT

The following points are worth noting in this definition:

- The emphasis is on structuring a system around the types of objects it manipulates (not the functions it performs on them) and on reusing whole data structures together with the associated operations (not isolated routines).

- Objects are described as instances of abstract data types – that is to say, data structures known from an official interface rather than through their representation.

- The basic modular unit, called the class, describes one implementation of an abstract data type (or, in the case of "deferred" classes, as studied below, a set of possible implementations of the same abstract data type).

- The word *collection* reflects how classes should be designed: as units which are interesting and useful on their own, independently of the systems to which they belong, and may be reused by many different systems. Software construction is viewed as the assembly of existing classes, not as a top-down process starting from scratch.

- Finally, the word *structured* reflects the existence of two important relations between classes: the client and inheritance relations.

Eiffel makes these techniques available to software developers in a simple and practical way.

1.4 Classes

A class, it was said above, is an implementation of an abstract data type. This means that it describes a set of run-time objects, characterized by the **features** (operations) applicable to them, and by the formal properties of these features.

→ *Chapters 4 and 5 discuss classes and their features.*

Such objects are called the **direct instances** of the class. Classes and objects should not be confused: "class" is a compile-time notion, whereas objects only exist at run time. This is similar to the difference that exists in classical programming between a program and one execution of that program, or between a type and a run-time value of that type.

"Object-Oriented" is a misnomer; "Class-Oriented Analysis, Design and Programming" would be a more accurate description of the method.

To see what a class looks like, let us look at a simple example, *ACCOUNT*, which describes bank accounts. But before exploring the class itself it is useful to study how it may be used by other classes, called its **clients**.

A class *X* may become a client of *ACCOUNT* by declaring one or more **entities** of type *ACCOUNT*. Such a declaration is of the form:

> *acc*: *ACCOUNT*

The term "entity" generalizes the more common notion of "variable". An entity declared of a reference type, such as *acc*, may at any time during execution become "attached to" an object; the type rules imply that this object must be a direct instance of *ACCOUNT* – or, as seen below, of a "descendant" of that class.

→ *Chapter 20 discusses the notion of attachment in detail.*

Entity of reference type and attached object

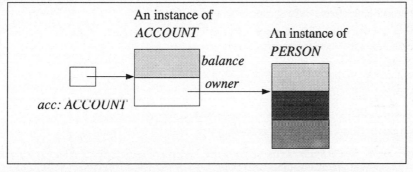

An instance of
ACCOUNT

An instance of
PERSON

balance

owner

acc: ACCOUNT

The 'owner' field of the ACCOUNT instance is itself a reference, attached to another object. See below.

An entity which is not attached to any object is said to be void. By default, entities are void at initialization. To obtain objects at run-time, a routine *r* of the client class *X* may use a **creation instruction** of the form

→ *Chapter 18 discusses creation instructions.*

> !! *acc*

which creates a new direct instance of *ACCOUNT*, attaches *acc* to that instance, and initializes all its fields to default values. A variant of this notation, studied below, makes it possible to override the default initializations.

Once the client has attached *acc* to an object, it may call on this object the features defined in class *ACCOUNT*. Here is an extract with some feature calls using *acc* as their target:

```
    acc.open ("Jill");
    acc.deposit (5000);
    if acc.may_withdraw (3000) then
        acc.withdraw (3000);
        print (acc.balance)
    end;
```

This is assumed to be part of the text of a class X.

These feature calls use dot notation, of the form *target.feature_name*. (Prefix and infix forms, described below, are also available.) Features are of two kinds:

- **Routines** (as *open*, *deposit*, *may_withdraw* or *withdraw*) represent computations applicable to instances of the class.

- **Attributes** represent data items associated with these instances.

An instance of a class is a direct instance of one of its descendants (which include the class itself).

Routines are further divided into **procedures** (actions, which do not return a value) and **functions** (returning a value). Here *may_withdraw* is a function returning a boolean result; the other three routines invoked are procedures.

The above extract of class *X* does not show whether, in class *ACCOUNT*, *balance* is an attribute or a function without argument. This ambiguity is intentional. A client of *ACCOUNT*, such as *X*, does not need to know how a balance is obtained: the balance could be stored as attribute of every account object, or computed by a function from other attributes. Choosing between these techniques is the business of class *ACCOUNT*, not anybody else's. Because such implementation choices are often changed over the lifetime of a project, it is essential to protect clients against their effects.

This technique of hiding from the client whether a feature is implemented by storage or by computation is known as the Principle of Uniform Access (or "Uniform Reference"). See "Object-Oriented Software Construction" and page 342 of this book.

Here now is a first sketch of how class *ACCOUNT* itself might look. Line segments beginning with -- are comments.

```
    class ACCOUNT feature
        balance: INTEGER;

        owner: PERSON;
        minimum_balance: INTEGER is 1000;

        open (who: PERSON) is
                -- Assign the account to owner who
            do
                owner := who
            end; -- open
        deposit (sum: INTEGER) is
                -- Deposit sum into the account
            do
                add (sum)
            end; -- deposit
        withdraw (sum: INTEGER) is
                -- Withdraw sum from the account
            do
                add (−sum)
            end; -- withdraw
```

```
        may_withdraw (sum: INTEGER): BOOLEAN is
            -- Is there enough to withdraw sum?
        do
            Result := (balance >= sum + minimum_balance)
        end -- may_withdraw

    feature {NONE}
        add (sum: INTEGER) is
            -- Add sum to the balance
            -- (Secret procedure)
        do
            balance := balance + sum
        end; -- add

    end -- class ACCOUNT
```

This class includes two **feature** clauses, introducing its features. The first begins with just the keyword **feature**, without further qualification; this means that the features declared in this clause are available (or "exported") to all clients of the class. The second clause is introduced by

```
    feature {NONE}
```

to indicate that the feature that follows, called *add*, is available to no client. What appears between the braces is a list of client classes to which the corresponding features are available; *NONE* is a special class of the Kernel Library, which has no instances, so that *add* is in effect a secret feature, available only locally to the other routines of class *ACCOUNT*. In a client class such as *X*, writing *acc.add* (*−3000*) would be invalid.

Let us examine the features in sequence. The **is** ... **do** ...**end** distinguishes routines from attributes. So here the class has implemented *balance* as an attribute, although, as noted, functions would also have been acceptable. Feature *owner* is also an attribute.

The language definition guarantees automatic initialization, so that the initial *balance* of an account object will be zero after a creation instruction. Each type has a default initial value, used for initialization: zero for *INTEGER* and *REAL*, false for *BOOLEAN*, null character for *CHARACTER*, and void references for reference types.

→ *The class designer may also provide clients with different initialization options, as shown below in a revised version of this example.*

The other public features, *open, deposit, withdraw* and *may_withdraw* are straightforward routines. The special variable *Result*, used in function *may_withdraw*, denotes the function result; it is initialized on function entry to the default value of the function's result type.

The secret procedure *add* serves for the implementation of the public procedures *deposit* and *withdraw*; the designer of *ACCOUNT* judged it too general to be exported by itself. The clause **is** *1000* introduces *minimum_balance* as a constant attribute, which will not occupy any space in instances of the class; in contrast, every instance has a field (similar to the components of a Pascal record) for each non-constant attribute such as *balance*.

To understand the routines fully, you must keep in mind that in Eiffel's object-oriented programming style any operation is relative to a certain object. In an external client invoking the operation, this object is specified by writing the corresponding entity on the left of the dot, as *acc* in *acc.open ("Jill")*. Within the class, however, the "current" instance to which operations apply usually remains implicit, so that unqualified feature names, such as *owner* in procedure *open* or *add* in *deposit*, mean "the *owner* attribute or *add* routine relative to the current instance".

If you need to denote the current object explicitly, you may use the special entity *Current*. For example the unqualified occurrences of *add* appearing in the above class are equivalent to *Current.add*.

In some cases, infix or prefix notation is more convenient. For example, if a class *VECTOR* offers an addition routine, most people will feel more comfortable with calls of the form *v + w* than with the dot-notation call *v.plus (w)*. To make this possible it suffices to give the routine a name of the form as **infix** "+" rather than *plus*; internally, however, the operation is still a normal routine call. Prefix operators are similarly available.

The above simple example has shown the basic structuring mechanism of the language: the class. A class describes a data structure, accessible to clients through an official interface comprising some of the class features. Features are implemented as attributes or routines; the implementation of exported features may rely on other, secret ones.

1.5 Types

Eiffel is strongly typed for readability and reliability.

Every entity is declared of a certain type, which may be either a reference type or an expanded type.

Any type *T* is based on a class, which defines the operations available on instances of *T*. The difference between the two categories of type affects the semantics of an entity *x* declared of type *T*: for a reference type, the most common case, possible values for *x* are references to objects; for an expanded type, the values are objects. In both cases, the type rules guarantee that the objects will be instances of *T*.

A (non-expanded) class such as *ACCOUNT* yields a reference type.

In contrast, the value of an entity *acc* declared of type **expanded** *ACCOUNT* is an object as shown below. No creation instruction is needed in this case.

→ *Chapter 12 discusses the notion of type, and chapter 13 the related notion of conformance.*

The "instances" of T are the direct instances of its descendants (T itself, its heirs, their own heirs etc.).

An entity of expanded type and a possible value

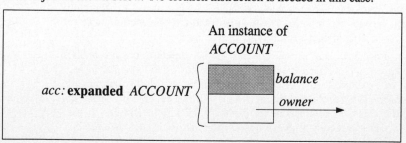

The only difference with the case illustrated on page 5 is the value of 'acc', now an ACCOUNT object, not a reference to such an object. Here the PERSON object attached to the 'owner' field has not been shown.

An important group of expanded types, based on library classes, includes the basic types *INTEGER*, *REAL*, *DOUBLE*, *CHARACTER* and *BOOLEAN*. Clearly, the value of an entity declared of type *INTEGER* should be an integer, not a reference to an object containing an integer value. Operations on these types are defined by prefix or infix operators such as "+" and "<".

As a result of these conventions, the type system is uniform and consistent: all types, including the basic types, are defined from classes, either as reference types or as expanded types. Of course, in the case of basic types, a good compiler or interpreter will implement the standard arithmetic and boolean operations directly, not through routine calls; but this is only a compiler optimization, which does not hamper the conceptual homogeneity of the type edifice.

1.6 Assertions

If classes are to deserve their definition as abstract data type implementations, they must be known not just by the available operations, but also by the formal properties of these operations, which did not appear in the above example.

→ *Chapter 9 discusses assertions.*

Eiffel encourages programmers to express formal properties of classes by writing **assertions**, which may in particular appear in the following roles:

- Routine **preconditions** express the requirements that clients must satisfy whenever they call a routine. For example the designer of *ACCOUNT* may wish to permit a withdrawal operation only if it keeps the account's balance on or above the minimum. Preconditions are introduced by the keyword **require**.

- Routine **postconditions**, introduced by the keyword **ensure**, express conditions that the routine (the supplier) guarantees on return, if the precondition was satisfied on entry.

- A class **invariant** must be satisfied by every instance of the class whenever the instance is externally accessible: after creation, and after any call to an exported routine of the class. The invariant appears in a clause introduced by the keyword **invariant**, and represents a general consistency constraint imposed on all routines of the class.

With appropriate assertions, the above *ACCOUNT* class becomes:

```
class ACCOUNT creation
    make
feature
    ... Attributes as before:
    ... balance, minimum_balance, owner

    open ... -- as before;
```

```
    deposit (sum: INTEGER) is
        -- Deposit sum into the account
      require
        sum >= 0
      do
        add (sum)
      ensure
        balance = old balance + sum
      end; -- deposit
    withdraw (sum: INTEGER) is
        -- Withdraw sum from the account
      require
        sum >= 0 ;
        sum <= balance – minimum_balance
      do
        add (–sum)
      ensure
        balance = old balance – sum
      end; -- withdraw
    may_withdraw ... -- as before

feature {NONE}

    add ... -- as before;

    make (initial: INTEGER) is
        -- Initialize account with balance initial.
      require
        initial >= minimum_balance
      do
        balance := initial
      end -- make
invariant
    balance >= minimum_balance
end -- class ACCOUNT
```

The notation **old** *attribute_name* may only be used in a routine postcondition. It denotes the value the attribute had on routine entry.

The class now includes a creation procedure, *make*. With the first version of *ACCOUNT*, clients used instructions such as !! *acc1* to create accounts; but then the default initialization, setting *balance* to zero, violated the invariant. By providing one or more creation procedures, listed in the **creation** clause, a class may provide a way to override the default initializations, possibly (as here) with client-supplied arguments. The effect of

The underscore _ in the integer constant 5_500 separates thousands from the rest of the number. It has no semantic effect. See the definition of construct Integer on page 420.

```
    !! acc1.make (5_500)
```

is then to allocate the object (as with the default creation) and to call procedure *make* on this object, with the given argument. This call is correct since it satisfies the precondition; it will ensure the invariant.

A procedure listed in the **creation** clause, such as *make*, otherwise enjoys the same properties as other routines, especially for calls. Here the creation procedure *make* is secret since it appears in a clause starting with **feature** {*NONE*}; so it would be invalid for a client to include a call of the form

```
acc.make (8_000)
```

WARNING: *not valid with the above form of the class (where 'make' is secret).*

To make such a call valid, it would suffice to move the declaration of *make* to the first **feature** clause of class *ACCOUNT*, which carries no export restriction. In contrast with the above Creation instruction, such a call does not create any new object, but simply resets the balance of a previously created account.

Syntactically, assertions are boolean expressions, with a few extensions such as the **old** notation. The semicolon (see the precondition to *withdraw*) is equivalent to an "and", but permits individual identification of the components.

Assertions play a central part in the Eiffel method for building reliable object-oriented software. They serve to make explicit the assumptions on which programmers rely when they write software elements that they believe are correct. Writing assertions, in particular preconditions and postconditions, amounts to spelling out the terms of the **contract** which governs the relationship between a routine and its callers. The precondition binds the callers; the postcondition binds the routine.

The underlying theory of *Design by Contract* views software construction as based on contracts between clients (callers) and suppliers (routines), relying on mutual obligations and advantages made explicit by the assertions. As will be seen below, this theory also explains much of the meaning of inheritance, and lies at the basis of Eiffel's disciplined exception mechanism.

The Design by Contract theory is discussed in "Object-Oriented Software Construction" and the article "Design by Contract". See references in appendix C.

Assertions are also an indispensable tool for the documentation of reusable software components: as with hardware components, one cannot expect large-scale reuse without a precise documentation of what every component expects (precondition), what it guarantees in return (postcondition) and what general conditions it maintains (invariant).

Documentation tools in a supporting environment, such as a class abstracter, use assertions to produce information for client programmers, describing classes in terms of observable behavior, not implementation.

*The class abstracter (also known as the **short** command) is discussed below.*

It is also possible to evaluate assertions at run time, so as to uncover potential errors ("bugs"). The implementation should provide several levels of assertion monitoring: preconditions only, postconditions etc. When monitoring is on, an assertion which evaluates to true has no further effect on the execution. An assertion which evaluates to false will trigger an exception, as described below; unless the programmer has written an appropriate exception handler, the exception will cause an error message and termination with an appropriate message.

This ability to check assertions provides a powerful testing and debugging mechanism, in particular because the classes of the Basic Libraries, widely used in Eiffel software development, are protected by carefully written assertions.

The Basic Libraries are described in the book "Eiffel: The Libraries". For an overview, see chapter 26 of the present book.

Run-time checking, however, is only one application of assertions, whose role as design and documentation aids, as part of the theory of Design by Contract, exerts a pervasive influence on the Eiffel style of software development.

1.7 Exceptions

Whenever there is a contract, the risk exists that someone will break it. This is where exceptions come in.

On exceptions, see the references mentioned above about assertions, the article "From Structured Programming ...", and chapter 15 of this book.

Exceptions – contract violations – may arise from several causes. One is assertion violations, if assertions are monitored. Another is the occurrence of a signal triggered by the hardware or operating system to indicate an abnormal condition such as arithmetic overflow or lack of memory to allocate a new object.

Unless a routine has made specific provision to handle exceptions, it will **fail** if an exception arises during its execution. Failure of a routine is a third cause of exception: a routine that fails triggers an exception in its caller.

A routine may, however, handle an exception through a **rescue** clause. This optional clause attempts to "patch things up" by bringing the current object to a stable state (one satisfying the class invariant). Then it can terminate in either of two ways:

- The rescue clause may execute a **retry** instruction, which causes the routine to restart its execution from the beginning, attempting again to fulfil its contract, usually through another strategy. This assumes that the instructions of the rescue clause, before the **retry**, have attempted to correct the cause of the exception.

- If the rescue clause does not end with **retry**, then the routine fails: it returns to its caller, immediately signaling an exception. (The caller's rescue clause will be executed according to the same rules.)

The principle is that **a routine must either succeed or fail**: either it fulfils its contract, or it does not; in the latter case it must notify its caller by triggering an exception.

Usually, only a few routines of a system will include explicit rescue clauses. An exception occurring during the execution of a routine with no rescue clause will trigger a default rescue procedure which, by default, does nothing, and so will cause the routine to fail immediately, propagating the exception to the routine's caller. A class may, however, provide a specific rescue procedure overriding this default.

→ The default rescue processing is provided by procedure 'default_rescue' from class ANY, which may be redefined. See 15.5, page 251.

An example of the exception mechanism is a routine *attempt_transmission* which tries to transmit a message over a phone line. The actual transmission is performed by an external, low-level routine *transmit*; once started, however, *transmit* may abruptly fail, triggering an exception, if the line is disconnected. Routine *attempt_transmission* tries the transmission at most 5 times; before returning to its caller, it sets a boolean attribute *successful* to **true** or **false** depending on the outcome. Here is the text of the routine:

```
attempt_transmission (message: STRING) is
        -- Attempt transmission of message,
        -- at most 5 times.
        -- Set successful accordingly.
    local
        failures: INTEGER
    do
```

```
        if failures < 5 then
            transmit (message);
            successful := true
        else
            successful := false
        end
    rescue
        failures := failures + 1;
        retry
    end; -- attempt_transmission
```

Initialization rules ensure that *failures*, a local entity, is set to zero on entry.

This example illustrates the simplicity of the mechanism: the rescue clause never attempts to achieve the routine's original intent; this is the sole responsibility of the body (the **do** clause). The only role of the rescue clause is to clean up the objects involved, and then either to fail or to retry.

This disciplined exception mechanism is essential for the software developers, who need a protection against unexpected events, but cannot be expected to sacrifice safety and simplicity to pay for this protection.

1.8 Genericity

Building software components (classes) as implementations of abstract data types yields systems with a solid architecture but does not in itself suffice to ensure reusability and extendibility. Two key techniques address the problem: genericity (unconstrained or constrained) and inheritance. Let us look first at the basic form of genericity.

To make a class generic is to give it **formal generic parameters** representing arbitrary types, as in these examples from the Kernel and Data Structure Libraries:

```
ARRAY [G]
LIST [G]
LINKED_LIST [G]
```

These classes describe data structures – arrays, lists without commitment to a specific representation, lists in linked representation – containing objects of a certain type. The formal generic parameter *G* represents this type.

Each of these classes describes a type template. To derive a directly usable type, you must provide a type corresponding to *G*, called an **actual generic parameter**; this may be either a basic expanded type (such as *INTEGER*) or a reference type. Here are some possible generic derivations:

```
il: LIST [INTEGER];
aa: ARRAY [ACCOUNT];
aal: LIST [ARRAY [ACCOUNT]]
```

As the last example indicates, an actual generic parameter may itself be generically derived.

Without genericity, it would be impossible to obtain static type checking in a realistic object-oriented language.

A variant of this mechanism, *constrained* genericity, will enable a class to place specific requirements on possible actual generic parameters.

→ *Constrained genericity will be introduced below, after inheritance.*

1.9 Inheritance

Inheritance, the other fundamental generalization mechanism, makes it possible to define a new class by combination and specialization of existing classes rather than from scratch.

→ *The inheritance relation is explored in chapter 6, with important developments in chapters 10 (redeclaration), 11 (repeated inheritance) and 21 (calls, introducing dynamic binding).*

The following simple example, from the Data Structure Library, is typical. *LIST*, as indicated, describes lists in any representation. One possible representation if the lists have a fixed number of elements uses an array. We may define the corresponding class by combination of *LIST* and *ARRAY*, as follows:

```
class FIXED_LIST [G] inherit
    LIST [G];
    ARRAY [G] export ... see below ...
feature
    ... Specific features of fixed-size lists ...
end -- class FIXED_LIST
```

The **inherit**... clause lists all the "parents" of the new class, which is said to be their "heir". (The "ancestors" of a class include the class itself, its parents, grandparents etc.; the reverse term is "descendant".) Declaring *FIXED_LIST* as shown ensures that all the features and properties of lists and arrays are applicable to fixed lists as well. Since the class has more than one parent, this is a case of *multiple* inheritance.

Standard graphical conventions serve to illustrate such inheritance structures:

A simple inheritance structure

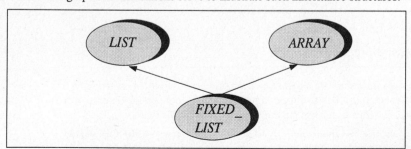

An heir class such as *FIXED_LIST* needs the ability to define its own export policy. By default, inherited features keep their export status (publicly available, secret, available to selected classes only); but this may be changed in the heir. Here, for example, *FIXED_LIST* will export only the exported features of *LIST*, making those of *ARRAY* unavailable directly to *FIXED_LIST*'s clients. The syntax to achieve this is straightforward:

→ *On the relation between exports and inheritance, and the consequences for type checking, see 22.6, page 360.*

```
class FIXED_LIST [G] inherit
    LIST [G];
    ARRAY [G]
        export
            {NONE} all
        end;
... The rest as above ...
```

With the **export**...
*subclause, FIXED_LIST
makes* **all** *of the features
inherited from ARRAY
available to NONE of its
clients. For details on this
subclause, called a*
New_exports *subclause in
the syntax specification, see
7.11, starting on page 98.*

Another example of multiple inheritance comes from a windowing system based on a class *WINDOW*, close to actual classes in the Graphics Library. Windows have **graphical** features: a height, a width, a position, routines to scale windows, move them, and other graphical operations. The system permits windows to be nested, so that a window also has **hierarchical** features: access to subwindows and the parent window, adding a subwindow, deleting a subwindow, attaching to another parent and so on. Rather than writing a complex class that would contain specific implementations for all of these features, it is preferable to inherit all hierarchical features from *TREE* (a class in the Data Structure Library describing trees), and all graphical features from a class *RECTANGLE*.

Inheritance yields remarkable economies of effort – whether for analysis, design, implementation or evolution – and has a profound effect on the entire software development process.

The very power of inheritance demands adequate means to keep it under control. Multiple inheritance, in particular, raises the question of name conflicts between features inherited from different parents; this case will inevitably arise in practice, especially for classes contributed by independent developers. Such a name conflict may be removed through **renaming**, as in

```
class C inherit
    A rename x as x1, y as y1 end,
    B rename x as x2, y as y2 end
feature...
```

Here, if both *A* and *B* have features named *x* and *y*, class *C* would be invalid without the renaming.

→ *On renaming see 6.9,
page 81.*

Renaming also serves to provide more appropriate feature names in descendants. For example, class *WINDOW* may inherit a routine *insert_subtree* from *TREE*. For clients of *WINDOW*, however, such a routine name is no longer adapted. An application using this class for window manipulation needs coherent window terminology, and should not be concerned with the inheritance structure that led to the implementation of the class. So you may wish to rename *insert_subtree* as *add_subwindow* in the inheritance clause of *WINDOW*.

As a further incentive not to misuse the multiple inheritance mechanism, the invariants of all parent classes automatically apply to a newly defined class. So classes may not be combined if their invariants are incompatible.

1.10 Polymorphism and dynamic binding

Inheritance is not just a module combination and enrichment mechanism. It also enables the definition of flexible entities that may become attached to objects of various forms at run time, a property known as polymorphism.

→ *Polymorphism and dynamic binding are discussed in chapters 13 (conformance), 20 (attachment) and 21 (calls).*

This remarkable facility must be reconciled with static typing. The language convention is simple: an assignment of the form $a := b$ is permitted not only if a and b are of the same type, but more generally if a and b are of reference types A and B based on classes A and B such that B is a descendant of A.

This corresponds to the intuitive idea that a value of a more specialized type may be assigned to an entity of a less specialized type – but not the reverse. (As an analogy, consider that if you request vegetables, getting green vegetables is fine, but if you ask for green vegetables, receiving a dish labeled just "vegetables" is not acceptable, as it could include, say, carrots.)

What makes this possibility particularly powerful is the complementary facility: **feature redefinition**. A class may redefine some or all of the features which it inherits from its parents. For an attribute or function, the redefinition may affect the type, replacing the original by a descendant; for a routine it may also affect the implementation, replacing the original's routine body by a new one.

Assume for example a class *POLYGON*, describing polygons, whose features include an array of points representing the vertices and a function *perimeter* which computes a polygon's perimeter by summing the successive distances between adjacent vertices. An heir of *POLYGON* may begin as:

```
class RECTANGLE inherit
    POLYGON redefine perimeter end
feature
    -- Specific features of rectangles, such as:
    side1: REAL; side2: REAL;

    perimeter: REAL is
        -- Rectangle-specific version
    do
        Result := 2 * (side1 + side2)
    end; -- perimeter

... other RECTANGLE features ...
```

Here it is appropriate to redefine *perimeter* for rectangles as there is a simpler and more efficient algorithm. Note the explicit **redefine** subclause (which would come after the **rename** if present).

Other descendants of *POLYGON* may also have their own redefinitions of *perimeter*. The version to use in any call is determined by the run-time form of the target. Consider the following class fragment:

```
p: POLYGON; r: RECTANGLE;

...
!! p ; !! r;
```

> ...
>
> **if** c **then** $p := r$ **end**;
>
> *print* $(p.perimeter)$

The assignment $p := r$ is valid because of the above rule. If condition c is false, p will be attached to an object of type *POLYGON* for the computation of $p.perimeter$, which will thus use the polygon algorithm. In the opposite case, however, p will be attached to a rectangle; then the computation will use the version redefined for *RECTANGLE*. This is known as **dynamic binding**.

Dynamic binding provides a high degree of flexibility. The advantage for clients is the ability to request an operation (such as perimeter computation) without explicitly selecting one of its variants; the choice only occurs at run-time. This is essential in large systems, where many variants may be available; each component must be protected against changes in other components.

This technique is particularly attractive when compared to its closest equivalent in traditional approaches. In Pascal or Ada, you would need records with variant components, and **case** instructions to discriminate between variants. This means every client must know about all possible cases, and that any extension may invalidate a large body of existing software. The Ada facilities for overloading and genericity do not bring any improvement in this respect, since they do not support a programming style in which a client module may issue a request meaning "compute the perimeter of p, using the algorithm appropriate for whatever form p happens to have when the request is executed", as permitted here by inheritance, redefinition, polymorphism and dynamic binding.

These techniques support a development mode in which every module is *open* and incremental. When you want to reuse an existing class but need to adapt it to a new context, you can always define a new descendant of that class (with new features, redefined ones, or both) without any change to the original. This facility is of great importance in software development, an activity which – whether by design or by circumstance – is invariably incremental.

The power of polymorphism and dynamic binding demand adequate controls. First, feature redefinition, as seen above, is explicit. Second, because the language is typed, a compiler can check statically whether a feature application $a.f$ is correct. In contrast, dynamically typed object-oriented languages defer checks until run-time and hope for the best: if an object "sends a message" to another (that is to say, calls one of its routines) one just expects that the corresponding class, or one of its ancestors, will happen to include an appropriate routine; if not, a run-time error will occur. Such errors may not happen during the execution of a type-checked Eiffel system.

In other words, the language reconciles dynamic *binding* with static *typing*. Dynamic binding guarantees that whenever more than one version of a routine is applicable the *right* version (the one most directly adapted to the target object) will be selected. Static typing means that the compiler makes sure there is *at least one* such version.

This policy also yields an important performance benefit: in contrast with the costly run-time searches that may be needed with dynamic typing (since a requested routine may not be defined in the class of the target object but inherited from a possibly remote ancestor), static typing will enable a good implementation to find the appropriate routine in constant-bounded time.

Assertions provide a further mechanism for controlling the power of redefinition. In the absence of specific precautions, redefinition may be dangerous: how can a client be sure that evaluation of *p.perimeter* will not in some cases return, say, the area? Preconditions and postconditions provide the answer by limiting the amount of freedom granted to eventual redefiners. The rule is that any redefined version must satisfy a weaker or equal precondition and ensure a stronger or equal postcondition than in the original. In other words, it must stay within the semantic boundaries set by the original assertions.

→ The rules on redefinition and assertions are discussed in 10.15, page 152.

These rules are part of the Design by Contract theory, where redefinition and dynamic binding introduce subcontracting. *POLYGON*, for example, subcontracts the implementation of *perimeter* to *RECTANGLE* when applied to any entity that is attached at run-time to a rectangle object. An honest subcontractor is bound to honor the contract accepted by the prime contractor. This means that it may not impose stronger requirements on the clients, but may accept more general requests, so that the precondition may be weaker; and that it must achieve at least as much as promised by the prime contractor, but may achieve more, so that the postcondition may be stronger.

1.11 Combining genericity and inheritance

Genericity and inheritance, the two fundamental mechanisms for generalizing classes, may be combined in two fruitful ways.

The first technique yields **polymorphic data structures**. Assume that in the generic class *LIST* [*G*] the insertion procedure *put* has a formal argument of type *G*, representing the element to be inserted. Then with a declaration such as

For a further assessment of genericity vis-à-vis inheritance see "Genericity versus Inheritance" (in "An Eiffel Collection") and "Object-Oriented Software Construction".

```
pl: LIST [POLYGON]
```

the type rules imply that in a call *pl.put* (...) the argument may be not just of type *POLYGON*, but also of type *RECTANGLE* (an heir of *POLYGON*) or any other type conforming to *POLYGON* through inheritance.

→ Conformance is the type compatibility rule; in simple cases, V conforms to T if V is a descendant of T. See chapter 13.

In other words, structures such as *pl* contain objects of different types, hence the name "polymorphic data structure". Such polymorphism is, again, made safe by the type rules: by choosing an actual generic parameter (*POLYGON* in the example) based higher or lower in the inheritance graph, you extend or restrict the permissible types of objects in *pl*. A fully general list would be declared as

```
LIST [ANY]
```

where ANY, a Kernel Library class, is automatically an ancestor of any class that you may write.

→ On class ANY see 6.12, page 85, and chapter 27.

The other mechanism for combining genericity and inheritance is **constrained genericity**. By indicating a class name after a formal generic parameter, as in

> *VECTOR [T –> ADDABLE]*

you express that only descendants of that class (here *ADDABLE*) may be used as the corresponding actual generic parameters. This makes it possible to use the corresponding operations. Here, for example, class *VECTOR* may define a routine **infix** "+" for adding vectors, based on the corresponding routine from *ADDABLE* for adding vector elements. Then by making *VECTOR* itself inherit from *ADDABLE*, you ensure that it satisfies its own generic constraint and enable the definition of types such as *VECTOR [VECTOR [T]]*.

As you have perhaps guessed, unconstrained genericity, as in *LIST [G]*, may be viewed as an abbreviation for genericity constrained by *ANY*, as in *LIST [G –> ANY]*.

1.12 Deferred classes

The inheritance mechanism includes one more major component: deferred routines and classes.

Declaring a routine *r* as deferred in a class *C* expresses that there is no default implementation of *r* in *C*; such implementations will appear in eventual proper descendants of *C*. A class which has one or more deferred routines is itself said to be deferred. A non-deferred routine or class is said to be **effective**.

A "proper" descendant of C is a descendant other than C itself.

For example, a system used by a Department of Motor Vehicles to register vehicles could include a class of the form

> **deferred class** *VEHICLE* **feature**
>   *dues_paid* (*year*: *INTEGER*): *BOOLEAN* **is**
>   ...
>   **end**; -- *dues_paid*
>   *valid_plate* (*year*: *INTEGER*): *BOOLEAN* **is**
>   ...
>   **end**; -- *valid_plate*
>   *register* (*year*: *INTEGER*) **is**
>   -- Register vehicle for *year*
>   **require**
>   *dues_paid* (*year*)
>   **deferred**
>   **ensure**
>   *valid_plate* (*year*)
>   **end**; -- *register*
>   ... Other features ...
>   **end** -- class *VEHICLE*

This example assumes that no single registration algorithm applies to all kinds of vehicle; passenger cars, motorcycles, trucks etc. are all registered differently. But the same precondition and postcondition apply in all cases. The solution is to treat *register* as a deferred routine, making *VEHICLE* a deferred class.

Effective versions of the routine are given in descendants of class *VEHICLE*, such as *CAR* or *TRUCK*. They are similar to redefined versions of a routine; only here there is no effective definition in the original class, just a specification in the form of a deferred routine.

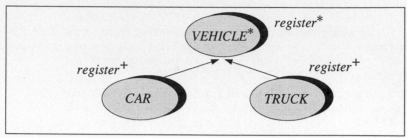

Vehicle hierarchy

*The asterisk * is the graphical marker for deferred features and classes, the plus sign means "redeclared". See chapter 10.*

Deferred classes describe a group of implementations of an abstract data type rather than just a single implementation. A deferred class may not be instantiated: !! *v* is invalid if *v* is an entity declared of type *VEHICLE*. But such an entity may be assigned a reference to an instance of a non-deferred descendant of *VEHICLE*. For example, assuming *CAR* and *TRUCK* provide effective definitions for all deferred routines of *VEHICLE*, the following will be valid:

> *v*: *VEHICLE*; *c*: *CAR*; *t*: *TRUCK*;
>
> ...
>
> !! *c* ...; !! *t* ...;
>
> ...
>
> **if** "Some test" **then** *v* := *c* **else** *v* := *t* **end**;
> *v.register* (*1988*)

This example fully exploits polymorphism: depending on the outcome of "Some test", *v* will be treated as a car or a truck, and the appropriate registration algorithm will be applied. Also, "Some test" may depend on some event whose outcome is impossible to predict until run-time, for example the user clicking with the mouse to select one among several vehicle icons displayed on the screen.

Deferred classes are particularly useful at the **design** stage. The first version of a module may be a deferred class, which will later be refined into one or more effective (non-deferred) classes. Particularly important for this application is the possibility to associate a precondition and a postcondition to a routine even though it is a deferred routine (as with *register* above), and an invariant to a class even though it is a deferred class. This enables the designer to attach precise semantics to a module at the design stage, long before making any implementation choices.

These possibilities make Eiffel an attractive alternative to PDLs (Program Design Languages) and other traditional design methods such as Structured Design. The combination of deferred classes to capture partially understood concepts, assertions to express what is known about their semantics, and the language's other structuring facilities (information hiding, inheritance, genericity) to obtain clear, convincing architectures, yields a higher-level design method. A further benefit, of course, is that the notation is also a programming language, making the development cycle smoother by reducing the gap between design and implementation.

The role of Eiffel in this cycle is not limited to design and implementation; you may also apply the language to the earliest stage of development, **analysis**. The deferred classes written at this step will describe not software objects, but objects from the external reality being modeled – documents, airplanes, investments. Here again the presence of assertions to express constraints and expectations, and the language's other structuring facilities, provide an attractive alternative to older methods and notations.

1.13 Implementation and environment aspects

This book discusses the Eiffel language, not a particular implementation. It should indeed be possible to talk about a programming language without referring to its implementations; this is especially true for Eiffel which doubles as an analysis and design language.

One should not, however, underestimate the importance of implementation; after all, when it comes to building software, developers will need not just a good language but also an equally good implementation.

Although the language definition does not prescribe any specific mode of implementation, it is useful to list the major components that seem appropriate in any environment meant to support the development of software in Eiffel.

This list of tools is directly inspired from what exists in ISE's current Eiffel environment.

First, a language processing tool must be available to execute Eiffel systems; this may be an interpreter (which directly executes Eiffel texts or an intermediate form) or a compiler (which translates the texts into another language for which an execution mechanism exists, or directly into machine code). Interpreters shorten the development-to-execution cycle, but compilers make it possible to generate efficient code, and may also perform a number of important tasks in advance of any execution.

If the implementation is based on a compiler, two essential requirements are that the compiler be **incremental** and **automatic**:

ISE's Version 3 implementation ensures quick reexecution after a change while retaining all the benefits of compilation.

- Incrementality means that it must be possible to recompile only those parts of a system that have actually been affected by a change, rather than the entire system.

- The second condition means that programmers should **not** be responsible for the analysis of what needs to be recompiled after a change. The compiler should take care of exploring class interconnection structures and deciding which classes, or class fragments, it must recompile.

Tools such as "Make", relying on programmer-supplied descriptions of module dependencies, are remnants of older software technology; they are not needed for Eiffel.

Beyond a compiler or interpreter, many tools are potentially useful in an Eiffel environment. Here are a few.

- A **run-time system** supports execution of Eiffel systems, in particular efficient memory allocation for creation operations.

- An important component of the run-time system should be a **garbage collector**, which reclaims the storage associated with unused objects, relieving programmers from this tedious and error-prone task. A good garbage collector is *incremental*; in other words, it wakes up every once in a while and goes back to sleep after a brief and partial outburst of collection activity, avoiding any interruption of the software's execution that would be detectable at the human level.

- A **cross-development system** is a variant of the compiler that will generate code in a portable assembly language such as C, supporting development in Eiffel on one platform and execution on another which may not have an Eiffel compiler of its own. Care must be taken to make sure that the generated code is self-contained, including a copy of the run-time system with, if appropriate, the garbage collector.

- A **class abstracter** produces an interface version of a class, providing client programmers with a specification of the exported features.

- A **class flattener** produces an inheritance-free version of a class, with all inherited features brought into the class itself, taking care of redefinition, renaming and invariant accumulation. This is useful for delivering classes independently of their inheritance context, and, in connection with the abstracter, for documentation.

*→ An abstracter yields the **short** form of a class, described in 7.14, page 103. A flattener, combined with an abstracter, yields the **flat-short** form, described in 7.15, page 106.*

- An **interactive browser** allows users to explore the available classes and their features.

- An **interactive debugger** makes it possible to follow and steer the execution of a system step-by-step. It should be compatible with the Eiffel approach by giving users access to the objects and their features. In general, Eiffel software is not debugged in the same way as traditional software; assertions play a central part in the effort.

- **Testing tools**, which may be in part the same as debugging tools, are also needed. Here too the proper use of assertions suggests a radical departure from older, less systematic techniques.

- **Notification tools**, which may be connected with both the compiler and the browser, make it possible to ascertain in advance the effect of contemplated changes.

Of course, many general-purpose software engineering tools, such as structural editors, configuration managers or project management tools may apply directly to the Eiffel context.

2

Syntax, validity and semantics

2.1 Overview

To dive into the details of Eiffel, you will need a few conventions and basic rules. In particular, you will need to understand the role of the three levels used for describing constructs: syntax (structure), validity (constraints) and semantics (effect).

For syntax, covering the textual form of Eiffel software, this chapter will introduce the notation used to present constructs in the rest of this book. It then explains the need for validity constraints, covering structural well-formedness conditions. Finally, it offers a brief view of correctness, covering the consistency of an implementation with its specification.

Before proceeding, you should have read the discussion entitled *About the language description* after the Preface.

2.2 Syntax, components, specimens and constructs

Eiffel's syntax is the set of rules describing the structure of class texts. It covers neither limitations on valid texts (described by validity constraints) nor the execution-time meaning or effect of these texts (described by semantic rules).

→ *See below 2.6 and 2.7, starting on page 26, about validity constraints, and 2.8, starting on page 28, about semantics.*

DEFINITION:
Component

Any class text, or syntactically meaningful part of that text, such as an instruction, an expression or an identifier, is called a **component**.

DEFINITION:
Construct,
Specimen

The structure of components of any one of these categories is described by a **construct**. A component conforming to a certain construct is called a **specimen** of that construct. For example, the construct Class describes the structure of class texts; any particular class text, built according to the rules given in this book, is a specimen of this construct.

Other important examples of constructs are:

Instruction
Expression
Call
Identifier

→ *See Appendix I for the alphabetical list of all Eiffel constructs.*

The specimens of these constructs are (respectively) instructions, expressions, feature calls and identifiers.

As illustrated by these examples, all constructs have names beginning with a capital letter and written in the default (roman) font. Each appears in the index with a reference to the page of its syntactical definition.

An important convention will simplify the discussions: the phrase "an X", where X is the name of a construct, serves as a shorthand for "a specimen of construct X". For example, "a Class" means "a specimen of construct Class", in other words a text built according to the syntactical specification of construct Class.

2.3 Terminals, non-terminals and tokens

Every construct is either a "terminal" or a "non-terminal":

DEFINITION:
Terminal
- Specimens of a terminal construct have no further syntactical structure. Examples include reserved words (such as **class**, *Result* etc.), constants such as integers, and identifiers used to denote classes, features and entities.

Non-terminal
- In contrast, the specimens of a non-terminal construct are defined in terms of other constructs. For example, a Class consists of an Indexing clause, a Class_header, and other construct specimens (some optional, some required).

Token
The specimens of terminal constructs are called **tokens** or **lexical components**. They form the basic vocabulary out of which you may build more complex texts – specimens of non-terminals.

→ *Chapter 25, which describes the lexical structure, explains the various forms of tokens.*

2.4 Productions

Since tokens have no syntactically identifiable subparts, their definition does not require a specific formalism. An example definition (given with more details in a later chapter) is: "An Integer is a sequence of one or more decimal digits, with possible intervening underscore (_) characters".

→ *See 25.12, page 420, about* Integer.

DEFINITION:
Production
In contrast, to understand a non-terminal, you need a formal description of the structure of its specimens. Such a description is called the **production** for the construct.

A production has the form

Construct ≜ right-hand-side

Every non-terminal construct appears on the left-hand side of exactly one such production. The symbol $\triangleq$ means "is defined as".

The right-hand-side of the production describes the structure of specimens of the left-hand-side construct. Three forms of right-hand-side are available:

- Aggregate, describing a construct made of a fixed number of parts (some of which may be optional) to be concatenated in a given order.

- Choice, describing a construct having a number of given variants.

- Repetition, describing a construct made of a variable number of parts, which are all specimens of a given construct.

An aggregate right-hand-side is a non-empty sequence of constructs, some of which may be in square brackets to indicate optional parts, as in the following production:

$\rightarrow$ *See page 235*

> Conditional $\triangleq$ **if** Then_part_list [Else_part] **end**

This indicates that a Conditional is made of the keyword **if**, followed by a Then_part_list, followed by zero or one Else_part, followed by the keyword **end**. More generally, an aggregate production for a construct A with a right-hand side of the form $a_1\ a_2\ ...\ a_n$ specifies that every specimen of A consists of one specimen of each of the a_i (zero or one if a_i is in square brackets, as [Else_part] in the example), in the order given.

As noted above, "a Conditional" is here a shorthand for "A specimen of the Conditional construct", and so on.

A choice right-hand side is a non-empty sequence of constructs separated by vertical bars, as in the following production:

$\rightarrow$ *See page 197*

> Type $\triangleq$ Class_type | Class_type_expanded |
> Formal_generic_name |
> Anchored | Bit_type

This indicates that a Type is a Class_type, or a Class_type_expanded, or an Anchored type, or a Formal_generic_name, or a Bit_type. More generally, a choice production for a construct C with a right-hand side of the form $c_1\ |\ c_2\ |\ ...\ |\ c_n$ specifies that a specimen of C is a specimen of any one of the c_i.

Finally, a repetition right-hand side is of one of the two forms

> {Construct § ...}
> {Construct § ...}$^+$

where §, the separator, is some construct – usually, but not necessarily, terminal. An example of a repetition production of the second form is

$\rightarrow$ *See page 235*

> Then_part_list $\triangleq$ {Then_part **elseif** ...}$^+$

This indicates that a specimen of Then_part_list (appearing as component of a Conditional instruction) the "then part list" of a conditional instruction is made of one or more Then_part clauses, separated, if more than one, by the keyword **elseif**. In other words, possible example specimens of Then_part_list are of one of the forms

> *t1*
> *t1* **elseif** *t2*
> *t1* **elseif** *t2* **elseif** *t3*

and so on, where *t1, t2, t3...* are specimens of Then_part. If no + sign had been present, the empty text would also have been an acceptable specimen of Then_part_list.

More generally, a repetition production for a construct R with a right-hand side involving construct B and separator § states that a specimen of R consists of zero or more specimens of B, separated, if more than one, by the separator §. In the first form, without a +, specimens of R may be empty; in the second form, with a +, they must include at least one B, as in the Then_part_list example.

2.5 Representing terminals

As shown by the above examples, the right-hand-sides of productions will usually refer to terminals. This raises a problem for reserved words, which might be mistaken for construct names, and special symbols, some of which (for example {, [and +) are also used as symbols of the syntax notation. The following conventions remove any ambiguity:

- Construct names, as already noted, appear in roman, with only their first letter in upper case, as in Class.
- Reserved words appear in boldface (for keywords such as **class**) or italics (for predefined names such as *Result*) and stand for themselves. This avoids any ambiguity for **if** and **end** in the above example production for Conditional.
- The double quote, one of the special symbols of the language, appears as '"' (a double quote character enclosed between two single quote characters).
- All other special symbols appear enclosed in double quotes, in roman: the comma as ",", the assignment symbol as ":=", the single quote as "'" etc.

As an example, here is the syntactic definition of construct Compound, given by a repetition production. A Compound is formed of zero or more Instruction, separated by semicolons:

> Compound   ≜   {Instruction ";" ...}

2.6 Validity

The productions and other elements labeled SYNTAX, as described so far, specify the structure of constructs. In many cases, however, adherence to the structural requirements does not suffice to guarantee that a specimen of a construct will be meaningful.

For example, the following Assignment is built according to the syntactical specification of the corresponding construct:

→ *The specification of* Assignment *is on page 311.*

$$x := f.func\ (a + b, x)$$

→ *The right-hand side in this example is a specimen of qualified* Call, *whose syntax appears on page 342.*

But this does not mean that the Assignment will be acceptable in every possible context. It must also satisfy certain rules regarding the types of the components involved, the number of arguments passed to a routine etc.

DEFINITION:
Validity
constraint

Such supplementary requirements on the syntactically well-formed specimens of a construct are called **validity constraints** on the construct. Paragraphs introducing them are labeled by the VALIDITY road sign.

Valid

A specimen which follows the syntactic rules and satisfies the constraints will be accepted by the language processing tools of any Eiffel environment and is said to be **valid**.

As an illustration, here is the validity constraint on assignments, which the above example must satisfy to be valid:

→ *See a full discussion of this constraint on page 311.*

VBAR

> **Assignment rule**
>
> An Assignment is valid if and only if its source expression conforms to its target entity.

("The "target entity" is the left-hand side, here *x*; the "source expression" is the right-hand side.)

Every validity constraint has a four-character code, here VBAR. You do not need to pay any attention to these codes as you are first reading this book. But implementors of language processing tools, especially compilers, should include the appropriate code in any error message that reports a constraint violation. Then, if you get one of these error messages during system development, you will be able to look up the code in the index of this book, where they all appear under the heading "validity codes", directing you to the detailed explanation of the language rule that you may have violated. (If you really want to know what the codes mean: the first letter is always V, the second one identifies the chapter, and the last two suggest the constraint's role, for example AR for Assignment Rule.)

Many constraints, such as the Feature Declaration rule on page 69 (code VFFD), list several conditions, each identified with a number. Error messages in this case should include not just the constraint code but also the number of the particular condition which was violated, for example VFFD (2).

2.7 Interpreting the constraints

A few of the constraints in this book are stated as necessary conditions, expressing that any specimen of a certain construct *must* satisfy a certain property, or *may not* be of a certain form.

Such constraints, however, are the rare exception. In all other cases, a constraint is given as a necessary and sufficient condition, stating that specimens of a certain construct will be valid *if and only if* a specified set of requirements are met. As discussed in the introduction to this book, such a form is much preferable, since it allows you not just to detect that certain specific components are not valid, but also to ascertain without doubt whether an arbitrary component *is* valid.

See the discussion on page xvi.

To understand and apply the validity constraints, you will need to keep in mind an important convention. In the above example of assignment instruction, you may have noted that the Assignment rule, VBAR, is blatantly insufficient to ensure the validity of the given assignment: what about the validity of the right-hand side, *f.func* (*a* + *b, c*), which must satisfy all the validity constraints on function calls (*func* a properly defined and exported function applicable to objects of *f*'s type, with number and type of formal arguments matching the actual arguments given)?

Spelling out all such conditions on the components of a construct would lead to needlessly complex and repetitive validity constraints. Instead, all validity discussions rely on a general rule:

VBGV

General Validity rule

Every validity constraint relative to a construct is considered to include an implicit supplementary condition stating that every component of the construct satisfies every validity constraint applicable to the component.

In the Assignment case, this means that constraint VBAR is considered to be automatically extended with the condition

"... and *x* satisfies all validity constraints on specimens of Writable, and *y* satisfies all validity constraints on specimens of Expression"

→ *The constraint on a* Writable *entity is the Entity rule, page 275.*

so that, for the example Assignment above, the Assignment rule implicitly requires that *f.func* (*a* + *b, c*) be a valid function call.

2.8 Semantics

A construct specimen which is syntactically legal and valid has an associated semantics, specifying its run-time effect in a system in which the specimen appears. That semantics may include executing certain actions, producing a value, or both. It is defined by the SEMANTICS paragraphs. For specimens made of further components, the specification usually refers recursively to the components' own semantics.

It is important to remember that the SEMANTICS paragraphs only apply to valid specimens. In many cases, the semantic rules would not even make sense otherwise. Clearly, attempting to describe the effect of an invalid component would be useless.

Most construct specifications cover syntax, validity and semantics in this order. In a few cases, however, the semantics comes before the validity; such departures from the normal sequence occur when the best way to understand the reason for a constraint is to look first at the construct's semantics in valid cases, and then find out what is required for that semantics to make sense. The change or order in such cases is, of course, only a pedagogical device; as everywhere else, the semantic specification is meaningless for invalid components.

→ *An example where the semantics appear before the validity is the presentation of the* Call *construct; chapter 21 covers syntax and semantics, and chapter 22 (type checking) covers validity.*

2.9 Correctness

Validity is only a structural property; valid Eiffel software is not guaranteed to perform according to any expected behavior. In fact, execution of valid software may lead to non-termination, or to exceptions and eventual failure.

For a valid component, then, we need a more advanced criterion: its ability to operate properly at run-time. This is called *correctness* and is a more elusive aim than validity, since it involves semantic properties.

Ascertaining the correctness of an executable software component, requires two elements of information: what the component does (its implementation), but also what it is expected to do (its specification). Eiffel supports the inclusion of both aspects: along with the executable elements of a class (the bodies of its routines, made of executable instructions), you may provide **assertions**, which describe the specification of the class. Then a class will be said to be correct if its features are guaranteed to perform according to its assertions.

→ "Failure" is a technical term defined precisely in the context of exceptions. See chapter 15.

→ Assertions, specifications and correctness are studied in chapter 9. As discussed there, it is usually not possible to check correctness by mere mechanical analysis of software texts.

2.10 The context of executing systems

As explained in the next chapter, the executable units of Eiffel software are called "systems". The following terminology will serve to discuss the context of system execution:

- *Run time* is the period during which a system is executed.
- The *machine* is the combination of hardware (one or more computers) and operating system which makes it possible to execute systems.
- The machine type, that is to say a certain kind of computer and a certain operating system, is called a *platform*.
- To make the text of an Eiffel system executable by a machine, you will need software tools such as compilers and interpreters, for which this book will use the term *language processing tool*, general enough to cover various implementation techniques.

2.11 Requirements on language processing tools

The definition of Eiffel syntax, validity and semantics contained in this book is also a specification of certain aspects of the corresponding language processing tools.

Not all aspects apply to all language processing tools. For example certain tools may perform tasks involving only syntactical aspects; examples are a syntax checker, an Eiffel-specific editor, or a class abstracter (producing the short form of a class). Other tools, such as a validity checker, may handle validity aspects only. Yet other tools, such as a compiler or an interpreter, will handle semantics as well.

→ On the short form, see 7.14, page 103. The **short** *command, mentioned there, is an example of class abstracter.*

A language processing tool that processes software components at a certain level (syntax, validity, semantics) is not required to perform the tasks associated with that level on components which do not not satisfy the requirements at the previous levels. In other words, a validity tool may assume that the input is syntactically legal, and a semantic tool may assume that the input is both syntactically legal and valid. This book does not specify what the tools should do for input texts which do not satisfy these properties: as was already noted above, validity rules always assume syntactically legal texts, and semantic specifications always assume valid texts.

In almost all cases, authors of tools should follow a stricter guideline and make sure that their tools **reject** any input that does not satisfy the rules applying to the earlier levels. Such rejection should include a clear error message. For syntax, the message should identify the production which is not properly observed; for validity it should give the code of the violated validity constraint (and the clause number for constraints divided into clauses).

Two special considerations may justify occasional departures from this general obligation of rejection:

1 • A semantic tool may be able to process valid parts of a text, even if other parts are invalid. For example, a compiler may generate code for some valid classes in a system, rejecting classes which are not valid.

2 • A tool author may have a particular reason for providing a tool or tool option which accepts input violating a specific validity constraint. A possible application would be for a prototyping mode which attempts to execute incomplete systems, or skips certain checks. Such tool variants are outside of the semantics of Eiffel proper and should be clearly labeled as such, reminding developers that acceptance of an input text provides no guarantee that the text satisfies the full language rules.

One final note, intended for implementors of Eiffel, and regarding what they might *not* find here. Although this book goes to great lengths to include every relevant validity and semantic property, it may of course have left an occasional one out. Such an oversight might be a case of *incompleteness* (a missing validity constraint or semantic specification) or *inconsistency* (ambiguous or contradictory answers).

If you run into such a case while trying to produce language processing tools, you should send a precise report to the Language Committee of the NICE consortium, which is in charge of controlling language evolution. (I will appreciate receiving a copy.) If, to proceed with your work, you need an immediate solution, you should choose the one that appears to be the most conservative (that is to say, involves the least amount of invention), the most in line with the rest of the language specification, and the most compatible with the spirit of Eiffel.

Part B

The structure

3

The architecture of Eiffel software

3.1 Overview

The constituents of Eiffel software are called *classes*. By extracting classes from a given *universe*, you may assemble them into executable *systems*. To keep your classes and your development organized, it is convenient to group classes into *clusters*.

These four concepts provide the basis for structuring Eiffel software:

- A class is a modular unit.
- A system results from the assembly of one or more classes to produce an executable unit.
- A cluster is a set of related classes.
- A universe is a set of clusters, out of which developers will pick classes to build systems.

Of these, only "class", describing the basic building blocks, corresponds directly to a construct of the language. To build systems out of classes, you will use not a language mechanism, but tools of the supporting environment. As to clusters and universes, they are not language constructs but mechanisms for grouping and storing classes using the facilities provided by the underlying operating system, such as files and directories.

The remaining chapters of this book concentrate almost exclusively on classes, which are the most important focus of Eiffel development. This is because in the Eiffel approach software construction is viewed as an industrial production activity: combining components, not writing one-of-a-kind applications.

This chapter introduces the overall structure of Eiffel software by discussing in turn the notions of class, system, cluster and universe.

3.2 Classes

Classes, defined above as the modular units of software decomposition, also have another role: they serve as a basis for the **types** of Eiffel.

The book "Object-Oriented Software Construction" discusses the notion of class in detail.

This dual view is essential to understanding the notion of class and, more generally, the principles of object-oriented software construction:

- As a decomposition unit, a class is a module, that is to say a group of related **services** packaged together under a single name.

- As a type, a class is the description of similar run-time data elements, or *objects*, called the **direct instances** of the class.

→ *The precise nature of objects is explained in chapter 17.*

Although these two roles may appear quite different at first, it is in fact natural to support them through a single concept – the class – on the basis of an important observation (which is the starting point for the theory of *Abstract Data Types*): a good method to characterize a set of similar objects without resorting to a description of their concrete implementation is to list the operations applicable to those objects. But then if the objects are all direct instances of the same class, we can build the class in such a way that the services it offers as a module are precisely the operations available on the objects.

This identification of services on modules to operations on direct instances is what makes it possible to merge the module and type views into the single concept of class. The **features** of a class are its services-operations.

For example, a document processing system could have classes such as *DOCUMENT*, *PARAGRAPH*, *FONT*, *TEXT_DISPLAY*. These are the modular units of the system; their texts can be processed by an Eiffel language processing tool, such as a compiler. They also describe possible run-time objects: documents, paragraphs, fonts, displayable views of text. Such objects may be created and modified by systems that include the given classes.

Each of theses classes will contain features; for example, *PARAGRAPH* may include features *indent*, describing an operation that indents a paragraph, *number_of_lines*, describing an operation used to determine the number of lines of a paragraph, and others.

To create a direct instance of a class, you may use a **creation instruction**; a typical form is

→ *Creation instructions are studied in chapter 18.*

> !! *x.cp* (...)

where *x* is the name of the entity which will denote the newly created object, and *cp* is one of the features of the class, which must have been designated as a **creation procedure**. For example you might create a direct instance of class *DOCUMENT* through the creation instruction

> !! *new_text.make* (*"Isabelle-Muriel", 100*)

assuming *DOCUMENT* has a creation procedure *make* with two arguments: a string representing the author's name, and an integer indicating the expected number of pages.

3.3 Class names and class texts

Every class has a name, such as *DOCUMENT* or *PARAGRAPH*, and a class text which describes the features of the class and its other properties.

→ *Chapter 4 explains how a class text is structured.*

For class names, as for all uses of identifiers, letter case is not significant: identifiers such as *DOCUMENT*, *document* and even *dOcUmEnT* have the same semantics when viewed as class names.

DEFINITION:
Upper Name

The standard recommended style in Eiffel texts is to write all class names using exclusively the **upper name** of the class, that is to say the name all in upper case (such as *DOCUMENT*).

→ *Style guidelines are the topic of appendix A.*

Language processing tools which need a class name outside of an Eiffel text may use a different convention. In ISE's Eiffel environment, for example, the compilation commands which require class names as arguments accept the lower name because it is more convenient for users when they type in the commands. In their output, however, the tools always use the recommended upper-case standard.

DEFINITION:
Class Name

The rest of this book uses the term "class name" to denote the upper name of a class. In particular, two classes are said to have the same class name if they have the same case-independent names, even if the names are written with different case conventions in the class texts.

3.4 Systems

By themselves, classes are only building blocks. To obtain an executable software element, you must assemble a set of one or more classes into a **system** and designate one of them as the "root".

The precise definitions are the following.

DEFINITION:
System,
Root

A **system** is a set of classes, one of which has been designated as the **root** of the system, such that all the classes on which the root depends belong to the system.

Dependency

Here a class *C* is said to **depend** on a class *A* if one of the following holds:

- *C* is an heir of *A*.
- *C* is a client of *A*.
- Recursively, there is a class *B* such that *C* depends on *B* and *B* depends on *A*.

In other words, *C* depends on *A* if it is connected to *A* directly or indirectly through some combination of the basic relations between classes – inheritance and client – studied in later chapters.

Chapter 6 explores the inheritance relation and chapter 7 the client relation, with a general definition on page 90.

A system, it was mentioned above, is executable. To execute (or "run") a system on a machine means to get the machine to apply a creation instruction to the system's root class.

If a routine is a creation procedure of a class used as root of a system, its execution will usually create other objects and call other features on these objects. In other words, the execution of any system is a chain of explosions – creations and calls –, each one firing off the next, and the creation procedure is the spark which detonates the first step.

See "Dynamite Binding and Other Explosive Developments" in Proceedings of BOOM! (Biennial of Object-Oriented Munitions), Monte-Carlo, 1991, pp. 1231-1456.

Any language processing tool used to assemble and execute systems must enable you to perform the following tasks:

1 • Selecting a root class.

2 • If the root class has two or more creation procedures, selecting one of them for the system's execution.

3 • If the creation procedure has an argument, enabling a user of your system to pass the corresponding values before an execution.

For tasks 1 and 2, the conventions fall beyond the scope of the Eiffel language, and depend on language processing tools. A standardized set of conventions is recommended: Lace (the Language for Assembling Classes in Eiffel), an Eiffel-like notation for specifying how to build and process a system. You will find a glimpse of Lace later in this chapter and a detailed description in an appendix.

→ See 3.8 below, page 40, for a look at Lace basics, and appendix D for a full description.

For task 3, two restrictions on root classes, part of the Root Class rule given below, will help. The first restriction states that any creation procedure of a class used as root for a system must have either no argument, or a single argument of type *ARRAY [STRING]*, describing an array of strings. If there is such an argument, it is the implementation's responsibility to initialize the array, starting at index 1, from a sequence of values provided by a user for a particular execution. The implementation will also define how users should enter these values (for example as command-line arguments, or by electronic form-filling). It is the creation procedure's responsibility to apply the appropriate processing to the values that it receives in string form from the environment. (Classes from the Lexical Library provide simple mechanisms for decoding string representations of such values as integer and real numbers.)

→ Classes ARRAY and STRING, describing arrays and character strings, are covered in chapter 28. On the Lexical Library see "Eiffel: The Libraries"; the reference is in appendix C.

The second restriction on using a class as root is that the class may not be generic. A generic class is a class parameterized by types; for example, the Data Structure Library class describing binary trees appears as *BINARY_TREE [G]* where *G*, the formal generic parameter, stands for the type of the information stored in a tree's nodes. To use such a class, you must provide a type, known as the actual generic parameter, for *G*. But this would not be appropriate for a root class, since the system's end users have no way of providing the necessary actual generic parameter at execution time.

→ On genericity, see the discussion of types in chapter 12, especially 12.7, page 200, and subsequent sections.

The constraint on root classes follows from these observations:

Root Class rule

A class *C* may be used as root of a system if and only if it satisfies the following two conditions:

1 • *C* is not generic.

2 • Any creation procedure of *C* has either no formal argument, or a single formal argument of type *ARRAY [STRING]*.

3.5 Clusters

As the number of classes in your systems grows, you will need to arrange these classes into groups, called clusters.

The figure below illustrates a typical system structure as a set of layers, each representing a cluster. Every cluster except *KERNEL* relies on others through pillars, representing the dependency relations, client and inheritance, between the clusters' classes. The lower clusters, which normally should be built first, provide the basic capabilities; the higher clusters are more specialized, including *APPLICATION* which is assumed to cover the application-specific facilities of the system. In practice, of course, a system may include several application clusters.

The analogy with a physical construction works only to a point, and you should probably not try to build a house with the architecture shown.

A possible cluster structure

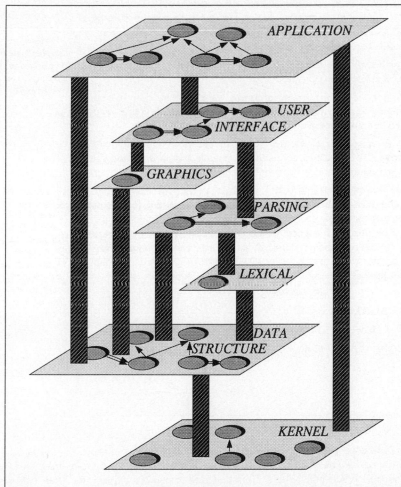

Here some of the clusters are taken from the Basic Libraries.

In each cluster, some classes are shown, with possible inheritance (single arrow) and client (double arrow) connections.

The classes of a cluster must satisfy a simple constraint:

> No two classes in a given cluster may have the same class name.

VSCN

Except for this restriction, there is no absolute rule governing the grouping of classes into clusters. It is usually wise to observe the following informal criteria:

- The classes in a cluster should be conceptually related.

- In most cases, the number of classes in a cluster should not exceed 20, although bigger clusters may be justified in some circumstances if there is a strong relationship between the classes.

- Cycles in the "client" relation should, in general, only involve classes which all belong to the same cluster. In other words, it is generally preferable to avoid cases in which *A* is a client of *B* and *B* a client of *A* unless *A* and *B* are in the same cluster.

- For every cluster, there should be at least one person who understands the cluster in its entirety.

→ *"Client" is a relation between classes. It is studied in chapter 7. Cycles in the relation are explicitly permitted, as explained in 7.4; see in particular the second figure on page 92.*

Clusters correspond to the major divisions of a system. For example, a compiling system may include a lexical cluster, a parsing cluster, a semantic analysis cluster, an optimization cluster, a generation cluster.

In the case of reusable classes, the notion of cluster is close to that of a library; the Basic Eiffel Libraries, for example, include a Data Structure Cluster, a Graphics cluster and so on.

Do not look, however, for a "cluster" construct in the Eiffel language. The highest-level construct is the class; clusters, although essential for organizing Eiffel software and managing its development, do not require specific language support. This is because such support would in most cases be redundant with the facilities provided by operating systems. If, as may be expected, classes are kept in files, then clusters will use the operating system mechanisms available to support the grouping of related files, such as:

Tools, in contrast with the language, should support the notion of cluster. See "Eiffel: The Environment". In particular, the Lace language, a suggested notation for tools which assemble Eiffel systems, supports the notion of cluster. See 3.8 below.

- "Directories" (Unix, VMS, MS-DOS).

- "Folders" (MacOS).

- "Partitioned Data Sets" (MVS).

Similar grouping capabilities are available in other operating systems.

3.6 Universes

DEFINITION:
Universe

A universe is a set of clusters.

Universes serve two related purposes:

- In building systems, you may need to use classes from different clusters – some developed by you, others by your group, yet others obtained from outside sources. When you write a class that refers to other classes, the language processing tools need to know where to look for those classes. The universe defines the search space. It is often convenient to define a universe by giving a list of directories and a convention stating which files in these directories contain class texts (for example, all files whose name

← *"Language processing tools" are tools of the supporting environment, such as compilers and interpreters. See 2.10, page 29.*

ends with .e); this enables the language processing tools to construct the
universe by searching all the appropriate files in the directories given.

→ *The Lace language, discussed in appendix D and previewed in 3.8 below, makes it possible to define a universe through a list of directories.*

- A class will be able to refer to other classes through their class names. But
a class name is ambiguous; it is not unlikely, for example, that in a given
installation many users will have developed at least one class called *TEST*.
The universe establishes the connection between class names and class texts
by resolving any such ambiguity.

The second observation raises the problem of multiple classes with the same
name. Let us take a closer look.

3.7 Class name conflicts

In most cases, the classes of a system should all have different names. But as
your systems grow bigger, and you combine classes from various sources, you
may run into class name clashes.

Because this issue only arises for advanced uses of Eiffel, and involves the
supporting development environment rather than the language, you may wish on
first reading to skip the rest of this chapter, if you are content enough with the
gist of the answer – that a full-fledged environment should provide a **renaming**
mechanism, enabling a class to be known to others, within a system, under a
name different from its actual class name. All you will miss is the details of this
mechanism.

Assuming you are not taking the shortcut, it is useful to ask first whether there
is really any need for a special mechanism. After all, we could try to impose a
unique class name rule, requiring that every universe contain at most one class
of any given name. This would guarantee that whenever you write a declaration
such as

*In mathematical terms, the unique class name rule would mean that every universe must define a **function** from class names to class texts.*

> *some_entity*: *TEST*

a language processing tool would be able to search the universe for the
appropriate class of name *TEST* – and find at most one such class.

In its strictest form, the unique class name rule is not realistic: when using
different clusters from various sources, you may expect that some class names
will appear in more than one cluster.

A less restrictive form of the rule would tolerate name clashes, with a
convention for disambiguating them. We might rely, for example, on the order
in which developers list the clusters to specify a universe, and select the class
from the first cluster that has one with the requested name. For example, if you
list clusters *a* and *b* in this order, and both contain a class called *TEST*, then the
name *TEST* will denote the class from *a*.

Although such a convention makes things easier, it fails to provide a full
answer. In the Eiffel method, based on the reuse of classes contributed by many
different sources, you may expect to encounter cases where one of your systems
will need to use two different classes from clusters contributed by different
authors, who happen to have chosen the same class names. In this case no
method for "disambiguating" the name clash is satisfactory, since you actually
want to use both classes in the same system.

Here is a typical example. You are writing a system for processing election results. Your design uses the following two clusters:

- Cluster *geography* handles information on political districts. One of its classes is *STATE*, denoting a country's administrative units (such as California or Ukraine).
- Cluster *lexical* offers mechanisms to perform analysis of input data. It contains a class *STATE* describing the states of the lexical analyzer's finite automaton.

Here, the name was a natural choice in each cluster's original context. But you cannot select one of the *STATE* classes over the other: your system actually needs both classes; even if your own classes do not directly refer to either of these classes, they will refer to classes of *lexical*, which need one version of *STATE*, and to classes of *geography*, which need the other.

In other words you cannot just get away by changing class names in *your* system: you would need to update class texts in at least one of the other clusters. This is a dangerous path to follow, especially if you have acquired the *lexical* and *geography* clusters from external sources. Adapting your software to remove a name clash is one thing; making extensive changes to externally procured software would be quite another. Should you be even willing to contemplate this possibility, the sheer prospect of having to start again whenever you receive a new release of *lexical* or *geography* should suffice to make you think again.

These observations indicate that, even in a project applying a good naming discipline, the practice of Eiffel software development may lead to systems that include two or more classes with the same name.

These observations do not affect the constraint, given above, that **within a given cluster** no two classes may have the same name: clusters should be under the control of one person, or a small group, and should not create any class name conflicts. But a cluster may need to refer to identically named classes from two or more other clusters.

← *See constraint VSCN, page 38.*

To provide a solution to this issue, it is necessary to know how clusters and classes are described and maintained on a certain computing platform (usually in directories and files). This is outside of the language definition, and depends on the supporting Eiffel environment.

Because the issue is important in large-scale Eiffel developments, the next section outlines a solution.

3.8 Class renaming in Lace

(This final section describes a way to address the problems described above, arising only for advanced uses of Eiffel. You may prefer to skip it on first reading.)

One way to describe a system is through the the **Language for Assembling Classes in Eiffel**, or Lace, which is not part of Eiffel, although it is recommended that Eiffel environments support at least part of Lace to facilitate the exchange of entire clusters and systems.

→ *Appendix D describes Lace in detail.*

You may use Lace to write an Assembly of Classes in Eiffel, or Ace, which specifies how to produce a system. For example, the Ace may indicate where to find the directories for the system's various clusters, and which class to use as the root. The Lace facility which will be of direct relevance to this discussion is how Lace makes it possible to build a system with two or more classes bearing the same name.

An Ace specifies a system through a sequence of cluster specifications, which may include class renaming clauses addressing the problem of name clashes. Here is a possible Ace for the election analysis system:

system *elections* **root**
 	
    ELECTION_ANALYSIS
default
    ... Default compilation options ...
cluster
    lexical: /*common*/*external*/*lexical*
        ... Compilation options for cluster *lexical* ...;
    geography: /*common*/*external*/*geo*
        ... Compilation options for cluster *geography* ...;
    my_cluster: ~/*elections*/*this_year*
        adapt
            lexical
                rename *STATE* **as** *AUTOMATON_STATE*;
            geography
                rename *STATE* **as** *COUNTRY_STATE*;
            ... Compilation options for cluster *my_cluster* ...
        end; -- *my_cluster*
    ... Other cluster specifications and other parts of system description ...
end -- system *elections*
	WARNING: This text is in Lace, not Eiffel.

The renaming specifications in the clause for *my_cluster* are self-explanatory; they allow the classes of that cluster to refer to both *STATE* classes, from clusters *lexical* and *geography*, under different names.

There is no need to change anything in the classes of *lexical* and *geography*, even though they may use their respective "state" classes under the same name: by default, a class name used in a class will refer to a class of the same cluster.

This example assumes that the two clusters do not refer to each other's *STATE* class. If they did, the entries for *lexical* and *geography* would need to include their own **rename** subclauses.

→ *Lace's class renaming mechanism is directly patterned after Eiffel's feature renaming, used for inheritance. See 6.9, page 81.*

4

Classes

4.1 Overview

Classes are the components used to build Eiffel software.

As already noted, classes serve two complementary purposes: they are the modular units of software decomposition; they also provide the basis for the type system of Eiffel.

This chapter explores the role of classes further and explains the structure of class texts.

4.2 Objects

Viewed as a type, a class describes the properties of a set of possible data structures, or **objects**, which may exist during the execution of a system that includes the class; these objects are called the **instances** of the class.

→ *The precise nature of objects is explained in chapter 17.*

An object may represent a real-world thing such as a signal in process control software, a document in text processing software or an electron in physics software. Objects may also be pure artefacts of computer programming, such as an abstract syntax tree in compilation software.

The classes corresponding to these examples might be:

- *SIGNAL*, whose instances represent signals transmitted by some sensing device.
- *DOCUMENT*, whose instances represent documents.
- *ELECTRON*, whose instances represent electrons.
- *ABSTRACT_NODE*, whose instances represent nodes of abstract syntax trees.

Every object that may exist during the execution of a system is an instance of some class of that system. This is an important property, since it means that the type system is simple and uniform, being entirely based on the notion of class.

→ See chapter 12 about types.

To be more precise, every object is a **direct instance** of only one class, called its generating class. It may, however, be an instance (direct or not) of more than one class; this is because the language defines the instances of a class C, without further qualification, as the direct instances not just of C but also of C's proper descendants – the classes which inherit from C directly or indirectly.

→ See 17.5, page 272, for the exact definitions of "instance" and "direct instance". "Generating class" is defined in 17.2, page 270.

Some classes, said to be **deferred**, have no direct instances; they provide incomplete object descriptions. If C is deferred, an instance of C is a direct instance of some effective (that is to say non-deferred) descendant of C.

All these concepts are studied in detail in subsequent chapters.

→ See chapters 6 and 10 about inheritance and deferred routines.

4.3 Features

Viewed as a module, a class introduces, through its class text, a set of **features**. Some features, called **attributes**, represent fields of the class's direct instances; others, called **routines**, represent computations applicable to those instances.

→ Features are studied in detail in the next chapter.

Since there is no other modular facility than the class, building a software system in Eiffel means analyzing the types of objects the system will manipulate, and writing a class for each of these types.

A system that includes a certain class may contain operations to create instances of that class (Creation instructions) and to apply features to those instances (feature calls).

→ See chapters 18 on creation instructions and 21 on calls.

4.4 Use of classes

In some cases, one of the two roles of classes is more important than the other.

- At one extreme, a class may be only interesting as a module encapsulating a number of routines. (It then resembles the "packages" of older programming languages.) Often, it will not have any attributes. A system that use such a class will not create any direct instance of it; instead, other classes of the system will make use of its features by inheriting from it.

Even though it has no direct instances, such a class will have instances – the direct instances of proper descendants.

- At the other extreme, you may want to introduce a class simply because you need to describe a new type of object, without necessarily thinking of its role in the system architecture, at least at first. (It then resembles the "records" or "structures" of older programming languages, although it will usually include routines along with attributes.)

Both of these uses of classes arise in practice and both are legitimate.

In most cases, however, classes live up to their reputation, making a name for themselves in both the module and type worlds.

4.5 Class text structure

A class text contains the class name, possibly followed by Formal_generics parameters, and a number of parts, all optional except for the Class_header, and all (except Formal_generics) introduced by a keyword:

- Indexing, beginning with **indexing**.
- Class_header, beginning with **class** or **deferred class**.
- Formal_generics, beginning with a bracket [.
- Obsolete, beginning with **obsolete**.
- Inheritance, beginning with **inherit**.
- Creators, beginning with **creation**.
- Features, beginning with **feature**.
- Invariant, beginning with **invariant**.

Here is an extract from a class describing hash tables, which illustrates all clauses except Obsolete:

This class is a simplified form of one in the Data Structure Library. A "hash table" is a table used to record a number of elements, each identified by an individual key.

```
-- Hash tables used to store items associated with
-- "hashable" keys.

indexing

    names: h_table;
    access: key, direct;
    representation: array;
    size: fixed, resizable

class HASH_TABLE [T, V –> HASHABLE] inherit

    TABLE [T, V]
        redefine
            load
        end

creation

    make

feature

    remove (k: V) is
            -- Remove entry of key k
        require
            valid_key: is_valid (k)
        do
            ... Procedure implementation omitted ...
        ensure
            not has (k)
        end; -- remove

    make (n: INTEGER): BOOLEAN is
            -- Allocate space for n items
        ... Procedure body omitted ...

    load ... Rest of procedure omitted
```

```
        ok: BOOLEAN is
            -- Was last operation successful?
          do
            Result := control = 0
          end; -- ok

      control: INTEGER;

      Max_control: INTEGER is 5;

      ... Other features omitted ...

    invariant

      0 <= control; control <= Max_control

    end -- class HASH_TABLE
```

This abbreviated example is a specimen of a Class_declaration, whose general syntax is:

Class_declaration	≜	[Indexing]
		Class_header
		[Formal_generics]
		[Obsolete]
		[Inheritance]
		[Creators]
		[Features]
		[Invariant]
		end ["--" **class** Class_name]

The next section offers an informal overview of the various parts and their role, using *HASH_TABLE* as illustration. The subsequent sections of this chapter will only cover in detail Indexing, Class_header parts, Formal_generics, Obsolete and the closing **end**.

→ *Inheritance is discussed in chapters 6, 10 and 11, Creators in chapter 18, Features in chapter 5, and Invariant in chapter 9.*

4.6 Parts of a class text

As noted, class *HASH_TABLE* includes all of the possible parts save for Obsolete. Let us look informally at each of them.

The Indexing part, studied in the next section, serves to associate indexing information with the class, for the benefit of any query-based class archival and retrieval tools which the environment may support. It is organized as a sequence of clauses, each containing an optional Index term, such as *names* or *access*, and one or more associated values. Here the *names* clause mentions an alternate name (*h_table*) for the class; the *access* clause lists possible modes of accessing the corresponding objects; the *representation* clauses indicates an array representation; and the *size* clause states that hash tables are of fixed size, but resizable.

The Index terms and values are free, but this example uses the terms and values recommended as part of the style guidelines for the Basic Libraries.

→ *For indexing guidelines, see next section and A.12, page 494.*

The Class_header introduces the class name, *HASH_TABLE* in the example.

Instead of just **class**, the class name could begin with **deferred class** or **expanded class**, making the class "deferred" in the first case and "expanded" in the second case. These correspond to variants of the basic notion of class:

- A deferred class describes an incompletely implemented abstraction, which other classes (its proper descendants) will use as a basis for further refinement.

→ 10.9 and the following sections, beginning on page 144, explore deferred classes in detail.

- Declaring a class as expanded indicates that entities declared of the corresponding type will have objects as their run-time values. (By default, values are *references* to objects.)

Expanded classes and the resulting types are discussed in chapter 12.

As the syntax below will express, these two options are exclusive: a class may not be both deferred and expanded.

The Formal_generics part, if present, makes the class "generic", which means it is parameterized by types. Here *HASH_TABLE* has two formal generic parameters: *T*, representing the type of the elements in a hash table; and *V*, representing the type of the keys which serve to retrieve these elements. To obtain a type from a generic class, you must provide types, called **actual generic parameters**. For example, you may declare an entity denoting a possible hash-table as

> *ownership_record*: *HASH_TABLE* [*CAR, STRING*]

using *CAR* and *STRING* as actual generic parameters for *T* and *V*. As a result, *ownership_record* may at run-time become attached to an object representing a table of cars; the table entries may be retrieved through keys, which are strings (perhaps the license plate numbers). A type obtained in this way is called a **generic derivation** of the base class, here *HASH_TABLE*.

The notation *V* –> in class *HASH_TABLE* indicates that second formal generic parameter, *V*, is "constrained" by the library class *HASHABLE*. This means that any corresponding actual generic parameter must be a descendant of *HASHABLE*; this is indeed the case with class *STRING*.

→ *On unconstrained and constrained generic derivations, see 12.7 and 12.8, starting on page 200.*

The Obsolete part, if present, indicates that the class is an older version which should no longer be used except for compatibility with existing systems. For example, along with *HASH_TABLE*, a library may contain a class beginning with

> **class** *H_TABLE* [*T, V* –> *HASHABLE*] **obsolete**
>
>   *"You should use HASH_TABLE, which relies on improved algorithms"*
>
> **inherit**
>
>   ... Rest of class text omitted ...

The only effect of such a clause is that some language processing tools may produce a warning when they process such a class. The warning should reproduce the String listed after the **obsolete** keyword.

The Inheritance part, beginning with **inherit**, lists the parents of the class and any **feature adaptation** applied to the inherited feature. *HASH_TABLE* has only one parent, *TABLE*; its Feature_adaptation part, beginning with **redefine**, simply indicates that the new class will redefine the inherited procedure *load*. There is indeed a new declaration of *load* in the class text.

The Creators part, beginning with **creation**, lists the procedures which may be used by clients to create direct instances of the class. Here there is just one: *make*. A client may create a direct instance of *HASH_TABLE* by executing a creation instruction such as

> !! *ownership_record.make* (5_000)

which will allocate a new table with room for 5000 items.

The Features part introduces the features of the class. It is made of zero or more subparts, each called a Feature_clause and introduced by the keyword **feature**; the reason for having more than one is that each may make different features available to different clients. Here there is only one Feature_clause, introducing features available to all clients: the procedures *remove* and *load*, the function *ok*, the variable attribute *control* and the constant attribute *Max_control*. Calls from clients will use dot notation, as in

> *ownership_record.remove* ("1745 BB 75");
>
> -- Assuming a Writable entity *status* of type *INTEGER*:
> *status* := *ownership_record.control*;
> *ownership_record.make* (10_000)

The last of these calls applies to *make*, which is also a creation procedure but here is just used as a normal exported procedure. (Compare this call instruction with the Creation instruction above, using the !! notation.) Of course, in deciding to make *make* an exported procedure, the designer of *HASH_TABLE* should make sure that calls occurring after the initial Creation instruction will have the proper effect; this probably means using a new size which is greater than or equal to the original one (in other words, keeping the original if the argument to the call is smaller), and writing the routine so that resizing does not lose any of the previously inserted elements.

→ A feature is "exported" if it is available to all clients. See the definition on page 100.

To ensure that *make* is not available for outside calls, it would suffice to add a second Feature_clause with an empty Clients list, beginning with **feature** { }, and move the declaration of *make* there. This is explained in detail by the chapters on features and exports.

→ On how to restrict the availability of a feature see 7.8, page 96. A full example appears in 5.4, page 56.

The Invariant part, beginning with **invariant**, introduces consistency conditions on the features of the class; here the condition simply gives the bounds for attribute *control*.

→ 9.11, page 126, covers class invariants.

After this general survey of the structure of a class text, the rest of this chapter examine five clauses which apply to the class as a whole: Indexing, Class_header, Formal_generics, Obsolete and ending comment.

4.7 Indexing a class

The optional Indexing part has no direct effect on the semantics of the class. It serves to associate information with the class, for use by tools for archiving and retrieving classes based on their properties.

This is particularly important in the approach to software construction promoted by Eiffel, based on libraries of reusable classes: the designer of a class should help future users find out about the availability of classes fulfilling particular needs.

We may imagine the author of a class *DOCUMENT* writing the class text beginning as follows:

> **indexing**
>   *text, text_processing, TeX*;
>   *author*: *"Tatiana Sergeevna Krasnojivotnaya"*;
>   *approved_by*: *"Giovanni Giacomo della Gambagialla"*;
>   *original*: *21, March, 1988*;
>   *last*: *12, July, 1992*
> **class** *DOCUMENT* **inherit**
>   ...

More generally, an Indexing part has the following form:

→ Manifest_constant *is introduced in 23.13, page 386, and subsequent sections.*

Indexing	≜	**indexing** Index_list
Index_list	≜	{Index_clause ";" ...}
Index_clause	≜	[Index] Index_terms
Index	≜	Identifier ":"
Index_terms	≜	{Index_value "," ...}$^{+}$
Index_value	≜	Identifier | Manifest_constant

Each Index_clause (there are five in the example) may optionally be preceded by an Index_value, such as *author*, followed by a colon. In the example all entries except the first have an Index.

The rest of the Index_clause is a list of Index_value terms, each of which is an Identifier (such as *text_processing* or *July*) or a Manifest_constant, that is to say a value of a basic type: integer (such as *21*), string (such as *"Tatiana Sergeevna Krasnojivotnaya"*) etc.

By the very nature of the Indexing part, the choice of indices and values is free. Using consistent conventions will greatly facilitate the successful retrieval of reusable classes. Here you may wish to rely on the set of guidelines defined for the Basic Libraries.

→ *The standard Eiffel indexing guidelines are given in A.12, page 494.*

The Indexing part of *HASH_TABLE*, given above, illustrated these guidelines. Here is another example, the Indexing part from the Data Structure Library class *ARRAY_LIST*, which describes lists implemented by one or more arrays chained to each other:

indexing
    names: *block_list*;
    representation: *array, linked*; -- In this case it is both
    access: *fixed, cursor*;
    size: *resizable*;
    contents: *generic*

4.8 Class header

The Class_header introduces the name of the class; it also serves to indicate whether the class is deferred or expanded. Here are two Class_header examples from the Data Structure Library and one from the Kernel Library, illustrating the three possibilities:

class *LINKED_LIST*

deferred class *SEQUENCE*

expanded class *INTEGER*

The general form of the Class_header is simply:

Class_header	$\triangleq$	[Header_mark] **class** Class_name
Header_mark	$\triangleq$	**deferred** | **expanded**
Class_name	$\triangleq$	Identifier

The Class_name part gives the name of the class. Here and in any context where a class text refers to a class name, the recommended convention is to use the upper name.

← *The upper name is the name written all in upper case.*

You will declare a class as **deferred** if you plan to include one or more features which are specified but not implemented, with the expectation that proper descendants of the class will provide the implementations. This is useful to describe groups of related concepts, or not fully understood concepts. For example, *SEQUENCE* describes data structures managed sequentially, without prescribing any particular implementation. Proper descendants of this class, such as *LINKED_LIST*, describe concrete sequential structures. A non-deferred class such as *LINKED_LIST* is said to be **effective**.

→ *Deferred classes are studied in chapter 10, starting with 10.9, page 144.*

You will declare a class *C* as **expanded** if you wish entities of type *C* to have values which are instances of *C*. Otherwise, the values are references to such instances.

If C is generic, the entities and instances under consideration are of a type T "generically derived" from C. See chapter 12 about generic derivation.

As the syntax indicates, deferred status is incompatible with expansion.

Simple as it is, the Class_header must satisfy a validity constraint:

VCCH

> A Class_header appearing in the text of a class *C* is valid if and only if it satisfies either of the following two conditions:
>
> 1 • There is no header mark of the **deferred** form, and *C* is effective.
>
> 2 • There is a Header_mark of the **deferred** form, and *C* is deferred.

PREVIEW

A class is considered to be deferred if it has at least one deferred feature, either introduced as deferred in the class itself, or inherited as deferred and not "effected" (redeclared in non-deferred form). Condition 2 indicates that in such a case the Class_header must begin with **deferred class**.

→ The definition of "deferred class" is on page 161.

COMMENT

A class which is declared as **deferred** but has no deferred features is invalid since it violates condition 1. This case may be harmless (you have removed all the deferred features of a class but neglected to delete the keyword **deferred** from the Class_header), but it may also be a consequence of an error, such as a forgotten feature, so it is just as well to flag it as a validity violation.

4.9 Formal generic parameters

A class whose Class_header is followed by a Formal_generics part, as in

> ...
>
> **class** *HASH_TABLE* [*T, V –> HASHABLE*] ...

will be called a **generic class**. (If the Formal_generics part is absent, the class is, predictably, a **non-generic class**.) A generic class has one or more **formal generic parameters**, which are identifiers, here *T* and *V*, not conflicting with any name of a class in the surrounding universe. The mechanism which permits generic classes and the corresponding types is called **genericity**.

As noted, a generic class does not directly yield a type, although it is easy to derive a type from it: just provide a list of types, called **actual generic parameters**, one for each formal generic parameter. This was done above in the declaration of *ownership_record* to derive the type

> *HASH_TABLE* [*CAR, STRING*]

from *HASH_TABLE*, with an Actual_generics list made of the types *CAR* and *STRING*. Such a type is said to be **generically derived**.

PREVIEW

Genericity is one of the main reasons why classes and types are not identical notions: although any non-generic class is also a type, a generic class such as *HASH_TABLE* needs actual generic parameters to yield types such as the above. The notions of class and type are, of course, closely connected. More precisely, any type has a **base class** whose features provide the operations available on the type's instances; for a generically derived type such as the above, the base class is simply the type stripped of its actual generic parameters, here *HASH_TABLE*.

→ For the special case of Bit_type, the base class is defined by convention as a fictitious class of the form BIT_n. See 12.14, page 209.

The chapter on types will explore these notions further, giving all the details *→ Chapter 12 discusses* of genericity. For the moment, all we need is the precise syntax of *types and genericity.* Formal_generics parts and the straightforward associated constraint:

SYNTAX

Formal_generics	≜	"[" Formal_generic_list "]"
Formal_generic_list	≜	{Formal_generic ","...}
Formal_generic	≜	Formal_generic_name [Constraint]
Formal_generic_name	≜	Identifier
Constraint	≜	"−>" Class_type

VALIDITY

VCFG

A Formal_generics part of a Class_declaration is valid if and only if every Formal_generic_name *G* appearing in it satisfies the following two conditions:

1 • *G* is different from the name of any class in the surrounding universe.

2 • *G* is different from any other Formal_generic_name appearing in the same Formal_generics_part.

4.10 Obsolete clause

By including an Obsolete clause in a class, you indicate that the class does not meet current standards, and you advise developers against continuing to use it as supplier or parent – but you do not want to harm existing systems which rely on this class.

The decision to make an entire class obsolete is not a frequent one in well- *→ See 5.17, page 73, about* planned software development: through such facilities as information hiding, *making a feature obsolete* uniform access, dynamic binding and genericity, the language often enables *without making its class* developers to change a class with little or no impact on its clients and *obsolete.* descendants. Even when some aspects of a class are obsolete, the class as a whole often remains appropriate; this is why a related mechanism, through which you may make one or more individual **features** obsolete, is usually to be preferred. The next chapter explains how to do this, and presents further comments about software evolution and the obsolescence process.

In some cases, however, you may perceive that it is not possible to bring a class up to its ideal form without disturbing existing software, and you may simply decide to replace it by a new version. The civilized way to do this is to leave the old class, at least for some time, available under its original name, but to make it obsolete; this signals to developers of client and descendant classes that they should eventually adapt these classes to the new version, normally an easy task.

Here is the syntax of the clause, which comes after the Class_header and optional Formal_generics:

SYNTAX

Obsolete	≜	**obsolete** Message
Message	≜	Manifest_string

Declaring a class as Obsolete does not affect its semantics. But language processing tools, or at least some of them, should produce a warning when they process a class that relies, as client or descendant, on an obsolete class. The warning should include the Message.

Class obsolescence is **not** a way to cover up for bugs or flawed designs. If you realize that a class is incorrect or inadequate, you should face the consequences and repair the problem, even if this requires updating dependent classes. Any existing system using the flawed class cannot be functioning properly anyway. The Obsolete facility is meant for a different case: classes which were useful and sound, but cover needs for which you now have found improved solutions, based on a new design which is not upward-compatible with the original.

4.11 Ending comment

The structure of the Class_declaration given above includes an optional final comment (after the class's **end**) of the form

→ *Inclusion of this comment is part of the recommended style guidelines. See appendix A.*

```
    -- class Class_name
```

If present, this comment must repeat the Class_name given at the head of the class.

5

Features

5.1 Overview

A class is characterized by its features. Every feature describes an operation for accessing or modifying instances of the class.

A feature is either an attribute, describing information stored with each instance, or a routine, describing an algorithm. Clients of a class C may apply C's features to instances of C through **call** instructions or expressions.

A feature has a name, which may be an identifier or an operator (prefix or infix). With an identifier name, calls to the feature will use dot notation. With an operator name, calls will use the syntax of operator expressions.

This chapter discusses the role of features, introduces the various categories of feature, explains how to write feature declarations, and describes the form of feature names.

5.2 The role of features

A feature of a class describes an operation which is applicable to the instances of the class. For example:

- Class *SIGNAL* might have such features as *amplitude* (amplitude of a signal) or *compare* (compare a signal to another).
- Class *DOCUMENT* might have such features as *print* or *number_of_characters*.
- Class *ELECTRON* might have such features as *spin* or *valence*.
- Class *ABSTRACT_NODE* might have such features as *arity, is_leaf, is_root, add_child* or *remove_child*.

As these examples indicate, the operations represented by features may be of two kinds. Some are access operations, used to query objects about some of their properties ("What is the amplitude of this signal? How many characters does this document contain? Is this tree node a leaf?"). Others are modification operations, used to change objects or apply actions to them ("Print this document. Add a new child to this node.").

Queries are implemented as attributes or functions, commands as procedures.

5.3 Immediate and inherited features

The rest of this chapter will describe the Features part of a class, which introduces zero or more features of the class.

When thinking about features, we must be careful not to confuse two different notions:

- The features *introduced in* a class.
- The features *of* that class.

Why such a distinction? The reason is inheritance, which enables a class, in addition to the features declared in its own text, to obtain features declared in other classes – its parents.

→ *The notion of parent is studied in chapters 6, 10 and 11.*

DEFINITION:
Features of a class

Here is the precise terminology. The features of a class *C* include its **inherited** features and its **immediate** features, defined as follows:

Inherited 1 • The features obtained by *C* from its parents, if any, are its inherited features.

Immediate,
Origin,
Introduced

2 • In the Features part of *C*, consider a declaration describing a feature *f*. If *f* is inherited, the declaration is in fact a **redeclaration** of *f*, giving *f* new properties in *C*. If this is not the case, *f* is a new feature, said to be immediate in *C*. *C* is then the **class of origin** (or simply "origin") of *f*, which is also said to be **introduced in** *C*.

→ *This defines the origin of immediate features only. The full definition, also covering inherited features, appears on page 162.*

A feature "redeclaration", mentioned in case 2, is a declaration that locally changes an inherited feature. We will see the details of redeclaration as part of the study of inheritance; what is important here is that a declaration in the Features part only introduces a new feature if it is not a redeclaration of some feature obtained from a parent.

→ *Redeclaration is studied in chapter 10, especially 10.22, starting on page 163.*

Every feature of a class is immediate either in the class or in one of its proper ancestors (parents, grandparents and so on).

The rest of this chapter only discusses immediate features, by describing the Features part of a class declaration.

→ *Inherited features are studied in chapters 6, 10 and 11, with the full definition on page 187.*

5.4 Features part: example

A Features part is a sequence of one or more Feature_clause, as in the following sketch of a class from the Data Structure Library:

-- One-way linked lists

indexing

... Indexing clause omitted ...

class *LINKED_LIST* [*T*] **inherit**

   LIST [*T*]

      redefine

        first, start, return

      end

feature -- Number of elements

   count: *INTEGER*;

      -- Number of items in the list

feature -- Special elements

   first: *T* **is**

      -- Item at first position

    require

     not_empty: **not** *empty*

    do

     Result := *first_element*. *item*

    end; -- *first*

   ... Other feature declarations omitted ...

feature -- Cursor movement

   ... Feature declarations and other Feature_clauses omitted ...

feature {*LINKED_LIST*} -- Chaining

   previous, next: **like** *first_element*;

   make_sublist ... Rest of procedure omitted ...

   ... Other feature declarations omitted ...

feature {*NONE*} -- Representation

   first_element: *LINKABLE* [**like** *first*];

      -- First linkable element

   put_linkable_left (*new*: **like** *first_element*) **is**

      -- Insert *new* to the left of cursor position.

    require

     empty_if_before: *before* **implies** *empty*;

     new_exists: *new* /= *Void*

    do

     ... Implementation omitted ...

```
        ensure
            count = old count + 1;
            (position /= 1) implies (position = old position + 1);
            previous = new
        end; -- put_linkable_left

    ... Other feature declarations omitted ...

invariant

    empty = (first_element = Void)

    ... Other invariant clauses omitted ...
end -- class LINKED_LIST
```

A Features part contains zero or more Feature_clause. Each Feature_clause is introduced by the keyword **feature**, which may be followed, as in the last two cases above, by a Clients subclause, which is a list of class names in braces, as in {*A, B, C, ...*}.

All the features of a Feature_clause have the same **export status**. If the beginning of the Feature_clause gives a list of clients in braces, the clause's features are available to those clients only; otherwise they are available to all clients. Here, for example:

→ *Chapter 7 explains the details of the export policy and of Clients clauses.*

- *count* and *first* are available to all clients.

- *previous, next* and *make_sublist* are available only to *LINKED_LIST* itself, when used as its own client.

- The remaining features are available only to class *NONE*; this means that they are secret (accessible within class *LINKED_LIST* only, without use of dot notation).

For a class including many features, you may want to use more than one Feature_clause even for features which all have the same export status. This separates features into feature categories. In this case every Feature_clause should begin (after the keyword **feature**) with a Header_comment indicating the feature category. Here, the comments indicating the various categories are

```
    -- Number of elements
    -- Special elements
    -- Cursor movement
    -- Chaining
    -- Representation
```

Because the inclusion of such a Header_comment is part of the recommended style, it appears as an optional component in the syntax for Feature_clause given below. Environment tools (such as the **short** class abstracter, or a "browser" used to explore a universe of available classes interactively) may rely on it for contents-based feature retrieval.

→ *See 7.14, page 103, about the* **short** *class abstracter.*

5.5 Graphical representation

In the suggested graphical representation for classes and system structures, the features introduced in a class should appear next to the ellipse representing that class.

If enough display space is available and you want a full representation of the class's features, the format is that of a **feature box** shown next to the class ellipse and shown below for part of the class sketched in the previous section.

Class ellipse with feature box

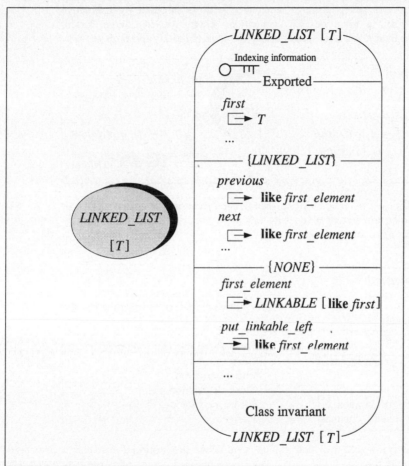

As in the textual form of the class, the features are grouped in successive divisions according to their export status.

For a routine, the open rectabgke with the arrow pointing inward indicates the types of the arguments. For an attribute or function, the open rectangle with the arrow pointing outward gives the result type.

The above notation takes up a large amount of space and is mostly suitable for examining and designing classes in an interactive graphical environment. For example, such an environment may let you display first the overall structure (ellipses representing classes and arrows representing the client and inheritance relations); then if you wish to obtain information about the features of a certain class, you will click on the corresponding ellipse, asking for feature information. A feature box will appear next to the class ellipse, as shown above. The box may temporarily overlay other display elements on the screen.

Because it uses so much space, the feature box format may not be appropriate for printing on paper, for drawing structures informally on a blackboard during design discussions, or for other situations in which you do not enjoy the luxury of showing and hiding display elements at will, as afforded by interactive systems. Then a more flexible convention, where you just write feature information in any available space close to the class ellipse, is appropriate:

A class with some features

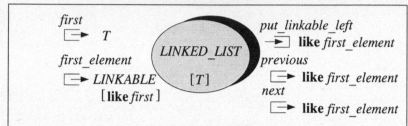

An additional convention will be seen in the discussion of attributes: if you know that a certain feature is an attribute, you may visualize this information by enclosing its name in a rectangle.

→ *The figure on page 262 shows the special convention for attributes.*

5.6 Features part: syntax

Here is the precise format of the Features part of a class text, as illustrated by the above example.

Features	≜	**feature** {Feature_clause **feature** ...}⁺
Feature_clause	≜	[Clients]
		[Header_comment]
		Feature_declaration_list
Feature_declaration_list	≜	{Feature_declaration ";" ...}
Header_comment	≜	Comment

→ *The syntax for the* Clients *part appears on page 101.*

As a general syntactical convention, semicolons are **optional** between a Feature_declaration and the next. The recommended style rule suggests including them.

The rest of this chapter concentrates on the Feature_declaration construct, explaining what kinds of feature may be declared in a class.

Semicolons are also optional between parent clauses (page 77), declarations of local entities (page 114), assertion clauses (page 121) and instructions (page 234). The style rule is on page 493.

5.7 Forms of features

Every feature of a class is either an **attribute** or a **routine**.

DEFINITION:
Field

By introducing an attribute in a class, you specify that at run-time every instance of the class will include a certain value, or **field**, corresponding to the attribute.

In other words, you may picture any instance of the class as an object made of a number of fields, each giving the value defined by the object for one of the attributes of the class. The figure illustrates a direct instance of a class C with three attributes, x, y and z. (To picture a non-direct instance, we would also need to consider attributes introduced in proper descendants.)

A class instance with its fields

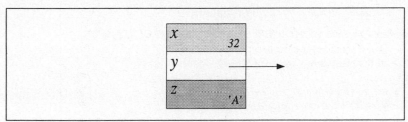

'x' is of type INTEGER, 'z' of type 'CHARACTER', and 'y' of some reference type. The corresponding field is attached to an object, which the figure does not show.

An attribute is either **constant** or **variable**:

- If an attribute is constant, the corresponding field is the same value for all instances, and may not change at run-time. This value appears in the class as part of the attribute declaration.

- If an attribute is variable, the corresponding fields may be different for various instances of the class and may change at run-time. As a consequence, the actual values must be stored in the representation of each instance.

By introducing a routine in a class, you specify that a certain computation (an algorithm) must be applicable to instances of the class.

A routine is either a **procedure** or a **function**:

- A procedure does not return a result; it may perform a number of operations, some of which may modify the instance to which the procedure is applied.

- A function returns a result and may also perform operations.

A function should not change any object, except if the change only affects an object's representation, not its abstract properties. Because compilers and other language processing tools cannot know which properties are abstract, the ban on object-modifying functions is a methodological guideline, not a language rule.

The problem of side effects in functions is discussed in detail in "Object-Oriented Software Construction".

5.8 Feature declarations: examples

To help you become familiar with the syntax of a Feature_declaration, here are a few artificial examples illustrating the various possibilities. The next sections give the precise syntax and detailed comments; for the most part, however, the examples should suffice as a guide for declaring features. The name of each example feature (such as *function_without_arguments*) suggests its nature.

```
variable_attribute: INTEGER;

other_variable_attribute: SOME_CLASS;

constant_attribute: REAL is 3.56;

other_constant_attribute: INTEGER is unique;

procedure (argument1: INTEGER; argument2: SOME_CLASS) is
        -- (Here should come the description
        -- of the procedure's intended effect)
    do
        some_attribute.some_procedure;
        other_attribute.other_procedure
    end; -- procedure

deferred_procedure (argument1: SOME_CLASS) is
        -- (Here should come the description
        -- of the procedure's intended effect)
    deferred
    end; -- deferred_procedure

function_with_arguments
    (argument1, argument2: SOME_CLASS): OTHER_CLASS
    is
        -- (Here should come the description
        -- of the result computed by the function)
    do
        !! Result;
        Result.some_procedure (argument2)
    end; -- function_with_arguments

function_without_arguments: INTEGER is
        -- (Here should come the description
        -- of the result computed by the function)
    do
        Result := some_value
    end; -- function_without_arguments

infix "+" (some_matrix: like Current): like Current is
        -- Matrix sum of Current and some_matrix
    do
        ... (Computation of the sum into Result) ...
    end; -- "+"
```

5.9 Feature declarations: syntax

With the above examples in mind, we can now look at the exact ingredients that make up a Features part.

The clause introduces the immediate features of a class. It is a sequence of individual Feature_declaration clauses, each of which introduces one feature, with the following pieces of information:

- The original name of the feature.
- The type of the feature, if it is an attribute or a function.
- The formal arguments, if the feature is a routine (procedure or function) with arguments.
- The actual value of the feature if it is a constant attribute.
- The computation associated with the feature if it is a routine.
- Possibly an Obsolete clause for a routine whose use is no longer recommended.

DEFINITION:
Frozen
Feature
- Possibly the keyword **frozen**, appearing before the feature name to express that the declaration is final (not subject to redefinition in descendants).

→ *More on frozen declarations in the discussion of the Feature rule page 70 below (condition 4), and of the Redefine Subclause rule, page 159 (condition 2).*

The precise syntax is:

Feature_declaration	≜	New_feature_list Declaration_body
Declaration_body	≜	[Formal_arguments]
		[Type_mark]
		[Constant_or_routine]
Constant_or_routine	≜	**is** Feature_value
Feature_value	≜	Manifest_constant | Unique | Routine

Of course, not all combinations of Formal_arguments, Type_mark and Constant_or_routine are possible. The above examples illustrate the valid combinations; the Feature Declaration rule will give the exact constraint.

→ *The Feature Declaration rule appears on page 69.*

5.10 Components of a feature declaration

Let us review the different subclauses that make up a Feature_declaration.

What appears before the Declaration_body is not just a Feature_name but a New_feature_list, with the syntax

→ *The form of a* Feature_name *and the rules on multiple feature declarations appear later in this chapter (5.16 and 5.13).*

New_feature_list	≜	{New_feature "," ...}⁺
New_feature	≜	[**frozen**] Feature_name

A Formal_arguments part, present only for a routine, describes the arguments to a routine and their types. An example is

→ *The syntax of* Formal_arguments *appears in 8.3, page 109.*

(arg1, arg2: TYPE1; arg3: TYPE2; arg4, arg5, arg6: TYPE3)

A Type_mark is present only for attributes and for functions. For an attribute, it gives the type of the corresponding field in instances of the class; for a function, it gives the function's result type. Examples of Type_mark are

> : *INTEGER*
>
> : *SOME_CLASS*

The Constant_or_routine is present only for constant attributes and for routines. Beginning with the keyword **is**, it gives the "value" of the feature, which is a literal value (integer, string etc.) for a constant attribute, and a routine text for a routine.

In the above example, the Constant_or_routine for *constant_attribute* defines the constant's value to be the real number 3.56; the Constant_or_routine for *procedure* is

> **is**
>   -- (Here should come the description
>   -- of the procedure's intended effect)
> **do**
>   *some_attribute.some_procedure*;
>   *other_attribute.other_procedure*
> **end** -- *procedure*

As indicated by the syntax on the previous page, a Constant_or_routine may introduce a Manifest_constant, a Unique constant or a Routine.

A Manifest_constant specifies the value of a constant attribute, as chosen by the author of the class.

Unique specifications are also reserved for constant attributes, but in this case the user lets the compiler or other language processing tool select different values for different Unique attributes introduced in a class. All must be integers.

→ *See 23.13 and subsequent sections, starting on page 386, about* Manifest_ constant, *and 16.6, page 264, about* Unique *specifications.*

A Routine part describes the algorithm associated with a routine and, in the case of a function, the computation of its result.

→ *The syntax for* Routine *is on page 112.*

5.11 How to recognize features

The precise form and properties of attributes and routines, as described by the syntax given above for Feature_declaration, are studied in later chapters. You should, however, learn right away how to recognize attributes (constant or variable) and routines (procedures or functions). This is not difficult and the above examples illustrate the most common cases.

A Feature_declaration is a **variable attribute** declaration if and only if it satisfies the following conditions:

• There is no Formal_arguments part.

• There is a Type_mark part.

• There is no Constant_or_routine part.

Here is an extract from a Feature_clause with two such variable attribute declarations:

> *count*: *INTEGER*;
>
> *backup*: *LINKED_LIST* [*STOCK*];

A Feature_declaration is a **constant attribute** declaration if and only if it satisfies the following conditions:

- There is no Formal_arguments part.
- There is a Type_mark part.
- There is a Constant_or_routine part, which is either a Manifest_constant or a Unique.

Three examples, introducing an Integer_constant, a Manifest_string and a Unique value, are:

> *maximum_discount*: *INTEGER* **is** *25*;
>
> *message*: *STRING* **is** *"No such site"*;
>
> *purple*: *INTEGER* **is unique**

A Feature_declaration is a **routine** declaration if and only if it satisfies the following condition:

- There is a Constant_or_routine part, whose Feature_value is a Routine.

In this case the following parts may or may not be present: Formal_arguments, Type_mark, Obsolete mark. If the Type_mark is present, the declaration describes a **function**; otherwise it describes a **procedure**.

In the example illustrating the various categories of feature, the features with the following names are routines:

← *The example started on page 62.*

> *procedure*
> *deferred_procedure*
> *function_with_arguments*
> *function_without_arguments*
> **infix** *"+"*

Why do we need such rules for recognizing various kinds of feature? To put it more critically, why doesn't the language distinguish more clearly between them – for example by requiring specific keywords such as **attribute** or **procedure** at the beginning of each declaration?

The reason is methodological. As seen by clients, a feature is an abstract property of the instances of the class. Whether it is implemented within the class as a procedure, a function or a routine is a subordinate concern. As a consequence, the syntax downplays the differences between these forms of features instead of emphasizing them.

Of course, it is sometimes necessary to check what category a feature really belongs to. As the above examples indicate, you should quickly become familiar with the various forms.

This discussion is closely related to the notion of Uniform Access, (or "Uniform Reference"), discussed in "Object-Oriented Software Construction"; see 21.5, page 342 in the present book. The same ideas also lead to the notion of short form, studied in 7.14, page 103.

5.12 The signature of a feature

As defined above, a feature which is an attribute or a function has a type, which is simply the type of the fields representing the attribute in instances of the class, or the type of the results to be returned by the function. But we often need a more complete characterization of the type requirements associated with any feature. In particular, a routine is characterized not just by the type of its result (if it is a function), but also by the type of its arguments.

The notion of signature covers the type properties associated with a feature. To define the signature of a feature, we need two sequences of types: the first sequence includes the types of all arguments (it is empty for an attribute); the second sequence includes the type of the result (it is empty for a procedure). For example, a function whose declaration begins with

> $f(a: INTEGER; b: X): LINKED\_LIST [STOCK]$ **is** ...

has signature

> $(<INTEGER, X>, <LINKED\_LIST [STOCK]>)$

A signature as illustrated here is a notation to talk about Eiffel, not a construct of Eiffel. In other words, you will not see such a signature in an Eiffel text.

using the notations (X, Y) for pairs and $<A, B, C, ...>$ for sequences.

We do not really need a sequence for the second component of a signature, which will have just one element for a function or attribute, and zero for a procedure. But the first component must be a sequence (representing routine arguments), and it is simpler to treat both arguments in a consistent way.

Here are the signatures of the features in the example at the beginning of this chapter. An empty sequence is shown as $<>$.

variable_attribute:	$(<>, <INTEGER>)$
other_variable_attribute:	$(<>, <SOME\_CLASS>)$
constant_attribute:	$(<>, <REAL>)$
another_constant_attribute:	$(<>, <INTEGER>)$
procedure:	$(<INTEGER, SOME\_CLASS>, <>)$
deferred_procedure:	$(<SOME\_CLASS>, <>)$
function_with_arguments:	$(<SOME\_CLASS, SOME\_CLASS>, <OTHER\_CLASS>)$
function_without_arguments:	$(<>, <INTEGER>)$
infix "+":	$(<$**like** $Current>, <$**like** $Current>)$

As you may have noted, the signatures of *variable_attribute* and *function_without_arguments* are identical, even though one is an attribute and the other a function. This is part of a more general guideline: downplaying, for the benefit of a class's clients, the difference between features implemented as attributes (that is to say, by storage) and those implemented by functions without arguments (that is to say, by an algorithm).

This is again the Principle of Uniform Access; see page 65 above and 21.5, page 342.

The precise definition of the notion of signature is the following:

DEFINITION:
Signature

> The **signature** of a feature f is a pair (*argument_types*, *result_type*) where both *argument_types* and *result_type* are sequences of types, defined as follows.
>
> - If f is a routine, *argument_types* is the possibly empty sequence of the types of its arguments. If f is an attribute, *argument_types* is an empty sequence.
>
> - If f is an attribute or a function, *result_type* is a one-element sequence, whose single element is the type of f. If f is a procedure, f is an empty sequence.

DEFINITION:
Argument
Signature

The first component of a feature's signature, written *argument_types* in this definition, is called the **argument signature** of the feature. The argument signature gives the types of the feature's arguments; it is an empty sequence for attributes and for routines without arguments.

In the above examples, the argument signature of *variable_attribute* is <> (empty sequence); the argument signature of *procedure* is <*INTEGER, SOME_CLASS*>.

5.13 Feature names

Feature names serve to identify features.

There are two kinds of feature names: identifiers and operator names. In the above example all but one of the features have identifier names: *variable_attribute, procedure* etc. Feature **infix** "+" has an operator name. Operator names can introduce infix features, as here, or prefix features.

The difference between identifiers and operator names does not affect any semantic properties of the features, but only the way in which clients may call them. For features with identifier names, calls use **dot notation**, as in the calls

→ *Calls are studied in chapter 21. See also chapter 23 about expressions.*

> *a. variable_attribute*
>
> *b. procedure* (b, c)

In contrast, calls to features of the Infix form use operator syntax, as in

> *matrix1 + matrix2*

and similarly for prefix operators. Here the advantage is obvious, although it is merely a notational one, devoid of any semantic consequence: for a class that manipulates matrices, the preceding syntax is more consistent with traditional arithmetic notation than dot notation which, in this case, would come out as

> *matrix1.plus* (*matrix2*)

Feature names are defined as follows.

Feature_name	≜	Identifier | Prefix | Infix
Prefix	≜	**prefix** '""' Prefix_operator '""'
Infix	≜	**infix** '""' Infix_operator '""'
Prefix_operator	≜	Unary | Free_operator
Infix_operator	≜	Binary | Free_operator

DEFINITION:
Identifier
Feature,
Operator
Feature

Features declared with a Feature_identifier are called **identifier features**. Features declared with an operator are called **operator features**.

As indicated by the above syntax, an operator is either a Free_operator of a **standard operator** (Unary or Binary). Here are the standard operators; they use special symbols, except for boolean operators which, following tradition, use keywords, simple (as **and**) or double (as **and then**).

Unary	≜	**not** | "+" | "–"
Binary	≜	"+" | "–" | "*" | "/" |
		"<" | ">" | "<=" | ">=" |
		"//" | "\\\\" | "^" |
		and | **or** | **xor** |
		and then | **or else** | **implies**

A Free_operator is a sequence of non-blank characters beginning with one of the characters @, #, | and &. Here are some possible free operators, illustrated by examples of expressions where they might appear as infix functions:

- $a @ i$ returns the i-th element of array a. (**infix** "@" is indeed one of the names of the corresponding function in the Kernel Library class *ARRAY*.)

  → *See chapter 28 about arrays.* **infix** *"@" is a synonym for 'item' on arrays.*

- $p|-|q$, which might be used to return the distance between graphical objects p and q in a graphical application.

  → *Such a distance function appears in 21.13, page 351.*

- $a|-f> b$, which might be used to return the set of partial functions from a to b in a symbolic mathematics application.

The precise rules on free operators appear in the description of the lexical structure. The main difference between standard and free operators involves precedence: all free operators have the same precedence (the highest), whereas standard operators have different levels of precedence, as given in the discussion of expressions. Furthermore, the basic classes such as *INTEGER* and *BOOLEAN* use the standard operators as feature names: + for addition, **and** and **and then** for boolean conjunction etc.

→ *See page 377 about the precedence of operators. The definition of* Free_operator *is on page 419, followed by a discussion on the proper use of free operators. Chapter 32 describes basic classes.*

Whether its operator is standard or free, an operator feature has no special properties other than the form of calls. In particular, its name (such as **infix** "+") may appear in any context requiring a feature name:

- As a Feature_list term in one of the following clauses: Creators, listing creation procedures; Redefine, listing features to be redefined; Undefine, listing features to be undefined; Select, resolving ambiguities for repeated inheritance; New_exports, giving a new export status to inherited features.

  → *Creators: 18.8, page 285. Redefine: 10.13, page 150. Undefine: 10.16, page 155. Select: 11.6, page 177. New_exports: 7.11, page 98. Rename_pair: 6.9, page 81.*

- As the first or second term of a Rename_pair. (In "**rename** ... $f1$ **as** $f2$", all four combinations are possible: renaming an operator feature into an identifier feature, an operator feature into an identifier feature and so on.)

- In the closing comment of a function declaration, if it is an operator feature. (For simplicity, only the operator in quotes, such as "+", is repeated there, not the keyword **prefix** or **infix**.)

→ *See 8.2, page 107, about closing routine comments.*

DEFINITION:
Same
Feature
Name

The Feature Declaration rule, given below, uses the notion of two feature names being "the same". By convention, two feature names are the same if and only if either of the following conditions holds:

- They are both identifier features, with identical lower name.
- They are both operator features, both Prefix or both Infix, and their operators are identical.

The lower name is the name all in lower case.

In other words, for identifier features as for other uses of identifiers, letter case is not significant: *my_name, MY_NAME* and *mY_nAMe* are considered to be the same feature name. The style standard uses a name with an initial capital and the rest in lower case (as in *My_name*) for constant attributes, and the lower name, all in lower case (as in *my_name*) for all other features.

→ *The style standard is discussed in appendix A.*

For identifier features, there is no limit on the length of identifiers or the number of significant characters.

5.14 Validity of feature declarations

To be valid, a Declaration_body must satisfy a constraint, known as the Feature Declaration rule. Here is the rule in full, followed by a detailed explanation of its various clauses.

← *The syntax of* Declaration_body *was given on page 63*

Feature Declaration rule

A Feature_declaration appearing in a class C, and whose New_feature_list contains one or more feature names f_1, ..., f_n, is valid if and only if it satisfies all of the following conditions:

1 • Its Declaration_body describes a feature which, according to the rules of 5.11, is one of: variable attribute, constant attribute, procedure, function.

2 • None of the f_i has the same name as another feature introduced in C (in particular, f_i is not the same name as f_j for different i and j).

3 • If the name of any of the f_i is the same as the final name of any inherited feature, the Declaration_body satisfies the Redeclaration rule.

4 • If the Declaration_body describes a deferred feature, then none of the f_i is preceded by the keyword **frozen**.

5 • If any of the f_i is a Prefix name, the Declaration_body describes an attribute or a function with no argument.

6 • If any of the f_i is an Infix name, the Declaration_body describes a function with exactly one argument.

7 • If the Declaration_body describes a once function, the result type is not a Formal_generic_name, and is not an Anchored type.

Conditions 1 and 2 are straightforward: the Declaration_body must make sense, and the name or names of the feature being introduced must not conflict with any other feature introduced in the class.

These names must also not conflict with names of inherited features. In some cases, however, as expressed by condition 3, a Feature_declaration may use an inherited name; this is permitted when the declaration is a *redeclaration* of inherited feature. A redeclaration is either a *redefinition* of an inherited feature (changing its implementation, its signature or both) or an *effecting* (an effective implementation of a feature inherited in deferred form). The exact requirements in this case are captured by the Redeclaration rule, which will be given when we complete the study of inheritance, redefinition and deferred features.

→ *The full Redeclaration rule is on page 163.*

In applying conditions 2 and 3, remember that (as defined at the end of the previous section) two feature names are "the same" not just if they are written identically in their class texts, but also if they only differ by letter case.

Condition 4 prohibits a frozen feature from being declared as deferred. This is an obvious restriction since frozen features, by their very purpose, may not be redeclared, whereas the purpose of deferred features is precisely to force redeclaration in proper descendants.

← *Frozen features were introduced on page 63.*

A companion constraint, seen as part of the Redefine Subclause rule in a later chapter, will prohibit the *redefinition* of a frozen feature.

→ *The Redefine Subclause rule is on page 159.*

Conditions 5 and 6 are the obvious consistency requirements on Prefix and Infix features. A feature **prefix** "§" will be called under the form § x; this is the equivalent of an identifier feature of name *feat* which would be called under the form $x.feat$, and so must be an attribute or, more commonly, a function without argument. Similarly, **infix** "‡" will be called under the form $x ‡ y$, equivalent to $x.feat$ (y), and so must have exactly one argument.

Condition 7 applies to once functions. A once routine only executes its body on its first call. Further calls have no effect; for a function, they yield the result computed by the first. If the class is generic, this result should not depend on the formal generic parameter, since successive calls could then apply to instances of types derived from the class through different actual generic parameters. Similarly, the result should not be anchored, which would mean that the type of the object returned by the first call could be unacceptable for further calls.

→ *The precise properties of once routines are covered by the semantics of calls; see 21.11, page 347. On generic derivation, see chapter 12. On Anchored types see 12.15, page 211.*

The Feature Declaration rule does not prohibit conflicts between feature names and class names. It is indeed possible for a feature to bear the same lower name as a class of the universe. You may sometimes find it convenient to write a feature declaration such as

> *error_window*: ERROR_WINDOW

in a class text which only needs one feature of a certain type (here given by class *ERROR_WINDOW*) if you consider that the type name provides enough information to describe the role of the feature.

5.15 Scope

Any feature of a class is accessible to the Routine_body, Precondition Postcondition and Rescue clauses of any routine of the class.

→ *See chapters 8 about* Routine_body, *9 about* Precondition *and* Postcondition *and 15 about* Rescue.

To avoid any ambiguity, constraints will prohibit giving a formal argument or local entity of a routine a name already used by a feature of the enclosing class.

5.16 Synonyms

Because the first part of a Feature_declaration is a Feature_list, not a Feature_name, each feature declaration may introduce more than one feature. This should be viewed as an abbreviation, according to the following rule:

Multiple Declaration rule

The semantics of a feature declaration applying to more than one feature name, as in

$f_1, f_2, \ldots, f_n$ *some_declaration_body*

is (except in one special case) defined as the semantics of the corresponding sequence of declarations naming only one feature each, and with identical declaration bodies, as in:

f_1 *some_declaration_body*;
f_2 *some_declaration_body*;
...
f_n *some_declaration_body*

The special case is that of a multiple declaration introducing Unique constant attributes, which is covered by the Unique Declaration rule.

→ *The Unique Declaration rule, given on page 266, specifies that a group of Unique constant attributes declared together have consecutive integer values.*

As a consequence of this rule, we may always assume, when studying the semantics of feature declarations, that each declaration applies to only one feature. This convention is used throughout the rest of this book.

A multiple declaration introduces the features as synonyms. But the synonymy only applies to the enclosing class; there is no permanent binding between the features. They simply have the same Declaration_body at the point of introduction, and are not otherwise related.

This means in particular that a proper descendant of the class may rename or redeclare one without affecting the other.

→ *See chapter 6 about renaming, and chapter 10 about redeclaration.*

When should we use multiple declarations? The last observation provides a clue. If you anticipate that a feature may have different variants in descendant classes, it may be better to introduce it as two features, initially identical, in its class of origin. This is in particular the case when you expect descendants to redefine the feature, but want to guarantee that the original will also be available to their clients. Then one of the two features should be declared as frozen.

Here is an example from *ANY*, the Kernel Library class which is an ancestor of all classes. *ANY* provides a general equality comparison, function *is_equal*. The original version tests two objects for field-by-field equality. (As explained in the presentation of object comparison, it is usually more convenient to use a companion function, *equal*, itself defined in terms of *is_equal*; but this is of no importance for the present discussion.)

→ *See 19.7, page 303, about the respective roles of functions 'is_equal' and 'equal'.*

Any class may redefine *is_equal* (with *equal* automatically following suit) to account for the specific semantics of equality desired for the class. For example, if objects *L1* and *L2* below are instances of a class *INTEGER_SET*, they are not field-by-field equal (since they contain references to different objects), but the author of *INTEGER_SET* may decide that *is_equal* must return true on these objects as they represent the same set. The class will then redefine *is_equal* to test for the desired notion of equality.

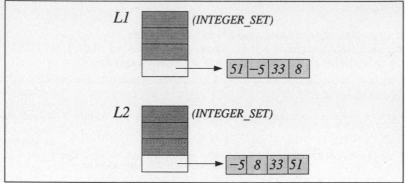

Equivalent objects not field-by-field equal

L1 and L2 are implemented as array descriptors; see 23.21, page 396.

Along with such redefinitions of *is_equal*, it is useful to keep the default version (performing field-by-field comparison) for all classes. This is why *ANY* introduces two equality functions, originally as synonyms:

> *is_equal*, **frozen** *standard_is_equal* (*x*: **like** *Current*): *BOOLEAN* **is** ...

with the consequence (enforced through the **frozen** keyword) that the second function will not be redefined, so that developers can rely on it having a fixed, universal semantics.

It is also important to understand when multiple declarations are **not** appropriate. This includes the following two situations:

- If you devise a better name for an existing feature, but wish to provide upward compatibility for existing clients and descendants, then a better mechanism, described in detail below, is available: "obsoleting" the feature. This has the advantage of facilitating the eventual phasing out of the obsolete version, whereas there is no incentive to remove a synonym.

  → 5.17 covers feature obsolescence.

- The availability of a synonym mechanism is usually not a good excuse for refusing to choose between possible names. Class designers, especially designers of reusable library classes, should not be fickle; even if two sets of names appear equally good, it is generally better to choose just one than to provide both. By passing on the choice to client developers, the latter solution would only confuse them, and make the class appear more complex than it is.

  "Eiffel: The Libraries" discusses how to choose the names of library features; see also Appendix A of the present book.

  *The Libraries have **one** example of fickleness: for array access, two names, 'item' and the more terse* **infix "@"**, *are available. See 28.4, page 439.*

These observations suggest that multiple declarations, although an important facility for cases such as the one mentioned above, should remain a relatively infrequent occurrence in normal Eiffel development.

The above example also suggests what kinds of use are proper for frozen features. The very idea of "freezing" a feature is, in general, contrary to the fundamental Eiffel concepts of software extendibility and adaptability, which the feature adaptation mechanisms (in particular redeclaration) support directly. When you inherit from a class, you should be able to adapt its features to the new context; you may use the assertion mechanism to guarantee that the specification remains compatible with the framework defined in the original, although the implementation may be different.

This mechanism is so central in the Eiffel method that it leaves only a limited role for frozen features: taking care of predefined, system-level operations such as *standard_is_equal*, for which we require not only the specification but the implementation to be determined once and for all.

5.17 Obsolete features

As classes evolve in the constantly changing world of software development, you may find that a feature is no longer satisfactory.

If all you need is to change its implementation, then you should be able to update the feature without impacting its dependent classes (clients and proper descendants). For example, you may change a Routine_body, replace an attribute by a function without arguments or conversely with minimum impact to dependents.

Unfortunately, this is not always the case. You may become unhappy with a feature's name, its signature or its specification.

The specification defines the routine's semantics. It is normally expressed by assertions; see chapter 9.

In such a situation, if you are certain that you have found a better replacement for the feature, you should perform the change without delay, for fear of carrying along inferior versions of your software. But you also need to take into consideration any existing dependent classes that relied on the feature. Clearly, you should avoid any change that would suddenly prevent such classes from functioning; but you may want to encourage their authors to adapt them to the new versions within a reasonable time.

The preceding chapter showed how to declare an entire **class** as obsolete. This is a rather drastic decision, however; more often, the class as a whole remains adequate, but you want to replace a few features by improved versions.

← See 4.10, page 52, about obsoleting an entire class.

The feature obsolescence mechanism supports this need. By declaring a feature as obsolete, you keep it usable exactly as it was, while alerting its users to the existence of a better version. This provides a graceful way to phase out a routine while remaining friends with the developers of client systems.

Only routines may be declared obsolete (but you may replace an attribute with an obsolete function). To make a routine obsolete, give it an Obsolete clause, of the form

> **obsolete** *Message*

where *Message* is a string. This serves to warn authors of dependent classes that the routine should no longer be used. The *Message* should direct readers to alternate features.

Here is an obsolete routine which once figured in class *ARRAY* of the Kernel Library:

```
enter (i: INTEGER; new_value: T) is
    obsolete "Use 'put (new_value, index)'"
        -- Replace by new_value the element at index i
    require
    i >= lower; i <= upper
```

```
        do
            ... (Appropriate algorithm) ...
        ensure
            item (i) = new_value
        end -- enter
```

In older versions of the library, this was the routine used to replace by *new_value* the value of the element at index *i* in an array. An examination of the consistency of names and conventions in the library resulted in a decision to update the routine; both the name (*put* rather than *enter*) and the interface (order of arguments) were changed. The Message explains this change.

To avoid cluttering up library classes with features that are no longer relevant, library administrators should not allow obsolete routines to remain forever. After a suitable grace period – time for one or two new releases of the software to displace the older generations – they will have fulfilled their duties as Client-Friendly Transition Facilitators and should be retired with honors. This indeed happened to the the above version of *enter*, which (although fondly remembered by old-timers) no longer appears in class *ARRAY*.

The syntax of class-level Obsolete clauses also applies to routine-level clauses; here it is again:

Obsolete	≜	**obsolete** Message
Message	≜	Manifest_string

← This syntax appeared originally on page 52.

Declaring a routine as Obsolete does not affect its semantics. But language processing tools, or at least some of them, should produce a warning when they process a client or descendant class that uses the routine. The warning should include the Message.

The abstract and flat-short forms of the class do not retain any feature marked as obsolete.

→ On the abstract and flat-short forms, see 7.14 and 7.15, beginning on page 103.

A compiler or other language processing tool may also go further and provide an option that, under some conditions, will automatically update the text of client classes, replacing all calls to an obsolete routine by the body of the routine with appropriate argument substitution.

As noted in the discussion of obsolete classes, the availability of a feature obsolescence mechanism is not an excuse to grant a reprieve to software components that are buggy or otherwise deficient. If you discover a specification, design or implementation flaw, only one reaction is reasonable: correcting the mistake. A routine is a candidate for obsolescence when, as originally written, it adequately covered a certain need, but is not up to the current state of your thinking. You prefer the new version, but the obsolete version is not *wrong*; it is simply not what you would like to keep for the future.

6

The inheritance relation

6.1 Overview

Inheritance is one of the most powerful facilities available to software developers. It addresses two key issues of software development, corresponding to the two roles of classes:

- As a *module extension* mechanism, inheritance makes it possible to define new classes from existing ones by adding or adapting features.
- As a *type refinement* mechanism, inheritance supports the definition of new types as specializations of existing ones, and plays a key role in defining the type system.

This chapter introduces the fundamental properties of inheritance, concentrating on the first view – the module aspect. The inheritance-based type system of Eiffel is discussed in later chapters.

→ *See chapters 12 on typing and 13 on conformance.*

6.2 An Inheritance part

To define a class as inheriting from one or more others, include an Inheritance part, introduced by the keyword **inherit**.

Below is an extract from class *FIXED_TREE* in the Data Structure Library. It shows a typical Inheritance part, indicating that *FIXED_TREE* obtains some of its features from three other classes:

- *TREE*, describing the general notion of tree, regardless of the representation.
- *CELL*, describing elements used to store an individual piece of information (such as a tree node).
- *FIXED_LIST*, providing some of the implementation.

```
class FIXED_TREE [T] inherit

    TREE [T]

        redefine
            attach_to_higher, higher
        end;

    CELL [T];

    FIXED_LIST [like Current]

        rename
            off as child_off,
            after as child_after,
            before as child_before
        redefine
            duplicate, first_child
        end

feature

    ... (Rest of class omitted) ...
```

The clause is reproduced only in part. Two feature names have been changed; the full class has more elements in the Rename *and* Redefine *subclauses.*

The classes listed in the Inheritance part, *TREE*, *CELL* and *FIXED_LIST*, are said to be the "parents" of *FIXED_TREE*. When, as here, there are two or more Parent clauses, inheritance is said to be **multiple**. With only one Parent clause, we would have "single" inheritance.

→ *"Parent" is defined precisely in the next section.*

DEFINITION:
*Multiple,
Single
Inheritance*

Multiple inheritance occurs as soon as there is more than one Parent clause (even if they all refer to the same parent class, a case called **repeated inheritance** and studied in chapter 11). Multiple inheritance is a frequent occurrence in Eiffel development; most of the effective classes in the Data Structure Library, for example, have two or more parents.

As this example shows, there is often a need to adapt the features of parents to a new class. This is achieved through the Feature_adaptation part of a Parent clause, of which an example was

```
rename
    off as child_off,
    after as child_after,
    before as child_before
redefine
    duplicate, first_child
end
```

A Feature_adaptation part may contain Rename and Redefine subclauses, as here. The other possible subclauses – New_exports, Undefine and Select – will appear in the syntax below.

6.3 Form of the inheritance part

Here is the structure of Inheritance parts:

Inheritance	≜	**inherit** Parent_list
Parent_list	≜	{Parent ";" ...}
Parent	≜	Class_type [Feature_adaptation]
Feature_adaptation	≜	[Rename]
		[New_exports]
		[Undefine]
		[Redefine]
		[Select]
		end

As with many other uses of semicolons, the semicolon separating successive Parent clauses is optional, although style guidelines suggest including it.

→ *The style rule is on page 493.*

DEFINITION:
Parent clause for a class

The Parent_list names a number of Parent clauses. Each Parent clause is relative to a Class_type, that is to say a class name *B* possibly followed by actual generic parameters (as in *B* [*T, U*]). *B* must be the name of a class in the universe to which the current class belongs. The clause is said to be a "Parent clause for *B*". For example, the above declaration of *FIXED_TREE* contains Parent clauses for *TREE, CELL* and *FIXED_LIST*.

→ *Class types are studied in chapter 12.*

In a Parent clause, the Class_type indicating the parent may be followed by a Feature_adaptation clause which indicates the modifications that the new class needs to perform on the features it inherits from its parents. These modifications may affect various properties of the features, each handled by a subclause of Feature_adaptation:

- Their names (Rename).
- Their export status (New_exports).
- Their effectiveness status, deferred or effective (Undefine).
- Their signature and implementation (Redefine).
- Conflict removal for dynamic binding under repeated inheritance (Select).

→ *See 6.9 below, page 81, on* Rename; *10.13, page 150, on* Redefine; *7.11, page 98, on* New_exports; *10.16, page 155, on* Undefine; *and 11.6, page 177, on* Select.

6.4 Relations induced by inheritance

Inheritance parts introduce the "parent" and "heir" relations between classes.

DEFINITION:
Heir, Parent

If class *C* has a Parent clause for *B*, then *C* is said to **inherit** from *B*; *B* is said to be a **parent** of *C*, and *C* is said to be an **heir** of *B*.

The reflexive transitive closures of these relations are also of interest:

DEFINITION:
Ancestor, Descendant

Class *A* is an **ancestor** of class *B* if and only if *A* is *B* itself or, recursively, an ancestor of one of *B*'s parents.

Class *B* is a **descendant** of class *A* if and only if *A* is an ancestor of *B*, in other words if *B* is *A* or (recursively) a descendant of one of its heirs.

Any class, then, is both one of its own descendants and one of its own ancestors. **Proper** descendants and ancestors exclude these cases:

DEFINITION:
Proper
Ancestor,
Descendant

> The **proper ancestors** of a class *C* are its ancestors other than *C* itself. The **proper descendants** of a class *B* are its descendants other than *B* itself.

6.5 Graphical convention

In pictorial representations of system structures, where classes appear as labeled ellipses, the inheritance relation is represented by single arrows pointing from heirs' ellipses to parents' ellipses.

Parent
and
heir

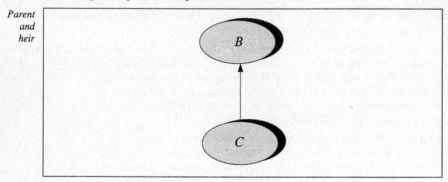

6.6 The inheritance structure

An important constraint governs the inheritance relation: no cycles are permitted.

Invalid
cycle
vs.
valid
repeated
inheritance

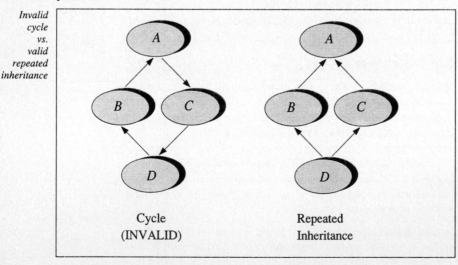

Cycle
(INVALID)

Repeated
Inheritance

In other words, you may not build a sequence of classes such as those on the left part of the preceding figure, where D inherits from C, C from A, A from B and B from D. More generally, it is invalid to have a set of classes C_0, C_1, ..., C_n ($n \geq 1$), where C_0 and C_n are the same class and each C_i is an heir of C_{i+1}.

→ *The structure on the right is not necessarily invalid. See below.*

The reason for this restriction is easy to understand: making C an heir to B means building the set of features of C as an extension of B's set of features; clearly, the relationship cannot be mutual.

Prohibiting cycles does not mean prohibiting a class D from being a descendant of another class A in more than one way. This case, known as **repeated inheritance** and studied in detail in a later chapter, is illustrated by the structure appearing on the right part of the figure, which may be valid if the appropriate conditions are met.

→ *Chapter 11 discusses repeated inheritance.*

These observations yield the validity constraint on Inheritance clauses, known as the Parent rule:

VHPR

> **Parent rule**
>
> The Inheritance clause of a class D is valid if and only if it meets the following two conditions:
>
> 1 • In every Parent clause for a class B, B is not a descendant of D.
>
> 2 • If two or more Parent clauses are for classes which have a common ancestor A, D meets the conditions of the Repeated Inheritance Consistency constraint for A.

The second condition corresponds to the case of repeated inheritance; the Repeated Inheritance Consistency constraint will guarantee that there is no ambiguity on features which are repeatedly inherited by D from A.

→ *The Repeated Inheritance Consistency constraint appears on page 191.*

A reminder on the meaning of validity constraints may be useful here. When applying the Parent rule, do not be misled by the "if and only if": to guarantee that an Inheritance clause is valid, you will also have to check conditions which do not appear explicitly in the rule. In particular:

- Every parent P must be a valid type; this means among other requirements that if P is generically derived, appearing as $B \lfloor X, ... \rfloor$, then B must be the name of a generic class in the surrounding universe and the actual parameters X, ... must be valid types matching the formal parameters of B.

→ *Chapter 12 gives the constraints on types, especially the Class Type rule, page 199, requiring P to be the name of a class in the universe, and the rules on generically derived types, pages 201 and 203.*

- Every Feature_adaptation clause (with its Rename, Redefine and other subclauses) must be valid.

The Parent Rule does not need, however, to express such requirements explicitly: The General Validity rule implicitly adds to the validity constraint on any construct the condition that all the components of any specimen are valid too. Be sure to remember this convention – without which the validity rules would become hopelessly complicated – whenever you see an "if and only if" validity constraint throughout this book. If you have the impression that the constraint does not cover every necessary condition, this is probably just because it omits the validity requirements on sub-components, as permitted by the General Validity rule.

← *The General Validity rule is on page 28.*

6.7 On inherited features

The major purpose of inheriting from one or more classes is to obtain their features as an addition to one's own. The features obtained by a class from its parents are called its inherited features. As already noted, this yields one of the two categories of features of a class; the others are "immediate" features, introduced in a class itself.

← *"Features of a class" and "inherited features" were first discussed on page 56.*

What does it mean to say that inherited features are the features "obtained from" parent classes? In simple cases, all the features of all parents will be "obtained" verbatim by the heir, yielding as many inherited features. Yet, because of the flexibility of inheritance, provided by mechanisms studied in later chapters, there is more to the story of obtaining features from parents. In particular:

- Two parent features may in some cases yield only one inherited feature, through sharing under repeated inheritance or the join of deferred features.

→ *See 10.17, starting on page 156, on the join mechanism and chapter 11 about repeated inheritance.*

- Conversely, a single parent feature may yield two or more inherited features; this is the replication case of multiple inheritance.

Until we have studied these mechanisms, we must content ourselves with the still somewhat vague definition of "inherited features" presented so far.

6.8 Adapting inherited features

The very notion of inherited features indicates how inheritance is used as an accumulation process enabling classes to use features defined in one or more previously existing classes – its proper ancestors.

Although a class inherits all its proper ancestors' features, it retains the flexibility to adapt them to its own context in various ways.

- A feature introduced in a certain class under a certain name may be known under different names in descendant classes. This is achieved through the **renaming** facility.

- A routine defined with a certain implementation may be redeclared with a new implementation. This is achieved through **redefinition**.

- A feature introduced with a certain signature may get a new signature. This is also achieved through redefinition, and through the associated mechanism of **anchored declaration**.

- A feature introduced in a proper ancestor with a specification but no implementation, known as a *deferred* feature, may be provided with an implementation. This is the process of **effecting**.

- If a class *C* inherits two or more deferred features with compatible signatures and specifications, it may merge them into a single feature. This is the **join** mechanism.

- When a class *C* inherits the same feature from two or more of its parents, which themselves inherit it from a common ancestor, simple techniques are available to ensure that the result in *C* is only one feature (sharing) or several (duplication). The rules to be applied are those of **repeated inheritance**.

The first of these techniques, renaming, is purely syntactical, affecting feature names rather than the features themselves. It is studied below. The others determine the semantic adaptation of features to the context of new descendants; later chapters explore them in detail.

→ *See chapters 10 on feature adaptation and 11 on repeated inheritance.*

6.9 Renaming

As part of its Feature_adaptation, any Parent clause may be followed by a Rename subclause, which serves to adapt names of inherited features to the local context of the new class.

The following Rename subclause is extracted from the previous example:

> **rename**
>   *off* **as** *child_off,*
>   *after* **as** *child_after,*
>   *before* **as** *child_before*

Renaming is especially useful in two cases:

- With renaming, you may correct any **name clash** occurring because of multiple inheritance. A name clash occurs when two or more parents of a class have a feature of the same name, and would usually make the class invalid if not removed by renaming.

→ *Name clashes, and the exact cases in which they are prohibited, are studied in chapter 11. See 11.10, page 185.*

- Renaming also enables a class to offer its inherited features to its clients and descendants under a terminology appropriate to its own context, rather than to the context of the parents from which it inherited them. In other words, it helps make sure that, beyond offering the right features, you also offer them under the right feature names.

→ *More on this at the end of this section.*

The general syntax of a Rename clause is:

Rename	≙	**rename** Rename_list
Rename_list	≙	{Rename_pair "," ...}
Rename_pair	≙	Feature_name **as** Feature_name

The Rename clause is subject to a constraint.

Rename Clause rule

It is valid to use *old_name* as first element of a Rename_pair, appearing in the Rename subclause of the Parent clause for *B* in a class *C*, if and only if the following two conditions are satisfied:

1 • *old_name* is the final name of a feature of *B*.

2 • *old_name* does not appear as the first element of any other Rename_pair in the same Rename subclause.

→ *The validity of using the second element, 'new_name', is governed by the Feature Name rule, page 188, expressing that no other feature of C must have 'new_name' as its final name.*

Renaming does not affect the semantics of an inherited feature, but simply gives it a new final name in an heir, as defined below.

6.10 Features and their names

To understand renaming, it is essential to understand the difference between a feature and a feature name.

A feature is a certain component (attribute or routine), characterized by a signature, an associated algorithm (for a routine), a value (for a constant attribute), and possibly other properties. Such a feature is "a feature of" one or more classes: the class which introduces it, and (barring redefinition) all the descendants of that class.

DEFINITION:
Name
of a
Feature
in a Class

Within the text of a class C, any feature of C is accessible through an identifier, or feature name, known as **the name of** f **in** C. As this expression suggests, the association between a feature and a feature name is not absolute but relative to a class. The same feature may well be denoted by different names in different classes.

This is precisely what happens through renaming. The presence of a Rename subclause of the form

> **rename** ..., f **as** g, ...

implies that the inherited feature known as f in the parent is known as g in the heir containing this subclause.

DEFINITION:
Original
Name

The precise definitions are the following.

> The **original name** of a feature is the name under which it is declared in its class of origin.

The notion of "class of origin" was first introduced on page 56. The full definition appears on page 162.

Final Name

> Every feature f of a class C has a final name in C, defined as follows:
>
> 1 • If f is immediate in C, its final name is its original name.
> 2 • If f is inherited, f is obtained from a feature of a parent B of C. Let *parent_name* be (recursively) the final name of that feature in B. Then:
>   - If the Parent clause for B in C contains a Rename_pair of the form **rename** *parent_name* **as** *new_name*, the final name of f in C is *new_name*.
>   - Otherwise, the final name is *parent_name*.

→ *Since an inherited feature may be obtained from two or more parent features, case 2 only makes sense if they are all inherited under the same name. This will be guaranteed by the full definition of "inherited feature" page 187.*

Final
Name Set

The final names of all the features of a class constitute the **final name set** of a class.

The notion of "inherited name" of an inherited feature is also convenient:

Inherited
Name

> The **inherited name** of a feature obtained from a feature f of a parent B is the final name of f in B.

→ *How the final name set is actually determined depends on renaming, redefinition and joining, as discussed in chapters 10 and 11. See some further comments about the final name set on page 188.*

Name of a
Feature

In this book, references to the "name" of a feature, if not further qualified, always denote the final name.

It is important to understand that renaming does not change any of the inherited features, but simply changes the names under which those features will be known by the clients and descendants of a class.

Consider for example a feature f, which has final name *old_name* in a class B. By writing an heir C of B under the form

> **class** C **inherit**
>   ...;
> B
>   **rename** ..., *old_name* **as** *new_name*, ...

you decide to make the inherited feature available to C, its clients and descendants under the name *new_name*.

As a consequence, you have also freed the inherited name of f, here *old_name*, so that another feature of C may now use this name. That other feature could come from various places:

1 • It could be a new feature introduced by C itself, for which you wish to use the name *old_name*.

2 • It could be a feature inherited from a parent of C other than B, and having the name *old_name* in that parent. Here, without renaming, you would have introduced an invalid name clash in C.

3 • It could even be a feature inherited from B or another parent under some other name, and renamed *old_name* in C. This case is somewhat contorted, but it may be justified in some circumstances.

Whatever the case, remember that if you do decide to reuse *old_name* for another feature of C, you do not introduce any connection between that feature and the original feature f, obtained from B under the inherited name *old_name*. The two are unrelated; for example one could be a procedure and the other an attribute.

The following example illustrates these properties. Assume a class *COLORS* with features of names *red, orange, black, white*, and *FRUITS* with a feature of name *orange_fruit*. Then you can write a class of the form

> **class** *FRUITS_AND_COLORS* **inherit**
>   *COLORS*
>   **rename**
>   *orange* **as** *orange_color*, *red* **as** *red_color*,
>   *black* **as** *white*, *white* **as** *black*
>   **end**;
>   *FRUITS*
>   **rename**
>   *orange_fruit* **as** *orange*
>   **end**
> **feature**
>   *red*: *INTEGER*
> **end** -- class *FRUITS_AND_COLORS*

The feature *orange* of class *COLORS* is known in *FRUITS_AND_COLORS* as *orange_color*; this makes the name *orange* available for the feature inherited from *FRUIT* under the name *orange_fruit*. The feature *red* of *COLORS* is known in *FRUITS_AND_COLORS* as *red_color*, making the name *red* free for a new attribute introduced in *FRUITS_AND_COLORS* with no connection to the original *red*. Finally each of *COLORS*'s features *black* and *white* is known in *FRUITS_AND_COLORS* under the other's name.

As you will have noticed from this example, the renaming induced by a Rename_pair of the form *old_name* **as** *new_name* only takes effect after the enclosing Rename clause. In other words, other occurrences of *old_name* or *new_name* in the same Rename clause must still be interpreted as they would be in the parent class.

Although the last case, which swaps the names of two inherited features, is rather extreme, this example illustrates the importance of renaming to the building of professional-quality reusable software components. Writing a class as heir to another means endowing the new class with a certain *functionality*, as provided by the parent's features. But this does not by itself make these features available under a *terminology* which is consistent with the heir's specific context. Renaming is there to guarantee that, for the heir, its clients and its descendants, the terminology is just as right as the functionality is.

6.11 Inheritance and expansion

The presence of inheritance raises the question of the expansion status of heirs of an expanded class.

As you may remember, a Class_header may begin with

← *Expanded class headers were introduced in 4.8, page 50.*

> **expanded class** *C* ...

as opposed to the more common **class** *C* or **deferred class** *C*. If the **expanded** mark is present, the class is said to be expanded; entities declared of a corresponding type, for example

> *x*: *C* ...

will have objects, rather than references to objects, as their possible values. What effect does this have on heirs of *C*?

The answer to this question is straightforward: no effect. The only consequence of the expansion status of a class is the semantics of entities of the corresponding types, such as *x* above. An expanded class may inherit from an non-expanded one, and conversely. The expansion status is not transmitted under inheritance; it is entirely determined by the presence or absence of the **expanded** mark in the class's own Class_header, not by any property of its parents.

6.12 *ANY*

No class that you write is an orphan. A general-purpose class, *ANY*, serves as parent to any class without an Inheritance clause, and hence as universal ancestor.

The inheritance structure

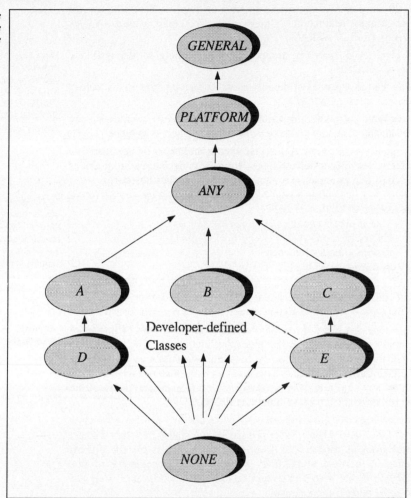

More precisely, the general inheritance structure, as shown above, reserves a special role to *ANY*, its acolytes *GENERAL* and *PLATFORM*, and also to class *NONE*. The details of *ANY*'s features are studied in a later chapter, but let us take a first look at how this class affects the inheritance structure.

→ *See chapter 27 about the features of GENERAL, ANY and PLATFORM.*

As illustrated by the figure, every class other than *GENERAL* and *PLATFORM* is a descendant of *ANY*. The precise rule is the following. Any class which does not include an explicitly written Inheritance clause is considered to have an implicit clause of the form

```
inherit
    ANY
```

Any class which after the application of this convention still does not include *ANY* among its ancestors is considered to have an implicit Parent clause for *ANY*, with no Feature_adaptation. (Otherwise a class could bypass *ANY* by inheriting directly from *GENERAL* or *PLATFORM*.)

This rule gives *ANY* two key properties, corresponding to the type and module views of inheritance:

A1 • *ANY* is the most general of directly useful types: any type that you may define will conform to *ANY*.

A2 • The features of *ANY*, describing general-purpose operations, are universal: any class that you may define will have access to them.

These properties suffer no exception. Even the classes describing the basic types BOOLEAN, INTEGER, CHARACTER, REAL, DOUBLE (chapter 32) are descendants of ANY.

As a consequence of property A1, if you want a routine to be applicable to objects of arbitrary developer-defined types, you should declare its argument as being of type *ANY*. An example is the routine which duplicates objects:

```
clone (other: ANY): like other is
        -- Void if other is void;
        -- Otherwise, new object field-by-field identical
        -- to object attached to other.
    ... Rest of routine omitted ...
```

→ *This declaration (which also includes the frozen synonym 'standard_clone') is itself in class GENERAL. See 19.3, page 298, about cloning. Anchored types are discussed in 12.15, starting on page 211.*

The result of this function is declared of the Anchored type **like** *other*, representing the type of the actual argument used in any given call for *other*.

Property A2 provides every developer-defined class with a set of important universal features coming from *ANY*. Examples include the above function *clone* for duplicating arbitrary objects, the function *default_rescue* which gives the default behavior after an exception, the function *out* which produces a string representation of any object, and the constant attribute *Integer_bits* whose value is the number of bits in the representation of an integer.

→ *See 15.5, page 251, about 'default_rescue'.*

The rule which adds the clause **inherit** *ANY* to a class only applies if the class has no explicit Inheritance clause, since if it has such a clause the class will get *ANY*'s features from its parents. (As seen next, it is harmless to inherit them more than once in the case of multiple parents.) As a consequence of this convention, any class that wishes to rename or redefine one or more features of *ANY* may do so by making the inheritance explicit, as in

```
class C inherit
    ANY
        redefine
            clone, default_rescue, ...
        end
feature
    ...
end
```

6.13 Repeated inheritance for *ANY*

You may have wondered about the effects of having *ANY* (as well as *GENERAL* and *PLATFORM*) as ancestor of classes who may have other parents – themselves descendants of *ANY*. What happens, for example, if *E* is, as on the figure of page 85, an heir of both *B* and *C*? In this case, *E* is a descendant of *ANY* in two ways.

Such situations do not, however, introduce any particular complexity; they are simply cases of **repeated inheritance**, the situation (studied in detail in a later chapter) in which a class is a proper descendant of another in more than one way. Unless you specify otherwise, repeated inheritance from *ANY* will produce the expected effect for a class such as *D*: *D* will have just one version of every feature inherited from the universal classes, as if it was connected to *ANY* through only one path of inheritance.

→ *Chapter 11 covers repeated inheritance; the case of "sharing", which will usually apply to features repeatedly inherited from GENERAL, PLATFORM and ANY, is presented first on page 170.*

6.14 *GENERAL* and *PLATFORM*

For convenience, universal features such as *clone* are not actually introduced in class *ANY*, but in its ancestors *GENERAL* and *PLATFORM*, with the inheritance structure shown on the above figure:

← *The inheritance figure was on page 85.*

- *GENERAL*, the only class with no parent, introduces the platform-independent universal features such as *clone* and *out*.
- *PLATFORM*, with *GENERAL* as its single parent, introduces a few constant attributes such as *Integer_bits* (the number of bits in an integer value) denoting constant values which depend on the local platform.

A "platform" is a type of machine (hardware plus operating system). See 2.10, page 29.

To simplify the discussion, this book usually refers to the universal features as the "features of class *ANY*", although they are introduced in proper ancestors of that class – *GENERAL* and *PLATFORM*.

6.15 Providing your own universal class

ANY, as delivered, does not introduce any features but simply inherits the features of *PLATFORM*, including those inherited from *GENERAL*. Its entire class text is:

```
class ANY inherit
    PLATFORM
end -- class ANY
```

This makes it possible for a project leader, a software manager or even an individual developer to write a new version of *ANY*, describing general-purpose operations which will be accessible to all classes developed locally. In contrast, you should not modify *GENERAL* and *PLATFORM*: *GENERAL* should remain the same for all Eiffel installations, and *PLATFORM* for all installations of a certain platform type.

You may, if you wish, get rid of all the standard universal features: just write a totally new version of *ANY*, with no connection to *GENERAL* and *PLATFORM*. But this is seldom appropriate. In most cases, it is preferable to write a new version of *ANY* which, as the standard version shown above, is an heir of *PLATFORM*. This will give your classes continued access to the features of *GENERAL* and *PLATFORM*.

If you write a new version of *ANY*, remember that all the classes in your system will be its descendants. This means in particular that you should think twice before using a **variable attribute** as one of the features of the new *ANY*, since this adds a field to all run-time objects. The default *ANY* only has routines and constant attributes, so as not to cause any such overhead.

You will need a way to direct the language processing tools to select your specific *ANY* over the default one. In Lace (the recommended Language for Assembling Classes in Eiffel) you may achieve this simply by writing an **exclude** clause for the default *ANY*. This is explained in the discussion of Lace. If your implementation does not support Lace, it will provide some other way of specifying that a class called *ANY* in a certain cluster must take precedence over *ANY* from the default universal cluster.

→ *See appendix D about Lace*; more specifically, *D.9, page 522, explains the* **exclude** *Lace clause and how to use it to replace the standard ANY by another version.*

Whether you use the default *ANY* or another one, any system will need to have a class of name *ANY*. This is a constraint on any valid universe.

VHAY

6.16 *NONE*

Another important special class appearing on the general inheritance figure is *NONE*. This class is considered to inherit from all classes – assuming appropriate renaming to remove any resulting name clashes. It does not actually exist as a class text in the library (if only because that text would need to be updated every time anyone, anywhere, writes a new class!), but serves as a convenient fiction to make the class structure and the type system complete.

← *The general inheritance figure was on page 85.*

NONE has no useful instance. In class *ANY*, there is a feature called *Void*, of type *NONE* (introduced in *GENERAL*); *Void* serves as initialization value for all entities of reference types. An entity which has the same value as *Void* is not attached to any object and is said to be void.

→ *Creation operations are studied in chapter 18, with the initialization rule on page 291.*

Since *NONE* is assumed to be an heir of every class, the parent rule implies that no class may be an heir of *NONE*. *NONE* does not export any feature; consequently, no feature call may have a void target when it is executed.

The parent rule was given on page 79. Calling a feature on a void target triggers an exception; see 21.8, starting on page 345. NONE also serves as the type of actual arguments of the Address form, studied in 24.6, page 404.

7

Clients and exports

7.1 Overview

Along with inheritance, the client relation is one of the two mechanisms for structuring software.

Although this relation has several cases, the simplest and most common way for a class C (the client) to be a client of S (the supplier) is for C to contain the declaration of an entity representing objects of type S. This occurs for example when C includes a declaration of the form

> x: S

The features that C may apply to an entity such as x are those which the designer of S has explicitly made *available* (has *exported*) to the clients of S. In other words, the client relation allows a class to rely on the facilities provided by another as part of its official interface.

This chapter defines precisely the various forms of the client relation, and studies how a class can export its features to others, and how these can use the exported features. The discussion ends with a solution, resulting from the export mechanism, to an important practical question: how to document a class.

7.2 Entities

Classes become clients of one another through the types of their **entities**. An entity of a class C is one of the following:

- A typed feature (attribute or function) of C.

- A formal argument to a routine of C.

- A local entity of a routine of C, including (for a function) the predefined entity *Result* denoting the result.

→ *Entities also include the predefined entity Current, representing the target of the latest routine call. The full definition of entities is in 17.9, page 275.*

7.3 Conventions

Together with the preceding notions, we need a few conventions to simplify the discussion of the client and supplier relations.

First, it will be convenient to distinguish between several variants of the client relation: simple client, expanded client and generic client relations. Each is studied in one of the following sections. The general client relation will be obtained as a union of these cases, according to the following definition:

DEFINITION:
Client

> A class *C* is a **client** of *S* if some ancestor of *C* is a simple client, an expanded client or a generic client of *S*.

(Recall that the ancestors of *C* include *C* itself.) The inclusion of *C*'s ancestors is necessary because the dependencies caused by inherited features are just as significant as those caused by the immediate features of *C*. For example, an inherited routine *r* of *C* could use a local entity *x* of type *S*; this means that *C* depends on *S*, even if the declaration of *r*, and hence of *x*, appears in a distant proper ancestor.

Next, we need to clarify a technical point: when does the discussion of clients and suppliers involve classes, and when is it about types? If, as above, you declare in class *C* the entity *x* as being of type *S*, *S* is a type. That type may be a class, but it may also be a less trivial type; for example, *S* may be the type

← *A similar problem arose for inheritance: syntactically, a* Parent *is a type, not a class, but the definitions in 6.4, page 77, made it possible to talk about parent classes.*

> *D* [*U*]

where *D* is a generic class and *U*, itself a type, is the actual generic parameter for this use of *D*. Such an *S* is called a **generic derivation** of class *D*.

As this example indicates, the client relation in its most basic form holds between a class and a type, not necessarily between a class and another class.

It generalizes immediately, however, to a relation between classes, since every type is derived from some class called its **base class**. In most cases, the base class of a type is obvious: for example, in a generic derivation such as *D* [*U*], the base class is *D*; and if a non-generic class such as *B* above is used as a type, it is of course its own base class.

→ *The complete and precise definition of "base class", for every possible category of type, appears in the chapter on types, chapter 12.*

This justifies the following convention:

DEFINITION:
Client relation between classes

> A class *C* is a client of a class *B* if *C* is a client of a type whose base class is *B*.

The above discussion avoided the issue by cheating: the definition of "client" began as "A class C is a client of S if...", without specifying what S is — class or type. With the present convention, the definition is correct in both cases.

A similar convention applies to every variant of the client relation (simple, expanded, generic). As a result of these conventions, the definitions of the following sections introduce the conditions for a class *C* to be a client (of some form) of a type *S*.

The next convention applies to the indirect forms of the relations. If *C* is a client of *S* and *S* is a client of *B*, we will say that *C* is an indirect client of *B*. *S* here is a class. The full definition reads:

*Direct
or Indirect
Client*

A class C is a **direct or indirect client** of a type S of base type B if there is a sequence of classes $C_1 = A, C_2, ..., C_n = B$ such that $n > 1$ and every C_i is a client of C_{i+1} for $1 \leq i < n$.

The "direct or indirect" forms of the simple client, expanded client and generic client relations are defined similarly.

Finally, we sometimes need to refer to the inverse of the client relation or one of its variants. This is the **supplier** relation, with all the corresponding variants: S is a supplier of C if and only if C is a client of S; similarly, S may be a simple supplier of C, a direct or indirect generic supplier and so on. As before, the basic notion applies to S being a type and C a class, but generalizes immediately to two classes.

7.4 Simple clients

The most immediate case of the client relation is for a class C to be a simple client of a type S, which is then said to be a simple supplier of C. This happens whenever C contains a declaration of the form

> $x: S$

Assume for example the following class skeletons:

```
class A feature
   x: B;
   y: C [D];
   ...
end
```

```
class B feature
   z: E;
   ...
end
```

Then A is a simple client of B and C and B is a simple client of E. B and C are, conversely, simple suppliers of A, etc.

In the preceding cases, a class becomes a client of certain types through the declarations of its entities. More generally, C will also be a client of S whenever it contains an expression of type S.

The suggested graphical representation, illustrated on the next page, shows the simple client relation with a double arrow. The arrow may be labeled above by the name of the corresponding entity, and below by the names of the actual generic parameters in brackets, as with $[D]$ for the relation between A and C.

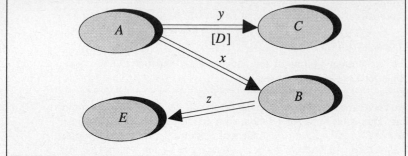

Here is the precise definition:

A class *C* is a **simple client** of a type *S* if some entity or expression of *C* is of type *S*.

As noted above, *S* is always derived from some base class *SC*, and *C* will also, by extension, be considered a client of *SC*. For example:

- A non-generic class *DOCUMENT* may be used as a type; the base class of that type is class *DOCUMENT* itself.
- The base class of *LIST* [*INTEGER*] is *LIST*. This base class is generic, and is used here with *INTEGER* as "actual generic parameter".

There is no constraint on how the classes of a system may be simple clients of one another.

This means in particular that a class may be its own simple client. For example you might need a class *PERSON* introducing attributes

mother, father: *PERSON*

This is an example of a direct cycle of the simple client relation. Cycles may also be indirect; for example, a class *HOUSE* might introduce an attribute

architect: *PERSON*

with class *PERSON* having an attribute *residence* of type *HOUSE*.

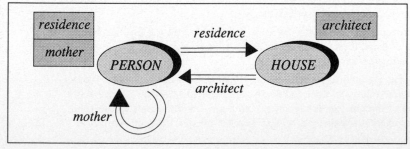

7.5 Expanded clients

Expanded types introduce a special variant of the client relation, called "expanded client".

Expanded types describe values which are themselves objects, without indirection. To specify that an entity is of an expanded type, you may declare it under the form

→ *See chapter 12 for the details of expanded types, starting with 12.10, page 204.*

> *y*: **expanded** *S*

for some Class_type *S*, or just

> *z*: *S1*

if the Class_header of *S1*'s base class begins with **expanded class** rather than just **class**. Assuming that class *S* is not expanded, the difference between the first of these declarations and

> *x*: *S*

is that possible values for *y* at run-time are not, as for *x*, references to instances of *S*, but those instances themselves. Similarly, the values of *z* at run-time will be instances of *S1*.

If either or both of *y* or *z* in the above declaration is an attribute of a class *C*, then instances of *C* will be **composite** objects; an object is composite if it contains sub-objects (other than values of basic types such as *INTEGER*). The figure below shows a composite object, which is an instance of a class that has some attributes of expanded types as well as others of reference types. All class names shown, except for *INTEGER*, are assumed to denote non-expanded, non-generic classes.

INTEGER, a basic class (and basic type), is expanded. See chapter 32 on basic types.

A reference type is a non-expanded type. See chapter 12.

Composite object

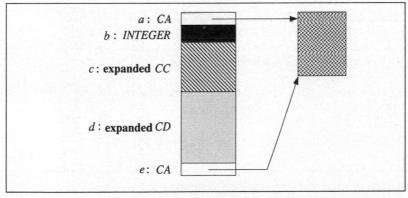

A declaration such as those of *y* and *z* above introduces a new variant of the client relation: expanded client. For this variant, in contrast with the previous one, cycles are not acceptable if they involve attributes. The reason is obvious: it would be absurd to expect every (composite) object of type *A* to have a sub-object of type *B* and every object of type *B* to have a sub-object of type *A*.

This leads to the following definition and constraint:

If C is an expanded client of S, C is also, according to the earlier definition, a simple client of S.

DEFINITION:
Expanded
Client

> A class *C* is an **expanded client** of a type *S* if *S* is an expanded type and some attribute of *C* is of type *S*.

> **Expanded Client rule**
>
> It is valid for a class *C* to be an expanded client of a class *SC* if and only if *SC* is not a direct or indirect expanded client of *C*.

(As with all the variants of the client relation, for *C* to be an expanded client of a class *SC* means to be an expanded client of a type *S* of base class *SC*.)

← *See "client relation between classes" page 90 above.*

The suggested graphical representation uses a double line, as with the simple client relation, but with a brace replacing the ending arrow, as shown below.

Expanded
client

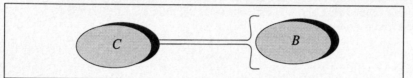

7.6 Generic clients

Assume that *B* is a generic class, and that class *C* contains a declaration of the form

> $x: B [S]$

using *S* as actual generic parameter for the generic derivation of *B*.

As seen above, this declaration makes *C* a simple client of *B*. But it also introduces a dependency between *C* and *S*. This dependency is in fact similar to what happens if *C* has an entity or expression of type *S*; this variant of the client relation is called **generic client**. Here is its precise definition:

DEFINITION:
Generic
Client,
Generic
Supplier

> A class *C* is a **generic client** of a type *S* if for some generically derived type *T* of the form *B* [..., *S*, ...] one of the following holds:
>
> 1 • *C* is a client of *T*.
> 2 • One of the Parent clauses of *C*, or of a proper ancestor of *C*, lists *T* as parent.

As the definition indicates, *C* may become a generic client of *S* by using *S* (or a type *T* based on *S*) as actual generic parameter not just in the type of an entity or expression (as with *x* above), but also in a Parent clause, as in

> **class** *C* **inherit**
>   *B* [..., *S*, ...];
>   ...
> **feature**
>   ...

The suggested graphical convention shows the generic client relation with a double arrow labeled with three dots in brackets [...] above the arrow, as in:

Generic client

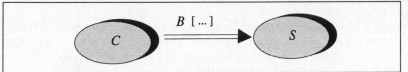

Do not confuse this with the notation expressing that C is a client of B, with S as actual generic parameter, through the declaration x: B [S]; in that case [S] will appear below the double arrow from C to B. See the relation between A and C on the first figure of page 92.

There is no restriction on how the classes of a system may be generic clients of each other.

7.7 Information hiding

Assume *C* is a simple or expanded client of *S*. In most cases, this means that *C* declares one or more entities of type *S*. Of course, just declaring these entities is not an end in itself. The main purpose of being a client is to call *S*'s features on these entities (and, more generally, on expressions of type *S*).

Let *C* be a client of *S*. The simplest form of call, occurring in *C*, is

> *x.f* (...)

→ See chapter 21 about the various forms, uses and properties of calls. Chapter 22 covers the conditions on call validity.

where *x* is of a type based on *S*, making *C* a client of *S*, and *f* is a feature of *S*. This form of call uses dot notation; forms using infix and prefix operators are also possible.

Not all such calls, however, are permitted; in particular, not all the features of a class need be callable by all clients. The designer of a supplier class may want to keep some features private, or available to some clients only, because they are only of internal use and subject to change; letting any client access them directly would jeopardize further evolution.

This is especially true of features that reflect not the primary services offered by a class to its clients, but particular choices of implementation of these services. By keeping such features private, the designer of the supplier class protects clients against the effects of later reversals of these choices. This policy is known as **information hiding**.

When designing a class, you may achieve information hiding through two mechanisms:

- For immediate features (those introduced in the class itself), you specify any needed export restrictions by listing clients in a Feature_clause. By default, in the absence of any explicit export restrictions, features are available to all possible clients.

- For inherited features (those obtained from parents), you may change the export policy specified by each parent through the New_exports subclauses of the corresponding Parent clauses. By default, inherited features not listed in an Export subclause keep the export status they had in the corresponding parent.

The next sections explain these two mechanisms in detail.

7.8 Restricting exports

The designer of a class achieves information hiding by specifying authorized clients in every Feature_clause of the class. As you may remember, a Feature_clause begins with the keyword **feature** followed by an optional Clients part; this Clients part, if present, lists those classes to which the feature is available.

If there is no Clients part, then every feature introduced in the Feature_clause is available to any client that cares to use it. So if class PARAGRAPH includes a Feature_clause of the form

To be quite accurate, the **feature** *keyword is not part of the* Feature_clause *but simply precedes it. This is because in the syntactical specification (page 60) the keyword is officially a list delimiter, belonging to the enclosing* Features *part.*

> **feature**
>   *indent* (*n*: *INTEGER*) **is**
>   -- Indent paragraph by *n* positions
>   ... Procedure body omitted ...

then any other class may declare an entity *p* of type *PARAGRAPH* and include a call such as

> *p.indent* (5)

If the Clients part of a Feature_clause is present, it consists of a list of classes in braces, and makes the features introduced by the clause available only to those classes and their descendants.

Here is such a Feature_clause, appearing in a class *LINKABLE* and listing three clients:

> **feature** {*LINKABLE, LINKED_LIST, TWO_WAY_TREE*}
>
>   *right*: **like** *Current*;
>
>   *put_right* (*other*: **like** *Current*) **is**
>   -- Replace by *other* the right neighbor of current element
>   ... Procedure body omitted ...

This Feature_clause introduces two features, *right* and *put_right*, which are available to clients *LINKABLE* (the class itself, viewed as its own client), *LINKED_LIST* and *TWO_WAY_TREE*. This means that, for *l* of type *LINKABLE*, calls of the form

> *l.right*
> *l.put_right (...)*

are permitted if they appear in descendants of one of the classes *LINKABLE, LINKED_LIST* and *TWO_WAY_TREE*.

The next two sections explore two properties which are visible on this example: a class may need to make features available to itself; and making a feature available to a class also makes it available to all of its proper descendants.

7.9 Exporting to oneself

The above Clients clause, appearing in class *LINKABLE*, listed *LINKABLE* itself among the classes to which *right* and *put_right* are available. This is required if the class contains a "qualified" call such as

> *l.put_right (...)*

with *l* of a type based on *LINKABLE*.

No such restriction exists, of course, for an "unqualified" call to a feature of a class, appearing in the class itself, as with

> *put_right (...)*

in class *LINKABLE*. This is permitted even if *put_right* is introduced in a Feature_clause whose Clients part does not include *LINKABLE*.

In contrast with the preceding qualified call, such unqualified calls are not considered to make the class a client of itself.

7.10 Exporting to descendants

As noted above, making a feature available to a class also makes it available to the proper descendants of that class. This is because a class needs the same privileges that its parents had; for example, it could redefine an inherited routine, replacing the original algorithm by a slightly different one, which still needs access to the same information from suppliers.

As a consequence, any features declared in a Feature_clause of the form

> **feature** {*ANY*}
>   ... Feature declarations ...

← See 6.12, page 85, for an introduction to class ANY, and chapter 27 for a detailed presentation.

are available to all classes, since every developer-defined class is a descendant of *ANY*. Such a clause has the same effect as no Clients part at all, as in

> **feature**
>   ... Feature declarations ...

Similarly, specifying

> **feature** *{NONE}*

has the same effect as an empty Clients clause, as in

> **feature** {}

 Do not confuse the effect of an empty Clients clause {} and that of no Clients clause: the first means features available to no useful clients and is equivalent to *{NONE}*; the second is equivalent to *{ANY}*, that is to say, features available to all potential clients.

7.11 Adapting the export status of inherited features

The above discussion has explained the export status of features introduced in a class (although the formal definitions have not yet been given). We also need to know what happens to inherited features.

If a feature is redeclared, its new declaration will appear in a Feature_clause, whose Clients clause, or absence thereof, will determine the export status as we have just seen. But what is the feature is not redeclared?

The rule is simple. By default, the feature will keep its export status. An heir can change that status, however, through a New_exports part, appearing as part of the Feature_adaptation subclause of a Parent clause.

→ A class "redeclares" a feature if it provides a new declaration for it. This may be either a redefinition of an effecting. See chapter 10 for details.

As an example, here is the beginning of a class of the Data Structure Library (excluding the Indexing clause):

> -- Stacks with a fixed physical size, implemented as arrays
> **class** *FIXED_STACK* [*T*] **inherit**
>   *STACK* [*T*] ;
>   *ARRAY* [*T*]
>   **rename**
>   *put* **as** *array_put,*
>   ... Other renaming pairs omitted ...
>   **export**
>   *{NONE}* **all**
>   **end**
> **feature**
>   ...

The New_exports part appears next to the other possible subclauses of a Feature_adaptation: Rename (as here), Undefine, Redefine, Join and Select. New_exports comes after Rename.

All these subclauses, and the Feature_adaptation *as a whole, are optional. The syntax is on page 77.*

In general, the New_exports subclause is of the form

$$\{A, B, C\}\, f1, f2, ...;$$
$$\{X, Y\}\, g1, g2, ...$$
$$...$$

and means: unless a redeclaration specifies a different status, make $f1$, $f2$, ... available to clients A, B, C and any of their descendants; make $g1$, $g2$, ... available to clients X, Y and any of their descendants; and so on.

If, instead of a feature list such as $f1$, $f2$, ..., a Clients list is followed by the keyword **all**, then all non-redeclared inherited features are available to the given clients and their descendants, except for any features for which other parts of the subclause specify a different policy. For example, *FIXED_STACK* above hides all features inherited from *ARRAY* from all clients (by exporting them to *NONE* only). This is a typical example of a class which inherits its interface from one parent (here *STACK*) and uses another parent (here *ARRAY*) for implementation purposes only.

If no part of the subclause mentions **all** in lieu of a feature list, any non-redeclared inherited feature which is not explicitly given a new export status keeps the exact export status that it had in the parent. Assume for example class declarations of the form:

```
class B feature
   x, y: INTEGER
feature {A}
   f, g, h: INTEGER
end
```

```
class C inherit
   B
      export
         {D} x;
         {ANY} f;
         {NONE} g;
      end
end -- class C
```

Then the features of C have the following status:

- y, available to all clients, and h, available to A and its descendants, keep the status they had in B.

- x is available to D and its descendants.

- f is available to all clients. (Re-exporting to *ANY* is the way to make generally available a feature which was selectively available, or secret, in a parent.)

- g is secret.

Such elaborate changes of export status in inheritance are uncommon. But the simpler cases do occur fairly often: in designing a new class, you may want to hide features that were exported by a parent, as in the case of all the features that *FIXED_STACK* inherits from *ARRAY*; or you may want to re-export a feature which was used in the parent for implementation purposes only, but turns out to be of direct value for the clients of the new class.

The ability of a class to change the export status of inherited features has important consequences for the type checking mechanism. See "notes on the type policy" in the discussion of type checking.

→ 22.6, Page 360.

7.12 The export status of features

The previous discussion allows us to give a precise definition of the "export status" of any feature of a class.

The status of any feature of final name *fn* in a class *C* will determine to what classes the feature is **available**. In turn, this determines what calls are valid: in a class *B*, if *x* is of type *C* a call of the form

→ *See chapter 22 on call validity. The precise requirement is condition 2 of export validity, page 368.*

$$x.fn \ (...)$$

or the equivalent using operator form, will only be valid if *fn* is available to *B*.

The status of a feature of a class is one of the following:

DEFINITION:
Exported

1 • The feature may be available to all classes. Such a feature is said to be **exported**, of **generally available**.

Selectively
Available

2 • The feature may be available to specific classes only. In that case it is also available to the descendants of all these classes. Such a feature is said to be **selectively available** to the given classes and their descendants.

Secret

3 • The feature may be available to no classes. Then it is said to be **secret**.

A feature is "available" to a class as a result of either case 1 or case 2:

DEFINITION:
Available

A feature of a class *S* is said to be **available** to a class *C* if and only if it is either selectively available to *S* or generally available.

C may be the same class as *S*: a feature from a class may or may not be "available to" the class itself.

A special variant of case 2 is a feature made selectively available to class *NONE* only. Since class *NONE* has neither instances nor proper descendants, this is equivalent to having the feature secret (case 3).

Another variant of case 2 is a feature made selectively available to class *ANY*. Since every class is a descendant of *ANY*, this is equivalent to having the feature generally available (case 1).

Be sure to remember that a feature available to a class is also available to all the proper descendants of that class.

7.13 Adapting the export status

(This section introduces no new concepts but gives a more formal presentation of ideas introduced above. You may wish to skip it on first reading.)

The two constructs that determine the export status of a feature are Clients and New_exports. To conclude this discussion of the export status, we need to express their precise syntax, constraints and semantics.

Here is the syntax of the Clients part:

| Clients | $\triangleq$ | "{" Class_list "}" |
| Class_list | $\triangleq$ | {Class_name "," ...} |

This construct may appear in two positions. One is in a New_exports, as seen next; the other is as an optional component of a Feature_clause, as in

feature $\{A, B, C\}$
... Feature declarations ...

A simple constraint applies:

A Clients part is valid if and only if every Class_name appearing in its Class_list is the name of a class in the surrounding universe.

VLCP

This is one of the two constraints on the use of an Identifier as Class_name. The other constraint, called the Class Type rule, addresses the only other possible use of a Class_name in the language: as part of a Class_type. Both constraints state the same property: the Identifier must be the name of a class in the universe.

→ *The Class Type rule is on page 199.*

The above rule does not restrict the classes that may be listed in the Class_list. In particular, one of them may be the enclosing class or one of its ancestors: as noted above, a class may wish to make a feature available selectively to itself.

Now for the New_exports part. It has the following form:

New_exports	$\triangleq$	**export** New_export_list
New_export_list	$\triangleq$	{New_export_item ";" ...}
New_export_item	$\triangleq$	Clients Feature_set
Feature_set	$\triangleq$	Feature_list | **all**
Feature_list	$\triangleq$	{Feature_name "," ...}

← *This appears as part of the* Inheritance *part; syntax page 77.*

It may appear in the Feature_adaptation part of a Parent clause, as illustrated by *FIXED_STACK* above.

A constraint applies to any New_exports clause:

VLEL

> **Export List rule**
>
> A New_exports parent appearing in class *C* in a Parent clause for a parent *B*, of the form
>
> **export**
>
> > {*class_list*$_1$} *feature_list*$_1$;
> >
> > ...
> >
> > {*class_list*$_n$} *feature_list*$_n$;
>
> is valid if and only if (for *i* in the interval $1..n$):
>
> 1 • At most one of the *feature_list*$_i$ is the keyword **all**.
>
> 2 • All the other *feature_list*$_i$ are lists of final names of features of *C* obtained from *B*.
>
> 3 • No final feature name appears twice in any such list, or appears in more than one list.

To obtain the export status of a feature, we need to look at the Feature_clause which introduces it if the feature is immediate, at the Feature_clause containing its redeclaration if its inherited and redeclared, and at the applicable New_exports clause, if any, if it is inherited feature but not redeclared. The rest of this section gives the corresponding semantic rules in each case.

An immediate feature of a class has the following export status:

A• If the Feature_clause which introduces it has no Clients part (that is to say, begins with the keyword **feature** with no further qualification), the feature is exported (generally available).

B• If the Feature_clause which introduces it has a Clients part (that is to say, begins with **feature** {*A, B, C* ...}), the feature is selectively available to the descendants of the classes listed in that Clients part, and to these descendants only.

Remember that the descendants of a class include the class itself.

Case B includes in particular the following situations:

DEFINITION:
Secret

• If the Feature_clause has an empty Clients list, that is to say, begins with **feature** {}, then the features it introduces are secret.

• A Feature_clause has a Clients list of the form {*NONE*}, making its features available only to *NONE* (which has no proper descendants), the practical effect is also to make the features secret.

• If the Clients list is of the form {*ANY*}, the effect is the same as an absent Clients list (features generally available), since every class is a descendant of *ANY*.

The next possibility to consider is that of an inherited feature *f* of a class *C*, for which *C* gives a redeclaration. The rule is the same as if *f* were immediate, as just defined: the Feature_clause containing the redeclaration determines the export status. New_exports clauses, if any, have no effect on *f*.

There remains to see the rule for non-redeclared inherited features. A feature *f* inherited by a class *C* from one of its parents *B* under the final name *fn*, and not redeclared in *C*, has the following status in *C*:

1 • If case 1 does not apply and *fn* appears in a list of feature names in the New_exports subclause of the Parent clause for *B*, then *f* is selectively available to the descendants of the classes listed in the corresponding Clients part, and to those descendants only.

2 • If case 1 does not apply, and the New_exports subclause for *B* includes a branch listing **all** in lieu of a list of feature names, then *f* is selectively available to the descendants of the classes listed in the corresponding Clients part, and to those descendants only.

3 • If none of the above cases applies (in particular, if there is no New_exports clause for *B* in *C*), *f* has the same export status that its precursor had in *B*.

The "precursor" of an inherited feature *f* is the version of that feature in the parent from which *f* is inherited, here *B*.

→ The definition of "precursor" is in chapter 10. See pages 140 and 165.

This rule is usually sufficient to determine the export status of an inherited feature, except for one special case that it does not address. The premise of the rule is that *C* inherits *f* "from *one* of its parents" – in other words, that *f* has only one precursor. This is by far the most common case. But under two circumstances studied in later chapters, it is possible for *f* to result from the merging of features coming from two or more different parents.

→ The two cases of merging inherited features are the Join of deferred features (10.17, page 156) and sharing under repeated inheritance (see Repeated Inheritance rule, page 170).

The extension of the above rule in this case is straightforward. If a non-redeclared inherited feature *f* has more than one precursor, it is available to all classes to which it would be available as a consequence of applying the preceding rule separately to each of its precursors.

In other words, if *f* has a precursor in each of B_1, B_2, ... B_n, you will pretend in turn that *C* inherits *f* only from B_1, only from B_2, ..., only from B_n. At each step you get a list of classes to which *f* would be available. Then *f* is in fact available to every one of the classes obtained at any step in this process, and to these classes only.

7.14 Describing a class for clients: the short form

Now that we have seen the details of the client and export mechanisms, we can obtain an answer to a central issue of Eiffel software development: how can the author of a class provide authors of client classes with a clear description of the facilities offered?

The full class text is not appropriate for this purpose, as it contains implementation details as well as interface information, in contradiction with the principle of information hiding.

DEFINITION:
Short Form,
Abstract Form

The proper description is provided by the **short form** of a class, also called its **abstract** form. This is a text which has the same structure as the class but does not include non-public elements. The short form is the one that should be used as interface documentation for the class.

The following shows the short form of class *LINKED_LIST* from the Data Structure Library.

-- One-way linked lists

class interface *LINKED_LIST* [*T*] **exported features**

put_right (*v*: **like** *first*)
-- Put *v* to the right of cursor position.
-- Do not move cursor.

put_left (*v*: **like** *first*)
-- Put *v* to the left of cursor position.
-- Do not move cursor.

remove
-- Remove item at cursor position
-- and move cursor to its right neighbor
-- (or after last item if no right neighbor).

remove_right (*n*: *INTEGER*)
-- Remove min (*n*, *count* − *position*) items
-- to the right of cursor position.
-- Do not move cursor.
require
non_negative_argument: *n* >= *0*

remove_left (*n*: *INTEGER*)
-- Remove min (*n*, *position* − 1) items
-- to the right of cursor position.
-- Do not move cursor
-- (but its index will be decreased by up to *n*).
require
non_negative_argument: *n* >= 0

remove_all_occurrences (*v*: **like** *first*)
-- Remove all items *v*;
-- Move cursor after last item.

merge_right (*other*: **like** *Current*)
-- Merge *other* into the current list after cursor position.
-- Do not move cursor.
require
argument_not_void: **not** *other*.*null*
ensure
other.*empty*

merge_left (*other*: **like** *Current*)
-- Merge *other* into the current list before cursor position.
-- Do not move cursor.
require
argument_not_void: **not** *other*.*null*
ensure
other.*empty*

sublist: **like** *Current*
-- Result produced by last *split*

split (*n*: *INTEGER*)
-- Remove from current list min (*n, position − count*) items
-- starting at cursor position.
-- Make extracted sublist accessible through attribute *sublist*.
require
valid_sublist: $n >= 0$
ensure
count = **old** *count* − min (*n*, (*count* − **old** *position* + *1*))

end interface -- class *LINKED_LIST*

The responsibility for producing such short forms should lie not with users but with automatic tools of the Eiffel environment. ISE's implementation, for example, includes a command **short** with various options, which will produce the short form of any class, generating a form close to the above. One may obtain the flat-short form (see below) by combining **short** with another command, **flat**.

See "Eiffel: The Environment" for details about commands **short** *and* **flat** *in ISE's implementation.*

As you will have noted, the short form relies on syntactical conventions which are slightly different from those of Eiffel, to avoid any confusion with actual Eiffel texts. For example, it uses the term **class interface** instead of the Eiffel keyword **class**.

The **short** *tool of ISE's implementation has, however, a* –e *option which generates a correct Eiffel output, with all features deferred.*

The precise specification of the short form is not part of the language definition. The general guidelines, as illustrated by the above example, are the following. The short form retains the following elements:

- The header of a Feature_declaration (Feature_list, Formal_arguments, Type_mark).
- The header comment of a routine.
- Those clauses of a routine's precondition and postcondition which only refer to exported features.
- Those clauses of a class invariant which only refer to exported features.

The short form omits implementation-dependent elements:

- The declarations of all non-exported features, and any other mention of such features.
- The Routine clauses of effective routine declarations (**do, once, deferred** or **external** clauses).
- Comments other than assertion and routine header comments.

Finally, note that features may be not just (generally) exported or secret, but also selectively exported to some classes. So it must be possible to produce a short form adapted to the view of a particular class *B*, or "short form for *B*". This will contain only the information available to *B*; in particular, the assertion clauses retained will be those available to *B*. An abstracting command such as **short** should support an option producing the short form for a given class.

→ *An* Assertion_clause *is "available" to a class if all the entities involved in the clause are available to the class. This notion is defined fully in the discussion of assertions, page 123.*

7.15 The flat-short form

DEFINITION:
Flat-Short
Form

The short form as seen above only includes information about the immediate features of a class. Often, developers of client classes will need more complete information, treating all features, immediate and inherited, on an equal footing.

To obtain such information, you need the **flat-short** form. The flat-short form is similar to the short form, but applies to the "reconstructed" full text of a class; you may view it as resulting from a shortening step that has been preceded by a "flattening" step, which expands the class text to unfold all the features obtained from proper ancestors, putting them at the same level as the immediate features of the class. Clearly, flattening must take both renaming and redefinition into account.

In ISE's Eiffel environment, flattening is the responsibility of the **flat** tool; to obtain the flat-short form, you may apply **short** to the result of **flat**. This is achieved by piping the two commands, as in

To "pipe" two commands is to use the output of one as input to the other. The notation using a vertical bar for piping comes from the Unix shell; other operating systems may use different conventions.

> **flat** *class* | **short**

The flat-short form normally does not list any information about the universal features that all classes inherit by default from the universal class *ANY*. This policy admits two exceptions:

• Environment tools in charge of producing flat-short forms should offer an option that will include the universal features.

• Whether or not you enable this option, any feature from *ANY* will appear in the flat-short form if it has been redefined.

*In ISE's implementation, command **flat** has an option -a (for "all") which will include features from ANY.*

8

Routines

8.1 Overview

Routines describe computations.

Syntactically, routines are one of the two kinds of feature of a class; the other kind is attributes, which describe data fields associated with instances of the class. Since every Eiffel operation applies to a specific object, a routine of a class describes a computation applicable to instances of that class. When applied to an instance, a routine may access some fields of the instance (corresponding to attributes of the class), and may also update some fields.

→ *Chapter 16 explores attributes.*

A routine is either a procedure, which does not return a result, or a function, which does. A routine may further be declared as **deferred**, meaning that the class introducing it only gives its specification, leaving it for descendants to provide implementations. A routine which is not deferred is said to be **effective**.

An effective routine has a *body*, which describes the computation to be performed by the routine. A body is a Compound, or sequence of instructions; each instruction is a step of the computation.

This chapter describes the structure of routine declarations. It also introduces the various forms of instructions, described in detail in subsequent chapters.

8.2 Routine declaration

A routine declaration describes the interface of a routine and (unless the routine is deferred) its implementation.

Here are two routine declarations; *total* is a function and *move* is a procedure.

```
total: INTEGER is
    -- The sum of attributes a, b and c
do
    Result := a + b + c
end; -- total
```

```
move (mice: MOUSE; men: MENU) is
    -- Move mouse cursor to first item in menu
require
    mice.move (men)
deferred
end -- move
```

As indicated by these examples, the optional ending comment, when present, should repeat the name of the routine.

More generally, remember that a Feature_declaration declares a routine if and only if the following condition is satisfied:

← The general form of feature declarations was given in 5.9, starting on page 63.

- There is a Constant_or_routine part, whose Feature_value is a Routine.

In this case the following parts may or may not be present: Formal_arguments, Type_mark, Obsolete mark. If the Type_mark is present, the declaration describes a **function**; otherwise it describes a **procedure**.

As with any other feature, a routine declaration may include more than one routine name, as in the following declaration of three procedures:

```
proc2, proc3, proc4 (x, y: REAL) is
    require
        x > y
    do
        print (sqrt (x − y))
    end -- proc2, proc3, proc4
```

Here the ending comment should list the names of all the routines declared together, separated by commas.

In such a case all the routines have the same Routine part and the same effect. They remain otherwise independent; in particular, redefining or renaming one in a descendant does not affect the others.

Renaming is studied in chapter 6, redefinition in chapter 10. The effect of multiple declarations ("synonyms") was discussed in 5.16, starting on page 71.

8.3 Formal arguments

A routine may have arguments, corresponding to information that callers will pass to every execution of the routine.

Within the routine, the arguments are represented by entities called **formal arguments**.

Any particular call will pass to the routines a list of expressions corresponding to each of the formal arguments; these expressions are called **actual arguments**. The number of actual arguments must be the same as the number of formal arguments, and the type of each actual argument must conform to the type of the formal argument at the same position in the list.

→ *The precise rule for validity of calls is studied in chapter 22. See below about achieving the effect of a variable number of arguments.*

A note on terminology: the arguments of a routine are always called that way – arguments. The word "parameter", never used in this context, is reserved for the formal and actual **generic parameters** of a generic class.

About genericity see chapter 12, especially 12.7 and the subsequent sections, starting on page 200.

Function *total* above has no arguments; its body only refers to attributes of the enclosing class. Procedure *move* has two formal arguments called *mice* and *men*.

Assume both *move* and *total* appear in a class *C*. Instructions using typical calls to these routines, appearing in some routine of a class *B*, might be

> *c1*.*move* (*mi*, *me*);
> *n* := *c1*.*total*

with *c1* of type *C*, *mi* of type *MOUSE*, *me* of type *MENU*, *n* of type *INTEGER*. Expressions *mi* and *me* are the actual arguments of the first call.

The formal arguments of *move* were all of different types. As with feature names in a Feature_declaration, you may group two or more arguments of the same type into an Entity_declaration_group. The comma serves as separator, as in this routine from class *TWO_WAY_LIST* in the Data Structure Library:

> *update_after_deletion*
>   (*one*, *other*: **like** *first_element*; *index*: *INTEGER*)
>   **is**
> ... Rest of routine omitted ...

This declares both *one* and *other* as being of type **like** *first_element*. The effect would have been the same with a routine header of the form

> *update_after_deletion*
>   (*one*: **like** *first_element*;
>   *other*: **like** *first_element*;
>   *index*: *INTEGER*)

The preceding examples illustrate the general form of the Formal_arguments part of a routine declaration.

Formal_arguments	≜	"(" Entity_declaration_list ")"
Entity_declaration_list	≜	{Entity_declaration_group ";" ...}
Entity_declaration_group	≜	Identifier_list Type_mark
Identifier_list	≜	{Identifier "," ...}⁺
Type_mark	≜	":" Type

A validity constraint mandates a choice of name avoiding any ambiguity:

Formal Argument rule

Let *fa* be the Formal_arguments part of a routine *r* in a class *C*. Let *formals* be the concatenation of every Identifier_list of every Entity_declaration_group in *fa*. Then *fa* is valid if and only if no Identifier *e* appearing in *formals* is the final name of a feature of *C*.

This is complemented by a general rule on any Entity_declaration_list, also applicable to the declaration of local entities, as studied later in this chapter:

→ *See 8.7, page 114, about local entities.*

Let *el* be an Entity_declaration_list. Let *identifiers* be the concatenation of every Identifier_list of every Entity_declaration_group in *fa*. Then *el* is valid if and only if no Identifier appears more than once in the list *identifiers*.

In other words, no identifier may be the target of more than one declaration in the entire Entity_declaration_group. Clearly, in

> *x*: *T1*;
> *x*, *y*, *y*: *T2*

WARNING: *not valid!*

the type of *x* would be ambiguous. The type of *y* would not be ambiguous since the two occurrences are part of the same Entity_declaration_group, but the duplicate listing of *y* is invalid all the same; it can serve no useful purpose.

8.4 Using a variable number of arguments

From the above syntax, and the previewed constraint on valid calls, it appears that every routine has a fixed number of arguments, which is the number of entities appearing in the Entity_declaration_list of its Formal_arguments part.

This restriction is indeed in force, but it does not prevent you from obtaining the effect of routines with variable numbers of arguments if you so desire. Just use a formal argument of type *ARRAY* [*T*] for some *T*. Then a corresponding actual argument may be a **manifest array**, written as a list of expressions enclosed in double angle brackets:

→ *See 23.20, page 393, about manifest arrays, and chapter 28 about class ARRAY.*

> $\ll e_1, e_2, ... e_n \gg$

where the type of every e_i conforms to *T*.

Assume for example that you need a procedure *formated_write* which writes any number of values of various types, using a specified format. The type of all these values must be based on *NUMERIC*, or on a proper descendant of that class. Then you may declare the procedure as

> *formated_write* (*values*: *ARRAY* [*NUMERIC*]; *format*: *STRING*) **is**
>   -- Print all the elements of *values*, under the given *format*
>   ... Procedure body omitted ...

and use calls of the form

$$c.formated\_write\ (\ll a, 34, 5.6, b + c\gg, my\_output\_format)$$

where the list in angle brackets is made of an arbitrary number of values, whose types all conform to *NUMERIC*. (This Kernel Library class is indeed such that basic types such as *INTEGER* and *REAL* conform to it.)

→ 'formated_write' may need to determine the precise type of each array element, especially for elements of basic types such as INTEGER. 32.4, page 477, explains how to do this.

The body of a procedure such as *formated_write* will access the elements of the *values* list through normal array accessing mechanisms.

For a routine which would need to manipulate an arbitrary number of values of arbitrary type, you could use the same scheme with a formal argument of type *ARRAY [ANY]*, where *ANY* is ancestor to all developer-defined classes.

→ About ANY, see 6.12, page 85, and chapter 27.

8.5 Routine structure

A Routine contains a Routine_body and a number of optional components. Here is a routine (from the Window cluster of the Graphics Library) which has all the optional components except for the Obsolete and Rescue clauses:

Obsolete *was discussed in 5.17, page 73. Chapter 15 covers* Rescue, *with a few words of preview below.*

```
imp_create (w: PIXMAP) is
    -- Create pixmap structure for w.
require
    pixmap_exists: w /= Void
local
    color: INTEGER
do
    color := White_color;
    e_ref := w;
    imp_reference :=
        c_createpixmap (w.width, w.height, imp_depth, color)
ensure
    imp_reference /= 0;
    e_ref = w
end -- imp_create
```

The various components and their respective roles are the following. All components except the Routine_body and the final **end** are optional.

- The text appearing immediately after the **is**, preceded by --, is a Header_comment explaining the purpose of the routine. Other comments may, of course, be inserted at the end of any line; but this one has a special role, documenting the routine's interface. The "short" form of a class retains header comments.

The notion of short form of a class was introduced in 7.14, page 103. See appendix A about recommended commenting styles.

- The keyword **require** introduces an Assertion, called the Precondition of the routine. This expresses the conditions under which a call to the routine is correct. Here clients must not call *imp_create* above unless they guarantee that the actual argument corresponding to *w* is a non-void reference. The Identifier *pixmap_exists* is a label identifying that assertion.

→ *Preconditions, postconditions and other assertions are studied in chapter 9.*

- The keyword **ensure** introduces an Assertion, called the Postcondition of the routine. This expresses the conditions that a routine call will ensure on return if called in a state satisfying the precondition. For example, *imp_create* guarantees that, on exit, *imp_reference* will be non-zero and *e_ref* will be a reference to the same object as *w*.

- The Local_declarations clause, studied below, declares local entities used only within the routine body, and initialized anew on each call. Here *imp_create* uses a local entity *color* of type *INTEGER*.

- The Routine_body, studied below, is either Deferred, making the routine deferred, or Effective. An Effective body may be External, meaning that the routine implementation is written separately (usually in another language), or Internal; an Internal body is the keyword **do** or **once**, followed by zero or more instructions. The example illustrates the most common case: Internal with **do**.

The example does not include a Rescue clause. If present, this describes what to do if an exception occurs during an execution of the routine. The absence of a Rescue clause has the same effect as the presence of an Rescue clause just consisting of a call to the procedure *default_rescue* of the universal class *ANY*. So the example routine could have been written equivalently as

→ *The* Rescue *clause and procedure 'default_rescue' are discussed in detail in chapter 15.*

```
imp_create (w: PIXMAP) is
    ... All other clauses as above ...
rescue
    default_rescue
end -- imp_create
```

In its original form, *default_rescue* has a null effect, but a class may redefine it to provide specific exception handling.

With this example in mind, we can now look at the general structure of a Routine part:

Routine	≜	[Obsolete]
		[Header_comment]
		[Precondition]
		[Local_declarations]
		Routine_body
		[Postcondition]
		[Rescue]
		end ["--" Feature_name]

Two of the clauses, Rescue (describing responses to exceptions occurring during the routine's execution) and Local_declarations, are only applicable to effective routines of the Internal form (**do** or **once**). This is because the clauses only make sense in reference to an actual computation described by the Routine_body; for a deferred routine the routine has no implementation, and for an external routine the implementation is described in another language, outside the scope of the routine declaration. These observations yield the constraint on Routine parts:

> **Routine rule**
>
> A Routine part of a routine declaration is valid if and only if one of the following conditions holds:
>
> 1 • Its Routine_body is an Internal body (beginning with **do** or **once**).
> 2 • In the other cases (where the Routine_body is External or Deferred), there is neither a Local_declarations part nor a Rescue part.

The remaining sections of this chapter examine the following parts of a Routine: Routine_body and Local_declarations. The chapter will conclude with a preview of the various types of Instruction. (An Instruction is the basic component in a Compound, used to build a Routine_body of the Internal form.)

8.6 Routine body

A Routine_body describes the computation, if any, that the routine will perform:

SYNTAX

Routine_body	$\triangleq$	Effective | Deferred
Effective	$\triangleq$	Internal | External
Internal	$\triangleq$	Routine_mark Compound
Routine_mark	$\triangleq$	**do** | **once**
Deferred	$\triangleq$	**deferred**

A Routine_body of the second possible form, Deferred, consists of the sole keyword **deferred**; this indicates that the routine is deferred (making the enclosing class deferred as well).

An Effective body may be External, indicating that the routine is implemented in another language. Otherwise (in the Internal case) it is a Compound, that is to say a sequence of instructions describing the algorithm to be executed after initialization of any local entities (including *Result* for a function), when the routine is called.

SEMANTICS

The introductory keywords **do** or **once** of an Internal body correspond to different semantics for calls to the routine:

1 • For a **do** body, as indicated above, the initialization and body are executed anew on each call.

2 • If routine *o* of class *C* has a **once** body (*o* is then called a "once routine"), the initialization and body of *o* are executed only for the first call to *o* applied to an instance of *C* during any given session. For every subsequent call to *o* applied to an instance of *C* during the same session, the routine call has no effect; if the routine is a function, the value it returns is the same as the value returned by the first call.

Once routines are useful for initialization actions which must be applied the first time a certain structure is accessed, and for shared information. They are instrumental in avoiding any need for the global variables of conventional programming languages.

→ Deferred routines and classes are studied in chapter 10. See in particular 10.9, page 144, and subsequent sections.

→ Compound and other control structures are studied in chapter 14.

*→ The presentation of call semantics in chapter 21 indicates how to execute a routine body, **do** or **once**. The precise specification is in 21.14, page 352.*

On how to use once functions to obtain shared objects, see the example of function 'shared' on page 387.

A constraint on once functions was introduced as part of the Feature Declaration rule (condition 7): if the enclosing class is generic, the result of a once function may not be one of the formal generic parameters. This is necessary for the function to provide a consistent result: since the first client which calls the function will determine the result of all later calls, the once function's result type must be meaningful for all clients; but different clients may use different actual generic parameters for the class. The formal parameter, which stands for any possible actual generic parameter chosen by a client, would then represent incompatible types.

← *The Feature Declaration rule is on page 69.*

→ *On formal and actual generic parameters, see chapter 12, especially 12.7, page 200, and the subsequent sections.*

8.7 Local entities and *Result*

If present in a routine, a Local_declarations clause is the declaration of entities which are only available within the Routine_body.

Here is the beginning of a routine in class *AGGREGATE* from the Parsing Library, with its Local_declarations and some of its Routine_body:

```
parse_body is
        -- Attempt to find input matching the components of
        -- the aggregate starting at current position.
    require
        no_child: no_components
    local
        wrong: BOOLEAN;
        err: STRING
    do
        from
            expand
        until
            wrong or child_offright
        loop
            ... Rest of Routine omitted ...
```

To understand the semantics of such examples, you will need to look at the default initialization rules, which every routine call applies anew to the local entities. Here *wrong* will be initialized to false, the default value of type *BOOLEAN*, on each routine entry.

→ *The initialization of local entities comes from the semantics of calls, given in 21.14, page 352. Default initialization values are given in 18.13, page 291.*

The general structure of a Local_declarations clause is:

Local_declarations   ≜   **local** Entity_declaration_list

Following a general syntax convention, the semicolon is **optional** between an Entity_declaration_list and the next. The style guidelines, as followed in this book, suggest including the semicolon.

The style rule appears on page 493 with the list of contexts in which the semicolon is optional.

In addition to the constraint requiring all identifiers in an Entity_declaration_list to be different, we must avoid any ambiguity between local entities and features of the class:

← *The earlier constraint is VREG, page 110.*

Local Entity rule

Let *ld* be the Local_declarations part of a routine *r* in a class *C*. Let *locals* be the concatenation of every Identifier_list of every Entity_declaration_group in *ld*. Then *ld* is valid if and only if every Identifier *e* in *ld* satisfies the following two conditions:

1 • No feature of *C* has *e* as its final name.

2 • No formal argument of *r* has *e* as its Identifier.

DEFINITION:
Local *entity*

Most of the rules governing the validity and semantics of declared local entities also apply to a special predefined entity: *Result*, which may only appear in the Routine_body or Postcondition of a function, and denotes the result to be returned by the function. Reflecting this similarity, this book uses the term **local entity** to cover *Result* as well as declared local entities.

When applying validity and semantics rules, you must treat *Result* as an entity of the type declared for the enclosing function's result. For example, this function from class *CLOSED_FIGURE* in the Graphics Library treats *Result* as a local entity of type *INTEGER*:

```
fill_style_count: INTEGER is
    -- Number of defined fill styles for this figure
do
    Result := global_fill_style_count + local_fill_style_count
end -- fill_style
```

8.8 Externals

A routine may have a Routine_body of the External form, which means that its implementation is written in another language.

The following examples illustrate the form of an External body:

```
open_file (file_od: INTEGER; mode: CHARACTER) is
    -- Open file_od in mode mode
require
    file_status (file_od) <= 0
external
    "C"
end; -- open_file
```

```
file_status (file_od: INTEGER): INTEGER is
    -- Current status of file associated with file_od
external
    "C"
alias
    "_fstat"
end -- file_status
```

The "other" language may be Eiffel if, for some reason, it has been felt necessary to precompile some classes separately. Except under special circumstances, however, this solution is not justified, since it will prevent the Eiffel implementation from performing normal type checking and optimization.

The Routine_body that includes this clause will be able to call a C procedure under the name *open_file* and a C function under *file_status*.

Such routines are viewed by the rest of a system as normal Eiffel routines; their only special property is that their execution, instead of being under the control of the Eiffel system to which they belong, is a call to some precompiled code, generated by a compiler for the foreign language.

The second external routine of the example, a function, has a subclause of the form **alias** *external_name*, indicating that this function will be known through an Eiffel name, *file_status*, different from its name in the foreign language; by default the two would be the same. Here an alias is required since the C name, *_fstat*, begins with an underscore and so is not a valid Eiffel identifier.

The details of external routines are given in a later chapter, as part of a general discussion of interfaces with other languages. → *See chapter 24.*

8.9 Types of instructions

The Internal body of a non-deferred routine is a Compound, or sequence of instructions. As an introduction to the detailed study of instructions in part C, here is an overview of the various forms of instructions.

A Creation instruction creates a new object, initializes its fields to default values, calls on it one of the creation procedures of the class (if any), and attaches the object to an entity.

→ *Creation instructions are studied in chapter 18.*

Assignment and Assignment_attempt are reattachment instructions, which change the attachment of an entity to an object. They differ in the applicable typing constraints.

→ *Reattachment instructions are studied in chapter 20.*

Call applies a routine to the object attached to a non-void expression. For the Call to yield an instruction, the routine must be a procedure.

→ *Calls are studied (both as instructions and as expressions) in chapter 21.*

Conditional, Multi_branch and Loop describe complex instructions, or *control structures*, obtained by scheduling other instructions.

Debug, which may also be considered a control structure, is used for instructions that should only be part of the system when you enable the *debug* compilation option.

→ *Control structures, including Debug, are studied in chapter 14.*

Check is used to express that certain assertions are satisfied at run-time.

→ *Assertions and Check are studied in chapter 9.*

Finally, Retry is used in conjunction with the exception handling mechanism.

The syntax specification corresponding to these various possibilities is the following:

→ *The exception mechanism and Retry are studied in chapter 15.*

Instruction	≜	Creation |
		Call |
		Assignment |
		Assignment_attempt |
		Conditional | Multi_branch | Loop |
		Debug | Check | Retry

9

Correctness

9.1 Overview

Eiffel software texts – classes and their routines – may be equipped with elements of formal specification, called **assertions**, expressing correctness conditions.

Assertions play several roles: they help in the production of correct and robust software, yield high-level documentation, provide debugging support, and serve as a basis for exception handling.

This chapter describes assertions and the resulting notion of correctness of a class. It also specifies how the supporting development environment should help check correctness conditions at run time.

9.2 Why assertions?

One could write entire systems without including any assertions. Some Eiffel developers are even rumored to have done this in the past. In fact, assertions have no effect on the semantics of correct systems – which is the only one that theoretically matters.

Do not look, however, for a SHORTCUT sign suggesting that you skip this chapter on first reading. Assertions are a key element of software development in Eiffel and omitting them would be renouncing a major benefit of the method.

Assertions serve to express the specification of software components: indications of *what* a component does rather than *how* it does it. This is essential information for building the components so that they will perform reliably, for using the components, and for validating them.

See "Deviant Eiffel Programmers", in Proceedings of RACOON 13 (Report of the Annual Conference on Object-Oriented Neuropsychiatry), Tahiti, 1991, pp. 3456-3542.

The classes of the Data Structure Library provide many examples of the use of assertions to express abstract properties of classes and routines. Consider the many descendants of class *CHAIN*, describing sequential data structures ("chains") such as lists. They enable clients to manipulate a cursor, which is allowed to go one position off the right and left edges of a chain, but no further. This property is expressed by an assertion occurring in the **class invariant** of the corresponding classes:

Calls are required to maintain the invariant only if they are "qualified", that is to say of the form a.*rout*. *See 9.14 below.*

> $0 <= position; position <= count + 1$

where *position* is the index of the current cursor position, and *count* is the number of elements in the structure. The invariant must be guaranteed by every creation procedure of the class, and maintained by any non-secret routine.

In the same classes, a client may use exported procedures such as *start*, *finish*, *forth* and *back* to move the cursor. The bodies of these procedures depend on the implementation chosen (linked, array etc.) but many of their important properties are expressed by implementation-independent assertions, so that a version of *forth* will have the form

```
forth is
        -- Move forward one position.
    require
        not_after: not after
    do
        ... Some appropriate implementation ...
    ensure
        position = old position + 1
    end -- forth
```

The **require** and **ensure** clauses introduce assertions, a **precondition** and **postcondition**:

- The precondition states the condition under which *forth* is applicable: the cursor must not be "after" the right edge, as expressed by the boolean function *after*. Any client must guarantee this condition when calling *forth*.

The optional label 'not_after', called a Tag, *serves as documentation and also for error messages. See below.*

- The postcondition states the property which the procedure must guarantee at the completion of any correct call: the cursor position will have been increased by one. The expression **old** *position* denotes the value of *position* as captured on routine entry.

As these examples indicate, assertions are not instructions; they do not necessarily have an effect on the execution of the systems in which they appear. Instead, they express properties that should be satisfied by the implementation. In other words, an assertion is a *description*, not a *prescription*.

Assertions have three major roles:

- By helping developers to state precisely the formal properties of software elements, they may be used to enhance the correctness and reliability of the resulting software. The underlying theory, known as **design by contract**, views the construction of a software system as the fulfillment of many small and large contracts between clients and suppliers.

See "Object-Oriented Software Construction" and "Design by Contract". References in appendix C.

- Assertions serve as the basis for automatic documentation tools such as the **short** class abstracter, which produce abstract interface documentation of a class by extracting implementation-independent information from the class text.

← *The class abstracter was described in 7.14, starting page 103.*

- Assertions may also be monitored at run time, providing a powerful tool for **testing** and **debugging** software.

9.3 Graphical convention

The figure below illustrates the graphical representations that may be used to show routine preconditions, routine postconditions and class invariants.

The convention for pre- and postconditions is easy to remember: each "drawer" figuratively opens on only one side; the routine may obtain an input condition from the left drawer and deliver a condition through the right drawer.

Representing assertions

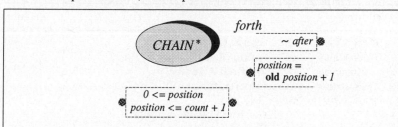

9.4 Uses of assertions

Assertions appear in the following constructs:

- The Precondition and Postcondition parts of a Routine.
- The Invariant clause of a class.
- The Check instruction.
- The Invariant of a Loop instruction.

← *See* Routine, *page 112*; Class_declaration, *page 46.*

→ *Page 129.*

→ Loop, *page 243.*

In addition, loops may have variants, which are integer expressions rather than assertions but play a closely related role.

All the constructs involving assertions are optional.

9.5 Form of assertions

An Assertion, introduced by such keywords as **require** (for preconditions), **ensure** (for postconditions), **invariant** (for class and loop invariants) and **check** (for Check instructions) is made of one or more Assertion_clause, each based on a boolean expression. For example, the precondition of the creation procedure *make* in class *CIRCLE* of the Graphics Library has two specimens of Assertion_clause, separated by a semicolon:

```
make (ce: POINT; ra: REAL) is
        -- Set circle to have center ce and radius ra.
    require
        point_exists: ce /= Void;
        positive_radius: ra > 0.0
    ... Rest of routine declaration omitted ...
```

This expresses that for a call to *make* to be correct the first argument must be non-void and the second argument must be positive. On this example each Assertion_clause is labeled by a Tag (*point_exists, positive_radius*).

The general form of an Assertion, and the syntax of constructs where it may appear, are the following.

→ *A related construct is the loop* Variant, *described later in this chapter (9.14).*

← *On* Tag_mark, *see page 397.*

Precondition	≜	**require** [**else**] Assertion
Postcondition	≜	**ensure** [**then**] Assertion
Invariant	≜	**invariant** Assertion
Assertion	≜	{Assertion_clause ";" ...}
Assertion_clause	≜	[Tag_mark]
		Unlabeled_assertion_clause
Unlabeled_assertion_clause	≜	Boolean_expression | Comment
Tag_mark	≜	Tag ":"
Tag	≜	Identifier

A Boolean_expression, as used in this syntax definition, is simply an Expression constrained to be of type *BOOLEAN*.

In an Assertion, the semicolon separating each Assertion from the next has the same semantics as the **and then** infix boolean operator. This means that the order of the clauses may be meaningful:

→ *The syntax for* Expression, *followed by the constraint on* Boolean_expression, *appears in 23.2, page 373.*

→ *See 23.9, page 381, about the semi-strict semantics of* **and then**.

1 • The value of an Assertion is true if and only if every Assertion_clause in the Assertion has value true.

2 • If an Assertion_clause has value false, the whole Assertion in which it appears has value false, even if the value of a subsequent clause is not defined.

The practical consequence of property 2 is that if an Assertion_clause *b* only makes sense when another, *a*, is true, you should write *a* before *b*. For example, the following Precondition may be appropriate:

```
    require
        table.meaningful_position (i);
        table.item (i).some_property
```

The extract does not show whether the table index 'i' is an integer or if the indexing mechanism uses a more elaborate type of index.

This extract assumes that *table* is an indexed data structure which may or may not have an element at index *i*, as determined by function *meaningful_position*. If this function yields value true, then *item* returns the element, which may or may not satisfy *some_property*. Since the second Assertion_clause has a value only if the first has value true, it would be incorrect to reverse their order.

As with many other uses of semicolons, the semicolon separating Assertion clauses is in fact optional, with one exception: the semicolon is required between to clauses if the second one begins with an opening parenthesis (which could cause an ambiguity).

The style standard, page 493, suggests including the semicolons for readability. This book always includes them.

An Assertion_clause may be preceded by a Tag, such as *point_exists* and *positive_radius* above. Such tags are identifiers, with no specific validity constraints. They do not affect the semantics of the enclosing text, but are useful for documentation purposes and may be used by environment tools to produce clear messages if they detect an assertion violation at run time (or are able to discover certain correctness violations statically).

→ What happens in the case of assertion violations at run time is discussed in 9.17 below, page 132.

An Unlabeled_assertion_clause consisting of a Comment serves documentation purposes only.

The next sections explore the various constructs using assertions.

9.6 Assertions on routines

The declaration of a Routine of any kind – deferred, effective with a **do** or **once** body, external – may be equipped with a Precondition, a Postcondition or both.

Here is an example from class *CHAIN* in the Data Structure Library:

> *put_i_th* (*v*: **like** *first*; *i*: *INTEGER*) **is**
>   -- Put item *v* at *i*-th position.
> **require**
>   *index_large_enough*: $i >= 1$;
>   *index_small_enough*: $i <= count$
> **deferred**
> **ensure**
>   **not** *empty*
> **end** -- *put_i_th*

The precondition expresses that no client should call the routine unless the actual argument for *i* is between 1 and *count*. The postcondition expresses that, after a successfully completed execution of the routine, *empty* (a boolean function of the same class) will yield false.

Each of the Assertion_clause components of the Precondition has been labeled with a Tag such as *index_large_enough*.

9.7 The specification of a routine

DEFINITION: Specification

Let *pre* and *post* be the precondition and postcondition of a routine *rout*. The **specification** of *rout* is the pair of assertions < *pre*, *post*>.

Sub-specification

A specification < *pre'*, *post'* > is said to be a **subspecification** of <*pre, post*> if and only if *pre* implies *pre'* and *post'* implies *post*. Here "implies" is boolean implication.

The notion of subspecification is important because it defines the clients' perspective on permissible changes in a routine's implementation. For a client of a class offering a routine

```
rout (...) is
    require
        pre
    do
        ...
    ensure
        post
    end -- rout
```

what counts is the contract defined by the assertions: a client which achieves *pre* at call time is entitled to obtain *post* on return. Another routine *other_rout* may be acceptable as a substitute for *rout* if it still satisfies that contract. This does not necessarily mean that the specification of *other_rout* must be the same as that of *rout*: it may also be a subspecification < *pre'*, *post'* >, since in that case any client's call that satisfies the obligation defined by the original contract (*pre*) also satisfies the obligation of the new contract (*pre'*), and the benefits guaranteed by the new contract (*post'*) also entitle the clients to those guaranteed by the original (*post*).

The constraint on routine redeclaration will ensure that whenever a routine is redeclared (redefined, or "effected" if the original was deferred), the new specification is a subspecification of the original.

→ *See "Redeclaration and assertions", page 152, and the Redeclaration rule, page 163.*

9.8 Constraints on routine assertions

For the contracts to be honest and enforceable, preconditions and postconditions must satisfy constraints which are usable by their clients.

The first constraint affects preconditions:

> A Precondition of a routine *r* of a class *C* is valid if and only if every feature whose final name appears in any Assertion_clause is available to every class to which *r* is available.

If *r* were available to a class *B* but its precondition involved a feature not available to *B*, *r* would be imposing to *B* a condition that *B* would not be able to check for itself; this would amount to a secret clause in the contract, preventing the designer of *B* from guaranteeing the correctness of calls.

→ *More on avoiding secret clauses below.*

The features mentioned in the constraint may include features of *C* and, for a complex precondition, features of other classes; for example, if the precondition of *r* includes the expression

$$a.b\,(c) + d * (e.f\,(g).h)$$

where *b*, *f*, *h* are features of other classes, all these features must be available to *B* – as well as *a*, *c*, *d*, **infix** *"* * *"*, *e* and *g* if all of these are features of *C*.

In addition to the above constraint, the Entity rule, studied as part of the discussion of entities, will require every entity appearing in a precondition to be an attribute of the enclosing class, a Local entity declared in the routine or a formal argument.

For postconditions, there is no need for a special constraint; the Entity rule, which in this case also allows the Local entity *Result* if the Postcondition appears in a function, is sufficient. In particular, there is no condition on availability: an Assertion_clause of a Postcondition may refer to features with a different availability status. For example, the postcondition for routine *put_right* in class *LINKED_LIST* of the Data Structure Library reads:

→ *The Entity rule is on page 276.*

> count = **old** count + 1;
> active = **old** active;
> position = **old** position;
> next /= Void;
> next. item = v

In the last clause, *v* is a formal argument of the routine, and so is available to all clients, but *next* is only available to *LINKED_LIST* itself.

Why prohibit the Precondition of a routine *r* from referring to features which are not available to clients that use *r*, but permit this for a Postcondition? The reason is methodological, and comes from the theory of Design by Contract. Including a non-available feature in a Precondition would mean imposing **secret clauses** on clients – conditions that they have no way to enforce. Clearly, no contractual collaboration between parties is possible if the supplier requires input conditions which the client has no way of checking or even knowing. For postconditions, the situation is different: you may wish to include properties affecting only features that are local to the class. This causes no harm to clients: according to the above rule, these extra properties will simply not be available to them, and the interface form will indeed not list them.

See *"Design by Contract" (reference in appendix C).*

The difference in export status of the various entities involved in a precondition or postcondition explains the need for the following notion:

DEFINITION: Availability of an Assertion Clause

> An Assertion_clause *a* of a routine Precondition or Postcondition is **available** to a class *B* if and only if all the entities involved in *a* are available to *B*, with the convention that formal arguments and *Result* are available to all classes.

This notion is necessary to define interface forms of a class adapted to individual clients, as was discussed in the presentation of the **short** class abstracter.

← *See 7.14, starting page 103, about* **short**.

9.9 Old expression

A special form of expression, the Old expression, is available in routine postconditions only.

→ *The general form of expressions is discussed in chapter 23.*

In a postcondition clause, the expression **old** *exp* has the same type as *exp*; its value at execution time, on routine exit, is the value of *exp* as evaluated on routine entry in the current call.

An example appeared in the postcondition for *forth* above. Here is another, from routine *put* in class *FIXED_QUEUE* of the Data Structure Library; the routine inserts an element into a queue:

← *See page 118 for the specification of 'forth'.*

```
put (v: T) is
    -- Add item v to queue.
  require
    not_full: not full
  do
    ...
  ensure
    count = old count + 1;
    (old empty) implies (item = v);
    not empty;
    array_item ((last − 1 + capacity) \\ capacity) = v
  end -- put
```

\\ is the remainder operator on integers. See 23.10, page 384.

The first postcondition clause indicates that any call to *put* increases the queue size, *count*, by one. The second indicates that if the queue was initially empty (as expressed by **old** *empty*), then the value at cursor position (as given by function *item*) will be the one just inserted. Operator **implies** is boolean implication.

The syntax of an Old expression is simply

Old ≙ **old** Expression

In expressions involving other symbols, the precedence of the **old** symbol is higher than that of any operator. So the second Assertion_clause of *put* above could have been written as

old *empty* **implies** *item* = v

the other parentheses being also optional since = (equality) has a higher precedence than **implies** (implication). Using extra parentheses does not hurt, of course, and may enhance readability.

→ See 23.5, page 376, on operator precedence.

The validity constraint expresses that a Postcondition is the only permitted context for an Old expression:

VAOL

An Old expression of the form **old** *e*, where *e* is an expression of type *TE*, is valid if and only if it satisfies the following two conditions:

1 • It appears in a Postcondition clause of a Routine *r*.

2 • Transforming *r* into a function with result type *TE* (by adding a result type if *r* is procedure, or changing its result type if it is already a function) and replacing its entire Routine part by

  do
    Result := *e*
  end

would yield a valid routine.

The second condition indicates that *e* must be an expression that would be valid in a "do" or "once" body for *r*, but does not involve any local entities. A more indirect formulation is necessary because *r* does necessarily have such a body (it could be of the External or Deferred form). The device of making *r* a function provides us with a suitable syntactical stage for *e*'s guest appearance in the simplified routine.

As a consequence, 'e' may not itself be of the Old *form.*

The value of an Old expression **old** *e* is defined only at the end of the execution of a call to *r*, just before the call returns; it is the result that would have been produced by evaluating *e* just before the call's execution began.

9.10 Strip expressions

The mechanisms introduced so far enable postconditions to describe the changes performed by routine calls. It may also be useful to express what a routine call will **not** change. The Strip form of expression is of particular interest here when used in an Old expression of a Postcondition.

A Strip expression describes a part of an object, possibly stripped of some of its fields. If *a, b...* are attributes of a class *C*, a routine of *C* may contain (particularly, but not exclusively, in its postcondition) a Strip expression of the form

→ See 23.21, page 396, about the details of Strip.

> **strip** (*a, b, ...*)

which, when evaluated on a direct instance of *C*, denotes an array whose entries are the fields of the current object, except for those explicitly named in the expression (here *a, b, ...*). In particular, the Strip expression

> **strip** ()

denotes an array which contains all the fields of the current object.

The above informal definitions assume that the Strip expression is evaluated on a direct instance of *C* itself – the class where the expression appears. It could also be evaluated, of course, on a direct instance of a proper descendant of *C*. In this case the resulting array only includes fields corresponding to attributes of *C*, and is stripped of any field that comes from an attribute introduced in a proper descendant. For details, see the formal presentation of Strip in the chapter on expressions. To simplify the discussion, the rest of this section continues to assume that the instance of *C* is direct.

→ The formal presentation of the grammar, validity and semantics of Strip *is in 23.21.*

With the help of Strip expressions you can express that a certain routine is only allowed to modify certain fields of its target object. A Postcondition which includes an Assertion_clause of the form

> *equal* (**strip** (*a, b, ...*), **old strip** (*a, b, ...*))

expresses that the routine may not change any field of *C* other than those given. Function *equal* is used here to test for the element-by-element equality of two arrays; the order of fields in an array produced by a Strip expression, deduced from the attributes as declared in the class text, is always the same for a given class.

→ *Applied to arrays, the call 'equal (a, b)' compares two arrays element by element. As explained in the discussion of arrays, 28.5, page 441, this is because 'equal' relies on function 'is_equal', redefined for class ARRAY to compare actual array values rather than array descriptors. See also 19.7, page 303.*

Similarly, a Postcondition of the form

> (*some_property* **and** *equal* (**strip** (), **old strip** ())) **or** *other_property*

expresses that only two situations are possible on routine exit: either condition *some_property* holds, in which case no change has been made to the object; or *other_property* holds.

9.11 Class invariants

The next category of assertion use is the class invariant, determined by the last clause of a class text, Invariant.

The invariant specifies properties which any instance of the class must satisfy at every instant at which the instance is observable by clients.

The class *CHAIN* quoted above has the following Invariant clause

> **deferred class** *CHAIN* **feature**
>   ...
> **invariant**
>   -- Definitions:
>   *empty* = (*count* = 0);
>   *off* = ((*position* = 0) **or** (*position* = *count* + 1));
>   *isfirst* = (*position* = 1);
>   *islast* = (**not** *empty* **and** (*position* = *count*));
>
>   -- Axioms:
>   *count* >= 0;
>   *position* >= 0; *position* <= *count* + 1;
>   *empty* => (*position* = 0);
>   (**not** *off*) => (*item* = *i_th* (*position*));
>
>   -- Theorems:
>   (*isfirst* **or** *islast*) **implies not** *empty*
> **end** -- class *CHAIN*

This particular Invariant has been divided into definitions, expressing that certain functions may be defined in terms of others, axioms, expressing constraints on the features, and theorems, which may be deduced from other clauses. This classification is meant for readability but has no semantic consequence.

In the actual class text, each Assertion_clause of the Invariant has a label such as 'empty_is_zero_count,' 'off_is_offleft_or_offright' etc. Here these labels have been removed for brevity.

As an example, the first Assertion_clause states that in all observable states the result of *empty* (a boolean function) called on a chain is true if and only if the value of *count* called on the same chain is zero. The second and third of those marked as "Axioms" state that the value of *position*, an integer attribute, always remains between 0 and the value of *count* plus one.

To obtain the full invariant associated with a class, you must add the invariants of all its parents (and also the postconditions of any function redefined as attribute, a rather fine point). This is captured by a definition, of which you may ignore clause 2 for the moment, concentrating on clauses 1 and 3:

→ *On clause 2, see below and page 154.*

DEFINITION:
Invariant
of a class

The invariant of a class C is an assertion obtained by concatenating the following assertions (omitting any one which is absent or empty):

1 • The invariants of all parents (determined recursively through the present rule), in the order of the corresponding Parent clauses.

2 • The postconditions of any inherited functions which C redefines as an attribute, with every occurrence of *Result* replaced by the attribute's final name. (If there are two or more such redefinitions, include them in the order in which their new declarations appear in C.)

3 • The Assertion in C's own Invariant clause, if any.

This prescribes a precise order for concatenating the assertions. This order is almost irrelevant semantically, but the definition must yield an assertion specified without any ambiguity.

This definition expresses an important property of the inheritance mechanism: a class inherits from its parents not only their features, but also the global properties applicable to their instances, as expressed by Invariant clauses. This is needed to ensure the consistency of the type view of inheritance. In particular, inheritance permits substitution of instances: if C is a descendant of B, instances of C will also be instances of B. But the soundness of this notion requires any semantic obligation on instances of B, as expressed by B's invariant, to be also applicable to instances of C. The above definition guarantees this.

→ The notion of instance of a class is defined in 17.4, page 271.

Clause 2 takes care of a fine point: a class may redefine an inherited function without arguments into an attribute. In such a case the original function's postcondition, if any, cannot remain attached to the feature, since an attribute has no associated assertions. Clause 2 indicates that the assertion then becomes part of the class invariant, after replacement of any occurrence of the predefined entity *Result*, denoting the function's result, by the attribute's name.

→ Chapter 10 discusses the details of redefinition, including the redefinition of a function into an attribute. The end of 10.15, on page 154, explains clause 2 of the above rule as part of the discussion of the fate of assertions in a redeclaration.

Throughout this book, because of the above definition, the phrase "the invariant of a class" means not just the Assertion of its Invariant clause, but the complete reconstructed assertion, including parents' invariants.

9.12 Consistency of a class

Invariants and the notion of routine specification make it possible to define the consistency of a class.

A class will be said to be consistent if its implementation satisfies the correctness requirements expressed by the preconditions on the routines of the class, the postconditions, and the class invariant.

The following notations serve to define this notion precisely. (These notations, of course, are not part of Eiffel, but mathematical conventions used to talk **about** Eiffel classes and their semantic properties.)

- If r is a routine, do_r denotes its body, pre_r its precondition, and $post_r$ its postcondition.

- If C is a class, INV_C denotes its class invariant.

- If P and Q are assertions and A is an instruction or compound, the notation
  $$\{P\}\ A\ \{Q\}$$
  expresses the property that whenever A is executed in a state in which P is true, the execution will terminate in a state in which Q is true.

WARNING: These are mathematical notations, not Eiffel text.

• In the preceding notation, if P, A and Q are extracted from the text of a routine with arguments, $\{P\}\ A\ \{Q\}$ will be considered to hold if and only if it holds for all possible values of the formal arguments.

Also, we assume that every Routine_body has both a Precondition and a Postcondition, and that every Class has an Invariant, by considering any missing clause as an implicit form for **require true**, **ensure true** or **invariant true**.

These conventions make it possible to define class consistency:

<table>
<tr><td>

DEFINITION:
Consistency

</td><td>

A class C is **consistent** if and only if it satisfies the following two conditions:

1 • For every creation procedure p of C:

$\{\ pre_p\}\ do_p\ \{INV_C\}$

2 • For every routine r of C exported generally or selectively:

$\{\ pre_r \wedge INV_C\}\ do_r\ \{\ post_r \wedge INV_C\}$

</td><td>

The mathematical symbol $\wedge$ represents boolean conjunction.

</td></tr>
</table>

Class consistency is one of the most important aspects of the *correctness* of a class: adequacy of routine implementations to the specification. The other aspects of correctness, studied below, involve Check instructions, Loop instructions and Rescue clauses.

→ *The definition of class correctness is on page 132.*

9.13 Check instructions

A list of assertions may be packaged into a Check instruction.

A Check instruction helps express a property that you believe will be satisfied whenever system execution reaches the instruction. As the name indicates, then, the instruction is there to require that some mechanism "check" that the property indeed holds. The mechanism in question may be a human reader, a mechanical program prover (if at all possible), or the system's execution. (We have not seen yet what effect, if any, assertion constructs may have on system execution; the reader is requested to wait a few more sections for an answer.)

→ *The reader who does not want to wait may look at section 9.17, page 132.*

A common use is to write a Check instruction just before a routine call, to express the two conditions which must be met for the call to execute correctly:

1 • For a remote call, the target must not be void.

2 • The routine's precondition must be satisfied.

As an example of condition 1, the body of procedure *remove_left* in class *LINKED_LIST* from the Data Structure Library contains the following extract:

```
previous := item (position − n − 1);
   check
      previous /= Void
   end;
previous.put_right (active);
```

The examples follow the convention of indenting the Check instructions to separate them from the instructions which perform actual actions.

Here *item* is the function such that $l.item\ (i)$ is the element at position i in list l. The Check instruction expresses that the value at *position* − n − 1 is not void, and so can be used as the target of the call to *put_right* which follows.

As an example of condition 2, the body of procedure *put* in the same class contains the following extract:

```
if i = 1 then
    lt.put_right (first_element)
else
        check
          i -1 >= 1;
          i -1 <= count
        end;
    left_neighbor := item (i - 1)
    ...
```

*The context of this extract
guarantees
i >= 1.*

This should be understood in light of the precondition for *item* applied to *j*:

```
require
    index_large_enough: j >= 1;
    index_small_enough: j <= count
```

In the Check *instruction,
the reason for using the
apparently strange
i−1 >= 1 rather than the
simpler i >= 2, and
similarly for the second
clause, is precisely to
express clearly that the call
satisfies the precondition of
'item', with i−1 substituted
for the formal argument 'j'.*

The Check instruction expresses that the context of the call to *item* in *put* will satisfy the precondition because of the context (the Conditional instruction).

More generally, a Check instruction is useful in the following situation. You know that that the proper execution of a certain computation requires some initial consistency condition. (In the examples above, the computation is a routine call, and the consistency condition is the routine's precondition.) To do your job properly, you design the context of the computation so as to guarantee the desired condition. If your reasoning and its consequence (that the consistency condition will be satisfied) are not obvious to readers of that context, a Check instruction will remind them that you did not overlook your obligations. As explained below, it will also help detect the mistake if you did make one after all.

The general form of a Check instruction is:

> Check   ≙   **check** Assertion **end**

The following definition expresses the semantics of a Check instruction:

> An effective routine *r* is **check-correct** if, for every Check instruction *c* in *r*, any execution of *c* (as part of an execution of *r*) satisfies all its assertions.

9.14 Loop invariants and variants

Correctness conditions on a loop may be expressed in the form of a loop invariant and a loop variant. The invariant determines the properties ensured by the loop on exit; the variant serves to guarantee that the loop's execution terminates.

Here is an example of these constructs in a loop from routine *search_child* (which looks for a certain node among the children of the current node) in the Data Structure Library class *LINKED_TREE*:

```
from
    go_before
invariant
    0 <= child_position; child_position <= arity + 1
variant
    arity − child_position + 1
until
    child_after or else (j = i)
loop
    child_forth;
    if (sought = child) then
        j := j + 1
    end
end
```

The invariant expresses a property of *child_position*, the index of the child being looked at: *child_position* will remain between 0 and *arity* (the number of children) plus one. Stating that this property is a loop invariant means asserting that the loop Initialization ensures it, and that every iteration preserves it. This is indeed the case:

- The Initialization, *go_before*, moves the child cursor to the node's first child, or to position 0 if there is no child.

- The iteration, *child_forth*, which moves the child cursor right by one position, is only executed when the property *child_after* is not satisfied (since this condition is part of the Exit_condition).

The variant is an integer expression, *arity − child_position + 1*, which is always non-negative and decreases on every iteration. This guarantees that the loop will terminate.

Here now are the precise rules governing these constructs.

First, the syntax. A loop invariant is a specimen of Invariant, also applicable to class invariants and given earlier in this chapter. A loop Variant (which contains an integer expression, not an assertion) has the following syntax:

← *The syntax for* Invariant *was on page 120.*

→ Invariant *and* Variant *clauses appear in the right-hand side for the production for* Loop *on page 243.*

| Variant | ≙ | **variant** [Tag_mark] Expression |

The optional Tag_mark labels the variant in the same way as an Assertion_clause.

A Variant is valid if and only if its Expression is of type *INTEGER*.

The assertion introduced by the Invariant clause of a loop is called the **invariant assertion** of the loop. The expression introduced by the Variant clause is called the **variant expression** of the loop.

As illustrated by the above example, the invariant assertion of a loop must have the following two properties:

- The loop's Initialization (**from** clause) ensures the truth of *INV*.

- Any execution of the Loop_body, when started in a state that does not satisfy the Exit_condition, preserves the truth of *INV* (in other words, leaves *INV* true if it finds *INV* originally true).

As a result of these properties, the invariant will still be satisfied on loop exit, together with the Exit_condition. Their conjunction is the output condition of the loop. From a theoretical viewpoint, the goal of the loop is to achieve this condition, and the looping process reaches it by successive approximations. You may view the variant as an estimate of the remaining distance to the goal.

A loop variant serves to guarantee that this process terminates. It is an integer-valued expression with the following two properties:

- The Initialization sets it to a non-negative value.

- Any execution of the Loop_body (at least when started in a state that does not satisfy the Exit_condition) decreases its value, but maintains it non-negative.

As a result of these properties, since the variant is an integer expression, the iterations may not go on forever.

The precise semantics is given by the following definition.

← *The notation {P} A {Q}, expressing that A, when started in a state satisfying P, will terminate in a state satisfying Q, was introduced page 127 above.*

DEFINITION: Loop-Correct

> A routine is **loop-correct** if every loop it contains satisfies the following four conditions:
>
> 1 • {**true**} *INIT* {*INV*}
>
> 2 • {**true**} *INIT* {*VAR* ≥ 0}
>
> 3 • {*INV* **and then not** *EXIT*} *BODY* {*INV*}
>
> 4 • {*INV* **and then not** *EXIT* **and then** (*VAR* = *v*)} *BODY* {*0 $\leq$ VAR < v*}
>
> where *INV* is the loop's invariant, *VAR* its variant, *INIT* its Initialization, *EXIT* its Exit condition, and *BODY* its Loop_body.

Conditions 1 and 2 express that the initialization yields a state in which the invariant is satisfied and the variant is non-negative. Conditions 3 and 4 express that the body, when executed in a state where the invariant is satisfied but not the exit condition, will preserve the invariant and decrease the variant, while keeping it non-negative. (*v* is an auxiliary variable used to refer to the value of *VAR* before *BODY*'s execution.)

9.15 Exception correctness

We now have almost all the ingredients (consistency, check-correctness, loop-correctness) to define the correctness of a class. One aspect has been left out, however: the properties of rescue blocks, which handle exceptional cases.

As described in a later chapter, every routine has a rescue block, syntactically a Compound, which takes over whenever an execution of the routine triggers an abnormal condition (an exception). The rescue block is the contents of the routine's Rescue clause, if any; otherwise it consists of a call to the routine *default_rescue*, which has a null effect in its default version (from class *ANY*) but may be redefined by any class.

The execution of the rescue block may end in either of two ways:

→ *Chapter 15.*

1 • A rescue block which executes a Retry instruction causes the Routine_body to be executed again.

2 • If it terminates without executing a Retry, the rescue block causes the routine execution to fail, triggering an exception in the routine's caller (which will handle it in one of the same two ways).

To be correct, the rescue block must be such that any branch terminating with a Retry (case 1) ensures the precondition and the invariant, and that any other branch (case 2) ensures the invariant.

A routine satisfying these conditions, which will be made more formal in the discussion of exceptions, is said to be **exception-correct**.

→ *See 15.10, page 258, for a precise definition of exception correctness.*

9.16 Correctness of a class

In connection with the various uses of assertions, we have seen how a class may be "correct" in several partial ways: consistent (every exported routine and creation procedure compatible with the assertions), check-correct, loop-correct, exception-correct. The combination of these properties yields the full notion of class correctness:

DEFINITION:
Correctness
(Class)

> A class is **correct** if and only if it is consistent and every routine of the class is check-correct, loop-correct and exception-correct.

Do not confuse correctness and validity. Correctness is a semantic notion, expressing that the implementation of a class matches its specification. Validity is simply the property that a construct is well-formed, such as a routine call with the proper number and type of actual arguments. The correctness of a software element is a meaningless notion unless the element is valid.

Ideally, an Eiffel environment should come with tools which can prove or disprove the correctness of a class as defined here. Unfortunately, the needed theorem and program proving facilities remain, in spite of encouraging research advances, beyond the reach of current technology.

As the next best thing to proofs, the environment should support run-time monitoring of assertions, as described in the next section.

9.17 Semantics of assertions

Assertions and the associated variant facility express correctness requirements on software texts. This has an interesting consequence on any attempt at defining the semantics of assertions: in the execution of a correct system, every assertion will always be satisfied at the times when it has to (a precondition on every call to its routine, a postcondition on return etc.). So in theory it should not be necessary to define the semantics of assertions evaluation: for a correct class, the effect of evaluating an assertion is irrelevant, since the value is always the same! This may be called the paradox of assertion semantics.

The paradox is only theoretical. In practice, short of proofs as discussed above, one must often accept the prospect that a system may contain errors – may not be correct. Then assertions provide crucial help in detecting these errors and suggesting corrections. By directing the run-time system to evaluate assertions and variant clauses, and to trigger an exception if it detects a violation, you check the consistency between what the software does (the routine bodies) and what you think it does (the assertions): you let the tools call your bluff. This gives a remarkable tool for debugging, testing and maintaining software systems.

For a correct system, assertions, in all cases, will have no effect on the semantics of system execution (except through possible side effects of the functions called by assertions). For an incorrect system, the effect depends on compilation or execution options. Various options of the environment will make it possible to evaluate assertions. If an assertion evaluates to true, it has no further effect on the outcome of the computation. If it evaluates to false, it will trigger an exception, disrupting the normal flow of computation, as discussed in the chapter on exception handling.

→ See chapter 15 about exceptions.

The implementation should enable developers to set various evaluation levels for assertions. The choice should be independent for the various classes *C* of a system. The possible levels (which also affect the semantics of variant clauses) are the following for a class *C*.

→ These options are available as part of Lace, the Language for Eiffel System Specification, a recommended interface for compilers and other language processing tools. See appendix D.

- **no**: no assertion checking of any kind.

- **require**: evaluate preconditions whenever the execution of a routine of *C* begins. This should be the default.

- **ensure**: also evaluate postconditions on return from routines of the class.

- **invariant**: also evaluate the class invariant on entry to and return from qualified calls to routines of *C*.

- **loop**: also evaluate the Variant and Invariant of every loop in *C* (after execution of the Initialization, and after every iteration of the Loop_body); after every iteration, check that the variant has decreased while remaining non-negative.

- **check** or **all**: also evaluate every Check instruction whenever the flow of control reaches it.

*The name **invariant** stands for class, not loop invariant (handled by **loop**). On why it is necessary to check the invariant on both entry and return, see "Object-Oriented Software Construction".*

Each of these levels implies the preceding ones; this is for simplicity, and also because the postcondition of a routine does not make sense unless the precondition is satisfied on entry, class invariants do not make sense unless preconditions and postconditions are also satisfied, etc.

As noted, **require** (precondition checking only) should be the default. Checking preconditions on routine entry avoids disasters (since a Routine_body might attempt to perform erroneous or impossible actions when executed in a state which does not satisfy the routine's precondition), but normally entails only a modest performance penalty. For this reason it is appropriate in normal development mode. The subsequent levels are especially useful for quality assurance, maintenance, debugging, testing and regression analysis.

The above specification indicates that assertion monitoring, when enabled at the **invariant** level or higher, evaluates invariants for qualified calls only. If *r* is a routine of a class *C*, a call is qualified if it is of the form

2c A qualified call may also be written in operator form. See 23.7, page 380.

$$a.r \ (...)$$

with an explicit target, here *a*. Whether it appears in the text of a routine of *C* or in another class, such a qualified call will cause the invariant to be evaluated (both before and after the call). The text of a routine of *C* may also contain an unqualified call, written just

```
r (...)
```

where the target (*a* in the previous example) is the current object. Such an unqualified call will not cause an invariant check. (The form *Current.r* (...), which has the same semantics in the absence of assertions, is qualified and so will trigger an invariant check.)

→ *The notion of current object is defined on page 349, as part of 21.12.*

An assertion violation detected as a result of enabling assertion monitoring at one of the above levels triggers an exception. An exception will also result, at level **loop** or higher, if a loop iteration fails to decrease the variant or gives it a negative value.

As will be seen in the discussion of exceptions, each possible type of exception has an integer code, corresponding to a constant attribute declared in the Kernel Library class *EXCEPTIONS*. The codes for assertion and variant violations will be seen in the description of that class.

→ *See chapter 15 on exceptions. On class EXCEPTIONS, see 15.11, page 258, and chapter 29.*

Another concept associated with exceptions is the notion of **recipient** of an exception. The recipient is the routine whose execution will be interrupted as a result of the exception. It is the recipient routine which determines the response to possible exceptions (through its Rescue clause, if any); in the absence of any specific provision, the recipient routine will simply fail, and trigger a new exception in its own caller.

→ *The notion of recipient is defined in the discussion of exceptions, page 250.*

Here is the rule for determining the recipient of an exception resulting from an assertion violation:

1 • For postconditions, class invariants, loop invariants, variants and Check instructions, the recipient is the routine whose text contains the violated assertion or variant.

2 • For a violated precondition, the recipient is the calling routine. In this case no component of the routine's body is executed; the routine fails immediately, not performing any of its normal actions, and triggering an exception in the caller.

This rule follows naturally from the contract model of computation. If a routine's precondition is violated, the client has not observed its obligations, and any attempt to execute the routine would be meaningless, and perhaps harmful. The routine's body will not even see the call. In this case, the error – the *bug* – is in the client. In all other cases, the routine has been called under the agreed clauses, and is unable to fulfil its duty: either it does not ensure the promised postcondition, or some part of its execution violates one of its own internal correctness conditions (class invariant, loop invariant, variant, Check). In this case the bug is in the routine itself or its enclosing class.

10

Feature adaptation

10.1 Overview

Chapter 6 introduced inheritance as a module enrichment technique. But to inherit from a class does not necessarily mean to accept all of its features at face value.

A key part of the inheritance mechanism is the ability to adapt some of the inherited features to the context of the new class. This is known as feature adaptation, and is the topic of this chapter, with some important complements, arising from the use of repeated inheritance, left to the next one.

This chapter is the longest of this book, which should not be a surprise since it explores in full detail some of the most fascinating aspects of the Eiffel technology: how to play mix and match with software components, taking advantage of the best features of existing classes while refining, adapting or overriding what is not exactly suited to your new need. Only a few basic concepts are involved, but they interact in diverse and powerful ways.

So make sure you have a comfortable armchair and a big cup of coffee, and for the next 31 pages be prepared to question, implement, override, rename, merge or otherwise wring all those features that your ancestors, for better or worse, bequeathed to you.

There are actually 26 more pages of wringing in the next chapter.

The major focus of the discussion will be the two *redeclaration* mechanisms which help adapt inherited features to the local context of a class:

- **Redefinition**, which may change an inherited feature's original implementation, signature or specification.

- **Effecting**, which provides an implementation (or "effective" version) for a feature which did not have one in the parent. The parent's version, deprived of any implementation (but with a signature and specification) is said to be **deferred**; deferred features play an important role in analysis and design, which this chapter will explain.

Two closely related facilities, which the discussion will address in detail, are the possibility of **joining** two or more deferred routines inherited from various parents, to merge abstractions, and of **undefining** an inherited feature, to forget its original implementation.

"Effecting" is not a very pleasant term. It has the advantage, however, of providing a consistent terminology: effecting a feature makes it effective.

Another adjacent concept is **repeated inheritance**, which enables a class to inherit twice or more from a given ancestor, letting the designer control what happens to the common feature heritage. This topic is important enough to have a separate chapter, the next one, devoted to it.

Although with the present chapter the major language constructs involving inheritance will have been introduced, we are still missing an important part of the picture. To grasp the full extent and practicality of the techniques introduced below, you will need to understand polymorphism and dynamic binding, studied in subsequent chapters. Together, these notions are responsible for some of the most powerful characteristics of the object-oriented method.

→ *See 20.9, page 323, on polymorphism, and 21.9, page 345, on dynamic binding.*

10.2 Redeclaring inherited features: why and how

A class inheriting from another may add new features of its own. But what about the old ones? So far the presentation has assumed that an heir will be happy enough to obtain every inherited feature "as is" from a parent. To be sure, the heir may rename the feature, but this does not change it; the effect is simply to make it available to the client's dependents under a name that is better suited to the local context.

← *Renaming was studied in 6.9, page 81*

In its full power, however, inheritance is more flexible than that. When you inherit a set of features, you may want to adapt those whose original specification or implementation does not take advantage of the specific properties of the heir.

The basic method for achieving such an adaptation is feature redefinition, thanks to which you may give an inherited feature a new implementation, a new signature or a new set of assertions, as long as you follow the applicable rules to ensure that the new version remains compatible with the old one for the purposes of their clients. You may even redefine a function into an attribute, switching from an algorithmic representation to a storage-based one. Of course, the various proper descendants of a class may provide alternative redefinitions of the same features.

In some cases, the original form of a routine does not provide any default implementation at all; this is an explicit signal to proper descendants, prompting them to offer various implementations. Such unimplemented features, and the classes that introduce them, are said to be deferred; proper descendants may then **effect** those features (make them **effective**). In the software construction process, classes and features may in fact remain deferred for a long time, providing a high-level notation for system analysis and design.

DEFINITION:
Redeclaration   A class that contains a redefinition or effecting of an inherited feature will be said to **redeclare** that feature.

Be sure to distinguish *redeclaration* from *redefinition*; redeclaration is the more general notion, which includes redefinition as a special case, but also applies to the effecting of a deferred feature. In both cases, a redeclaration never introduces a new feature, but simply overrides the original declaration of an inherited feature, deferred or not.

Getting the full power of deferred features requires two more mechanisms:

- Sometimes a class will be able to merge two or more features that it inherits as deferred; in other words, the class combines several abstractions into one. This is the join mechanism.

- In some cases, as you inherit an effective feature from a parent, you may want to discard the inherited implementation altogether, recanting all the sins of its earlier effective life. This is the process of undefinition, which turns an effective feature into a born-again one – deferred.

The following sections explore redefinition, deferred features, undefinition and join. The discussion will first explain these facilities and their role in software analysis, design and implementation. The second part of the chapter, which may be skipped on first reading, gives the more formal set of corresponding syntactic rules and validity constraints, together with the resulting semantic definitions.

→ *The formal part starts with 10.19, on page 159.*

10.3 Feature adaptation clauses

For a start, let us just refresh our memory as to the syntactical context of this discussion: the Inheritance clause of a class declaration, which may contain one or more Parent parts. As an illustration, here is (in slightly simplified form) the beginning of class *TWO_WAY_TREE* in the Data Structure Library:

← *Another descendant of TREE, class FIXED_TREE, served as illustration of inheritance basics in 6.2, page 75.*

> **indexing**
>   ... (Indexing clause omitted) ...
> **class** *TWO_WAY_TREE* [*T*] **inherit**
>   *TREE* [*T*]
>   **redefine**
>   *higher, ...*
>   **end**;
>
>   *BI_LINKABLE* [*T*];
>   **rename**
>   ... (Rename subclause omitted) ...
>   **redefine**
>   *put_between*
>   **end**;
>
>   *TWO_WAY_LIST* [**like** *Current*]
>   **rename**
>   ... (Rename subclause omitted) ...

> **redefine**
> > *first_child, update_after_insertion,*
> > *duplicate, merge_right, merge_left*
> **end**
> **feature**
>
> ... Rest of class omitted ...

As you can see, each Parent clause is relative to one of the class's parents and may include a Feature_adaptation subclause (optional, but present for all three parents above). The corresponding syntax is worth repeating:

Inheritance	≜	**inherit** Parent_list
Parent_list	≜	{Parent ";" ...}
Parent	≜	Class_type [Feature_adaptation]
Feature_adaptation	≜	[Rename]
		[New_exports]
		[Undefine]
		[Redefine]
		[Select]
		end

← *The original presentation of this syntax is on page 77.*

The Rename and New_exports clauses have been discussed in previous chapters. The next sections explain Redefine and Undefine.

← *See 6.9, starting on page 81, about* Rename, *and 7.11, starting on page 98, about* New_exports.

10.4 Why redefine?

The first important mechanism is feature redefinition, which makes it possible to change some aspects of an inherited feature.

Assume you write a class *C* which describes a specific variant of the concepts covered by an existing class *B*. *C* will be an heir of *B*. You may find that, for that variant, the inherited version of a certain feature *f* is not appropriate any more. This sets the stage for redefining *f* in *C*.

Besides its name, a feature is characterized by three properties: its signature (type of arguments and results, if any); its implementation (which includes the choice between having an attribute or a routine and, in the latter case, the Routine_body, Local_declarations and Rescue); and its specification (Precondition and Postcondition, for routines only). A feature redefinition may affect one or more of these three aspects. In general, a change of specification implies a change of implementation. (The exceptions to this observation arise from replacing a specification by a weaker one, or by a stronger one which the old implementation happened to satisfy already.)

The syntax of Feature_declaration *is on page 63, with the* Routine *case on page 112.*

A routine may also have a Header_comment *and an* Obsolete *clause, which a redefinition may change.*

There are two possible reasons, correctness and efficiency, for redefining a feature:

- The original version may perform actions or compute results which are incorrect for the new class, for example because they do not update some of the new attributes.

- If the original version is still appropriate, it may not be efficient enough, because it does not take advantage of the specific properties of that class.

Signature redefinition falls in the correctness category: the types of arguments or results, as originally declared, are not appropriate for the new class. Implementation redefinition may be for correctness, efficiency or both. For a change of specification, correctness must be involved (the change means that the redefined version offers a new "contract", as represented by the new assertions, to its clients.)

10.5 Two simple examples

To get a good intuitive feeling for redefinition, let us take a look at two examples illustrating each of the two purposes mentioned above.

As a case of redefinition for correctness, assume an implementation of *CIRCLE*, inheriting from *ELLIPSE* and adding an attribute *radius*:

Inheritance structure for circles and ellipses

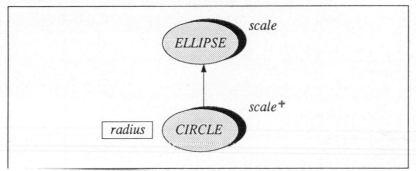

Let *scale* be the procedure that scales a figure by a certain ratio. Since attribute *radius* is not present in *ELLIPSE*, the version of *scale* inherited from *ELLIPSE* does not update the value of that attribute. Class *CIRCLE* must redefine *scale* to make sure that it updates not just the attributes inherited from *ELLIPSE*, but also the specific *CIRCLE* attributes such as *radius*. (Here the problem would not arise if *radius* was a function, defined in terms of attributes inherited from *ELLIPSE*, rather than an attribute.)

As illustrated above, the graphical convention for a redefined feature will be to write a plus sign after the feature's name (as in *scale*$^+$). This convention will also apply to effecting (the other case of redeclaration).

As an example of redefinition for efficiency, here is the redefined version of function *contains* in class *CIRCLE* from the Graphics Library:

```
contains (p: POINT): BOOLEAN is
    -- Is p inside the circle?
require
    point_exists: p /= Void
do
    Result := (origin.distance (p) <= radius)
ensure
    ... Postcondition omitted ...
end -- contains
```

Function *contains* determines whether a point *p* is inside a closed figure. There is of course a version of that routine in *ELLIPSE*. Because an ellipse is a more general figure than a circle, however, the *ELLIPSE* version is more complex than the above; it would still be correct for circles, but less efficient since it does not take advantage of the special properties of circles. Redefinition solves the problem.

10.6 The Redefinition clause

Whether for correctness or for efficiency, the redefinition of a feature must be explicitly announced in a Redefine subclause of the Feature_adaptation for the corresponding parent, as in

```
...
class CIRCLE inherit
    ...;
    ELLIPSE
        rename
            ...
        redefine
            scale, contains, ...
        ...
        end
    ... Rest of class omitted ...
```

The names given in the Redefine subclause must be the final names of features inherited from the given parent.

Such a Redefine subclause allows class *CIRCLE* to include (in a Feature_clause) new feature declarations, as given above, for *scale, contains* and other features listed after the keyword **redefine**. These new declarations will override the ones inherited from the parent, here *ELLIPSE*.

Without the Redefine subclause, such new declarations would make *CIRCLE* invalid, since it would now have two features called *scale*, *contains* etc., a case of invalid **name clash**.

→ *For the full discussion of name clashes and when they may be valid, see 11.10, page 185.*

DEFINITION: If a class inherits a feature from a parent, either keeping the feature
Precursor   unchanged or redefining it, the parent's version of the feature is called the **precursor** of the feature. For example the precursor of the *CIRCLE* version of *scale* is the *ELLIPSE* version of that procedure.

With the mechanisms seen so far, each feature of a parent yields a separate feature in the heir; as a result, an inherited feature has one precursor. Mechanisms which we will explore later – joining of deferred features, and sharing under repeated inheritance – may result in the merging of two or more parent features into just one heir feature. This will require extending the definition of "precursor" to account for features having more than one precursor.

→ *For the extension of precursors to joined features, see page 165; for the full definition including repeated inheritance, see the discussion after the definition of "inherited features" on page 187.*

10.7 Redefinition in the software process

Before proceeding with more technical aspects of redefinition, it is useful to reflect a little on the implications of this notion for object-oriented software engineering.

Feature redefinition is part of the answer to a major software engineering issue: reconciling reusability with extendibility.

In software, it is seldom satisfactory to reuse an element exactly as it is; often, you must also adapt it to a specific context. With redefinition, as suggested by the simple examples above, you can keep those features that are still appropriate for the new context, while overriding the implementations of those which need to be adapted.

The ability to change the signature of an inherited routine, studied below, is also essential to the smooth functioning of Eiffel's type system.

← *The discussion of renaming was in 6.9, starting on page 81.*

To understand redefinition further, it is useful to contrast this technique with another mechanism open to classes for "adapting" inherited features: renaming. The distinction to keep in mind is that between a *feature* and a *feature name*:

- A feature of a class is a certain operation (routine or attribute) applicable to instances of the class. The feature is normally passed on to heirs, except for redeclaration, which allows an heir to substitute another feature.

- Every feature of a class has a final name relative to that class. This is the name used by the class, its clients and heirs to refer to the feature. The name is normally passed on to heirs, except for renaming, which allows an heir to substitute another name for the same feature.

Let B be a class and f the final name of one of its features. A class C that inherits from B may rename f, or it may redefine it, or both. The purposes are different, and complementary:

- By renaming f, you do not change the feature, but you change its final name in C.

- By redefining f, you do not change the name, but you change the feature (some of its implementation, signature, specification).

You may combine the two mechanisms if you want to change both the feature and its name:

```
class C inherit
   B
      rename
         f as new_name
      redefine
         new_name
      end
feature
   new_name ... is ...

   ...
end -- class C
```

Remember that if you have renamed a feature the only name that makes sense for it in the rest of the class, beyond the Rename clause, is the new name, which becomes its final name in *C*, here *new_name*. In particular, the Redefine subclause (as every other subclause of the Feature_adaptation, such as Undefine and Select) only refers to the new name. So in this example it would have been invalid to write

> **redefine** *f*

since *f* is not the name of a feature that *C* inherits from *B* (unless the Rename subclause separately renames another inherited feature as *f*).

One more point is worth noting about the connection between renaming and redefinition. In all the examples of redefinition seen so far, with or without renaming, the precursor of *f* (its version in the parent) is not usable in *C* any more. For such examples this does not raise any problem; for example the *ELLIPSE* version of *scale* or *contains* is of no interest to *CIRCLE*, its descendants or clients. In other contexts, however, you might want to keep the old version along with the redefined one. Here are two typical reasons:

The definition of "precursor" for redefined routines was on page 140.

- If *f* is a routine, the *C* version of *f* may need to do *more* than the old one. Its body might then have to call the original at some point. This assumes that the original is still usable by *C*.

- You may also in some cases want to provide *C*'s clients with both the old and new implementations, giving them an explicit choice.

With the mechanisms introduced so far, we cannot achieve these goals. The solution will involve **repeated inheritance**, studied in the next chapter. Roughly speaking, *C* will inherit twice from *B*, getting one version of *f* from each of the inheritance paths. One of the paths redefines *f*; the other renames *f* without redefining it, keeping the old version usable by *C* under a new name.

→ *The solution is given in 11.4.*

10.8 Changing the signature

The preceding example redefinitions affected the implementation, for either correctness or efficiency reasons. Here now is an example where we need to change the signature of an inherited feature. That feature is an attribute, so its signature only includes the attribute's type.

Consider class *LINKED_LIST* [*T*] in the Data Structure library, representing one-way linked lists of objects of type *T* (the formal generic parameter).

One-way linked list

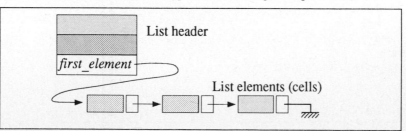

One of the attributes of class *LINKED_LIST* is a reference to the first element of a list:

> *first_element*: *LINKABLE* [*T*]

The type of the corresponding objects, *LINKABLE* [*T*], represents list cells, chained to their right neighbors:

*Linkable
list
cell*

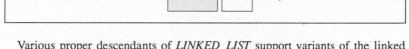

Various proper descendants of *LINKED_LIST* support variants of the linked list data structure. An immediate heir is *TWO_WAY_LIST*, which, instead of linkables, uses "bi-linkables", chained not just to their successors but also to their predecessors:

*Bi-linkable
list
cell*

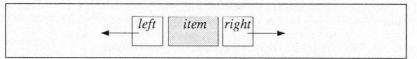

Clearly, the *first_element* of a *TWO_WAY_LIST* should not just be a linkable any more, but a bi-linkable. Hence the need to redefine that attribute, which will appear in *TWO_WAY_LIST* as

> *first_element*: *BI_LINKABLE* [*T*]

Class *BI_LINKABLE* is itself an heir from *LINKABLE*. This is in line with the general rule, given in detail below, which requires that any change of type in a redeclaration replace the original with a type that conforms to it (that is to say, roughly speaking, is based on a descendant class, as *BI_LINKABLE* is with respect to *LINKABLE*).

In this example, the redefined feature is just an attribute. There is often a concomitant need to change the types of routine arguments. For example, the insertion routine *put_element* may be declared in *LINKED_LIST* as

> *put_element* (*lt*: *LINKABLE* [*T*]; *i*: *INTEGER*)

Clearly, class *TWO_WAY_LIST* needs to adapt *put_element* so as to have a first argument *lt* of type *BI_LINKABLE* [*T*]. A redefinition of *put_element* would achieve this.

Such cases are so frequent, however, that they have warranted a special mechanism, bypassing the need for explicit redefinition. Rather than the above, *put_element* is declared in *LINKED_LIST* as

> *put_element* (*lt*: **like** *first_element*; *i*: *INTEGER*)

In the original class text the actual generic parameter used for LINKABLE is of type 'like first' rather than T. This does not affect the present discussion. See below on the like (anchored) form of declaration.

→ See 10.14, beginning on page 151, on the rules governing type redeclaration, and chapter 13 on the full conformance rules.

Routine 'put_element' is secret since clients of the list classes never explicitly manipulate linkables, only objects of type T.

meaning that *lt* has the same type as *first_element*: type *LINKABLE* [*T*] in *LINKED_LIST* and, in any proper descendant of this class, the new type, if any, to which *first_element* has been redefined. This mechanism, known as anchored declaration, is discussed in detail in a subsequent chapter. It is semantically equivalent to a signature redefinition, but avoids any explicit redefinition.

→ *See 12.15, starting on page 211, about anchored declarations.*

10.9 Deferred features

Feature redefinition, as we have just studied it, makes it possible to override the implementation, signature or specification of a feature that already had an implementation in a proper ancestor.

In some cases, however, the designer of that ancestor could not provide such a default implementation, or did not want to. It is possible to declare a feature without choosing an implementation by making it a **deferred** feature. This transfers to proper descendants the responsibility for providing an implementation through a new declaration, called an **effecting** of the feature.

Although similar in many ways to redefinition, this case is more a "definition" (without the *re*) of the feature, since there was no original implementation in the parent. Accordingly, a class that effects a feature inherited as deferred will not list it in the corresponding Redefine clause.

Some terminology: a feature which is not deferred (that is to say, has an implementation, either as an attribute or as a non-deferred routine) is said to be **effective**. A class which has at least one deferred feature is itself said to be deferred; a non-deferred class is called an effective class. These definitions, although sufficient for the time being, will be made more rigorous below.

In graphical representations of system structures, both deferred features and deferred classes will be marked by an asterisk *. Their effectings, as other forms of redeclaration, are marked with a plus sign.

→ *A feature is "inherited as deferred" in two cases: it may come from a feature (a precursor) which is deferred in the parent; or, as seen below, the* Parent *clause may undefine it. See page 156.*

The full definition of effective and deferred features of a class is on page 160.

Deferred class, deferred feature, and effectings

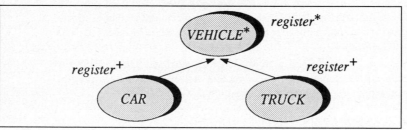

← *This figure already appeared in chapter 1.*

As noted above, a class designer may decide to declare a feature as deferred because of either *inability* or *refusal* to provide an implementation. These two cases correspond to the two major uses of deferred routines and classes:

1 • You may want to write a class describing an abstract notion, covering several possible implementations. Then you cannot write an effective class, which would require that you provide full implementation information. Some of the features of such a class will have to be deferred.

2 • In other cases, whether or not you have enough information to give the implementation, you prefer to concentrate on the abstract properties of a class and its features, postponing implementation concerns to a later stage.

The next two sections explore these two applications.

10.10 Deferred classes for describing abstractions

The first application of deferred classes supports a central aspect of the Eiffel method, resulting from the use of inheritance as a classification mechanism. Often, classes appearing towards the top of inheritance hierarchies represent general categories, of which certain proper descendants will provide specific implementations. The more general classes should then be deferred.

The Basic Libraries contain numerous such classes. A typical example, taken from the Data Structure Library, is class *TREE*, which describes the most general notion of tree, independent of any representation. Specific implementations are described by proper descendants of that class, such as *FIXED_TREE* and *TWO_WAY_TREE*, both sketched earlier. Class *TREE* contains a number of deferred features describing operations that cannot be made more precise without committing to a representation. Typical of these is the deferred procedure

← *On FIXED_TREE see 6.2, page 75. On TWO_WAY_TREE see 10.3 above, page 137.*

```
child_put (v: like item) is
    -- Put item v at active child position.
require
    not_child_off: not child_off
deferred
ensure
    child.item = v
end -- child_put
```

which replaces by *v* the value stored in the "active child" (that is to say, the child at current cursor position) of the current node.

The keyword **deferred**, indicating that the routine is deferred, comes in lieu of an Effective body introduced by **do**, **once** or **external**. As the example shows, the Precondition and Postcondition clauses may still be present; they characterize the semantics of the routine, which must be preserved by all implementations in proper descendants (in a manner explained below).

← *See page 113 for the syntax of a* Routine_body.

Here are two further examples from the Basic Libraries.

The Graphics Library contains numerous classes representing various geometrical figures, some simple, some composite. They are all descendants of a deferred class *FIGURE*, usually through one of its heirs *OPEN_FIGURE* and *CLOSED_FIGURE*, still deferred themselves.

See "Eiffel: The Libraries" for details about these examples.

The Parsing Library provides tools for analyzing programs or other structured texts. To build a parser for a particular language, you write classes describing the abstract structure of that language's constructs; for example, a parser for Eiffel will contain classes *EIFFEL_CLASS, ROUTINE, INSTRUCTION* etc. All such classes are descendants of the deferred class *CONSTRUCT*, through one of three heirs of *CONSTRUCT* describing three kinds of construct:

← *The three kinds of construct are also used in the productions describing Eiffel syntax in this book, as explained in 2.4, page 24.*

- *AGGREGATE* describes constructs with a fixed number of parts. For example, in a parser for Eiffel, a class describing the syntax of a Loop (where the parts are an Initialization, an Invariant, a Variant and a Loop_body) would be written as an heir to *AGGREGATE*.

→ *The syntax for* Loop *is on page 243.*

- *CHOICE* describes constructs whose specimens are chosen from a number of possible constructs. For example an Eiffel Instruction is a Creation, or a

Call, or an Assignment etc.; the corresponding class in a parser would be an heir of *CHOICE*.

← *The syntax for* Instruction *is on page 116.*

- *SEQUENCE* describes constructs with a variable number of components of the same kind, such as an Eiffel Feature_declaration_list, which may consist of zero or more Feature_declaration.

← *The syntax for* Feature_declaration_list *is on page 60.*

CONSTRUCT is almost fully deferred. Its heirs, although still deferred, are "less" deferred since they provide effective routines for parsing the corresponding types of constructs.

As you will remember, it is not possible to have a feature both deferred and frozen, since frozen features may never be redeclared, and deferred features are born for the very purpose of redeclaration.

← *The incompatibility between frozen and deferred status is part of the Feature Declaration rule, page 70.*

10.11 Deferred classes for system design and analysis

In the preceding examples, deferred classes were "abstracted" from effective ones, by removing implementation aspects. In other cases, deferred classes may be written independently of any implementation, at least at first. This is the second of the two major applications of deferred classes mentioned above.

This situation − mentioned above as a case of the designer not *wanting* to consider any implementation − arises in particular out of the use of Eiffel as a tool for system analysis and design.

At **design** time, you are concerned with the architecture of a system, not its implementation; deferred classes provide an ideal tool for expressing the abstract properties of an architecture, including assertions, without making decisions about representation or algorithms

At a level even more remote from implementation concerns, deferred classes are an **analysis** tool: to model and analyze a certain category of real world objects, you may write fully deferred classes which capture the abstract properties of those objects. Not only are such classes independent of any implementation; they may in fact be independent of any computerization. Many natural or artificial systems, whether or not they include some components implemented by computer software, may be described by sets of deferred classes as long as their structure and semantics are well understood.

A "fully deferred" class is a class whose features are all deferred. In general, a class is deferred as soon as it has one deferred feature, even if some of its other features are effective.

Object-oriented systems analysis may be defined as the discipline of describing systems of any kind through collections of fully deferred classes, connected by client and heir relations (capturing system structure) and characterized by preconditions, postconditions and invariants (capturing system semantics). Although a detailed presentation of these topics falls far beyond the goal of this book, the following class sketch should enable you to form a general idea of object-oriented system analysis.

Extracted from the hypothetical description of a chemical plant, it illustrates the gist of the method, in particular its use of assertions to characterize the known abstract properties of a set of objects. As noted, such a specification is independent from any computer implementation − although it will of course serve as an ideal basis for the software design and implementation process if computerization does occur.

```
deferred class TANK feature
    fill is
            -- Fill tank with liquid
        require
            in_valve.open;
            out_valve.closed
        deferred
        ensure
            in_valve.closed;
            out_valve.closed;
            is_full
        end; -- fill
    ... Other deferred features, such as:
        fill, empty, is_full, is_empty,
        in_valve, out_valve,
        gauge, maximum ...

invariant
    is_full = ((0.97 * maximum <= gauge )
                and (gauge <= 1.03 * maximum));

    ... Other invariant clauses ...
end -- class TANK
```

10.12 Effecting a deferred feature

Unless you are using Eiffel just as a modeling language, and do not plan to implement the classes that you have first described as deferred, you will eventually write proper descendants which **effect** (redeclare as effective) the features inherited in deferred form.

Any class C that inherits a deferred feature from one of its parents may provide a declaration making the feature effective in C. (This is a possibility, not an obligation; if the designer of C elects to leave some or all of the inherited features deferred, C itself will still be a deferred class.)

Effecting a feature is similar to redefining an inherited feature. Here the feature should not be listed in the corresponding Redefine clause since it was not "defined" in the first place.

→ The Redeclaration rule, page 163, states what exactly must appear in the Redefine clause.

As an example of effecting, one of the many proper descendants of *TREE* which effect *child_put* above is *TWO_WAY_TREE*, where the redeclaration, describing the routine's implementation for this particular representation, is:

← The deferred version of 'child_put' was on page 145.

```
child_put (v: like item) is
        -- Put item v at active child position;
        -- create one active child with item v if current node is a leaf.
    require else
        is_leaf_or_not_off: (not is_leaf) => (not child_off)
    local
```

```
        node: like parent
    do
        if is_leaf then
            !! node.make (v);
            put_child (node);
            child_start
        else
            child.put (v)
        end
    ensure then
        child_item = v
    end -- child_put
```

Note the new form of the precondition and postcondition clauses. The precondition of the effective version is the boolean "or" of the original (deferred) routine's precondition and of the assertion given in the **require else** clause; the new postcondition is the boolean "and" of the original postcondition and of the assertion given in the **ensure then** clause. This is part of the general Redeclaration rule, as given below.

→ *On adapting assertions in a redeclaration, see 10.15 below and clause 3 of the Redeclaration rule, page 163.*

For an effecting of the above form it is not necessary to list the feature in a Redefine clause. If, however, the redeclared version of an inherited feature is still deferred, then, as expressed formally by the Redeclaration rule below, you do need to include the feature in the Redefine clause. This is the case in which you write a class C which inherits a deferred feature f from B and want to let f remain deferred in f, but with a different signature. Then you must list f in the Redefine subclause for B in C.

10.13 Partially deferred classes and programmed iteration

As defined above, a class is deferred as soon as it has at least one deferred feature. But nothing requires it to be all deferred: it may contain a combination of deferred and effective features.

This yields one of the most powerful techniques of Eiffel development: producing partially deferred classes which capture what you know for sure about the behaviors and data structures characterizing a certain application area, while leaving open what you do not yet know and what is open to individual variation. You will describe the known aspects through effective features, the variable ones through deferred routines. In particular, an effective routine, covering a known general behavior, may call one or more deferred features, which stand for the variable components of that behavior.

This technique is studied in detail in "Object-Oriented Software Construction", under the heading **Factoring out common behaviors.**

A typical application of this technique appears in many user-interface building systems, where the application software is under the control of an outside loop, sometimes called an **event loop**, which controls the overall scheduling of individual operations: detecting input events, processing these events, updating the screen etc. The event loop is the same for all applications, but each application will define its own version of the individual operations. To implement this scheme elegantly, you may write a deferred class covering the properties of all applications of a certain type, with an effective routine which serves as event loop and calls deferred routines representing the individual operations. Each specific application will then effect these routines, according to its own needs, in a proper descendant of the deferred class.

This scheme is an attractive alternative to the "call-back" mechanisms present in lower-level programming languages.

→ *On call-back mechanisms see also 24.6, page 404, indicating how to enable an existing call-back mechanism, implemented in another language, to call Eiffel routines.*

Another important application of the same idea is illustrated by the **iteration** classes of the Iteration Library. These classes provide various iteration mechanisms on arbitrary structures: linear iteration (forward only), two-way iteration, tree iteration (preorder, inorder, postorder). For example, class *LINEAR_ITERATION* [*T*] has iteration procedures such as

The body of this routine has been slightly simplified for this presentation. In the actual class, 's' is declared of type 'like anchor', with 'anchor' of type TRAVERSABLE [T], and the loop is written not directly in 'do_until' but in a procedure 'continue_until', called by 'do_until', 'do_while' and others. 'continue_until' appears on page 383.

```
do_until (s: TRAVERSABLE [T]) is
        -- Starting at the beginning of s, apply action to every item of s
        -- up to and including the first one satisfying test.
    require
        traversable_exists: s /= Void;
        invariant_satisfied: invariant_value (s)
    do
        from
            start (s); prepare (s)
        invariant
            invariant_value (s)
        until
            off (s) or else test (s)
        loop
            action (s);
            forth (s)
        end;
        if not off (s) then action (s) end;
        wrapup (s)
    ensure
        not off implies test (s)
    end -- do_until
```

and, similarly, *do_all, do_while, do_for, do_if, exists* etc. *TRAVERSABLE* is a very general deferred class, requiring its effective descendants to provide features representing basic traversing steps (start traversal, advance by one position etc.). All library classes that describe traversable data structures such as chains, lists and many others are descendants of *TRAVERSABLE*.

The effective procedures such as *do_until* define traversal patterns. Deferred features describe the ingredients to be used in any particular application of these patterns:

1 • Iteration mechanisms on the data structure: *start* (position the cursor on the first element), *forth* (advance to the next element), *off* (find out if the cursor has moved beyond the last element).

2 • Specific operations to apply during the traversal: *prepare* (action to be applied before processing the first element), *action* (action to be applied to each successive element, accessed as *s.item*), *test* (condition defining the element that stops the iteration, if any), *wrapup* (final action).

To iterate over a certain structure, then, it suffices to inherit from one of the iteration classes and to define the specifics of the desired iteration by effecting the deferred features of that class. For example, if a routine *decode_header* of a class *NETWORK_CONTROL* needs to process a list *cpl* of communication packets, applying a certain operation to successive packets until the first that meets a specific criterion, it may do so simply by calling

> *do_until* (*cpl*)

provided that *NETWORK_CONTROL* is a descendant of *LINEAR_ITERATION* and effects routines *start, forth* and *off* to traverse the given data structure, and routines *prepare, action, wrapup* to perform the desired action and tests on each packet.

In simple cases it is not even necessary to write 'decode_header' as a new procedure: just rename 'do_until' as 'decode_header' in the Parent part for CHAIN_ITERATION in NETWORK_CONTROL.

Two-step effecting for iteration classes

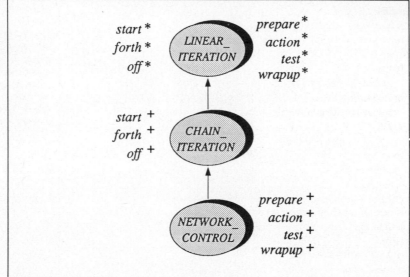

The effecting of a high-level iteration class such as *LINEAR_ITERATION* will usually proceed in two steps, as shown on the figure: first define an heir which only effects the traversal routines, specializing them for a certain data structure, for example *CHAIN_ITERATION* for chains; then, in a descendant of that heir, effect the action and test routines to cover a particular application, such as the packet list processing.

Chains include lists as a special case. Class CHAIN_ITERATION, and its equivalents for other important data structures, are available as part of the Iteration Library.

As presented so far, the iteration mechanism seems to limit every descendant of an iteration class to just one form of iteration (corresponding to the effecting of the deferred routines). To overcome this limitation, however, it suffices to use repeated inheritance and replication, as studied in the next chapter: just inherit from *LINEAR_ITERATION* or another iteration class as many times as there are variants of the iteration process.

→ To obtain two or more iteration variants, each Parent part will rename 'do_until' and other iteration features. For the full details see 11.5, page 174.

10.14 Redeclaration and typing

The two redeclaration mechanisms studied so far in this chapter, redefinition and effecting, share many properties; both are ways to refine the original declaration of an inherited feature, and both are subject to the same constraints.

Two important properties apply in both cases:

- The type constraint, which we will now explore informally.
- The rule on semantics of updated assertions, studied in the next section.

The formal version of these combined properties is the Redeclaration rule, given in full later.

→ *The Redeclaration rule is on page 163.*

As you had probably guessed, there are type constraints on redefining a feature. They are given formally below, but here are the key concepts. Let f be a precursor (parent's feature) of signature

$$(<A, B>, <C>)$$

Recall that the first part, here $<A, B>$, describes the types of the arguments for a routine (it is empty for an attribute), and that the second part, here C, describes the type of the result for an attribute or a function (it is empty for a procedure).

← *Signatures were studied in 5.12, page 66.*

Then the Redeclaration rule states that if you redeclare f into a new feature, the new signature must conform to the precursor's signature.

Conformance, a key concept of the type system, is discussed in detail in a later chapter; an example of signature conformance is shown on the figure page 166. Roughly speaking, a type conforms to another if its base class is a descendant of the other's; a signature conforms to another if it has the same number of arguments and results and every type in the first signature conforms to its counterpart in the other. For example, the signature

→ *Chapter 13 studies conformance rules. Signature conformance is in 13.3, page 218.*

$$(<X, Y>, <Z>)$$

will conform to the above if type X conforms to A, Y to B and Z to C.

This rule means in particular that a redeclaration may not change the number of arguments and may only replace types of arguments or results by conformant types.

‹ *You may usually obtain the effect of changing the number of arguments by using a "manifest array" argument. See 8.4, page 110.*

The Redeclaration rule also prohibits the redeclaration of an attribute into a function. It is permitted, however, to redeclare a function into an attribute; in this case the preceding constraint implies that the precursor function must have been without arguments (otherwise the new signature could not conform). The attribute used for the redeclaration may be variable or constant.

Redeclaring a function into an attribute is a useful and common practice. Here is a typical case. Feature *count*, present in most classes of the Data Structure Library, gives the number of elements of a structure. Classes high in the inheritance graph, such as *LIST*, the deferred class describing lists independently of any representation choice, declare *count* as a function, which traverses a structure to count its elements. The implementation of Effective descendants such as *LINKED_LIST* keeps a record of a list's element count in the list header; so they redefine *count* as an attribute.

This example illustrates why you may want to redefine a function into an attribute. In the general case, assume C is a proper descendant of B, and B has a function f returning some information about instances of B. (In the example B was *LIST*, C was *LINKED_LIST* and f was *count*.) At the B level, this information must be computed whenever a client requests it; so f is a function. At the C level, however, you have made further implementation decisions; in particular, you have added an attribute which corresponds directly to the value of f, now kept within each instance of C (which means that procedures modifying instances of C may need to update it). In such a case, you will redefine f into an attribute in C.

Sometimes the B version of f is deferred; this is the case in the above example if instead of *LIST* we consider its ancestor *SEQUENTIAL*, where *count* is deferred. (Deferred features are syntactically treated as routines, although if they have no arguments they are precisely features for which we have refused to choose yet between attribute and routine implementations.)

Why then does the type constraint prohibit the reverse form of redefinition — changing an attribute into a function? One of the reasons is that we would be unable, were this permitted, to make sense of certain routines inherited from parents. Assume class B with features

> a: *INTEGER*;   -- a is an attribute
>
> *set_a* **is do** $a := 0$ **end**   -- *set_a* assigns to a

→ *The Redeclaration rule will also prohibit redeclaring an external routine (implemented in another language) into an internal one and conversely. See below 10.22, page 163.*

Then if C, an heir of B, were allowed to redefine a into a function, but did not redefine *set_a*, there would be no way to execute *set_a* applied to instances of C, since one may not assign to a function. For the same reason, it is not permitted to redefine a variable attribute into a constant attribute.

10.15 Redeclaration and assertions

The other fundamental property of redeclaration governs the Precondition and Postcondition clauses of a redeclared routine. Such assertions, if present, may not be of the basic forms using just **require** and **ensure**; instead they must use the respective forms

← *See 9.6, starting on page 121, about* Precondition *and* Postcondition *clauses and their semantics in the absence of redeclaration.*

> **require else** *alternative_precondition*
>
> **ensure then** *extra_postcondition*

expressing the new assertions as a variation on the precursors' assertions.

More precisely, let $pre_1, ... \ pre_n$ be the precursors' preconditions and $post_1, \ post_n$ be the precursors' postconditions. (Remember that in most practical cases there is only one precursor, so that n is 1; only with a join of deferred features may there be two or more precursors.) If the above clauses are present, the redeclared routine will be considered to have the precondition and postcondition

With sharing in repeated inheritance, there may also be two or more precursors, but this is not a case of redeclaration. See the definition of "inherited features" on page 187.

> *alternative_precondition* **or else** pre_1 **or else** ... **or else** pre_n
>
> *extra_postcondition* **and then** $post_1$ **and then** ... **and then** $post_n$

In other words, the precondition is or-ed with the original preconditions, and the postcondition is and-ed with the original postconditions. For the precondition, the use of operator **or else** rather than plain **or** guarantees that the assertion is defined, with value true, whenever one of the operands has value true, even if a subsequent one is not defined; similarly, **and then** for postconditions guarantees that any false operand makes the whole assertion false even if a subsequent one is not defined.

→ **or else** *and* **and then** *are the "semi-strict" versions of plain* **or** *and* **and**. *They are discussed in detail in 23.9, page 381.*

If the Precondition part is absent, the redeclared routine is considered to have **false** as its *alternative_precondition*; if the Postcondition part is absent, the redeclared routine is considered to have **true** as its *extra_postcondition*. Because of the rules of boolean algebra, the absence of one of these assertions means that the corresponding precursor assertion is kept as it was. (Or-ing a boolean value with **false**, or and-ing it with **true**, does not change the condition.)

This rule reflects a key part of the Eiffel approach to the construction of correct software, based on the theory of design by contract. Redefining a routine means subcontracting to a descendant the job which clients originally entrusted to the precursor. An honest subcontractor will do as well or better for clients as agreed in the original contract (involving the precursor). This means:

See "Object-Oriented Software Construction" and "Design by Contract" (references in appendix C) and the notion of subspecification in 9.7, page 121.

- Keeping or weakening the precondition, so as not to impose any new requirements on the original clients.

- Keeping or strengthening the postcondition, so as to return a result that is as good as what was originally promised to the clients.

The or-ing and and-ing automatically guarantee these rules, since p **or else** q is always weaker than or equal to p, and p **and then** q is always stronger than or equal to p.

A condition is stronger than or equal to another if it implies it, in the sense of boolean implication. "Weaker than or equal" is the inverse relation.

Examples of strengthening the postcondition in a redeclared routine are very common. In fact, almost any redefinition of a routine's implementation, or effecting of a deferred routine, will do something more (update new attributes, etc.), so that its postcondition will be naturally stronger than the original. The added properties should appear in the **ensure then** ... clause.

As an example of weakening the precondition, assume the inheritance hierarchy illustrated on the next page. Procedure *write*, in *DEVICE*, has two clauses in its Precondition: the device must be open, and it must not be protected. Examples of devices are output devices, interactive devices and files. Assume for this discussion that printers, a special case of output device, may not be write-protected. (The invariant of class *PRINTER* should then include the clause **not** *protected*.) The precondition of *write* for *PRINTER* may then be weakened to just *open*.

To achieve this, just include in the redefined version of *write* in *PRINTER* the Precondition

> **require else** *open*

Weakening a precondition

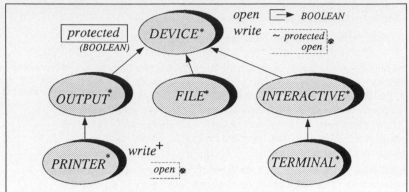

The resulting precondition is, according to the above rule:

> *open* **or else** (**not** *protected* **and then** *open*)

Since 'protected' has value **false** *here, this has the same boolean value as 'open'.*

This discussion complements another property involving the combination of assertions and inheritance: the definition of "invariant of a class" as containing not only the local Invariant clause, but also any others inherited from parents. Together with the rules just seen on assertions of redeclared routines, this ensures that inheritance and redeclaration maintain the fundamental semantic properties of a class and its features, as expressed by the assertions.

← *See 9.11, page 126.*

We need to consider one more case in the combination of redeclaration and assertions. As noted, it is permitted to redefine a function without arguments into an attribute. What then happens of the function's assertions, if any? Since an attribute has no precondition, you may consider that the precondition is changed to **true**; this is consistent with the preceding discussion since **true** is weaker than any other assertion. For a postcondition, the situation is different: the only way to express that the attribute's possible values will satisfy the corresponding condition (with the attribute's name substituted for *Result*) is to make it part of the invariant of the class. The definition of class invariants took care of this by stating that the redefinition of a function into an attribute automatically adds the adapted postcondition to the invariant of the redefining class, replacing any occurrence of *Current* by the attribute name. So if a function was of the form

← *The rule on postconditions was part of the definition of the invariant of a class in 9.11.*

```
last_value: INTEGER is
    do
        ...
    ensure
        Result >= 0
    end -- last_value
```

and is redefined into an attribute by a descendant *C* of its class of origin, the invariant of *C* will automatically include the clause

```
last_value >= 0
```

Remember that the invariant of a class, as defined on page 126, always includes the parents' invariants.

10.16 Undefining a feature

One specific form of feature adaptation, not covered by redeclaration, requires a complementary mechanism: undefinition.

As the Redeclaration rule will express precisely, you may not use redeclaration to turn an effective feature into a deferred one, discarding its inherited implementation. In other words, redeclaration cannot decrease the effectiveness level of a feature: it can take the status of an inherited feature from deferred to deferred (redefinition), effective to effective (redefinition), or deferred to effective (effecting), but never from effective to deferred.

→ *See clause 5 of the Redeclaration rule, page 163.*

In some cases, however, this is desirable; when inheriting a feature, you may wish to give it back its virginity, by pretending you inherited it as deferred, even though its precursor (the parent's version) is in fact effective.

Undefinition serves this goal. To undefine one or more effective features inherited from a parent, just list them in the Undefine subclause of the corresponding Parent part, as in

```
class C inherit
    B
        rename
            ...
        undefine
            f, g, h
        redefine
            ...
        ... Other subclauses of Feature_adaptation ...
        end;
    ... Other parents ...
```

In the order of the optional subclauses of a Feature_adaptation, Undefine comes after Rename and New_exports, and before Redefine and Select.

Here f, g, h must be features which are effective in B. The result of the above Undefine subclause is that C obtains these features from B as if they had been deferred rather than effective in that class; the process does not change the features' signature and specification.

To remember this order, note that all subclauses except Rename *refer to features by their final names, so that* Rename *should come first. Since, as seen below, an undefined feature may then be redefined,* Undefine *must come before* Redefine.

It is possible to apply both undefinition and redefinition to the same inherited feature; this is useful if you want to make an inherited feature deferred and at the same time to change its signature or specification, as in

```
        class C inherit
            B
                undefine
                    f
                redefine
                    f
                end
        feature
            f (x: U) is deferred end
        end -- class C
```

where the *B* version of *f* had an argument of type *T* rather than *U*. (The Redeclaration rule implies that *U* must conform to *T*.)

DEFINITION:
Inherited
as effective,
as deferred

In the rest of this discussion, an inherited feature is said to be **inherited as effective** if it has at least one effective precursor and the corresponding Parent part does not undefine it. Otherwise the feature is **inherited as deferred**.

10.17 The join mechanism

One more useful property is associated with deferred features: the join mechanism.

This facility allows a class to merge several features, inherited as deferred, into just one feature.

The join mechanism supports an important aspect of object-oriented architecture design: the fusion of abstractions. The abstractions that need to be combined will come from different hierarchies of deferred classes.

The Data Structure Library is based on combinations of three such hierarchies, provides typical opportunities for such fusion. The hierarchies correspond to various classification mechanisms for general-purpose "container" data structures:

A container data structure, such as a queue or a hash table, serves to store and retrieve objects. Some of the most important kinds of container data structure are covered by the classes of the Data Structure Library. See "Eiffel: The Libraries" for details.

- Storage, characterizing the storage properties of a data structure (fixed size, variable size but bounded, unbounded but finite, potentially infinite).

- Access, characterizing the methods through which clients may store and retrieve elements (in last-in-first-out fashion for stacks, through a key in hash tables etc.).

- Traversal, characterizing the available mechanisms for exploring the data structure exhaustively (forward, backward, postorder, preorder etc.).

A given effective class of the library is obtained by multiple inheritance from classes of these three categories. For example, a "fixed list" has a fixed-size storage, access by index and other techniques, and forward traversal.

In this process of combining abstractions, it will often be useful to merge inherited deferred routines if they correspond to the same notion in the descendant. For example, the deferred Data Structure Library class *CHAIN* (describing sequential structures such as lists) inherits from two deferred classes which both have an *item* function returning the item at cursor position:

- *ACTIVE*, from the Access hierarchy, describe structures with a client-controlled "cursor" position. Procedures are available to move the cursor to various elements. In this class, *item* denotes the value of the element at cursor position.

- *BIDIRECTIONAL*, from the Traversal hierarchy, describe structures which are sequentially traversable both forward and backward. In this class, *item* denotes the value of the current element at each step of a traversal operation.

Class *CHAIN*, which combines these two concepts, inherits both *item* functions. Normally, this would be considered a name clash, which would have to be removed through renaming. But here the clash is harmless, and in fact desired, since at the level of *CHAIN* the two concepts may be merged into one.

It is valid, then, to write *CHAIN* as heir to both *BIDIRECTIONAL* and *ACTIVE* even without renaming the deferred *item* routines, which will yield a single deferred routine in *CHAIN*:

→ *See page 188 about name clashes.*

```
deferred class CHAIN [T] inherit
    BIDIRECTIONAL [T]
        ...
            -- BIDIRECTIONAL has a deferred routine item
    ACTIVE [T]
        ...
            -- ACTIVE has a deferred routine item
    ... Other parents and rest of class text omitted ...
```

To be joined, inherited features must have the same final name in the class that performs the join. In the above case both precursors were called *item* in the parents, so no particular action was required from the designer of class *CHAIN* with respect to their names. In some cases, of course, you might want to join two deferred features which have different names, say *f* and *g*, in the parents from which they come. To achieve this, you should use renaming to make sure that the features are inherited under the same final name:

```
        -- C may be deferred or not (see below)
... class C inherit
    B
        rename
            f as new_name
        ...
        end;
    A
        rename
            g as new_name
        ...
        end;
```

If *C* inherits and joins two or more deferred features, the net result for *C* is as if it had inherited a single deferred feature. In the absence of further action from *C*, that feature remains deferred. Of course, *C* may also provide an effective declaration for the feature, killing several abstract birds with one concrete stone by using a single redeclaration to effect several features inherited as deferred.

← *"Inherited as deferred" (see the definition on page 156) means either coming from deferred precursors, or explicitly undefined.*

More generally, *C* may treat the result of the join as it would any other inherited deferred feature. This means in particular that *C* may also redefine the feature to change its signature while leaving it deferred. In that case the inherited features must all be listed in the Redefine subclauses of their Parent parts.

The join mechanism imposes easily justifiable conditions on features to be joined: they must be deferred (after possible undefinition, as seen in the next section), inherited under the same name (after possible renaming), and equipped with the same signature (after possible redeclaration). The formal rule expressing these requirements is the Join rule, described later in this chapter.

→ *The Join rule appears on page 165.*

10.18 Merging effective features

(This section describes a specialized application of the undefinition and join mechanisms and may be skipped on first reading.)

As introduced above, the join mechanism applies only to deferred routines. The reason is obvious: an attempt by a class D to join two effective features inherited from parents of D would yield an ambiguous result in the absence of a clear universal criterion for choosing one of the two inherited implementations over the other.

What happens, however, if when you design D you *do* know which of the two versions you want to override the other in D? Then merging the two versions into one should not raise any particular problem.

The undefinition mechanism makes this possible. Here is an illustration of the general scheme:

← *Undefinition was studied in 10.16, on page 155.*

Merging and overriding

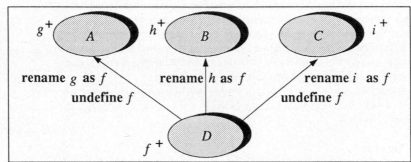

To discard the unwanted versions (the ones from A and C on the figure), D undefines them, and joins them if there are two or more. These versions and the overriding one (coming from B on the figure) must all be inherited under the same name; this requires renaming if the names are different in the parents.

In the simplest case, there are only two competing features in parents B and C, and they already had the same name f in these parents. Then if you want the B version to take over in D all you need to do is to undefine the C version:

```
class D inherit
    B;
    C
        undefine
            f
        end
feature
    ...
end -- class D
```

Even though f's precursor in B was effective, f is inherited as deferred from C because of the undefinition. Then the B version simply provides an effecting.

An application of this technique will appear in repeated inheritance when a class inherits conflicting versions of the same feature, and the class designer wants to retain only one of these versions.

→ *See policy R2 in 11.8, page 182.*

10.19 Redefinition and undefinition rules

With this discussion of feature merging we have now covered all the practical uses of redeclaration, join and undefinition. What remains for this chapter to provide is the precise rules for syntax, validity and semantics of the corresponding constructs. Because this will only be a more formal examination of concepts already introduced, you may prefer on first reading to skip the rest of this chapter.

Let us begin with the straightforward syntax and validity of Undefine and Redefine subclauses. It will do no harm to repeat here (again) the general structure of Inheritance clauses:

Inheritance	≙	**inherit** Parent_list
Parent_list	≙	{Parent ";" ...}
Parent	≙	Class_type [Feature_adaptation]
Feature_adaptation	≙	[Rename]
		[New_exports]
		[Undefine]
		[Redefine]
		[Select]
		end

← This syntax appeared first on page 77.

The clauses involved in this discussion are Undefine and Redefine.

Here is the syntax of the Redefine clause:

See page 81 for the syntax of Rename, *101 for* New_exports, *and 192 for* Select.

Redefine	≙	**redefine** Feature_list

The following constraint applies to Redefine subclauses:

Redefine Subclause rule

Consider a class *C* with a parent *B*. If a Parent part for *B* in *C* contains a Redefine subclause, that clause is valid if and only if every Feature_identifier *fname* that it lists (in its Feature_list) satisfies the following conditions:

1 • *fname* is the final name in *C* of a feature inherited from *B*.

2 • That feature was not frozen, and was not a constant attribute.

3 • *fname* appears only once in the Feature_list.

4 • The Features part of *C* contains one Feature_declaration for *fname*, which is a valid redeclaration, but not an effecting, of the original feature.

In this definition:

- The final name of an inherited feature is its name as it results from possible renaming.

- A feature is "frozen" if it has been declared with the keyword **frozen** in its class of origin. The purpose of such a declaration is precisely to forbid any redefinition of the feature in descendants, guaranteeing that the exact original implementation remains in place.

← See 5.9, page 63.

- A constant attribute is declared with a clause of the form **is** v, where v is Manifest_constant or Unique.

← *See "How to recognize features", 5.11, page 64.*

- The condition for a redeclaration to be valid appear later in this chapter; in particular, the new signature must conform to the original's, and you may not redeclare an attribute into a function.

→ *See 10.22, starting page 163, about valid redeclarations.*

- If C provides an effective version of a feature which it inherits as deferred, this is a case of effecting, and hence of redeclaration, but not of redefinition; as a consequence, condition 4 indicates that the feature must not appear in the Redefine subclause.

→ *Effecting is defined precisely below. See condition 3 of the definition at the bottom of this page.*

The effect of redefining a feature in a class is that any use of the feature in the class, its clients or (barring further redefinitions) its proper descendants will refer to the redefined version rather than the original.

→ *This also applies to the clients of proper ancestors, under polymorphism and dynamic binding. See 21.9, page 345.*

The syntax of an Undefine clause is similar to that of a Redefine:

$$\text{Undefine} \quad \triangleq \quad \textbf{undefine}\ \text{Feature\_list}$$

and the constraint is also similar:

Undefine Subclause rule

Consider a class C that inherits from a class B. If a Parent part for B in C contains an Undefine subclause, that clause is valid if and only if, for every Feature_identifier *fname* that it lists (in its Feature_list):

1 • *fname* is the final name in C of a feature inherited from B.

2 • That feature was not frozen, and was not an attribute.

3 • That feature was effective in B.

4 • *fname* appears only once in the Feature_list.

10.20 Deferred and effective features and classes

The discussion has already referred informally to features being deferred in a class. The following makes this notion precise in terms of the reverse, "effective feature"; it also defines the "effecting" of a feature.

DEFINITION:
Effective,
Deferred
Feature;

Effecting

A feature f of a class C is said to be an **effective feature** of C if and only if any of the following conditions holds.

1 • f is introduced in C as an attribute or a routine whose Routine_body is of the Effective form (that is to say, not the keyword **deferred** but beginning with **do**, **once** or **external**).

2 • f is an inherited feature, coming from a parent B of C where it is (recursively) effective, and C does not undefine it.

3 • Another feature of C with the same final name is (recursively) effective. That feature is then said to **effect** f in C.

A feature of C is a **deferred feature** of C if and only if it is not an effective feature of C.

As a result of this definition, a feature is deferred in C not only if it is introduced or redefined in C as deferred, but also if its precursor was deferred and C does not redeclare it effectively. In the latter case, as you may remember, the feature is "inherited as deferred".

← *"Inherited as deferred" was defined on page 156.*

The definition captures the semantics of deferred features and of their effecting. Condition 1 yields the simplest form of effective feature of C: a new feature introduced in C as non-deferred. Condition 2 corresponds to an inherited feature which was already effective, unless C (using an undefinition as introduced earlier) makes it explicitly deferred.

← *Undefinition was discussed in 10.16, starting on page 155.*

Condition 3 defines the effecting case: an effective feature, which has the same final name as one or more deferred features, serves as effecting for all of them. Of course, some validity constraints, seen below, apply to this case: the effective feature must satisfy the Redeclaration rule, and if there are two or more deferred features among the lot, this is a join, governed by the Join rule.

→ *See page 163 about the Redeclaration rule and page 165 about the Join rule.*

Condition 3 raises the possibility of two or more features of a class having the same final name. Here all except at most one are deferred. The only other case in which such name clashes are permitted is sharing under repeated inheritance.

→ *On the other case, see the Repeated Inheritance Consistency constraint on page 191.*

One interesting aspect of condition 3 is that an effective feature C will serve as effecting of any deferred feature f with the same final name in C as long as they have the same final name and the two applicable rules (Redeclaration and Join) are satisfied. Four schemes are possible:

1 • You may write C as heir to a class B where f is deferred, and provide an effecting of f in the form of a Feature_declaration in the Features part of C. This is the most common use of deferred features and effecting.

← *This is the case illustrated in the example of 10.12.*

2 • You may want to inherit a specification from one parent A and the corresponding implementation from another B. In this case A will provide a deferred feature and B an effective feature with compatible signature; if they have the same final name in C, the B version will serve as effecting of the A version. In this case there is no new feature declaration in C.

3 • C may also undefine a parent's effective feature, and use an effective feature (inherited from a parent, or introduced or redefined in C itself) to provide an implementation. This is less common, but provides the mechanism for merging effective features, with one of the implementations overriding the others, as explained above.

← *See 10.18, page 158.*

4 • Finally, C could introduce a deferred feature and use an effective feature to effect it on the spot. This case is permitted by the rules but appears useless.

The above defines the meaning of "deferred" and "effective" for features. These qualifiers carry over to the classes that contain these features:

DEFINITION:
Deferred,
Effective
Class

> A class is **deferred** if it has at least one deferred feature. It is **effective** otherwise.

Be sure to remember that a class C is deferred as soon as it has one deferred feature f, and that f does not need to be introduced in C as deferred: it may also be inherited as deferred, and not effected in C.

If a class is deferred according to the above definition, then its Class_header must be marked with the **deferred** Header_mark. This was part of the validity constraint on Class_header. In other words, a class which either introduces a deferred feature, or inherits one from a parent without redeclaring it effectively, must have a Class_header beginning with

← Class_header, *the* **deferred** Header_mark *and the corresponding validity constraint were introduced in 4.8, starting on page 50.*

> **deferred class** *C* ...

whereas the Class_header of an effective class simply begins with one of

This is not necessarily the beginning of the class text itself since there may be an Indexing *clause first.*

> **class** *C* ...
>
> **expanded class** *C* ...

10.21 Origin and seed

Two useful definitions follow from the discussion of redeclaration. Chapter 5 defined the "origin" of a feature introduced in class *C* as *C* itself. We can now generalize this to arbitrary features – inherited as well as immediate. The associated notion is a feature's "seed", its original version. These notions, which will be especially useful in the discussion of repeated inheritance (next chapter), are defined as follows.

← *This is a refinement of the initial definition of "origin" on page 56, which only covered case 1 of the present definition.*

If this is your first reading, do not let yourself be troubled by case 2, which refers to repeated inheritance. As soon as you have read the first three sections of the next chapter, the context in which case 2 occurs should be quite clear.

DEFINITION:
Origin,
Seed

> Every feature of a class *C* has a seed, which is a feature, and an origin, which is a class, defined as follows.
>
> 1 • Any immediate feature of *C* (in other words, any feature introduced in *C* rather than inherited) is its own seed, and has *C* as its origin.
>
> 2 • An inherited feature of *C* with two or more precursors, all of which have (recursively) the same seed *s*, also has *s* as its seed. (This is the case of sharing under repeated inheritance.)
>
> 3 • If *C* joins a set of inherited deferred features, yielding (as explained above) a single feature of *C* to which case 2 does not apply, that feature is its own seed and its origin is *C*.
>
> 4 • Any feature of *C* to which none of the previous cases applies is inherited, and has exactly one precursor; then its seed and origin are (recursively) the seed and origin of that precursor.

The origin of a feature is the most remote ancestor from which the feature "comes", and its seed is its original form in that ancestor.

None of the reincarnations that the feature may have gone through along the inheritance part as a result of redefinition, effecting or renaming ffect its seed or its origin.

10.22 Redeclaration rules

(The rest of this chapter gives the formal rules applying to feature redeclaration. The essential concepts have already been seen, so you may safely skip to the next chapter on first reading.)

First, we need a precise definition of what is meant by redeclaration:

DEFINITION:
Redeclaration,
Redefinition,
Effecting

A class C **redeclares** an inherited feature f if and only if one of the following two conditions holds:

R1 • C contains a Feature_declaration for a feature g with the same final name as f.

R2 • C inherits f as deferred, and inherits as effective another feature g with the same final name as f.

A **redefinition** is a redeclaration which is not an effecting.

← *Two feature names are "the same" if they are identical or differ only by letter case. See page 69.*

Case R2 is an effecting. R1 is an effecting for deferred f and effective g, a redefinition if they are both deferred or both effective. Clause 6 of the constraint below will preclude the other apparent possibility: f effective, g deferred.

← *Effecting was defined in 10.20, page 160. Case R2 of the present definition is part of case 3 of the earlier definition of effecting.*

In case R2, the text of C does not contain any declaration for f, but some other inherited feature g (which must come from a different parent) effects f. It is convenient to treat this implicit and somewhat special case as a redeclaration, along with the explicit and more common case R1.

The above definition says nothing about validity: case R1 simply states that if a declaration uses the name of an inherited feature, we must treat it as a redeclaration (valid or not) of that feature, not as the declaration of a new, or *immediate*, feature. Here is the rule which determines when a redeclaration (explicit or implicit) is valid:

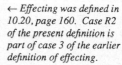

VDRD

Redeclaration rule

Let C be a class and g a feature of C. It is valid for g to be a redeclaration of a feature f inherited from a parent B of C if and only if the following conditions are satisfied.

1 • No effective feature of C other than f and g has the same final name.

2 • The signature of g conforms to the signature of f.

3 • If g is a routine, its Precondition, if any, begins with **require else** (not just **require**), and its Postcondition, if any, begins with **ensure then** (not just **ensure**).

4 • If the redeclaration is a redefinition (rather than an effecting) the Redefine subclause of the Parent part for B lists the final name of f in its Feature_list.

5 • If f is inherited as effective, then g is also effective.

6 • If f is an attribute, g is an attribute, f and g are both variable, and their types are either both expanded or both non-expanded.

7 • If either one of f and g is an External routine, so is the other.

Condition 6 prohibits name clashes between effective features. No invalidity results, however, if f is deferred. Then if g is itself deferred, the redeclaration is simply a redefinition of a deferred feature by another (to change the signature or specification). If g is effective, the redeclaration is an effecting of f. If g plays this role for more than one inherited f, it both joins and effects these features: this is the case, mentioned above, in which C kills several deferred birds with one effective stone.

← *The bird-shooting was on page 157.*

Condition 2 is the fundamental type compatibility rule: signature conformance. In the case of a join, g may be the redeclaration of more than one f; then g's signature must conform to all of the precursors' signatures. This is discussed in detail below.

← *On signature conformance see 13.3, page 218.*

→ *About the application of condition 1 to joins, see below, particularly the figure on page 166.*

Condition 3 requires adapting the assertions of a redeclared routine.

Condition 4 requires listing f in the appropriate Redefine subclause, but only for a redefinition, not for an effecting. (As noted above, we have a redefinition if g and the inherited form of f are both deferred or both effective.) If two or more features inherited as deferred are joined and then redefined together, each must appear in the Redefine subclause for the corresponding parent.

Condition 5 bars the use of redeclaration for turning an effective feature into a deferred one. This is because a specific mechanism is available for that purpose: undefinition. As noted, it is possible to apply both undefinition and redefinition to the same feature to make it deferred and at the same time change its signature.

← *See 10.16, starting on page 155, on undefinition.*

Condition 6 prohibits redeclaring a constant attribute, or redeclaring a variable attribute into a function or constant attribute. It also precludes redeclaring a (variable) attribute of an expanded type into one of reference type or conversely. You may, however, redeclare a function into an attribute — variable or constant.

Finally, condition 7 prohibits a redeclaration from changing an External routine into a non-external feature, or conversely. An External routine is implemented in another language. In contrast with a non-external feature, it does not automatically have access to the "current object", hence this condition.

→ *On* External *routines, see chapter 24, especially 24.4, page 402. On the semantics of non-external feature calls, see chapter 21.*

This discussion yields another useful notion:

DEFINITION:
Declared
Type

> Any feature or entity of a class C has a **declared type** as follows:
>
> A• For a feature which is immediate in C or redeclared in C, dt is the type given by the declaration or redeclaration.
>
> B• For an inherited feature which is not redeclared in C, dt is (recursively) the declared type of its precursors in the corresponding parents.
>
> C• For the predefined entity *Current*, dt is C with its formal generic parameters if any.
>
> D• For the predefined entity *Result*, appearing in a function, dt is the return type declared for the function.
>
> E• For any other entity e, dt is the type used in the declaration of e.

→ *A complementary notion is the* **base type**, *which results from unfolding any anchored declaration: for an anchored type 'like anchor', the base type is the type declared for 'anchor'. See page 215 for the definition of the base type of an anchored type.*

DEFINITION:
Type of a
Feature

In this book, the "type" of a feature or entity, without further qualification, always means its declared type (rather than its base type).

In case B, there is no ambiguity when f has more than one precursor: this can only occur as a result of a join of deferred features, in which the Join rule requires all inherited versions to have the same type, or sharing under repeated inheritance, in which the precursors are in fact all the same feature.

Join rule: page 165 below. Repeated Inheritance rule: page 170, next chapter.

10.23 Rules on joining features

The last constraint that we need to examine governs the validity and semantics of the join mechanism, used to merge two or more deferred features by inheriting them under the same name.

DEFINITION:
Precursor
(Joined
Features)

It is useful first to extend the notion of **precursor**. A precursor of an inherited feature is a version of the feature in the parent from which it is inherited. Without the join mechanism there was just one precursor; but a feature which results from the join of two or more deferred features will have all of them as precursors.

← The definition of "precursor" in the non-join case is on page 140.

Here now is the validity constraint for joining features:

> **Join rule**
>
> It is valid for a class C to inherit two different features as deferred under the same final name if and only if, after possible redeclaration in C, they have identical signatures.

VDJR

The assumption that the features are "different" is important: they could in fact be the same feature, appearing in two parents of C which have inherited it from a common ancestor, without any intervening redeclaration. This would be a valid case of repeated inheritance; here the rule which determines validity is the Repeated Inheritance Consistency constraint. The semantic specification (sharing under the Repeated Inheritance rule) indicates that C will have just one version of the feature.

→ The Repeated Inheritance rule is on page 170 and the Repeated Inheritance Consistency constraint on page 191.

The Join rule indicates that joined features must have exactly the same signature – argument and result types. What is taken into account, however, is the signature after possible redefinition or effecting. So in practice you may join precursor features with different signatures: it suffices to redefine them using a feature which (as required by clause 2 of the Redeclaration rule) must have a signature conforming to all of the precursors' signatures.

← The Redeclaration rule appears on page 163.

› A signature conforms to another (13.3, page 218) if every type in it conforms to the corresponding type in the other. Details in chapter 13.

If the redeclaration describes an effective feature, this is the case in which you are both joining and effecting the precursors. If the redeclaration describes a feature which is still deferred, it is a redefinition, used to adapt the signature and possibly the specification. In this case, clause 4 of the Redeclaration rule requires every one of the precursors to appear in the Redefine subclause for the corresponding parent.

← Join-cum-effecting was described on page 157.

In either case, nothing requires the precursors' signatures to conform to each other – as long as the signature of the redeclared version conforms to all of them. This means you may write a class inheriting two deferred features of the form

> $f(p: P; q: Q): R$ **is** ...
>
> $f(u: U; v: V): W$ **is** ...

and redeclaring them with

> $f(x: X; y: Y): Z$ **is** ...

provided X conforms to both P and U, Y to both Q and V and Z to both R and W. No conformance is required between the types appearing in the precursors' signatures (P and U, Q and V, R and W).

The figure below illustrates a valid case, in which all types involved are non-generic classes (so that conformance is just inheritance). U is an heir of P, but for the second argument the relation is in the other direction: Q is an heir of V. Then a redeclaration into a feature of signature $<< U, Q>, <R>>$ will be valid.

Conforming to two incompatible signatures

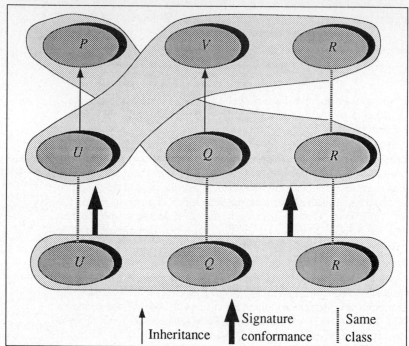

This takes care of the validity of the join mechanism. The last rule gives the precise properties of the resulting feature:

Clause 5 leaves the concatenation order unspecified.

In clause 6 (corresponding to a rare case) language processing tools should produce an obsolescence message for the class performing the join, but the resulting feature is not itself obsolete. See 5.17, page 73, about obsolete features.

Join Semantics rule

Joining deferred features with the same final name yields a non-obsolete deferred feature defined as follows:

1 • Its name is the final name of all its precursors.

2 • Its signature is the precursors' signature, which the Join rule indicates must be the same for all precursors after possible redeclaration.

3 • Its precondition is the **or** of all the precursors' preconditions.

4 • Its postcondition is the **and** of all the precursors' postconditions.

5 • Its Header_comment is the concatenation of those of all precursors.

6 • It is not obsolete (even if some of the precursors are obsolete).

11

Repeated inheritance

11.1 Overview

Inheritance may of course be *multiple*: a class may have any number of parents. Any more restrictive solution would severely limit the benefits of inheritance, so central to object-oriented software engineering.

Because of multiple inheritance, it is possible for a class to be a descendant of another in more than one way, as illustrated on the next page for two typical schemes. This case is known as *repeated* inheritance; it raises interesting issues and yields useful techniques, which this chapter studies in detail.

This is the last of three chapters devoted to inheritance. It introduces the remaining linguistic constructs associated with this notion. As a result, it will complete our study of two important notions, whose complete definition must cover all aspects of the inheritance mechanism: the notions of inherited feature and of name clash.

← *The other two chapters on inheritance are 6 and 10.*

As already remarked, however, our view of inheritance will only be final when we have grasped the semantics of reattachment and feature call, involving the powerful techniques of polymorphism and dynamic binding.

→ *On polymorphism see 20.9, page 323; on dynamic binding see 21.9, page 345.*

11.2 Cases of repeated inheritance

The Parent rule indicates that the inheritance graph of a set of classes may not contain any cycles. It is perfectly possible, however, for two classes to be connected through more than one path. The figure on the next page provides two examples.

← *The Parent rule was given on page 79.*

Repeated inheritance

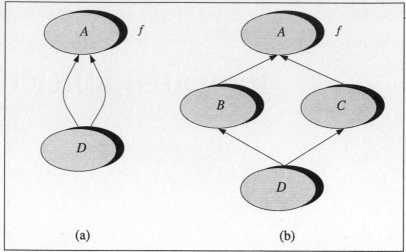

(a)   (b)

More precisely:

Why does the first sentence of the definition use the word "ancestor" rather than "proper ancestor"?

DEFINITION:
Repeated
Inheritance,
Ancestor,
Descendant

> Repeated inheritance occurs whenever (as a result of multiple inheritance) two or more of the ancestors of a class *D* have a common parent *A*.
>
> *D* is then called a repeated descendant of *A*, and *A* a repeated ancestor of *D*.

As shown by the two examples in the figure, *D* can repeatedly inherit from *A* directly (a) as well as indirectly (b).

DEFINITION:
Direct
Repeated
Inheritance

The simplest case (a), called **direct repeated inheritance**, corresponds to the following scheme (where *D* is a "repeated heir" of *A*):

```
class D inherit
    A
        rename ... redefine ... end;
    A
        rename ... redefine ... end
    ... Rest of class omitted ...
```

DEFINITION:
Indirect
Repeated
Inheritance

The second case (b), **indirect repeated inheritance**, arises when one parent of *D* is a proper descendant of *A*, and one or more other parents are descendants of *A*. (Some of the paths may be direct.)

The discussion so far has neglected the generic parameters, if any, of the repeated ancestor *A*. In reality, a Parent is not just a class but a Class_type – a class name possibly followed by actual generic parameters. Uses of *A* as repeated ancestor with different actual generic parameters still cause repeated inheritance (*D*'s ancestors have a common parent class even though the corresponding Parent types are different); this case will be subject to a consistency constraint.

→ *See 11.9, page 184.*

11.3 Sharing and replication

Repeated inheritance raises an important question: what happens to features inherited more than once?

In the absence of repeated inheritance, the situation was simple: if Y is a proper descendant of X, every feature of X yields at most one feature of Y. With repeated inheritance, things are not so clear any more. In any of the above pictures, what should D get out of a feature f of A: one feature, or two?

Because uses of inheritance are so diverse, choosing one of these solutions as the universal, language-imposed answer would not be appropriate. Depending on the context, either solution may be the right one, and you will need some leeway for choosing between them in any particular case:

1 • In some circumstances you may use repeated inheritance precisely because you like a feature of an ancestor so much that you want two of it.

2 • Often, however, one copy is enough. For example, the indirect scheme (b) illustrated above may arise when you write both B and C (the intermediate ancestors) as heirs of A because each needs A's features, such as f; D needs the new features introduced by B and C, but only one copy of A's features.

An extreme example of the case 2 is the universal class *ANY* of the Kernel Library, which is an obligatory ancestor of all Eiffel classes. For any non-trivial Eiffel system, the repeated inheritance structure induced by *ANY*, if we ever tried to draw it, would be rather luxuriant. In most cases, useful as the features of *ANY* are, you would not want your classes to inherit multiple copies of all of them.

→ *See 6.12, page 85, and chapter 27 on class ANY.*

Not only would it be too restrictive for the language definition to specify either solution 1 or solution 2 for all cases of repeated inheritance; forcing developers, for each case of repeated inheritance from a class A, to select either one of these solutions for all the features of A would also be impractical. In reality, you may need replication for some features and sharing for some others.

The need for both sharing and replication

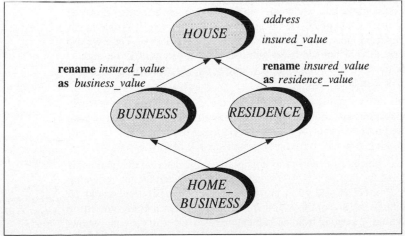

*The **rename** subclauses as shown will produce the desired effect: sharing for 'street_address', replication for 'insured_value'. See below.*

As a simple example, illustrated by the figure, assume that in a system used by an insurance company a class *HOUSE* has heirs *RESIDENCE* and *BUSINESS*. A special class *HOME_BUSINESS* handles the case of people (such as consultants) who run a business from their house; this class may be written as an heir to both of the previous two. Two of the features of *HOUSE* are attributes *street_address* and *insured_value*. For the street address, an instance of *HOME_BUSINESS* should inherit a single attribute; but for *insured_value* it needs two, since the insured value may be different for the two viewpoints.

The same reasoning would apply to routines, such as 'update_street_address' or 'change_insured_value'.

To obtain the desired flexibility, then, we need a way to tune the repeated inheritance mechanism so that any feature of a repeated ancestor may yield one feature or several in the repeated descendant.

The Repeated Inheritance rule provides this flexibility. It is simple: variants of a repeatedly inherited feature will be merged if they are inherited under the **same final name**, and replicated otherwise. More precisely:

Repeated Inheritance rule

Let D be a class and $B_1, \ldots B_n$ ($n \geq 2$) be parents of D having a common ancestor A. Let $f_1, \ldots f_n$ be features of these respective parents, all having as their seed the same feature f of A. Then:

1 • Any subset of these features inherited by D under the same final name yields a single feature of D.

2 • Any two of these features inherited under a different name yield two features of D.

Since A may be any ancestor, not just a proper one, the rule applies to direct repeated inheritance, where $B_1 \ldots B_n$ are all the same as A, as well as to the indirect case.

DEFINITION: Shared, Replicated   Features will be said to be **shared** if case 1 of the rule applies, and **replicated** if case 2 applies.

The Repeated Inheritance rule applies to attributes as well as to routines. It provides the designer of a repeatedly inheriting class with all the needed flexibility through proper choice of names:

• If two or more of the parents of D happen to have a common ancestor A, and you do not take any particular renaming action, each feature of A will yield just one feature of D. This is usually what is wanted in simple cases, such as repeated inheritance from *ANY*, as mentioned above. The rule also renders harmless a common oversight: making A a parent of D because D needs the features of A, forgetting that among the other parents of D one is already a descendant of A.

• If, on the other hand, you want two or more versions of a repeatedly inherited feature, just make sure that it is inherited under different names. This is the modern version of the loaves and fishes miracle: if you have one of a good thing, you may turn it into as many as you like – just ask.

"They took up twelve baskets full of the loaves, and of the fishes", Mark 6:43. Scholars believe Loaf and Fish to be ancient Aramean for attribute and routine. See Proc. ALOOF 3 (Archaeo-Linguistic Object-Oriented Forum), Acapulco, 1991, pp. 798-923.

To determine which of the two cases applies, the only criterion that matters is the final name of the feature in D. This name will be affected by any renaming performed in D itself as well as in intermediate ancestors between A and D. This means that, as the author of D, you are the master when it comes to setting the fate of a feature f coming from an indirect repeated ancestor through parents B and C:

- If f has the same name in B and C, f will normally be shared, but you may force replication by renaming one of the inherited versions, or renaming both forms with different names.
- If there has been some renaming between A and D's parents, f will normally be replicated, but you may force sharing by renaming both inherited versions to the same name.

REMINDER

As you will have noted from the definition, the Repeated Inheritance rule only applies if f is the common seed of the features under consideration or, equivalently, if A is their origin. Remember that the seed of a feature is its original version in the most remote ancestor (the feature's origin) where it appears, regardless of any redeclaration or renaming that it may have endured between that ancestor and the current class.

← The precise definition of "seed" and "origin" was on page 162.

Only the seed and the origin matter for repeated inheritance

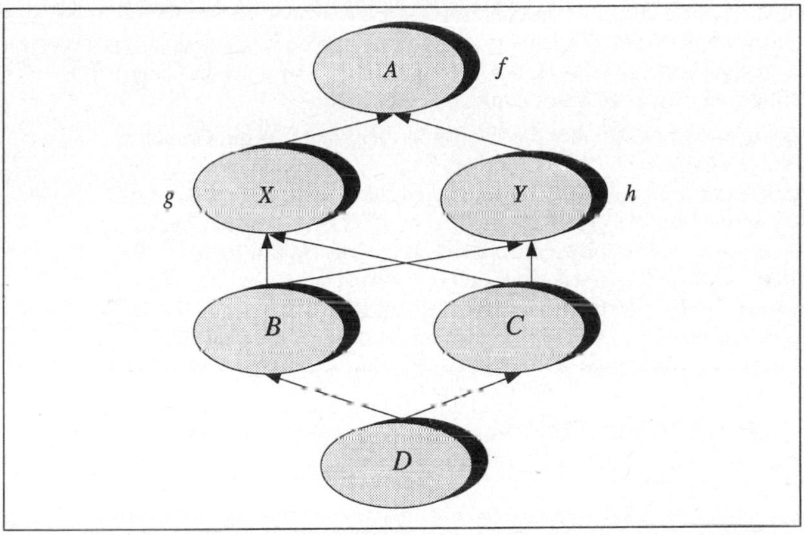

CAVEAT

This requirement that A be the origin of f is an important one. Without it, as illustrated by the above figure, the Repeated Inheritance rule would be ambiguous. On the figure, f is a feature of A, but it is also a feature (an inherited one) of X and Y. All three classes are repeated ancestors of D. To infer sharing or replication from the rule, we need to know what repeated ancestor to consider. The rule's phrasing answers this question precisely: for f, the only relevant ancestor is class A, the origin of that feature. Similarly, to determine the fate of g and h, you must apply the rule (respectively) to X and Y, assumed to be the origins of these features.

PREVIEW

As you may have guessed, the application of the Repeated Inheritance rule raises some potential problems, especially in the case of conflicting redeclarations on separate branches, or conflicting actual generic parameters in the repeated ancestor. Accordingly, we will need a validity constraint, the Repeated Inheritance Consistency constraint, to clarify the mechanism. Before exploring that constraint, it will be useful to examine two important applications of repeated inheritance:

→ The discussion of the Repeated Inheritance Consistency constraint begins in 11.6, page 177; the precise formulation is on page 191.

- How to keep the original version of a feature along with a redefined version.

- How to apply an iterating mechanism to different choices of actions to be iterated.

Of course, both applications only make sense if the validity constraint is satisfied.

11.4 Keeping the original version of a redefined feature

The most novel aspect of the Repeated Inheritance rule is case 1: here for the first time there is a way for one feature of a parent to yield two or more features in an heir.

Among other applications, this mechanism serves to solve an important practical problem of inheritance, mentioned in the last chapter's discussion of redeclaration: keeping the inherited version – the precursor – of a feature along with the redefined one. The need arises in particular for routines.

Here is a simple example of why the facility is important. In the Graphics Library, class *COMMAND_BUTTON* describes buttons, which are small boxes that you can associate with a certain command, and then display on the screen, enabling users to execute the command simply by "clicking" on the button. Since a button is a special kind of window, the class inherits from *WINDOW*. To display a button, however, you must do a little more than for a window of the most general kind. To describe the extra work, *COMMAND_BUTTON* redefines procedure *display* as inherited from *WINDOW*. Here is the new implementation:

← The problem was mentioned towards the end of 10.7, on page 142.

```
display is
      -- Set up button and display it.
   do
      if changed then
         rebuild_button;
      end;
      window_display;
      display_label
   end; -- display
```

Here *window_display* represents *WINDOW*'s original *display* procedure. The extra work for a button is to rebuild the button (if its dimensions have changed due to some user action) and to display its label.

This is typical of a frequent case in which a redefined version of a routine performs the same actions as those of its precursor, adding, however, some actions of its own before, after, or (as in this example) both. Since no two features of a class may have the same name, we must be able to refer to the two variants through different names. The example assumes that we have been able to keep the old procedure under the name *window_display*.

How do we achieve this goal? Normally, if we redefine a feature, we lose the precursors' version. Here, we redefine *display*, but we still need access to the precursor (*WINDOW*) implementation.

By now, you have probably guessed the answer. Since we must get two features of *COMMAND_BUTTON* out of one feature of *WINDOW*, the proper mechanism (and the only possible one) is repeated inheritance. The direct form is applicable: one of the branches will rename, and the other one will redefine. Here is the complete scheme:

> **class** *COMMAND_BUTTON* **inherit**
>   *WINDOW*
>   **rename**
>   *display* **as** *window_display,* ...
>   ...
>   **end**;
>   *WINDOW*
>   **redefine**
>   *display,* ...
>   **select**
>   *display*
>   ...
>   **end**;
>   ...
> **feature**
>   *display* **is**
>   ... See above ...
>   ...
> **end** -- class *COMMAND_BUTTON*

→ *The* **select** ... *subclause is needed to avoid any ambiguity in the context of dynamic binding. See 11.6, page 177, for an informal presentation of the* Select *clause, and the Repeated Inheritance Consistency constraint on page 191 for the precise rule.*

More generally, assume *D* inherits twice from *A* and, through renaming, obtains two variants of *f*, one of *D*'s features. *A* may redefine none of these variants, one of them, or both:

> **class** *D* **inherit**
>   *A*
>   **rename**
>   *f* **as** *f1*
>   **redefine**
>   ... *f1* may or may not appear here ...
>   **select**
>   *f1*
>   **end**;
>   *A*
>   **rename**
>   *f* **as** *f2*
>   **redefine**
>   ... *f2* may or may not appear here ...
>   **end**;
>   ...

Class *D* now has two variants of the original *f*, which are known to *D*, its clients and its heirs under the names *f1* and *f2*. (Of course, to achieve this replication, it suffices to rename just one of them.)

The lists are sorted by increasing mass. The application needs the following two operations on an arbitrary list of particles:

1 • Print the mass of all particles in the list up to and including the first positively charged one.

2 • Compute the total vector speed of the first 50 particles in the list and store it into an attribute *total_speed*. To add speeds, you may use procedure *increase* of class *VECTOR*.

Here is a solution:

→ *The* **select**... *clause removes ambiguities for dynamic binding. See 11.6, page 177 below.*

```
class PARTICLE_LIST_PROPERTIES inherit
    LIST_ITERATION [PARTICLE]
        rename
            do_until as print_masses,
            prepare as nothing,
            test as positive_test,
            action as print_one_mass,
            wrapup as nothing
        end;
    LIST_ITERATION [PARTICLE]
        rename
            do_until as add_speeds,
            prepare as set_speed,
            test as at_threshold,
            action as add_one_speed,
            wrapup as nothing
        select
            set_speed, at_threshold, add_one_speed
        end
feature

    nothing (s: FIXED_LIST [PARTICLE]) is
            -- Do nothing.
        do
        end; -- nothing

    positive_test (s: FIXED_LIST [PARTICLE]): BOOLEAN is
            -- Is particle at current cursor position in s positive?
        do
            Result := s.item.positively_charged
        end; -- positive_test

    print_one_mass (s: FIXED_LIST [PARTICLE]) is
            -- Print the mass of particle at cursor position in s.
        do
            print (s.item.mass)
        end -- print_one_mass

    counted: INTEGER;

    Threshold: INTEGER is 50;

    sum: VECTOR;
```

```
        set_speed (s: FIXED_LIST [PARTICLE]) is
            -- Create sum as zero vector
        do
            !! sum
        end; -- set_speed
        at_threshold (s: FIXED_LIST [PARTICLE]): BOOLEAN is
            -- Have Threshold particles been counted?
        do
            Result := (counted = Threshold)
        end; -- at_threshold
        add_one_speed (s: FIXED_LIST [PARTICLE]) is
            -- Add to sum the speed of particle at cursor position in s.
        do
            sum. increase (s. item);
            counted := counted + 1
        end -- add_one_speed
    end -- class PARTICLE_LIST_PROPERTIES
```

The routines describing individual traversal steps (*start, forth, off*) have been effected at the level of *LIST_ITERATION* and are inherited without further adaptation; for them, the Repeated Inheritance rule yields sharing. For the features of which *PARTICLE_LIST_PROPERTIES* needs two versions, the rule achieves replication; the class then effects these versions separately to yield the required semantics in each case.

There is no need in such a class to write any loops; the iteration structure is entirely inherited from a general-purpose iteration class, normally drawn from the Iteration Library, such as *LIST_ITERATION*.

In this example, an empty implementation (a procedure which does nothing) is appropriate for *prepare*, the initial action, in one of the two variants, and for *wrapup*, the final action, in both variants. All of these features, being inherited under the same name *nothing*, are shared; then the redeclaration of *nothing* as an empty effective procedure effects them all.

11.6 Redeclaration and replication

Back now to the details of the repeated inheritance machinery. The rest of this chapter examines the conditions that are required for repeated inheritance will to work properly; it culminates in a validity rule, the Repeated Inheritance Consistency constraint.

→ *The Repeated Inheritance Consistency constraint appears in 11.13, on page 191.*

To understand the formal rule, however, we must first probe what could possibly go wrong in the application of the desirable semantics of repeated inheritance, as defined above – the sharing and replication mechanism. Three possibilities turn out to cause potential problems:

• Redeclaration on separate paths of repeated inheritance.

• Attribute duplication.

• Conflicting generic derivations.

This section and the next three examine these problems and the solutions.

The first way to run into trouble, illustrated below, appears immediately if we consider the combination of repeated inheritance with redeclaration. The Repeated Inheritance rule, based on the renaming mechanism, remained silent on redeclaration. What happens if a feature f has been redeclared on two separate paths between an ancestor and a repeated descendant?

Redeclaration under repeated inheritance with replication

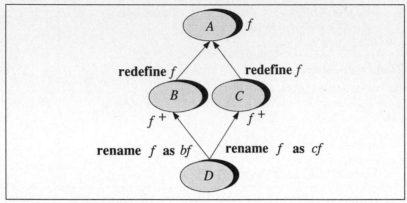

As defined on page 136, redeclaration covers two cases: redefinition and effecting. The problem described here may occur for both forms, although the examples below emphasize redefinition.

The figure shows this happening in a case for which f is replicated, having two versions bf and cf in D as a result of separate redeclarations. The problem also arises if only one branch, for example the B branch, redeclares f. Then bf is the redeclared form and cf the original. This is what happens for *display* in class *COMMAND_BUTTON* above.

← *The class COMMAND_BUTTON appeared on page 173.*

In the absence of renaming, f would be shared; this second case will in fact be prohibited, and the discussion will show that this limitation has no unpleasant consequence. But for the moment let us concentrate on the replication case, using as working example the situation illustrated on the above figure.

→ *The sharing case is discussed below in 11.8, page 182.*

Why is there a problem? After all, nothing is ambiguous about the calls in the following extract:

```
d1: D;
...
!! d1;        -- Attach d1 to an object
d1.bf;
d1.cf
```

A call of the form d1.f would be invalid since D, from the information given here, has no feature called f.

The first call will trigger execution of the version of f redefined in B, and the second will use the C version. No difficulty seems to arise either with polymorphism and dynamic binding applied to entities of types B or C:

```
b1: B; c1: C;
...           -- The rest as before
b1 := d1; c1 := d1;
b1.f;   -- [1]
c1.f;   -- [2]
```

To keep things simple, this example assumes that f is a procedure without arguments, that the classes involved are all non-generic – in other words, are also types – and that D has no creation procedure.

Here the two assignments are polymorphic, allowing *b1* and *c1*, although declared of types *B* and *C*, to become attached to an object which is of type *D*. The type rules permit this since *D* conforms to both *B* and *C*. Complementing polymorphism, **dynamic binding** would then normally determine that the version executed in each case is the one redefined by the closest ancestor; this means that call [1] should trigger the *B* version and call [2] the *C* version.

→ *On polymorphism see 20.9, page 323; on dynamic binding see 21.9, page 345.*

The exact effect of cases [1] and [2] will be affected by the Select *clause; see the end of this section.*

The situation is different, however, if you use polymorphism and dynamic binding to call *f* on an entity *a1* of type *A*, the repeated ancestor, as in

```
a1 : A;
...        --   The rest as before
a1 := d1;

a1.f
```

How should we understand such a call? Dynamic binding rules indicate that it should trigger a version of *f* applicable to the actual object, which here is an instance of *D*. But there are two such versions of *f*, resulting from the *B* and *C* redefinitions, and none of them is a priori better than the other.

Here is for example how *B*, *C* and *D* might appear:

```
class B inherit
    A redefine f end
feature
    f is do print ("Yes!") end
end -- class B
```

```
class C inherit
    A redefine f end
feature
    f is do print ("No!") end
end -- class B
```

```
class D inherit
    B
        rename f as bf end;
    C
        rename f as df end
end -- class D
```

WARNING: the text of D as given is invalid. As explained below, addition of a Select *subclause will make it valid.*

Will the call *a1.f* obey *B* and print *Yes!*, or will it print *No!*, obeying *C*?

Using a convention based on the order of the Parent clauses for *B* and *C* in *D* would be dangerous: by reversing the order of parents, an innocuous editing change, you would change the semantics of the class. Besides, such a convention only makes sense for simple cases such as the above; with more levels of repeated inheritance, the "order" of ancestors becomes murky. In the structure illustrated on page 171, if *B* lists its parents in the order *X*, *Y* and *C* in the reverse order, what is the order of *X* and *Y* as ancestors of *D*?

Faced with these difficulties, we might decide to prohibit such situations. But there is nothing fundamentally wrong here; the problem is not that we cannot find an interpretation for the resulting structure, but that we have *too many* interpretations (the *B* one and the *C* one).

What we need, then, is a way to dispel the ambiguity caused by such cases. This is made possible by a new subclause of Feature_adaptation – the last unexplored inheritance construct: Select. Whenever repeatedly inherited features would cause a conflict for dynamic binding, the Repeated Inheritance Consistency constraint requires the author of *D* to include a Select subclause specifying which of the conflicting variants takes precedence.

← The other subclauses of Feature_adaptation are: Rename, *6.9, page 81;* New_exports, *7.11, page 98;* Undefine, *10.16, page 155; and* Redefine, *10.6, page 140.* Select *comes last, after* Redefine.

The syntax is straightforward. To make the above example valid, it suffices to update the declaration of *D* so that it reads

```
class D inherit
    B
        rename
            f as bf
        select
            bf
        end;
    C
        rename
            f as df
        end
    end -- class D
```

The '**select** *f*' *could be in the* Parent *part for C rather than B, but it must be in one of them, and may not be in both.*

More generally, whenever a repeated descendant *D* inherits two or more separately redeclared versions of a feature, or the original and a redeclared version, the Repeated Inheritance Consistency constraint requires *D* to select exactly one of them in its Feature_adaptation clause, as illustrated here.

→ The precise statement of the Repeated Inheritance Consistency constraint is on page 191.

The Select subclause acts as a redefinition of **all** the conflicting inherited versions – here the *f* features from *B* and *C*. This means that calls [1] and [2], for which the target entity is of type *B* or *C*, but dynamically attached to an object of type *D*, will both cause the execution of the "selected" version *bf*, in other words the version redefined in *B*.

← Cases [1] and [2] appear on page 178.

11.7 The case of attributes

The above example involved a feature *f* which was a routine. For attributes, a similar problem arises even in the absence of redefinition.

The cause of ambiguity here is that a replicated attribute will yield two fields rather than one in the repeated descendant. Then, with dynamic binding, a reference to such a replicated attribute may become ambiguous in the same way that a reference to a multiply redeclared routine was ambiguous.

This may occur even with direct repeated inheritance of a class *D* from a class *A*, with a scheme such as this:

← An attribute (which may not be effected since it is necessarily effective) may be redefined; but this is only useful for type redefinition, since the redefined version must still be an attribute. See condition 6 of the Redeclaration rule, page 163.

```
class A feature
    attr: SOME_TYPE
    some_proc is do print (attr) end
end -- class A
```

```
class D inherit
    A
        rename attr as attr1 end;
    A
        rename attr as attr2 end
end -- class D
```

WARNING: D as shown is invalid. Adding a Select subclause will make it valid. See below.

Here a direct instance of *A* has only one field, corresponding to *attr*. In an instance of *D*, however, *attr* yields two fields, corresponding to *attr1* and *attr2*:

Field replication under repeated inheritance

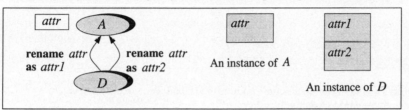

As in the case of conflicting redeclarations, it is not clear which one of the fields the following should print:

```
a1: A; d1: D;
...
!! d1; a1 := d1; a1.some_proc
```

Similar problem, same solution: whenever the Repeated Inheritance rule implies replication of an attribute, the Repeated Inheritance Consistency constraint will require a Select in this case too:

→ The Repeated Inheritance Consistency constraint appears on page 191.

```
class D inherit
    A
        rename
            attr as attr1
        select
            attr1
        end;
    A
        rename attr as attr2 end
end -- class D
```

In this example, you may of course "select" attr1 rather than attr2.

COMMENT

An important consequence of the use of Select, mandated by the Repeated Inheritance Consistency constraint, is that for any feature *f* of a class *A*, every descendant *D* of *A* has exactly one feature which corresponds most closely to *f*. This feature is called **the version of** *f* **in** *D*. The Select subclause removes any ambiguity if, because of repeated inheritance, two or more features could vie for the role.

→ This definition of the version of a feature in a descendant is accurate but not fully rigorous. A more precise definition appears below in 11.12, page 189.

11.8 Redeclaration and sharing

We know now how to resolve the conflict between conflicting versions of a repeatedly inherited feature (routine or attribute) in the case of replication. But what about the other case – sharing?

Redeclaration under repeated inheritance with sharing

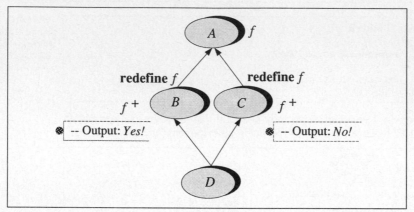

The earlier example of conflicting routine redeclarations becomes even simpler since no renaming need be involved:

```
class B inherit
    A
        redefine f end
feature
    f is do print ("Yes!") end
end -- class B
```

```
class C inherit
    A
        redefine f end
feature
    f is do print ("No!") end
end -- class B
```

```
class D inherit
    B;
    C
end -- class D
```

WARNING: the declaration of D as given is invalid. To make it valid, use renaming and a Select, or undefine one of the inherited versions, as explained below.

Here the ambiguity arises even in the absence of dynamic binding: it is not clear whether a call $d1.f$, for $d1$ of type D, should trigger the B or the C version.

In this case the Repeated Inheritance Consistency constraint provides the answer by making D invalid. D may not inherit f repeatedly if the Repeated Inheritance rule would yield sharing and two parents of D have different versions of f as a result of redeclaration.

This rule might appear too restrictive at first, but it is not. To decide the fate of f in D, only two policies make sense:

R1 • Keeping both the A and the B versions in D.

R2 • Discarding one in favor of the other.

For R1, you will need different names to distinguish between the two versions. It suffices, then, to use the scheme described in the previous section, where renaming ensures replication and a Select clause resolves the ambiguity for dynamic binding.

For R2, the **undefinition** mechanism, studied in the previous chapter, provides the solution. Assume you want to retain only the B version in D. Then you may for example update D's declaration as follows:

← See 10.16, page 155, about undefinition.

```
class D inherit
    B;
    C
        undefine f end
    end -- class D
```

What happens here is that, at the point of inheritance, the Undefine subclause turns the version of f inherited from B into a deferred feature. Then under the normal mechanism of effecting, as made possible by the Join rule, the B version will override the deferred version inherited from C.

← The Join rule is on page 165. The general use of undefinition for merging features, with one version overriding the other, is discussed in 10.18, page 158.

This scheme only works if the B version is a valid redeclaration of the C version. This will not be true if a redeclaration has changed the signature of the C version into one which does not conform to that of the B version. In such a case you may need to undefine both inherited versions, replacing them by a fresh one:

← Valid redeclarations are covered by the Redeclaration rule, page 163.

```
class D inherit
    B
        undefine f end;
    C
        undefine f end
feature
    f ... Rest of redeclaration omitted
    end -- class D
```

Here the redeclaration must be valid for both the B and C versions.

One more problem seems to arise from sharing in repeated inheritance: what happens if a shared feature refers to a replicated one? Assume that D has a repeated ancestor A of the form

```
class A feature
    attr: SOME_TYPE;
    proc is do ... end;
    rout is do proc; print (attr) end
    end -- class A
```

Here *rout* refers to features *proc* and *attr*. Assume that, as a result of repeated inheritance from *A*, *rout* is shared in *D*. But what if *proc* or *attr* is replicated? For a call of *rout* on an instance of *D*, how do we know what *proc* to call, and what *attr* field to print?

On closer look, however, there is no new problem here:

- If *proc* is redefined along one or more of the inheritance paths, then the Repeated Inheritance Consistency constraint requires a Select in *D*; this removes any potential ambiguity for the call.

- Feature *attr*, being an attribute, must also appear in a Select subclause.

The previous rules suffice, then, to resolve any difficulty in such cases of combined sharing and replication.

11.9 Conflicting generic derivations

(This section, which clarifies the semantics of a rare case, may be skipped on first reading.)

The above techniques have addressed the two principal cases of conflict between versions of a repeatedly inherited feature: redeclaration and attribute duplication. One more case, although not frequent, is possible. It arises from conflicting generic derivations of the repeated ancestor, yielding features which are different (because of their signatures) even without any redeclaration.

→ *Generic classes and generic derivations are studied in chapter 12, especially in 12.7, page 200, and subsequent sections.*

It is not hard to devise a simple example. Assume that *A* is generic, with one formal generic parameter *G*, and has a feature *f* whose signature involves *G*:

← *See 5.12, page 66, about signatures.*

```
class A [G] feature
    f (x: G) is ... Routine body omitted ... end
end -- class A
```

```
class B inherit
    A [INTEGER]
end -- class B
```

```
class C inherit
    A [REAL]
end -- class C
```

What the body of *f* does is irrelevant; so is the exact nature of *f* – procedure as above, attribute or function – as long as *f*'s signature depends on *G*.

The different generic derivations of *A* used in the Parent parts of *B* and *C* cause *f* to have different signatures in these classes:

```
in B: (<>, <INTEGER>)
in C: (<>, <REAL>)
```

This means that the features are different: a feature is defined not only by its specification (assertions) and its implementation, but also by its signature.

What then if you want to write a class *D* as heir to both *B* and *C*? This is a case of conflict, similar to the two cases studied previously, although the cause of the conflict is different – different generic derivation rather than redeclaration or field duplication. The solution is also similar:

1 • Sharing is clearly impossible. As with conflicting redeclarations, no good criterion exists to choose one feature over the other as the shared version in *D*; besides, any such choice would cause type incompatibities for dynamic binding in examples such as the above. The Repeated Inheritance consistency constraint will prohibit sharing in the case of different generic derivations.

2 • It may be possible to let one of the versions override the other through undefinition. This technique was also available for conflicting redeclarations, where it was called policy R2.

← *Merging through undefinition was studied in 11.8, page 182, which introduced policy R2.*

3 • Replication may be possible, provided a Select clause removes any ambiguity for dynamic binding.

Here, because the signatures are different, solution 2 requires some care. The problem (similar to the case of signature redeclaration, studied as part of policy R2) is that if a version overrides the other it must have a conforming signature; but this may not be true because of conflicting generic derivations. In the above example, indeed, the signatures of the *B* and *C* versions are incompatible since neither of the types *INTEGER* and *REAL* conforms to the other. The only solution is to undefine both features and provide a fresh redeclaration in *D*. Here, in the absence of a useful common descendant to *INTEGER* and *REAL*, that fresh feature may only be of the form

$f(x: NONE)$ **is do** ... Some routine body ... **end**

← *On NONE, see 6.16, page 88.*

and hence cannot do anything useful with its argument *x*. (Recall that *NONE* is a common descendant of all classes, but has no exported feature.)

In more favorable cases, one of the actual generic parameters used for generic derivations of *A* in *B* or *C* will conform to the other; then you may select the corresponding version of *f* in *D*.

11.10 Name clashes

We have now seen all the properties of inheritance-related constructs (although a few are still awaiting their formal presentation). One interesting consequence is a precise definition of the intuitively clear notion of name clash between features, and of exactly which clashes are permitted.

DEFINITION:
Name
Clash

A name clash occurs for a certain feature name *fname* in a class *C* if, for two different parents *A* and *B* of *C*, both *A* and *B* have a feature of name *fname*.

In most cases, a name clash would make the heir class invalid and you must remove it by renaming at least one of the conflicting features, as in

---

class *C* **inherit**
   A
      rename *fname* **as** *name1* **end**;
   B
      rename *fname* **as** *name2* **end**
  ... Rest of class text omitted ...

In three precisely defined cases, however, a name clash causes no invalidity; instead, the rules of the previous chapter and this one explicitly prescribe the merging of features with the same name. Here are these three cases:

A • The effecting of a deferred feature (possibly joined from two or more), as covered by case 3 of the definition of effective features.

B • Joining of deferred features, as permitted by the Join rule.

C • Sharing under repeated inheritance, as permitted by the Repeated Inheritance Consistency constraint.

← Definition of effecting: page 160. Join rule: page 165. Repeated Inheritance Consistency constraint: page 191.

A fine point: if B and C both apply (a class inherits two or more deferred features coming from a common seed), the interpretation is technically C. If you have been reading very carefully, you may have noticed that this property follows from the order of rules 2 and 3 in the definition of "seed"; it will be confirmed by the order of steps in the definition of "inherited features". Not that taking the other interpretation would make much difference – but the rules must leave no ambiguity.

The notion of seed was defined on page 162. In the definition of inherited features, page 187, step 1 achieves sharing under repeated inheritance before step 3 joins any deferred features.

This is a time for celebration: by now you know all the important concepts of inheritance and feature adaptation. The remainder of this chapter only provides some more formal definitions associated with these concepts. On first reading, you may prefer to skip directly to the next chapter.

On the other hand, you are only saving yourself little more than 6 pages. Is it really worth it?

The concepts which deserve a more precise definition are:

• The inherited features of a class (a concept needed for the more general notion of "features of a class"), also yielding the precise definition of the final name set of a class and the Feature Name rule.

• The version of a feature in a descendant of its class of origin.

• The Repeated Inheritance Consistency constraint, which is the major constraint on the use of repeated inheritance.

11.11 The inherited features of a class

(This section and the remainder of this chapter may be skipped on first reading.)

As defined in chapter 5, the "features of a class" include its immediate features (those introduced in the class itself), and its inherited features, defined informally as the features "obtained from" the parents' features.

← The definition of "features of a class" is on page 56.

The reason for being informal at that earlier stage is now clear: two mechanisms, repeated inheritance and join, affect how a class "obtains" features from its parents. Without these mechanisms, every feature from a parent (every **precursor**) would yield one feature in the heir. But:

- With sharing under repeated inheritance, two or more precursors, inherited from different parents but coming from the same feature of a common ancestor, yield a single feature of D.

- Conversely, with replication under direct repeated inheritance (D has two or more Parent clauses listing the same parent), a single precursor will yield two or more features of D. This is in particular the technique used to keep the original version of a feature along with the redefined one.

← *See 11.9 above on keeping the original version along with the redefined one.*

- Finally, one or more deferred precursors, inherited under one name, may yield only one feature of D under the join mechanism.

D may or may not effect the feature. See 10.17, page 156 on join.

These observations yield a final definition of "inherited features". To obtain the list of inherited features of a class D, you may start from the list made of all features of all parents, and remove unneeded elements in successive steps accounting for various cases: the joining of deferred features; the effecting of a deferred feature by an effective one; sharing under repeated inheritance. Finally you must take into account any redefinition, effecting or undefinition that D applies to the remaining features.

Here is the precise description of this process.

DEFINITION:
Inherited
Features

Let D be a class. The list *inherited* of inherited features of D is obtained as follows. Let *precursors* be the list obtained by concatenating the lists of features of every parent of D; this list may contain duplicates in the case of repeated inheritance. Then *inherited* is obtained from *precursors* as follows:

1 • In list *precursors*, for any set of two or more elements representing features that are repeatedly inherited in D under the same name, so that the Repeated Inheritance rule yields sharing, keep only one of these elements. The Repeated Inheritance Consistency Constraint (sharing case) indicates that these elements must all represent the same feature, so that it does not matter which one is kept.

→ *The repeated Inheritance consistency constraint is on page 191.*

2 • For every feature f in the resulting list, if D undefines f, replace f by a deferred feature with the same signature and specification.

3 • In the resulting list, for any set of deferred features with the same final name in D, keep only one of these features, with assertions joined as per the Join Semantics rule. (Keep the signature, which the Join rule requires to be the same for all the features involved.)

← *The Join Semantics rule is on page 166.*

4 • In the resulting list, remove any deferred feature such that there is an effective feature with the same final name in the list. (This is the case in which a feature f inherited as effective effects one or more deferred features: of the whole group, only f remains.)

5 • Let *merged_features* be the resulting list. All its elements have different feature names; they are the inherited features of D in their parent form. From this list, produce a new one as follows: for any feature which D redeclares (by redefinition or effecting), replace the feature by the result of the redeclaration; keep any other feature as it is in *merged_features*.

6 • The result is the list *inherited* of inherited features of D.

To understand this definition, you must remember that the lists under consideration are lists of **features**, not of feature names, although the features that remain at the end all have different final names in D. The list *inherited* obtained under 6 may still contain duplicate features: this is the result of repeated inheritance with duplication; such duplicate features in the list have different feature names.

The presence of duplicates is the reason why 'inherited' is defined as a list and not as a set.

As a consequence, if an inherited feature of D has two or more precursors they all have the same final name in D; indeed, any merging of elements of the *precursors* list under steps 1 and 3 of the definition only occurs under this condition.

This gives the rigorous definition of the precursors of a feature. An informal definition appeared on page 140, extended to joined features on page 165.

This is an important property because without it the earlier definition of the final name of an inherited feature would not make sense. Recall that according to this definition the final name m of a feature f obtained from a precursor of name n in a parent B is n in the absence of renaming, and otherwise is the m appearing in a Rename_pair of the form **rename** n **as** m in the Parent clause for B in D. Obviously, if f is obtained from two or more precursors, all this is meaningless unless we are sure that m is the same for all these precursors.

← The definition of "final name" is on page 82.

This also clarifies the definition of the **final name set** of a class. The final name set was introduced as the set of final names of all the features of a class. These final names are obtained as follows:

← The definition of the final name set is on page 82.

- For immediate features, they are the names under which the features are declared in the class.

- For inherited features, they are the inherited names except as overridden by renaming.

- Two or more precursors merged into one as a result of either the join mechanism or sharing under repeated inheritance yield just one element of the final name set.

- If a feature from a repeated ancestor yields several features under replication, then all the corresponding names are added to the final name set.

Both the Repeated Inheritance rule and the Join rule require all the merged features to have the same final name.

Finally, the various rules on choosing feature names may now be summarized by a simple constraint, the Feature Name rule:

VMFN

Feature Name rule

It is valid for a class C to introduce a feature with the Feature_identifier *fname*, or to inherit a feature under the final name *fname*, if and only if no other feature of C has that same name.

Two feature names are the same if their lower-case version is the same (for identifier features), or their operator and number of arguments are the same (for operator features).

← See the definition of "same feature name", page 69.

The important notion here is that of "other feature", which results from the above definition of inherited features. When do we consider g to be a feature "other" than f? This is the case whenever g has been declared distinctly from f, unless the definition of inherited features causes the features to be merged into just one feature of D. Such merging may only happen as a result of sharing features under repeated inheritance, or of joining deferred features.

Also, remember that if D redeclares an inherited feature (possibly resulting from the joining of two or more), this does not introduce any new ("other") feature. This was explicitly stated by the definition of "introducing" a feature.

← *See the definition of features introduced in a class, page 56.*

Specific consequences of the Feature Name rule include the following important constraints.

1 • A class may not introduce two different features, both deferred or both effective, with the same name.

2 • If a class introduces a feature with the same name as a feature it inherits in effective form, it must rename the inherited version.

3 • If a class inherits two features as effective from different parents and they have the same name, the class must also (except under sharing for repeated inheritance) remove the name clash through renaming.

These constraints do not bring anything new; they just follow from previous constraints. Because of their practical importance, they deserve a code of their own.

11.12 Versions of a feature

The definition of inherited features yields a precise definition for yet another important notion used informally so far: the **version** of a feature in a descendant.

← *This notion appeared originally on page 181.*

It is convenient to define first the **potential versions**. If a feature has two or more potential versions in a class, one of them will be *the* version.

Informally, a potential version of a feature f is any feature which, in a descendant of f's class, comes from f after possible redeclarations and generic derivations. More precisely:

DEFINITION:
Potential
Version

> Let f be a feature of a class A and D a descendant of A. A potential version of f in D is any inherited feature of D which is either:
>
> F1 • f itself.
>
> F2 • A feature resulting (recursively) from a redeclaration of a potential version of f.
>
> F3 • (Recursively) a potential version of a feature of which f is a redeclaration.
>
> F4 • A feature resulting (recursively) from a generic derivation of A.

To understand this definition better, it is useful to look again at the above construction of the list *inherited* of inherited features. There was a one-to-one correspondence between the final list *inherited* and the list *merged_features* obtained at the end of step 4: for every feature f in *inherited* there is a unique element *pf* of *merged_features* such that f is one of:

← *The construction of the 'inherited' list appeared on page 187.*

• *pf* itself.

• The result of redeclaring *pf* in D.

Feature *pf* corresponds to one or more precursors $pf_1, ..., pf_n$ of D's parents (usually just one, but possibly more as a result of join, effecting and sharing). Then f is a potential version of itself and (recursively) of any feature s of which any of the pf_i is a potential version. In addition (case F3), if s has another potential version *pf'* among the parent features from other parents, then f is also a potential version of *pf'*.

The notion of potential version yields a precise definition of *the* version of a feature in a class. Every feature f of A has at least one potential version in D. Can it have more than one? In the absence of repeated inheritance, the answer is no; but the effect of replication under repeated inheritance is precisely to yield two or more potential versions of f. (They correspond to several occurrences of f, under different names, in the list *inherited*.) In such a case, a Select subclause of D must list one of the potential versions, to remove any ambiguity for dynamic binding. The feature listed is the version of f in D. In brief:

DEFINITION:
Version

> Let f be a feature of a class A and D a descendant of A. The version of f in D is the feature df defined as follows:
>
> V1 • If D has only one potential version of f, then df is that feature.
>
> V2 • If D has two or more potential versions of f, the Repeated Inheritance Consistency constraint, seen below, states that exactly one of them must appear, under its final D name, as part of a Select clause in D; then df is that feature.

In case V2, the potential versions may be different because of redeclaration or generic derivation.

From this definition comes a a closely related notion. A feature is **potentially ambiguous** in a repeated descendant if it presents more than one choice for dynamic binding – and so requires a Select to remove the potential ambiguity:

DEFINITION:
Potentially
Ambiguous

> Let D be a repeated descendant of a class A. A feature f of A is potentially ambiguous in D if and only if one of the following two conditions holds:
>
> A1 • f is an attribute.
>
> A2 • D has two or more potential versions of f.

Case A2 is the same as V2 above.

A final consequence of the notion of version affects dynamic binding for entities of intermediate types in repeated inheritance – a property which was mentioned in the earlier informal discussion but may now be shown precisely. Consider again a situation of repeated inheritance with redeclaration and replication:

← This is the situation discussed in 11.6, more specifically cases [1] and [2] appearing on page 178. The property under discussion was stated in the last paragraph of 11.6, page 180.

Repeated
inheritance
with
redeclaration
and
replication

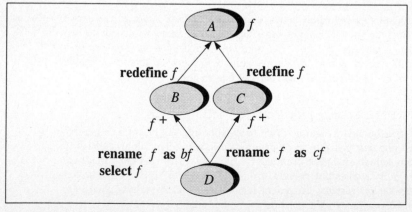

The inclusion of a Select for *bf* makes this scheme valid; the text of the classes, sketched here in graphical form, was given above.

← *The text of class D, with the* Select, *appears on page 180.*

Because of the Select, a call of the form *a1.f*, for *a* of type *A* but dynamically attached to an object of type *D*, will trigger the *B* version, *bf*. What is perhaps less obvious is that this version is also the one that will be triggered for a call of the form

> *c1.f*

for *c1* of type *C*, dynamically attached to an object of type *D*. (Of course, *b1.f*, where *b1* is of type *B* and attached to an object of type *D*, will also trigger *bf*.) In other words, the Select affects not just the original feature *f* whose conflicting redeclarations required it, but also any versions of *f* appearing in intermediate descendants – for example *cf*, the *C* version of *f*, in the above scheme. For such intermediate versions the Select has the same effect as a redefinition in *D*.

To see how this property follows from the above specification, note that *bf* is a potential version of *cf* in *D*: this follows from case F3 of the definition of potential versions, since *bf* is a feature of *D* and is a potential version of *f* (from *A*), of which *cf* is also a potential version. Since *D* selects *bf* over *cf*, clause V2 of the above definition of "version" makes *bf* the version in *D* not just of *f* but also of *bf*.

11.13 The Repeated Inheritance Consistency constraint

This chapter has explained informally the two conditions required for valid uses of repeated inheritance: the sharing of a feature must not cause any ambiguity; and, in the replication case, a Select subclause must remove any potential ambiguity arising from conflicting redeclaration, attribute replication, or different generic derivation.

The precise definitions of the last few sections, especially the notion of versions of a feature, provide all the elements needed for a full statement of these conditions – the Repeated Inheritance Consistency Constraint:

VMRC

> It is valid for a class *D* to be a repeated descendant of a class *A* if and only if *D* satisfies the following two conditions for every feature *f* of *A*:
>
> 1 • If the Repeated Inheritance rule implies that *f* will be shared in *D*, then all the inherited versions of *f* are the same feature.
>
> 2 • If the Repeated Inheritance rule implies that *f* will be replicated in *D* and *f* is potentially ambiguous, then the Select subclause of exactly one of the Parent parts of *D* lists the corresponding version of *f*, under its final *D* name.

← *This constraint is one of the conditions imposed by the Parent rule, page 79, which determines whether it is valid for a class to list another as one of its parents.*

Condition 1 prohibits sharing if there is any difference between the inherited versions, because of redeclaration or generic derivation. In any such case you may rename the conflicting features, ensuring replication rather than sharing; then condition 2 will apply.

Condition 2 – which underlies case V2 of the above definition of "version" – applies if *f* is an attribute yielding two or more fields in instances of *D*, or has two or more potential versions in *D*. Again the potential versions may be due to conflicting redeclaration, or to different generic derivations. All these cases would cause an ambiguity at run time for a call *x. fname*, where *fname* is the name of *f* in *A*, *x* is of a type based on *A*, and *x* is attached dynamically to an object of a type based on *D*. The Select subclause solves the problem.

As you may have noticed, condition 2 covers the special case in which the cause for potential ambiguity is a redeclaration not in a parent of *D*, but in *D* itself. Here is the simplest possible example of this scheme, using direct repeated inheritance:

```
class D inherit
    A
        rename
            fname as original
        end;
    A
        rename
            fname as new_version
        redefine
            new_version
        select
            new_version
        end;
feature
    new_version is
        do
            ... Redefined routine body omitted ...
        end -- new_version
end -- class D
```

Instead of the new version, D could select the original, by having 'select original' in the first Parent clause.

Without the Select, we would not know whether dynamic binding (for the call *x. fname* under the conditions discussed above) should trigger *original*, the version of *f* in *A*, or *new_version*, the version redefined in *D*.

There remains to give without further comment the straightforward syntax and validity constraint of the Select subclause itself:

SYNTAX

$$\text{Select} \triangleq \textbf{select } \text{Feature\_list}$$

Select Subclause rule

A Select subclause appearing in the Parent part for a class *B* in a class *D* is valid if and only if, for every Feature_identifier *fname* in its Feature_list, *fname* is the final name in *D* of a feature that has two or more potential versions in *D*, and *fname* appears only once in the Feature_list.

VMSS

12

Types

12.1 Overview

Types describe the form and properties of objects that can be created during the execution of a system.

Every such object is an instance of some type. (More precisely, it is a *direct instance* of exactly one type but, because of the inheritance mechanism, may also be an instance of other, more general types.) Class texts refer to eventual run-time objects through the software components which denote values: constants, attributes, function calls, formal routine arguments, local entities, and expressions built from such components.

Typing in Eiffel is static. For software developers, this means four practical properties:

- Every component denoting run-time values is **typed**: it has an explicit type limiting the possible types of the attached run-time objects.

- The type of every typed component is immediately clear – to a human reader or to a language processing tool – from the component's context. For a manifest constant such as the Integer *421* the type follows from the constant's lexical form; in all other cases it is a consequence of a type declaration, made compulsory by the validity rules of the language.

- Non-atomic constructs impose complementary validity constraints, defining admissible **type combinations**. For example, an assignment requires the type of the source to conform to the type of the target.

- Since the constraints are defined as conditions on the software text, language processing tools such as compilers or static analyzers may check the type consistency of a system **statically**, that is to say, just by examining the system's text, without making any attempt at execution.

This explicit and static approach to typing has a number of advantages. It makes software texts easier to read and understand, since developers, by declaring the types of entities, reveal how they intend to use them. It enables compilers and other tools to catch many potential errors by detecting inconsistencies between declarations and actual uses. It gives compilers information that helps them generate much more efficient code than would be possible with an untyped (or more weakly typed) language.

Typing, if taken seriously, also means that there is no way to bypass the type system. Many languages which claim to be statically (sometimes even "strongly") typed also allow developers to cheat the type system, enticing them into sordid back-alley deals sometimes known as *casts*. No such cheating exists in Eiffel, where the typing rules suffer no exception. This is essential if we want to have any trust in our software. The only price to pay for this added security is the need to declare entities explicitly and to observe validity constraints – obligations which are even easier to justify if you observe that the type system, far from being a hindrance to the developer's power of expression, helps in the production of powerful and readable software systems.

This chapter explores the different forms of types and their properties. It does not exhaust, however, the issue of typing, which pervades most of the discussions of this book. To understand the type system fully, you will need important complements provided by two chapters closely related to this one:

- The discussion of **conformance** will explain how a type may be used in lieu of another, and its instances in lieu of that other's instances.

- The presentation of **type checking** policy will show how the typing policy defines the fundamental validity constraints on the most important computational construct – feature call.

→ *Conformance is the topic of chapter 13. Chapter 21 covers calls; on type checking, see chapter 22.*

12.2 Categories of types

The Eiffel type system is entirely based on the notion of class. Every type is based on a class, called the type's **base class**.

A type may be of one of three kinds: **reference type**, **expanded type** and Formal_generic_name. The difference between the first two possibilities comes from the values the type describes:

- The possible run-time values of an entity declared of a reference type are references to potential objects – instances of the type – which may be created at run-time through explicit creation instructions.

- For an entity declared of an expanded type, the possible values are not references to objects but the objects themselves, which do not require creation instructions.

Expanded types include two special cases: the basic types *INTEGER, REAL, CHARACTER, BOOLEAN, DOUBLE*, covering simple mathematical objects, and *POINTER*, covering addresses of features to be passed to external (non-Eiffel) routines; and Bit_type, whose instances are bit sequences, useful for low-level manipulations and interfacing with other languages.

→ *On POINTER and how to pass feature addresses to external routines see 24.6, page 404.*

How should you choose between reference types and expanded types? Here are a few general guidelines:

- Apart from basic types, reference types are the most frequently used in typical Eiffel applications because of their flexibility: dynamic object creation allows developers to produce objects whenever they need them, but only then; and reference semantics supports sophisticated data structures whose elements are chained to each other. In particular, reference types are the only possibility for structures that may be cyclic, such as a circular chain; this is the reason why the Expanded Client rule specifically prohibited any cycles in the expanded client relation.

← *The Expanded Client rule was given on page 94.*

• Expanded types are useful when you want to avoid run-time indirections, since the entities will give you access to objects directly rather than through references. As noted, they also cover the basic types such as *INTEGER*; clearly, an entity of integer type should give us an integer value, not a reference to a dynamically allocated integer. The same holds for a Bit_type, for which the values are bit sequences.

A special case of reference types is provided by **anchored** types, which tie the type of an entity to the type of another.

Genericity brings in the third kind of type, Formal_generic_name, representing a type parameter to be provided in actual uses of the class by parents or proper descendants. The corresponding values may be references as well as objects.

The rest of this chapter discusses these various concepts and mechanisms in detail.

The important notion of **conformance** is closely connected to the type system. Conformance determines when a type is compatible with another for assignment, argument passing or signature redefinition. This topic deserves a chapter of its own – the next chapter.

→ *Chapter 13 starts on page 217.*

12.3 Where to use types

You will need to write a type – a specimen of the construct Type – in the following contexts:

1 • To declare the result type of an attribute or function: construct Declaration body.

Syntax: page 63.

2 • To declare a routine's arguments: construct Formal_arguments, defined in terms of Entity_declaration_list.

Page 109.

3 • To declare a local routine entity: construct Local_declarations (also defined in terms of Entity_declaration_list).

Page 114.

4 • To indicate that a class has a certain parent: construct Parent, as part of Inheritance.

Page 77.

5 • To specify actual generic parameters, as explained later in this chapter: construct Actual_generics.

Page 197.

6 • To specify a generic Constraint, also explained below: construct Constraint, as part of Formal_generics.

Page 201.

7 • To indicate an explicit creation type in a Creation instruction: construct Creation.

Page 285.

As an example of the first three cases, here is the beginning of a possible function declaration:

> *total_occupied_area* (*wl*: *LIST* [*WINDOW*]): *RECTANGLE* **is**
>   -- Smallest rectangle that covers the representations
>   -- of all windows in *wl*
> **local**
>   *xmin, ymin, xmax, ymax*: *REAL*
> ... Rest of routine omitted ...

This indicates that the function has one argument (case 1) of type *LIST* [*WINDOW*], a "generically derived" reference type, and one result (case 2) of type *RECTANGLE*, probably a reference type. It uses four local entities (case 3) of type *REAL*, a basic expanded type. The use of *WINDOW* as actual generic parameter to *LIST* provides an example of case 5.

→ *See page 12.7 and 12.8 below, starting on page 200, about generically derived types.*

The following class beginning uses types in its two Parent parts (case 4):

> **class** *DISPLAY_STATE* **inherit**
>   *LIST* [*WINDOW*];
>   *INPUT_MODE*; ...

An example of case 6 is the use of type *ADDABLE* in a class text beginning with

> **class** *MATRIX* [*G –> ADDABLE*] ...

which states that any actual generic parameter must conform to *ADDABLE* (which means roughly that it must be based on a descendant of that class).

Finally, an example of case 7 is the Creation instruction

> ! *WINDOW* ! *a.set* (*x_corner, y_corner*)

which creates a direct instance of *WINDOW*, initializes it using a call to *set* with the given arguments, and attaches it to *a*.

→ *See chapter 18 about Creation instructions. As explained there, this explicit form is useful only if 'a' is of a type other than WINDOW. For 'a' of type WINDOW, you can omit the type from the instruction.*

12.4 How to declare a type

The distinction between reference types and expanded types, introduced at the beginning of this chapter, is the only one that matters at run-time, since it determines whether a value will be an object, or a reference to a dynamically created object.

Syntactically, however, the notation for specimens of the Type construct offers more flexibility than afforded just by this distinction. Each of the following facilities yields a form of type:

- Certain classes, known as *generic* classes, do not immediately describe a type (reference or expanded); instead, they describe a type pattern, with one or more variable parts that must be filled in to yield an actual type. For example, the generic Data Structure Library class *LIST* has a formal generic parameter representing the (arbitrary) type of list elements. The class is indeed declared as *LIST* [*G*], where *G* is the formal generic parameter. To obtain a type, you must provide an **actual generic parameter** corresponding to *G*. An example of a type built this way is *LIST* [*WINDOW*], where *WINDOW* (itself a type) is the actual generic parameter. Such a type is said to be **generically derived** from *LIST* (or a **generic derivation** of *LIST*).

• Within the text of a generic class such as *LIST*, the formal generic parameters such as *G* themselves represent types (the possible actual generic parameters). The class may for example introduce an attribute of type *G*, or a routine with an argument or result of type *G*. Syntactically, then, a formal generic parameter is a type, although the exact nature of that type is not known in the class itself; only when a client or a descendant provides the corresponding actual generic parameter (such as *WINDOW* above) can we know for sure what *G* represents.

• Finally, you may declare an entity *x* in a class *C* by using an **anchored** type of the form **like** *anchor* for some other entity *anchor*. This mechanism avoids tedious redeclarations by tying the fate of the entity's type to that of *anchor*: in *C*, *x* is treated as if you had declared it with the type used for the declaration of *anchor*; if a proper descendant of *C* redeclares *anchor* with a new type, *x* will automatically follow.

Here is the syntactical specification covering all the possibilities.

SYNTAX

Type	≜	Class_type |
		Class_type_expanded |
		Formal_generic_name |
		Anchored |
		Bit_type
Class_type	≜	Class_name [Actual_generics]
Actual_generics	≜	"[" Type_list "]"
Type_list	≜	{Type "," ...}
Class_type_expanded	≜	**expanded** Class_type
Bit_type	≜	*BIT* Constant
Anchored	≜	**like** Anchor
Anchor	≜	Identifier | *Current*

The first form of type, Class_type, covers types described by a class name, followed by actual generic parameters if the class is generic. The class name gives the type's base class. If the base class is expanded, the Class_type itself is an expanded type; if the base class is non-expanded, the Class_type is a reference type.

*← A class is an "expanded class" if its Class_header begins with **expanded** class, and a non-expanded class otherwise.*

The second form, Class_type_expanded, is written

expanded *CT*

for some Class_type *CT*. The result is an expanded type, even if *CT* was a reference type. The base class is *CT*.

The third syntactical form, Formal_generic_name, covers the formal generic parameters of a class. If *C* has been declared as

> ... **class** C [..., G, ...] ...

then, within the text of C, G denotes a type. As noted above, you cannot know the precise nature of this type just by looking at class C; G represents whatever actual generic parameter is provided in an actual use of the class by a client or descendant.

The next form, **like** *anchor*, covers anchored declarations.

The fifth and last form, *BIT* N, describes bit sequences of length N. As noted, this is useful for low-level, machine-dependent manipulations, and for exchanging binary information with other languages.

The rest of this chapter examines the detailed properties of these type categories.

12.5 Base class, base type

A type T of any category is derived, directly or indirectly, from a class, called the base class of the type.

If T is a Class_type the derivation is direct: T is either the name of a non-generic class, such as *PARAGRAPH*, or the name of a generic class followed by Actual_generics, such as *LIST* [*WINDOW*]. In both cases the base class of T is the class whose name is used to obtain T, with any Actual_generics removed: *PARAGRAPH* and *LIST* in the examples.

For other categories of type the derivation from a class will be indirect but just as clear: for example if T is an Anchored type of the form **like** *anchor*, and *anchor* is of type *LIST* [*WINDOW*], then the base class of that type, *LIST*, is also the base class of T. More generally, if T is anchored, the type of its anchor is the **base type** of T, and the base class of T's base type also serves as the base class of T.

The following sections will define the base class and base type for each of the possible kinds of type. The base class of a type is always the same as the base class of its base type.

Why are these notions important? Many of a type's key properties (such as the features applicable to the corresponding entities) are defined by its base class. Furthermore, class texts almost never directly refer to classes: they refer to types based on these classes. For example, assuming that C is generic:

There is only one case in which a class text refers to a class, not a type: the Clients *part (syntax on page 101) lists the classes to which a feature is available for call or creation.*

- If D is an heir of C, the Inheritance part of D will list as Parent not just C, but a type of the form C [*ACTUAL1*, ...].

- To describe objects to which C's features are applicable, D will declare an entity e using not just C but, again, a type generically derived from C.

In such situations (and all other uses of types listed above) the base class provides the essential information: what features are associated with C. In the first case, they give the list of features that D inherits from C; in the second case, they provide the features which D may call on e.

As for the base type, besides its role in defining the base class, it appears in many of the conformance rules, and determines what kind of object a Creation instruction will create at run time.

→ *See chapters 13 about conformance and 18 about Creation instructions.*

Clearly, you may only build a class type, generically derived or not, if the base class is a class of the universe. A constraint states this requirement:

> **Class Type rule**
>
> An Identifier *CC* is valid as the Class_name part of a Class_type if and only if it is the name of a class in the surrounding universe.

The class of name *CC* will be the type's base class. For generically derived types, that class will have to satisfy further constraints, given below.

This is one of the two constraints on the use of an Identifier as Class_name. The other constraint addresses the only possible use of a Class_name other than as part of a Class_type: in a Clients clause, listing the classes to which certain features are available.

← *The validity constraint on* Clients *parts is on page 101.*

12.6 Class types without genericlty

We start our exploration of the type categories with the simplest way of defining a type: using a class without generic parameters. In this case there is no difference between class and type. Assume for example a class text of the form

> **class** *PARAGRAPH* **feature**
>
>   *first_line_indent*: *INTEGER*;
>
>   *other_lines_indent*: *INTEGER*;
>
>   *set_first_line_indent* (*n*: *INTEGER*) **is**
>   ... Procedure body omitted ...
>
>   ... Other features omitted ...
>
> **end** -- class *PARAGRAPH*

Then a class of the same universe (including *PARAGRAPH* itself) may use *PARAGRAPH* as a type, for example to declare entities.

Here *PARAGRAPH* is declared as a non-expanded class, so the corresponding type is a reference type. At run-time, entities of that type will represent references which, if not void, are attached to instances of *PARAGRAPH*, obtained through creation instructions.

If class *PARAGRAPH* had been declared a **expanded class** ..., then the resulting type would be expanded.

In either case, *PARAGRAPH* is its own base type, and class *PARAGRAPH* is its base class. These are not fascinating notions yet, but we need have a base class and base type for every type, and they will get less trivial as we move on.

Clients of the class may call exported features such as *first_line_indent* and others on entities of type *PARAGRAPH*.

→ *See chapter 21 about calling features on entities.*

There is no constraint on a non-generic Class_type other than the Class Type rule given above (the Identifier used must be the name of a class of the universe).

12.7 Unconstrained genericity

The next case arises from **generic classes**. A generic class is a class declared with formal generic parameters; this mechanism supports type parameterization. This section introduces the unconstrained form of genericity; the next one will add the constrained form.

Generic classes describe flexible structures having variants parameterized by types. Often these are **container data structures**, used to gather objects of various possible types; examples include lists, stacks, arrays and the like, which contain objects of arbitrary type. The generic parameters of such classes specify the types of objects to be kept in the container structures, such as the elements of an array.

← *Container data structures were mentioned in 10.17, page 156.*

The following examples, extracted from the Data Structure Library, show beginnings (Class_header parts followed by Formal_generics parts) of classes with unconstrained generic parameters:

> **deferred class** *TREE* [*G*] ...
> **class** *LINKED_LIST* [*G*] ...
> **class** *ARRAY* [*G*] ...

In each case, *G* is a **formal generic parameter** of the class, representing the types of objects to be kept in an instance of the class – a tree, a linked stack, an array. Classes may have more than one formal generic parameter; the next section will give an example with two parameters.

To derive a type from a generic class, you must provide a type, called an **actual generic parameter**, for each of the formal generic parameters. This will yield a **generically derived** type.

Generic derivation, applied to the above classes, will yield types such as

> *TREE* [*INTEGER*]
> *TREE* [*PARAGRAPH*]
> *LINKED_LIST* [*PARAGRAPH*]
> *TREE* [*TREE* [*TREE* [*PARAGRAPH*]]]
> *ARRAY* [*LINKED_LIST* [*TREE* [*LINKED_LIST* [*PARAGRAPH*]]]]

Instances of the first type represent trees of integers; instances of the second one represent trees of paragraphs (that is to say, trees of instances of the reference type *PARAGRAPH*); and so on.

Since all the classes used in these examples have exactly one formal generic parameter, each of the above generically derived types is obtained by providing one actual generic parameter. The actual generic parameters are *INTEGER* for the first example, *PARAGRAPH* for the second and third, *TREE* [*TREE* [*PARAGRAPH*]] for the fourth, *LINKED_LIST* [*TREE* [*LINKED_LIST* [*PARAGRAPH*]]] for the last.

An actual generic parameter, corresponding as here to an unconstrained formal generic parameter, is an arbitrary type. This means in particular that it may itself be generically derived; the last two examples illustrate this possibility, which leads to nested genericity without any limit on the depth of nesting.

DEFINITION:
Base Class,
Base Type
(Class Type)

The base class of a generically derived type is the class used to derive it by providing actual generic parameters. In the above examples the successive base classes are *TREE, TREE, LINKED_LIST, TREE* and *ARRAY*. A generically derived type is its own base type.

As before, we will get an expanded type if the base class is expanded, a reference type otherwise.

It is time now to state the exact properties of unconstrained generically derived types in a more formal way. (Since this will only be a more detailed exposé of the concepts introduced above, you may skip to the next section if this is your first reading.)

The construct that determines whether a class is generic or not is the Formal_generics part which optionally appears after the Class_header of a Class_declaration. Here is its structure:

← The form of a Class_declaration was given in chapter 4. The syntax reproduced here appeared first on page 52.

SYNTAX

Formal_generics	≜	"[" Formal_generic_list "]"
Formal_generic_list	≜	{Formal_generic ","...}
Formal_generic	≜	Formal_generic_name [Constraint]
Formal_generic_name	≜	Identifier
Constraint	≜	"->" Class_type

DEFINITION:
Constrained,
Unconstrained
Generic

This grammar includes an optional Constraint part after every formal generic parameter. If present, this part makes the parameter **constrained**; if not, the parameter is **unconstrained**. A generic class is constrained if it has at least one constrained parameter, unconstrained otherwise. The above examples were unconstrained; constrained genericity is studied in the next section.

Generic
Class,
Generic
Derivation,
Non-generic

Any class declared with a non-empty Formal_generics part (constrained or not) is said to be a **generic class**. A generic class does not describe a type but a template for a set of possible types. To derive an actual type from this template, you must provide an Actual_generics list, whose elements are themselves types. The result is called a **generic derivation**.

A type which is not generically derived, such as *PARAGRAPH* above, is called a **non-generic** type, and its base class is a non-generic class.

A straightforward constraint applies to unconstrained genericity:

This is a "constraint" on "unconstrained" genericity. Sometimes language meets metalanguage.

VALIDITY
VTUG

Unconstrained Genericity rule

Let *C* be an unconstrained generic class. A Class_type *CT* having *C* as base class is valid if and only if it satisfies the following two conditions:

1 • *C* is a generic class.
2 • The number of Type components in *CT*'s Actual_generics list is the same as the number of Formal_generic parameters in the Formal_generic_list of *C*'s declaration.

In addition, of course, the base class must exist in the universe; this is a consequence of the Class Type rule.

← The Class Type rule appeared on page 199.

SEMANTICS

A generically derived type is expanded if its base class is an expanded class; otherwise it is a reference type.

12.8 Constrained genericity

In the above unconstrained examples of genericity, any type was acceptable as actual generic parameter; this is because we do not require any special property of the objects to be entered into an array, inserted into a tree or pushed onto a stack. As long as operations applicable to all objects (such as assignment, copying or equality testing) are available, we can write the generic class, for example *TREE* [*T*], without any specific knowledge about the actual types to be used for *T*.

In some cases, however, you will need a guarantee that these types possess specific properties, so that the class text may apply certain operations to the corresponding objects. A typical example is a generic class *VECTOR* [*T*...] describing vectors, which must support an addition operation. To add two vectors, you need the ability to add two vector elements; in other words, you need an addition operation on *T*. Then *T* cannot be an arbitrary type.

With constrained genericity, you can guarantee that *T* supports addition, by requiring any actual generic parameter for *T* to be based on a descendant of a class that includes an addition routine.

Class *HASH_TABLE* of the Data Structure Library provides another example of constrained generic class. This class describes tables of elements, retrievable through associated keys. Its text begins with

> **class** *HASH_TABLE* [*G, KEY −> HASHABLE*] ...

This is a generic class with two parameters. The first one, *T*, plays the same role as those encountered in the previous section; it stands for the type of table elements, and is unconstrained. The second one, *KEY*, is constrained by the Kernel Library class *HASHABLE*.

The constraint means that the base class of any actual generic parameter used for *KEY* must be a descendant of the constraining class, *HASHABLE*. *HASHABLE* is a simple class introducing a function

The −> symbol is reminiscent of the arrow used in inheritance diagrams.

> *hash_code*: *INTEGER* **is**
>   -- Hash_code value
>   **deferred**
>   **end** -- *hash_code*

In other words, keys must be "hashable" into integer values. An example of a class that inherits from *HASHABLE* is the Kernel Library class *STRING*, describing character strings, for which a standard *hash_code* function is provided. An example of a type generically derived from *HASH_TABLE* is

> *HASH_TABLE* [*PARAGRAPH, STRING*]

The general syntax for constrained formal generic parameters was given above: such a parameter is accompanied by a Constraint of the form

SYNTAX

> "−>" Class_type

The effect of such a Constraint is to restrict allowable actual generic parameters to types that conform to the Class_type given.

In elementary terms, a type C conforms to a type B if the base class of C is a descendant of the base class of B; also, if C is generically derived, its actual generic parameters must (recursively) conform to the corresponding ones in B.

→ The next chapter covers conformance.

In the simple example above, *HASHABLE* and *STRING* are both non-generic class types, and conformance simply means that *STRING* is a descendant of *HASHABLE*.

The rule for generic derivations, given above for unconstrained genericity, includes an extra condition for constrained genericity: not only must the number of actual parameters match the number of formal parameters; the conformance requirements must also be met. More precisely:

Constrained Genericity rule

Let C be a constrained generic class. A Class_type CT having C as base class is valid if and only if CT satisfies the Unconstrained Genericity rule (VTUG, page 201) and, in addition:

3 • For any Formal_generic parameter in the declaration of C having a constraint of the form $\rightarrow D$, the corresponding Type in the Actual_generics list of CT conforms to D.

Again, the existence of the base class in the surrounding universe will be ensured by the Class Type rule.

← The Class Type rule appeared on page 199.

12.9 Using formal generic parameters as types

In a generic class C [..., G, ...], a formal generic parameter G, constrained or unconstrained (and syntactically known as a Formal_generic_name), stands for any actual generic parameter to be provided in generic derivations of the class. Within the text of C, you may use G wherever the syntax requires a type.

For example, the text of

---

class *HASH_TABLE* [G, *KEY* $\rightarrow$ *HASHABLE*] ...

---

declares a number of features using G or *KEY* as type of an argument, result or local entity. Typical is the function

---

item (*access_key*: *KEY*): G **is**
　　　　　-- Item associated with *access_key*, if present;
　　　　　-- otherwise default value of type G.
　　do ... Routine body omitted ... **end**

The type of the function result in the actual class is not exactly G but 'like last_put', where 'last_put' is an attribute of type G. See 12.15 below, page 211, on such "anchored" types.

which uses both of the formal generic parameters as Formal_generic_name types.

As with every other category of type, we need to define the "base class" and "base type" of a Formal_generic_name such as G and *KEY*, viewed as a type in the text of the enclosing class. Such types have few properties of their own: they just stand for actual generic parameters, unknown in the class text.

For a constrained parameter, such as *KEY*, the only available information is provided by the constraining type, here *HASHABLE*; the features of that type's base class are the only operations that we know can be applied to entities of the Formal_generic_name type.

DEFINITION:
*Base Class,
Base Type
(Constrained
Generic)*

As a consequence, we consider the base type of such a type, in the constrained case, to be its constraining type, with the associated base class. So *HASHABLE* serves as base class and base type for *KEY* used as a type in the text of class *HASH_TABLE*.

What about an unconstrained Formal_generic_name such as *G*? Every object ever manipulated by a system is an instance of some class, and every class is a descendant of the universal library class *ANY*. In other words, *HASH_TABLE* could be equivalently declared as

See 6.12, page 85, and chapter 27 on ANY. ANY is a descendant of GENERAL, providing basic features applicable to all types, and may be customized by individual projects.

> **class** *HASH_TABLE* [*G −> ANY, KEY −> HASHABLE*] ...

DEFINITION:
*Base Class,
Base Type
Unconstrained
Generic)*

As a result of this convention, *ANY* serves as both the base type and the base class of any unconstrained Formal_generic_name.

12.10 Using expanded types

The next few sections describe expanded types (Class_type_expanded, basic types, Bit_type). Before looking at the details, it is useful to recall when expanded types are useful.

In most Eiffel systems, the vast majority of types used are reference types, based on non-expanded classes similar to the last examples discussed (*KEY, HASH_TABLE, HASHABLE* and others). This is because reference types offer two major advantages, briefly noted at the beginning of this chapter:

- The dynamic creation of objects provides a high degree of flexibility, which is a key element of the object-oriented method. Your systems will create objects if they need them, when they need them, and as many of them as they need.

- Reference types are indispensable for most non-trivial data structures, which involve chained elements, possible cycles etc.

Expanded types, for their part, make it possible to describe composite objects (objects with sub-objects), as discussed in an earlier chapter. Some of the (non-exclusive) cases that justify the use of composite objects are:

← A first view of expanded types appeared in 7.5, page 93.

- Realism in modeling external world objects.
- Possible efficiency gain.
- Basic types.
- Interface with other languages.
- Machine-dependent operations.

The first case arises when we use Eiffel objects to model external world objects which are composite, rather than containing references to other objects.

For example, in a Computer-Aided Design application, we may view a car as containing, among others, four "wheel" sub-objects, rather than four references to such objects. Such a decision, illustrated below, is only legitimate for objects which may never share sub-objects: in this example, a wheel may not be part of two different cars.

← *The notions of composite object and sub-object were introduced on page 93.*

Composite car object

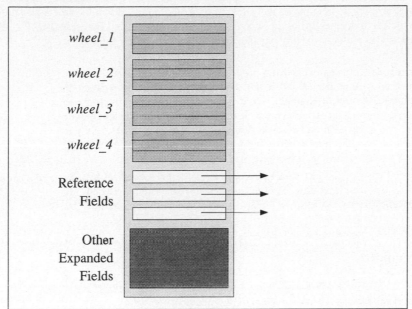

The second reason is, in some circumstances, a modest gain in efficiency: composite objects save some space (by avoiding pointers) and time (by avoiding indirections). For example, if every instance of *PERSON* has a *head*, declaring *head* of an expanded type will give the structure illustrated by (a) on the figure below, avoiding the indirection of (b). Here again, this only applies because there is no sharing of sub-objects, at least if we exclude the case of Siamese twins.

Subobject vs. reference to another object

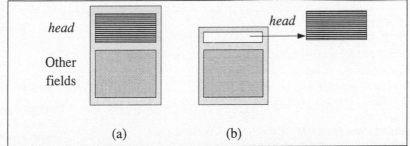

You must realize, however, that the possible efficiency gain is not guaranteed. The above figure, and similar illustrations of expanded attributes and composite objects, are only conceptual descriptions, not implementation diagrams. The authors of an Eiffel compiler or interpreter may choose any representation they wish as long as they guarantee the *semantics* of expanded values, according to which (as explained in the discussion of reattachment in a later chapter) an assignment $x := y$ must copy the object attached to y onto the object attached to x, and an equality test $x = y$ must compare the objects field by field.)

→ *The semantics of reattachment instructions and equality tests for entities of expanded types is discussed in chapter 20.*

A case where the previous two reasons apply is that of basic types such as integers or characters; to manipulate the value 3, we should not need to allocate an integer object dynamically, or to access it through a reference. For that reason, basic types are described by expanded classes of the Kernel Library, as explained below.

→ *See 12.13, beginning on page 209, about basic types.*

Another motive for using expanded types is the need to store in Eiffel objects some data structures produced and handled by software elements written in other languages. A typical example would be control information associated with a database management system, which Eiffel routines will not manipulate directly, but will pass back and forth to foreign (non-Eiffel) routines. As you have no control over the format and size of such data structures, the best way may be simply to keep them as sub-objects within your objects.

As a special case of the last situation, you may sometimes need, especially when taking care of operating system or machine-dependent aspects, to manipulate information which the Eiffel side views as unstructured bit sequences. The expanded Bit_type, studied below, supports this.

→ *Bit_type is discussed in 12.14, starting on page 209.*

12.11 Class types expanded

How do we obtain an expanded type from a class?

The class types seen so far may or may not be expanded:

- A Class_type whose base class is expanded is itself an expanded type; in other words, values of that type are objects (instances of the type).

- A Class_type whose base class is not expanded is a reference type; in other words, values of that type are references to potential objects, created dynamically.

In some cases we may also need to produce an expanded type from a non-expanded class. Assume for example that *HEAD* is a non-expanded class. In *PERSON*, you may declare the attribute

> *head*: *HEAD*

But this will give you the second variant of the figure (b), not the first (a).

You could achieve the effect of (a) by introducing a special expanded class *EXPANDED_HEAD* just for this purpose and declaring *head* to be of type *EXPANDED_HEAD*. The class declaration, using inheritance, is trivial:

> **expanded class** *EXPANDED_HEAD* **inherit** *HEAD* **end**

← *See 7.11, page 98, about the influence of inheritance on the export status, and 6.11, page 84, on the non-transmission of expansion status to heirs.*

Remember that by default the export policy of *HEAD* will be passed on to *EXPANDED_HEAD*, and that the "expansion" status of a class (whether or not it is declared as **expanded class**) does not affect that of its heirs. (It only affects the semantics of entities declared of the corresponding class types.)

Although it produces the desired result, this technique requires introducing extra classes such as *EXPANDED_HEAD*, which play no other role than to provide the basis for expanded types. This could soon become tedious.

The notion of Class_type_expanded solves the problem. If class *EXPANDED_HEAD* serves no other role than to declare entities such as *head*, you can avoid introducing the class altogether, by declaring the entities under the form

> *head*: **expanded** *HEAD*

The convention is simple: if *T* is a valid Class_type, generically derived or not, **expanded** *T* is a valid Class_type_expanded, and the possible values for entities of that type are instances of *T*.

It is not an error to use the type **expanded** *T* if the base class of *T* is already an expanded class; such a type is simply equivalent to *T*. For example, using the Kernel Library expanded class *INTEGER*, the following two declarations are equivalent:

Declaring 'n' under the second form given serves no useful purpose. But in general, it is convenient to know that **expanded** *T will have the intended effect, whether T is a reference type or already an expanded type.*

> *n*: *INTEGER*
> *n*: **expanded** *INTEGER*

This technique for obtaining expanded types by adding **expanded** to a Class_type also works for generically derived types. For example, you may declare

> *pls*: **expanded** *LINKED_LIST* [*PARAGRAPH*]

The expansion only applies to the object corresponding to *pls*; there is no recursive expansion of the data structure. An object of type *LINKED_LIST* (a class from the Data Structure Library) is not an entire list but a list header, with references to list cells; an example is the object marked "List header" on the figure below. Such an object contains references to actual list cells, which of course will not be expanded. So the only effect of the above declaration is to make the value of *pls* be an object such as the illustrated list header, rather than a reference to such a header.

List header and list cells

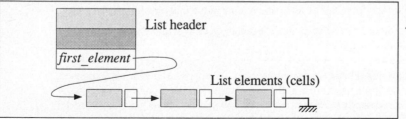

This is a repetition of the figure on page 143.

A Class_type_expanded of the form **expanded** *T* is its own base type; its base class is the base class of *T*.

Two important validity constraints, formalized below, apply to an expanded type (both a Class_type based on an expanded class, and a type of the form **expanded** *T*):

- An expanded type may not be based on a deferred class. This is natural since deferred classes are not fully implemented. In particular, assume that instead of *LINKED_LIST* above you had attempted to use *LIST*, an ancestor which is deferred. *LIST* [*T*] has, among others, a deferred feature *last* without arguments, of type *T*, which its descendants may choose to implement (to "effect") as either an attribute or a function. This means that in some client class we could not handle an attribute such as *pls* since we do not know how many fields (representing attributes) to set aside for *pls*.

- The base class of an expanded type must have either no Creators part, or a Creators part listing only one creation procedure, with no argument. This comes from the automatic initialization rule: when you apply a creation instruction to an object, all of its fields will first be initialized to universal, language-defined default values. For composite objects as they appear on the figures of page 205, this must be applied to all sub-objects; to avoid any ambiguity, there must be just one possible initialization for every such sub-object. This rules out having to choose between creation procedures or to supply arguments to such a procedure.

→ If the base class has a creation procedure, it must not make it unavailable for creation from the class that uses the expanded type. See condition 2 of the constraint in the next section.

In addition, you will remember the constraint on expanded classes (base classes of expanded types): the Expanded Client rule, which prohibits cycles in the client relation between expanded classes.

← The Expanded Client rule is on page 94.

12.12 Rules on expanded types

(This section only formalizes previous concepts, and may be skipped on first reading.)

To express precisely the properties of expanded types we will need to know exactly what the "base class" and "base type" of such a type are. The following definition also states precisely when a type is expanded and when it is not.

DEFINITION:
Expanded
Type,
Reference
Type

A type *T* is expanded if and only if one of the following conditions holds:

1 • *T* is a Class_type whose base class *C* is an expanded class.

2 • *T* is of the form **expanded** *CT*. (As noted, it is redundant but not erroneous for the base class of *CT* to be an expanded class.)

3 • *T* is of the form *BIT* M for some non-negative integer M.

T is a reference type if it is not a Formal_generic_name and none of the above condition applies.

This definition characterizes every type as either reference or expanded, except for one case mentioned in the last clause: formal generic parameters. A Formal_generic_name stands for any type to be used as actual generic parameter in a generic derivation; since an actual generic parameter may be an expanded type as well as a reference type, it would be premature to classify the Formal_generic_name in either of these two categories.

The following constraint applies to expanded types:

Expanded Type rule

It is valid to use an expanded type of base class *C* in the text of a class *B* if and only if it satisfies the following two conditions:

1 • *C* is not a deferred class.

2 • *C* either has no Creators part, or has a Creators part containing exactly one creation procedure, with no argument, available to *B* for creation.

The reason for the last part of clause 2 is that using an expanded type for an entity requires the same privileges as applying a creation instruction to an entity of the corresponding reference type. So a class which restricts creation availability also restricts the ability to declare expanded entities.

→ *18.6, page 283, explains how to restrict creation availability.*

Any entity declared of an expanded type has run-time values which are instances of the corresponding base type.

12.13 Basic types

As an important case of expanded types, the basic types *BOOLEAN, CHARACTER, INTEGER, REAL* and *DOUBLE* cover some of the most common types of values: booleans, characters, integers, real numbers in simple and double precision. The other basic type, *POINTER*, covers feature addresses intended for transmission to non-Eiffel routines.

Three types also enjoy special properties but are not considered basic types: Bit_type, covered in the next section, *ARRAY* and *STRING*.

→ *See chapter 28 about ARRAY and STRING.*

The basic types are class types, defined by non-generic classes of the Kernel Library called basic classes. To help implementors achieve the highest possible efficiency for simple arithmetic and boolean operations, the names of the six basic types, which are also the names of their base classes, are reserved words.

The basic types will need some special conformance properties. In general, a type *U* conforms to a type *T* only if *U*'s base class is a descendant of *T*'s base class. But then *INTEGER*, for example, is not a descendant of *REAL*. Since mathematical tradition suggests allowing the assignment *r := i* for *r* of type *REAL* and *i* of type *INTEGER*, the definition of conformance will need to include a small number of special cases for basic types.

→ *The special rules appear in the discussion of conformance for expanded types, 13.10, page 226.*

Except for *POINTER* which has no exported feature, each of the basic classes describes the operations applicable to values of the corresponding type (booleans, characters etc.). A chapter of part C gives the flat-short form of these classes. For compatibility with traditional arithmetic notation, many of the feature identifiers are of the Prefix or Infix form.

→ *The chapter on basic classes is chapter 32.*

12.14 *BIT* types

In some cases it is useful to manipulate raw data, viewed simply as sequences of bits. This may occur for platform-dependent manipulations, for other low-level operations, and for sharing objects with by non-Eiffel software.

The Bit_type predefined expanded types serve this need. Examples of Bit_type are

EXAMPLES

> BIT 256
> BIT Real_bits

denoting types whose values are sequences of bits of fixed length: 256 in the first case; the value of *Real_bits* in the second case. *Real_bits* is a constant, introduced in the universal class *PLATFORM*, which gives the number of bits needed for the representation of a real number.

About PLATFORM see 6.12, page 85, and 27.5, page 433.

More generally, the syntax for Bit_type, given at the beginning of this chapter, requires a Bit_type to be of the form

← *The syntax for* Bit_type *appeared with the syntax of* Type *on page 197.*

> BIT N

where *N* is a Constant. It may be a Manifest_constant, as with *256*, or it may be a Constant_attribute, as with *Real_bits*. In all cases, the value of *N* must be a positive integer, as expressed by the associated constraint:

VALIDITY

VTBT

> A Bit_type declaration is valid if and only if its Constant is of type *INTEGER*, and has a positive value.

SEMANTICS

The possible values of an entity declared as *BIT N* for some *N* are bit sequences of exactly *N* bits.

To assign a value to a Bit_type entity, you may use bit sequence constants – specimens of Bit_sequence. Such a constant is a sequence of zeros and ones terminated by the letter *B*, as in the assignment

→ *About bit sequences see 23.16, page 388, and 25.14, page 421.*

> *mask*: BIT 8;
> ...
> *mask* := 00100100B

For consistency with the rest of the type system, it is convenient to postulate an infinite set of expanded library classes *BIT_1*, *BIT_2* etc., all with the same operations. *BIT N* is then viewed as a notation for *BIT_n*, where n is the value of *N*. The flat-short form of a typical *BIT_n* class appears in the chapter on basic classes. Operations on Bit_type objects, described there, include:

→ *See 32.10, page 480, for the text of a BIT class.*

- The boolean operations **not**, **and**, **or** and **xor**.
- Shift operations, using the ∧ operator (*b*∧*s* is *b* shifted by *s* positions; positive *s* shifts right, negative shifts left, bits falling off the sequence's bounds are lost, and new positions are filled with zeros).
- Rotate operations, using the # operator.

The *BIT_n* classes only play a theoretical role, providing *BIT* types, like other types, with base classes. They need not exist physically in the library.

12.15 Anchored types

The originality of an Anchored type, the next category on our list, is that it carries a provision for automatic redefinition in descendants of the class where it appears.

An Anchored type is of the form

> **like** *anchor*

DEFINITION: *Anchor*

where *anchor*, called the anchor of the type, is an entity, or *Current*. If it is an entity, *anchor* must be the final name of a feature of the enclosing class, or, in the text of a routine, a formal argument.

A declaration using an Anchored type is an "anchored declaration", and the entities it declares are "anchored entities".

We already encountered anchored declarations in the discussion of redeclaration; the example was that of a routine in the Data Structure Library class *LINKED_LIST*:

← The encounter was towards the end of 10.8, on page 143.

> *put_element* (*lc*: **like** *first_element*; *i*: *INTEGER*)

whose argument *lc* represents a list cell. As a result of this declaration, *lc* is considered in class *LINKED_LIST* to have the same type as *first_element*, declared as a *LINKABLE* [*G*], the type representing list cells. Thanks to the anchored declaration, a descendant of *LINKED_LIST* which redefines *first_element* to a new type, taking into account more specific forms of list cells (such as cells chained both ways, or tree nodes), does not need to redefine *lc* and all similar entities of the class: their types will automatically follow the redeclared type of their anchor, *first_element*.

Here is another example, from the Graphics Library. A command button is a displayable box with which a graphical application will have associated a certain command, so as to execute the command whenever an interactive user "clicks" on the button. Class *COMMAND_BUTTON* has the corresponding attribute and procedure:

> *associated_command*: *COMMAND*
>   -- Command associated with current button
>
> *bind_command* (*c*: **like** *associated_command*) **is**
>   -- Associate command *c* with current button.
>   **require**
>   *command_exists*: *c* /= *Void*
>   **do**
>   *associated_command* := *c*
>   **ensure**
>   *associated_command* = *c*
>   **end** -- *bind_command*

Here *COMMAND* is a deferred class representing the abstract notion of command; specific commands (representing actions to be executed as a result of input events, such as saving a file, displaying a new window, or any other action defined by the application) are described by effective descendants of *COMMAND*.

Descendants of *COMMAND_BUTTON*, representing specific kinds of command button, may redefine *associated_command* to a type which is one of the effective descendants of *COMMAND*. In such a case, we need to be sure that the type of *c*, the argument to *bind_command*, remains tied to the type of *associated_command*.

As noted, the anchor may be *Current*. Declaring *x* in a class *C* as being of type **like** *Current* is equivalent to declaring it of type *C* in *C*, and redefining it as being of type *D* in any proper descendant *D* of *C*.

Simply chained list element

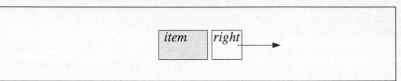

← *This figure and the next appeared previously on page 143.*

This mechanism is commonly used to avoid lengthy redefinitions. An example of its use is class *LINKABLE*, mentioned above. As shown on the above figure, any linkable element has a reference to its right neighbor, declared as an attribute

> *right*: **like** *Current*

This declaration guarantees that in any more specialized version of *LINKABLE*, described by a proper descendant class, *right* will automatically be constrained to refer to objects of the descendant type.

An example of such a proper descendant class is *BI_LINKABLE*, representing elements chained both ways:

Doubly chained list element

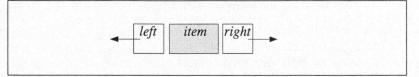

In this case the anchored declaration guarantees that a "doubly linked" list element is only used in conjunction with other elements of the same (or a more specialized) type. Another possible descendant of *LINKABLE* is a class describing tree nodes; here again anchored declaration will guarantee that tree nodes only refer to other tree nodes, not to simple *LINKABLE* elements.

There is a third possibility for an *anchor* besides *Current* and the name of a feature: it may also be, in a routine, one of the formal arguments of that routine. This is useful in particular for guaranteeing that two arguments of a routine, or an argument and the result (for a function) must have compatible types. A good example is provided by two features of the universal library class *ANY*, and hence passed on to every other class:

→ *See 19.2, starting on page 295, on "clone", and 19.7, starting on page 303, on "equal".*

> **frozen** *equal* (*some*: *ANY*; *other*: **like** *some*): *BOOLEAN* **is**
>   -- Are *some* and *other* either both void or attached to
>   -- objects field-by-field identical (on the fields of *some*)?
> **do**
>   *Result* :=
>   (*some* = *Void* **and** *other* = *Void*) **or**
>   (*some* /= *Void* **and** *other* /= *Void* **and then** *some.is_equal* (*other*))
> **end** -- *equal*

> **frozen** *clone* (*other*: *ANY*): **like** *other* **is**
>   -- Void if *other* is void;
>   -- Otherwise, new object field-by-field identical
>   -- to object attached to *other*.
>   **do ... end**

Function *equal* takes two objects and compares them field by field by calling the more elementary function *is_equal*. The second argument of *equal* is anchored to the first.

→ *On the need for two functions 'equal' and 'is_equal', see 19.7, page 303.*

Function *clone*, if called with a non-void argument, produces a fresh copy of the attached object; it relies internally on *copy* just like *equal* relies on *is_equal*. Since *clone* is applicable to objects of arbitrary type, the type declared for the argument *other* may only be *ANY*. Then without anchored types we would be reduced to using *ANY* as result type; but this would make normal uses of *clone* impossible, as in

> *x, y*: *SOME_TYPE*;
>
> ...
>   -- Create an object and attach it to *y*:
> !! *y* ...
>
> *x* :- *clone* (*y*)

where the last assignment would violate the type conformance rules since the source is of type *ANY* and the target of type *SOME_TYPE*, and the normal relation for assignment is the reverse one (the source type's base class must be a descendant of the target type's).

→ *The exact conformance rules are given in the next chapter.*

Anchored declaration solves the problem; without this mechanism we would have to redefine the function in every class.

If a routine has a formal argument or result anchored to another of its formal arguments (this is the case with *other* anchored to *some* in *equal*, and the result of *clone* anchored to *other*), the type rules on routine calls will require that, in a call, the type of the associated actual argument or result conform to the type of the actual argument corresponding to the anchor. For example, in

> **if** *equal* (*a, b*) **then** ... **end**;
> *u* := *clone* (*v*)

the type of *b* must conform to the type of *a*, and the type of the object returned by the second call must conform to that of *u*. These rules will be given precisely in the study of conformance and reattachment.

→ *See 13.9, page 225, defining expression conformance. On validity rules for direct reattachment see the Assignment rule, page 311, and the definition of argument validity, page 369.*

Another apparent solution would be to use *clone* not with an assignment as above, but with an Assignment_attempt, an instruction which indeed works when conformance is from target to source. But this would be inappropriate: the assignment attempt is meant for cases in which the author of a class cannot guarantee the type of an object statically (for example with a persistent object retrieved from a file or database), not for cases such as the above whose type validity may be statically ascertained without any difficulty.

→ *On* Assignment_attempt *see 20.13, page 330, and the subsequent sections.*

Let us now see the precise constraint and semantics on anchored types. First, we must know where anchored types fit in the classification of types into three kinds: reference, expanded and Formal_generic_name. The answer is clear: it follows from earlier definitions that an anchored type is a reference type.

← *See the definition of expanded and reference types on page 208.*

The following rule applies to the choice of anchor.

An anchored type of the form **like** *anchor* appearing in a class *C* is valid if and only if one of the following holds:

1 • *anchor* is the final name of an attribute or function of *C*, whose declared type is a non-Anchored reference type.

2 • The type appears in the text of a routine *r* of *C*, and *anchor* is a formal argument of *r*, whose declared type is a non-Anchored reference type.

3 • *anchor* is the reserved word *Current*.

The phrasing of cases 1 and 2 indicates that the anchor's type may not be an expanded type or a Formal_generic_name, and may not itself be anchored. The reason for this restriction is mainly simplicity and readability: when you see *x* declared as **like** *anchor*, you only have one more place to consult – the declaration of *anchor* – to know everything about the type properties of *x*. Were *anchor* permitted to be of type **like** *other_anchor*, you might have to embark on a search along a chain of mutually anchored declarations.

Although the type of the anchor may not itself be anchored, it may be defined in terms of an anchored type. An example was encountered in the sketch of class *LINKED_LIST* of the Data Structure Library:

> *put_linkable_left* (*new*: **like** *first_element*) **is** ...
>
> ...
>
> *first_element*: *LINKABLE* [**like** *first*];

---

where the type of *first_element* (serving as anchor for the argument *new* of *put_linkable_left*), although not anchored, uses a generic derivation of *LINKABLE*, with an anchored type as actual generic parameter.

Now for the semantics. Part of the effect of an anchored declaration is captured by the definition of the base type in this case. The base type *BT* of an anchored type **like** *anchor* appearing in a class *C* is determined as follows:

→ *The rest of the semantics of anchored declarations is covered by the notion of expression conformance, 13.9, page 225.*

DEFINITION:
Base Class,
Base Type
(Anchored)

1 • If *anchor* is the final name of some feature of *C*, then *BT* is the declared type of that feature in *C*.

2 • If *anchor* is a formal routine argument, then *BT* is the type declared for that argument in the Formal_arguments list.

3 • If *anchor* is *Current*, then *BT* is *C* followed by its Formal_generics, if any, with any Constraint removed.

As an example of case 1, the base type of function *bind_command* given above is *COMMAND*, the type of its anchor *associated_command*.

← *'bind_command' was part of the example on page 211.*

As an example of case 2, the base type of *Result* in *clone* is *ANY*.

As an example of case 3, the base type of an entity declared as **like** *Current* in class

← *The predefined entity Result, in a function, is considered to have the function's result type. See 8.7, on page 114.*

> **class** *HASH_TABLE* [*G, KEY –> HASHABLE*] ... **end**

is simply

> *HASH_TABLE* [*G, KEY*]

a generic derivation obtained by using as actual generic parameters two cases of Formal_generic_name, *G* and *KEY*, which, as noted, stand for types in the class text.

In the rule for case 3, the base type of an entity of type **like** *Current* in a class *C* does not include the keyword **expanded** even if class *C* is expanded. As a result, an entity of anchored type will always denote a reference.

Anchored declaration is a purely syntactical facility: you may always replace it by explicit redefinition. But it is extremely useful in practice, avoiding much code duplication when you must deal with a set of entities (attributes, function results, routine arguments) which should all follow suit whenever a proper descendant redefines the type of one of them, to take advantage of the descendant's more specific context.

13

Conformance

13.1 Overview

Conformance, a relation between types, is the most important characteristic of the Eiffel type system: it determines when a type may be usable in lieu of another, and when it may not.

The most obvious use of conformance is its application to assignments and other reattachment operations: $x := y$, for x of type T and y of type V, will not be valid unless V conforms to T. The next section will detail all the other cases when conformance governs the validity of a construct.

Conformance, as the rest of the type system, is based on inheritance. The basic condition for V to conform to T is straightforward:

- The base class of V must be a descendant of the base class of T.

- If V is a generically derived type, its actual generic parameters must conform to the corresponding ones in T.

- Also, if T is expanded, no inheritance may be involved: V can only be T itself, or its base type. (Otherwise the above assignment would be physically impossible.)

If this is your first reading, this simple explanation is probably sufficient to understand the references to conformance in the rest of this book, and you may want to move on right away to the next chapter.

For a thorough understanding of conformance, you will need the formal rules explained below, which take into account the details of the type system (constrained and unconstrained genericity, anchored types, predefined types).

13.2 Applications of conformance

Conformance governs the valid use of types in quite diverse situations. For any of the following to be valid, V must conform to T (with x of type T and y of type V):

- The assignment $x := y$.

- The routine call r (..., y, ...), where x is the formal argument declared in r at the position that y has in the call.

- The creation instruction ! V ! x ..., which creates an instance of V and attaches x to it.

- The redeclaration of x as being of type V in a proper descendant, where x is an attribute, a function, or a routine argument.

- Any use of C [..., V, ...] with V as actual generic parameter, where the corresponding formal generic parameter of C is constrained by T – in other words, the class is declared as C [..., $G \rightarrow T$, ...].

→ In the first three cases, the exact rule is that 'y' must conform to 'x'; this uses the generalization of conformance as a relation between expressions. See "expression conformance" page 225 below.

The discussion will first explain how to infer the conformance rules for *signatures* from those for types. It then introduces a simpler relation, direct conformance, from which general conformance may be inferred. Specific rules are then given for the various cases: class types, first without genericity, then with genericity added to the picture; formal generic parameters; anchored types (**like** *anchor*), which justify extending conformance from a relation between types to a relation between expressions and entities; expanded types. The chapter ends with a few special rules on basic types and Bit_type, made available as a concession to established arithmetic practice (for example, an integer value may be assigned to a real entity).

This chapter introduces no validity constraint but covers the various cases of conformance as successive "DEFINITIONS". To enable language processing tools such as compilers to make precise references to these cases in their error messages, the definitions have codes of the form VN*XX*, similar to those used in other chapters for validity constraints, and appearing with them in the index under "validity codes".

13.3 Signature conformance

The basic notion of conformance applies to types; the following sections will explain when a type conforms to another and when it does not.

In many cases, however, we need to determine conformance not just between types but between **signatures**. A signature gives the full type information associated with a feature: the types of its arguments, if any, and of its result, if any. Conformance of signatures is important because it governs redeclaration: whenever a feature is redeclared, the signature of the new version must conform to the signature of the original.

← The conformance constraint for signatures is clause 2 of the Redeclaration rule, page 163.

The definition of conformance for signatures will follow immediately from the definition for types: a signature t conforms to a signature s if and only if every element of t (the type of an argument or result) conforms to the corresponding element of s.

More precisely, recall that a signature is a pair of sequences of the form

← *Signatures were defined in 5.12, page 66.*

$$(<A_1, ..., A_n>, <R>)$$

where all elements involved are types; the A_i are the types of the formal arguments (for a routine) and R is the result type (for a function or an attribute). Either component of the pair, or both, may be empty (the first is empty for an attribute or a routine without arguments; the second, for a procedure). The second component has at most one element.

Then from a definition of type conformance, as explored in the rest of this chapter, we may immediately obtain a definition of signature conformance:

DEFINITION:
Signature
Conformance
VNCS

> A signature $t = (<B_1, ..., B_n>, <S>)$ conforms to a signature $s = (<A_1, ..., A_n>, <R>)$ if and only if it satisfies the following conditions:
>
> 1 • Each of the two sequence components of t has the same number of elements as the corresponding component of s.
>
> 2 • Every type T_i in each of the two sequence components of t conforms to the corresponding type S_i in the corresponding component of s.

In other words, the argument types must conform (for a routine), and so must the result type for a function or attribute.

13.4 Direct and indirect conformance

Conformance is, with one restriction, a reflexive and transitive relation. In other words, any type conforms to itself, and if V conforms to U and U to T, then V conforms to T. (The restriction is that T must not be expanded; see below.)

Also, replacing an actual generic parameter by a conforming type yields a conforming type: in other words, if Y conforms to X, then $B [Y]$ conforms to $B [X]$ for a class B with one generic parameter; this generalizes to an arbitrary number of parameters.

We may use these properties to simplify the study of conformance rules. By considering the relation **direct conformance**, which only covers the case of a class conforming to a different one through no intermediary, we can define general conformance by reflexive transitive closure:

DEFINITION:
General
Conformance
VNCC

> Let T and V be two types. V **conforms to** T if and only if one of the following holds:
>
> 1 • V and T are identical.
>
> 2 • V conforms directly to T.
>
> 3 • V is *NONE* and T is a reference type.
>
> 4 • V is $B [Y_1, ... Y_n]$ for some generic class B, T is $B [X_1, ... X_n]$, and every one of the Y_i conforms (recursively) to the corresponding X_i.
>
> 5 • T is a reference type and, for some type U, V conforms to U and U conforms (recursively) to T.

Cases 1 and 2 are immediate: a type conforms to itself, and direct conformance is a case of conformance.

Case 3 introduces the class *NONE* describing void values for references. Such a value may be assigned to a writable entity of any reference type, but since there is no associated object it may not be assigned to an expanded entity.

← See 6.16, page 88, about NONE.

Case 4 covers the replacement of one or more generic parameters by conforming ones, keeping the same base class: as noted, $B\,[Y]$ conforms to $B\,[X]$ if Y conforms to X. This does not address conformance to $B\,[Y_1, \ldots Y_n]$ of a type *CT* based on a class C different from B, a case discussed below.

Finally, case 5 is indirect conformance through an intermediate type U. Note the restriction that T must be a reference type: conformance to an expanded type may only be direct. This stems from the constraints on assignment to entities of expanded types, and is explained in the discussion of expanded types at the end of this chapter.

→ See 13.10, page 226, about conformance to and from expanded types. The restriction also excludes indirect conformance to a Formal_generic_name, which is just identity (13.10, page 226).

Thanks to the above definition of conformance in terms of direct conformance, the rules below concentrate on defining direct conformance. Conformance rules follow immediately: for any type T, direct conformance rules will yield the (possibly empty) set *ST* of types which conform directly to T; then the types that conform to T are T itself, the members of *ST*, and, recursively, if T is a reference type, any type conforming to a member of *ST*.

The next two sections introduce the basic direct conformance rules for reference (non-expanded) types: direct conformance to a non-generic type (which is just inheritance), and to a generically derived type (which takes parameterization into account). The subsequent sections apply these rules to the special cases of formal generic parameters, when used as types, and anchored types. The last sections deal with expanded types, ending with Bit_type.

13.5 Conformance to a non-generic reference type

Let us begin with the simple but common and important case of conformance to a reference type B obtained directly from a non-generic class. Then direct conformance is essentially inheritance: C conforms directly to B if C is an heir of B – which means that D conforms to B, directly or indirectly, if D is a descendant of B. In these examples C and D may be generically derived or not.

Assume for example class declarations beginning with

> **class** *C1* ... **inherit** *A1* ...
> **class** *C2* [*G*] ... **inherit** *A2* ...
> **expanded class** *C3* [*G, H* –> *HASHABLE*] ... **inherit** *A3* ...

Then, if X is an arbitrary type and Y is any type that conforms to *HASHABLE*:

- *C1* conforms directly to *A1*.

- *C2* [*X*] conforms directly to *A2*.

- *C3* [*X, Y*] conforms directly to *A3*.

Here is the precise rule:

C3 is expanded, C1 and C2 are not; this has no influence on the discussion. But A1, A2 and A3 must not be expanded. See 13.10, page 226, on conformance to expanded types.

DEFINITION:
*Direct
Conformance
(Non-generic)*
VNCN

> Let *CT* be a Class_type of base class *C*, and *BT* be a reference type whose base class *B* is not generic. *CT* conforms directly to *BT* if and only if the Inheritance clause of *C* lists *B* in one or more of its Parent items.

The restriction to non-generic reference types in this rule applies only to the target of the conformance, *BT*. The source, *CT*, may be expanded, as in the last example, or generically derived, as in the last two.

13.6 Generically derived reference types

The next typing mechanism to take into account is genericity. A generic class such as

> **class** *B* [*G, H* –> *DT, I* ...] ... **end**

raises two kinds of conformance issues. One is the conformance to a generically derived type *BT* based on *B*, of the form *B* [*TK, TL, TM*]. The other concerns the conformance properties of the formal parameters *G, H, I* ... themselves, which within the class text represent types. This section deals with the first issue; the next one will cover formal parameters.

← Conformance **of** *a generically derived type such as BT to a non-generic one raises no particular problem and is covered by the above rule on non-generic conformance.*

In considering conformance of a type *CT* to a type *BT* of the form *B* [*TK, TL, TM*], we may assume right away that the base class *C* of *CT* is not *B*, since condition 4 of the General Conformance rule takes care of identical *B* and *C*: in this case *CT* must be of the form *B* [*TR, TS, TT*] with the same number of parameters, and the rule simply states that *TR* must conform to *TK*, *TS* to *TL* and *TT* to *TM*.

← The general conformance rule is on page 219.

Thanks to this first rule, it suffices to examine the case of different base classes, but the same actual generic parameters. Then to check conformance of, say, *C* [*Y*] to *B* [*X*], you will check separately the conformance of *C* [*Y*] to *B* [*Y*], using the rule given below, and then show that *Y* conforms to *X*, which will complete the deduction thanks to case 4 of General Conformance.

This discussion is relevant only if B and C are non-expanded classes. See 13.10, page 226, for the expanded case, for which conformance is very limited.

Here the full rule is a little more delicate because of all the parameterization involved, but the idea is easy to understand intuitively.

The only delicate aspect is that the two classes involved, here *C* and *B*, may have different formal generic parameters – different in role, number or both. For example, given class declarations of the form

> **class** *B* [*I, J, K*] ... **end**

> **class** *C* [*P, Q*] **inherit**
>
>   *B* [*TK, P, TM*]
>
>   ...
>
> **end**

we will want the type *CT* defined as

$$C \; [TL, TN]$$

to conform to the type *BT* defined above as

$$B \; [TK, TL, TM]$$

even though the number of generic parameters is different for each class. Why *CT* should conform to *BT* is intuitively clear: if we interpret the text of *C* for the actual generic parameters *TL*, corresponding to *P*, and *TN*, corresponding to *Q*, the Parent *B* [*TK, P, TM*] listed in its Inheritance clause really stands for *B* [*TK, TL, TM*], which is precisely *BT*.

On first reading, if you find this example sufficient to give an intuitive understanding of conformance in such cases, you may wish to skip to the next section.

As the example shows, we will need to use substitutions (of actual to formal generic parameters) to ascertain direct conformance rigorously. If $\{x_1, \ldots, x_n\}$ and $\{y_1, \ldots, y_n\}$ are sets with the same number of elements, a substitution from the first set to the second is a one-to-one correspondence between them, associating a different element of the second to every element of the first. For example, a substitution (among many possible ones) from $\{T, U, V\}$ to $\{L, M, N\}$ is given by the table

$$
\begin{aligned}
T &\rightarrow M \\
U &\rightarrow N \\
V &\rightarrow L
\end{aligned}
$$

The number of possible substitutions between two sets of n elements is the factorial of n. In the example there are 3! = 6 possible substitutions.

With these notions the remaining rule for generically derived types is:

DEFINITION:
Direct
Conformance
(Generic
Substitution)
VNCG

Let *BT* be a generically derived reference type of base type $B \; [X_1, \ldots X_n]$ for some $n \geq 1$, where the formal generic parameters of *B* are $G_1, \ldots G_n$. Let *CT* be a Class_type of base class *C* different from *B*. To determine whether *CT* conforms directly to *BT*, define the substitution σ as follows:

* If *CT* is non-generic, σ is the identity substitution.
* If *CT* is a a generically derived type, of the form $C \; [Y_1, \ldots Y_m]$, and class *C* is declared with formal generic parameters $H_1, \ldots H_m$, then σ applied to any of the H_i (for $1 \leq i \leq m$) is Y_i, and σ applied to any other element is the element itself.

Then *CT* conforms directly to *BT* if and only if the Inheritance clause of *C* lists $B \; [Z_1, \ldots Z_n]$ as one of its Parent items and, for every *j* such that $1 \leq j \leq n$, applying substitution σ to Z_j yields X_j.

This rule is less formidable than it may look at first. The notion of substitution serves to specify actual-formal correspondence rigorously.

To see that the rule is in fact easy to apply, let us use it to check that the type CT defined in the above example as C [TL, TN] indeed conforms to BT, defined as B [TK, TL, TM]. The assumption is that B is declared as B [I, J, K], with three formal parameters, and that C [P, Q], with two formal parameters, lists B [TK, P, TM] as Parent.

The application is straightforward. Here $n = 3$ and $m = 2$; the types and Formal_generic names appearing in the definition are:

$$X_1 : TK \qquad X_2 : TL \qquad X_3 : TM$$

$$G_1 : I \qquad G_2 : J \qquad G_3 : K$$

$$Y_1 : TL \qquad Y_2 : TN$$

$$H_1 : P \qquad H_2 : Q$$

$$Z_1 : TK \qquad Z_2 : P \qquad Z_3 : TM$$

The substitution σ associates Y_1 to H_1 and Y_2 to H_2. In other words, it defines the associations

$$P \to TL$$
$$Q \to TN$$

and leaves other elements unchanged. As a result, applying σ to the Z_j yields

TK	(σ leaves Z_1, that is to say TK, unchanged.)
TL	(This is the result of applying σ to Z_2, that is to say P.)
TM	(σ leaves Z_3, that is to say TM, unchanged.)

The three resulting types TK, TL and TM are indeed, respectively, X_1, X_2 and X_3. This shows that C [TL, TN] does conform directly to B [TK, TL, TM].

To show that C [TL, TN] conforms to B [SK, SL, SM] given that TK conforms to SK, TL to SL and TM to SM, we would first use the Generic Substitution rule, as was just done, to show conformance to B [TK, TL, TM], and then apply case 4 of the General Conformance rule to obtain the required actual generic parameters.

13.7 Formal generic parameters

The next case is that of a type which is a Formal_generic_name, that is to say a formal generic parameter to the enclosing class. Consider the generic class

class C [$G, H \to CT, ...$] ... **end**

where G and H illustrate the two kinds of generic parameters, placing different requirements on the types to be used as the corresponding actual generic parameters: the Formal_generic_name G, unconstrained, stands for arbitrary types, and H, constrained by CT, stands for types that conform to CT.

As noted in the previous chapter, the base type of a constrained Formal_generic_name such as H is the constraining type, here CT, and its base class is the base class of CT. An unconstrained generic Formal_generic_name such as G is considered to be constrained by the universal class ANY, which then is both its base class and its base type.

← *Unconstrained genericity was studied in 12.7 and constrained genericity in 12.8. The use of generic parameters as types was addressed in 12.9, which defined the base type and base class for such types (page 204).*

In both cases, the Formal_generic_name will conform directly to its constraining type (CT or ANY). In the reverse direction, however, no direct conformance is possible: if we allowed any assignment to an entity of type G or H, with the assignment's source being of different type from that of the target, we would have no way of guaranteeing that this type would always be compatible for every possible actual generic parameter.

The rule for conformance to and from generic parameters follows from these observations:

DEFINITION:
Direct Conformance (Formal Generic)
VNCF

> Let G be a formal generic parameter of a class, which in the class may be used as a type of the Formal_generic_name category. No type conforms directly to G. If G is not constrained, it conforms directly to the type ANY (based on the corresponding universal class) and to no other type. If G is constrained by CT, G conforms directly to CT and to no other type.

Remember that a type that conforms directly to "no other type" still conforms (not directly) to itself. This follows from the general definition of conformance given above.

← *See case 1 of General Conformance, page 219.*

13.8 Anchored types

We must now look at anchored types, defined in the previous chapter as a form of reference type which provides an important notational simplification for groups of entities that must be redefined together in descendants.

An anchored type is of the form

← *Anchored types were introduced on page 211.*

> **like** *anchor*

where *anchor* is the name of an attribute or function, or *Current*. Such a declaration describes a type which is the same as the type of *anchor* but will automatically follow any redefinition of the type of *anchor* in a proper descendant. Using *Current* as anchor means that the type will be given by the class itself, possibly followed by its formal parameters (used here as actuals since we are in the text class itself).

The base type of an anchored type is the type BT of the *anchor*. BT must be a Class_type (it may not itself be anchored). If *anchor* is *Current*, BT is the class name followed by any formal generic parameters (used here as actual generic parameters).

The anchored type conforms directly to its base type BT. In the reverse direction, we cannot have any direct conformance: since a proper descendant may redefine the *anchor* to any type *NT* conforming to *BT*, we can never be sure that a given type *U* would conform to all such possible *NT*, except if *U* is the anchored type itself or *NONE* – two cases covered by the general definition of conformance from direct conformance. Hence the rule:

DEFINITION:
Direct
Conformance
(Anchored)
VNCH

> In a class *C*, type **like** *Current* conforms directly to its base type *CT*, where *CT* is *C* followed by its Formal_generic_list, if any, with any Constraint removed.
>
> Type **like** *anchor*, where *anchor* is a feature of *C* or a formal argument of a routine of *C*, conforms directly to the type of *anchor* in *C*.
>
> An anchored type conforms directly to no type other than implied by these rules. No type conforms directly to an anchored type.

13.9 Expression conformance

The preceding definition of conformance for anchored types does not suffice to cover the type properties of the corresponding entities. For example, the following should clearly be valid:

> *x*: *CT*; *y*: **like** *x*;
> ...
> *y* := *x*

The conformance rule indicates that *CT* does not conform to **like** *x* since it is not **like** *x* itself; but surely nothing can go wrong here since the actual types of *x* and *y* are, by construction, guaranteed to be the same after possible redefinition. The problem is that a conformance rule on **types** is not sufficient in this case: the reason for considering the assignment as valid is not the type of the right-hand side (since an entity of type *CT*, other than *x*, would not be acceptable) but that right-hand side itself. In other words we need in this case a conformance rule on **entities**, and more generally on expressions.

The same need arises in a case which is more important in practice: anchoring to a formal argument. Consider for example function *equal* from class *ANY*. It tests for the equality and is declared as

→ *See 19.7, page 303,*
about object equality, and
chapter 27 about class
ANY.

> **frozen** *equal* (*some*: *ANY*; *other*: **like** *some*): *BOOLEAN* **is**
>   ... Rest of routine omitted ...

The purpose of declaring *other* of type **like** *some* is to make the following kind of call valid if type *DT* conforms to *CT*:

> *x*: *CT*; *y*: *DT*;
> ...
> **if** *equal* (*x*, *y*) **then** ...

but the conformance rule for anchored types does not suffice to make this pattern valid: *DT*, the type of the actual argument *y*, does not conform to **like** *some*, the type of the corresponding formal argument *other*. And indeed we cannot always accept a second actual argument of type *DT*: what the routine declaration means is that the second argument's type must conform to that of the first.

This shows the need for defining conformance not just between types but between expressions. A reattachment (such as assignment, as in the above $y := x$, or actual-formal argument association, as in the call to *equal*) will require its source expression *s* to conform to its target entity *t*. In the absence of anchored types, this simply means that the type of *s* conforms to the type of *t*, according to the conformance rules between types defined in this chapter. But expression conformance will also permit the reattachment in cases involving anchored declarations; the simplest of these, as discussed in the first above example, is when *s* is of type **like** *t*.

Here is the precise rule resulting from this discussion:

DEFINITION:
Conformance
(Expression)
VNCX

An expression *v* of type *VT* conforms to an expression *t* of type *TT* if and only if they satisfy any one of the following four conditions.

1 • *VT* conforms to *TT*.

2 • *TT* is **like** *v* (*v* in this case must be an entity).

3 • *VT* and *TT* are both of the form **like** *x* for the same *x*.

4 • *TT* is **like** *x* where *x* is a formal argument to a routine *r*, *v* is an actual argument in a call to *r*, and *VT* conforms to the type of the actual argument corresponding to *x* in the call.

---

*If VT is '**like** t' (the inverse of case 2) conformance also holds. This is covered by case 1 since, because of rule VNCH as given on the previous page, '**like** t' conforms to the type of 't'.*

This definition will yield the basic type rule for an assignment $y := x$ and for the validity of *r* (*y*) where the formal argument is *x*: in both cases, *y* must conform to *x*. An equality test $x = y$ will be valid if either of the operands conforms to the other.

→ Assignment validity: Assignment rule, page 311. Actual-formal association: clause 2 of argument validity, page 369. Equality testing: 23.3, page 374.

This also makes it possible to express many properties using simpler language: rather than "the type of *y* must conform to the type of *x*", we can usually say just "y must conform to *x*".

13.10 Expanded types

There remains to cover the case of conformance to and from expanded types. The case of Bit_type will be studied separately in the next section.

First, consider conformance to an expanded type *T*. Clause 5 of the definition of General Conformance severely limits the possibilities here since it excludes any indirect conformance to *T*; so the only types that conform to *T*, other than *T* itself, are those which conform directly to *T*. There are two cases, based on the two categories of expanded types other than Bit_type:

← The definition of General Conformance was on page 219.

• *T* may be of the form **expanded** *BT* for some Class_type *BT*. Then only *BT* conforms directly to *T*.

• *T* may be based on an expanded class. Then, except for a special extension covering *REAL* and *DOUBLE*, as seen below, no type conforms directly to *T*.

The reason for these rules is clear if you remember that the assignment $t := v$ is valid whenever the type V of v conforms to the type T of t. If T is expanded, the effect of such an assignment, as studied in detail in a later chapter, is to copy, field by field, the object attached to v onto the object attached to t. But then if we allowed indirect conformance in this case, the base class of V could be a proper descendant of the base class of T, and hence it could have more attributes. As a result, we would have more fields in the source object than in the target, which could not accommodate the result of the field-by-field copy.

→ *The effect of assignment on an expanded target, which explains in part the reasons for the rules given here, appears in the discussion of reattachment in chapter 20. See 20.5, starting on page 313, on the semantics of direct reattachment, especially the table on page 317.*

What about conformance in the reverse direction – an expanded type ET conforming to a reference type RT? Here there is no implementation constraint since it is always physically possible to reattach a reference to an object of arbitrary size. But of course the attachment must be compatible with the type system; in other words, the base type of ET must conform to RT.

These are the essential ideas. Let us see now the unsurprising details.

First let us review the two forms of expanded type other than Bit_type. Examples of the first case are

> **expanded** C
> **expanded** D $[X, Y, Z]$

where classes C and D need not have been declared as expanded. Here the base types are C and D $[X, Y, Z]$), and the base classes are C and D.

Examples of the second case are

> A
> B $[X, Y, Z]$

where A and B have been declared as **expanded class** (A non-generic, B generic). These types are their own base types; the base classes are A and B. The basic types *BOOLEAN, CHARACTER, INTEGER, REAL, DOUBLE* and *POINTER* fall into this category.

Conformance to an expanded type of one of the above forms is limited to the type itself and its base type.

As a result, if T is a reference Class_type, the assignment below will be valid:

> *ref*: T;
> *exp*: **expanded** T;
> ...
> *exp* := *ref*

The semantics of this assignment is to copy onto the value of *exp* the fields of the object attached to *ref*, if not void (and to trigger an exception otherwise). This is studied in detail in a later chapter.

→ *See chapter 20; precise references above.*

DEFINITION:
Heavier
arithmetic
type

A special extension, ensuring compatibility with mathematical and programming language tradition, applies to the arithmetic types *INTEGER*, *REAL* and *DOUBLE*: any arithmetic type conforms to **heavier** ones, where *DOUBLE* is heavier than *REAL* and *INTEGER*, and *REAL* is heavier than *INTEGER*. This makes it possible to accept such assignments as

> *integer_entity*: *INTEGER*;
> *real_entity*: *REAL*;
> ...
> *real_entity* := *integer_entity*
>   -- May be understood as an abbreviation for an explicit conversion:
>   -- *real_entity* := *integer_entity*.*to_real*

as well as mixed expressions such as *4.5 + 3*, which is in fact a feature call – to function **infix** *"+"* of class *REAL*, having a formal argument of type *REAL*.

The rule is also important in connection with constrained genericity: if you declare a class as

> **class** *MATRIX* [*G* –> *DOUBLE*] ... **end**

→ *Yes, will you ask if you are following carefully, but what about 3 + 4.5? Compatibility with traditional notation will indeed require another special rule, the Arithmetic Expression Balancing rule, 23.10, page 385.*

you know that you can use this class in a client to declare a *MATRIX* [*REAL*] or a *MATRIX* [*INTEGER*].

This takes care of conformance to an expanded type. In the reverse direction:

• For a type based on an expanded class *EC*, the earlier discussion of this chapter has given the conformance rules, based on inheritance from non-expanded classes.

← *13.5, page 220, and 13.6, page 221.*

• A type of the form **expanded** *BT* conforms directly to its base type *BT*, and to no other type.

In either case, assignments or other reattachments from an expanded source to a reference (non-expanded) target will have the semantics of cloning. This means that in

→ *The semantics of assignment, which is the same as the semantics of other reattachment operations such as argument passing, is studied in detail in chapter 20.*

> *ref*: *T*;
> *exp*: **expanded** *T*;
> ...
> *ref* := *exp*

the effect of the assignment is to create a duplicate of the value of *exp*, which is an object, and assign to *ref* a reference to the new object.

This discussion yields the precise rule for conformance to and from expanded types:

DEFINITION:
Direct
Conformance
(Expanded
Types)
VNCE

Let T be an expanded type other than a Bit_type. A type U conforms directly to T if and only if they satisfy any one of the following three conditions:

1 • T is of the form **expanded** BT, and U is BT.

2 • T is *REAL* and U is *INTEGER*.

3 • T is *DOUBLE* and U is *REAL* or *INTEGER*.

In case 1 T also conforms directly to U.

An expanded type conforms directly to no type other than implied by this rule and the rules of 13.5 and 13.6.

Combined with the general definition of conformance in terms of direct conformance, this rule indicates that a type defined as **expanded** RT, where RT is a reference Class_type (generically derived or not), conforms to itself, to RT, to any class type to which RT conforms, and to no other type. No other type except RT conforms to it.

13.11 Bit types

The last category of type is Bit_type, meant for manipulations of information representable as bit sequences.

Bit_type, describing bit sequences of fixed length, is often used for machine-dependent manipulations. Clearly, few Eiffel applications need it; those that do should confine its use to a small number of classes (normally one per system), so as to facilitate portability between various platforms by limiting the amount of adaptation to be done in each case.

For Bit_type, conformance rules reflect a very simple notion: a Bit_type $BT1$ will conform to another Bit_type $BT2$ if and only if we may guarantee that there is "enough room" in an instance of $BT2$ to accommodate an instance of $BT1$. In addition, a Bit_type, like any other type, should conform to *ANY*. More precisely:

DEFINITION:
Direct
Conformance
(Bit_Type)
VNCB

The possible direct conformance cases involving a Bit_type are the following for any positive integers N and P:

1 • *BIT N* conforms directly to *ANY*.

2 • *BIT N* conforms directly to *BIT P* for $N \leq P$.

Other than implied by these rules, no type conforms directly to a Bit_type, and a Bit_type conforms directly to no type.

Case 1 is necessary here because Bit_type is not deduced from a class. For any other type CT, there was no need to state conformance to *ANY* explicitly since CT has a base class which, by a universal property, is automatically a descendant of *ANY*. (The discussion of Bit_type did use an infinite set of base classes *Bit_1, Bit_2* and so on, but these classes are only a convenient fiction and need not actually exist.)

← *The property that every class is a descendant of ANY is given by the semantics rule on page 85.*

The fictitious classes BIT_N appear in 12.14, page 209; their features are in 32.10, page 480.

As an example of case 2, in

> *x*: *BIT 261*;
> *y*: *BIT 107*;
> ...
> *x* := *y*

→ *More on the semantics of assignment in 20.5, page 313. Since bit sequences are expanded, the table on page 317 shows the effect to be a copy, specified by case 1 of the semantics of 'copy', page 297.*

the assignment is valid. The shorter bit sequence will be extended with leading zeros.

Part C

The contents

14

Control structures

14.1 Overview

The previous chapters have described the "bones" of Eiffel software: the module and type structure of systems. With this chapter we begin studying the "meat": the elements that govern the execution of applications.

Control structures are constructs used to schedule the execution of instructions at run-time. There are five control mechanisms: sequencing, null instruction, conditional, multi-branch choice and loop. A complementary construct is the Debug instruction.

As given below, the description of the semantics of the various control structures involved assumes that none of the instructions executed as part of a control structure triggers an exception. If an exception occurs, the normal flow of control is interrupted, as described by the chapter that specifically deals with exception handling.

→ *Exceptions are studied in chapter 15.*

14.2 Compound

The first control structure, sequencing, is not very visible in the syntax even though it plays an important role: executing instructions sequentially.

The supporting syntax involves the semicolon operator and appears in the description of construct Compound. An example specimen of this construct is:

```
window1.display; mouse.wait_for_click (middle);
if not last_event.is_null then
    last_event.handle; screen.refresh
end
```

This expresses that the three instructions given, separated by semicolons, must be executed in the order given. Notice how the last instruction (a conditional instruction, as studied below) itself includes a two-instruction Compound.

The syntax description for Compound is:

> Compound   ≜   {Instruction ";" ...}

A special syntactical convention reinforces the natural shyness of the sequencing control structure: the semicolon is **optional** as a separator between any two instructions, except if the second begins with an opening parenthesis (which could cause ambiguity).

Semicolons are also optional between parent clauses (page 77), feature declarations (page 60), declarations of local entities (page 114), Parent clauses (page 77) and assertion clauses (page 121).

This does not detract, however, from the role of sequencing as a control structure – even if the only syntactical trace left in the software text is the textual order of instructions in a compound, indicating the temporal order in which they should be executed at run time.

Aside from its role as a control structure, the Compound construct serves an important syntactical purpose: ensuring that any construct which involves an instruction (so that the effect of the construct may include executing this instruction) is permitted to involve any number of instructions, including zero. This rule is observed consistently in the syntax of Eiffel: no production of the syntax defining a construct other than Compound uses Instruction directly on the right-hand side; every such production uses Compound instead. This includes:

The style guidelines of appendix A, page 493, do suggest including the semicolon anyway, as consistently does this book.

- The body of a non-deferred routine (construct Internal).
- The Initialization and Loop_body of a Loop instruction.
- The Then_part and Else_part of a Conditional instruction.
- The When_part and Else_part of a Multi_branch instruction.
- The Rescue clause of a non-deferred routine.
- The Debug instruction.

← *Syntax: page 113.*

→ *Page 243.*

→ *Page 235.*

→ *Page 239.*

→ *Page 256.*

→ *Page 245.*

The effect of executing a Compound may be defined as follows.

- If the Compound has zero instructions, the effect is to leave the state of the computation unchanged.
- If the Compound has one or more instructions, its effect is that of executing the first instruction of the Compound and then (recursively) to execute the Compound obtained by removing the first instruction.

Expressed less formally, this means executing the constituent instructions in the order in which they appear in the Compound, each being started only when the previous one has been completed.

14.3 Null instruction

The form of the null instruction does not appear explicitly in the syntax specification but may be illustrated as follows.

The effect of the null instruction is to leave the state of the computation unchanged.

This instruction has a purely syntactical role: making sure that extra semicolons added by oversight to a compound, are harmless, as in

As noted above, semicolons in compounds are optional anyway.

> **if** *c* **then**; *i1* ;;; *i2*; **else** *i3*;;; **end**

14.4 Conditional

A Conditional instruction serves to prescribe that one among a number of possible compounds must be executed, the choice being made on the basis of boolean conditions associated with each compound.

Although the Conditional is a useful and frequently used construct, you should remain alert to an important aspect of the Eiffel method, which de-emphasizes explicit programmed choices between a fixed set of alternatives, in favor of automatic selection at run-time based on the type of the objects to which an operation may be applied. This automatic selection is made possible by the object-oriented techniques of inheritance and dynamic binding. This methodological guideline, discussed in more detail below, does not detract from the usefulness of Conditional instructions, but should make you wary of complicated decision structures with too many **elseif** branches. This applies even more to the Multi_branch instruction studied next.

→ *More on how to avoid complicated choice structures in 14.6, page 240.*

An example Conditional is

> **if** *x* > *0* **then**
>   *i1*; *i2*
> **elseif** *x* = *0* **then**
>   *i3*
> **else**
>   *i4*; *i5*; *i6*
> **end**

whose execution is one among the following: execution of the compound *i1*; *i2* (if $x > 0$ evaluates to true); execution of *i3* if the first condition does not hold and $x = 0$ evaluates to true; execution of *i4*; *i5*; *i6* if none of the previous two conditions holds.

There can be zero or more "**elseif** Compound" clauses. The "**else** Compound" clause is optional; if it is absent, no instruction will be executed if all boolean conditions are false.

The general form of the construct is

Conditional	$\triangleq$	**if** Then_part_list [Else_part] **end**
Then_part_list	$\triangleq$	{Then_part **elseif** ...}$^+$
Then_part	$\triangleq$	Boolean_expression **then** Compound
Else_part	$\triangleq$	**else** Compound

To define precisely the semantics of this construct, a few auxiliary notions are useful. As the syntactical specification shows, a Conditional begins with

> **if** *condition*$_1$ **then** *compound*$_1$

where *condition*$_1$ is a boolean expression and *compound*$_1$ is a Compound.

DEFINITION:
Secondary
Part

The remaining part may optionally begin with **elseif**. If so, replacing the first **elseif** by **if** would transform the remaining part into a new, syntactically correct, Conditional; such an instruction is called the **secondary part** of the enclosing Conditional. For example, the secondary part of the above Conditional is

> **if** *x = 0* **then**
>   *i3*
> **else**
>   *i4*; *i5*; *i6*
> **end**

The final part, also optional, is of the form **else** *compound*$_n$.

DEFINITION:
Prevail
Immediately

If the value of *condition*$_1$ is true when the instruction is executed, then the Conditional is said to **prevail immediately**.

Finally, we may consider that every Conditional has an Else_part if we understand an empty Else_part to stand for one with an empty Compound.

With these conventions, the effect of a Conditional may be defined as follows. If the Conditional prevails immediately, then its effect is that of its *compound*$_1$ part, as defined above. Otherwise:

- If it has a secondary part, the effect of the entire Conditional is (recursively) the effect of the secondary part.

- If it has no secondary part, its effect is that of the (possibly empty) Compound in its Else part.

The above three-branch Conditional will execute the Compound *i1*; *i2* if *x* is found to be positive, *i3* if *x* is zero, and *i4*; *i5*; *i6* otherwise.

Like the instruction studied next, the Conditional is a "multi-branch" choice instruction, thanks to the presence of an arbitrary number of **elseif** clauses. These branches do not have "equal rights", however; as the preceding discussion implies, their conditions are evaluated in the order of their appearance in the text, until one is found to evaluate to true. If two or more conditions are true, the one selected will be the first in the syntactical order of the clauses.

14.5 Multi-branch choice

Like the conditional, the Multi_branch supports a selection between a number of possible instructions. In contrast with the Conditional, however, the order in which the branches are written does not influence the effect of the instruction. Indeed, the validity constraints seen below guarantee that at most one of the selecting conditions may evaluate to true.

Like the Conditional, the Multi_branch instruction is less commonly used in proper Eiffel style than its counterparts in traditional design and programming languages. This is explained in more detail below.

→ *See the methodological guidelines in 14.6, page 240.*

You may use a Multi_branch if the conditions are all of the form

$$exp = v_i$$

where *exp* is an expression, the same for every branch, and the v_i are constant values, different for each branch. In this case, the Multi_branch provides a more compact notation than the Conditional, and makes a more efficient implementation possible.

Here is an example of Multi_branch, which assumes an entity *last_input* of type *CHARACTER*:

```
inspect
    last_input
when 'a' .. 'z', 'A' .. 'Z', '_' then
    command_table. item (upper (last_input)). execute;
    screen. refresh
when '0' .. '9' then
    history. item (last_input). display
when Control_L then
    screen. refresh
when Control_C, Control_Q then
    confirmation. ask;
    if confirmation. ok then
        cleanup; exit
    end
else
    display_proper_usage
end
```

Depending on the value of *last_input*, this instruction selects and executes one Compound among five possible ones. It selects the first (*command_table...*) if *last_input* is a lower-case or upper-case letter, that is to say, belongs to one of the two intervals *'a' .. 'z'* and *'A' .. 'Z'*, or is an underscore *'_'*. It selects the second if *last_input* is a digit. It selects the third (refresh the screen) for the character *Control_L*, and the fourth (exit after confirmation) for either one of two other control characters; here *Control_L, Control_C* and Control_Q must be constant attributes. In all other cases, the instruction executes the fifth compound given (*display_proper_usage*).

DEFINITION: A Multi_branch instruction contains a Expression, called the "inspect
Inspect expression" appearing after the keyword **inspect**. The inspect expression,
Expression *last_input* in the example, may only be of type *INTEGER* or, as here,
CHARACTER. It includes one or more When_part, each of which indicates a list of one or more Choice, separated by commas, and a Compound to be executed when the value of the Expression is one of the given Choice values.

DEFINITION:
Inspect
Constant
Every Choice specifies one or more values, called **inspect constants**. More precisely, a Choice is either a single constant (Manifest_constant such as the character constant '_', or constant attribute such as *Control_L*) or an interval of consecutive constants, such as *'a' .. 'z'*, yielding all the interval's elements as inspect constants. If present, the instruction's optional Else_part is executed when the inspect expression is not equal to any of the inspect constants.

As the validity constraint will state precisely, all the inspect constants must be of the same type as the inspect expression (all characters, or all integers) and constant values appearing in different When_part branches must be different.

Every constant in the preceding example is either a Manifest_constant such as *'a'*, whose value is an immediate consequence of the way it is written, or a constant attribute such as *Control_L* whose value is given in a constant attribute declaration such as

→ *See 16.6, page 264, about Unique attributes. and 25.15, page 422, about character codes such as %/217/.*

> *Control_L*: *CHARACTER* **is** *'%/217/'*

In some cases, however, you may just want to use a set of integer constants to distinguish between several possibilities, for example possible marital statuses (single, married etc.), without any need to know their actual values as long as they are guaranteed to be different. **Unique attributes** serve this purpose, and may be used in Multi_branch instructions. A typical declaration is

→ *16.6, page 264, discusses unique attributes.*

> *Single, Married, Divorced, Widowed*: *INTEGER* **is unique**;

which yields four integer constants. The only official properties of these constants is that their values are all different, all positive, and, for Unique constants introduced in the same declaration, as here, consecutive. The language definition provides no other information on the values.

One or more of the inspect constants of a Multi_branch may be Unique, as in

```
inspect
    n
when Single, Divorced then
    ...
when Married then
    ...
when Widowed then
    ...
end
```

If any Unique constants are involved, the validity constraint seen below in its precise form will guarantee that all values are different in this case too. All Unique constants must have been introduced in the same class (otherwise they could have conflicting values), and that if any non-Unique integer constants are also used they must have negative or zero values to ensure that they don't coincide with one of the Unique.

Here now are the formal rules. First, the syntax of Multi_branch:

Multi_branch	≜	**inspect** Expression
		[When_part_list] [Else_part] **end**
When_part_list	≜	**when** {When_part **when** ...}⁺
When_part	≜	Choices **then** Compound
Choices	≜	{Choice "," ...}
Choice	≜	Constant | Interval
Interval	≜	Integer_interval | Character_interval
Integer_interval	≜	Integer_constant " **..** " Integer_constant
Character_interval	≜	Character_constant
		" **..** " Character_constant

→ Construct Constant *describes manifest or symbolic constants, including Unique constants, and is studied in 23.13, starting on page 386.*

DEFINITION:
Unfolded
Form of a
Multi_branch

To discuss the constraints and the semantics, it is convenient to consider the **unfolded form** of a Multi_branch. To obtain it, just replace any integer or character Interval, in the Choices of a When_part, by a Choices list made up of all constants between the interval's bounds, or empty if the second bound is smaller than the first. Integer order is used for an Integer_interval, and character code order for a Character_interval.

For example, of the intervals

> *3 .. 5*
> *'i' .. 'n'*
> *5 .. 3*

the first two unfold into

> *3, 4, 5*
> *'i', 'j', 'k', 'l', 'm' 'n'*

and the third into an empty Choices list. Thanks to unfolding, the constraint and semantics may consider that every Choice is of the Constant form.

A Multi_branch must satisfy a validity constraint:

VOMB

Multi_branch rule

A Multi_branch instruction is valid if and only if its unfolded form satisfies the following conditions.

1 • The inspect expression is of type *INTEGER* or *CHARACTER*.

2 • The inspect constants (the values in the various Choices parts) are constant attributes of the same type as the inspect expression.

3 • Any two non-Unique inspect constants have different values.

4 • Any two Unique inspect constants have different names.

5 • If any inspect constant is Unique, then every other inspect constant in the instruction is either Unique or has a negative or zero value.

6 • All Unique inspect constants, if any, have the same class of origin (the enclosing class or a proper ancestor).

This is the precise form of the requirements introduced above, guaranteeing (in clauses 3 to 6) that values in different branches are different. The last three clauses address this problem for a Multi_branch instruction containing one or more Unique constants, possibly in conjunction with non-Unique ones (which must then be of type *INTEGER*).

The effect of executing a Multi_branch instruction is defined as the effect of executing its unfolded form, as follows. The value of the inspect expression is computed. Because of the above validity constraint, that value may be equal to at most one of the inspect constants. If there is indeed one such constant, the effect of the Multi_branch is that of the Compound appearing after the **then** in the When_part of the matching inspect constant. If there is no such constant:

1 • If the Else_part is present, the effect of the Compound is that of the Compound appearing in the Else_part.

2 • Otherwise an exception is triggered and the current routine execution fails.

The integer code for the exception in case 2 is given by the constant attribute *Invalid_inspect_value* in the Kernel Library class *EXCEPTIONS*.

→ *See 15.11, page 258, about class EXCEPTIONS and exception codes.*

Note the difference between Conditional and Multi_branch as regards the meaning of an absent Else_part when none of the selection conditions is satisfied. A Conditional just amounts to a null instruction in this case; but a Multi_branch will fail (triggering an exception).

The reason is a difference in the nature of the instructions. A Conditional tries a number of possibilities in sequence until it finds one that holds. A Multi_branch selects a Compound by comparing the value of an expression with a fixed set of constants; the Else_branch, if present, catches any other values.

If you expect such values to occur and want them to produce a null effect, you should use an Else_part with an empty Compound. By writing a Multi_branch without an Else_part, you state that you do *not* expect the expression ever to take on a value not covered by the inspect constants. If your expectations prove wrong, the effect is to trigger an exception – not to smile, do nothing, and pretend that everything is proceeding according to plan.

14.6 A note on selection instructions

If you have accumulated some experience with some of the traditional design or programming languages, many of which include a "case" or "switch" instruction, you will recognize the Multi_branch as similar in syntax and semantics. But when it comes to writing Eiffel applications, you should be careful to not misuse this instruction. This warning extends to Conditional instructions with many branches.

Staying away from explicit discrimination is an important part of the Eiffel approach to software construction. When a system needs to execute one of several possible actions, the appropriate technique is usually not an explicit test for all cases, as with Multi_branch or Conditional, but a more flexible inheritance-based mechanism: **dynamic binding**. With explicit tests, every discriminating software element must list all the available choices – a dangerous practice since the evolution of a software project inevitably causes choices to be added or removed. Dynamic binding avoids this pitfall.

→ *See 21.9, beginning on page 345, about dynamic binding.*

The use of Multi_branch instructions should be reserved, then, to simple situations where a single operation depends on a set of fixed and well-understood choices, representable as integers or characters.

When the choices represent variants of a data type (for example different categories of employees, for which a certain operation, such as paying the salary, is executed differently), then Multi_branch is *not* appropriate: instead, you should define different classes that inherit from a common ancestor (for example *MANAGER*, *ENGINEER* etc. inheriting from *EMPLOYEE*) and redefine one or more features (such as *pay_salary*) to take care of the local context. Then dynamic binding guarantees application of the proper variant: the call

```
Caroline.pay_salary
```

will automatically use the variant of *pay_salary* adapted to the exact type of the object attached to *Caroline* at run time (which may be an instance of *MANAGER*, or *ENGINEER* etc.).

This is much more flexible than a Conditional or Multi_branch which would have to list the choices explicitly, especially if other operations besides *pay_salary* have variants for the given categories. To add a new variant, it suffices to write a new class (for example *SECRETARY*), heir to *EMPLOYEE*, equipped with the new versions of the operations that differ from the default version defined at the level of *EMPLOYEE*. In contrast with a system that makes explicit choices through Conditional or Multi_branch instructions, a system built using this method will only have to undergo minimal changes for such an extension.

There does remain a role, of course, for explicit choices. As an example of legitimate Multi_branch, let us look again at the extract already shown above:

```
inspect
    last_input
when 'a' .. 'z', 'A' .. 'Z', '_' then
    command_table.item (upper (last_input)).execute;
    screen.refresh
when '0' .. '9' then
    history.item (last_input).display
when Control_L then
    screen.refresh
when Control_C, Control_Q then
    confirmation.ask;
    if confirmation.ok then
        cleanup; exit
    end
else
    display_proper_usage
end
```

This decodes a user input consisting of a single character and executes an action depending on that character, What is interesting is that the Multi_branch does only the "easy" part: separating the major categories of characters (letters, digits, control characters).

In the branches for letters and characters, however, the finer choice is made not through explicit instructions but through dynamic binding. For example, letters are used to index a table *command_table* of objects representing command objects; here we must assume a class *COMMAND*, perhaps deferred, representing the general notion of command, with one or more effective descendants (such as *DELETE* or *UPDATE*) representing the various types of command, each with its specific version of procedure *execute* to execute the corresponding command. Every "command object" appearing in *command_table* is an instance of one of these effective descendants. To execute the action associated with the upper-case version of a given letter, the above instruction gets a command object by looking up the appropriate table entry, *command_table.item* (*upper* (*last_input*)), and applies *execute* to it, relying on dynamic binding to ensure that the proper action will be selected.

Using a Multi_branch to discriminate between the actions associated with individual letters *'A'*, *'B'* etc. would have resulted in a more complicated and inflexible architecture. At the outermost level, however, the above extract does use a Multi_branch, which appears justified because of the small number of cases involved and the diversity of actions in each case, which do not fall into a single category such as "execute the command attached to the selected object".

→ *As a complement to this discussion, see the Single Choice principle, page 283, and the clonable array technique, 19.5, page 301.*

14.7 Loop

The next control structure is the only construct (apart from recursive routine calls) supporting iterative computation. This is the Loop instruction, describing iterative computations that obtain their result through successive approximations.

The following example of a routine from class *LINKED_TREE* of the Data Structure Library illustrates the Loop construct with all possible clauses:

```
search_same_child (sought: like first_child) is
        -- Move cursor to first child position, at or after current
        -- cursor position where sought appears.
        -- If no such position, move cursor after last item.
    require
        sought_child_exists: sought /= Void
    do
        from
            child_start
        invariant
            0 <= position;
            position <= arity + 1
        variant
            arity – child_position
```

```
        until
            child_off or else (sought = child)
        loop
            child_forth
        end
    ensure
        (not child_off) implies (sought = child)
    end -- search_same_child
```

The loop construct extends from the keyword **from** to the first **end**.

The Initialization clause (**from**...) introduces the loop initialization, here a call to procedure *child_start*. The Loop_body (**loop**...) introduces the instruction to be iterated, here a call to *child_forth*; this will be executed zero or more times, after the Initialization, until the Exit condition, introduced in the **until**... clause, is satisfied. The Invariant clause introduces an assertion, describing a property that must be satisfied by the initialization and maintained by every execution of the loop body if the exit condition is not satisfied. The Variant clause introduces an integer expression which must be non-negative after the initialization and will decrease whenever the body is executed, but will remain non-negative; these properties of the variant ensure that the loop terminates.

Here is the general form of the Loop construct.

Loop	≜	Initialization
		[Invariant]
		[Variant]
		Loop_body
		end

The following components are involved:

Initialization	≜	**from** Compound
Loop_body	≜	Exit **loop** Compound
Exit	≜	**until** Boolean_expression

← Invariant *and* Variant
were studied in 9.14.

The Initialization (**from** clause) is required. If no specific initialization is desired, the corresponding Compound may be absent, as in

```
    from
    until
        printer.ready
    loop
        printer.output_job
    end
```

In general, however, the Initialization introduces a Compound of one or more instructions, as in this example from routine *duplicate* in class *FIXED_LIST* in the Data Structure Library:

```
from
    mark;
    Result.start
until
    Result.off
loop
    Result.put (item);
    forth;
    Result.forth
end
```

The effect of a Loop is the effect of executing its Initialization followed by the effect of executing its Loop_body. The effect of executing an Initialization clause is the effect of executing its Compound. The effect of executing a Loop_body is to leave the state of the computation unchanged if the Boolean_expression of its Exit clause evaluates to false; otherwise, it is the effect of executing the Compound clause, followed (recursively) by the effect of executing the Loop_body again in the resulting state.

The optional Invariant and Variant parts have no effect on the execution of a correct loop; they describe correctness conditions. Their precise use was explained in the discussion of assertions and correctness. As a reminder:

← *See 9.14, starting on page 129, about the formal semantics of* Invariant *and* Variant *clauses in loops.*

- The Invariant must be ensured by the Initialization; and any execution of the Loop_body started in a state where the Invariant is satisfied, but the Exit condition is not, must produce a state that again satisfies the Invariant.

- The Initialization must produce a state where the Variant expression is non-negative; and any execution of the Loop_body started in a state where the Variant has a non-negative value v and the Exit condition is not satisfied must produce a state in which the Variant is still non-negative, but its new value is less than v. Since the Variant is an integer expression, this guarantees termination.

14.8 The Debug instruction

The Debug instruction serves to request the conditional execution of a certain sequence of operations, depending on a compilation option.

A Debug instruction such as

```
debug
    instruction₁;
    ...
    instructionₙ;
end
```

will be ignored at execution time if the *debug* option is off; if the option is on, the execution of the Debug is the execution of all the *instruction$_i$*, in sequence, as with a Compound.

The supporting Eiffel environment must make it possible for developers to turn the *debug* option on or off, with "off" being the default. The option may apply to an entire system, to all the classes of a cluster, or to an individual class.

A variant of the instruction uses a Manifest_string as Debug_key. For example:

> **debug** (*"GRAPHICS_DEBUG"*)
>   *instruction*$_1$;
>   ...
>   *instruction*$_n$;
> **end**

This means that developers must be able to turn *debug* on specifically for a certain Debug_key, as well as generally for all possible keys.

Here is the syntax of the instruction:

Debug	$\triangleq$	**debug** [Debug_keys] Compound **end**
Debug_keys	$\triangleq$	"(" Debug_key_list ")"
Debug_key_list	$\triangleq$	{Debug_key "," ...}
Debug_key	$\triangleq$	Manifest_string

The effect of a Debug instruction depends on the mode that has been chosen for the enclosing class:

- If the *debug* option is on generally, or if the instruction includes a Debug_key_list and the option is on for at least one Debug_key in the list, the effect of the Debug instruction is the same as that of its Compound.

- Otherwise the effect is that of a Null instruction.

Letter case is not significant for a Debug_key: *"GRAPHICS_DEBUG"* is the same as *"graphics_debug"*.

15

Exceptions

15.1 Overview

During the execution of an Eiffel system, various abnormal events may occur. A hardware or operating system component may be unable to do its job; an arithmetic operation may result in overflow; an improperly written software element may produce an unacceptable outcome.

Such events will usually trigger a signal, or exception, which interrupts the normal flow of execution. If the system's text does not include any provision for the exception, execution will terminate. The system may, however, be programmed so as to *handle* exceptions, which means that it will respond by executing specified actions and, if possible, resuming execution after correcting the cause of the exception.

This chapter presents the exception mechanism by explaining what conditions lead to exceptions, and how systems can be written so as to handle exceptions.

It also introduces the *EXCEPTIONS* Kernel Library class, which provides tools for fine-tuning the exception mechanism.

When using the exception facility, remember to take its name literally. The constructs discussed in this chapter – Rescue clause, Retry instruction – are not control structures on a par with those of the previous chapter; they should be reserved for those unexpected cases which cannot be detected a priori. Complex algorithmic structures, if any, should appear in Routine_body parts, not in exception handlers. If your system has many sophisticated exception handling clauses, it is probably misusing the mechanism.

15.2 What is an exception?

DEFINITION: Under certain circumstances, the execution of a construct (such as an   *"Failure" is in fact the*
Failure instruction) may be unable to terminate as you normally expect it to. The   *more primitive notion; an*
execution is then said to result in a **failure**.   *exception is the*
                                                                                        consequence of a failure.

Exception   If a routine executes a component and that component fails, this will prevent
the routine's execution from proceeding as planned; such an event is called an
exception.

The following categories of exception may occur (be **triggered**) during the
execution of a routine:

1 • Assertion violation (in an assertion monitoring mode).   ← *See chapter 9 about*
                                                                                       assertions.

2 • Failure of a called routine.   → *See below about routine*
                                                                                       failure.

3 • Using an entity with a void value for an operation which requires an object;   → *See 21.8, page 345, on*
   examples include feature call, for which the target must be non-void, or   *Call with a void target, and*
   assignment to an entity of expanded type, for which the source must be   *the table on page 317 on*
   non-void.   *assigning void to an*
                                                                                       expanded. Chapter 18
4 • Impossible operation, such as a Creation instruction attempted when not   *covers Creation.*
   enough memory is available, or an arithmetic operation which would cause
   an overflow or underflow in the computer's number system.

5 • Interruption signal sent by the machine for example after a user has hit the   ← *"Machine" means*
   "break" key or the window of the current process has been resized. Events   *hardware combined with*
   which conceptually fall under category 1, such as an attempt to read from a   *operating system. See 2.10,*
   non-existent process, are often caught first by the machine in this way.   *page 29.*

6 • An exception raised by the software itself, through the facilities offered in   → *The software may raise*
   the Kernel Library class *EXCEPTIONS*, as explained below.   *an exception through*
                                                                                       procedure 'raise' in class
These categories distinguish the manifestation of the exception, not its real   *EXCEPTIONS. See 15.11,*
cause. Causes of exceptions essentially boil down to two possibilities: an error   *page 258 below.*
(a bug) in the software, or the inability of the underlying machine to carry out a
certain operation. Assertion violations are a clear example of the first cause – a
correct program always satisfies its assertions at run time – whereas running out
of memory for a Creation is an example of the second.

In a way, the second of these types of cause is a variant of the first: if systems   → *In an environment*
never executed an operation without checking first that it is feasible, then a   *supporting virtual memory*
correct system would never run into an exception. But it would be hardly   *and a garbage collector,*
practical to have every Creation instruction preceded by a check for available   *unsuccessful Creation only*
space, or every addition preceded by a check that the result will fit in the   *occurs when the system has*
machine's number system – assuming such checks were possible.   *exhausted virtual memory*
                                                                                       and the collector is unable
In cases like these, a priori checking is expensive, and only a small percentage   *to reclaim any space. See*
of executions are likely not to pass the checks. These are the cases requiring   *20.16, page 334.*
exceptions – ways to detect an abnormal situation, and possibly recover from it,
after it has occurred.

15.3 Exception handling policy

What can happen after an exception? In other words, what can we do when the unexpected occurs?

To answer this question properly, we must remember that a routine or other software component is not just the description of some computation. What transcends that particular computation is the goal that it is meant to achieve – what in the Eiffel theory is called the **contract**. The component provides just one way to achieve the contract; often, other implementations are possible. For simple components the contract is defined by the language: for example the contract of a Creation instruction is to create an object, initialize its fields and attach it to an entity. For more complex components you may express the contract through assertions: for example, a routine's contract may be defined by a precondition, a postcondition, and the class invariant. Even if there are no explicit assertions, the contract implicitly exists, perhaps expressed informally by the routine's Header_comment.

See "Object-Oriented Software Construction" and "Design by Contract" for more in-depth discussions of exception handling principles. References in appendix C.

If we want to remain in control of what our software does, we must concentrate on the notion of contract to define possible responses to an exception. The contract of a software component defines the observable aspects of its behavior, those which its clients expect. Any exception handling policy must be compatible with that expectation.

An exception is the occurrence of an event which prevents a component from fulfilling the current execution of its contract. An unacceptable reaction would be to terminate the component's execution and to return silently to the client, which would then proceed on the wrong assumption that everything is normal. Since things are *not* normal – the client's expectations were not fulfilled – such a policy would almost inevitably lead to disaster in the client's execution.

What then is an acceptable reaction? Depending on the context, only three possibilities make sense:

E1 • A favorable albeit unlikely case is one in which the exception was in fact not justified. For example, an operating system signal (such as window resizing) caused an exception, but that exception did not reflect any problem that would prevent the execution from proceeding normally, perhaps after taking some cleanup actions. This is called the **false alarm**.

E2 • When writing the component, you may have anticipated the possibility of an exception, and provided for an alternative way to fulfil the contract. Then the execution will try that alternative. In other words, you have lost a battle, but have not lost the war yet. This case is called **resumption**.

E3 • If you have indeed lost the war, in other words if you have no way of fulfilling the contract, then you should surrender but with honors: try to return the objects involved into an acceptable state, and signal your failure to the client. This is called **organized panic**.

The language mechanism described below – Rescue clauses and Retry instructions – directly supports resumption and organized panic. The rather infrequent case of false alarm is handled through features of the Kernel Library class *EXCEPTIONS*.

These mechanisms are defined at the routine level. For components at a lower level, such as an instruction or a call, you have no language mechanism to specify potential recovery. This means that for an unsuccessful attempt at executing such a component (for example an attempt at object creation when there is not enough memory, or at feature call on a void target) only policy E3 is possible: the component's execution will fail immediately.

→ *See page 349 for a precise definition of the "current routine".*

DEFINITION:
Recipient

What happens next? Any execution of a software component is part of the execution of a call to a certain routine, known as the *current routine*. When the component's execution fails, this will trigger an exception in the current routine, which becomes the **recipient** of the exception. Depending on how the software has been written, the exception will be handled through one of the three techniques listed above.

← *In the case of an assertion violation, the rule for determining the recipient appears on page 134.*

For the rest of this chapter, then, the unit of discourse is the routine. Any exception has a recipient, which is a routine. By writing an appropriate Rescue clause, you may specify the routine's response as resumption or organized panic; through the appropriate calls to library features, you may in some cases proceed with the routine's execution after a false alarm.

The next sections explain how to specify one of these three possibilities as your choice for exception handling.

15.4 Rescue clauses and organized panic

The construct which specifies a routine's response to exceptions that may occur during an execution of the routine is the Rescue clause.

This is an optional part of a Routine declaration, introduced by the keyword **rescue**.

Here is a sketch of a routine with a Rescue clause:

```
attempt_transaction (arg: CONTEXT) is
        -- Try transaction with arg; if impossible,
        -- reset current object
    require
        ...
    do
        ...
    ensure
        ...
    rescue
        reset (arg)
    end -- attemp_transaction
```

Any exception triggered during the execution of the Routine_body (**do**... clause) will cause execution of the Rescue clause. Here this clause calls procedure *reset*, meant to restore the current object to a stable state; such a state should satisfy the class invariant.

Termination of the Rescue clause also terminates the routine execution; in this case, however, as opposed to what would happen if the **do**.. clause was executed to the end with no exception, the call to *attempt_transaction* will fail. This is indeed the only way for a routine call to fail: being the recipient of an exception and executing its Rescue clause to the end, not ending with a Retry instruction (described below).

In other words, the routine illustrates the policy defined above as organized panic – put back the object in an acceptable state (satisfying the invariant) and terminate, notifying your caller, if any, of the failure. The technique used for this notification is to trigger a new exception, with the caller as recipient.

As noted, organized panic should restore the invariant. The formal version of this requirement, given below as part of the definition of exception correctness, is that any branch of a Rescue clause not terminating with a Retry should yield a state satisfying the invariant, independently of the state in which it is triggered.

As you may remember from the definition of class consistency, this requirement of ensuring the invariant also applies in another context: creation procedures of a class. This suggests that it is sometimes possible to write a Rescue clause as a call to a creation procedure, which will reset the object to a state which it could have reached just after creation. Of course, other situations may require more specific Rescue clauses, taking into account the routine that failed and the context of the failure.

← Class consistency is defined on page 128.

15.5 The default Rescue

In most systems, the vast majority of routines will not have an explicit Rescue clause. What happens if an exception is triggered during the execution of such a routine?

The convention a routine of a class *C* is considered, if it has no explicit Rescue clause, to have an implicit Rescue of the form

> **rescue**
>   *def_resc*

where *def_resc* is the version of *default_rescue* in the enclosing class. Procedure *default_rescue* is introduced in the universal class *ANY*, where it is defined so as to have no effect:

> *default_rescue* **is**
>   **do**
>   **end** *-- default_rescue*

On ANY, see 6.12, page 85, and chapter 27. The "version" of a routine in a descendant of its class of origin is the result of any redefinition and renaming that may have occurred along the inheritance path; see 11.12, page 189.

Any developer-defined class, which is automatically a descendant of *ANY*, may redefine this routine to serve in case of organized panic. The redefined version will be called by any routine of the class which does not have a specific Rescue clause. Like any other routine, the redefined version is passed on to every heir, which will use it as default Rescue clause unless there is a new redefinition in the heir.

The reason for using the name *def_resc* rather than *default_rescue* in expressing the above equivalence is that in the process of inheriting from *ANY*, directly or indirectly, classes may rename features. For clarity, however, it is recommended to keep the original name *default_rescue*.

If, following the possibility suggested above, you use a creation procedure as default Rescue, you may rely on the following scheme, where *default_rescue* and the creation procedure are declared as synonym features:

← *Synonyms were discussed in 5.16, page 71. Recall that to redefine a feature from ANY you must explicitly list ANY as parent in the* Inheritance *clause; see the end of 6.12.*

---

class *C* **creation**

   make, ... other creation procedures if any ...

inherit

   ANY
      redefine *default_rescue* **end**

   ...

feature

   make, *default_rescue* **is**
      -- No precondition
      do
         ... Appropriate implementation;
         ... must ensure the invariant.
      end; -- *make*, *default_rescue*

   ... Other features ...

end -- class *C*

It is also possible to undefine 'default_rescue' and rename it as 'make'. This, however, would lose the original name.

With this scheme, since *default_rescue* has no argument, there must also be no argument for the creation procedure chosen as synonym, here *make*.

The *default_rescue* convention explains what happens if a routine such as *attempt_transaction* above fails and its caller had no explicit Rescue. The caller will simply execute its version of *default_rescue* – which means doing nothing at all if it still has the original version inherited from *ANY*. Then it will fail and trigger an exception in its client, which will itself be faced with the same situation. The effect of executing this Rescue chain all the way to the original root call will be described below.

← *'attempt_transaction' was on page 250.*

15.6 Retry instructions and resumption

Sometimes you can do better than just conceding defeat and cutting your losses. This is where the Retry instruction is useful.

This instruction, which supports the resumption policy, may only appear in a Rescue clause. It has a very simple form, being just the keyword

---

retry

The effect of a Retry is to execute again the body of the routine. A Rescue clause which executes a Retry escapes failure – perhaps only temporarily, of course, since the body may again cause an exception.

Here is a general scheme that covers many uses of Retry. To solve a problem, you normally use method 1; if that method does not work, however, it may trigger an exception, and method 2 may yield the desired result.

```
try_once_or_twice is
        -- Solve problem using method 1 or, if unsuccessful, method 2
    local
        already_tried: BOOLEAN
    do
        if not already_tried then
            method_1
        else
            method_2
        end
    rescue
        if not already_tried then
            already_tried := true;
            retry
        end
    end -- try_once_or_twice
```

This example relies on the default initialization rules for local entities: *already_tried*, being of type *BOOLEAN*, is initialized to **false** on routine entry. This initialization is not repeated if the rescue block executes a Retry.

→ *Local entity initialization is specified in the discussion of call semantics, 21.14, starting on page 352.*

If *method_2* triggers an exception, that is to say if both methods have failed, the Rescue clause will execute an empty Compound (since the Conditional has no Else_part). So the routine execution will fail, triggering an exception in the caller. This is because *try_once_or_twice* had two methods to reach a goal, and neither succeeded.

You may of course prefer a routine that behaves less dramatically when it cannot produce a result. Rather than sending an exception to the caller, it will just record the result in a boolean attribute *impossible* of the enclosing class:

```
try_and_record is
        -- Attempt to solve problem using method 1 or,
        -- if unsuccessful, method 2. Set impossible to true
        -- if neither method succeeded, false otherwise.
    local
        already_tried: BOOLEAN
    do
        if not already_tried then
            method_1
        elseif not impossible then
            method_2
        end
    rescue
        if already_tried then
            impossible := true
        end;
        already_tried := true;
        retry
    end -- try_and_record
```

This routine will never fail, since its Rescue clause always terminates with a Retry. This is not a paradox: the contract here is simply broader. As opposed to the contract for *try_once_or_twice*, it does not require the routine to solve the problem, but, more tolerantly, either to solve the problem (and set attribute *impossible* to true) or to set *impossible* to false if it is unable to solve the problem. Clearly, it is always possible to satisfy such a requirement; so there is no cause for failure.

You may easily generalize either version – *try_once_or_twice*, which may fail, and *try_and_record*, which never fails but sets a boolean success indicator – to try more than two alternative methods: just replace *already_tried* by a local entity *attempts* of type *INTEGER*, which will be initialized to zero.

As a special case, the resumption may in some situations simply amount to trying the same policy again. This applies when the exception was caused by an intermittent malfunction in external device, for example a busy communication line, or by an erroneous human input; by trying the line again, or outputting an error message asking the user to correct his input, you may hope to succeed. Here is the general scheme:

```
try_repeatedly_and_record is
        -- Attempt to solve problem in at most Maximum trials.
    local
        attempts: INTEGER
    do
        if attempts <= Maximum then
            attempt_to_solve
        else
            impossible := true
        end
    rescue
        attempts := attempts + 1;
        ... Other corrective actions, such as outputting an error message ...
        retry
    end -- try_repeatedly_and_record
```

Maximum is a constant attribute with a positive value. The integer attribute *attempts* will be initialized to zero on routine entry.

The strategy used by *try_repeatedly_and_record* derives from *try_and_record* rather than *try_once_or_more*: if unable to perform its duty, it does not fail but simply sets attribute *impossible* to true. Adapting to the other style, which causes the routine to fail and trigger an exception in its caller, is easy and is left as an exercise.

15.7 System failure and the exception history table

In the organized panic case, a failed execution of a routine *r* triggers an exception in the caller. But what if there is no caller?

This can occur only if the execution that fails is the "original call": the execution of the root's creation procedure which started system execution. Remember that executing a system means creating an instance of its root class and applying a creation procedure to that instance. The creation procedure usually calls other routines, which themselves execute further calls. This means that any routine execution except the original call has a caller.

← The semantics of system execution was defined on page 35.

A failure of the original call produces a **system failure**. Execution of the system terminates, producing an appropriate diagnostic about the system's inability to fulfil its task.

This rule does not just apply to exceptions triggered directly by the original call – an infrequent case since root creation procedures tend in practice to perform only simple actions before creating other objects or calling other routines. The more interesting case is the failure of a routine execution deep down in the call sequence, for which all direct and indirect callers eventually fail because they are not able to apply resumption. Then the failure bubbles up the call chain until it finally causes system failure.

This scenario in fact applies to the simplest case, in which no routine of the system has a Rescue clause, and no class redefines *default_rescue*: then any exception occurring during execution will propagate to the root's creation procedure, and result in a system failure.

What happens after a system failure? As noted, the tool that handles execution (the run-time system) should produce a diagnostic. The exact form of that diagnostic is not part of the language specification. Here is the format used in one particular implementation. After a system failure, that implementation prints an error message and an **exception history table** such as the following:

This is the format used by ISE's implementation. Others may use different conventions.

An exception history table

Object	Class	Routine	Nature of exception	Effect
2FB44	INTERFACE	m_creation	Feature "quasi_inverse": Called on void reference.	Retry
2F188	MATH	quasi_inverse (from BASIC_MATH)	"positive_or_null": Precondition violated.	Fail
2F188	MATH	raise (from EXCEPTIONS)	"Negative_value": Developer exception.	Fail
2F188	MATH	filter	"Negative_value": Developer exception.	Retry
2F32	MATH	new_matrix (from BASIC_MATH)	"enough_memory": Check violated.	Fail
2FB44	INTERFACE	set	Routine failure	Fail

For an exception whose recipient was a routine *r*, during a call on an object OBJ, the first column identifies OBJ (through an internal object identifier), the second column identifies the generating class of OBJ (the base class of its type), and the "Routine" column identifies r. The next column indicates the nature of the exception; for developer-defined exceptions and assertion violations this includes a tag (the Assertion_tag for assertions clauses). The last column indicates the effect of the exception: resumption (appearing as *Retry*) or organized panic (appearing as *Fail*).

The table contains not just a trace of the calls that led to the final failure but also the entire history of recent exceptions. Some exceptions may have been caught and handled through resumption, only to lead to further exceptions. This is why the exception history is divided into periods, each terminated by a Retry. The table shows these periods separated by a double line; exceptions appear in the order in which they occurred, which is the reverse of the order of the calls.

The case illustrated on the table, which resulted from a specially contrived system meant to illustrate the various possibilities – involving exceptions of many kinds, and resumptions that trigger new exceptions – is unusual. Exception handling in well-written systems should remain simple, and as much effort as possible should go into avoiding exceptions rather than handling them a posteriori. Exception handling does play a crucial role, however, for those hard to prevent cases which, in the absence of an appropriate exception mechanism, would leave defenseless the system, its users and its developers.

15.8 Syntax and validity of the exception constructs

It is time now to look at the precise properties of the two constructs associated with exceptions: Rescue clauses of routines and Retry instructions.

The grammar is straightforward:

Rescue	≜	**rescue** Compound
Retry	≜	**retry**

A Rescue clause is part of a Routine. A Retry instruction is one of the choices for the Instruction construct.

← *See page 112 for the syntax of* Routine *and page 256 for the syntax of* Instruction.

A constraint applies to Rescue clauses:

VXRC

> It is valid for a Routine to include a Rescue clause if and only if its Routine_body is of the Internal form.

An Internal body is one which begins with either **do** or **once**. The other possibilities are Deferred, for which it would be improper to define an exception handler since the body does not specify an algorithm, and an External body, where the algorithm is specified outside of the Eiffel system, which then lacks the information it would need to handle exceptions.

← *The various kinds of* Routine_body *are discussed in 8.6, page 113.*

The constraint on Retry instructions has already been mentioned:

VXRT

> A Retry instruction is valid if and only if it appears in a Rescue clause.

Because this constraint requires the Retry to appear physically within the Rescue clause, it is not possible for a Rescue to call a procedure containing a Retry. This means in particular that a redefined version of *default_rescue* may not contain a Retry. In other words, the default exception processing may not lead to resumption. The reason for this rule is one of simplicity and readability: outside of the Rescue clause to which it applies directly, a Retry would be little more informative than an arbitrary branch instruction.

15.9 Semantics of exception handling

To define the semantics of exception handling, it is convenient to consider that every routine has an implicit or explicit "rescue block":

DEFINITION:
Rescue
Block

> Any Internal routine *r* of a class *C* has a **rescue block** *rb*, which is a Compound defined as follows:
>
> 1 • If *r* has a Rescue clause, *rb* is the Compound contained in that clause.
>
> 2 • If *r* has no Rescue clause, *rb* is a Compound made of a single instruction: a call to the version of *default_rescue* in *C*.

SEMANTICS

An exception triggered during an execution of a routine *r* leads, if it is neither ignored nor continued, to the following sequence of events.

1 • Some or all of the remaining instructions are not executed.

2 • The rescue block of the routine is executed.

3 • If the rescue block executes a Retry, the body of the routine is executed again. This terminates processing of the current exception. Any new triggering of an exception is a new occurrence, which will (recursively) be handled according to the present semantics.

4 • If the rescue block is executed to the end without executing a Retry, this terminates the processing of the current exception and the current execution of *r*, causing a **failure** of that execution. If there is a calling routine, this failure triggers an exception in the calling routine, which will be handled (recursively) according to the same semantics. If there is no calling routine, *r* is the root's creation procedure; its execution will terminate.

After failure and termination, the run-time should normally produce a diagnostic similar to the exception history table of page 255.

DEFINITION:
Success

The definition mentions that it applies only to a routine which is neither ignored nor continued. This corresponds to two facilities provided through features of the Kernel Library class *EXCEPTIONS*, studied below and implementing the false alarm response:

← False alarm was response E1 introduced on page 249 as part of the exception handling policy discussed in 15.3.

• You may specify that a certain type exception must be altogether ignored.

• You may specify that a certain type of exception must cause execution of a designated procedure and then continuation.

In step 3, the Retry will only re-execute the Routine_body of *r*; it does not repeat argument passing and local entity initialization. This may be used to take a different path on a new attempt.

15.10 Exception correctness

The role of Rescue clauses is to cope with unexpected events. Although in a well-designed system Rescue clauses will only be executed in rare, special conditions, they still have an obligation to maintain the consistency of objects.

In particular, a routine failure should leave the current object (corresponding to the target of the latest call) in a consistent state, satisfying the invariant, so as not to hamper further attempts to use the object if another routine is able, through resumption, to recover from the failure. Also, a Retry instruction, which will restart the Routine_body, should re-establish the routine's precondition, if any, since the precondition is required for the Routine_body to operate properly.

These two requirements yield the notion of **exception correctness**, one of the conditions which make up class correctness. As you may recall, a class is correct if it is consistent (every Routine_body, started in a state satisfying the precondition and the invariant, terminates in a state satisfying the postcondition and the invariant), loop-correct (loops maintain their invariant and every iteration decreases the variant), check-correct (the conditions of Check instructions are satisfied) and exception correct, a notion which was sketched in the general discussion of correctness but may now be made more precise.

← Chapter 9 addressed correctness, with the full definition on page 132, as part of 9.16.

DEFINITION: Exception-Correct

A routine r of a class C is **exception-correct** if and only if, for every branch b of its rescue block:

1 • If b ends with a Retry:

$$\{\textbf{true}\}\ b\ \{INV_C\ \wedge\ pre_r\}$$

2 • If b does not end with a Retry:

$$\{\textbf{true}\}\ b\ \{INV_C\}$$

The notation $\{P\}\ A\ \{Q\}$, expressing that A, when started in a state satisfying P, will terminate in a state satisfying Q, was introduced in 9.12, page 127. The symbol $\wedge$ denotes boolean conjunction. These are mathematical notations, not Eiffel.

Here INV_C is the class invariant and pre_r is the precondition of r.

The definition involves the rescue block of a routine. Remember that the rescue block always exists: if the routine has a Rescue clause, then its Compound is the rescue block; otherwise the rescue block is the local version of *ANY*'s procedure *default_rescue*.

As with other correctness conditions, exception correctness should ideally be provable automatically, but in practice you will most likely have to ascertain it through informal means.

15.11 Fine-tuning the mechanism

In some cases it is useful to have finer control over the handling of exceptions. Features from the Kernel Library class *EXCEPTIONS* address this need. These features will be available to any descendant of *EXCEPTIONS*: to use them in a class C which is not already a descendant, just add a Parent part for *EXCEPTIONS* to the Inheritance clause of C.

Let us take a look at the facilities offered. A later chapter gives the full short-flat form of *EXCEPTIONS*.

→ See chapter 29 about the details of class EXCEPTIONS.

First, *EXCEPTIONS* introduces an integer code for every possible type of exception. Examples include

> *Precondition*   (code for a violated precondition)
> *Routine_failure*
> *Incorrect_inspect_value*
> *Void_call_target*
> *No_more_memory*

The integer-valued feature *exception* is then guaranteed, after an exception occurs, to have the value of the code for that exception. This makes it possible to write Rescue clauses such as

> **rescue**
>   **if** *exception = No_more_memory* **then**
>   ... Specific treatment ...
>   **else**
>   *default_rescue*
>   **end**

The call to *default_rescue* in the Else_part is not required, of course, but as a general guideline if you do need to treat certain categories of exception in a special way then such treatment should remain simple and apply to a small number of categories. You should handle the remaining categories through *default_rescue* or another general-purpose mechanism.

Another integer-valued feature, *original_exception*, complements the information given by *exception*. It yields the "real" cause of an exception, disregarding any resulting failures of intermediate routines. Consider for an example a Postcondition violation which causes a routine *t* to fail, triggering an exception whose recipient is *t*'s caller, *s*; the Rescue clause of *s*, if any, does not execute a Retry, so *s* in turn fails, sending an exception to its own caller, *r*. If the Rescue clause of *r* looks at *exception* to determine what happened, it will find as exception code the value of *Routine_failure*. This gives the immediate cause of *r*'s exception (the failure of *s*) but not the real source of the problem – *t*'s Postcondition violation. Feature *original_exception* provides more precise information in such cases. Its value is the code of the oldest exception not handled by a Retry. In the example, this will be the value of *Precondition*.

Features which provide further information about the original exception include *routine_name* (name of the original recipient) and *tag_name* (tag of the violated Assertion_clause, for an assertion violation).

Class *EXCEPTION* also provides a way to raise an exception on purpose. This is called a **developer exception** and is triggered by the procedure call

> *raise (code, name)*

whose arguments are an exception code *code*, which must be a negative integer (non-negative values are reserved for predefined exceptions), and a string *name* describing the nature of the exception. To obtain that string when handling the exception, use feature *developer_exception_name*.

To know the general category of an exception given of a given *code* (usually *exception* or *original_exception*), use one of the boolean functions

> *is_assertion_violation* (*code*)
> *is_developer_exception* (*code*)
> *is_signal* (*code*)

To prescribe a **false alarm** response you may use one of the procedure calls

> *ignore* (*code*)
>
> *continue* (*code*)

A call to *ignore* simply prescribes that later occurrences of the event with the given *code* must not cause an exception.

After a call to *continue* with *code* as argument, any occurrence of the corresponding signal will cause execution of the appropriate version of procedure *continue_action*, followed by continuation of the Routine_body which was the signal's recipient. Procedure *continue_action* is introduced in class *EXCEPTIONS* with an empty body, but (like *default_rescue*) may be redefined in any class to yield specific behavior. The procedure has an integer argument *code* to which the exception handling mechanism, when calling *continue_action* as a response to an exception for which "continue" status has been prescribed, will attach the code of that exception.

The false alarm policy would not make sense for exceptions which cause irrecoverable damage to the current routine execution. For example, an assertion violation indicates a breach of some consistency condition, making it impossible to continue normal execution. For this reason, *continue* has the precondition *is_signal* (*code*). No such precondition has been imposed on *ignore* in deference to the potential needs of developers of low-level systems software; except in very special cases, however, *ignore* must only be applied to signals.

To restore the default behavior after a call to *ignore* or *continue*, use the call

> *catch* (*code*)

To know the behavior specified for *code*, use

> *status* (*code*)

whose result, an integer, is given by one of the Unique constants *Caught* (the default), *Continued* and *Ignored*.

As a final comment, it is useful to note once again that the best exception handling is simple and modest. The facilities of class *EXCEPTIONS* are there to give you full access to the context of exceptions if you need it; remember, however, that if you are trying to do something complicated in a Rescue clause, you are probably misusing the mechanism.

Non-trivial algorithms belong in the Routine_body; the Rescue clause is there to recover in a simple and non-committing way from abnormal situations which it was absolutely impossible to avoid.

16

Attributes

16.1 Overview

Attributes are one of the two kinds of feature.

← *The other kind is routines, studied in chapter 8.*

When, in the declaration of a class, you introduce an attribute of a certain type, you specify that, for every instance of the class that may exist at execution time, there will be an associated value of that type.

There are two kinds of attribute: **variable** and **constant**. The difference affects what may happen at run time to the corresponding attribute values: for a variable attribute, it is possible to write routines that will change the attribute values associated with particular instances; for a constant attribute, the value is the same for every instance, and it cannot be changed at run time.

This chapter introduces the two kinds of attribute and discusses their properties.

16.2 Graphical representation

In graphical system representations, you may mark a feature that you know is a variable attribute by putting its name in a box.

The figure on the next page illustrates this convention for attributes *first* and *first_element* in the informal representation of features for class *LINKED_LIST* from the Data Structure Library. (This is a partial representation of the class.)

← *The "informal" variant is one of the two possible representations for features of a class; see page 60.*

As illustrated by this example, attributes boxed in adjacent rectangles suggest the form of instances of the class, each rectangle representing a field.

Showing attributes separately

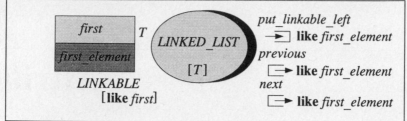

Not boxing a feature does not mean that it is not a attribute. In some cases, you may choose to preserve the uncertainty about whether a particular feature is an attribute or a routine. Then the standard representation for features, unboxed, is appropriate. In the example illustrated above, *previous* and *next* may be attributes just as well as they may be functions without arguments.

→ *See the "principle of uniform access", 21.5, page 342.*

16.3 Variable attributes

Declaring a variable attribute in a class prescribes that every instance of the class should contain a field of the corresponding type. This field can be set to variable values through the instructions executed by the routines of the class.

The following are examples of variable attribute declarations:

> *n*: INTEGER;
> *a, b, c*: WINDOW

The first introduces a single attribute *n* of type *INTEGER*. The second (equivalent, because of the Multiple Declaration rule, to three separate declarations) introduces three attributes, all of type *WINDOW*.

← *The Multiple Declaration rule was given in chapter 5.*

If these declarations appear in the Features clause of a class *C*, all instances of *C* will have associated values of the corresponding types.

More generally, as you may remember, a feature declaration is a variable attribute declaration if it satisfies the following conditions:

← *The general form of feature declarations was given in 5.11, beginning on page 64.*

• There is no Formal_arguments part.
• There is a Type_mark part.
• There is no Constant_or_routine part.

16.4 Constant attributes

Declaring a constant attribute in a class prescribes that a certain value be associated with every instance of the class. The value is the same for every instance; as a consequence, it does not need to be physically stored with the instance.

→ *The construct Constant_attribute is introduced in 23.13, page 386, as part of the discussion of expressions.*

Because you must specify the value together with the attribute, the type of a constant attribute may only be one of the types for which the language offers a lexical mechanism for denoting values explicitly. The following types satisfy this property:

- *BOOLEAN*, with values written **true** and **false**.

- *CHARACTER*, with values written as characters in single quotes, such as *'A'*.

- *INTEGER*, with values written using decimal digits possibly preceded by a sign, such as *−889*.

- *REAL*, with values such as *−889.72*.

- *DOUBLE*, with values written in the same way as for *REAL*.

- Bit_type, with values consisting of sequences of zeros and ones followed by the letter B, such as 100100B.

- *STRING*, with values made of strings in double quotes such as *"A SEQUENCE OF $CHARACTERS#"*.

→ *All these types except STRING and* Bit_type *are called basic types. See 12.13, page 209.*

All these examples use "manifest" constants; see below.

For types other than these, you may obtain an effect similar to that of constants by using a once function. For example, assuming a class

← *See 21.11, page 347, about the effect of calling a once function.*

```
class COMPLEX creation
    cartesian, ...
feature
    x, y: REAL

    cartesian (a, b: REAL) is
            -- Initialize to real part a, imaginary part b
        do
            x := a; y := b
        end; -- cartesian
    ...
end -- class COMPLEX
```

you may, in another class, define the once function

```
i: COMPLEX is
        -- Complex number of real part 0, imaginary part 1
    once
        !! Result.cartesian (0, 1)
    end -- i
```

which creates a *COMPLEX* object on its first call; this call and any subsequent one return a reference to that object.

Returning to true constant attributes: the declaration of a constant attribute must determine the attribute's value. You may specify such a constant value in either of two ways:

- If you want to choose the value yourself, you will use a **manifest** constant.

- You may also let language processing tools select an appropriate value. This is the policy for **unique** values.

The next sections examine these two cases.

16.5 Constant attributes with manifest values

A Manifest_constant is a constant given by its explicit value. It may be a Boolean_constant, Character_constant, Integer_constant, Real_constant or Manifest_string.

→ Chapter 25 describes the precise form of manifest constants.

Here are some constant attribute declarations using Manifest_constant values:

There is no lexical difference between a real constant and a double constant.

> *Terminal_count*: INTEGER **is** *247*;
> *Cross*: CHARACTER **is** *'X'*;
> *No*: BOOLEAN **is false**;
> *Height*: REAL **is** *1.78*;
> *Message*: STRING **is** *"No such file"*

More generally, a feature declaration is a constant attribute declaration if it satisfies the following conditions:

← See "How to recognize features", 5.11, page 64.

- There is no Formal_arguments part.
- There is a Type_mark part.
- There is a Constant_or_routine part, which is either a Manifest_constant or a Unique.

An obvious validity constraint governs such declarations:

VQMC

> A declaration of a feature *f* introducing a manifest constant is valid if and only if the Manifest_constant *m* used in the declaration matches the type *T* declared for *f* in one of the following ways:
>
> - *m* is a Boolean_constant and *T* is BOOLEAN.
> - *m* is a Character_constant and *T* is CHARACTER.
> - *m* is an Integer_constant and *T* is INTEGER.
> - *m* is a Real_constant and *T* is REAL or DOUBLE.
> - *m* is a Manifest_string and *T* is STRING.
> - *m* is a Bit_constant and *T* is a Bit_type.

16.6 Unique attributes

Unique constants describe positive integer values chosen by the language processing tool (for example a compiler) rather than by the software developer.

Unique attributes are useful for sets of codes describing different variants of a certain phenomenon. You are guaranteed to get different values for all unique attributes declared in the same class, without having to choose – or know – these values.

You may for example use declarations of the following form:

> *Full_time, Part_time*: INTEGER **is unique**;
> *Blue, Red, Green, Yellow*: INTEGER **is unique**

Such features are constant attributes of type *INTEGER*. The difference with a Manifest_constant declaration is that here the constant values are chosen by the language processing tool; so you avoid the need to invent integer codes, as in

WARNING: Not necessary.

> *Blue*: *INTEGER* **is** *1*;
> *Red*: *INTEGER* **is** *2*;
> *Green*: *INTEGER* **is** *3*;
> *Yellow*: *INTEGER* **is** *4*

To discriminate between unique values, you may use a Multi_branch instruction. An example, assuming *n* is an expression of type *INTEGER*, is the instruction

← *The Multi_branch instruction was studied in 14.6, page 240.*

> **inspect**
>   *n*
> **when** *Blue* **then**
>   *some_action*
> **when** *Red, Green, Yellow* **then**
>   *other_action*
> **else**
>   *default_action*
> **end**

This will execute *some_action* if *n* has the value of *Blue*, *other_action* if it has any of the values *Red, Green, Yellow*, and *default_action* otherwise.

Unique values are guaranteed to be positive, and different for all unique attributes introduced in a given class. Furthermore, for unique attributes declared as part of the same Feature_declaration, such as *Blue, Red, Green, Yellow* above, the values are guaranteed to be consecutive; this means that you can safely use intervals in a Multi_branch instruction, and rewrite the above as

> **inspect**
>   *n*
> **when** *Blue* **then**
>   *some_action*
> **when** *Red* .. *Yellow* **then**
>   *other_action*
> **else**
>   *default_action*
> **end**

Here now are the precise rules. A unique attribute is an integer constant attribute whose value is simply expressed by the keyword **unique**:

> Unique   ≜   **unique**

VQUI

A declaration of a feature *f* introducing a Unique constant is valid if and only if the type *T* declared for *f* is *INTEGER*.

The effect is defined by a rule which provides the missing case of the Multiple Declaration rule:

← *As mentioned in the Multiple Declaration rule, page 71, this is the only case in which a multiple declaration has more properties than the corresponding sequence o individual declarations.*

Unique Declaration rule

The value of an attribute declared as unique is a positive integer. If two unique attributes are introduced in the same class, their values are different. Furthermore, unique attributes declared as part of the same Feature_declaration are guaranteed to have consecutive values, in the order given.

Because of this guarantee of consecutiveness, you may for example use the first and last elements of a list of unique attributes declared together to set the dimensions of an array, as in

A Unique declaration does not introduce an "enumerated type". Nothing binds the different attributes together; they are simply integer constants whose values are not chosen by the author of the class.

```
a: ARRAY [INTENSITY];
...
!! a.make (Blue, Yellow)
```

which declares and creates an array *a*, using the creation procedure *make* to set the bounds to *Blue* and *Yellow*. Then you know that the legal indices for *a* are *Blue, Red, Green* and *Yellow* as declared above.

Another example that relies on the consecutiveness of values is their use in an interval for a Multi_branch instruction, as in the branch **when** *Red .. Yellow* above.

Because the values of unique attributes are guaranteed to be positive, you can safely use a set of unique attributes to handle a number of specific cases, and zero or negative codes to handle other cases. For example, if *n* is an integer entity, a conditional instruction of the form

```
if n <= 0 then
    action
end
```

will not execute *action* if *n* has been assigned any one among the values of *Blue, Red, Green* and *Yellow*.

The only properties that you may expect of the values of unique attributes are those specified above: uniqueness of the values of all unique attributes introduced in a given class; all values positive; consecutive values for unique attributes declared as part of the same Feature_declaration. Any further properties are dependent on the implementation of unique values in a particular language processing tool, and you may not rely on them. In particular:

- A unique attribute introduced in a class may have the same value as some unique attribute inherited from a parent.

- Two unique attributes inherited from different parents may have the same value.

- You may not make any assumption on the values of unique attributes declared in separate Feature_declaration clauses, even if the declarations are in the same class and appear consecutively. For example, the above declaration of *Full_time* and *Part_time* was separate from that of *Blue, Red, Green, Yellow*; this means that, although the values of *Full_time* and *Part_time* will be consecutive, and so will be those of *Blue, Red, Green, Yellow*, you may not assume any connection between those two sets of values.

- The implementation may choose any positive values for unique attributes as long as they satisfy the above constraints. In particular, it does not have to start at 1.

Unique attributes and the Multi_branch instruction should only be used in cases of simple multi-value discriminations where the set of choices is frozen. As soon as there is any chance that the choices could change, using this mechanism would defeat the goals of extendibility and reusability, which are at the heart of the Eiffel method. For more advanced situations, you should rely on the dynamic binding of redefined routines, as explained in chapter 21.

← *See the methodological guidelines in 14.6, page 240.*

17

Objects, values and entities

17.1 Overview

The execution of an Eiffel system consists in creating, accessing and modifying *objects*.

This chapter discusses the structure of objects and explains the relation between these objects and the syntactical constructs which denote them in software texts: *expressions*.

At run time, an expression may take on various *values*; every value is either an object or a reference to an object.

Among expressions, a particular role is played by *entities*. An entity is a name in the software text, meant to become associated at run-time with one or more successive values, under the control of attachment and reattachment operations such as creation, assignment and argument passing.

The description of objects and their properties actually introduces the **dynamic model** of Eiffel software execution: the run-time structures of the data manipulated by an Eiffel system.

This chapter and the following one will illustrate the dynamic model through figures representing values and objects. These figures and the conventions only serve explanatory purposes. In particular:

- Although they may suggest the actual implementation techniques used to represent values and objects at run time, they should not be construed as *prescribing* any specific implementation.

- Do not confuse these conventions for representing *dynamic* (that is to say, run-time) properties of systems with the graphical conventions used in part B to represent classes, features, the client relation, inheritance, and other *static* properties of software texts.

17.2 Objects

During its execution, an Eiffel system will create one or more objects.

There are two kinds of object, **standard** and **special**:

DEFINITION:
Standard
Object,
Special
Object

- A standard object is the direct result of a Creation instruction or clone operation executed by the system.
- A special object is a sequence of values, all compatible with a given type. It may be a **string** or an **array**. In a string, the values are all characters; in an array, they are either all references, or all direct instances of a single type.

→ *See chapter 28 about special objects and classes STRING and ARRAY.*

Software texts do not manipulate special objects directly, but access and modify them through standard objects – instances of the Kernel Library classes *STRING* and *ARRAY*. The rest of this discussion concentrates on standard objects.

Generating
Class,
Generating
Type,
Generator

Every standard object is a **direct instance** of some type of the system, called the **generating type** for the object, or just "the type of the object" if there is no ambiguity. The base class of the generating type is called the object's **generating class**, or **generator** for short.

*An object may be an instance of many types: if it is an instance of TC, it is also an instance of any type TB to which TC conforms. But it is a **direct** instance of only one type, and so has just one generating type. See below.*

There are two kinds of standard object: basic and complex.

A basic object is an instance of a basic type or Bit_type, and is one of the following:

- A boolean object (there are exactly two such objects, representing the two boolean truth values true and false).
- A character.
- An integer.
- A real number in single precision floating-point representation.
- A real number in double precision floating-point representation.
- A feature address (for passing to a non-Eiffel routine).
- A bit sequence (sequence made of bit values, zero or one).

Function 'generator' from class ANY yields the name of an object's generator. See 27.4, page 433.

A complex object is made of zero or more values, called **fields**. All direct instances of a given type *T* are made of a fixed number of fields, each corresponding to one attribute of *T*'s base class.

→ *The notions of value and field are defined precisely in the next sections.*

To make the definition of complex objects more precise, it is necessary first to examine in detail the notions of value and instance.

17.3 Values

As introduced above, the fields of a complex object are values. This deserves closer examination.

Value,
Reference,
Void, Attached

A value is either an object or a *reference*.

A **reference** is a value which is either **void** or **attached**. If a reference is void, no further information is available on it. If it is attached, it gives access to an object; it is said to be attached to that object. The object will also be said to be attached to the reference.

A reference is attached to zero or one object. An object may be attached to zero, one or more references.

To know whether a reference is void or not, it suffices to compare it to the feature *Void* of the universal class *ANY*. The test

$$e = Void$$

→ *See chapter 27 about the features of class ANY. 'Void' may be implemented as an attribute or a once function.*

will return true if and only if the value of *e* is void. If the type of *e* is expanded, the result will always be false, since *e* will always be attached to an object.

References and other values

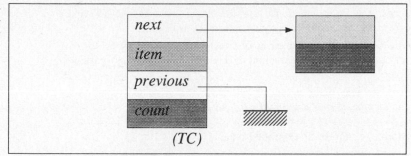

(TC)

The figure shows conventions for representing a reference (by an arrow if attached to an object, by a special symbol if void). Also, you may write the generating type of an object, here *TC*, in parentheses next to the object.

The four values on the figure are the fields of the object on the left. The first and the third value from the top, labeled *next* and *previous*, are references; *next* is attached to the object on the right, and *previous* is void. The figure does not give any information about the values in fields *item* and *count* or about the fields of the object on the right.

It is essential for the consistency of the Eiffel type system and dynamic model that **all values are objects or references to objects**. In particular, simple values such as integers, booleans or bit sequences are also objects.

With one exception, then, every data element ever manipulated by an Eiffel system is closely connected with an object: either it is that object, or it is a reference to it. The single exception is a void reference (such as the above *previous* field) which, by definition, is not attached to any object.

17.4 Instances of a class

This chapter defines the notions of instance and direct instance for the various categories of types.

DEFINITION: Instance of a Class

It is also sometimes convenient to talk about the instances (or direct instances) of a class. The extension is immediate: an instance of a class *C* is an instance of any type *T* based on *C*, and similarly for direct instances.

For non-generic classes the difference between *C* and *T* is irrelevant, but for a generic class you must remember that by itself the class does not fully determine the shape of its direct instances: you need a type, which requires providing a set of actual generic parameters.

17.5 Instances and direct instances

Every object is an instance of one or more types. More precisely:

DEFINITION:
Instance

> **Instances of a type**
>
> The instances of a type *TX* are the direct instances of any type conforming to *TX*.

In other words, the instances of *TX* are the direct instances of *TX* and, recursively, the instances of any other type conforming to *TX*.

Because this defines instances in terms of direct instances, it suffices, for the rest of this discussion, to define the notion of direct instance for every possible category of type.

Furthermore, we may avoid a special discussion for expanded types other than basic and bit types thanks to the following rule:

> **Direct instances of non-basic expanded types**
>
> Let *TX* be an expanded type which is neither one of the basic types (*BOOLEAN*, *CHARACTER*, *INTEGER*, *REAL*, *DOUBLE*, *POINTER*) nor a Bit_type. The direct instances of *TX* are the the direct instances of the base type of *TX*.

This means that the direct instances of a type of the form **expanded** *T* will be those of *T*. The remaining case, which will be covered below, is that of a Class_type based on an expanded class.

This advance work will enable us to characterize every object that may exist during the execution of a system as a direct instance of exactly one type.

What about the reverse property – does every type have direct instances? Almost, but not quite. More precisely, all types have direct instances but for the following categories:

- Formal_generic_name.
- Anchored.
- Any type whose base class is deferred.

The reason for these special cases is clear: a Formal_generic_name does not really define a type (in the sense of object structure) by itself, but only stands for the potential corresponding actual parameters. Similarly, an anchored type, of the form **like** *x*, stands for the type of *x*, as adapted to the enclosing class. Finally, a deferred class is incompletely implemented; if we tried to create a direct instance, we might omit certain fields (since some deferred functions may be eventually implemented as attributes) and we would get objects for which certain features (declared as deferred) have no implementation.

In all three cases, the types at hand may have instances, although not direct ones. In particular (using non-generic types for simplicity) if *T* is deferred and a descendant *V* of *T* is effective, a direct instance of *V* is an instance of *T*.

The next two sections define direct instances for the two categories of types that remain to cover as a result of this preparatory discussion: basic types and reference types.

→ *The impossibility of direct instances of* Formal_generic_name *and deferred types follows from conditions 1 and 2 of the Creation Instruction rule, page 286, which prohibit creation instructions having such creation types. A anchored creation type is permitted, but will produce a direct instance of the base type, which is not anchored.*

17.6 Direct instances of basic types

Here first is the definition for basic types.

> **Direct instances of basic types**
>
> The direct instances of the basic types are the following.
> - For *BOOLEAN*: the boolean values true and false.
> - For *CHARACTER*: any character.
> - For *INTEGER*: all the integer values which may be represented on *Integer_bits* bits.
> - For *REAL*: all floating-point values which may be represented on *Real_bits* bits.
> - For *DOUBLE*: all the floating-point values which may be represented on *Double_bits* bits.
> - For *POINTER*: all possible feature addresses, for transmission to non-Eiffel routines.
> - For *BIT n*, with $n \geq 0$: all the sequences of n binary (zero or one) values (none if $n = 0$).

This definition reflects the reason for calling the above types "basic": their instances, instead of being defined by specific language rules, are atomic values of a predefined form, such as integers and boolean values.

The constants mentioned in the definition (*Integer_bits, Real_bits*) have values defined in the universal class *PLATFORM*. The precise definition of "character" will be given in the presentation of lexical conventions.

→ *See chapter 27 about PLATFORM, and 25.15, starting on page 422, on the character set.*

17.7 Fields of complex objects

There remains to cover the case of non-basic class types.

DEFINITION:
Complex Class, Complex Type Field

Every class other than *BOOLEAN*, *CHARACTER*, *INTEGER*, *REAL*, *DOUBLE* and *POINTER* is said to be a **complex class**. Any type whose base class is complex is itself a **complex type**, and its instances are **complex objects**.

A direct instance of a complex type is a sequence of zero or more values, called **fields**. There is one field for every attribute of the type's base class.

→ *This definition makes no difference between variable and constant attributes. See the end of this section.*

Consider a class type *TC*, of base class *C*, and an attribute *a* of class *C*, with *TA* being the type of *a*. The possible values for the field corresponding to attribute *a* in a direct instance of *TC* depend on the nature of *TA*. There are three possible cases for *TA*:

1 • Reference type. (This also covers the case of an anchored type, of the form **like** *x*, which has a class type as base type.)

2 • Expanded type.

3 • Formal generic parameter of class *C*.

In case 1, illustrated by the top three fields of the object called O1 on the figure on the next page, the field corresponding to attribute *a* is a reference. That reference may be void, as in the second field of the figure, or it may be attached to an instance of *TA*'s base type – not necessarily a direct instance. In the figure, the first and third fields are attached to the same object, called O2.

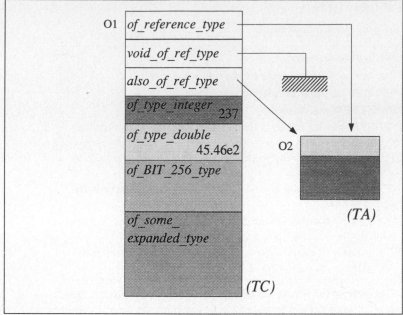

Run-time object structures

O1

of_reference_type

void_of_ref_type

also_of_ref_type

of_type_integer   237

of_type_double   45.46e2

of_BIT_256_type

of_some_expanded_type

(TC)

O2

(TA)

This represents a partial snapshot taken during the execution of a possible system, illustrating some of the various kinds of field.

DEFINITION:
Sub-object

In case 2, illustrated by the bottom four fields of O1, the field corresponding to attribute *a* is an instance of the expanded type *TA*. In other words, the field is itself an object, called a **sub-object** of the enclosing object. Depending on the precise nature of *TA*, the sub-object may be of various forms:

- *TA* may be a basic type, in which case the sub-object is a basic object of the corresponding type; the figure shows fields of type *INTEGER*, *DOUBLE* and Bit_type.

DEFINITION:
Composite Object

- If *TA* is a non-basic expanded type, the sub-object is itself a complex object. This applies to the last field of the left object on the figure. In this case the enclosing complex object is said to be **composite**.

Do not confuse "complex object", which means non-basic object, made of zero or more fields, and "composite object" which means complex object with at least one complex sub-object.

Finally, in case 3, *TA* is a formal generic parameter of class *C*, the base class of *TC*. Depending on whether the actual generic parameter is a reference type or an expanded type, this will in fact yield either case 1 or case 2.

The above definition of fields makes no difference between constant and variable attributes: an attribute of either kind yields a field in every instance. In a reasonable implementation, of course, the fields corresponding to constant attributes, being the same value for every instance of a class, will not occupy any run-time space. This indicates again that figures representing objects (such as the ones in this chapter) do not necessary show actual object implementations. This book uses "field" in the precise sense defined above, which does not always imply an actual memory area in an object's representation.

17.8 Reference atomicity

The dynamic model as illustrated above has both composite objects, containing sub-objects, and references to objects. How do these notions combine? In other words, can a system produce the run-time situation illustrated below, where a reference is attached to a sub-object of another object?

Reference attached to sub-object

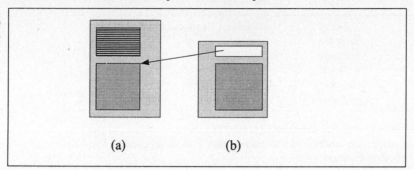

WARNING: This illustrates an impossible situation.

(a)   (b)

The answer is no. The semantics of reattachment operations (Assignment, formal-actual argument association), which will be studied in a later chapter, guarantees that a reference can only become attached to a full object. In other words, although objects are not "atomic" when it comes to accessing their properties (since clients can access exported attributes, and modify attributes through exported routines), the level of atomicity for attaching references is an entire object.

→ *The precise rule that precludes references from becoming attached to sub-objects is the absence of a "Reference attachment" mention in case [3] of the table on page 316; see the discussion that follows the table.*

Although it is possible to conceive of a model which supports references to sub-objects, this does not appear to bring a useful improvement in expressive power, but significantly complicates the dynamic model and the implementation.

17.9 Expressions and entities

The above discussion has defined the object structures that can be created during the execution of a system. To refer to the objects and their fields in the software texts, you may use expressions – specimens of the construct Expression.

There are several forms of expression, which subsequent chapters cover in detail. One form of expression, the simplest, will be of immediate interest: entities.

An entity is a name used by a class text to refer to values which may at run-time become associated in some way to the instances of the class.

DEFINITION: Entity

In a class text, four kinds of entity may appear:

1 • Attributes of the class.

2 • Local entities of routines, including the predefined entity *Result* for functions.

← *See 8.7, page 114, about local entities and Result.*

3 • Formal routine arguments.

4 • *Current*, the predefined entity used to represent a reference to the current object (the target of the latest not yet completed routine call).

Two operations, Creation and reattachment, may modify the value of an entity; both accept only attributes (category 1) and local entities (category 2) as targets. Attributes and local entities are therefore called **writable** entities. Formal arguments (category 3) and *Current* (category 4) are **read-only** entities, which may not be used as targets of Creation or reattachment operations.

→ *See chapters 18 about Creation instructions and 20 about reattachment. The simplest form of reattachment is assignment.*

Here is the syntactic description of these notions:

Entity	≜	Writable | Read_only
Writable	≜	Attribute | Local
Attribute	≜	Identifier
Local	≜	Identifier | *Result*
Read_only	≜	Formal | *Current*
Formal	≜	Identifier

The constraint on entities indicates that an entity must be of one of the four forms listed above; in addition, local entities and formal arguments are only permitted in certain contexts:

Entity rule

An occurrence of an entity *e* in the text of a class *C* (other than as feature of a qualified call) is valid if and only if it satisfies one of the following conditions:

1 • *e* is the final name of an attribute of *C*.

2A • The occurrence is in a Local_declarations, Routine_body, Postcondition or Rescue part of a Routine text for a function, and *e* is the Local entity *Result*.

2B • The occurrence is in a Local_declarations, Routine_body or Rescue part of a Routine text for a routine *r*, and the Local_declarations part for *r* contains an Entity_declaration_list including *e* as part of its Identifier_list.

3 • The occurrence is in a Feature_declaration for a routine *r*, and the Formal_arguments part for *r* contains an Entity_declaration_list including *e* as part of its Identifier_list.

4 • *e* is *Current*.

The constraint retains the case numbering of the definition of "entity" on the previous page, case 2 being split into subcases 2A and 2B.

The phrase "other than as feature of a qualified call" excludes from the scope of the rule any attribute, possibly of another class, used as feature of a call in dot notation. For example in *a.b* the rule applies to *a* but not to *b*. The constraint on *b* is the Call rule, here requiring *b* to be the name of an attribute or function with no arguments in *D*'s base class.

→ *The Call rule is on page 367.*

The semantics of entities involves two aspects:

• When evaluated as part of an expression, an entity will yield a value. This will be studied as part of the semantics of expressions.

• A Creation or Call may initialize the value of Writable entity, and a reattachment constructs may change it. This will be part of the study of Creation, Call and reattachment.

→ *Entities as expressions: 23.12, page 385. Creation: chapter 18. Call: chapter 21. Reattachment: chapter 20.*

18

Creating objects

18.1 Overview

The dynamic model, whose major properties were explored in the preceding chapter, is highly flexible: your systems may create objects and attach them to objects at will, according to the demands of their execution.

The Creation instruction is the principal mechanism used to produce new objects, and the topic of this chapter.

A closely related mechanism – **cloning** – exists for duplicating objects. This will be studied in the next chapter together with the mechanism for copying the contents of an object onto another.

18.2 Forms of object creation

You may use a Creation instruction to produce a totally new object, initialize its variable fields to preset values, and attach it to a Writable entity called the **target** of the creation and named in the instruction.

See 18.7 below (page 284) about Creation instructions applied to expanded types.

The examples which follow assume that the target is of a reference (non-expanded) type. As will be seen below, the Creation instruction also applies to expanded types, although with a less interesting effect.

Syntactically, a Creation instruction always contains two exclamation marks (!), followed by the target. Here are some examples:

```
!! x
!! point1.make_polar (1, Pi/4)
! SEGMENT ! fig.make (point1, point2)
! LINKED_TREE ! ast
```

The respective targets are x, point1, fig and ast.

18.3 Procedure-less form

The first and simplest form, !! *x*, is only valid if class *C* (the base class of *x*'s type) has no Creators part. Then the effect of the instruction is as follows:

The Creators *part comes at the beginning of a class. It was introduced in 4.6, page 46, and is discussed in detail below.*

1 • Creating a new object which is a direct instance of *T*.
2 • Initializing all the variable fields of that object to default values.
3 • Attaching *x* to the object.

The default initialization values used in step 2 are adapted to the type of each field corresponding to a variable attribute: zero for numbers, false for booleans, void for references and so on. The full rule is given below.

→ *On the default initialization rule see 18.13, page 291.*

The figure illustrates the result of a simple creation instruction of the above form. The attributes have received names suggesting their types.

Entity attached to newly created object

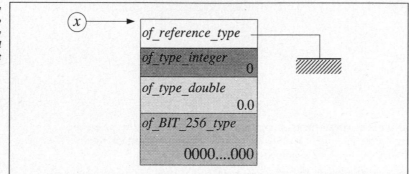

18.4 Using a creation procedure

The above form is not applicable if class *C* has a Creators part.

Recall that such a part consists of at least one Creation_clause, each beginning with the keyword **creation** followed by a list of zero or more procedures of the class. It comes just before the Features part (but after Inheritance), as in

More than one Creation_clause *may be present; also, each one may restrict the list of clients with creation privileges. See 18.6 below, starting on page 283, for the full details.*

```
class C ... inherit
    ...
creation
    make, execute, ...
feature
    ...
end -- class C
```

where *make, execute* ... are procedures of *C*.

By including such a Creators part, the author of *C* has explicitly specified that any corresponding Creation instruction (for producing direct instances of types based on *C*) must execute one of the procedures listed in the Creators part instead of just relying on the default initializations.

If *C* has such a Creators part, then you may use the following form of the instruction:

> !! *x.cp* (...)

where *cp* is the name of one of the creation procedures of *C* (*make, execute, ...* in the example), and, if that procedure has been declared in *C* with formal arguments, *cp* is followed by a list of matching actual arguments.

With this form of the instruction, the effect is the following:

- Steps 1 and 2 as above (creating an object and applying the default initializations).
- Calling *cp* on that object, with the actual arguments given.
- Step 3 above (attaching *x* to the object).

A creation procedure serves to apply initializations beyond the default ones if these do not suffice. For example, the author of a class *POINT* in a graphics system may wish to offer a creation mechanism that not only allocates a new object but also initializes its fields according to coordinates provided by the client. Here is an outline of such a class:

```
class POINT inherit
    TRIGONOMETRY
creation
    make_polar, make_cartesian
feature
    ro, theta: REAL;
    x, y: REAL;

    make_polar (r, t: REAL) is
        -- Set to polar coordinates r, t
      do
        ro := r; theta := t;
        reset_from_polar
      end; -- make_polar

    make_cartesian (a, b: REAL) is
        -- Set to cartesian coordinates a, b
      do
        x := a; y := b
        reset_from_cartesian
      end; -- make_cartesian

    ... Other exported features ...

feature {NONE}

    consistent_attributes: BOOLEAN is
        -- Do polar and cartesian attributes represent the same point?
      do
        Result := (x = ro * cos (theta)) and (y = ro * sin (theta))
      end; -- consistent_attributes
```

This assumes a library class TRIGONOMETRY offering functions such as 'cos' and 'sin'. The equality in 'consistent_attributes' should be changed to an approximate equality to account for numerical inaccuracy.

```
    reset_from_polar is
        -- Update cartesian coordinates from polar ones
    do
        x := ro * cos (theta);
        y := ro * sin (theta)
    ensure
        consistent_attributes
    end; -- reset_from_polar
    reset_from_cartesian is
        -- Update polar coordinates from cartesian ones
    do
        ...
    ensure
        consistent_attributes
    end; -- reset_from_cartesian
invariant
    consistent_attributes
end -- class POINT
```

With this design, the author of class *POINT* provides clients with two creation mechanisms, one which initializes a point by its polar coordinates, the other by its cartesian coordinates. Possible Creation instructions, assuming that *point1* is a Writable entity of type *POINT*, are

```
!! point.make_polar (2, Pi/4)
!! point.make_cartesian (Sqrt2, Sqrt2)
```

If Pi and Sqrt2 are real constants with the values suggested by their names, these instructions will have the same effect.

Because the class has a Creators part, the earlier form of the instruction, without a procedure (as in !! *point1*), would be invalid. Here you should note the difference between the absence of a Creators part, which means that the procedure-less form of the Creation instruction is applicable, and the presence of an empty Creators part, which means that no Creation instruction is possible at all. In other words, with *x* of type *C* and *C* declared as

```
class C feature        -- No Creators part
    ...
end -- class C
```

the instruction !! *x* will be valid; but with *C* declared as

```
class C creation
    -- Nothing here: present but empty Creators part
feature
    ...
end -- class C
```

the author of *C* is expressly including a Creators part, making the !! *x* form invalid; the Creators part is empty, however, so that the form with a creation procedure is also impossible. You can use this technique if you want to prevent clients from creating any direct instances of a given class.

As the example of *POINT* indicates, the author of a class may provide two or more initialization mechanisms through different creation procedures. In practice, many classes have just one creation procedure, or have a creation procedure which covers the simplest form of creation and is used more frequently than the others. For such a procedure, you may choose a name which clearly suggests the form of initialization which it performs, but in the absence of such an obvious specific name the recommended convention is to call such a creation procedure *make*. The consistency will help client programmers recognize quickly the basic creation procedure, although the number and type of its arguments depend of course on the specifics of the class.

→ *See appendix A and* "Eiffel: The Libraries" *about other recommended naming conventions.*

18.5 Using an explicit type

In the examples seen so far, the type of the object created is the type *T* declared for the instruction's target, *x* in the last example.

In some cases, you may want to use another type *V* instead; this will be permitted if *V* conforms to *T*. The form of the instruction in this case is one of

```
! V ! x
! V ! x. cp (...)
```

with the first one valid only if *V* has no Creators part, and the second one if *cp* is a creation procedure of *V*.

As an example, assume class *SEGMENT* is a descendant of *FIGURE*, and has a creation procedure *make*, with two formal arguments of type *POINT* (corresponding to the end points of a segment). Then the following will be valid:

```
[1]
    fig: FIGURE;
    point1, point2: POINT;

    ...

    ! SEGMENT ! fig. make (point1, point2)
```

and will have exactly the same effect on *fig* as

```
[2]
    fig: FIGURE; seg: SEGMENT;
    point1, point2: POINT;

    ...

    !! seg. make (point1, point2);
    fig := seg
```

where the last instruction is a polymorphic assignment, permitted by the Assignment rule since *seg* conforms to *fig*.

→ *The Assignment rule is on page 311.*

The explicitly typed form [1] brings no new facility since it is just an abbreviation for the implicitly typed form [2]. It avoids the need for declaring intermediate entities such as *seg*.

To become really useful the example should include more than one case: after all, if all you ever want to obtain is an instance of *SEGMENT*, then you do not need *fig* in the first place; *seg* suffices. Things become more interesting with a scheme of the following kind:

```
[3]
    fig: FIGURE; selected_icon_type: INTEGER;
    ...
    selected_icon_type := interface.icon_selected (mouse_position);
    inspect
        selected_icon_type
    when Segment_icon then
        ! SEGMENT ! fig.make (point1, point2)
    when Triangle_icon then
        ! TRIANGLE ! fig.make (point1, point2, point3)
    when Circle_icon then
        ! CIRCLE ! fig.make (point1, radius)
    when ...
        ...
    end
```

Here *SEGMENT*, *TRIANGLE*, *CIRCLE*, ... are descendants of *FIGURE*, all with specific Creation procedures, and *Segment_icon*, *Triangle_icon*, *Circle_icon*, ... are integer constants (perhaps Unique) with different values. Depending on the type of icon selected by an interactive user, the above fragment creates an object of the appropriate type, and attaches *fig* to it.

Were the explicitly typed form of the creation instruction not available, you could still use the equivalence illustrated by [2], which here is somewhat unpleasant because of the need to declare a temporary entity (*seg*, *tri*, *circ*, ...) for each of the possible icon types.

The scheme illustrated by [3] is particularly interesting in connection with the **dynamic binding** mechanism: after executing the above Multi_branch instruction, you normally should never have to discriminate again on the type of *fig*; instead, to apply an operation with different variants for the figures involved, you should use a call of the form

```
    fig.display
```

where the procedure, here *display*, is redefined in various ways in the proper descendants of *FIGURE*. This will select the appropriate version depending on the exact type of the object to which *fig* is attached, as a result of the variable-type creation achieved by [3].

This example illustrates an important concept of Eiffel software development: the **Single Choice principle**. The principle states that in a software system which has to handle a number of variants of the same notion (such as the various commands of a text editor, the various programming language constructs to be handled by a compiler, or, as here, the various figure types in a graphics system) any exhaustive knowledge of the set of possible variants should be confined to just **one component** of the system. This is essential to prevent future additions and modifications from requiring extensive system restructuring.

See also 14.6, page 240, on explicit discrimination. For further discussion of these issues see "Object-Oriented Software Construction", in particular the Open-Closed Principle.

Often, the component that performs the "Single Choice" will be the one that initially creates instances of the appropriate objects, and [3] illustrates one of the typical modes of operation of such a component.

→ *Another typical Single Choice technique uses a clonable array; see 19.5, page 301.*

18.6 Restricting creation availability

All the preceding examples had at most one Creation_clause, and all clients could use the procedures listed there for creating direct instances. In some cases, it may be appropriate, for purposes of information hiding, to define more restrictive creation privileges for clients.

← *See 7.7, page 95, on information hiding.*

To achieve this, you may write a Creators part that has one or more Creation_clause listing procedures available for creation by specific clients, as in

```
class C ... creation
    make
creation {A, B}
    jump_start, bootstrap
feature
    ...
end -- class C
```

Here the first Creation_clause has no restriction, so that any client can create a direct instance of C through an instruction of the form !! *x. make* (...) for *x* of type C. Because of the restriction in the second clause, however, only the descendants of A and B may use *jump_start* and *bootstrap* for creation.

Remember that descendants of a class include the class itself.

The convention is the same as for defining the export status of features: one or more clauses (beginning with **feature** in one case and **creation** in others), optionally followed by a Clients restriction in braces. The features given are available (for export or creation respectively) to all potential clients if there is no Clients restriction, and otherwise to the classes listed and their proper descendants.

The export and creation status of a procedure are independent. This means in particular that if you list procedure *cp* in a Creation_clause, enabling clients to include instructions of the form

```
!! x. cp (...)
```

you are free to export *cp* or not, so that calls of the form

$$x. cp \ (...)$$

may or may not be valid. The first instruction creates an object and initializes it using *cp*; the second uses *cp* to reinitialize an existing object – a right which, as the designer of a class, you may decide to grant or not to grant to clients.

18.7 The case of expanded types

The preceding examples assumed that the type of the target entity was a reference (non-expanded) type. What if it is expanded?

In this case there is no need to create an object, since the value of the target is already an object, not a reference to an object that a Creation instruction must allocate dynamically.

Rather than disallowing Creation for expanded targets, it is convenient to define a simple semantics for the instruction in this case, limited to the steps of the above process that still make sense: the instruction will execute the default initializations on the object attached to the target and, if it includes a creation procedure, it will call that procedure on the resulting object.

As a consequence of this rule, if we have a class whose instances contain sub-objects, as in

> **class** *COMPOSITE* **feature**
>   *a*: *SOME_REFERENCE_TYPE*;
>   *b*: *SOME_EXPANDED_TYPE*
>   ...
> **end** -- class *COMPOSITE*

then the default initialization rule for the field associated with *b* in an instance of *COMPOSITE* will be to apply a Creation, recursively, to the corresponding sub-object.

This semantic rule justifies two basic constraints on expanded types:

- To avoid any ambiguity, it is not valid for the base class of an expanded type to have more than one creation procedure.

- If the base class does have a creation procedure, it is not valid for that procedure to have arguments.

If any of these requirements was violated, it would be impossible to initialize a sub-object such as *b* without further information from the client (choice of creation procedure, actual arguments to the procedure).

This requirement appears in two rules: the Class_type_expanded rule, introduced in the chapter on types, and the Creators rule, discussed next.

See page 209 for the Expanded Type rule, and the next section, page 285, for the Creators rule (condition 4).

18.8 Creation syntax

Here now are the precise syntax, validity and semantic rules applying to Creators parts and Creation instructions.

First, the syntax of a Creators part, an optional component of the Class text, appearing towards the beginning of a class, after Inheritance and before Features:

← *The structure of a Class text, with all its parts, is on page 46.*

Creators	≜	**creation** {Creation_clause **creation** ...}⁺
Creation_clause	≜	[Clients] [Header_comment] Feature_list

The optional Header_comment *emphasizes the similarity with the syntax of a* Feature_clause, *given page 60.*

A constraint applies to the Creators part:

> ### Creation_clause rule
>
> A Creation_clause appearing in the Creators part of a class C is valid if and only if it satisfies the following four conditions, the last three for every Feature_identifier *fname* in the clause's Feature_list:
>
> 1 • C is effective.
>
> 2 • *fname* is the final name of a procedure of C.
>
> 3 • *fname* appears only once in the Feature_list.
>
> 4 • If C is expanded, that procedure has no arguments, and no other Feature_identifier appears in the Feature_list.

Condition 4 ensures that we can give an appropriate semantics to creation instructions for sub-objects, as just explained.

As noted above, the Expanded Type rule imposed the same condition on the base class of a type U if the type **expanded** U is to be valid.

← *Page 209.*

DEFINITION:
Creation
Procedure

This constraint being satisfied, we may define the **creation procedures** of a class: they are all the procedures listed in any Creation_clause of its Creators part. A creation procedure appearing in a Creation_clause is **available for creation** to the descendants of the classes given in the Clients restriction if there is one, and otherwise to all classes. If there is no Clients restriction, the procedure is also said to be a **general creation procedure**.

As with a Feature_clause, *the absence of a* Clients *restriction is equivalent to a restriction of the form* {ANY}.

Now for the Creation instruction itself. Its general syntax is the following:

Creation	≜	"!" [Type] "!" Writable [Creation_call]
Creation_call	≜	"**.**" Unqualified_call

If the Type is absent, the two exclamation marks may be written with or without an intervening break. In the style standard, the recommend form is the one without breaks, which makes !! appear as a single lexical symbol.

→ *A break is a sequence made only of blank, new line and tab characters; see 25.3, page 412. See appendix A about the style standard.*

DEFINITION:
Creation
Type

To discuss the validity and semantics of this instruction it is useful to introduce the notion of **creation type** of a Creation instruction. The creation type is the optional Type appearing in the instruction (between exclamation marks) if present; otherwise it is the base type of the target. So in

EXAMPLE

> *x*: *A*;
> *point1*: *POINT*;
>
> ...
>
> !! *x*
> !! *point1.make_polar* (*1*, *Pi*/4)
> ! *SEGMENT* ! *fig.make* (*point1*, *point2*)
> ! *LINKED_TREE* ! *ast*

the creation types for the four instructions are *A*, *POINT*, *SEGMENT* and *LINKED_TREE*. As you have guessed, the creation type is the type of the object that the instruction will create, if any.

In two cases, the instruction will not create an object: for an expanded creation type, and if a "no more memory" exception occurs (see below).

18.9 Creation validity (class-level)

The validity of Creation instructions is defined as the conjunction of two notions: class-level validity and system-level validity. This two-step definition comes from the flexibility of the type system, as will be explained in detail in the discussion of type checking.

$\rightarrow$ *See chapter 22 on type checking, with special emphasis on calls. Calls have the same two levels of validity as creation instructions.*

The more immediately relevant notion is class-level validity. Here is its definition:

The next section covers system-level validity.

VALIDITY

VGCC

Creation Instruction rule

Consider a Creation instruction appearing in a class *X*. Let *x* be the target of the instruction, *T* its creation type, and *C* the base class of *T*.

The instruction is **class-valid** if and only if it satisfies the following conditions:

1 • *T* is not a Formal_generic_name (that is to say, a formal parameter of the class where the instruction appears).

2 • *C* is an effective class.

3 • If the Type part is present, the type that it contains (which is *T*) conforms to the type of *x*, and is a reference type.

4 • If *C* does not have a Creators part, there is no Creation_call part.

5 • If *C* has a Creators part, there is a Creation_call part, and the call would be argument-valid if it appeared in the text of *C*.

6 • If case 5 holds and *f* is the feature of the Creation_call, then *f* is a procedure, its Routine_body is not of the **once**... form, and *f* is available for creation to *X*.

Condition 1 makes it invalid to write a class such as

```
class INVALID [FORMAL] feature

    x: FORMAL;

    routine_with_creation is
        do
            !! x;        -- Not permitted
            ... Instructions using x ...
        end -- routine_with_creation
end -- class INVALID
```

WARNING: not valid.

since it is generally impossible to know statically what actual type *FORMAL* may represent. More on the reasons for this restriction below, with an explanation of how to get the desired effect anyway.

→ See 18.14, page 291.

Condition 2 makes it impossible to create a direct instance of a type based on a deferred class. Recall that a class is deferred as soon as it has at least one deferred feature, effective otherwise. If creation was permitted on deferred classes, it would be possible to call deferred routines on the resulting objects; but such routines cannot be executed.

← "Direct instance" is not defined anyway for a deferred class; see page 272. The definition of "effective" and "deferred" for classes is on page 161.

Condition 3 is the obvious conformance requirement, justifying the informal semantic definition of the form with a Type in terms of the form using implicit typing.

← The informal definition is [3] above, page 282. The other part of condition 3 (ruling out an expanded T) just keeps the semantics simple.

Conditions 4 to 6 are the consistency requirements on the presence of a Creators part. Condition 5 refers to the validity rule for routine calls, given in the discussion of calls in a later chapter; informally, the call will be argument-valid if its actual arguments conform, in number and type, to the formal arguments declared for the creation procedure in *C*. In condition 6, the "feature of the call" will be the procedure used in the creation instruction, for example *cp* in the instruction !! *x.cp* (...). Its Routine_body, not being of the **once** form, must be either of the **do** form (the most common case) or External.

→ "Argument-valid" is defined on page 369.

← The various forms of Routine_body appear in the syntax for this construct, page 113.

18.10 Creation validity (system-level)

(This section explores a specialized type-checking issue and may be skipped at first reading. Even if you want all the details, you will probably have to come back after you have read the chapter on type checking, which is necessary for a full understanding of this discussion.)

→ Chapter 22 explains the type checking policy, with special emphasis on calls.

Although class-level validity generally suffices to determine the validity of a Creation, the complete definition will require system-level validity as well.

For our immediate purposes it suffices to note that some invalid cases may escape class-level validity checks. The reason is polymorphism. As a result of assignments of the form

→ Polymorphism is studied in 20.9, page 323.

$$x := y$$

a Writable entity *x* of type *T* may become attached to objects of *y*'s type (which the Assignment rule requires to be a descendant of *T*). These types, for all possible *y*, make up the set of all **possible dynamic types** of *x*, also called its

dynamic type set. The dynamic type set may contain types other than x's declared type, T.

 ← *The rigorous definition of the dynamic type set is on page 370.*

But a Creation instruction involving x

> !! $x.make$ (...)

may be invalid even if it is class-valid. This will be the case, for example, if in the above assignment y is of a type U based on a class D (a proper descendant of T's base class), and D fails to list its version of *make* as a creation procedure.

System-level validity avoids any such problem:

VGCS

> A Creation instruction is **system-valid** if and only if it satisfies one of the following two conditions:
>
> 1 • The creation type is explicit (in other words, the instruction begins with ! T ! ... for some type T).
>
> 2 • The creation type is implicit (in other words, the instruction begins with !!...) and every possible dynamic type T for x, with base class C, satisfies conditions 1 to 6 of the Creation Instruction rule (page 286). In applying conditions 5 and 6, the feature of the call, f, must be replaced by its version in C.

In other words, system-level validity is the same property as its class-level counterpart, but applied to all possible dynamic types of the target x. In interpreting conditions on the creation procedure f, we must take into account the version of that procedure in a descendant class, which may be different from the original because of redeclaration, and may have a different name because of renaming.

← *The "version" of a feature in a class was defined in 11.12, page 189.*

As condition 1 of the definition indicates, the problem of system-level validity only arises for Creation instructions with an implicit type. If the type is explicit, as in ! T ! x ..., the possible dynamic types of x do not affect the validity of the instruction, which in this case is entirely covered by class-level validity.

CAVEAT

System-level validity, as all other validity properties, is a **static** requirement, which a human reader or language processing tool may ascertain simply by looking at the software text. Checking it does not require any control flow analysis: whenever a given context contains both an assignment $x := y$ and a Creation with target x which would be invalid for y's type, the Creation will be system-invalid – even if clever control flow analysis would in fact show that no control flow path will ever execute the assignment and the Creation in sequence. Static validity checking does not need to be clever; it needs to be safe. This discussion will be generalized to calls in the discussion of type checking.

To be valid, a Creation must satisfy the requirements at both levels:

VGCI

> A Creation instruction is valid if and only if it is both class-valid and system-valid.

18.11 Creation semantics

With the above validity rules, we can define the precise semantics of a Creation instruction. Consider such an instruction with target x and creation type T. If T is a reference type, the effect of executing the instruction is the following sequence of steps:

1 • If there is not enough memory available to create a new direct instance of T, trigger an exception in the routine that executed the instruction. Steps 2 to 5 do not apply in this case.

2 • Create a new direct instance of TC.

3 • Assign a value to every field of the new instance: for a field corresponding to a constant attribute, the value defined in the class text; for a field corresponding to a variable attribute, the default value of the attribute's type, according to the rules given below.

→ 18.13, page 291, gives the default initialization rules.

4 • If the Creation instruction includes a Creation_call, that is to say an Unqualified_call, execute that call on the resulting object.

5 • Attach x to the object.

← See page 270 about a reference being attached to an object.

The integer value of the code for the exception raised in step 1 if creation is impossible is the value of the constant attribute *No_more_memory* in the Kernel Library class *EXCEPTIONS*.

See chapters 15 on exceptions and 29 on class EXCEPTIONS.

If T is an expanded type, the value of x is an object; then the effect of the instructions is to apply steps 3 and 4 above to the object attached to x.

18.12 Properties of creation

Three properties of Creation instructions follow from the previous syntactic and semantic rules.

First, the creation type of a Creation instruction must be effective. This does not prevent the target from being of a deferred type, but does mean that in such a case the instruction must be of the form with explicit Type (! *ET* ! *x* ...), with *ET* effective. One of the above examples, with creation instructions of the form

"Effective type" is here an abbreviation for "type based on an effective class"; "deferred type" is the inverse notion.

```
! TRIANGLE ! fig.make (point1, point2, point3)
! SEGMENT ! fig.make (point1, point2)
```

illustrated this case, with *fig* of type *FIGURE*, most likely deferred, having *TRIANGLE* and *SEGMENT* as effective descendants.

The second observation, a consequence of the syntax given for Creation instructions, is that you may **not** write "remote creation" instructions of the form exemplified by the last line below (assuming that *y1*, of type *Y*, is an attribute of class *X*):

For simplicity, X is assumed to be non-generic, and hence its own base type.

```
x1: X;
...
!! x1.y1.cp (...)
```

WARNING: Syntactically illegal!

To obtain an equivalent effect, you must introduce a specific procedure in X, of the form

```
class X feature
    make_y (arguments: ...) is
        do
            !! y.cp (arguments)
        end; make_y
    ...
end -- class X
```

so that instead of the above attempt at remote creation clients will use the instruction

```
x1.make_y (...)
```

This is in line with the principle of information hiding: deciding whether or not clients of X may directly "create" the y field of an object is the privilege of the designer of X who, if the answer is positive, will write a specific procedure to grant this privilege. The designer may of course restrict the export availability of that procedure (*make_y* in the example).

The third interesting property of Creation instructions is their connection with inheritance – or rather the lack of a connection. The designer of a class C that inherits from a class B is free to choose any appropriate procedures of C as creation procedures; a creation procedure of B, or its C redefined version, may or may not be selected as creation procedure for C.

The reason for this policy is that since an heir represents a more specialized version of the notions described by its parents, the information needed to create a direct instance may be different. A standard example is the creation procedures for a class *RECTANGLE* and its heir *SQUARE*: to create a rectangle object, a client may be requested to supply the location of the center, the orientation, and the two side lengths; squares, however, need only one side length. Reusing *RECTANGLE*'s creation procedure in *SQUARE* would be incorrect. Redefining it would only lead to trouble: since the number of arguments must remain the same, the redefined version would need to check that the two side lengths are equal, and it is not clear what the procedure should do when they are not. The only reasonable solution is to have each class define its own creation procedure.

Of course it also happens that a creation procedure cp of a class B remains appropriate as creation procedure for an heir C of B. This case is easy to handle: since creation procedures are otherwise normal features, C will inherit cp from B; it suffices for C to list cp in a Creation_clause of its Creators part.

It is interesting to relate this discussion to the question of how the **export** status (rather than the creation status) of a feature fares with respect to inheritance. The answer is essentially the same: a class is free to change the status (for export or creation) of its inherited features, and is not constrained by the choices made in its parents' design. The only difference affects the default policy:

- Inherited features retain their original export status unless the heir explicitly overrides it (through a New_exports clause).

← *See page 101 about the* New_exports *clause.*

- In contrast, a creation procedure loses its creation status unless the heir explicitly reaffirms it (by listing the procedure in its own Creators part).

The reason for this difference is the pragmatic consideration of what designers of heir classes most commonly need.

18.13 Default initialization values

As noted in the above semantic definition, a successful Creation instruction always performs default initializations (which may then be overridden by the creation procedure) on the variable attribute fields of the resulting object. Let us see the precise default rules.

The same default rules will also apply to the initialization of local routine entities (on every call to a routine) and of the *Result* of a function.

→ *See the semantics of calls, 21.14, page 352.*

Consider a field of a newly created object, corresponding to an attribute of type *FT* in the base class of the object's type. The default initialization value *init* for the field is determined as follows according to the nature of *FT*.

A• For a reference type: a void reference.

B• For *BOOLEAN*: the boolean value false.

C• For *CHARACTER*: the null character.

D• For *INTEGER, REAL* or *DOUBLE*: the integer, single precision or double precision zero.

E• For *POINTER*: a null pointer.

F• For a Bit_type of the form *BIT* N: a sequence of N zeros.

G• For an expanded type other than one of the basic types listed so far, *init* will be the content of a sub-object of the newly created object. Let *FC* be the base class of *FT*. To obtain *init*, apply (recursively) the default initialization rule to every field of the sub-object. Then if *FC* has a creation procedure, apply that procedure to the sub-object. The Creation_clause rule implies that there is only one creation procedure, and that it has no argument.

← *The Creation_ clause rule was on page 285.*

H• The only remaining possibility is for *FT* to be a formal generic parameter of the class where the Creation instruction appears. This case is prohibited, however, by condition 1 of the Creation Instruction rule.

← *The Creation Instruction rule was on page 286.*

18.14 The case of formal generics

(This section discusses a fairly fine point of the Creation Instruction rule, explaining why a restriction is justified and how to get around it. On first reading, you should probably go directly to the next section.)

The last case discussed deserves further explanation. Look again at the invalid example brought up above:

WARNING: not valid.

Using constrained rather
than unconstrained
genericity would not affect
this discussion.

```
class INVALID [FORMAL] feature
    x: FORMAL;

    routine_with_creation is
        do
            !! x;        -- Not permitted
            ... Instructions using x ...
        end -- routine_with_creation
end -- class INVALID
```

It would in fact be possible to give a perfectly consistent semantics to the prohibited Creation instruction. If permitted, that instruction would only be executed as a result of the execution of some other routine *calling_routine*, from a class *CLIENT* of the general form

```
class CLIENT feature
    ...
    some_instance: INVALID [ACTUAL]
        -- Could also be a local entity of calling_routine

    calling_routine is
        do
            ... Make sure some_instance is attached
            ... (to an instance of INVALID [ACTUAL])

            some_instance.routine_with_creation

        end -- routine_with_creation
end -- class INVALID
```

At run time, then, it would be possible to know what actual type the Formal_generic_name *FORMAL* represents for the call to *routine_with_creation* on the specific object to which *some_instance* is attached: that type is *ACTUAL* unless *ACTUAL* is itself a formal generic parameter of *CLIENT*, in which case it may be determined by applying the same reasoning recursively to the client of *CLIENT* which created the relevant instance of *CLIENT*. (The process is bound to terminate since, by the Root Class rule, the original execution object must be an instance of a non-generic class.)

← The Root Class rule is
on page 36.

In principle, then, we could remove the restriction of condition 1 of the Creation Instruction rule (prohibition of targets whose type is a Formal_generic_name) by extending the semantics given: in case G of the semantic rule above, the semantics would be obtained by applying the rule recursively to the type used as actual generic parameter for the particular object from which the Creation instruction emanates (*ACTUAL* in the example). As noted, the recursion will always terminate.

← The Creation Instruction
rule is on page 286. The
semantic rule is on page
291.

This possible extension to the rule is logically consistent. It is not difficult to explain the major reason for not retaining it in the language specification: that reason is the associated implementation overhead. Supporting the extension would require that instances of a generically derived type have an extra field for every generic parameter.

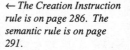

This seems unacceptable, especially for small objects; you may for example think of the instances of the Data Structure Library's generic class *LINKABLE*, representing list cells.

← *See page 143 (particularly the first figure on that page) for an explanation of LINKABLE.*

One may imagine a clever implementation, avoiding the space overhead if it is not strictly necessary. But the practical benefit remains dubious.

Fortunately, this constraint does not really limit the expressive power of the language. A simple way to obtain the desired effect is available; it follows the time-honored technique of passing the buck to your client. Let us see how it applies to the preceding example. You may replace *INVALID* by

```
class VALID [FORMAL] feature
  x: FORMAL;

  routine_without_creation (a: like x) is
    require
      a /= Void
    do
      x := a ;
      ... Instructions using x ...
    end -- routine_with_creation
end -- class VALID
```

In other words, you add an argument to the routine that would otherwise have performed the creation, and you expect a client class such as *CLIENT* above to do the creation before a call, passing as new actual argument a reference to the created object.

It is usually not a good idea, however, to rely on implicit requirements (such as "always create an object for the first argument before calling me.") If the text of *CLIENT* as originally written contained two or more calls of the form

```
some_instance.routine_with_creation
```

you may prefer to encapsulate the requirement (the need to create before a call) in a routine of *CLIENT*, such as

```
create_and_call (v: VALID [ACTUAL]) is
  local
    a: ACTUAL
  do
    !! a;
    v.routine_without_creation (a)
  end
```

Of course, the 'routine_without_creation' could have other arguments, and the creation of 'a' could involve a creation procedure.

so that *CLIENT* will obtain the requested creation through the call

```
create_and_call (some_instance)
```

19

Duplicating and comparing objects

19.1 Overview

The Creation instruction, studied in the previous chapter, is the basic language mechanism for obtaining new objects at run time; it produces fresh direct instances of a given class, initialized from scratch.

Sometimes you will need instead to copy the contents of an existing object onto those of another. This is the **copy** operation, which exists both in a *shallow* version, copying only one object, and in a *deep* version, copying an entire data structure.

A variant of copy is **clone**, which produces a fresh object by duplicating an existing one. Here too both shallow and deep forms are available.

A closely related problem is that of *comparing* two objects for shallow or deep equality.

The copying, cloning and comparison operations studied in this chapter are obtained not through language constructs but through routines of the universal class *ANY*, which are automatically available to any software element since every developer-defined class is a descendant of *ANY*.

→ *The universal class ANY is studied in chapter 27. For an introduction, see 6.12, page 85.*

19.2 Copying an object

The first operation copies the fields of an object onto those of another. It is provided by the procedure *copy* from class *ANY*; *copy* may be redefined but has a frozen synonym, *standard_copy*.

For the copy operation to succeed, both the source and the target must be attached to objects. (In contrast, cloning will work for void sources or targets.)

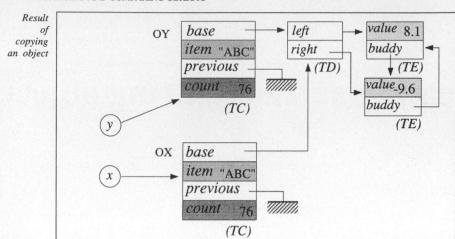

Result of copying an object

The figure illustrates the effect of a copy operation with x as target and y as source. If *copy* has not been redefined for the generating class of the object OX attached to x, you may obtain this effect through the call

x. *copy* (y)

Before the call, y was attached to the object labeled OY; x was attached to the object labeled OX. What the fields of OX contained then does not matter (since the call overwrites them), but this object must exist. The call copies every field of OY onto the corresponding field of OX. Since the argument of *copy* is declared of type **like** *Current*, the type of OY conforms to the type of OX, so that in the general case OY could have more fields than OX. The operation will only copy the fields which are meaningful for OX – those which correspond to attributes of x's generating class. On the figure, OX and OY are of an identical type *TC*.

The fields of OY include expanded values, such as the integer *count*, of value 76, and references such as *base* and *previous*. In both cases, the copy operation will simply copy the field. For reference fields, no attempt is made to duplicate the data structure recursively: as a result, the *base* fields of both OX and OY will, after the call, be attached to the same object of type *TD*. Later in this chapter we will encounter recursive copy routines, *deep_copy* and *deep_clone*, which duplicate an entire object structure, following references recursively.

→ *See 19.6 below, page 302, about deep copy and clone.*

As noted, *copy* requires a non-void source and target. For the target, this is simply part of the general requirement on Call instructions: in the above example, x, like the target of any other call, must be non-void under penalty of raising an exception. For the source, the requirement is expressed by the precondition of *copy*. A void source will trigger an exception if if the execution monitors preconditions.

→ *On the effect of a void target in a call, see 21.8, page 345. On run-time assertion monitoring, see 9.17, page 132.*

It is time now to look at the exact specification of *copy*. First, the short form of the procedure's version in class *ANY*:

> copy, **frozen** standard_copy (other: **like** Current)
>   -- Copy every field of other onto
>   -- corresponding field of current object.
> **require**
>   other_not_void: other /= Void;
>   other_conforming: other.conforms_to (Current)
> **ensure**
>   is_equal (other)

ANY inherits these features from GENERAL; see 6.12, page 85, and subsequent sections. See below about the function 'conforms_to' used in the precondition and 19.7, page 303, about the function 'is_equal' used in the postcondition.

Setting the style for other duplication and comparison routines, *copy* has two versions: one redefinable, the other (whose name begins with *standard_*) frozen.

← *Chapter 5 discussed frozen features.*

The second precondition clause uses function *conforms_to* of *ANY*. For *a* and *b* attached to objects OA and OB, *b.conforms_to* (*a*) has value true if and only if the type of OB conforms to the type of OA.

→ *'conforms_to' is discussed in 27.4, page 433.*

Here now is the precise effect of the standard version. Assume *copy* has not been redefined and consider a call *x.copy* (*y*). As with any call, the target *x* must be non-void; the first precondition clause of *copy* states that *y* must also be non-void. Let OX and OY be the attached objects at the time of the call.

1 • If OX and OY are bit sequences, the conformance rule on Bit_type requires OX to be at least as long as OY. The call then copies onto OX the contents of OY, extended with zeros on the left if OY is shorter than OX. Cases 2 to 4 assume that OX and OY are not bit sequences.

← *Conformance on Bit_type: 13.11, p. 229.*

2 • If the types of OX and OY are basic types (*BOOLEAN*, *CHARACTER*, *INTEGER*, *REAL*, *DOUBLE* or *POINTER*), then OX is identical to OY or is a heavier type. Then the call copies the value of OY onto OX, after conversion to the heavier type if necessary.

← *DOUBLE is heavier than REAL and REAL than INTEGER. See page 227.*

3 • If OX and OY are special objects, that is to say sequences of values (strings or arrays), the call copies the value of OY onto OX. The implementation must ensure that whenever this occurs the size of OX is at least as large as the size of OY.

Special objects are not directly accessible to software texts. See 17.2, page 270.

4 • In the remaining cases OX and OY are standard objects, made of zero or more fields, and the second precondition clause implies that the type of OY is a descendant of the type of OX; as a result, for every field of OX there is a corresponding field in OY. Then the call copies onto every field of OX the corresponding field of OY.

← *With repeated inheritance, an attribute of TX may yield two fields in OY. The Select subclause, 11.6, page 177, determines which one is the field "corresponding" to the relevant OX field.*

Any class may redefine *copy* to describe a form of duplication reflecting the specific properties of the class. Classes *ARRAY* and *STRING*, studied in a later chapter, provide an example. A direct instance of *ARRAY* or *STRING* is a descriptor, containing a reference to the sequence of values making up an array or string. Here *standard_copy* will copy the descriptor, not the sequence of values. Since this is usually not the desired copy semantics, both *ARRAY* and *STRING* redefine *copy* to duplicate the sequence of values as well as the descriptor. You may always use *standard_copy* to bypass the redefinition.

→ *Arrays, strings and the supporting Kernel Library classes are covered in chapter 28.*

Any redefinition of *copy* must still satisfy the postcondition *is_equal* (*other*). Function *is_equal*, another feature of *ANY* covered in detail later in this chapter, expresses the equality of two objects. Clearly, if you redefine either one of *copy* and *is_equal*, you must redefine the other as well, so as to maintain consistent semantics for copying and equality.

← *Any redeclaration must maintain the postcondition; see 10.15, page 152.*

19.3 Cloning an object

A variant of copying is cloning. The call

> *clone* (*y*)

is syntactically an expression; evaluating it will return a new object, which is a field-by-field copy of the object attached to *y*, if any. If *y* is void, the result is void.

This mechanism is often, although not exclusively, used in assignments of the form

> *x* := *clone* (*y*)

where the type of *y* must be a descendant of the type of *x*. The figure used to illustrate *x*.*copy* (*y*) also describes the effect of this assignment; only now the object OX represents a new object created by the assignment.

← *The figure is on page 296.*

It is also possible to use *clone* to pass a fresh copy of an existing object as argument to a call, as in

> *some_routine* (..., *clone* (*y*), ...)

Although closely related, the copy and clone operations differ in three respects:

1 • Copy modifies an existing object, whereas clone creates a new object. In the above assignment, any earlier attachment between *x* and some object is lost.

2 • For copy to work, the target must be non-void; this is expressed syntactically by the nature of *copy*, a procedure in *ANY*. In contrast, *clone* is a function and does not by itself have a target; it simply produces a result. When used as part of an assignment of target *x* as above, it does not care whether *x* is void or attached.

3 • Finally, because *clone* does not presuppose an existing target object, it can handle a void source. The result in this case is simply a void reference.

Like *copy*, *clone* does not attempt to follow references for fields of reference types, but simply copies the fields. A "deep" version of the operation will be described below.

→ *See 19.6, page 302, about deep cloning.*

As with a Creation instruction, a call to *clone* will fail, returning a void reference and triggering an exception (the same one, of code *No_more_memory* in the Kernel Library class *EXCEPTIONS*) if it attempts to create a new object and no memory is available for it.

← *The precise semantics of Creation instructions appears in 18.11, page 289.*

Here is the short form of function *clone*:

> **frozen** *clone* (*other*: ANY): **like** *other*
>   -- Void if *other* is void;
>   -- Otherwise, new object field-by-field identical
>   -- to object attached to *other*.
> **ensure**
>   *equal* (*Result*, *other*)

→ *The function 'equal' used in the postcondition is derived from 'is_equal'. See below.*

Why is *clone* frozen? The reason is not that its effect is immutable, but that there is no need to redefine this function. To guarantee compatible semantics for cloning and copying, *clone* is defined in terms of *copy*, and so its effect will follow any redefinition of *copy*.

A frozen routine may, of course, call routines which are not frozen; it will then be affected by their redefinitions.

More precisely, here is the definition of the semantics of a call *clone* (*y*):

1 • If the value of *y* is void, the call returns a void value.

2 • If the value of *y* is attached to an object OY, the call returns a newly created object of the same type as OY, initialized by applying *copy* to that object with OY as source.

In exactly the same way, function *equal*, used in the postcondition of *clone*, will automatically follow any redefinition of *is_equal*, used in the postcondition of *copy*, as seen in the discussion of equality below. The reason for having two functions is that *x. is_equal* (*y*) only applies to non-void *x* and *y* (returning true if the attached objects are field-by-field equal), whereas *equal* (*x, y*) works for arbitrary *x* and *y*, returning true if they are either both void or attached to objects satisfying *is_equal*. These different properties precisely match the different requirements of *copy* and *clone*.

→ *19.7, page 303 below, covers equality.*

To guarantee the original semantics of field-by-field duplication and ignore any redefinition of *copy*, you may use function *standard_clone*, which has the same signature as *clone*, and is defined in terms of *standard_copy* exactly as *clone* is defined from *copy*.

The semantics of cloning deserve a few more observations. As noted, *clone* does not require its argument to have a non-void value. Although "cloning" a non-existent object is not very interesting, this convention avoids the need to precede clone assignments by tests for void references, as in

> **if** *y* = *Void* **then**
>   *x* := *Void*
> **else**
>   *x* := *clone* (*y*)
> **end**

WARNING: not necessary!

since the straightforward *x* := *clone* (*y*) does the job just as well.

The desire to handle gently the case of a void reference, freeing clients from such tedious tests, is the reason why *clone* takes the source as an argument, as in *clone* (*y*). It would also have been possible to define a function without argument, *other_clone*, duplicating the object attached to the call's target, as in *x* := *y. other_clone*. Such a function, although perhaps more in line with the object-oriented style of calling features, would only work for non-void *y*, triggering an exception for void *y*, and forcing clients to use frequent tests of the above form.

→ *See chapter 21 about the details of the* Call *mechanism. The notion of target of a call is defined on page 340.*

Whenever one of the routines of this chapter handles a certain type of value and it is possible to define a reasonable default response for cases in which that value is void, the routine follows the example of *clone* and treats that value as an argument, not as the target of calls.

In principle, *clone* is superfluous: you may in most cases use a Creation and copy instead, replacing $y := clone (x)$ by

> ! ... ! y ...;
> y.copy (x)

In practice, however, several reasons justify retaining *clone* as a separate mechanism:

- The form using *copy* is more verbose, especially if the call to *clone* appears not as right-hand side of an Assignment instruction, but as part of an expression. For example, as noted above, you may use cloning for an actual routine argument in a call r (..., clone (x), ...)); the form using *copy* requires declaring an intermediate entity y and adding the above two intermediate instructions.

- If the base class of the underlying type has two or more creation procedures, a Creation instruction forces you to choose one among them, although the choice is irrelevant.

- A creation procedure may do some extra work which is justified when you actually create a first copy of a certain object, but unneeded or harmful when all you need is a duplicate of an existing object.

- Finally and perhaps most importantly, a Creation forces the client to specify the exact type of the new object, whereas a call to *clone*, as emphasized next, may dynamically produce an object of one among several possible types, depending on the type of the source, selected at run time. (This means in particular that *clone* is applicable to a Formal_generic_name type, for which the above equivalence does not work, since the Creation instruction is not applicable in this case.)

← On the prohibition of Creation instructions for Formal_generic_ name, see clause 1 of the Creation Instruction rule, page 286, and the discussion in 18.14, starting on page 291.

19.4 Cloning and types

If x is an expression of type T, and its value is not void, the generating type of the object created by a call to *clone* (x) is not necessarily T: it is the type of the object to which x is attached – which will always conform to T, but may be based on a proper descendant. In fact T may very well be deferred, in which case there are no objects of generating type T. For example, with *fig* and *fig1* of the deferred type *FIGURE*, you may execute

← The generating type of an object is the type of which it is a direct instance. See 17.2, page 270.

> fig1 := clone (fig)

which, if *fig* is attached to a direct instance of some descendant of *FIGURE* such as *TRIANGLE* or *CIRCLE*, will attach *fig1* to a direct instance of the same type. Here you do not need to know, when writing the instruction, what the type will be; it may be different for successive executions of the same instruction if the value of *fig* has changed in the meantime.

19.5 The clonable array technique

The last observation yields an important practical design technique, directly addressing one of the Eiffel developer's constant concerns: how to avoid unneeded explicit discriminations.

The Single Choice principle, introduced in the previous chapter, suggests that a system supporting a set of alternative possibilities (such as various kinds of figures) should concentrate any explicit choice between them in just one place. Often, this single place of explicit choice will be an instruction that creates a direct instance of one among a specified set of types, corresponding to the set of alternatives; these types will all be based on descendants of a general class, usually deferred (such as *FIGURE*).

← *See page 283 about the Single Choice principle. See also the comments on explicit discrimination instructions in 14.6, page 240.*

A scheme which achieves this was presented earlier, using a Multi_branch and Creation instructions:

← *See [3], page 282.*

```
[4]
   x: GENERAL_TYPE;
      -- GENERAL_TYPE is based on a deferred class;
      -- FIRST_TYPE, SECOND_TYPE etc. conform to GENERAL_TYPE.
   ...
   inspect
      discriminant
   when First_possibility then
      ! FIRST_TYPE ! x ...
   when Second_possibility then
      ! SECOND_TYPE ! x ...
   when
      (etc.)
   end
```

An equivalent but slightly more elegant technique, which avoids any explicit discriminating control structure such as Multi_branch or Conditional, uses a pre-filled array of templates. In a routine used at initialization time you will fill an array with one direct instance of each possible variant:

→ *The creation procedure 'make' of class ARRAY sets the bounds of the array from the arguments. See 28.4, page 439.*

```
template: ARRAY [GENERAL_TYPE];
...
!! template.make (1, Number_of_variants);

! FIRST_TYPE ! x ...; template.put (x, 1);

! SECOND_TYPE ! x ...; template.put (x, 2);
(etc.)
```

Then, when you actually need to select an alternative, you can avoid the explicit discrimination of [4]: instead of the *discriminant*, use an integer code to index directly into the array, and clone the object found there. [4] becomes just:

> [5]
>   x := clone (template @ code)

"template @ code" is the
element of index "code" in
array "template". This may
also be written
template.item (code). See
28.4, page 439.

Note how important it is to declare x of the more abstract GENERAL_TYPE, even though the actual object produced by clone will be of one of the specialized types (FIRST_TYPE etc.).

19.6 Deep copy and clone

As noted, clone and copy are "shallow": they do not follow references, just copy fields of the source object as they appear.

You may in some cases need deep versions of these operations, which will recursively duplicate an entire structure. The routines deep_clone and deep_copy of class ANY, with the same signatures as clone and copy respectively, fulfil this need. They will replicate an entire data structure, starting at the source and creating new objects as needed.

As an illustration, starting from the value that y has on the figure page 296 (which showed the value of x resulting from x := clone (y)), the instruction z := deep_clone (y) will lead to the situation shown below.

*Result
of
deep
cloning*

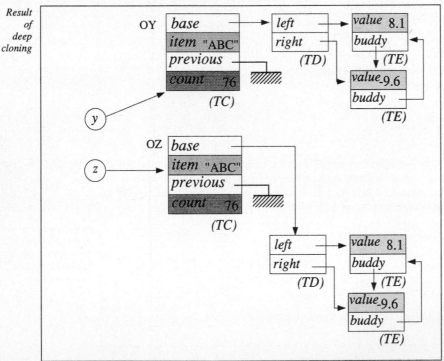

Your usual supplier of memory upgrades and discount disks will be happy to provide your staff, at no charge, with a full training session on the use of 'deep_copy' and 'deep_clone'.

In contrast with clone and copy, deep_clone and deep_copy may not introduce sharing of references between source and target.

Like their shallow counterparts, they are subject to redefinition, so that you can write adjustable-depth duplication procedures adapted to a specific data structure. The frozen synonyms *standard_deep_clone* and *standard_deep_copy* are there for clients who need the guaranteed original versions.

The postconditions of the four deep duplication routines involve *deep_equal*, studied below. As with *clone* and *copy*, redefined versions of *deep_copy* and *deep_clone* will need to be accompanied by redefinitions of *deep_equal* to satisfy the Assertion Redefinition rule.

→ *Function "deep_equal" appears in 19.8, starting on page 305.*

19.7 Object equality

The discussion of cloning and copying transposes readily to the problem of comparing objects for equality. To determine if the objects attached to *x* and *y* are field-by-field identical, you may use the Call

> *equal* (*x*, *y*)

which returns a boolean value (and so must be used as an expression). As noted, *is_equal*, a variant of *equal*, appears in the postcondition of *copy* and *clone* to express the properties of the result.

Here is the precise result that the standard version of this function must return when applied to two values *x* and *y*.

1 • If any one of *x* and *y* is void, the result is true if the other is also void too, and false otherwise. Cases 2 to 6 assume that both arguments are attached to respective objects OX and OY of types *TX* and *TY*.

2 • If OX and OY are bit sequences, the result is true if and only if the two sequences, with the shorter one being extended with zeros on the left to match the length of the longer one if necessary, are bit-by-bit identical. Cases 3 to 6 assume that OX and OY are not bit sequences.

3 • If *TY* does not conform to *TX*, the result is false. Cases 4 to 6 assume that *TY* conforms to *TX*.

4 • If *TX* is *BOOLEAN*, *CHARACTER*, *INTEGER*, *REAL*, *DOUBLE* or *POINTER*, the result is true if and only if OX and OY are the same value, after possible conversion to the heavier type if OX and OY are different arithmetic types.

→ *DOUBLE is heavier than REAL and REAL than INTEGER. See page 227.*

5 • If OX and OY are special objects (strings or arrays), that is to say, sequences of values, the result is true if and only if the sequences have the same length, and every field in one is (recursively) equal to the field at the same position in the other.

Special objects are strings (sequences of characters) arrays (sequences of fields, all references or all of exactly the same type). See page 270.

6 • Otherwise OX and OY are standard complex objects, and conformance of *TY* to *TX* implies that for every field of OX there is a corresponding field in OY. Then the result is true if and only if every reference field of OX is attached to the same object as the corresponding field in OY, and every object field of OX, coming from an expanded attribute in *TX*'s base class, is (recursively) equal to the corresponding field in OY.

← *A "field", as defined on page 273, is one of the values that constitute a complex object.*

In the comparison of two standard complex objects for case 6, the arguments play non-symmetric roles, as reflected by the signature of function *equal*:

> **frozen** *equal* (*some*: *ANY*; *other*: **like** *some*)*:*

← *With repeated inheritance, an attribute of TX may yield two fields in OY. The* Select *subclause, 11.6, page 177, determines which one is the field "corresponding to" the relevant OX field.*

The function will yield true not just if OY is identical to OX but more generally if the *TX* part of OY is identical to OX, *TX* being the type of OX. Here "the *TX* part of OY" denotes the set of fields corresponding to attributes of *TX*'s base class; these fields are guaranteed to exist since *TY* (the type of OY) conforms to *TX*.

← *See case 4 in the definition of copy semantics, page 297.*

This is compatible with the semantics of *copy*: as noted above, a call of the form *x.copy* (*y*) only copies the *TX* fields of the object attached to *y*. Accordingly, such a call ensures the postcondition *equal* (*x, y*).

The interesting part of function *equal*'s job is done not by the function itself, but by an associated function called *is_equal*. The reason for having two functions is convenience. Experience shows that developers often want to have an equality test of the form

> *equal* (*a, b*)

which is applicable to all possible values of *a* and *b*, including void. This is indeed ensured by the signature and semantics defined above.

→ *See 28.5, page 441, about equality of arrays.*

Defined just by itself, however, a function *equal* with the above signature would make it impossible to benefit from redefinitions describing local versions of equality testing; for example, the Kernel Library classes *ARRAY* and *STRING* need versions comparing two arrays or strings rather than the array or string descriptors. To make this work, we need calls of the form

> *a.is_equal* (*b*)

where dynamic binding ensures that if a class *C* redefines *is_equal*, the call will use the redefined version if *a* is attached to a direct instance of *C*. But then a call of this form requires *a* to be non-void, forcing clients to test for *a = Void* before the call, and threatening with an exception and run-time failure if they forget.

To get us out of this dilemma, we accept that *ANY* needs both *equal* and *is_equal*. In most cases, you will probably want to use *equal*, which has the broader applicability; internally, however, *equal* is defined in terms of *is_equal*, so as to guarantee the following postcondition:

> **frozen** *equal* (*some*: *ANY*; *other*: **like** *some*): *BOOLEAN* **is**
>   -- Are *some* and *other* either both void or attached
>   -- to objects field-by-field identical (on fields of *some*)?
> **ensure**
>   *Result* = (*some* = *Void* **and** *other* = *Void*) **or**
>   (*some* /= *Void* **and** *other* /= *Void* **and then**
>   *some.is_equal* (*other*))
> **end** -- *equal*

This postcondition directly suggests an implementation of 'equal' using tests and a call to 'is_equal'. Any other implementation which satisfies the postcondition is acceptable.

As a result of this definition, a call *equal* (*a, b*) will benefit from any redefinition of *is_equal* applicable to the type of *a*. Function *equal* itself is frozen to guarantee this semantics.

As with earlier examples involving *copy* and *clone*, the original version of *is_equal* has a frozen synonym *standard_is_equal*. A function *standard_equal*, defined in terms of *standard_is_equal* exactly as *equal* is defined from *is_equal*, guarantees the original semantics of field-by-field comparison for calls written under the form *standard_equal* (*a, b*).

In practice, you will probably want to use *equal* or its *standard_* counterpart rather than *is_equal* for most equality tests. Remember, however, that if you want to override the default equality test for the instances of a certain class, the function to redefine is not *equal* but *is_equal*; *equal* will automatically use the redefined version because of its above definition in terms of *is_equal*. There is no risk of getting the wrong effect, however, if you forget this rule and attempt to redefine *equal*: because *equal* is frozen, such a redefinition is invalid and will be rejected by the language processing tools.

19.8 Deep equality

Predictably, the just explored shallow form of equality testing has a deep counterpart, with both a redefinable version and a frozen one, from *ANY*:

> *deep_equal*, **frozen** *standard_deep_equal*
>   (*some*: *ANY*; *other*: **like** *some*): *BOOLEAN*
>   -- Are *some* and *other* either both void
>   -- or attached to recursively isomorphic object structures?

The declaration is in GENERAL.

What exactly are recursively isomorphic structures? Clearly, *deep_equal* should yield true if one of the arguments results from a *deep_clone* or *deep_copy* applied to the other, as *x* and *y* on the figure of page 302. But this case appears too restrictive because it excludes any sharing between the two object structures, as in the figure below where you probably expect *deep_equal* to yield true for *x* and *y*.

A case of deep equality

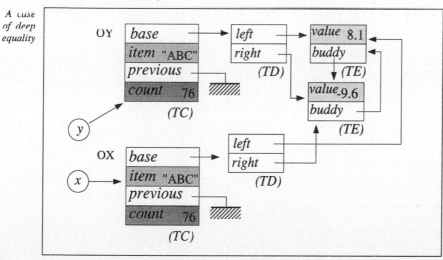

Here is the definition of deep equality which has been retained for the standard version of this function, yielding true for cases such as the above. It is convenient to define the notion separately for references and for objects.

Two references *x* and *y* are deep-equal if and only if they are either both void or attached to deep-equal objects.

Two objects OX and OY are deep-equal and only if they satisfy the following four conditions:

1 • OX and OY have the same exact type.

2 • The objects obtained by setting all the reference fields of OX and OY (if any) to void references are equal.

3 • For every void reference field of OX, the corresponding field of OY is void.

4 • For every non-void reference field of OX, attached to an object PX, the corresponding field of OY is attached to an object PY, and it is possible (recursively) to show, under the assumption that OX is deep-equal to OY, that PX is deep-equal to PY.

Condition 1 excludes indirect conformance. This is in contrast with *equal*: remember that OX may be "equal" to OY if OY is of a conforming type, provided the common parts are identical. Here, however, the definition is recursive and so will be applied to any object reachable from OX and the corresponding one reachable from OY, for example the two object of type *TD* on the figure. Type rules require one of these objects to conform to the other, but there is no guarantee that the conformance relation will be in the same direction for all such object pairs.

← See point 3 in the definition of 'equal', page 303, and the CAVEAT following the definition.

Conditions 2 and 3 express that every expanded or void field must be equal to the field in the other object.

Condition 4 handles the non-void reference fields. It is a bit subtle, as often when recursion is involved. The phrasing seems strange: why not just state that in this case PX must recursively be deep-equal to PY?

Another case of deep equality

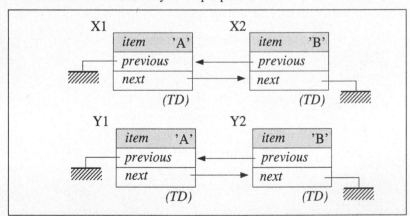

The problem is that such a condition, although not wrong, would be impossible to prove, or disprove, for any cyclic data structures. This appears readily on the two identical structures illustrated above, which might be the result of a *deep_clone* operation.

How can we check that the objects labeled X1 and Y1 are deep-equal – which they clearly should be?

Condition 1 will raise no problem since all objects are of the same type. Condition 2 is readily satisfied since the only non-reference fields in X1 and Y1, the *item* fields, are equal. Condition 3 is also immediate since both *previous* fields are void. For condition 4, we must check recursively that the objects X2 and Y2 are deep-equal.

Conditions 2 and 3 again hold trivially, covering fields *item* and *next*. There remains to check condition 4, in other words, that the *previous* fields of X2 and Y2 are attached to deep-equal objects. But now you see the problem: those attached objects are none other than X1 and Y1, and we are back to square one.

The phrasing of condition 4 gets us out of this apparently endless reasoning loop: when checking condition 4 on the original objects X1 and Y1, we only have to check that X2 and Y2 are deep-equal **under the assumption** that X1 and Y1 are themselves deep-equal. So here the equality of the *item* and *next* fields suffices to terminate the proof.

If you are looking at this with a programmer's rather than a mathematician's eyes, you will have understood this clause as meaning that in an abstract traversal algorithm designed to check deep-equality of objects, you may *mark* every previously encountered object so as not to explore it again, avoiding infinite looping.

If, on the other hand, you also master the theoretical background, you will have recognized the idea of self-conditional recursive proof (a technique whereby, to prove a property R, you must first prove a property of the form "if R holds, then P holds" for some other property P). This is exactly the scheme used, in *axiomatic* specifications of programming language semantics, to prove the correctness of a recursive routine.

On this theoretical perspective, see the book "Introduction to the Theory of Programming Languages": 9.10.6 and the example in 9.10.9.

20

Reattaching entities

20.1 Overview

At any instant of a system's execution, every entity of the system has a certain *attachment status*: it is either attached to a certain object, or void (attached to no object). At the beginning of execution, all entities of reference types are void; one of the effects of a Creation instruction, as studied in chapter 18, is to attach the instruction's target an object.

The attachment status of an entity is not eternal. It may be changed one or more times during system execution by any of the following four **reattachment** operations:

- The association of an actual argument of a routine to the corresponding formal argument at the time of a call.
- The Assignment instruction, which may attach an entity to a new object, or remove the attachment.
- The Assignment_attempt instruction, which conditionally performs the job of assignment in cases where the Assignment instruction would be prohibited by the type rules.
- The Creation instruction, which attaches its target to a newly created object (detaching it from its previous attachment if the target was not void).

You already know everything about the last case. This chapter explores the other three. It will also examine a closely related problem, for which the last chapter did the advance work: how to determine that two entities have the same attachment, or are **equal**, in any of the possible interpretations of this general notion.

20.2 Role of reattachment operations

It is convenient to divide reattachment operations into two categories: Assignment and actual-formal association are cases of **direct reattachment**; Assignment_attempt may be called a **reverse reattachment** instruction.

"Direct" is used here in opposition not to "indirect" but to "reverse".

The reason for examining the first two mechanisms under the common umbrella of direct reattachment is their great conceptual similarity. They are governed by the same constraint, which defines one of the fundamental properties of the inheritance-based type system: the type of the source must conform to the type of the target. They also follow the same semantics: for reference types, make the target a reference to the object attached to the source, if any, and otherwise make it void; for expanded types, copy the contents.

The Assignment_attempt applies only to reference types, for which its semantics is a conditional form of direct reattachment; but it it is free from type conformance constraints, making it possible to perform assignments which go against the normal direction of conformance (hence the use of the term "reverse") if they are safe.

A sharp contrast exists between these two categories of reattachment. Both of the direct forms, assignment and actual-formal association, are basic staples of Eiffel software; there are few routine bodies, even small ones, which do not use one or the other. The Assignment_attempt is at the other end of the statistical spectrum: it is hard to conceive of a well-written Eiffel system, even a very large one, which needs more than a very few specimens of this construct. But let this not lead you to file it under the exotic or marginal category. Assignment_attempt is one of those language mechanisms which, although they account for a negligible percentage of software texts, are in fact indispensable in those places where they do appear; removing them would produce an almost fatal conceptual gap in the language.

This chapter explores direct and reverse reattachment operations: their constraints, semantics, and syntactic forms.

20.3 Forms of direct reattachment

As noted, the two forms of direct reattachment, Assignment instructions and actual-formal association, have similar constraints and essentially identical semantics, studied in the following sections.

The syntax is different, of course. An assignment appears as

$$x := y$$

where x, the target, is a writable entity and y, the source, is an expression.

Very informally, the semantics of this instruction is to replace the value of x by the current value of y; x will keep its new value until the next execution, if any, of a reattachment (direct, reverse or new Creation) of which it is the target.

Actual-formal association arises as a byproduct of routine calls. A Call to a non-external routine r with one or more arguments induces a direct reattachment for each of the argument positions.

Consider any one of these positions, where the routine declaration (appearing in a class *C*) gives a formal argument *x*:

For an external routine, written in another language, the exact semantics depends on the other language's rules.

> *r* (..., *x*: *T*, ...) **is** ...

Then consider a call to *r*, where the actual argument at the given position is *y*, again an expression. The call must be of one of the following two forms, known as unqualified and qualified:

→ *See chapter 21 for the details of* Call *instructions and expressions.*

> *r* (..., *y*, ...)
> *t.r* (..., *y*, ...)
>   -- In this second form, *t* must conform to a type based on *C*

Note that a qualified Call *also has a "target", appearing to the left of the period, 't' in the second example. Do not confuse this with the target of the attachment induced by the call, 'x' in this discussion.*

Qualified or not, the call causes a direct reattachment of target *x* and source *y* for the position shown, and similarly for every other position.

Informally again, the semantics of this direct reattachment is to set the value of *x*, for the whole duration of the routine's execution caused by this particular call, to the value of *y* at the time of call. No further reattachment may occur during that execution of the routine; any new call that is later executed will, however, start by setting the value of *x* to the value of the new actual argument.

20.4 Syntax and validity of direct reattachment

Here is the syntax of an Assignment instruction:

> Assignment   ≜   Writable ":=" Expression

Actual-formal association does not have a syntax of its own; it is part of the Call construct.

→ *See chapter 21 about* Call. *Syntax page 342.*

The major validity constraint in both cases is simply conformance of source to target. For Assignment this is covered by the following rule:

VJAR

> **Assignment rule**
>
> An Assignment is valid if and only if its source expression conforms to its target entity.

As you will remember from the discussion of conformance, to say that *y* conforms to *x* (where *y* is an expression and *x* and entity) is usually to say that the type of *y* conforms to the type of *x*, but also covers cases of anchored declaration: for example, *x* of type *CT* conforms to an entity of type **like** *x* even though, as a type, *CT* does not conform to any anchored type.

← *See 13.9, page 225, about expression conformance.*

The syntax requires the target to be a Writable. Recall that a Writable entity is either an attribute of the enclosing class or a local entity of the enclosing routine. The latter case includes, in a function, the predefined entity *Result*.

← *17.9 introduced* Writable *entities; the syntax is on page 276.*

The restriction to writable entities excludes the formal arguments of a routine. Indeed, in the body of a routine

```
r (..., x, ...) is
    ...
    do
        ...
    end -- r
```

an assignment $x := y$, for some expression y, would not be valid. The only reattachments to a formal argument occur at call time, through the actual-formal association mechanism.

As a result of this rule, it is not possible for the instructions of a routine's body to change the value of any of the routine's formal arguments. If that argument is of a reference type, however, it is still possible to update fields of the **object** to which the corresponding reference is attached. So in the situation pictured below, where x is a formal argument of a routine r, the Routine_body of r may include a procedure call such as

```
x.set_attrib1 (2)
```

where *set_attrib1* will update the value of the integer field *attrib1*. What is **not** permitted is an Assignment of target x, which would affect the reference rather than the object.

Object may change, reference may not change

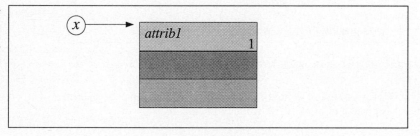

The validity constraint for the other form of direct reattachment, actual-formal association, also involves conformance of source to target: the type of every actual argument of a routine call must conform to the type declared in the routine for the corresponding formal argument. This is the notion of **argument validity** of a call, part of the general discussion of call validity, which the chapter on the Call construct will discuss in full detail.

→ *Argument validity is defined on page 369, as part of the discussion on call validity in chapter 22.*

20.5 Semantics of direct reattachment

We must now examine the precise effect of executing a direct reattachment of either of the two forms at run time.

In fact the semantics of a direct reattachment of target entity x and source expression y is exactly the same when the reattachment is an assignment of left-hand side x and right-hand side y and when it occurs as a result of a routine call with x as formal argument and y as corresponding actual argument. As a result, we only need one of the two forms as working example; let us choose the Assignment

$$x := y$$

where x is of type TX and y of type TY, which must conform to TX.

The effect depends on the nature of TX and TY: reference types, or expanded?

Here is a simple rule covering the vast majority of practical uses of assignment. If both TX and TY are expanded, the assignment copies the value of the object attached to the source onto the object attached to the target; if both are reference types, the operation attaches x to the object attached to y, or makes it void if y is void.

As an example of the first case, in

> x, y: INTEGER
> ...
> $y := 4$;
> $x := y$

the resulting value of x will be 4, but the last Assignment does not introduce any long-lasting association between x and y; this is because INTEGER is an expanded type. As an example of the second case, if TC is a reference type, then

> x, y: TC
> ...
> !! y ...
> $x := y$

will result in x and y being attached to the same object:

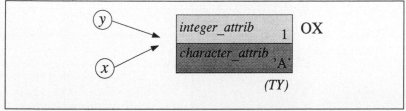

This is the basic rule, covering what most applications need. There remains, of course, to see what happens when one of TX and TY is expanded and the other is a reference type. But it is more important to understand first the reasons for the rule by exploring what potential interpretations make sense in each case.

Consider first the case of references. Assume you have the run-time situation pictured below, with two objects labeled OX and OY, assumed for simplicity to be of the same type *TY*, and accessible through two references *x* and *y*. Of course, since the Eiffel dynamic model is fully based on objects, *x* and *y* themselves will often be reference fields of some other objects, or of the same object; these objects, however, are of no interest for the present discussion and so they will not appear explicitly.

Before a reattachment

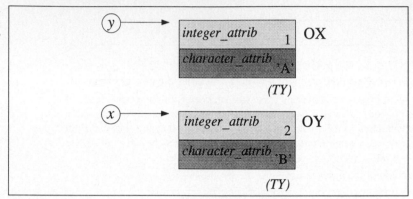

With a very broad view of reattachment, there are three possible variants of an operation that may update *x* from *y*: copying, cloning and reference reattachment.

The first operation, copying, makes sense only if both *x* and *y* are attached (non-void). Its semantics is to copy every field of the source object onto the corresponding field of the target object. It does not create a new object, but only updates an existing one. We know how to achieve it: through procedure *copy* of the universal class *ANY* or, more precisely, its frozen version *standard_copy*, ensuring identical semantics for all types (whereas *copy* may be redefined). The next figure illustrates the effect of a call *x.standard_copy* (*y*) starting in the above situation.

← *See 19.2, page 295, on 'copy' and its frozen version 'standard_copy'.*

Effect of standard copy

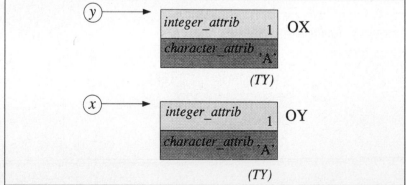

The second operation is a close variant of the first: cloning also has the semantics of field-by-field copy, but applied to a newly created object. No existing object is affected. Here too a general mechanism is available to achieve this: a call to function *clone* which (anticipating on this section) we have learned to use in an assignment *x := clone (y)*. Again, as a precaution against redefinition, we may use the frozen version *standard_clone*. The result is shown below; the cloning creates a new object, OZ, a carbon copy of OX.

← *See 19.3, page 298, about 'clone' and 'standard_clone'.*

Effect of standard clone

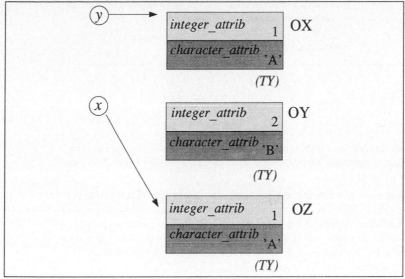

A natural question here is: "what happens to the object OY?". This will be discussed below.

→ *See "Memory management", 20.16, page 334.*

The third possible operation is reference reattachment. This does not affect any object, but simply reattaches the target reference to a different object. The result (already illustrated above) may be represented as follows:

Effect of reference reattachment

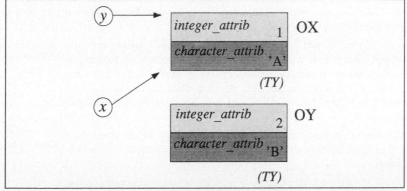

To obtain the proper rule for semantics of reattachment, we must study which of these operations make sense in every possible case. Since the source and target types may each be either expanded or reference, there will be four cases:

Possible shallow reattachment semantics

SOURCE TYPE →	Reference	Expanded
TARGET TYPE ↓		
Reference	[1] Copy (if neither source nor target is void) Clone Reference reattachment	[3] Copy (if target is not void) Clone
Expanded	[2] Copy (if source is not void)	[4] Copy

← This list only takes into account shallow operations. Deep variants were discussed in 19.6, page 302.

If all we were interested in was copying and cloning, we would not need any new mechanism: routines *standard_copy* and *standard_clone*, from *ANY*, are available for these purposes.

The missing case is reference reattachment, corresponding to the last figure shown (page 315). This only makes sense for case 1, when both target and source are of reference types: if the target is expanded, as in cases 2 and 4, there is no reference to reattach; and if the source is expanded, as in case 3 and 4, a reattachment would introduce a **reference to a sub-object**, a case discussed and rejected in the discussion of the dynamic model.

← On the absence of references to sub-objects, see the discussion in 17.8; the excluded case is illustrated by the figure on page 275.

In case 1, however, we do need the ability to specify reference reattachment, not covered by *copy*, *clone* or their frozen variants. This will be the semantics of the Assignment $x := y$ and of the corresponding actual-formal association when both x and y are of reference types.

We now have notations for expressing meaningful operations in every possible case: reference assignment in case 1, routines *standard_copy* and *standard_clone* in the other cases. At least two reasons, however, indicate that in addition to these case-specific operations we also need a single notation which will be applicable to all four cases:

- In a generic class, *TX* and *TY* may be a Formal_generic_name; then the class text does not reveal whether x and y denote objects or references, since this depends on the actual parameter used in each generic derivation of the class. But it must be possible for this class text to include an Assignment $x := y$, or a call $r (..., y, ...)$, with a clearly defined meaning in all possible cases.

If the formal generic is TX, conformance requires TY to be identical to TX. If the formal is TY, TX is either TY or an ancestor of TY's constraint (ANY if TY is unconstrained). See direct conformance rule (Formal Generic), page 224.

- The availability of general-purpose copying and cloning mechanisms does not relieve us from the need to define a clear, universal semantics for actual-formal association.

Examination of the above table suggests a uniform notation addressing these requirements. What default semantics is most useful in each case?

- In case 1, where both x and y denote references, the semantics should be reference reattachment, if only (as discussed above) because no other notation is available for reference assignment.

- In case 4, with both x and y denoting objects, only one semantics makes sense for a reattachment operation: copying the fields of the source onto those of the target.

- In case 3, with x denoting a reference and y an object, both copying and cloning are possible. But copying only works if x is not void (since there must be an object on which to copy the source's fields). If x is void, copying will fail, triggering an exception. It would be unpleasant to force class designers to test for void references before any such assignment. Cloning, much less likely to fail, is the preferable default semantics in this case.

  Cloning may also fail, triggering an exception, if there is no more memory available (19.2). But this is a much less frequent situation than the target being a void reference.

- In case 2, as in case 4, the target x is an object, so copying is again the only possible operation. In this case it will fail if y is void (since there is no object to copy), but then there is no operation that would always work.

This analysis leads to the following definition of the semantics of direct reattachment.

SOURCE TYPE →	Reference	Expanded
TARGET TYPE ↓		
Reference	[1] Reference reattachment	[3] Clone
Expanded	[2] Copy (will fail if source is void)	[4] Copy

→ The table giving equality semantics on page 336 will be organized along similar lines.

In this semantic specification, "Copy" and "Clone" refer to the frozen versions *standard_copy* and *standard_clone* that every class inherits from the universal class *ANY*.

True, a rationale could be found for using instead the redefinable version *copy*, and *clone* which is defined in terms of *copy*: after all, if the author of a class redefined these routines, there must have been a reason. But it is more prudent to stick to the frozen versions, so that the language defines a simple and uniform semantics for assignment and argument passing on entities of all types. If you do want to take advantage of redefinition, you can always use the call $x.copy\ (y)$ instead of the assignment $x := y$, or pass *clone* (y) instead of y as an actual argument to a call. These alternatives to direct reattachment apply of course to reference types as well as expanded ones.

For the exception raised in case 2 if the value of y is void, the Kernel Library class *EXCEPTIONS* introduces the integer code *Void_assigned_to_expanded*.

See chapters 15 on exceptions and 29 on class EXCEPTIONS.

Here are a few simple consequences of the above definition. As noted at the beginning of this chapter, if x and y are of type *INTEGER* (an expanded type), the instruction

$$x := y$$

assigns to x the value of y; if, however, x and y are of a reference type, the effect is a reference reattachment.

If the type of x and y is a formal generic parameter of the enclosing class, as in

```
class GENERIC_EXAMPLE [G] feature
    example_routine is
        local
            x, y: G
        do
            x := y
        end
end -- GENERIC_EXAMPLE
```

the effect of the Assignment may be reference reattachment or copying depending on the actual generic parameter used for G in the current generic derivation. (Cloning, which only occurs for reference target and expanded source, does not apply to this case since, by construction, x and y are of the same type.)

The reasoning that led to the definition of direct reattachment semantics yields the most commonly needed effect in each case. This applies in particular to cases 1 and 4, which account for the vast majority of reattachments occurring in practice: for an integer variable (case 4), it is pleasant to be able to write

$$n := 3$$

rather than

$$n.copy\ (3)$$

Here 'copy' and 'standard_copy' are the same.

which would have the same effect in this case. For a reference variable y, it is normal to expect the call

$$some\_routine\ (y)$$

simply to pass to *some_routine* a reference to the object attached to y, if any, rather than to duplicate that object for the purposes of the call. If you do wish duplication – shallow or deep – to occur, you may make your exact intentions clear by using one of the calls

$$some\_routine\ (clone\ (y))$$

$$some\_routine\ (standard\_clone\ (y))$$

$$some\_routine\ (deep\_clone\ (y))$$

20.6 An example

EXAMPLE

To illustrate the effect of reattachment in various cases, consider the run-time situation pictured below.

Type T2 may in fact be **expanded** *T1.*

A run-time system snapshot

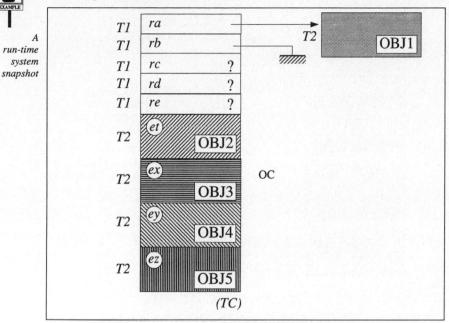

To keep matters simple, all the entities considered are attributes of a class *C*. OC, the complex object on the left, is a direct instance of type *TC*, of base class *C*.

OC is not only complex but composite.

The first five attributes (*ra, rb, rc, rd, re*), whose names begin with *r*, are of a reference type *T1*. The corresponding fields of OC are references. The four others (*et, ex, ey, ez*), whose name begins with *e*, are of type **expanded** *T2*, for some reference type *T2*. The corresponding fields are sub-objects of OC, which have been given the names OBJ2 to OBJ5. The reference field *ra* is originally attached to another object OBJ1, also of type *T2*.

Assume that class *C* has the following routine, using Assignment instructions to perform a number of reattachments:

```
assignments is
      -- Change various fields
   do
      rc := rb;
      rd := ra;
      re := et;
      ex := ey;
      ez := ra
   end -- assignments
```

If applied to the above OC, this procedure will produce the following situation:

Snapshot after assignments

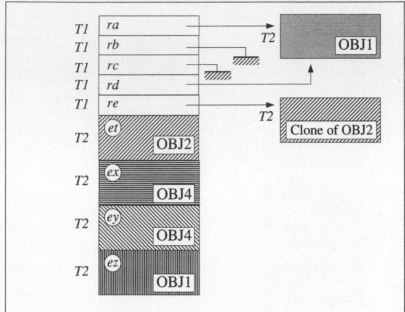

The assignment *re := et*, with reference target and expanded source, produces a duplicate of object OBJ2.

An attempt to execute *et := rb*, with an expanded target and a void source, would trigger an exception.

20.7 Comments on direct reattachment

(This section brings no new Eiffel concept. It will only be of interest to readers who wish to relate the above concepts to the argument passing conventions of earlier programming languages.)

It may be useful to compare the semantics of direct reattachment to the mechanisms provided by other languages, in particular to traditional variants of argument passing semantics.

Consider a call of the form

$$r\ (...,\ y,\ ...)$$

This causes an attachment as a result of actual-formal association between the expression *y*, of type *TY*, and the corresponding formal argument *x*, of type *TX*.

An examination of the semantics defined above in light of other argument passing conventions yields the following observations:

- If both TX and TY are reference types (case 1), the reattachment causes sharing of objects through references, also known as **aliasing**. For actual-formal association this achieves the effect of **call by reference**, with the target being protected against further reattachment for the duration of the call.

- If both TX and TY are expanded types (case 4), reattachment copies the content of y, an object, onto x. This achieves the effect of **call by value**.

- If TX is an expanded type and TY a reference type (case 2), the operation copies onto x the content of the object attached to y (y must be non-void). This achieves what is often called **dereferencing**.

- If TX is a reference type and TY an expanded type (case 3), the operation attaches to x a newly created copy of y. This case has no direct equivalent in traditional contexts; it may be viewed as a form of call by value combined with call by reference.

20.8 Effect on generic programming

More important to the practice of Eiffel software development is the effect of the above semantics on both the production and the use of generic classes – a cornerstone of reusable software production.

For a generic class such as $GENERIC\_EXAMPLE$ above, it may seem surprising to see a given syntactical notation, the assignment symbol :=, denote different operations depending on the context, and similarly for argument passing.

This convention corresponds, however, to the most common needs of generic programming. The container classes of the Data Structure library, such as $LINKED\_LIST$, TWO_WAY_LIST, $HASH\_TABLE$ and many others, used to store and retrieve values of various types, provide numerous examples. These classes are all generic and, depending on their generic derivations, the values they store may be references or objects.

← The notion of container data structure was presented in 10.17, page 156, and 12.7, page 200.

All of these classes have one or more procedures for adding an element to a data structure; for example, to insert an element to the left of the current cursor position in a linked list l a client will execute

> $some\_list.put\_left\ (x)$

Almost all of these procedures use assignment for fulfilling their task. Many do this not directly but through a call of the form

← See page 143 for an illustration of a LINKABLE list cell.

> $some\_cell.put\ (x)$

where $some\_cell$, representing some individual entry of the data structure, is of a type based on some effective descendant of the deferred generic class $CELL$; for example, $LINKED\_LIST$ uses the descendant $LINKABLE$, describing cells of linked lists. Procedure put comes from $CELL$, where it appears (in effective form) as

```
class CELL [G] feature
    item: G;
    put (new: G) is
            -- Replace the cell value by new.
        do
            item := new
        ensure
            item = new
        end; -- put
    ... Other features ...
```

*This is a slight simplification; the type of the argument 'new' is actually **like** item, which has the same immediate effect since item is of type G.*

Because the addition of an element x by *put* uses assignment, what will be added to the data structure is an object value if x is of expanded type, and otherwise a reference to an object.

This policy means that if you are a "generic programmer" (a developer or user of generic classes) you must exercise some care, when dealing with data structures having diverse possible generic derivations, to make sure you know what is involved in each case: objects or references to objects. But it provides the most commonly defaults: a call

```
some_list_of_integers.put_left (25)
```

should insert the actual value 25, whereas

```
some_list_of_integers.put_left (her_bank_account)
```

should not by itself duplicate the object representing the bank account. Storing a reference in this case is the most conservative default policy. As in earlier examples, you can always obtain a different policy by using such calls as

```
some_list_of_integers.put_left (clone (her_bank_account))
some_list_of_integers.put_left (deep_clone (her_bank_account))
```

which guarantee uniform semantics (duplication, shallow in the first case and deep in the second) across the spectrum of possible types.

The discussion also applies to the problem of **searching** a data structure, as discussed below.

→ *See the end of 20.17.*

20.9 Polymorphism

The only type constraint applying to direct reattachment is that the type of the source must conform to the type of the target.

If the target is expanded, this means that the types must essentially be the same; the only permitted flexibility is that one may describe objects of a certain form and the other references to objects of exactly the same form. This follows directly from the rules defining conformance when an expanded type is involved.

← See the General Conformance rule, page 219, and the conformance rule for expanded types, page 228.

If the target is a reference, however, the situation is much more interesting. (This is cases 1 and 3 of the above tables, and the only ones of interest for this section.) If the target's base type is based on a class C, the validity rules mean that the base class of the source may be not just C but any proper descendant of C. This gives a remarkable flexibility to the type system, while preserving safety thanks to the conformance restrictions.

As a consequence, an entity declared of type TC may refer at run time to objects which are not just of type TC but of many other types, all based on descendants of the base class of TC. This also applies to expressions containing such entities.

DEFINITION:
Dynamic
type

The **dynamic type** of an entity or expression x, at some instant of execution when x is not void, is the type of the object to which x is attached. This should not be confused with the "type" of x (called its *static type* if there is any ambiguity), which for an entity is the type with which it is declared, and for an expression is the type deduced from the types of its constituents.

DEFINITION:
Polymorphism

This ability to have more than one dynamic type is called **polymorphism**; an entity or expression which has two or more possible dynamic types (that is to say, which may become attached at run time to objects of two or more types) is itself a polymorphic entity. Only entities or expressions of reference types may be polymorphic.

"Poly", many, "morphë", shape. See SCROOGE 27 (Symposium on Current Research in Object-Oriented Greek Etymology), Bali, 1991, pp. 341-465.

The conformance rules mean that possible dynamic types for x all conform to the (static) type of x. This is how polymorphism is kept under control by the type system.

DEFINITION:
Dynamic
Type Set,
Dynamic
Class Set

The set of possible dynamic types for an entity or expression x is called the **dynamic type set** of x. The set of base classes of these types is called the **dynamic class set** of x.

It is possible to determine the dynamic type set of x through analysis of the classes in the system to which x belongs, by considering all the attachment and reattachment instructions involving x or its entities.

The dynamic type set is an important notion because of its role in expressing the validity constraints on calls and Creation instructions and, more generally, in permitting full static type checking. For example a call of the form

$$x.\,proc\ (...)$$

will not execute correctly unless, for the base class B of every possible dynamic type of x, *proc* is a procedure of B which is available to the class containing this call. Similarly, the creation instruction

$$!! \; x. creat \; (...)$$

requires that *creat* be a creation procedure of every possible *B*. So to check the validity of calls and Creation instructions it is necessary to consider not just the type of an entity but its dynamic type set. This will be done in the discussion of validity constraints for both Creation instructions and calls.

→ *See 18.9, starting on page 286, for the rules on* Creation *instructions, and chapter 22 on the validity of calls.*

To avoid any confusion on the notion of dynamic type set, we need two observations, one on void values, the other on why no flow analysis is necessary.

First, the definition of the possible dynamic types of *x* only considers attachment of **non-void** values to *x*. This means that an assignment of the form

$$x := Void$$

does not affect the dynamic type set of *x*. Without this rule, the assignment would add *NONE* to that type set. (*NONE*, the type of *Void*, is the "most constrained" class, descendant of all other classes but with no usable features.)

← *See 6.16, page 88, about* NONE.

The other observation is that the dynamic type set does not take into account control flow analysis: if an attachment instruction such as $x := y$ appears in the system, you must register its effect on the dynamic type set of *x*, even though the instruction may be on a control flow path that a certain system execution, or even all executions, will never follow. For example, the fragment

```
a1: A; b1: B;
...
if b1 = Void then a1 := b1 end
```

B must be a proper descendant of A. A and B are assumed to be non-generic classes.

may not, at run time, attach to *a1* an object of type *B* (in fact, using *Void* rather than *b1* as right-hand side would yield the same effect); yet its presence in a system's text adds *B* to the dynamic type set of *a1*. In other words, we accept that whenever the system contains a reattachment instruction of target *x*, any possible type *T* of the source expression is also a possible type for *x*. We do not require our language processing tool to perform the kind of exhaustive control flow analysis that would be needed to determine whether *x* can actually become attached to an object of type *T* in a particular execution.

20.10 Semi-strictness

(This section and the next are only for the benefit of readers with a taste for theory, and may be skipped. They bring new light on earlier concepts, but introduce no new language rules, and have little influence on the practice of software development.)

One more interesting property follows from the semantic specification of direct reattachment, in one of its two forms – actual-formal association. The property is that semi-strict implementations of argument passing are possible, depending on the arguments' expansion status. Let us look at what this means.

DEFINITION:
Strict   In programming theory, an operation is **strict** on one of its operands if it cannot execute without computing the value of that argument. It is non-strict if it may in some cases yield a result without needing to evaluate the argument.

Many common operations are strict on all arguments: for example you cannot compute the sum of two integers m and n unless you know their values, so this operation is strict on both arguments.

Not all possible operations are strict on all arguments, however. Consider a conditional operation

> **test** c **yes** m **no** n **end**

WARNING: this is a mathematical notation, not Eiffel syntax!

which yields m if the value of c (a boolean) is true, n otherwise. This is strict on c, but not on the other two arguments, since it does not need to evaluate m when it finds that c is false, or to evaluate n when c is true.

Detecting that an operation is non-strict on an argument may be interesting for performance reasons (since this may avoid unnecessary computations); more importantly, however, non-strict operations may be more broadly applicable than their strict counterparts. This is immediately visible on the previous example: a fully strict version of the **test** operation would always start by evaluating c, m and n; but then it would fail to yield a result when c is true and n not defined, and when c is false and m not defined. A "semi-strict" version (strict on c but not on m and n) may, however, yield results in these cases, provided m is defined in the first and n in the second.

How does this apply to Eiffel? Here the operations of interest are calls, of the general form

> $t.r\ (...,\ y,\ ...)$

and the operands are the target t and the actual arguments such as y, if any. Such a call is always strict on its target (which must be attached to an object). In a literal sense, it is also strict on its actual arguments, since it will need to pass their values to the routine r.

When considering an actual argument such as y, however, it is more interesting to analyze strictness not for the value of y but for the attached object, if any. Then the specification of direct reattachment semantics yields two cases, depending on the types of y and of the corresponding formal argument in r:

A • If both are reference types, the call passes to r a reference, not the attached object (which does not exist anyway if the value of y is void).

B • If either type is expanded, the call passes the attached object. (The value of y may not be void in this case.)

← A *is case 1 of the table of direct reattachment semantics, page 317.* B *is cases 2, 3 and 4.*

In other words, considering the object as operand, actual-formal association is non-strict on y in case A, and is strict in case B.

If the target is a reference and the source is expanded (case 3 of the table), actual-formal association results in reference reattachment, but the source must first be cloned, so that the operation is indeed strict on y.

DEFINITION:
Semi-strict

The call as a whole will be said to be strict if it is strict on all arguments, and **semi-strict** if it is non-strict on at least one argument. (Remember that it is always strict on its target.)

If a call may be semi-strict and you want to guarantee strictness on a particular argument without changing anything in the routine's text, this is easy: just use cloning on the actual argument, passing *clone* (y) rather than y. The reverse adaptation is not possible: if the routine has a formal argument of expanded type, it will always be strict on the corresponding actuals.

What does semi-strictness mean in practice? Essentially that if both an actual argument *y* and the corresponding formal argument are of reference types the implementation **may** choose a non-strict argument passing mechanism, which evaluates *y* when and only when the routine actually needs *y*'s value.

Such a semi-strict implementation is possible, but, except in one case, it is **not guaranteed**. Implementations are not required to use a non-strict argument passing mechanism even if the formal and actual arguments are both references. This means that when you write a call of the form

→ *The exception is semi-strict boolean operators, as explained below.*

> *t*. *r* (..., *y*, ...)

you must make sure that the value of *y*, which may be a complex expression, is always defined at the time of call execution – even in cases for which *r* does not actually need that value. The call may evaluate *y* anyway.

Consider for example a routine

> *too_strict_for_me* (*i*: *INTEGER*; *arr*: *ARRAY* [*REAL*]; *val*: *REAL*): *REAL* **is**
>   **do**
>   **if** *i* >= *arr*. *lower* **and** *i* <= *arr*. *upper* **then**
>   *Result* := *val*
>   **end**
>   **end** -- *too_strict_for_me*

which returns the value of its last argument if its first argument, *i*, is within the bounds of the middle argument, an array, and returns 0.0 (the default value for *REAL*) otherwise. Then consider a call in the same class:

WARNING: *potentially incorrect!*

> *arr1*: *ARRAY* [*REAL*]; *a*: *REAL*; *n*: *INTEGER*;
>
> ...
>
> *a* := *too_strict_for_me* (*n*, *arr1*, *arr1*. *item* (*n*))

If the value of *n* may be outside of the bounds of *arr1*, then this call is not correct since *arr1*. *item* (*n*), denoting the *n*-th element of *arr1*, is not defined in this case. Semi-strict implementation (non-strict on the last argument) would avoid evaluation of *arr1*. *item* (*n*) and hence ensure proper execution of the call; but you may **not** assume that the implementation uses this policy.

There is one exception, however. As will be seen in detail in the discussion of operator expressions, three functions of the Kernel Library class *BOOLEAN*, are required to be semi-strict (that is to say, non-strict on their single argument). These are infix functions representing a variant of the common boolean operations: and, or, implies. Their declarations in class *BOOLEAN* appear as

→ *See 23.9, page 381, about semi-strict boolean operators and their semi-strictness.*

> **infix** *"and then"* (*other*: *BOOLEAN*): *BOOLEAN* **is do** ... **end**;
>
> **infix** *"or else"* (*other*: *BOOLEAN*): *BOOLEAN* **is do** ... **end**;
>
> **infix** *"implies"* (*other*: *BOOLEAN*): *BOOLEAN* **is do** ... **end**;

The semantics of these functions readily admits a semi-strict interpretation: *a* **and then** *b* should yield false whenever *a* is false, regardless of the value of *b*, and similarly for the others. To state this property concisely for all three operations, it is useful to express the value of each, as applied to arguments *a* and *b*, in terms of the above **test** notation, which yields successively:

---

test not *a* **yes false no** *b* **end**

test *a* **yes true no** *b* **end**

test not *a* **yes true no** *b* **end**

---

*Remember that an operator expression such as 'a **and then** b' stands for a call of target 'a' and actual argument 'b'. This explains why all the expressions considered here are strict on 'a', since a call is always strict on its target.*

This semi-strictness of these boolean operators is important in practice because it makes it possible to use them as conditional operators. As a typical example, again using arrays, it is often convenient to write instructions of the form

---

if
  i >= *arr*. *lower* **and then**
  i <= *arr*. *upper* **and then**
  arr. *item* (*i*). *some_property*
then
  ...

---

where the last condition is not defined unless the first two are true (because *i* would then be outside of the bounds of *arr*). In the absence of a semi-strict version of "and", it would be much more cumbersome to express such examples.

The discussion of boolean operators will show further uses of this semi-strict policy, especially for writing iterators on data structures, with an example from the Iteration Library.

→ See in particular the example of procedure 'continue_until' from class LINEAR_ITERATION on page 383.

20.11 More on strictness

(This more theoretical section may be skipped on first reading.)

What about the ordinary boolean operators **and** and **or**? You may expect them to have a strict semantics, but this is not the case – at least not necessarily. Here the language definition is simply less tolerant: it makes it incorrect to evaluate expressions *a* **and** *b* and *a* **or** *b* when *b* is not defined, even if *a* has value false in the first case and if *b* has value true in the second case. There is nothing surprising in this convention, which has its counterpart in all other forms of expression except those involving semi-strict operators: no rule in this book will tell you how to compute the value of *m* + *n* if the value of the integer expression *n* is not defined.

Because the language definition does not cover cases in which the second operand of **or** or **and** does not have a value, an implementation that computes **and** using **and then** and **or** using **or else** is legitimate; it may produce results in cases for which a strict implementation would not, but these cases are incorrect anyway. The reverse is not true: a correct implementation of **and** and **or** does not necessarily provide a correct implementation of **and then** and **or else** since it may be strict. In other words: non-semi-strict does not necessarily mean strict! If you want to guarantee strictness, it does not suffice to use **and** or **or**; you should use cloning as suggested above. (For **implies**, which is semi-strict, there is no equivalent non-semi-strict operator, but you can use the form **not** *a* **or else** *b*.)

It is legitimate to ask why the semi-strict property of three boolean operators – **and then**, **or else**, **implies** – is not expressed as part of the language syntax. One could indeed envision a special optional qualifier **nonstrict** applicable to formal arguments of reference type:

> **infix** *"and then"* (**nonstrict** *other*: *BOOLEAN*): *BOOLEAN*

WARNING: not legal Eiffel!

Such a facility was not, however, deemed worth the trouble, since the common practice of software development seldom requires semi-strictness outside of the special case of boolean operators. A possible exception is concurrent computation which, however, falls beyond the scope of this book.

For a discussion of a possible model for concurrent computation in Eiffel, based on ideas of semi-strictness, see the article "Sequential and Concurrent Object-Oriented Programming", reproduced as part of "An Eiffel Collection" (the reference is in the bibliography of appendix C).

20.12 Limitations of direct reattachment

To complete the study of reattachment, there remains to see one mechanism which, like the operations examined so far, may reattach a reference to a different object. The semantics will in fact be one of reference reattachment; what differs is the validity constraint under which you may apply this mechanism, and also the conditional nature of its effect.

The need for such a facility arises when you must access an object of a certain type *TX*, but the only name you have to denote that object is an expression of type *TY*, for two different types with the "wrong" conformance (*TX* conforms to *TY* rather than the reverse), or even no conformance at all. Normally, you would use the assignment

> *x* := *y*

with *x* of type *TX*; but this will not work because the fundamental constraint of direct reattachment, expressed in the Assignment rule, assumes conformance in the other direction: source should conform to target. Calling a routine with *y* as actual argument corresponding to a formal argument *x* of type *TX* would also be invalid for the same reason. This conformance property is essential to ensure the soundness of the type system.

When would such a need ever arise? The typical situation is one in which you have lost the appropriate type information, so that you may only declare the source expression as being of a type which is too general to be useful in the new context.

Type TA is "more general" than type TB if TB conforms to TA.

This happens sometimes as a result of genericity. Assume a data structure declared as

> *account_list*: *LIST* [*ACCOUNT*]

where *ACCOUNT* has heirs *SAVING* and *CHECKING*:

Inheritance
structure
for
accounts

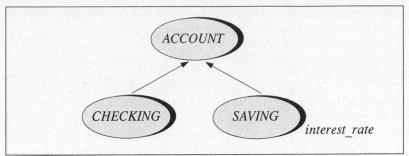

A feature *interest_rate* is introduced at the level of *SAVING*, with no precursor in the parent (only saving accounts pay interest). What if you know, or think you know, that the first element in the list is an instance of *SAVING* and need to obtain its interest rate? The following will not do the job:

> *account_list*: LIST [*ACCOUNT*];
>
> *my_saving_account*: *SAVING*; *my_rate*: *RATE*;
>
> ...
>
>   -- The following assignment is not valid:
> *my_saving_account* := *account_list*. *item* (*1*);
>
> *my_rate* := *my_saving_account*. *interest_rate*

→ *WARNING: this extract is not valid. A valid rephrasing, solving the given problem, appears below (page 331).*

because the first assignment violates the conformance property implied by the Assignment rule.

Since such examples are easy to envision, beginners in object-oriented technology tend to think that they typify a huge immediate problem. This is inaccurate. In well-designed Eiffel software, the problem seldom arises unless the software has reached a level of sophistication far beyond the elementary. After all, if you use a generic structure, it is precisely because you want to forget the details of specific variants, and concentrate on what is common to all of them. If you know that an element of such a structure (such as the first list item in the above example) has special properties, then you can probably access it separately anyway, through an entity of the right type (such as an entity *first_saving* of type *SAVING*, whose value is a reference to the first list item).

Even in fairly elementary uses of Eiffel, however, the problem does arise, and could risk creating a serious obstacle, in one particular context: **persistence**.

Persistence is the presence of a mechanism enabling a session of a system to store objects on a permanent medium, so that another session of the same or another system may eventually retrieve them.

When a new session retrieves a persistent object, the type information of the original entities associated with it has been lost; the new system can only "guess" at the type of the object, and needs a mechanism to check the validity of such guesses.

Consider for example a persistence mechanism offering a procedure *store* to file away objects, and a function *retrieved* to access previously stored objects. If the persistence facility is truly general-purpose, *store* must apply to objects of arbitrary types. Consequently, the argument representing the object to be stored may only be declared of the most general type *ANY*:

→ *Such general-purpose retrieval facilities are introduced in chapter 30. ANY is presented in chapter 27.*

> *store* (*object*: *ANY*; *k*: *KEY*)

Because all user-defined types conform to *ANY*, this enables *store* to accept arguments of any type.

The routine is assumed to have a second argument representing a storage key. In practice it may need to take various arguments representing files, data base, or other information needed to store and retrieve the object.

The *retrieved* function, however, raises a serious problem. By the reasoning applied to *store*, if *retrieved* is a general-purpose function, it can only return a result of type *ANY*. But then we can do nothing useful with that result! In the assignment

> *x* := *retrieved* (*my_saving_account_key*)

x may only be of type *ANY*. Then the only applicable features are those which work for every Eiffel class. If what the system has stored is your savings account and you want to know the balance, you will soon start hating the type system, which prevents you from using *x* of type *SAVING*.

Such cases are not a reason, of course, to throw away the typing with the bath water: typing constraints provide an important safeguard against serious potential errors. Even here, in fact, we would not want to renounce these constraints: what if the object associated with *my_key* is in fact **not** of the expected type? Clearly, the assignment cannot succeed and you need to find that out before you attempt to apply to *x* a feature of class *SAVING*.

Such, then, is the problem: how to "force" the typing of a certain object, without destroying the consistency of the type system.

20.13 The assignment attempt

What is needed is a way to perform the assignment, but conditional on its applicability: if the type of the source object turns out *not* to be compatible with the type of the target entity, then no reattachment should occur. The effect of such a reattachment would be to attach an entity to an object of a type that does not conform to the entity's type (*SAVING* in the example); as a result, further feature calls (such as *x.interest_rate*) could wreak total chaos.

The Assignment_attempt instruction provides such a form of conditional reattachment. Its syntax uses a symbol resembling the := of normal Assignment, but with a question mark replacing the colon to suggest the conditional nature of the operation:

> *x* ?= *retrieved* (*my_saving_account_key*)

If, at execution time, the source is attached to an object of a type conforming to that of the target, the instruction will have the same effect as an Assignment.

What if the type does not conform? As noted, we must avoid any erroneous call $x.f$ where f is a feature of x's generating class. The validity constraints on calls permit such calls: this is the very basis of a class-based type system. In one case, however, the call would not be applicable at run time: if the value of x is void. Then there is no object to which f may be applied.

This suggests what the Assignment_attempt should do if it fails to find a source object whose type is compatible with the target's requirements: make the target void.

As a result, the effect of the above Assignment_attempt, assuming x to be of type *SAVING*, is the following:

- If the call to *retrieved* returns a reference to an object whose type conforms to *SAVING*, then attach x to that object.

- Otherwise, make x void.

The second case also includes the possibility that the source is void; then it is natural that the target should become void too.

When using an Assignment_attempt such as the above, you will usually want to check that the operation did attach a reference to the target – in other words, that the source was attached to an object of the expected type. The scheme for doing this is:

```
x: SAVING;
...
x ?= retrieved (my_saving_account_key);
if x = Void then
    ... No object was retrieved, or the object retrieved
    is not of the expected type; take appropriate actions ...
else
    -- Here everything is as expected.
    -- You may apply SAVING features to x, for example:
    x.set_interest_rate (new_rate); ...
end
```

This scheme also yields an immediate solution to the problem left unsolved above: you believe that the first item of *account_list* is a *SAVING* object, and you want to know its interest rate. Here is how to get it:

```
account_list: LIST [ACCOUNT];
my_saving_account: SAVING; my_rate: RATE;
...
my_saving_account ?= account_list.item (1);
if my_saving_account /= Void then
    my_rate := my_saving_account.interest_rate
else
    ... What we found is not what we were looking for! ...
end
```

As a related example, assume you need to compute the number of instances of *SAVING* in the *account_list*. You may use the following function:

```
saving_count: INTEGER is
        -- Number of instances of SAVING in account_list
    local
        next_saving: SAVING
    do
        from
            account_list.start
        until
            account_list.off
        loop
            next_saving ?= account_list.item;
            if not next_saving = Void then
                Result := Result + 1
            end;
            account_list.forth
        end
    end -- saving_count
```

This will count direct as well as indirect instances; in other words, direct instances of proper descendants of SAVING are included.

The algorithm relies on mechanisms to traverse a list: 'start' moves the cursor to the first element; 'forth' advances it by one position; 'off' indicates if it is beyond the last element. See 10.13, page 148, and "Eiffel: The Libraries".

The Assignment_attempt will produce a non-void result whenever the source yields an object conforming to *SAVING*. This means that (as implied by the header comment) this function counts instances of *SAVING*, not just direct instances. An object which is a direct instance of a type based on a proper descendant of *SAVING* and conforming to *SAVING* will be included.

20.14 Rules on assignment attempt

Let us see now the precise syntax, validity and semantics of the Assignment_attempt instruction.

Here is the form of the instruction:

> Assignment_attempt   ≙   Writable "?=" Expression

The instruction is subject to a single restriction:

VJRV

> **Assignment Attempt rule**
>
> An Assignment_attempt is valid if and only if the type of the target entity is a reference type.

This condition rules out a target whose type is expanded, or a Formal_generic_name – cases for which the instruction would not play any useful role. If *x* is of an expanded type, the test *x* = *Void* could only yield false; a Formal_generic_name may stand for both reference and expanded types. The target may, however, be of an Anchored type since this falls under the category of reference types.

← The precise definition of "reference type" is on page 208.

There is no such restriction on the source type, which may be a reference, expanded or formal generic type.

The effect of an Assignment_attempt of source y and target x, of type TX, is the following:

M1 • If y is attached to an object whose type conforms to TX, then the effect is that of a direct reattachment of y to x, as given earlier in this chapter.

← The semantics of direct reattachment is given by the table on page 317.

M2 • If y is void or attached to an object whose type does not conform to TX, the effect is to make the value of x void.

If the source y is expanded, then y will never be void, and its type TY must have TX as its base type (since TX must conform to TY, and the only reference type that conforms to an expanded type is its base type). As given by the first case (M1) of the semantics, the effect is a direct reattachment, which yields a clone operation (box [3] of the table defining direct reattachment semantics) since the source is expanded, and condition 2 of the above constraint requires the target to be a reference.

← See 13.10, page 226, about conformance to an expanded type. The table of direct reattachment semantics was given on page 317.

20.15 Notes on assignment attempt

A frequently asked question by newcomers to Eiffel is whether it is possible to test at run time for the dynamic type of an object (through an attached entity).

In principle, the assignment attempt addresses this request if the entity is expected to be one of a set of known types (for example types based on descendants of a known class). For example:

```
Checking_type, Account_type: INTEGER is unique;

Unknown_type: INTEGER is 0;

what_exact_type (a: ACCOUNT): INTEGER is
        -- Precise type of a: checking, saving or unknown
    local
        as_checking: CHECKING;
        as_saving: SAVING
    do
        as_checking ?= a;
        as_saving ?= a;
        if as_checking /= Void then
            Result := Checking_type
        end;
        if as_saving /= Void then
            Result := Saving_type
        end
    end -- what_exact_type
```

At most one of the assignment attempts will produce a non-void target. A more nested conditional structure (executing the second assignment attempt only if the first one produces a void target) would save some tests, especially if there were more than two cases. If all yield a void target, the function's result is 0, that is to say Unknown_type.

This technique becomes cumbersome as soon as there is more than a few possible types, since you must include an entity declaration and an assignment attempt for each of them. Better techniques are available for the same purpose:

• Function *conforms_to* from the universal class *ANY* makes it possible to determine whether the type of an object conforms to the type of another.

→ See 27.4, page 433, about 'conforms_to'.

- The kernel class *INTERNAL* provides a simpler way to access the dynamic type of an entity through a function *dynamic_type*.

See "Eiffel: The Libraries" about INTERNAL.

- More fundamentally, if you need to test an entity for its possible dynamic types, it is because you will perform different computations based on the result of this test. Here the recommended technique, which lies at the very heart of the Eiffel software design method, is **not** to specify the set of choices explicitly, as this would freeze the system's architecture and make future extensions painful.

Instead, you should usually describe the different cases by multiple proper descendants to a common heir class, and the different computations by definitions or redefinitions of a common original routine. Then dynamic binding will automatically achieve the required effect and keep the system open to future additions, removal or changes of individual cases, preserving the extendibility and reusability of the corresponding software architectures.

See "Object-Oriented Software Construction", in particular the discussions of the "Open-closed Principle", for a presentation of the underlying methodological concepts. See also in the present book the single choice principle (page 283) and dynamic binding (chapter 21).

The assignment attempt is most useful in cases when you know more about the dynamic type of an entity than what the entity's declaration implies – but may still want to check that the actual objects do satisfy your expectations. Such cases occur especially, although not exclusively, in the context of persistence, as illustrated above.

20.16 Memory management

A practical consequence of the reference reattachment mechanism, both in the direct form (assignment, argument passing) and in the reverse form (assignment attempt), is that some objects may become useless. This raises the question of how, if in any way, the memory space they used may be reclaimed for later use by newly created objects.

For example, the reference reattachment illustrated by the figure below may make the object labeled OY unreachable from any useful object.

Effect of reference reattachment

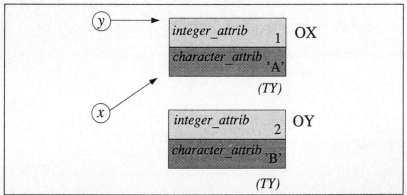

← *This is the same figure as on page 315.*

In a similar way, the result of a cloning operation may make an object unreachable. This may be the case with the middle object (also labeled OY) in the earlier illustration of cloning.

The illustration of cloning is also on page 315.

What does it mean for an object to be "useful"? Remember that the execution of a system is the execution of a creation procedure on an object. That object, which will remain in place for the duration of the system's execution, and is an instance of the system's root class, may be called the root object. Then a useful object is one that may be reached directly or indirectly, following references, from the root object. Objects that are not useful may not influence the system's execution; it is appropriate, then, to reclaim the memory space they use.

← See the definition of executing a system on page 35.

Should a reattachment such as the one illustrated above (or its clone variant) automatically result in freeing the associated storage? Of course not. The object labeled OY may still be reachable from the root through other reference paths.

It would indeed be both dangerous and unacceptably tedious to lay the burden of object memory reclamation on developers. Dangerous because it is easy for a developer to forget a reference, and to recycle an object's storage space wrongly while the object is still reachable, resulting in disaster when a client later tries to access it; and unacceptably tedious because, even if you know for sure that an object is unreachable, you should not just recycle its own storage but also analyze all its references to other objects to determine recursively whether other objects have not also become unreachable as a result. This makes the prospect of manual reclamation rather formidable.

Authors of Eiffel implementation are encouraged (although not required) to provide a **garbage collection** mechanism which will take care of detecting unreachable objects. Although many policies are possible for garbage collection, the following properties are often deemed desirable.

This list matches the design goals for the garbage collector in ISE's implementation. See "Eiffel: The Environment".

- Efficiency: the overhead on system execution should be low.

- Incrementality: it is desirable to have a collector which works in small bursts of activity, being triggered at specified intervals, rather than one which waits for memory to fill up and then takes over for a possibly long full collection cycle. Interactive applications require bursts to be (at least on average) of a short enough duration to make them undetectable at the human scale.

- Tunability. library facilities should allow systems to turn collection off (for example during a critical section of a real-time application) and on again, to request a full collection cycle, and to control the duration of the bursts if the collector is incremental.

Such facilities may be found in the Support Library class MEMORY.

20.17 Semantics of equality

The previous discussions have shown how to reattach values. A closely related problem, whose study will conclude this chapter, is to **compare** values, for example to see if they are attached to the same object. This raises the question of the semantics of the equality operator = and its opposite the inequality operator /=.

Class MEMORY also offers a procedure 'free' which explicitly reclaims an object's storage space. In view of the above discussion, use of this procedure is strictly reserved for low-level system programming. An example of a possibly legitimate use is in an Eiffel garbage collector written in Eiffel.

If you remember how the study of object duplication (*copy*, *clone* and their variants) led us to object comparison (*equal* and its variants), you will probably have anticipated the current section: just as the assignment operator := has the semantics of reference attachment, copy or clone depending on the expansion status of its operands, so will the equality operator = have the semantics of reference or object equality.

There are in fact two operators to consider here: equality = and inequality /=. However only one semantic definition is needed, since the effect of x /= y is defined in all cases to be that of

> **not** $(x = y)$

For =, two tests are a priori possible: reference equality, which returns true if and only if two references are attached to the same object; and object equality.

The previous chapter has introduced a function to test object equality: function *equal* from the universal class *ANY*, which in its original version will return true if and only if two objects are field-by-field equal. As with copying and cloning operations, it is more prudent to rely on the frozen version *standard_equal*, guaranteeing uniform semantics. (By redefining *is_equal*, you may provide another version of *equal* for a specific class.) For convenience, *standard_equal* (like *equal*) also applies to void values. In the present discussion, "object equality" denotes an operation that can only compare two objects, and so must be applied to attached (non-void) values.

← On the equality functions 'equal' and 'is_equal', see 19.7, page 303.

Here is the table of possibilities, which closely parallels the corresponding table for direct reattachment:

Possible shallow equality semantics

TYPE OF FIRST → TYPE OF SECOND ↓	Reference	Expanded
Reference	[1] Reference equality Object equality (if neither is void)	[3] Object equality (if second is not void)
Expanded	[2] Object equality (if first is not void)	[4] Object equality

← See the table on page 316.

For each of the four cases, we must give a reasonable meaning to the equality operator =. The line of reasoning applied earlier to direct reattachment yields the following semantics, which again parallels the table for direct reattachment.

TYPE OF FIRST → TYPE OF SECOND ↓	Reference	Expanded
Reference	[1] Reference equality	[3] *standard_equal*
Expanded	[2] *standard_equal*	[4] *standard_equal*

← Compare with the table giving assignment semantics on page 317.

In other words, if *x* and *y* are references, the result of a test

$$x = y$$

is true if and only if *x* and *y* are either both void or both attached to the same object; if either or both of *x* and *y* are objects, then the test yields true if and only if they are attached to field-by-field equal objects, as indicated by function *standard_equal* from class *ANY*.

As with direct reattachment, the semantics given is the most frequently needed one for each case, and in particular is usually appropriate for operations on arguments of a Formal_generic_name type. For more specific semantics, you may use one of the calls

equal (*x*, *y*)

deep_equal (*x*, *y*)

standard_equal (*x*, *y*)

standard_deep_equal (*x*, *y*)

Many container classes of the Data Structures library offer functions to ask whether a value appears in a certain a data structure such as a list, a set, a hash table etc. Usually, these classes provide two variants: one, normally called *has*, uses = to test whether an element stored in the data structure "is" the value sought; the other, normally called *has_equal*, uses *equal* to test whether a stored element is "equal to" the sought value.

See "Eiffel: The Libraries". The notion of container data structure was presented in 10.17, page 156, and 12.7, page 200.

21

Feature call

21.1 Overview

How does a software system perform its job – its computations?

It must first set the stage: create the needed objects, attach them to the appropriate entities. The preceding chapters discussed how to do this. But once it has the objects in place and knows how to access them, the system should do something useful with them.

In Eiffel's model of computation, the fundamental way to do something with an object is to apply to it an operation which – because the model is class-based, and behind every run-time object lurks some class of the system's text – must be a feature of the appropriate class.

This is feature call, one of the most important constructs in Eiffel's object-oriented approach to computation, and the topic of this chapter.

Two closely related topics are important enough to deserve separate chapters:

- The validity of calls raises the general question of **type checking**: how to make sure that the target of every call will be an object equipped with the appropriate feature. $\rightarrow$ *Chapter 22.*

- Operator expressions are conceptually calls, but use traditional mathematical syntax. They are discussed as part of the chapter on expressions, although there will be little new to say about their validity and semantic properties, which are those of calls. $\rightarrow$ *Chapter 23.*

21.2 Parts of a call

A call is the application of a certain feature to a certain object, possibly with arguments. As a consequence, it has three components:

- The *target* of the call, an expression whose value is attached to the object.
- The *feature* of the call, which must be a feature of the base class of the object's type.
- An *actual argument list*.

The target and argument list are optional; the feature is required.

Here is a typical example showing these components:

> remote_bank.transfer_by_wire (20000, today)

This particular call uses one of the two syntactical possibilities, **dot notation**. (The other one, relying on prefix or infix operators, is discussed below.) The target of the call is *remote_bank*; the feature of the call is *transfer_by_wire*; and the actual argument list contains the two elements *20000* and *today*.

The target is separated from the feature of the call by a period, or dot, hence the name dot notation.

If the target is the predefined entity *Current*, representing the "current object" of system execution, as explained below, you may write the call as

→ *The definition of "current object" is on page 349*.

> Current.print (message)

but in this case you may also leave the target implicit, as in the equivalent form

> print (message)

which is still considered to be a case of dot notation in spite of the absence of an explicit dot. If a dot is present, the call is **qualified**; otherwise, it is **unqualified**.

A qualified call may have more than one level of qualification and is then said to be a **multidot** call, as in

> paragraph (2).line (3).second_word.set_font (Bold)

For a feature without arguments, the actual argument list will be absent, as in the source expression of the Assignment

> code := remote_bank.authorization

where *authorization* must be either an attribute or a function without arguments.

21.3 Uses of calls

Syntactically, a call may play either of two roles: instruction and expression.

A call is a specimen of construct Call (in dot notation) or Operator_expression (in prefix or infix notation). Operator expressions, as their name indicates, are always used as expressions, but a Call in dot notation may be either an instruction or an expression. The syntax productions for both the Instruction and Expression constructs indeed include Call as one of the choices.

The production for Instruction appears on page 116, and the production for Expression on page 373.

The above examples used calls to *transfer_by_wire*, *print* and *set_font* as instructions, and a call to *authorization* as an expression.

Whether a particular call is an instruction or an expression depends on the nature of the feature of the call:

VKCN

- If the feature is an attribute or a function, the Call is syntactically an expression.

- If the feature is a procedure, the Call is an instruction.

Since this rule has a constraint code, a language processing tool may refer to it when detecting an error such as the use of a procedure call in an expression.

21.4 The two syntactic forms

A call serving as an expression may use, instead of dot notation, the Operator_expression form based on prefix or infix operators. For example, both of the two operator expressions

```
    –1
    4 – 3
```

are in fact calls to functions of the Kernel Library class *INTEGER*: the first is a call to function **prefix** *"–"*; the second, to function **infix** *"–"*. The Feature Declaration rule requires a prefix feature to be a function without argument or an attribute, and an infix feature to be a function with one argument.

← The Feature Declaration rule is on page 69; see clauses 5 and 6.

It is important to realize that the difference between the two notations is only syntactical. With a different choice of feature names in class *INTEGER*, the above two expressions would have been written

```
    (1).minus
    (4).subtract (3)
```

The syntax of Call requires the parentheses. See page 342 below.

and the calls would have been subject to exactly the same validity constraints and semantics. In such a case, of course, most people prefer the above prefix and infix forms.

The discussion of expressions will formalize the correspondence between the two syntactic forms by defining an **equivalent dot form** for any operator expression.

→ 23.7, page 380.

21.5 Uniform access

An important property applies to feature calls written in dot notation and used as expressions: the notation is exactly the same for a Call involving a function with no arguments and one involving an attribute. So the expression

> *p1.age*

where entity *p1* is of type *PERSON*, is applicable both if the feature *age* of class *PERSON* is an attribute or if it is a function.

If *age* is an attribute, every instance of *PERSON* has a field which gives the value of *age* for the instance. If *age* is a function, that value is obtained, when requested, through some computation, presumably of the difference between the current date and a "birth date" field.

For a client containing the above call, however, this makes no difference.

This property of **uniform access** facilitates smooth evolution of software projects by protecting classes from internal implementation changes in their suppliers.

← The Uniform Access property was first discussed on page 65.

21.6 Form of a call

The syntax of calls in prefix or infix form is part of the syntax of construct Expression and will be studied separately. Construct Call describes calls in dot notation (qualified or not) and has the following syntax.

→ *See page 373 for the syntax of* Expression.

Call	≜	[Parenthesized_qualifier] Call_chain
Parenthesized_qualifier	≜	Parenthesized "."
Call_chain	≜	{Unqualified_call "." ...}⁺
Unqualified_call	≜	Entity [Actuals]

When present, the optional Actuals part gives the list of actual arguments:

Actuals	≜	"(" Actual_list ")"
Actual_list	≜	{Actual "," ...}
Actual	≜	Expression | Address
Address	≜	"$" Identifier

→ *The* Address *form for* Actual *serves to pass the address of an Eiffel feature to a foreign (non-Eiffel) routine. See 24.6, page 404.*

A Call is **qualified** if it includes at least one dot – in other words, if the optional Call_chain component is present, or if the required Call_chain component has two or more elements (separated by a dot), or both of these properties hold.

Here are two calls serving as instructions. The first is unqualified, the second qualified:

> *print (message)*;
> *paragraph (2).line (3).second_word.set_font (Bold)*

The intermediate components of the second example:

> *paragraph* (*2*)
> *paragraph* (*2*). *line* (*3*)
> *paragraph* (*2*). *line* (*3*). *second_word*

are all specimens of construct Call_chain. They may themselves be viewed as calls; any such intermediate call must be an expression (rather than an instruction) so that it may serve as the target of further calls.

The following instructions use calls which are expressions:

> *second_paragraph* := *paragraph* (*2*);
> *output* (*second_paragraph*. *line* (*3*). *second_word*. *letter* (*3*))

The features of all the above calls have arguments. Here are two examples where the feature has no argument:

> *paragraph* (*2*). *indent*;
> *f* := *that_word*. *current_font*

These examples assume that *indent* is a procedure with no arguments and that *current_font* is an attribute or function without arguments.

The syntax indicates that a qualified Call may begin (before the Call_chain) with a Parenthesized_qualifier, that is to say a Parenthesized expression followed by a dot. This explains why earlier examples

> (*1*). *minus*
>
> (*4*). *subtract* (*3*)

WARNING: will not work with the standard INTEGER class.

would be valid if *INTEGER* had routines with the names given. As a more useful example, assume a class *VECTOR* of the form

> **class** *VECTOR* [*G* –> *X*] **feature**
>
>   *norm*: *G* **is do** ... **end**;
>
>   **infix** "+" (*other*: **like** *Current*): **like** *Current* **is**
>   **do** ... **end** -- "+"
>
>   ...
> **end** -- class *VECTOR*

Then with *u* and *v* of type *VECTOR* [*T*] for some appropriate *T* you may use the expressions

'f' must be a feature of class X, hence applicable to (*u* + *v*). *norm since the type G of this expression, a formal generic parameter of VECTOR, is constrained by X.*

> (*u* + *v*). *norm*
> (*u* + *v*). *norm.f.h.*

both of which apply function *norm* to the result of applying function **infix** "+" to *u* with argument *v*. As indicated by the above syntax, there may be at most one

Parenthesized_qualifier, and it must appear at the beginning of the Call. In the second example the Parenthesized_qualifier is followed by the Call_chain *norm.f.h.*

Thanks to this mechanism, you may use any expression as qualifier (if the validity constraints are satisfied, of course) by parenthesizing the expression. Without parentheses, the Call would be syntactically illegal, as in *3.minus*, or legal but with the wrong semantics, as with *u+v.norm* which applies *norm* to *v*, not to the sum.

The dot has the highest precedence of all operators except parentheses, so in the second case it applies to v, not to u + v. Operator precedence is given by the table on page 377.

21.7 Introduction to call semantics

Let us now examine the semantics of calls. As usual, we try to understand the concepts first, and then we examine the formal rules.

No, you have not missed the validity constraints: exceptionally, they will come only after the semantics, in the next chapter. Why depart from the immemorial order of things, and put the third horse of the sacred troika – syntax, validity, semantics – ahead of the second one? Simply for clarity: once we have seen the semantics we will better understand the need for the constraints.

The validity constraints on calls are studied in chapter 22.

It will suffice to consider as working example a qualified Call of the form

$$target.fname\ (y_1, ..., y_n)$$

where *target* is an expression, *fname* is a feature name of the appropriate class, and the y_i are expressions.

Let us further assume that *target* is either a Parenthesized expression or a single Unqualified_call, in other words that the Call is not a multi-dot of the form *a.b.c. ... . fname (...)*.

Concentrating on this example will simplify the discussion; it may seem that we are losing generality, but in fact this is not the case:

- By not considering multi-dot expressions we are simply accepting that (for example) an instruction of the form *a.b.proc*, for some procedure *proc*, is an equivalent to the following Compound (using an auxiliary entity *x* of the appropriate type):

  $x := a.b;$
  $x.proc$

  an equivalence which the formal semantic definition will justify.

- The example uses dot notation, which makes the call's components more visible. But this loses no generality: the semantics presented will also apply to calls in prefix or infix form; the only difference is how we obtain the feature and arguments of a call from its syntactic form.

- If there are no arguments, we may simply consider that *n* is zero.

- Lastly, the above call is qualified; what of unqualified calls? It turns out that we do not need to handle this case explicitly; its semantics will come out as a special case of the qualified case. This may appear a trifle mysterious, but the mystery will not last long.

21.8 Void targets

So we want to execute or evaluate *target.fname* (...) at a certain instant of system execution.

"Execute" for an instruction, "evaluate" for an expression. The rest of the discussion uses the first of these terms for simplicity, except when the context implies an expression.

Expression *target* has a certain value *target_value*. The call can only proceed if *target_value* is not void.

This is a universal and fundamental requirement on calls: it is impossible to execute a call on a void target. The reason is immediate: a call is the application of a feature to an object; if there is no object, there can be no meaningful call. So any attempt to execute the call if *target_value* is void is the result of an error in the software and will trigger an exception.

This property means that if you want a function to work for a void value of one of its operands, you must treat that operand as an argument, not as the target of the call. As an example, this is the reason why the general-purpose function *equal*, from class *ANY*, is called under the form

← *See 19.7, page 303, about 'equal' and 'is_equal'.*

> *equal* (*x*, *y*)

and is usually more convenient to use than *x.is_equal* (*y*), which does not work for void *x*. The same applies to *clone*.

If an operand is treated as target of the call, it is the caller's responsibility to make sure that the target is never void at the time of a call. If it is indeed possible for *x* to be void in the context of the call, you may test for this condition through an equality comparison to feature *Void* of class *ANY*:

← *Feature Void was introduced in 17.3, page 270. See chapter 27 for the detail of ANY's features.*

> **if** *x* /= *Void* **then**
>   *x.f* ...
> **else**
>   ...
> **end**

21.9 Dynamic binding

Now assume *target_value* is not void. It is attached to an object OD. This object is a direct instance of some type *DT*, of base class *D*. *D* (the generating class of OD) must be effective: otherwise *DT* could not have any direct instance.

The D in the type and class names stands for "dynamic", the S for "static".

Expression *target_value* has a certain type *ST*, of base class *S*. You may recall that *ST* is also called the static type of *target*, and *DT* its dynamic type at the time the call is executed. The static type is obvious from the software text and is fixed; polymorphism means that the dynamic type may change at run time as a result of reattachments.

← *"Generating class" was defined in 17.2, page 270. Static and dynamic types were defined in the discussion of polymorphism, on page 323.*

The typing constraints imply that *DT* will always conform to *ST*, and hence that *D* is a descendant of *S*. The validity rules seen below imply that the feature of the call, *fname*, must be the final name in *S* of a feature of *S*, available to the class which includes the call. Let *sf* be that feature.

But, as you have certainly guessed, we are not interested in *sf*. Using *sf* for the call would be committing the gravest possible crime in object-oriented technology: **static binding**. What matters is not the type of *target* (what was declared in the software text) but the type of the object attached to *target_value* (what is actually found at run time). Using that type, *DT*, to determine the appropriate feature, yields the appropriate policy: **dynamic binding**.

The feature to be used, *df*, is the version of *sf* that applies to class *D*. The two features will be different if *D* or some intermediate class has redefined *sf*. The purpose of such a redefinition is precisely to ensure that the feature performs for instances of *D* in a way that differs from its default behavior for instances of *S*. Not using the redefined version would be equivalent to renouncing the whole power of the inheritance mechanism.

An object is, properly speaking, an instance of a type, not of a class. For convenience, however, 17.4 (page 271) has defined the instances of a class as the instances of any type based on that class.

The word "version", as used here, has a precise meaning, defined in the discussion of inheritance. Every feature of a class has a version in any descendant of that class; that version is the result of applying any redefinition, undefinition or effecting that may have occurred since the original introduction of the feature. The definition takes into account the case of repeated inheritance, for which the Select subclause removes any ambiguity that could be caused by conflicting redefinitions on different inheritance paths, or by the replication of an attribute.

← See page 181 for an informal presentation of "version", and page 189 for the precise definition.

21.10 The importance of being dynamic

Dynamic binding is not just a useful convention but a major condition of correctness. The correctness of a class requires every exported routine to preserve the class's invariant, so that calls will never produce an inconsistent object – an object which does not satisfy the invariant of its own generating class. This means that *sf* must preserve the invariant *SI* of *S*, and *df* the invariant *DI* of *D* (which is a possibly strengthened form of *SI*). But there is of course no requirement that *sf* preserve *DI*; in fact, the designer of *S* usually did not even know about class *D*, which may have be written much later by someone else. Static binding could then apply to an object, OD, a feature, *sf*, which does not preserve the invariant of the generating class – the ultimate disaster in the execution of a software system.

← The invariant preservation requirement is part of class consistency, defined page 128.

Dynamic binding, then, is the only meaningful policy. In some cases, of course, *sf* and *df* are the same feature because no redefinition has occurred between *S* and *D*, or simply because *S* and *D* are the same class. Then static and dynamic binding trivially have the same semantics. A compiler or other language processing tool which is able to detect such situations through careful (and correct) analysis of a system's source text may apply this analysis to generate slightly more efficient object code. This is perfectly acceptable as long as the system's run-time behavior implements the semantics of dynamic binding.

Beyond its theoretical necessity, dynamic binding plays an essential role in the Eiffel approach to software structuring. It means that clients of a number of classes providing alternative implementations of a certain facility can let the mechanisms of Eiffel execution select the appropriate implementation automatically, based on the form of each polymorphic entity at the time of execution.

*Customers
and
invoices*

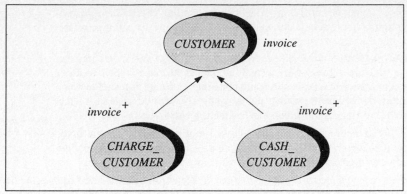

As a typical example, assume a class *CUSTOMER* with a procedure *invoice* used to bill customers. Heirs *CHARGE_CUSTOMER* and *CASH_CUSTOMER* may redefine this procedure in two different ways to account for different forms of invoicing. Then, if *c* is a writable entity of type *CUSTOMER*, *c* may be attached, at some run-time instant, to an instance of *CHARGE_CUSTOMER* or *CASH_CUSTOMER*. A call of the form

> *c.invoice*

will, thanks to dynamic binding, be treated appropriately in each case.

This is a great advantage for the authors of client classes containing such calls, since they do not need to test explicitly for every possible case (charge customer, cash customer), and may integrate the introduction of a new case (such as check customers) at minimal change in the client classes.

21.11 Applying the feature

So now we have a value, *target_value*, attached to an object OD; we have a feature, *df*, determined through the dynamic binding mechanism; and we have a possibly empty list of expressions, containing the expressions $y_1, \ldots, y_n$ to be used as actual arguments. It remains to apply the feature to the object, using the arguments.

From the discussion of routines, *df* may be one of the following:

A • An attribute

B • An external routine (whose implementation is outside the system's direct reach, being written in another language).

C • A once routine.

D • A normal (non-once, non-external) routine.

Examination of the syntax for Routine_body suggests a fifth case: a routine with a **deferred** body. Here, however, this case is impossible since, as noted above, *D* has a direct instance and hence must be effective.

← *The syntax for* Routine_body *is on page 113.*

If *df* is an attribute, object OD has a field corresponding to *df*. Then the call is an expression, whose value is that field. The sole effect of the call is to return that value.

If *df* is an external routine, execution of the call will mean passing the *target_value* and the values of the actual arguments to that external routine, waiting for it to complete its execution, and obtaining its result if it is a function. The semantics of argument passing and of routine execution depend on the conventions of the language in which that routine is written.

→ *See chapter 24 about external calls. The external routine must be prepared to handle an extra argument, representing what appears in an Eiffel call as the target.*

In case C, *df* is a once routine (that is to say, a routine with an Internal body beginning with the Body_mark **once** rather than **do**). That routine is designed to have its body executed only once during the entire system execution. Then:

← *See syntax page 113.*

- If the current call to *df* is not the first one in the current execution of the system, it has no effect if *df* is a procedure; if *df* is a function, the sole effect is to return the value of *Result* computed by the first call to *df*.

→ *The "value of Result computed by the first call" means almost the same as "the result of the first call". See the last section of this chapter.*

- If this is the first call, the effect is the same as for a non-once routine, as described next.

It remains, then, to cover the case D of a routine *df* which is not "once" (its Internal body begins with the Body_mark **do**.) Then the execution must yield the same effect as the following sequence of steps.

D1 • Using the semantics of direct reattachment, attach every formal argument of *df* to the value of the corresponding actual argument y_i. The validity constraints imply that the actuals must match the formals in number of arguments and type conformance. Of course, this step is not needed if there are no arguments.

← *The semantics of direct reattachment is defined in 20.5, page 313. It yields reference reattachment, clone or copy according to the table on page 317.*

D2 • If *df* has any local entities, save the current values of these entities if any call to *df* has been started but not yet terminated; then initialize each local entity to the default value of its base type.

← *Default initialization values were specified in 18.13, page 291.*

D3 • If *df* is a function, initialize the predefined entity *Result* to the default value for the function's return type. The default initialization values are the same as for the initialization of attributes in a Creation instruction.

D4 • Execute the Compound of *df*'s Internal body, according to the conventions described in the next section.

D5 • If *df* is a function, the call is an expression. The value returned for that expression is the value of *Result* after D4.

D6 • If the values of any local entities have been saved under D2, restore these entities to their earlier values. This terminates the execution.

The saving of local entities under D2, and their restoring under D6, are necessary because routines may be directly or indirectly recursive: the body of *df* may contain a call to another routine, and that routine may turn out at run time to be *df*, or it may recursively call *df*. As a result, step D4 may recursively start the whole process again on the same routine. The saving and restoring ensure that each incarnation of *df* recovers its local entities when it is resumed after a recursive call.

← *Remember that for a function the local entities include Result, which will contain the return value. See 17.9, page 275.*

21.12 Executing the body

We are almost done with understanding the effect of a call, but we must see how to interpret the Compound of a routine's Internal body in step D4.

A little mystery remains. Assume the text of routine *df*, in class *D*, has the following simple form:

> ```
>              -- If there had been any renaming, df's name would not
>              -- be fname any more.
> fname is
>     do
>         some_proc;
>         x.other_proc
>     end -- fname
> ```

where *x* is an attribute of *D*, *some_proc* a procedure of *D*, and *other_proc* is a procedure of the base class of *x*'s type. The core of the call's execution, step D4, consists of executing the two instructions of the Compound.

But what exactly do they mean? What does *x* represent? To what object should the computation apply *some_proc*?

To answer these questions we must put ourselves in the global context of system execution and remember how anything ever gets executed. Quoting from a very early part of this book:

← *See page 35.*

> To execute (or "run") a system on a machine means to get the machine to apply a creation instruction to the system's root class.

DEFINITION:
Current
Object

In all but trivial cases, of course, the root's creation procedure will create more objects and execute more calls. This extremely simple semantic definition of system execution has as its immediate consequence to yield a precise definition of the **current object** and **current routine**. At any time during execution, the current object CO is the object to which the latest non-completed routine call applies, and the current routine *cr* is the feature of that call. They may be defined precisely as follows:

1 • At the start of the execution of a system, CO is the **root object** (the instance of the root class whose creation is the first act of system execution) and *cr* is the selected creation procedure. (If the root class has no creation procedure, execution terminates immediately.)

2 • If *cr* executes any construct other than a call, the current object and current routine remain the same.

3 • If *cr* executes a qualified call of the form *target.fname* (...) where the value *target_value* of *target* is attached to an object OD, then for the duration of the call OD becomes the new current object and *df*, the routine deduced from *fname* as discussed earlier, becomes the new current routine. When the qualified call terminates, the earlier CO and *cr* resume their roles as current object and current routine.

4 • When *cr* executes an unqualified call, the current object remains the same, and there is a new current routine for the duration of the call as in case 3.

Note the hidden recursion in the definition for case 3: to evaluate *target_value*, we will need to perform a call, whose result is evaluated relative to the current object according to the above definition, used recursively.

This need to use Call semantics recursively to evaluate the target of a call is not just true of multi-dot calls (such as *t1.t2.fname*, where the *target* is the qualified call *t1.t2*), but in fact of all qualified calls: in the above example, the target *x* of *x.other_proc*, representing an attribute of the enclosing class *D*, is in fact syntactically an Unqualified_call. This comes from the way the syntax has been defined:

Call	$\triangleq$	[Parenthesized_qualifier] Call_chain
Parenthesized_qualifier	$\triangleq$	Parenthesized "."
Call_chain	$\triangleq$	{Unqualified_call "." ...}⁺
Unqualified_call	$\triangleq$	Entity [Actuals]

← *This syntax appeared initially on page 342.*

meaning that attribute *x*, as it appears in *x.other_proc*, is itself an Unqualified_call which must be evaluated with respect to the current object. Also, in a call that includes a Parenthesized_qualifier, the Parenthesized expression is in fact another syntactic form of Call, so in this case too evaluating the target requires recursive application of Call semantics.

→ *See chapter 23 about operator expressions and the equivalence with calls.*

All that remains to complete this discussion of call execution, then, is to define how the execution of a routine *df* (of name *fname* in the above example) should evaluate an Unqualified_call *unqual* (such as *x* or *some_proc* in the example). As before, let OD be the current object and *D* the underlying class. The rules are straightforward:

- If *unqual* is an attribute of *D* (such as *x* in the example) it returns the value of the corresponding field of OD.

- If *unqual* is a local entity of *df*, or the predefined entity *Result*, it returns the current value of that entity, as initialized on entry to the current call according to the default rules, and possibly updated by previously executed instructions of *df*.

- If *unqual* is a routine of *df* (such as *some_proc* in the example), possibly followed by an Actuals list, then its effect is that of a call to the corresponding routine, recursively determined by the present discussion, and still using OD as current object.

So in the example the call *some_proc* will execute the procedure of final name *some_proc* in *D*, using OD as current object. The call *x.other_proc*, assuming *x* is an attribute of type *STX*, and the base class of *STX* is *SCX*, will have the following effect:

1 • Execute a call to *x* to obtain an object OX, of some type *DTX* (conforming to *STX*), of base class *DCX* (a descendant of *SCX*).

2 • Execute the *DCX* version of the procedure of final name *some_proc* in *DCX*, using OX as current object for the duration of this execution.

In step 1, the result OX of the call is the object attached to the field of OD corresponding to attribute *x*.

21.13 Naming the current object

At any time during the execution of a system, there is a current object CO and a current routine. In the class text, most calls in dot notation do not need to refer explicitly to the current object, since if a Call has CO as its target you may write it as an Unqualified_call, which does not name its target.

For operations other than dot-notation calls, however, you may need an explicit name for referring to the current object.

An example is equality comparison. Assume a function computing the distance between two points, which might be written in a class *POINT* with the name **infix** "|−|" as

EXAMPLE

> **infix** "|−|" (*other*: *POINT*): *REAL* **is**
>   -- Distance of current point to *other*.
>   **do**
>   ...
>   **end**

(Using an infix operator makes it possible to write a typical call under the form *point1* |−| *point2* rather than *point1.distance* (*point2*).) The routine's Internal body (the **do** clause) may need to check whether *other* is not in fact the same point as the current object.

The predefined entity

> *Current*

is available to denote the current object in such cases. The value of *Current*, evaluated as part of a call to a routine *df* of a class *D*, is a reference attached to the current object OD if *D* is not an expanded class, and OD itself if *D* is expanded.

Using the above function, then, the Internal body of **infix** "|−|" could include one of the tests

POINT is assumed to be non-expanded.

> *other* = *Current*
>
> *equal* (*other*, *Current*)

depending on what form of equality comparison is desired.

As noted above, an Unqualified_call such as *some_proc* or *x* does not need to use explicitly *Current* as its target, although it is harmless to write it with *Current*, giving

> *Current.some_proc*
>
> *Current.x*

One form of call, however, may need *Current* to refer to the target: calls written using prefix or infix features. For example, if some routine of class *POINT* above must refer to the distance of the current point to some other point *point1*, it will have to do so, using the above infix function, under the notation

$$Current \;|\!-\!|\; point1$$

whereas if the feature had been an identifier feature, with a name such as *distance*, this could have been written just as the Unqualified_call

$$distance \; (point1)$$

Be sure to remember that *Current*, which is one of the choices for the construct Unqualified_call, is a **read-only** entity. As a consequence, it cannot be the target of an attachment or reattachment operation such as creation or assignment. Instructions such as !! *Current* ... or *Current* := ... would be invalid.

← Entities are either read-only or writable. See 17.9, page 275.

Similarly, if x is an attribute, the equivalence of the notations x and *Current*.x only applies to contexts in which x is a call. So if x is an integer attribute and a routine contains the assignment

$$x := x + 1$$

you may replace the right-hand side x by *Current*.x since it is syntactically a call; this does not apply to the left-hand side x, which syntactically is a Writable entity, as implied by the syntax for Assignment.

← The syntax for Assignment appears on page 311.

21.14 Semantics of calls

(This section formalizes the semantics of call, repeating the above description in more compact and precise form. It introduces no new concept and you should probably skip it on first reading.)

The brave among us will now examine the precise definition of call semantics. Consider the execution, at a certain run-time instant, of a call

$$target.fname \; (y_1, ..., y_n)$$

To define its effect, call *target_value* the value of *target* at that instant. We can only determine *target_value* by applying recursively this definition of call semantics to *target*, which (as noted above) may itself be viewed as a call. This use of recursion in the definition is appropriate since *target* will have one less level of qualification (one dot less) than the original call, so that the recursion cannot go on forever.

The first possibility is for *target_value* to be void. Then the call cannot be executed correctly; it will fail, triggering an exception.

For the exception raised in this case, the Kernel Library class *EXCEPTIONS* introduces the integer code *Void_call_target*.

← See chapter 15 about exceptions, and chapter 29 about class EXCEPTIONS.

The rest of this section assumes that *target_value* is not void. Then *target_value* is attached to some object OD, which must be a direct instance of some type *DT* (for "dynamic type") based on some class *D*. Let *ST* be the type of expression *target* and *S* the base class of *ST*. The rules of reattachment indicate that *DT* conforms to *ST*, and that *D* is a descendant of *S*. Also, because *DT* has a direct instance OD, *D* must be an effective class.

If the call is valid, the constraint on calls (seen in the next chapter) implies that *fname* is the final name of a feature *sf* of class *S*, available to the class which contains the call. Let *df* be the version of *sf* in *D*; dynamic binding means that the effect of the call is determined by *df*, not *sf*.

→ *See 22.9, starting page 367, for the validity constraint on calls.*

There are four possibilities depending on whether *df* is an attribute, an external routine, a once routine or a normal (non-external, non-once) effective routine.

← *These are the cases called* A, B, C, D *in 21.11.*

If *df* is an attribute, the call is an expression; the value of that expression is the field corresponding to *df* in OD. The sole effect of the call in this case is to return this value.

Otherwise *f* is a routine. This routine may not be deferred since *D* is an effective class. But it may be external, and if it is internal it may or may not be a once routine.

If *df* is an external routine, the effect of the call is to execute that routine on the actual arguments given, if any, according to the rules of the language in which it is written.

If *df* is a once routine, the effect depends on whether the current system execution included an earlier call to that routine. If so, the call has no effect if *df* is a procedure; if *df* is a function, its sole effect is to return the value of *Result* as computed by the first call to *df*. If, however, this is the first call to *df* in the current system execution, the effect is exactly the same as for a non-once routine, as described next.

There is a little subtlety in the previous paragraph. The specification does not state, for a once function, that subsequent calls return the result of the first one, but that they yield the value of the predefined entity *Result*. In most cases this is the same thing, since the first call returns its value, of course, through *Result*. But if the function is **recursive**, a new call to *df* may be spawned before the first one has terminated, so the "result of the first call" would not be a meaningful notion. The preceding paragraph indicates that in this case the recursive call will return whatever value the first call has obtained so far for *Result* (starting with the default initialization). Clearly, a recursive once function is rather bizarre, and of little apparent use, but no validity constraint disallows it, and the semantics must leave no stone unturned.

Had you detected this case?

Coming back to the mainstream, there remains to cover the case in which *df* is a non-external non-once routine (with a Routine_body beginning with the keyword **do**). Then the effect of the call is the effect of the following sequence of steps, which for the most part has already been described and explained.

D1 • If *df* has arguments, attach every formal argument to the value of the corresponding actual argument, applying the semantics of direct reattachment.

← *The semantics of direct reattachment is defined in 20.5, page 313; see the table on page 317.*

D2 • If *df* has any local entities, save the current values of these entities if any call to *df* has been started but not yet terminated; then initialize each local entity to the default value of its base type.

D3 • If *df* is a function, initialize the predefined entity *Result*, again according to the default initialization rules.

D4 • Execute the body of *df*. In this execution, evaluation of the entity *Current* will return *target_value*; the effect of an Unqualified_call *u*, where *u* is neither *Current* nor *Result*, is defined (recursively) as the effect of the qualified call *target.u*; and the effect of a qualified call of the form *s.u*, where *s* is an expression and *u* is an Unqualified_call, is defined (recursively) as the effect of a call of the form *v.u*, executed after the assignment

← This definition of the semantics of Current agrees with the earlier informal presentation, page 351, which distinguished explicitly between expanded and non-expanded classes.

$$v := target.s$$

v being a Writable entity used only for this definition.

D5 • If *df* is a function, the call is syntactically an expression; the value of that expression is the value of the entity *Result* on termination of the function's execution.

D6 • If the values of any local entities have been saved under D2, restore these entities to their earlier values. This terminates the execution.

22

Type checking

22.1 Overview

In discussing calls, the previous chapter covered syntax and semantics, but set aside any consideration of validity – even though its semantic definitions only apply to valid constructs. It is time now to come back to the second horse of our troika and examine what it takes to make a call meaningful.

Calling features, it was already noted, is the principal means of performing computations in Eiffel. This is why the title of this chapter does not just read "validity of calls", but "type checking", since the type safety of a system is essentially defined by the validity of its calls. This is also why, in an approach that places so much emphasis on helping developers produce correct and robust software, it is crucial to ask what could go wrong at run time with a call – and see what we can do *before* run time to prevent it from going wrong.

Consider the basic form of a call in dot notation:

$$target.fname \, (\, y_1, ..., y_n)$$

For this to be properly executed, *target* must be attached to an object DO, and DO must be equipped with a feature corresponding to *fname*; that feature must have a signature (types of arguments and result, if any) and a specification (precondition and postcondition) compatible with what the caller expects.

Not all of these requirements may be handled statically by mere analysis of the software text. To ascertain statically that DO will always exist (that is to say, that *target* will never have a void value) and that the assertions will always be satisfied, we would need theorem and program provers beyond the reach of current software technology. For these properties, the presentation has reluctantly settled for run-time checks which, if not satisfied, may trigger exceptions.

For the remaining properties, however, the picture is brighter. Assuming the object DO exists, it is a direct instance of a certain class *D*, and if we have enough information about the possible *D* we will know statically what features they have. Determining the possible classes and checking that their features match the corresponding calls will enable us to perform static type checking. This chapter explains how to achieve this goal.

As usual, we will take an informal look first, then examine the precise rules.

22.2 Syntax variants

As noted in the previous chapter, dot notation is only one possible form of call. Operator expressions provide the other variant, meant for compatibility with traditional mathematical and programming language notation. The difference is just syntactical, however; an Operator_expression of the form

> *a* + *b*

→ The notion of equivalent dot form will serve to formalize the correspondence between dot notation and operator expressions; see 23.7, page 380. The ability to treat mixed arithmetic expressions according to mathematical tradition will require a specific rule, balancing; see 23.10, page 384.

is semantically a call having *a* as its target, **infix** *"+"* as its feature, and *b* as its single argument.

For simplicity, this chapter will (like the discussion of call semantics in the previous one) rely on dot notation calls of the basic form shown in the previous section. Its results immediately carry over to operator expressions.

22.3 Class-level validity

At first sight, the conditions which will make a call valid appear straightforward. After all, *target*, like every expression, has a type; because all entities must be explicitly declared, the type of any expression is immediately obvious from the class text. Like any other type, it is based on a class; the properties of that class should tell us whether a certain feature is applicable to the expression.

Consider a typical context for the above call:

```
class C feature
    ...
    target: S;
    y: SOME_TYPE;
    routine is
        do
            ...
            target.fname (y);
            ...
        end; -- routine
    ...
end -- class C
```

Here the type of *target* is a non-generic class *S*, and there is a single argument *y*. The elementary type rule seems clear: *S* must have a feature of final name *fname*; this feature must be available to *C* (in other words, *S* must export it either generally or to a set of classes that includes an ancestor of *C*); and it must have the requested signature, which means that it must be a procedure with a single formal argument, to which *y* conforms.

← *"Available" was defined on page 100.*

For example if class *C* uses the following call as expression:

> *next_paragraph.line* (3)

then *C* must have a feature (attribute or function without argument) of final name *next_paragraph*, available to class *C*, and if *next_paragraph* is of type *PARAGRAPH*, class *PARAGRAPH* must have a function of final name *line*, with one formal argument of type *INTEGER* (the type of *3*, the actual argument), or perhaps of another type to which *INTEGER* conforms.

These conditions at first sight appear not only necessary but also sufficient to guarantee that the call will always make sense at run time.

The rule as sketched is still partial: we will need to extend it to account for zero-dot (Unqualified_call) and multi-dot calls, for targets whose type is anchored or generically derived, and for features with no arguments or more than one argument. But these extensions do not raise any particular difficulty.

DEFINITION:
Class-level
validity

Properly formalized, this is indeed a fundamental type rule, which will be defined below as **class-level validity**. Calls which satisfy this condition will be said to be **class-valid**.

22.4 System-level validity

Although class-level validity may at first appear sufficient, the typing problem is in fact less trivial than the above would suggest. The reason is polymorphism and dynamic binding, which forces us to take into account not just the declared types of entities, but also their possible dynamic types (their dynamic type set).

Polymorphism means that the type used to declare the *target* (*S* above) is not the only possible type for the object DO to which the call will apply. To see this, let us extend the context introduced above:

```
class C feature
    target: S; other: D;    -- D must be a descendant of S
    y: SOME_TYPE; ...
    routine is
        do
            if some_test then target := other end; ...
            target.fname (y); ...
        end; -- routine
    ...
end -- class C
```

where the Assignment rule requires *D* to be a descendant of *S*. Because of the possible polymorphism resulting from the assignment of *other* to *target*, the type of the object DO may now be not just *S* but *T* as well.

In other words, we need to consider not only the type of *target* as it results from the declarations, called the **static type** if there is any ambiguity, but also the set of all the types that *target* may assume at run-time as a result of polymorphic attachments. This set was defined in the discussion of polymorphism as the **dynamic type set** of *target*; a member of that set is said to be a possible **dynamic type** for *target*.

← The Assignment rule is on page 311. Since the classes are non-generic, conformance is the same relation as "descendant of".

The base classes of the possible dynamic types constitute the **dynamic class set** of *target*.

In this example all types are classes, so that the dynamic type set and dynamic class set are the same, but with generic derivation, expansion and anchored types we will need to reintroduce the distinction between types and classes.

Dynamic type sets and dynamic class sets were defined in 20.9, page 323, and are covered more extensively below: first in 22.8, page 364, and then in 22.9, page 367 for the precise rules.

What then is the actual type constraint? It still applies to a class D the conditions defined above for class-level validity:

1 • D must have a feature corresponding to *fname*, available to C.

2 • That feature must have the required signature.

But there is an important difference: whereas for class-level validity, the only D of interest was S, the static type of *target*, here, as a result of polymorphism, we must enforce these two conditions **for any D in the dynamic class set of** *target*.

DEFINITION:
System-level
validity

This requirement is called **system-level validity**. Calls which satisfy it will be said to be **system-valid**.

A call will be valid, without further qualifier, if it is both class-valid and system-valid.

A class-valid call is not necessarily system-valid. This is because of two important properties of the inheritance mechanism:

← On P1, see "adapting the export status of inherited features", page 98. On P2, see the informal discussion on "typing and redeclaration", page 151, and the Redeclaration rule, page 163, clause 2.

P1 • A class may override the export policies of its parents; it may for example make secret its version of a feature which the parent exported.

P2 • A routine redefinition may replace the type of a formal argument by a type conforming to the original. This is know as the **covariant** argument typing policy.

Properties P1 and P2 may seem surprising at first; the rationale for these important aspects of the typing policy is discussed in detail below. First, we must convince ourselves, if need be, that these properties can have unpleasant consequences if we limit ourselves to class-level validity checking.

→ 22.6 below, page 360, explains why P1 and P2 are essential for realistic uses of object-oriented concepts.

22.5 Violating system validity

(If this is your first reading, you may be content with the realization that type checking is less trivial than it appears at first, and that a systemwide type checker will detect the non-trivial errors. You may then want to skip the rest of this chapter.)

It is indeed not hard to put together an example where P1 prevents a class-valid system from working properly. Similar examples relying on P2 would be almost as immediate.

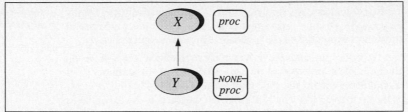

Hiding an inherited feature

Consider a class X which exports a procedure *proc* without arguments, and its heir Y which makes *proc* secret, as shown by the above figure. To hide *proc*, class Y will use the New_exports clause:

← *The* New_exports *clause of a* Feature_adaptation *part enables a class to override the export policies of its parents. See 7.11, page 98.*

> **class** Y **inherit**
> X
>   **export** {$NONE$} *proc* **end**;
>   ... Rest of class omitted ...

Then consider a class C which calls *proc* on a polymorphic entity which at run time may become attached to an object of type Y. This will be the case if C contains the following declarations and instructions, in some order:

> a: X
> b: Y -- Y is an heir of X
> !! b -- Instruction β
> $a := b$ -- Instruction δ
> $a.proc$

WARNING: this is not a contiguous extract, just some lines which may appear anywhere in a class text in any order satisfying the constraints on declarations and instructions.

The call $a.proc$ is class-valid since X exports *proc*. But it is not system-valid: the instruction labeled β may attach to b an object of type Y (the declared type of b); the instruction labeled δ may attach a to the same object as b; then the last instruction may call *proc* on that object, even though it is an instance of Y, and *proc* is secret in Y.

This example – or any similar one using P1 or P2 to violate system-level validity in the presence of polymorphism – immediately brings four important comments.

First, the example is not affected by the order of the offending instructions (β, δ and the call). As long as they appear in the same system and may all potentially be executed, the call is system-invalid. For obvious reasons of simplicity, system-level validity does **not** involve any flow analysis; even in the extreme case in which the polymorphic assignment δ would be replaced by

> **if false then** $a := b$ **end**

we would still consider the call to be invalid.

The second comment is that system-level invalidity in such an example is a serious problem, not just a matter of style. If the author of Y did not export *proc*, we must presume that this was for a good reason. Remember in particular that an exported routine must preserve the class invariant. So *proc* preserved the invariant of X, but perhaps the invariant of Y is stronger and *proc* does not preserve it any more. In this case, applying *proc* to an object of type Y may produce an inconsistent object – one which does not satisfy the fundamental consistency constraints expressed by the invariant. This is a potential disaster.

← *The invariant preservation requirement is part of class consistency, page 128.*

Third, neither the call $a.\,proc$ nor the polymorphic assignment $a := b$ is wrong by itself. The call applies an exported procedure of class X to an entity a of type X; the assignment satisfies the type conformance rule. What is wrong is the possibility for these two individually legitimate constructs to be executed as part of an execution of the same system. To be more precise, even that combination would be harmless were it not for the presence of a third accomplice, the Creation instruction labeled β, which raises the possibility for b, and hence for a as well, to become attached to an object of type Y.

This brings the last comment, addressing a question that may well have been troubling you for some time now: isn't the type policy *wrong*? Why do we allow a class to hide some of its parent's exported features, or to replace an argument type by a more specific (conforming) one? Shouldn't we have a stricter policy, guaranteeing that class-level validity implies system-level validity?

As it turns out, however, the type policy, although perhaps surprising at first, is essential to support the practice of object-oriented software development. Let us take a closer look at the underlying issues.

22.6 Notes on the type policy

You may indeed have wondered what all the fuss was about. Shouldn't class-level validity imply system-level validity? Then type checking would be trivial, involving only local properties of classes.

The culprits were identified above: the two properties P1 and P2, which free heirs from some of the export and typing decisions made by their parents. We should really ask ourselves whether these properties are appropriate.

Here they are again:

← *A third related property is that a creation procedure of a class may not enjoy the status of creation procedure any more in a proper descendant. See the Creation rule, page 286.*

P1 • A class may override the export policies of its parents; it may for example make secret its version of a feature which the parent exported.

P2 • A routine redefinition may replace the type of a formal argument by a type conforming to the original (covariant argument policy).

Then if S has an exported routine *sf* of name *fname* with a formal argument of type *SOME_TYPE* the call used earlier as example will be class-valid. Here it is again, with some of the enclosing class text omitted:

```
target: S; other: D;    -- D must be a descendant of S
y: SOME_TYPE; ...
routine is
    do
        if some_test then target := other end; ...
        target.fname (y); ... Rest of routine omitted ...
```

But that call is not necessarily system-valid. *D* may redefine *target* to be of some type *D*; or it may make its version of *sf* secret; or it may redefine this routine to take an argument of type *B*, a proper descendant of *SOME_TYPE*. Any of these cases makes the above call system-invalid since the dynamic class set of *target*, as a result of the polymorphic assignment *target* := *other*, includes *D*.

System-level checking will detect the problem and flag the system as invalid.

The above two properties (P1 and P2) often seem surprising at first. Why make type checking more difficult, and introduce the distinction between class-level and system-level validity by allowing classes to choose export and argument typing policies different from those of its parents?

The answer is that this flexibility is indispensable to the practice of object-oriented design. Without it, designers would constantly have to reshuffle inheritance hierarchies, and would have much difficulty observing the constraints of a typed object-oriented language. P1 and P2 serve to acknowledge the inescapable difficulty of reconciling the goals of orderly classification (as implemented through inheritance) and safety (as implemented through typing) with the irregularities and instability of the real-world situations which our software systems attempt to model through their inheritance hierarchies.

Although a full discussion of this question falls beyond the scope of this book, a simple example will serve to illustrate the need for properties P1 and P2.

Vehicles and drivers

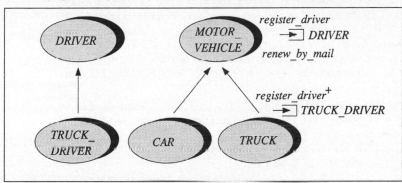

Assume the two inheritance hierarchies represented above, with *MOTOR_VEHICLE* having heirs *CAR* and *TRUCK*, and *DRIVER* having *TRUCK_DRIVER* as heir. These classes could be part of the system used by a company to manage its fleet of vehicles, or by a Department of Motor Vehicles to keep track of driver registration.

To begin, this raises an obvious case of P2 (covariant argument type redefinition). Class *MOTOR_VEHICLE* has a procedure

```
register_driver (d: DRIVER) is ...
```

which naturally takes an argument of type *DRIVER*. For trucks, however, the driver must be approved for truck driving; accordingly, class *TRUCK* redefines *register_driver* to take an argument of type *TRUCK_DRIVER*.

The type constraints in such a case permit the above inheritance structure and the redefinition of *register_driver* – a case of possibility P2. They even permit such polymorphic assignments as the one in

---

a: *MOTOR_VEHICLE*; *t*: *TRUCK*;

...

a := *t*

---

or Creation instructions such as ! *TRUCK* ! *a* ..., with the same declarations. What system-level validity will reject is the only case that could lead to an erroneous call at run time: the presence in the same system of a polymorphic reattachment such as the above and a Call such as

---

a.register_driver (*dr1*)

---

where *dr1* is of type *DRIVER* (not *TRUCK_DRIVER*). Clearly, the presence of this Call in a system that may also attach an instance of *TRUCK* to *a* is erroneous, and will be flagged as invalid. This, however, does not affect the need for P2-like covariant argument redefinition; in fact, the system-level validity rule is what makes P2 possible.

Examples of this kind, with two parallel inheritance hierarchies, are a constant occurrence in the development of systems and their class hierarchies. Many appear in the Data Structure Library. For example, to describe doubly linked lists, *TWO_WAY_LIST* inherits from *LINKED_LIST*; to describe two-way chained linked cells, *BI_LINKABLE* inherits from *LINKABLE*. The list classes have procedures manipulating list cells, such as *put_linkable_left*, which quite naturally take arguments of type *LINKABLE* in *LINKED_LIST* and *BI_LINKABLE* in *TWO_WAY_LIST*.

← *LINKED_LIST and its use of LINKABLE and 'put_linkable_left' are sketched in 5.4, starting on page 56.*

In this case, however, there is no explicit redefinition such as that of *register_driver* in *TRUCK*. The reason is the presence of the Anchored form of type declaration. Class *LINKED_LIST* contains the declarations

---

first_element: *LINKABLE* [**like** *first*];

put_linkable_left (*new*: **like** *first_element*) **is** ...

---

so that *TWO_WAY_LIST* only needs to redefine *first_element* (to be of a type based on *BI_LINKABLE*); the argument *new* of *put_linkable_left*, and all the other entities declared **like** *first_element* in *LINKED_LIST*, follow automatically. As this example shows, the whole idea of anchored declarations is based on the principle of covariant argument redefinition.

The example of motor vehicles, trucks and drivers may also provide an example of the need for policy P1 (independence of heirs' and parents' export policies. Assume the permits for motor vehicles can normally be renewed by mail, hence the presence in *MOTOR_VEHICLE* of an exported procedure *renew_by_mail*. For trucks, however, this does not apply (the truck must be inspected for safety, every year at the time of re-registration). So *TRUCK* does not export *renew_by_mail* (which might violate an invariant of this class, although it preserves the invariant of *MOTOR_VEHICLE*).

In a case like this, one may always argue that the inheritance hierarchy was improperly designed, and should have separated renewable-by-mail vehicles from others, with *renew_by_mail* introduced not in class *MOTOR_VEHICLE* but one level down:

*Not all
registrations
may be
renewed
by mail*

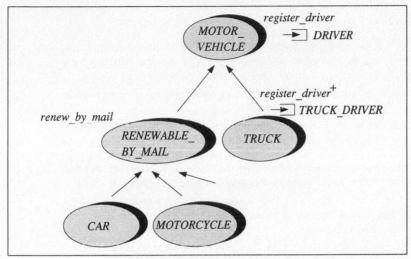

But forcing this as the only acceptable choice would make the practice of object-oriented software development almost impossible.

In any practical problem, there will be many possible criteria for classification; what will happen if, after you have taken apart the original hierarchy because of the registration-by-mail problem, you must take into account other, independent criteria? For example, some vehicles will be for personal use and others for professional use; some will have two wheels and others will have more; some will pay a road tax and some will not; some will require smog inspections every three years; and so on. Since the original designers could not, without perfect foresight, have come up with the ideal inheritance hierarchy, the developers will find themselves constantly redoing the structure. The conflicting criteria may in fact make it impossible to obtain any acceptable inheritance structure at all.

The flexibility of policy P1 makes it possible to handle this problem by allowing a class to be selective about its inheritance – exporting or hiding inherited features to its own clients according to its own local properties. As before, this is an example of transferring part of the burden from developers (in the form of constant architecture redesign) to the supporting implementation (in the form of the more sophisticated form of type checking required by system-level validity).

It should be clear from this discussion that a well-designed inheritance hierarchy will include few occurrences of classes hiding some of their parent's features. If you find yourself constantly at odds with the parent designers' decisions, then you should probably consider improving the inheritance structure (assuming you are permitted to do so). This is why the default policy for inherited features is to retain the parents' export status; to override it, you must include an explicit New_exports clause. But the ability to do this in the minority of cases which call for it is a key component in the effort to make object-oriented software construction not just a pleasant theoretical idea but a practical way to produce real systems.

22.7 Why distinguish?

If we accept that system-level validity is the appropriate notion of validity, it is fair to ask why one should bother at all with class-level validity. Why not have a single validity condition, as for the other constructs studied in this book?

The reason is pragmatic, and involves two complementary observations on possible violations of the validity constraints:

- First, it is easier (for a language processing tool as well as a human reader) to detect violations of class-level validity, since they only involve a local analysis of the features one class – S, the base class of *target*'s type. In contrast, checking system-level validity may involve systemwide analysis. The names "class-level" and "system-level" reflect this difference.

- Second, a study of errors as they occur in actual system development reveals that system-level validity violations which are not also class-level violations occur very rarely.

For these reasons, implementors may choose to design class-level and system-level checking as separate facilities. Class-level checking will detect a vast majority of errors; the remaining ones will be found by applying system-level checking.

Of course, to guarantee fully the type safety of a system, you must check both kinds.

Class-level checking is straightforward. The only non-trivial part of system-level validity is to determine the dynamic class set. Let us see concretely how this can be done.

22.8 A look at the dynamic class set

The dynamic class set of an entity is the set of base classes of all types that the entity may take on at run-time, as a result of polymorphic reattachements and creation instructions.

The call validity rule, appearing in the precise discussion at the end of this chapter, will give a full definition. It is important, however, to get first an intuitive view of what the base class represents. (Although "intuitive" this view is not incorrect; it simply misses some details and does not cover all cases.)

The idea will be to determine in a single process the dynamic class sets of *all* entities. The process is iterative; if you have a background in numerical mathematics, it will remind you of algorithms which compute the solution to a vector or matrix equation by successive iteration (for example over a grid); if you are familiar with the theory of programming languages, it will remind you of fixpoint methods for approximating the high-level functions and domains of denotational semantics.

Fixpoint methods for denotational semantics are covered in "Introduction to the Theory of Programming Languages". See bibliography.

An example will serve to illustrate the process. Consider a class extract containing the following four instructions, in some order:

← *This is a variant of the example on page 359.*

$$! X ! a \qquad -- \alpha$$
$$! Y ! b \qquad -- \beta$$
$$c := a \qquad -- \gamma$$
$$a := b \qquad -- \delta$$
$$a.proc$$

Each instruction has been identified by a Greek letter. The context is missing, in particular the declarations; the Creation instructions have an explicit creation type for clarity, although α, for example, could appear as just !! a if a is of type X.

As before, the order of these instructions is irrelevant. If they appear in the same context, then a, as discussed above, may become attached to an object of type Y; this means that, for system validity, any routine *rout* appearing in a call $a.rout$ using a must meet the appropriate conditions not just for X but also for Y.

System-level validity analysis will need to determine the base class sets of a, b and c. The result, obtained through a process explained below, will be the following:

→ *The complete form of this result, given page 366, will include more information, in particular references to iteration steps.*

$$a \qquad \boxed{X\,[\alpha]\;;\;Y\,[\delta]}$$

$$b \qquad \boxed{Y\,[\beta]}$$

$$c \qquad \boxed{X\,[\gamma]\;;\;Y\,[\gamma]}$$

This shows a vector of dynamic class sets, one for each entity. Each class set contains a list of types. Any type which appears in one of these lists is there because of one of the instructions; to make this justification clear, the instruction's identifying greek letter appears in brackets next to the type.

For b, the class set includes just Y, resulting from the Creation instruction β. For a, it includes X, resulting from the Creation instruction α, and Y, resulting from the polymorphic assignment δ which adds all of b's class set to the class set of a. For c, assignment γ means that the class set is the same as that of a.

In the rest of this section "class set" is an abbreviation for "dynamic class set".

How do we determine this result? An iterative process will provide the solution. Starting from the types given by Creation instructions, we may repeatedly extend the current sets by adding to the class set of every entity e the class set of any other entity f such that there is a reattachment of f to e somewhere. We stop when we have reached a "fixpoint", that is to say when our vector of class sets is stable.

Here is this process applied to the above example. To obtain the initial vector v_0 of class sets, just look at the creation instructions:

$$a_0 \quad \boxed{X[\alpha]}$$

$$b_0 \quad \boxed{Y[\beta]}$$

$$c_0 \quad \boxed{}$$

For each type appearing in a class set, a comment in brackets identifies the instruction which causes the class to be there: the Creation instruction α puts X in the class set of a, and β puts Y in the class set of b. Entity c is not the target of any Creation, so its class set is empty for the moment.

On each iteration, we will look at every reattachment and extend the target's class set with all the classes obtained so far in the source's class set. For the first iteration, this gives the new class set vector v_1:

$$a_1 \quad \boxed{X[\alpha] \; ; \; Y[\delta : b_0]}$$

$$b_1 \quad \boxed{Y[\beta]}$$

$$c_1 \quad \boxed{X[\gamma : a_0]}$$

The class set of a now contains Y, again identified, for clarity, by its origin: the comment $[\delta : b_0]$ means that Y comes from b_0, the earlier class set for b, and has be added to a_1, the new class set of a, because of the polymorphic assignment $a := b \; (\delta)$. In the same way, X now appears in the class set of c because of its presence in a_0 and of the assignment $c := a \; (\gamma)$. You may be tempted to add Y, which appears in a_1, but this would be cheating: to update a vector at any step, we may only use vector elements from the previous step.

The next step, producing vector v_2, will indeed use a_1 and γ to add Y to the class set of c:

$$a_2 \quad \boxed{X[\alpha] \; ; \; Y[\delta : b_0]}$$

$$b_2 \quad \boxed{Y[\beta]}$$

$$c_2 \quad \boxed{X[\gamma : a_0] \; ; \; Y[\gamma : a_1]}$$

If you apply the mechanism once more, you will find that it does not bring anything new: v_3 is the same as v_2. We have put all the available type information to good use; v_2 gives the complete class sets for all entities involved. (In technical terms v_2 is a fixpoint.)

The process as illustrated on this example is not hard to generalize to the full language. The extension must integrate expressions which are function calls rather than simple entities; it must also account for the two other forms of reattachment beside Assignment: actual-formal association, which raises no particular problem, and Assignment_attempt. For this last case, the effect of

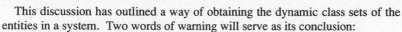

> $b: Y$;
>
> ...
>
> $b\ ?= a$

to extend b's class set not with all elements of a's class set (as with normal Assignment), but only with those which are descendants of Y.

This discussion has outlined a way of obtaining the dynamic class sets of the entities in a system. Two words of warning will serve as its conclusion:

- The precise specification of dynamic class sets appears as part of the call validity rule below. The iterative process that we have just discussed is only one concrete interpretation of that specification, although of course it satisfies that specification.

- Although you may view the description of that process as an abstract algorithm for language processing tools that perform type checking, its purpose is explanatory only. Implementors of compilers and other type checking tools may well rely on totally different methods.

By now you should have a good understanding of the practical implications of type checking. All that remains is to give the rules in their full and precise form.

22.9 The call validity rule

(This last section formalizes the previous discussion of validity, but does not introduce any new concepts, so that you may safely skip to the next chapter. In fact this section will be mostly of interest to implementors of language processing tools.)

Let us now make the definition of validity precise.

VUGV

> ### Call rule
>
> A call is valid if and only if it is both class-valid and system-valid.

Since this general validity rule is very abstract, the successive definitions of this section, introducing the different aspects of call validity, have received separate validity codes for ease of reference.

This is very general and means that we must now define class-level and system-level validity. Like the above validity constraint, the definition relies on further notions to be defined next: export validity, argument validity and the dynamic class set.

VUCS

> Consider a single-dot call with target x, appearing in a class C. Let S be the type of x. Then:
>
> 1 • The call is **class-valid** if it is export-valid and argument-valid for S.
>
> 2 • The call is **system-valid** if for any element D of the dynamic class set of x it is export-valid and argument-valid for D.

PREVIEW

Export validity will require suppliers to make the needed features available to *C*; argument validity will require every actual argument to conform to the corresponding formal argument.

The validity of a call at either level – class or system – will require both export and argument validity. The only difference is that for class validity you need only apply these criteria to *S*, the type declared for the target *x* of the call, whereas for system-level checking you will need to consider all possible dynamic classes of *x*.

First, export validity:

VALIDITY

VUEX

> A call appearing in a class *C*, having *fname* as the feature of the call, is export-valid for a class *D* if and only if it satisfies either of the following two conditions.
>
> 1 • The call is an Unqualified_call and *fname* is the final name of a feature of *C*.
>
> 2 • The call has at least one dot, *D* has a feature of name *fname* which is available to *C*, and the call's target is either a valid entity of *C* or (recursively) a call which is export-valid for *D*.

A call's target may be a Parenthesized expression, which is equivalent to a call. See 23.7, page 380.

Condition 1 takes care of unqualified calls. Condition 2 is the basic requirement: *D* must make the feature available to *C* – that is to say, export it generally, or selectively to *C* or one of its ancestors. Condition 2 also takes care of the multi-dot case: in *a.b.c*, the target, here *a.b*, must itself satisfy the same condition. This use of recursion is justified since the target has one more level of dot notation than the original Call, so the recursion cannot go on forever.

CAVEAT

For the export validity of multi-dot calls, be sure to note that all that counts is availability to the class *C* where the call appears; availability to intermediate classes is irrelevant. For example, if *C* contains the call

> *next_paragraph.line (3). second_word. set_font (Bold)*

where the successive features are of types *PARAGRAPH, LINE and WORD*, export validity means that *PARAGRAPH* must make function *line* available to *C*, *LINE* must make *second_word* available to *C*, and *WORD* must make *set_font* available to *C*. If some of the exports are selective, it does not matter whether *second_word* is available to *PARAGRAPH*, or *set_font* is available to *LINE*. To understand why, it suffices to realize that the above call may be rephrased with just one level of dot notation as

> *l: LINE*; *w: WORD*;
> ...
> *l := next_paragraph.line (3)*;
> *w := l.second_word*;
> *w.set_font (Bold)*

This shows multi-dot notation as essentially a notational facility – although of course an important one in practice, avoiding the need for intermediate entities such as *l* and *w*.

Here now is argument validity. The definition will be simpler if we assume export validity as a prerequisite:

Condition 4 applies to external calls and will be examined in the discussion of the foreign language interface in chapter 24; see page 405. The Address *form of argument, '$ fn', is part of the syntax for* Call, *page 342. It serves to pass addresses of Eiffel features to foreign (non-Eiffel) routines.*

> Consider an export-valid call of target *target* and feature name *fname* appearing in a class *C*. (For an Unqualified_call take *target* to be *Current*.) Let *ST* be the type of *target*, *S* the base class of *ST*, and *sf* the feature of final name *fname* in *S*. Let *D* be a descendant of *S*, and *df* the version of *sf* in *D*. The call is argument-valid for *D* if and only if it satisfies the following four conditions:
>
> 1 • The number of actual arguments is the same as the number of formal arguments declared for *df*.
>
> 2 • Every actual argument, if any, conforms to the the corresponding formal argument of *df*.
>
> 3 • If *target* is itself a Call, it is (recursively) argument-valid for *D*.
>
> 4 • If any of the actual arguments is of the Address form *$ fn*, *fn* is the final name of a feature of *C* which is not a constant attribute.

Export validity ensures that *df* exists. Condition 2 is the fundamental type rule on argument passing, which allowed the discussion of direct reattachment to treat Assignment and actual-formal association in the same way. Condition 3 handles, as before, the case of multi-dot calls.

In condition 2, remember from the discussion of expression conformance an actual argument *y* will conform to the corresponding formal argument *x* if the type of *y* conforms to the type of *x*, but also if *x* is of type **like** *z* and the type of *y* conforms to the type of *z*; also, if *x* is anchored to another final argument, as in

← See 13.9, page 225, about expression conformance and the exact type rules which explain why a routine call as given is argument-valid.

> $r (z: T; x:$ **like** $z)$ **is** ...

then *y* of type *YT* conforms to *x* in a call *r* (*u*, *y*) if *u* is of type *UT* (conforming to *T*) and *YT* conforms to *UT*.

The argument validity rule assumes that *D* is a descendant of *S*. This is always the case whenever you need this rule to ascertain argument validity as part of the requirements on call validity: for class-level checking, *D* will be *S*; for system-level checking, the validity constraints on reattachment indicate that all the dynamic types of an entity conform to its static type (and so are based on descendant classes). This is also clear from the definition of the dynamic type set below.

This gives the full validity rule on calls.

To remove any ambiguity, we must provide an equally precise definition of the **dynamic class set** of an expression. This is the set of base classes of all elements in the **dynamic type set** of the expression; the dynamic type set was itself defined as the set of all possible dynamic types of the expression, where a possible dynamic type for an expression is the type of any object to which it may become attached at run time. This definition is correct, but it does not enable us to determine easily the dynamic type set, or the dynamic class set, from the software text.

← The original definitions are in 20.9; see page 323.

The above informal illustration constructed dynamic class sets through successive vector approximations, until it reached a fixpoint. Since it assumed all classes to be non-generic, its results were both dynamic classes and dynamic types. The full definition, which covers anchored and generically derived types, will yield the the dynamic *type* sets; to obtain the corresponding class sets, just replace every type by its base class.

← *The iterative process was described in 22.8, starting on page 364.*

The definition needs the following two notions to deal with genericity. Let T be a Class_type based on a class C. If C is a generic class C $[G_1, ...]$, T is C $[A_1, ...]$ for some types $A_1, ...$; if C is not generic, T is just C. Then:

- If e is an entity or expression appearing in a feature of C, the "dynamic type set of e for T" is the set of dynamic types of objects that may become attached to e as a result of calls to C's features on direct instances of T. The "dynamic type set of e", with no further qualification, is the dynamic type set of e for C $[G_1, ...]$, or just C if C is not generic.

- If U is a type, the notation U_T will stand for the type obtained from U by substituting A_i for any occurrence of G_i – or just U if C is not generic. For example, if U is X $[G, INTEGER]$ appearing in a feature of class D $[G]$, and T is D $[REAL]$, then U_T is X $[REAL, INTEGER]$.

Here is the full definition of dynamic type sets:

The dynamic type sets of the expressions, entities and functions of a system result from performing all possible applications of the following rules to every Class_type T, of base class C, used in the system.

1 • If a routine of C contains a creation instruction, with target x and creation type U, the dynamic type set of x for T is $\{U_T\}$.

2 • The dynamic type set for T of an occurrence of *Current* in the text of a routine of C is $\{T\}$.

3 • For any entity or expression e of expanded type appearing in the text of C, if the type ET of e is expanded, the dynamic type set of e for T is $\{ET_T\}$. (Rules 4 to 7, when used to determine elements of the dynamic type set of some e, assume that e's type is not expanded.)

4 • If a routine of C contains an Assignment of target x and source e, the dynamic type set of x for T includes (recursively) every member of the dynamic type set of e for T.

5 • If a routine of C contains an Assignment_attempt of target x, with type U, and source e, the dynamic type set of x for T includes (recursively) every type conforming to U_T which is also a member of the dynamic type set of e for T.

6 • If a routine of C contains a call h of target ta, U is (recursively) a member of the dynamic type set of ta for T, and tf is the version of the call's feature in the base class of U, then the dynamic type set for U of any formal argument of tf includes every member of the dynamic type set for U_T of the corresponding actual argument in h.

7 • If h, tf and U are as in case 6 and tf is an attribute or function, the dynamic type set of h for T includes (recursively) every member of the dynamic type set for U_T of the *Result* entity in tf.

Each of the seven cases of this definition, explained in detail below, is a rule which you may use to bring new elements to the possible dynamic type sets of the expressions, entities and functions of a system. More precisely:

- Rules 1, 2 and 3 are non-recursive: they yield elements of the dynamic type sets without further ado.

- Rules 3 to 7 are recursive: given known elements of the dynamic type sets of the expressions of a system, they may add new elements.

In other words, you may view the definition as describing an iterative process, generalized from the earlier discussion, for building the dynamic type sets: first apply rules 1 to 3 to every possible case, obtaining v_0, the initial vector of dynamic type sets; then, at each successive step i, apply rules 3 to 7 to every possible case, obtaining new elements of the type sets in v_i from elements of the type sets in v_{i-1}. The process terminates if the resulting v_i is the same as v_{i-1} — that is to say, the last iteration has brought nothing new.

This process is finite since the set of types in the system is finite. To get an upper bound to the number of iterations, call DEPTH be the maximum depth of a call (number of dots in Call form, number of operators in Operator_expression form) and ATTACH the maximum length of a non-cyclic sequence e_i such that there is a reattachment from e_{i+1} to e_i; then the process will terminate in at most DEPTH + ATTACH steps.

Let us now make sure we understand the seven rules. Rule 1 addresses creation instructions. It considers that an instruction of the form

$$! U ! x$$

adds the creation type, here U, to the dynamic type set of x. (If U is absent, the creation type is x's base type.) If C is generic, the rule pertains to the dynamic type sets relative to some generic derivation T of C; then we must perform the corresponding substitution of actual for formal generics, so the rule uses U_T rather than just U.

← Creation instructions were discussed in 18.8, with the definition of "creation type" appearing on page 285.

Rule 2 indicates that *Current*, when used in C, represents an object of type T that is to say C, with the requested generic derivation if applicable.

Rules 1 and 2 reflect the pragmatism of system-level validity checking. Class-level checking considers the developer's intentions (the declarations); but system-level checking only considers deeds: the types of the objects that Creation and reattachement instructions may actually attach to entities.

Rule 3 takes care of expressions of expanded types, which are never polymorphic. In this case we just take the declarations at face value.

As you may remember, the conformance rule for expanded types allows for some tolerance in the case of basic arithmetic types. For example you may attach the integer value *3* to an entity r of type *REAL*. But this has no effect on the dynamic type set of r: such an assignment causes a conversion, and attaches to r a real value, here *3.0*. So there is no polymorphism in this case.

See 13.10, page 226, about conformance for basic types. Assignment semantics in this case ([4] on the table page 317) is copy, implying conversion to the "heavier" type (case 2 of copy semantics, page 297).

Rules 4, 5 and 6 covers the three forms of possibly polymorphic reattachment: Assignment, Assignment_attempt, and actual-formal association in a call. For a reattachment of a value e to an entity x, we must add all of e's possible dynamic types to those of x. In addition:

- For an Assignment_attempt of the form $x \mathrel{?}= e$ (rule 5), we must only consider those possible types for e which conform to the type of x: any other one would result, in accordance with the semantics of Assignment_attempt, in no object attachment for ta.
- For a call (rule 6), e is an actual argument and x is the corresponding formal argument in the appropriate version of the routine.

In rule 6, a member U of the dynamic type set of ta, the call's target, may be generically derived; then when need to perform the corresponding type substitutions in adding the members of the actual argument's dynamic type set to the dynamic type set of the formal argument. This is why the rule considers the dynamic type set of e (the actual argument) for U_T.

A call whose feature is a function is itself an expression, with its own dynamic type set. Since the expression's value is the final value of *Result* as used in the function, rule 7 defines the dynamic type set of the expression as that of *Result*. As with rule 6, we must perform the appropriate substitution if the type of the call's target is generic, hence the use of U_T.

We need one more convention to make the above rule fully applicable in practice: how to handle the dynamic type sets of array elements. The relevant features in the Kernel Library class *ARRAY* are *put* and *force*, which set an element's value, and *item*, which returns an element's value, as in

> *Arrays require a specific convention since the language specification defines the interface of class ARRAY (28.7, page 443) but not its implementation.*

> x, *some_entity*: T; i, j: *INTEGER*; a: *ARRAY* [T];
> ...
>   -- Assign the value of *some_entity* to the i-th element of a:
> a.*put* (*some_entity*, i);
> ...
>   -- Assign to x the value of the j-th element of a:
> $x := a$.*item* (j)

> *'put' assumes that the index, 'i' in the example, is within bounds; 'force' resizes the array if necessary. Details in chapter 28.*

To find out the dynamic type set of a.*item* (j) (and hence of x), note that the software text usually does not suffice to determine whether i and j will have the same value at execution time. So we must treat every *put* or *force* operation as affecting potentially every array element. Hence the rule:

Array type rule

To study the effect of array manipulations on dynamic type sets, assume that in class *ARRAY* feature *item* is an attribute, and that *put* (v, i) and *force* (v, i) are both implemented as

> *item* := v

The rule also applies to manifest arrays. A manifest array is an expression of the form $\langle\langle a_1, ..., a_n \rangle\rangle$, denoting an array of n elements, containing the values given. For typing purposes, it will be treated as it had been initialized explicitly by n calls to *put*, each of the form

> *$\rightarrow$ See 23.20, page 393, about manifest arrays.*

> a. *put* (a_i, i)

23

Expressions and constants

23.1 Overview

The variants of the Expression construct make it possible for a software text to denote run-time values – objects and references. Previous chapters have already introduced some of the available forms: Call and Old.

← *See chapter 21 on* Call *and 9.9, page 123, on* Old.

This chapter gives the full list of permissible expressions and the precise form of the remaining categories: operator, equality, locals, constants, Strip and manifest arrays.

23.2 General form of expressions

The following possibilities are available for expressions.

Expression	≜	Call | Operator_expression | Equality | Manifest_constant | Manifest_array | Old | Strip
Boolean_expression	≜	Expression

The previous two chapters explored the notion of Call, which covers feature calls using dot notation. A Call is an expression if and only if its feature is an attribute or a function (otherwise it is an expression).

← *Chapter 22 covered the validity constraints on* Call.

As a special case of Call, an entity x (attribute, local entity including *Result, Current*) may be used as expression in the text of that class. (This is obtained from the syntax of Call by taking x as Entity of an Unqualified_call without Parenthesized_qualifier or Actuals.)

← *The syntax of* Call *is on page 342.*

Operator expressions are built using operators, prefix and infix, and parentheses. They have the semantics of calls, but raise different syntactical questions, in particular the issue of operator precedence.

Equality expressions cover both equality and inequality tests, using the symbols = and /=. Although they are syntactically similar to operator expressions, with = and /= being used in infix form, it is preferable to treat them separately because here the semantics is not that of a call.

A Manifest_constant has a fixed value, given by the form of the constant, as in the Integer_constant −87. A special case is that of a Manifest_string, which may be viewed as constant in the sense that it denotes a fixed string descriptor object, but gives access to a character sequence which may in fact change. (This is a potential source of confusion and is explained in detail later in this chapter.)

→ See 23.19, page 391, on the semantics of Manifest_string.

Not all constants are manifest: by declaring a constant attribute you may use an Identifier to denote a constant value. Syntactically, as noted above, constant attributes used as expressions are a special case of Call, but it will be convenient to study them together with manifest constants.

Manifest arrays are arrays given by the list of their elements.

An Old expression, usable only in a postcondition, denotes the earlier value of an expression. This was studied in the discussion of assertions.

← See 9.9, page 123, about Old.

A Strip expression, most commonly used in a postcondition, yields an array consisting of the contents of an object possibly stripped of some of its fields.

The following sections explore these various cases in the order given, except for Call and Old on which nothing more need be said.

The above syntax definition also covers Boolean_expression, used in the grammar whenever a construct needs a boolean value: Then_part (conditional instructions), Exit (loops), Unlabeled_assertion_clause (assertions). An Expression is valid as Boolean expression if it satisfies the obvious constraint:

← Unlabeled_assertion_ clause: page 120. Then_ part: page 235. Exit: page 243.

VWBE

> A Boolean_expression is valid if and only if it is an Expression of type *BOOLEAN*.

23.3 Equality expressions

PURPOSE

An Equality expression serves to test equality (with the = symbol) or inequality (with the /= symbol) of values. Typical examples are

> *border_color = Black_color*
> *window.extent /= 0*

The syntax is straightforward:

SYNTAX

> Equality $\triangleq$ Expression Comparison Expression
> Comparison $\triangleq$ "=" | "/="

PREVIEW

Vis-à-vis other operators, = and /= have the same precedence as relational operators such as < and >=, higher than the boolean operators such as **and** and **or**, and lower than arithmetic operators such as + and *. The full precedence table appears below.

→ See 23.5, page 376, on operator precedence.

Equality expressions are subject to a type constraint:

VWEQ

> An Equality expression is valid if and only if either of its operand conforms to the other.

The operands need not have identical types, but conformance must hold either from the first to the second or conversely. As you may recall, two expressions conform to each other not only if their types conform, but also, for example, if one is an entity x and the other is of type **like** x.

← Expression conformance was covered in 13.9, page 225.

The semantics of the equality operator = was explored in detail as part of the discussion on reattachment. As a summary of that presentation, the expression $e = f$ has two possible meanings:

← See 20.17, starting on page 335, and particularly the second table on page 336.

1 • If both e and f are of reference types, the expression denotes reference equality. In other words, it returns true if and only if e and f are either both void or attached to the same object.

2 • If either e or f is of an expanded type, the expression denotes object equality; more precisely, it returns the same result as *equal* (e, f), based on the equality function from class *ANY*, which here yields true if and only if e and f are attached to field-by-field equal objects (unless *is_equal* has been redefined to account for a local version of equality).

SEMANTICS

The expression $e\ /= f$ has value true if and only if $e = f$ has value false.

23.4 Operator expressions

You may build operator expressions by combining simpler expressions through prefix and infix operators, using parentheses to remove ambiguities if necessary. An example, from the postcondition of procedure *put_child_left* in class *LINKABLE* of the Data Structure Library, is

> **not** (*child_position* = 2) **implies** *child_position* = **old** *child_position* + 1

This expression appears in class LINKABLE with some extra parentheses for clarity. The effect is the same, however, because of the precedence rules given below.

This uses the infix operators **implies** and + and the prefix operator **not**, applied to subexpressions involving Old and Equality.

An important property of operator expressions is that semantically they bring nothing new to the picture: they are simply a different way to write calls, using conventional operator notation rather than dot notation. This means that if the Kernel Library classes *BOOLEAN* and *INTEGER* had used identifiers such as *unary_not*, *binary_implies* and *unary_plus* rather than prefix and infix operator names for some of their features, the above call would have to be written

> ((*child_position* = 2). *unary_not*). *binary_implies*
> (*child_position* = **old** (*child_position*. *binary_plus* (1)))

In spite of this direct equivalence with calls, however, we have a few more properties to explore about operator expressions: understanding their syntax requires the notion of precedence, without which any non-trivial expression would have to include an unpleasant number of parentheses, and the equivalence with Call needs to be made precise through the notion of equivalent dot form, taking into account a few special cases for arithmetic and boolean operators.

23.5 Operator expression syntax and precedence rules

Here is the general form of operator expressions:

Operator_expression	≜	Parenthesized |
		Unary_expression | Binary_expression
Parenthesized	≜	"(" Expression ")"
Unary_expression	≜	Prefix_operator Expression
Binary_expression	≜	Expression Infix_operator Expression

A Prefix_operator is either a Unary or a Free_operator; an Infix_operator is either a Binary or a Free_operator. The list of Unary and Binary operators, already given in the discussion of feature names, is:

→ *See page 419 for the definition of* Free_operator.

Unary	≜	**not** | "+" | "−"
Binary	≜	"+" | "−" | "∗" | "/" |
		"<" | ">" | "<=" | ">=" |
		"//" | "\\" | "^" |
		and | **or** | **xor** |
		and then | **or else** | **implies**

← This syntax appeared originally on page 68.

The syntax for Operator_expression, as given, is of course highly ambiguous. It would make it possible to understand an expression such as

$$a + b + c * d$$

in several different ways (expressed with full parenthesization):

[I1]	$a + (b + (c * d))$
[I2]	$a + ((b + c) * d)$
[I3]	$(a + b) + (c * d)$
[I4]	$(a + (b + c)) * d$
[I5]	$((a + b) + c) * d$

The correct interpretation, according to the precedence rules given below, is I3.

This means that to get a practically usable syntactical definition we must complement the above syntax productions by **precedence rules**. Every possible operator has a precedence, determined by the table given below. Precedences are numerical values on a scale from 1 to 12. The numerical values themselves are not important; what matters is the comparison of the precedence values of any two operators appearing consecutively in an expression. In the absence of intervening parentheses, the one with the higher value binds tighter.

For example, the value denoted by $a + b * c$ is the sum of two terms, one of which is the value of a and the other the value of the product $b * c$. This is because the operator $*$ has higher precedence than the operator $+$.

Here is the table of operator precedence. It includes the operators that may appear in an Operator_expression, the equality and inequality symbols used in Equality expressions, as well as other symbols and keywords which may also occur in expressions and hence require disambiguating: the semicolon in its role as separator for Assertion_clause; the **old** operator which may appear in an Old expression as part of a Postcondition; the dot **.** of dot notation, which binds tighter than any other operator; the **strip** keyword of Strip expressions.

Operator precedence

Level	Symbols
12	**.** (Dot notation for Unqualified_call expressions)
11	**old** (in postconditions) **strip** **not** unary + unary − All free unary operators
10	All free binary operators
9	^ (power)
8	* / // (integer division) \\ (integer remainder)
7	binary + binary −
6	= /= (not equal) < > <= >=
5	**and and then**
4	**or or else xor**
3	**implies**
2	<< >> (for manifest arrays).
1	; (semicolon as separator between an Assertion_clause and the next)

You may use parentheses to override the grouping implied by operator precedence. If *exp* and *other_exp* are arbitrary expressions, and § an arbitrary Binary operator, the first operand of § in the expression

> (*exp*) § *other_exp*

is always the value of *exp*, regardless of the precedence of § relative to the operators appearing in *exp*. Similarly, the second operand of § in the expression

> *other_exp* § (*exp*)

is always the value of *exp*. For a unary operator †, the expression

> † (*exp*)

always denotes the application of † to the value of *exp*.

The rules given so far only resolve potential conflicts between different operators. There remains to see how to interpret expressions containing two or more consecutive operators § and ‡, with no intervening parentheses. The relevant cases are:

1 • § and ‡ are the same binary operator, as in *a* § *b* § *c*.

2 • § and ‡ are different binary operators, as in *a* § *b* ‡ *c*.

3 • § and ‡ are different unary operators, as in § ‡ *a*.

4 • One of the operators is binary and the other one is unary, as in ‡ *a* § *b* or *a* § ‡ *b* (where § is binary and ‡ unary).

For two or more consecutive occurrences of the same binary operator § (case 1), left-to-right association always applies, except if § is the operator ∧, for which the association is right-to-left. This means that

$$a \; \S \; b \; \S \; c$$

is understood as

$$(a \; \S \; b) \; \S \; c$$

unless § is ∧, whereas $a \wedge b \wedge c$ means $a \wedge (b \wedge c)$. The reason for this special case is that basic arithmetic types (*INTEGER*, *REAL*, *DOUBLE*) use ∧ as power operator; the mathematical notation a^{b^c} is traditionally understood as meaning $a^{(b^c)}$. This is the only interesting interpretation since $(a^b)^c$ is simply a^{b*c}.

For different binary operators (case 2), precedence determines the grouping unless it is the same for both operators. So the expression

$$a \; \S \; b \; \ddagger \; c$$

is understood as

$$a \; \S \; (b \; \ddagger \; c)$$

if the precedence of ‡ is higher than the precedence of §, and

$$(a \; \S \; b) \; \ddagger \; c$$

otherwise. If the two operators have the same precedence, left-to-right association applies, so that the grouping is the second one.

As reflected in the above precedence table, all unary operators have the same precedence. This means that if § and ‡ are unary operators (case 3) then § ‡ a is understood as § (‡ a)

The table also shows that all unary operators bind tighter than all binary operators, so that if § is binary and ‡ unary (case 4) then

$$\ddagger \; a \; \S \; b$$
$$a \; \S \; \ddagger \; b$$

are respectively understood as

$$(\ddagger \; a) \; \S \; b$$
$$a \; \S \; (\ddagger \; b)$$

This applies in particular when § and ‡ are the same operator, used as infix in one case and prefix in the other. So $a - - b$ means the same as $a - (- b)$.

Special cases in rules are unpleasant, of course, and developers may always use parentheses; but it is dangerous to go against time-honored mathematical conventions. Here the left-to-right rule could cause errors in classes written by people trained in mathematics or physics.

Here this is in fact the only interpretation that makes sense.

→ *Two adjacent uses of the same operator, the first binary and the second unary, as in − −, must be separated by a blank or other separator. Two consecutive minus signs, as in --, would yield the symbol introducing comments. See 25.5, page 414, for the precise rules on separators.*

23.6 Validity and semantics of operator expressions

Once no syntactical ambiguity remains, the validity and semantic properties of an Operator_expression are essentially those of a corresponding Call.

For every Operator_expression there will be an **equivalent dot form,** syntactically a Call, illustrated above for a postcondition clause of class *LINKABLE*. As another example, here is the equivalent dot form of the expression used to discuss precedence:

← *The example refers to the expression in 23.5, page 376, understood under interpretation I3.*

> (*a*. *binary_plus* (*b*)). *binary_plus* (*c*. *binary_times* (*d*))

The earlier example of equivalent dot form, from LINKABLE, was in 23.4, page 375.

This assumes that if *x*'s type has a base class *C*, the operator features **infix** "+" and **infix** "∗" of *C* have been replaced by identifier features of names *binary_plus* and *binary_times*, all other aspects of these functions (Routine_body, Precondition etc.) remaining unchanged.

← *A feature is either an operator feature, whose name is of the Prefix or Infix form, or an identifier feature, whose name is an Identifier. See 5.13, page 67.*

The next section gives a precise definition of the equivalent dot form, although the above examples suffice to make the idea clear. Then the validity constraint on operator expressions is straightforward:

VWOE

> An Operator_expression is valid if and only if its equivalent dot form is a valid Call.

← *The validity of calls was the subject of chapter 22.*

This rule ensures that every operator is used with the proper number of arguments. For example *INTEGER* and other basic arithmetic classes have a function **infix** "∗", but not prefix version. Then of the expressions

> *2 ∗ 2*
>
> *∗ 2*

WARNING: *second expression not valid.*

the first is valid but not the second. To see this it suffices to produce the equivalent dot forms:

> *2. binary_times* (2)
>
> *unary_times* (2)

and observe that *unary_times* does not exist.

DEFINITION:
Multiary
Operator

The rule also explains why some binary operators are actually "multiary" – that is to say, may take three or more operands, whose types all conform to the type of the first – while other operators are limited to two arguments. An example of multiary operator is "+" on integers; relational operators such as "<", on the other hand, are binary but not multiary. This is clear from the equivalent dot forms. With integer operands, the Operator_expression

> *1 + 2 + 3 + 4*

has the valid equivalent dot form

$$((1.\mathit{binary\_plus}\ (2)).\mathit{binary\_plus}\ (3)).\mathit{binary\_plus}\ (4)$$

In contrast, the Operator_expression

$$1 < 2 < 3$$

WARNING: this expression is not valid!

is not valid since its operands do not yield a valid set of call targets and arguments for the corresponding function **infix** *"+"* in class *BOOLEAN*. This is immediately visible on the equivalent dot form:

$$(1.\mathit{binary\_less}\ (2)).\mathit{binary\_less}\ (3)$$

Here the last *binary_less* is applied to the preceding expression, which is of type *BOOLEAN* (and has value true since 1 is less than 2). Since *BOOLEAN* does not have a function **infix** *"<"*, the expression is invalid.

Of course, it is not inconceivable that *BOOLEAN* could have a function *"<"*, for example with **false** considered less than **true**. But this would not make the expression valid: such a function would then expect an argument of type *BOOLEAN*, whereas *c* is of type *INTEGER*. A true multiary operator, such as *"+"* on integers, must accept successive operands of the same type.

In summary, there is no need to define binary and multiary operators as separate syntactical categories. The grammar lists both kinds as binary (construct Binary); whether a given operator may be used in multiary form depends on the signature of the corresponding infix function.

← The syntax for Operator *was repeated on page 377.*

Finally, there remains to define the semantics of an Operator_expression. This is simply the semantics of calls: the value of an operator expression is the value that would be returned by the equivalent dot form. This is complemented by a special rule seen below, semi-strict evaluation, for boolean operators.

→ See 23.8 below about boolean operators and 23.9 about semi-strictness.

To understand the validity and semantics of operator expressions, then, is simply to understand the corresponding prefix and infix features; this applies in particular to arithmetic operators (for which the feature declarations are in the basic classes *INTEGER*, *REAL* and *DOUBLE*), to boolean operators (class *BOOLEAN*), and to operators on bit sequences (based on theoretical classes *BIT_N*). The next sections (after a digression, not needed on first reading, defining in full the notion of equivalent dot form) give more details on the specific semantics of these operators.

← The semantics of calls was the subject of 21.14, starting page 352, with less formal discussions in the preceding sections of that chapter.

→ See chapter 32 about the basic and BIT_N classes.

23.7 The equivalent dot form

(This section defines precisely the notion of equivalent dot form, already introduced informally through examples, and used extensively in the previous sections. It may be skipped on first reading.)

For a full specification of the validity and semantics of an Operator_expression, we need a precise description of how to obtain its equivalent dot form. Because an Operator_expression may involve components which are expressions of other kinds (such as calls or constants), the definition must in fact be applicable to any kind of expression.

To obtain the equivalent dot form, perform the following four steps:

1 • Replace every operator feature of every class by an identifier feature with a suitable **equivalent identifier name** (such as *unary_plus* or *binary_plus*).

2 • Replace every Unary_expression of the form

   § *e*

by the equivalent dot form

   e' . equiv_name

where *equiv_name* is the equivalent identifier name chosen for operator § and *e'* is (recursively) the equivalent dot form of *e*.

3 • Replace every Binary_expression of the form

   e § *f*

by the equivalent dot form

   e' . equiv_name (*f'*)

where *equiv_name* is the equivalent identifier name chosen for operator § and *e'* and *f'* are (recursively) the equivalent dot forms of *e* and *f*.

4 • Replace every Parenthesized expression (*e*) by *e'*, where *e'* is (recursively) the equivalent dot form of *e*.

This process only affects the Operator_expression parts of an expression *e*: If *e* is an identifier (local entity or attribute) or a Manifest_constant, it is its own equivalent dot form; if *e* is a complex expression of another kind, such as a Call or Equality, its equivalent dot form is obtained by applying the transformation recursively to *e*'s operator expression components.

Of course, these transformations need only be carried out mentally. A compiler, however, may internally process operator features in a similar way.

There is a special rule for INTEGER, REAL and DOUBLE operands, as explained below.

23.8 Ordinary boolean operators

The boolean operators **not**, **and**, **or** and **xor**, defined in the Kernel Library class *BOOLEAN*, define operations on boolean values.

The value of **not** *a* is true if and only if *a* has value false. The others are binary operators; the value they yield when applied to a first operand of value *v1* and a second operand of value *v2* is defined as follows:

• For **and**: true if and only if both *v1* and *v2* are false.

• For **or**: false if and only if either *v1* or *v2* is false.

• For **xor**: true if and only if *v1* and *v2* have different values. In other words, *a* **xor** *b* has the same value as (*a* **or** *b*) **and not** (*a* **and** *b*).

23.9 Semi-strict boolean operators

In addition to the above, three infix operators, also defined in *BOOLEAN*, have a special semantic property known as semi-strictness. These operators are **and then** (semi-strict conjunction), **or else** (semi-strict disjunction) and **implies** (semi-strict implication); they complement **and** and **or**.

For operands of values *v1* and *v2* these operators yield the following results:

- **and then**: false if *v1* is false, otherwise the value of *v2*.
- **or else**: true if *v1* is true, otherwise the value of *v2*.
- **implies**: true if *v1* is false, otherwise the value of *v2*. (In other words, *a* **implies** *b* has the same value as **not** *a* **or else** *b*.)

At first sight, **and then** may seem equivalent to **and**, **or else** to **or**, and *a* **implies** *b* to **not** *a* **or** *b*. The difference is that the semantics of the three new operators, as it has just been defined, is semi-strict. This means that any one of these operators may in some cases yield a result on the sole basis of its first argument *v1*, if the value of *v1* suffices to determine the outcome – even if the second argument does not have a value.

This happens for **and then** when *v1* is false (result: false), for **or else** when *v1* is true (result: true), and for **implies** when *v1* is false (result: true). In these three cases the implementation must not evaluate the second argument *v2*. No such rule applies to **and** and **or**, which are not required to produce any result for an undefined second argument, and so may use a strict implementation as well as a semi-strict one.

As a consequence, the semi-strict operators, in contrast with their counterparts in standard mathematical logic, are not commutative: they do not treat their operands symmetrically. For example, *a* **and then** *b* does not necessarily have the same effect as *b* **and then** *a*. To be more accurate, any values these expressions yield will be the same, but it is possible for the second to yield a value when the first does not.

Because they enable you to write two-operand boolean expressions whose second operand need not have a value if the first operand's value leaves only one possible result, semi-strict operators are particularly useful for a certain kind of loop used to traverse a data structure. Here is an example from a search routine in class *LINKED_LIST* in the Data Structure Library:

← A general presentation of semi-strictness appeared in 20.10, page 324. You should not have any trouble understanding the present section even if you skipped the earlier, more theoretical discussion.

For a more complete discussion of strictness see the book "Introduction to the Theory of Programming Languages". For a study of various degrees of strictness in boolean operators see H. Barringer, J.H. Cheng and Cliff B. Jones, "A Logic Covering Undefinedness in Program Proofs", Acta Informatica, 21, 3, October 1984, pp. 251-269.

```
search_same (v: like first) is
        -- Move cursor to first position (at or after current one)
        -- where v appears; move "off" if no such position.
    do
        from
            ... (Initialization omitted) ...
        variant
            count − position + 1
        until
            off or else (item = v)
        loop
            forth
        end
    ensure
        (not off) implies (item = v)
    end -- search_same
```

Here the loop will terminate whenever the cursor moves after the last element (*off*), or hits an element whose value, as given by *item*, is equal to the argument *v*. The Exit expression tests for either of these conditions to occur. When the first condition (*off*) is true, however, we definitely do not want to evaluate the second (*item = v*): not only would its contribution to the result be useless (since a disjunction with one true operand may have no value other than true); evaluating it would in fact be improper since function *item* is only defined when the cursor is on an actual element, which is not the case when it is *off*. (This is reflected in the precondition for *item*, which includes the condition **not** *off*.)

To guarantee the desired result, the Exit condition uses **or else** rather than **or**. In the same way, the postcondition only makes sense because of the semi-strictness of **implies**.

In other words, the semi-strict semantics of **or else** and **implies** guarantees that *search_same* will work properly even if *v* does not appear in the list.

This loop illustrates a common scheme, easy to implement thanks to the semi-strict semantics of **or else**: a loop traverses a certain data structure, and may terminate either by encountering an element that satisfies a certain property, or by going one step too far, having exhausted the potential candidate elements. Because this scheme is so general, it has been captured by a procedure of the Iteration Library:

```
    continue_until (s: like anchor) is
        -- Apply action to every item of s up to
        -- and excluding the first one satisfying test.
        -- (From the current cursor position in s)
    require
        traversable_exists: s /= Void;
        invariant_satisfied: invariant_value (s)
    do
      from
        start (s); prepare (s)
      invariant
        invariant_value (s)
      until
        off (s) or else test (s)
      loop
        action (s);
        forth (s)
      end;
      if not off (s) then action (s) end; wrapup (s)
    ensure
        not off (s) implies test (s)
    end -- continue_while
```

← *The scheme was encountered in the discussion of programmed iteration, 10.13, page 148. See 11.5, page 174, on how to use several variants of such an iteration scheme in a single class.*

To apply it to a particular data structure, just effect the deferred routines in a proper descendant of *LINEAR_ITERATION*.

← *The sections referenced above give examples of such effectings.*

23.10 Arithmetic operators and the Balancing rule

When applied to operands of types *INTEGER*, *REAL* or *DOUBLE*, operators such as +, −, *, / and ∧ (power) denote arithmetic operations, as defined by the corresponding prefix and infix features in the corresponding Kernel Library classes. Operators // and \\, defined only for integer operands, denote integer division and remainder.

On operands of type *INTEGER*, *REAL* or *DOUBLE*, the relational operators <, >, <= and >= denote the usual order relation. On character operands, they denote ASCII order.

As with other types of operands, the validity and semantics of arithmetic expressions follow from the equivalent dot form, obtained through the process described above. To ensure compatibility with the usual conventions of arithmetic and of programming languages, however, it is necessary to complement this process with a special rule for operands of the arithmetic types *INTEGER*, *REAL* and *BOOLEAN*.

The problem arises from the need to remain compatible with standard mathematical conventions, which accept mixed-type computation on arithmetic values when there is no ambiguity. For example, *d* being of type *DOUBLE*, you probably expect the expressions

> 3 + 4.5
> 4.5 + 3
> d + 3

to be all valid, and to yield results of type *REAL* (the type of *4.5*) for the first two cases and *DOUBLE* for the last. More generally, the usual convention is that the heaviest type in a mixed-type arithmetic expression determines both the type of the result and the operation variant to be applied, with *REAL* considered heavier than *INTEGER* and *DOUBLE* heavier than *REAL*.

← The notion of heavier type was introduced in 13.10, page 227. It served to define the conversions needed in copy operations (19.2, page 297) and equality comparisons (19.7, page 303).

As defined so far, the equivalent dot form would yield calls to features of class *INTEGER* in the first case, *REAL* in the second and *DOUBLE* in the third, since the corresponding features are declared as

> -- In class *INTEGER*:
>   **infix** *"+"* (*other*: *INTEGER*): *INTEGER* **is** ...
> -- In class *REAL*:
>   **infix** *"+"* (*other*: *REAL*): *REAL* **is** ...
> -- In class *DOUBLE*:
>   **infix** *"+"* (*other*: *DOUBLE*): *DOUBLE* **is** ...

→ Basic classes are covered in chapter 32. As explained there, "+" and similar features are introduced as deferred in class NUMERIC and effected with different argument and result types for NUMERIC's descendants INTEGER, REAL and DOUBLE.

These declarations are not appropriate for mixed-type expressions such as the above. For example, the equivalent dot form of the first expression is

> (*3*). *binary_plus* (*4.5*)

which is not valid since **infix** *"+"* for *INTEGER*, corresponding to *binary_plus*, expects an *INTEGER* argument.

The following rule addresses the problem:

> **Arithmetic Expression Balancing rule**
>
> In determining the equivalent dot form of a Binary expression involving operands of arithmetic types (one or more of *DOUBLE*, *REAL* and *INTEGER*), first convert all operands to the heaviest operand type occurring in the expression.

There is no ambiguity in defining the conversion to a heavier type; for example the integer *2* may be converted into the real *2.0*.

Conversions to a lighter type would require choosing between policies such as truncation or rounding.

23.11 Operations on bit sequences

A small number of operators are available on bit sequences. One – **not** – is unary; the others – **and, or, implies, xor** – are binary.

If *b* is a bit sequence, **not** *b* is a bit sequence of the same length, with a one at every position where *b* has a zero and conversely.

If *sa* and *sb* are bit sequences, each of the binary operators pads the shorter operand with zeros on the left if necessary to reach the number of bits, N, of the larger. For any position i $(1 \leq i \leq N)$ let a, b, c be the i-th bits of *sa*, *sb*, *sc*. Then c is a one if and only if:

- For **and**: a and b are ones.
- For **or**: a or b or both are ones.
- For **implies**: a is a zero, or b is a one, or both of these conditions.
- For **xor**: one among a and b is a one and the other is a zero.

An Equality expression involving two bit sequences yields true if and only if, after left-padding if necessary, they are bit-by-bit identical.

← See "Object equality", 19.7, page 303.

Although the bit operators have the same name as the corresponding boolean operators, and similar semantics if we match **true** with 1 and **false** with 0, the question of semi-strict semantics does not arise here.

← Semi-strictness for boolean operators was discussed in 23.9, page 381.

23.12 Entities

Entities do not appear as a separate case in the syntax for Expression because they form a special case of Call (more precisely Unqualified_call). But their role as expressions or components of expressions deserves a few comments.

The observation that an attribute is a Call by itself was made on page 350.

First, as a reminder, the syntactic definition:

← This syntax appeared initially on page 276.

Entity	≜	Writable | Read_only
Writable	≜	Attribute | Local
Attribute	≜	Identifier
Local	≜	Identifier | *Result*
Read_only	≜	Formal | *Current*
Formal	≜	Identifier

The associated constraint, called the Entity rule, required any entity appearing in a routine *r* to be one of: attribute; local entity of *r* (including *Result* if *r* is a function); formal argument of *r*; *Current*; feature of a call.

← *The Entity rule is also on page 276.*

Together with the Call rule, the Entity rule governs the use of identifiers in expressions. A simple consequence of these two constraints is:

← *The Call rule is on page 367.*

VWID

Identifier rule

An Identifier appearing in an expression as part of the text of a routine *r* in a class *C*, either by itself or as the target or actual argument of a Call, must be the name of a feature of *C*, a local entity of *r*, or a formal argument of *r*.

"By itself or as the target or actual argument of a Call" excludes an identifier appearing immediately after a dot and denoting the feature of a qualified Call. For example, in *a* + *b.c* (*d*), the rule applies to *a* ("by itself"), *b* (target of a Call) and *d* (actual argument), but not to *c* (feature of a qualified Call). For *c* the relevant constraint is the Call rule, which among other conditions requires *c* to be a feature of the base class of *b*'s type.

If the example is examined in equivalent dot form, 'a' actually appears as target of a call, and 'b' appears both as argument of a call and target of another.

SEMANTICS

The Identifier rule is not a full "if and only if" rule; in fact it is conceptually superfluous since it follows from the earlier, more complete constraints. Language processing tools may find it convenient, however, as a simple criterion for detecting the most common case of invalid Identifier in expression.

The value of an entity of each possible form, evaluated during a call to the enclosing routine, is straightforward:

- The value of a Local entity (including *Result*) results from the successive instructions that may have been applied to the entity since the default initializations, performed anew on each call.

← *The initialization of local entities comes from the semantics of calls, given in 21.14, page 352.*

- The value of a routine's Formal argument is obtained, according to the rules of direct reattachment, from the value of the corresponding actual argument at the time of the current call. This value may not change for the duration of that call (although fields of the attached object, if any, may change).

← *See "Semantics of direct reattachment", 20.5, page 313.*

- The value of *Current* is the current object.

← *The definition of "current object" is on page 349.*

23.13 Constants

PURPOSE

A Constant expression has a value which does not change at run time, and is the same for all instances of a class.

The form is:

← *A* Constant *is required as "inspect constant" in Multi_branch instructions (chapter 14), and as size for a Bit_type (12.14, page 209).*

SYNTAX

| Constant | = | Manifest_constant \| Constant_attribute |
| Constant_attribute | = | Entity |

A Constant_attribute denotes a constant value, specified in the attribute's declaration as either a Manifest_constant or a Unique. The use of an identifier as Constant_attribute is subject to an obvious constraint:

← Constant attributes were discussed in chapter 16, with the presentation of Unique attributes starting on page 264.

VWCA

> A Constant_attribute appearing in a class *C* is valid if and only if its Entity is the final name of a constant attribute of *C*.

To apply this rule, you must look at the declaration of the attribute and check that, according to the rules for distinguishing between various kinds of feature, it indeed defines a constant attribute.

← The rules for recognizing constant attributes and other feature categories appear in 5.11, page 64.

If not a Constant_attribute, a Constant will be a Manifest_constant, whose lexical form indicates both a type and a value:

Manifest_constant	≜	Boolean_constant | Character_constant | Integer_constant | Real_constant | Manifest_string | Bit_constant
Sign	≜	"+" | "−"
Integer_constant	≜	[Sign] Integer
Character_constant	≜	"'" Character "'"
Boolean_constant	≜	**true** | **false**
Real_constant	≜	[Sign] Real
Manifest_string	≜	'"' Simple_string '"'
Bit_constant	≜	Bit_sequence

The following sections study the various cases in detail – except for Boolean_constant, about which it suffices to note that this construct only has two specimens, **true** and **false**, whose values are different (when compared for equality).

Beyond basic types, there is also a need for specifying constant values of complex types. This is addressed through **once functions**. The body of a once function is executed at most once, to compute the result of the first call (if any). All subsequent calls return the same result as the first, without further computation.

← On once functions (and once routines in general) see 8.6, page 113, and the semantics of calls in chapter 21.

For functions of reference types, this yields constant references. The scheme is particularly useful for objects containing shared information and may be illustrated as follows:

> *shared*: *SOME_REFERENCE_TYPE* **is**
>   -- A reference to an object shared by
>   -- all instances of the enclosing class
> **once**
>   !! *Result* ... (...);
>   ... Operations on *Result*, to initialize the shared object ...
> **end** -- *shared*

Calls to *shared* always return a reference to the object created and initialized by the first call. The object itself is not actually constant, since its fields may be changed through procedure calls of the form

> *shared.some_procedure* (...)

23.14 Integer constants

An integer constant – a specimen of Integer_constant – consists of an Integer, possibly preceded by a sign. (Integer, a lexical construct, describes unsigned integers.) Example specimens of Integer_constant are:

→ *Construct* Integer *is described as part of the lexical specification in 25.12, page 420.*

```
0
253
−57
+253
```

23.15 Real constants

A real constant – a specimen of Real_constant – consists of a Real, possibly preceded by a sign.

Real, a lexical construct, describes floating-point numbers. Without scaling factor, the possible forms of Real are

→ Real *is described in 25.13, page 421.*

```
a.
.b
a.b
```

where *a* and *b* are integer constants. Any of these may be followed by the letter *E*, an optional sign and an Integer to indicate scaling by a power of ten.

Here are some example specimens of Real_constant:

```
46.
.54
24.36
−34.65
−34.65E−12
45.21E2
+45.21E2
```

23.16 Bit constants

A Bit_constant, of Bit_type, is simply a specimen of the lexical construct Bit_sequence, that is to say, a sequence of zeros and ones followed by the letter *B* or *b*, without intervening blanks. For example:

→ *See 25.14, page 421,* *about* Bit_sequence. *The recommended style standard uses B rather than b.*

```
0010001110101B
```

Such a constant is of type *BIT N*, where *N* is the number of zeros and ones (13 in the example).

23.17 Character constants

A Character_constant is a character enclosed in single quotes, as in

> *'c'*

The following constant attribute declarations define symbolic names for some specimens of Character_constant:

> *Upper_z*: *CHARACTER* **is** *'Z'*;
>
> *Dollar_sign*: *CHARACTER* **is** *'$'*;
>
> *blank* : *CHARACTER* **is** *' '*;

A Character_constant consists of exactly three characters: the first and the third are single quotes '; the middle one is a Character other than a single quote.

Allowing a quote would not cause any ambiguity (since there are always exactly three characters altogether), but the rule is consistent with the convention for double quotes in a Manifest_string, as studied in the next section.

The value of a Character_constant is its middle Character.

To understand the above syntactic definition, you must realize that a Character is either a key corresponding directly to a printable character (such as *A* or *$*) or one of a set of multiple-key special character codes beginning with the percent sign %. Examples of such codes are:

The full table of character codes appears on page 423, as part of the discussion of characters in 25.15, page 422.

- %*N* for a new-line.
- %' for a single quote.
- %*B* for a backspace.
- %/91/ for the character of ASCII code 91.

91 is the (decimal) code of the opening bracket [, which you may also write as %(.

For example, a class text may include constant attribute declarations such as

> *New_line*: *CHARACTER* **is** *'%N'*;
>
> *Single_quote*: *CHARACTER* **is** *'%''*

Because a new-line is not a Character, the three characters of a Character_constant must appear on the same line. Of course, you may define a constant whose value is a new-line character by using %*N* as middle Character.

In spite of appearances, the presence of %' in a Character_constant, as in the declaration of *Single_quote* above, does not violate the prohibition of the quote character as a constant's Character: %', as all the special character codes, is considered to be a single character, although it consists of two signs (percent and single quote). This is explained in detail in the specification of characters.

23.18 Manifest strings

A Manifest_string denotes an instance of the Kernel Library class *STRING*, studied in a later chapter.

→ *See 28.8, starting on page 445, about class STRING.*

An example Manifest_string is:

> *"This Manifest_string contains 43 characters"*

As explained in more detail below, the value of a Manifest_string is a *STRING* object, which represents a sequence of characters. In this example the sequence contains all the characters given except for the two enclosing double quotes, which play a purely syntactical role.

There are two forms of Manifest_string:

- The **basic** form, illustrated above, is a Simple_string (that is to say a sequence of Character values, hence not including any new-line character) enclosed in double quote characters.

- Since the basic form requires all the characters to fit on a single line, which may be inconvenient for long strings, you may also use the **extended** form to write a Manifest_string on two or more lines. This requires that you end every line but the last with a percent sign %, and begin every line but the first with a percent sign, possibly preceded by blank or tab characters.

Although a Simple_string *may not contain any new-line character, it may include the two-key character %N, which represents a new-line.*

An example of extended form is the Manifest_string

> *"ABCDEFGHIJKLM%*
> *%NOPQRSTUVWXYZ"* ;

The characters before the percent sign on the second line may include blanks, tabs, or both kinds.

The extended form is only a matter of convenience in writing a class text, and every Manifest_string, basic or extended, defines an associated Simple_string obtained as follows: remove the enclosing double quotes; if the Manifest_string is of the extended form, remove the terminating percent signs on all lines but the last, remove the prefixes (the line portions up to and including the percent sign) on all lines but the first, and concatenate the resulting lines.

A constraint applies to any Manifest_string:

VWMS

> A Manifest_string is valid if and only if it satisfies the following two conditions:
>
> 1 • None of the characters of its associated Simple_string is a double quote.
>
> 2 • In the extended form, no characters other than blanks or tabs may appear before the initial percent sign on the second and subsequent lines.

As with the value of a Character_constant, one or more of the characters in the Simple_string may be two-key characters, such as %N, representing a new-line, or %", representing a double quote.

→ *The table of special character codes appears on page 423.*

23.19 Semantics of manifest strings

As explained above, a Manifest_string *m* defines an associated Simple_string *s*. For example, in the Manifest_string appearing in the declaration

> *Message*: *STRING* **is** *"Example 1"*

m is *"Example 1"* and *s* is the String made of the nine characters *Example 1*.

For most practical purposes you may view *s* as the value of *m*. In a more precise specification of the semantics, however, this is not quite correct. Although the nuance is somewhat fine, you should understand it even if this is your first reading, because of a potential confusion that has been known to surprise newcomers.

The problem is that the value of *m*, like any other value, must be an object or a reference to an object, and that a String (a sequence of characters) is not appropriate for this purpose. The desired object should be an instance of some class, so that you can apply features to it: for example a routine to which you pass *message* as actual argument may need to access properties of *message*, such as its length, through the features of some appropriate class. But there is no class whose instances are just arbitrary sequences of characters.

There does exist a class meant for representing character strings: the Kernel Library class *STRING*, which indeed served as type for *Message* in the above example declaration. But an instance of *STRING* is not a sequence of characters: it is a string descriptor, which must of course provide access to the characters but may also include other information such as the string length. Most importantly, because a string descriptor is an instance of a class, all the features of that class are applicable to it. Class *STRING* offers many routines for operations on strings such as accessing the character at a given position, extracting a substring and appending another string.

→ *The details of class STRING, its representation and its features are given in 28.8, page 445.*

String descriptor and associated character sequence

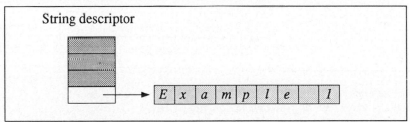

The details of string representation do not matter for this discussion, although the above figure shows a possible implementation, where the string descriptor includes, among various possible fields, a reference to the actual character sequence.

The character sequence is a "special object", as introduced in 17.2, page 270. See the discussion of strings in 28.8.

What does matter is that the value of an entity declared of *STRING* type, such as *Message* above, is a string descriptor, not a character sequence.

What difference does it make? Only one consequence is of practical concern: a Manifest_string is not a "constant" in the sense that most people would expect. It will always refer to the same string **descriptor**, but not necessarily to the same *character sequence*; this is because the contents of the descriptor may be changed through procedure calls.

Here is an example showing how this can happen:

> *Message*: *STRING* **is** *"Example 1"*
>
> ...
>
> *Message.put* *('2', 9)*

where the call to *put*, a procedure of class *STRING*, replaces the character at position 9 (originally *1*) by the character *2*. As a result, if a later instruction prints *Message*, the output will be

> *Example 2*

The same potential problem may arise through a feature call applying to another entity than the original "constant" if there has been an assignment; for example, the assignment

> *New_message* := *Message*;

produces a situation where both entities refer to the same character sequence:

String descriptors referring to the same character sequence

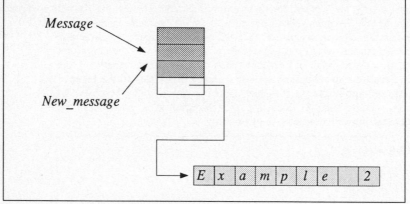

The characters are assumed to be Example 2 *as a result of the call to 'put' in the previous example.*

Then any operation on *Message* will have the same effect as the corresponding operation on *New_message*. For example, after

> *Message.put* *('3', 9)*

an instruction to print *New_message* will produce *Example 3*.

23.20 Manifest arrays

The next form of Expression is the Manifest_array, which makes it possible to describe an array by giving a list of expressions, corresponding to the array's successive elements.

An example of Manifest_array expression, of type *INTEGER*, is

$$<<27, n, -3, m + n>>$$

where *m* and *n* are entities of type *INTEGER*. The value of this expression is an array of four elements, having the values given. The lower bound of a Manifest_array is always 1, so that here the upper bound is 4.

If the list of expressions in a Manifest_array is empty, it describes an array with no elements:

$$<< >>$$

Among other applications, you may use a Manifest_array to obtain the effect   *← See 8.4, page 110.* of a variable number of arguments for a routine: if one of the formal arguments of a routine is declared with the type *ARRAY* [*T*] for some *T*, then an actual argument may be an expression list

$$<<e_1, e_2, ... e_n>>$$

such that every e_i is of a type conforming to *T*. The number *n* of elements in the list is arbitrary, so that you indeed obtain the same effect as if routines were permitted to have a variable number of arguments. Examples of this technique appeared in the discussion of routines.

The e_i do not need, of course, to be all of the same type, as long as their types all conform to *T*. By choosing a more specific or more general *T* (based on a class lower or higher in the inheritance graph), you restrict or extend the set of acceptable types for the e_i.

Here is the syntax of manifest arrays:

| Manifest_array | $\triangleq$ | "<<" Expression_list ">>" |
| Expression_list | $\triangleq$ | {Expression "," ...} |

Manifest arrays must obey a typing constraint:

VWMA

Manifest Array rule

A Manifest_array $<<e_1, e_2, ... e_n>>$ is a valid expression of type *ARRAY* [*T*] if and only if the type of every e_i conforms to *T*.

This is the rule that may be used in practice to ascertain whether a Manifest_array is appropriate as actual argument to a routine, or whether an assignment of the form

$$a := \langle\langle e_1, e_2, ... e_n \rangle\rangle$$

is valid. For example, with the routine specification

$$average\_age \ (group: ARRAY \ [PERSON]): INTEGER$$

then the call in

> *group_average* :=
>
>   *average_age* (<<*Fiordiligi, Dorabella, Guglielmo, Ferrando, Alfonso*>>)

is valid if *Fiordiligi* and *Dorabella* are of type *LADY*, *Guglielmo* and *Ferrando* of type *GENTLEMAN*, Alfonso of type *PHILOSOPHER*, and all these classes are descendants of *PERSON*. If you add to the Manifest_array an expression whose type does not conform to *PERSON*, the Manifest_array ceases to be a valid expression of type *ARRAY* [*PERSON*].

As another example of applying the Manifest Array rule, this time recursively, here is a valid expression of type *ARRAY* [*ARRAY* [*INTEGER*]]:

$$\langle\langle \ \langle\langle-3, 41\rangle\rangle, \ \langle\langle0\rangle\rangle, \ \langle\langle45, 31, -27\rangle\rangle, \ \langle\langle \ \rangle\rangle \ \rangle\rangle$$

describing an array whose elements are integer arrays of two, one, three and zero elements successively.

As you may have noted, the Manifest Array rule departs slightly from the style using elsewhere in this book to talk about types, since it does not define "the type of" a Manifest_array, but instead tells us how to ascertain whether a Manifest_array is "a valid expression of type" *ARRAY* [*T*] for given *T*. This is because, in contrast with the other expressions studied in this chapter (and any other Eiffel component that has a value), a Manifest_array does not have a single type of the form *ARRAY* [*T*] for a single *T*. You may see this by considering the Manifest_array in

> *v1: V; w1: W*
>
> ...
>
> *some_routine* (<<*v1, w1*>>)

where *V* and *W* are non-generic classes with the inheritance structure illustrated on the adjacent page.

Here the given Manifest_array is a valid argument for *some_routine* if the formal argument is declared either as *ARRAY* [*T*] or as *ARRAY* [*U*] (as well as *ARRAY* [*X*] for any *X* to which *T*, *U* or both conform). If we tried to define "the" type of the Manifest_array, however, *ARRAY* [*T*] and *ARRAY* [*U*] would be equally good candidates.

No single type

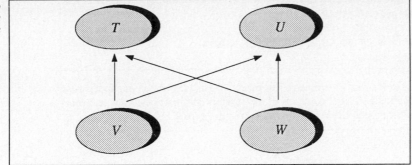

Fortunately, this inability to settle for a single type will not cause any difficulty in the two situations which require obtaining type information about a Manifest_array *ma*:

- The Manifest Array rule enables us to ascertain conformance of *ma* to a certain type (the type of the target in an assignment, or of a routine's formal argument) without any ambiguity, as illustrated by the above examples.

- The dynamic type set of *ma*, needed to ascertain system-level call validity, is the set of all types of the form *ARRAY* [*T*] for every type *T* in the dynamic type set of any of the elements of *ma*. This is in line with the handling of genericity in the definition of the dynamic type set.

← *See the final clause of the definition of the dynamic type set, page 370.*

The value of a Manifest_array made of N expressions is an array of bounds 1 and N, whose elements are the values of the successive expressions in the Manifest_array. In this definition, an "array" is an instance of the Kernel Library class *ARRAY*.

→ *Arrays and class ARRAY are discussed in 28.4, starting on page 439.*

The situation here is similar to what we encountered above for strings: an instance of *ARRAY* is in fact an array descriptor, which must of course provide access to the actual elements, but may also include other information such as the number of elements and the bounds. This also means that an array descriptor is a standard object − an instance of class *ARRAY*, with all the features of this class applicable to it.

← *A standard object is a direct instance of a class, as opposed to a special object, which is a sequence of values. See 17.2, page 270.*

Array descriptors sharing values

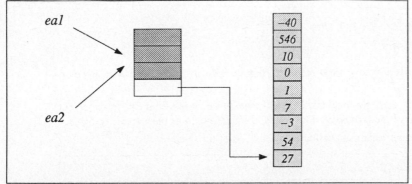

The last figure illustrates the notion of array descriptor; it is a conceptual representation of the situation resulting from

> *ea1, ea2: ARRAY [INTEGER];*
> ...
> *ea1 := <<27, 54, –3, 7, 1, 0, 10, 546, –40>>*
> *ea2 := ea1*

In this case the array's elements are objects (instances of the expanded type *INTEGER*). Below is an illustration of the effect of similar operations on arrays *ra1* and *ra2* of type *ARRAY [T]* for some reference type *T*.

Array descriptors sharing references

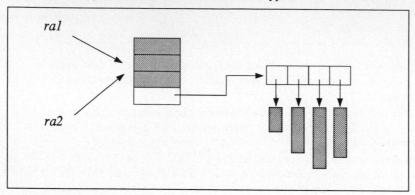

This could be the result of:

> *ra1, ra2: ARRAY [T];*
> *a, b, c, d: T;*
> ...
> *! T ! a ...*
> *! U ! b ...*
> *! V ! c ...*
> *! W ! d ...*
> *ra1 := <<a, b, c, d>>;*
> *ra2 := ra1*

U, V, W are types conforming to T.

23.21 Strip expressions

(This last section covers a specialized form of expression and may be skipped on first reading.)

The last form of expression, Strip, yields an array built from an object deprived (stripped) of some of its fields; the array contains the remaining fields.

A Strip expression appearing in a class *C* is of the form

> **strip** (*a, b, ...*)

where *a, b, ...*, are attributes of *C*. When evaluated for a direct instance of a type based on *C*, this denotes an array whose elements are the fields of that instance, except for the fields corresponding to *a, b, ...*

An important application of this construct is in postconditions, where it serves (in connection with the Old form of expression) to express that a routine may only change (reattach) certain fields of an object. For example, the Postcondition clause

← *This application of* Strip *was discussed in 9.10, page 125.*

> **ensure**
>   *equal* (**strip** (*a, b, c*), **old strip** (*a, b, c*))

expresses that the enclosing routine must not have reattached fields other than *a*, *b* and *c*.

Here is the syntax:

> Strip $\triangleq$ **strip** "(" Attribute_list ")"
> Attribute_list $\triangleq$ {Identifier "," ...}

A validity constraint applies:

VWST

> A Strip expression appearing in a class *C* is valid if and only if its Attribute_list satisfies the following two conditions:
>
> 1 • Every Identifier appearing in the list is the final name of an attribute of *C*.
>
> 2 • No Identifier appears twice in the list.

The type of a Strip expression is always *ARRAY* [*ANY*].

Consider the evaluation of a Strip expression as part of a call to a routine *r*, whose origin is a class *C*. Let $a_1, ..., a_n$ be the set containing all the attributes of *C* except for those listed in the Attribute_list, if present, of the Strip expression. Let CO be the current object for the call (CO is an instance, not necessarily direct, of a type based on *C*). Then the value of the expression is an array whose elements are the fields of CO corresponding to attributes $a_1, ..., a_n$, appearing in an order which only depends on class *C* (that is to say, is the same for all possible values of the object CO).

Every developer-defined type conforms to ANY. See 6.12, page 85.

← *The notion of current object is defined on page 349.*

The "attributes of C" include of course not just the attributes introduced in C itself but also those which C inherits from its ancestors. This is a special case of the notion of "features of a class", defined on page 56.

An important aspect of this definition is that the array will only include elements correspondings to attributes of *C*, even if CO is an instance of a type based on a strict descendant *D* of *C*. For example, with the class declarations

> **class** *C* **feature**
>   *c1, c2*: *INTEGER*
>
>   *rout* **is**
>   **local**
>   *extract*: *ARRAY* [*ANY*]
>   **do**
>   *extract* := **strip** (*c1*)
>   **end** -- *rout*
> **end** -- class *C*

```
class D inherit
    C
feature
    d1: REAL
end -- class D
```

a call to *rout* will always produce an array *extract* with exactly one element corresponding to the attribute *c2*. This is true even if the target of the call is of type *D* rather than *C*; attribute *d1*, not being present in the class of origin of *rout*, plays no part in the result.

In other words, to yield the same semantics on direct instances of *D*, a routine introduced in *D* rather than *C* would have to replace the Strip expression of *rout* by

```
strip (c1, d1)
```

This applies in particular to the semantics of a Strip expression with an empty Attribute_list, appearing in a class *C* as just **strip**. The value then is an array made of all the fields of CO (the current object) which correspond to attributes of *C*. The array does not include any field for the attributes introduced below *C* in the inheritance graph – even though CO may include such fields if its type is based on a proper descendant of *C*.

Since a Strip expression appearing in a class *C* drops all fields corresponding to attributes not present in *C*, you may redeclare a routine *r* with a Postcondition clause of the form illustrated above

```
ensure
    equal (strip (a, b, c), old strip (a, b, c))
```

as long as the redeclared version continues to leave fields *a*, *b*, *c* untouched. The redeclaration may, however, affect fields corresponding to attributes introduced in proper descendants of the class containing the original declaration of *r*. This will not violate the original postcondition, whose scope only extended to attributes of the original class.

← *On the rules governing how a redeclaration may affect a postcondition, see 10.15, starting page 152.*

24

Interfaces with other languages

24.1 Overview

Eiffel software systems may need to use software elements written in other languages. This chapter describes the techniques which may be used to achieve such communication.

 Many applications will be happy enough to use the pure Eiffel mechanisms described in the rest of this book, and will not require any direct interfaces with other languages. (The next section explains the circumstances which may justify the inclusion of foreign software in an Eiffel system.) If you are mostly interested in understanding the techniques of Eiffel proper, you should probably get familiar with the principles of external calls by reading this section and the next two, and move on to the next chapter.

Since Eiffel is of a higher level than common programming languages, and is particularly appropriate as an integration tool for combining software elements written in various languages, the more frequent need is for Eiffel routines to call non-Eiffel routines. The reverse need also exists, however. As a consequence, the mechanisms described in this chapter cover both *call-out* (Eiffel to foreign) and *call-in* (foreign to Eiffel) facilities. The call-in facilities depend heavily on the foreign language and, as a consequence, cannot be made part of the Eiffel description; they are presented in this chapter for illustration only.

In accordance with the terminology used for the different forms of Routine_body in the syntax specifications, this chapter will use the term **internal routine** for any Eiffel routine accessible to language processing tools, and **external routine** for other routines. The name "external" refers to the routine as viewed from the Eiffel text; for the form of the routine as it appears in its original language, the discussion will use the term **foreign routine**.

The notion of external routine, and the techniques described in this chapter, are clearly intended for routines written in other languages. True, if you have access to an Eiffel compiler, you could in principle precompile an Eiffel routine and then have other routines call it as an an external routine. But there is no need to do this in a well-designed implementation of Eiffel: as discussed at the end of chapter 1, a good compiler will be incremental, avoiding any unnecessary recompilation of previously compiled routines; similarly, an interpreter should support calls to precompiled routines. In both cases, you will still benefit from type checking, in particular conformance checking of actual arguments against formal arguments. By treating Eiffel routines as external, you would lose these important validity checks.

The semantic specifications presented in this chapter involve the semantics of languages other than Eiffel. Granting non-Eiffel software access to Eiffel objects may defeat the properties guaranteed by the semantic rules of this book. You should exercise care, then, to guarantee that foreign languages are confined to their proper role in the construction of Eiffel-based software.

24.2 When to use external software

What is this proper role? After all, Eiffel is a complete programming language, and many systems do not need any external software.

Four cases, however, may require interfacing Eiffel classes with software written in other languages:

1 • Reuse of older software elements.

2 • Use of libraries written in other languages.

3 • Access to low-level platform-dependent properties.

4 • Use of Eiffel as a tool for re-engineering of software.

Cases 1 and 2 are similar: they result from the obvious observation that Eiffel developments do not proceed alone in the software world, but must be combined with other products. In case 1, an organization may want to reuse previously developed elements as part of a new system. In case 2, the system will use existing primitives providing facilities in a specialized area – such as graphics, databases, user interfaces, expert systems, or any other for which an external library is available.

In case 3, you need to access primitives which depend on the hardware or the operating system, available through external routines.

In case 4, an older non-Eiffel system must be converted to more modern software technology, but you want to proceed in stages. A possible strategy is to start by isolating appropriate abstractions in the existing software, and to build classes around them; the architecture of the resulting system will be expressed in Eiffel, using the structural mechanisms described in this book – classes, information hiding, genericity, inheritance, assertions – but the actual computations will still be performed by external routine calls. Here Eiffel serves as a packaging mechanism more than as a down-to-details programming language. This effort may be a first step towards more thorough re-engineering of the software: once you have an acceptable Eiffel structure, you may start upgrading to full Eiffel status some of the foreign elements in that structure, for example those which will need to evolve anyway because of changes in requirements, or those which are known to be the most difficult to maintain.

24.3 External routines

As seen in the discussion of routines, the Routine_body of an Effective routine, instead of using the more common Internal form (beginning with **do** or **once**), may be of the External form, which indicates that a call to the routine is a call to some outside software component.

← Routine_body *was discussed in 8.6, starting on page 113. The syntax is on page 113. The syntax for* External *appeared on page 402; it is reproduced below.*

An External clause begins with the keyword **external**, followed by a Manifest_string indicating the language in which the routine is written. It may also contain an External_name subclause, beginning with **alias**, giving the routine's name in its language of origin.

Here is an example of external routine:

```
f_close (filedesc: INTEGER): INTEGER is
        -- Close file associated with filedesc; record status in result.
    require
        descriptor_exists: exists (associated_file (filedesc));
    external
        "C"
    ensure
        (Result = 0) implies closed (associated_file (filedesc))
    end -- f_close
```

As this example shows, an external routine may have a Precondition and a Postcondition.

Function *f_close* performs a certain action and returns a status report through its result. This interface technique is not normally employed by Eiffel routines, which should instead record the status in an attribute; in communicating with external software, however, there may be no better means available.

You may wish to refer to an external routine through a name other than its original name in the foreign language. In such a case you may use an External_name subclause, beginning with **alias**, as in

```
file_status (filedesc: INTEGER): INTEGER is
    external
        "C"
    alias
        "_fstat"
    end -- file_status
```

The **alias** specifies that any call to *file_status* will cause a call to the C function of name *_fstat*. Two possible reasons may raise the need for such a subclause:

- The name adaptation is required for foreign routines whose native name is legal in the foreign language but not in Eiffel, as in the above example where a C function has a name beginning with an underscore character _, not acceptable as the first character of an Eiffel identifier. Similarly, other languages permit special characters such as $ in identifiers.

- Even if the foreign name abides by Eiffel rules, it may be incompatible with the naming conventions that you have established for your project.

Here is the syntax of External routine bodies:

External	≜	**external** Language_name
		[External_name]
Language_name	≜	Manifest_string
External_name	≜	**alias** Manifest_string

24.4 Executing an external call

The effect of a call to an external routine f was previewed in the general discussion of call semantics. Only three aspects differ from the semantics of Internal routines:

1 • Actual-formal argument association.

2 • Execution of the Routine_body

3 • Value to be returned, if the routine is a function.

The next section will cover items 1 and 3. Item 2, the simplest, was handled by the general discussion of call semantics. Quoting:

← *See 21.11, page 347, about feature application in a* Call, *and 21.14, page 352, for the precise specification of call semantics.*

> If df is an external routine, the effect of the call is to execute that routine on the actual arguments given, if any, according to the rules of the language in which it is written.

Here df is the version of f to be applied to the given target, deduced from the rules of call semantics (dynamic binding).

In addition to its official arguments, an Eiffel routine has access to the **current object** – the target of the call. This important property does not necessarily hold for a foreign routine:

← *The notion of current object was explained on page 349.*

• If the foreign routine was written independently of Eiffel, it does not use the current object. Accordingly, the call, as specified by the above semantics, will not pass the current object. A typical case is a call to a primitive of a pre-existing graphics or database package.

• Another case is that of foreign routines specifically written for the needs of an Eiffel application. Such routines may need access to the current object; you must then explicitly pass $Current$ as one of the arguments.

← *The entity 'Current' was introduced in 21.13, page 351.*

24.5 Argument and result transmission

The semantics of passing arguments, and of returning the result for a function, raises the problem of attachment between Eiffel values and foreign entities.

For internal routines, the semantic rule was simple, being deduced (like the semantics of Assignment instructions) from the semantics of the direct reattachment mechanism: at call time, each formal argument becomes attached to the corresponding actual; at return time, the result of a function is the final value attached to the function's $Result$ entity.

← *See 21.11, page 347, and 21.14, page 352. The semantics of direct reattachment appears in 20.5, page 313.*

The semantic specification of a direct reattachment allowed flexible combinations of expanded and reference types in the source and target. Here is the table which gave the effect in all four possible cases:

SOURCE TYPE →	Reference	Expanded
TARGET TYPE ↓		
Reference	[1] Reference reattachment	[3] Clone
Expanded	[2] Copy (will fail if source is void)	[4] Copy

← This table appeared originally on page 317.

This specification takes both types – source and target – into account, particularly in cases 2 and 3 where one is expanded and the other is not.

For external calls, however, we cannot afford such semantic flexibility, since the target is the formal argument, and we have no way of knowing how the foreign routine has declared it. The semantic definition must rely on properties of the actual argument alone.

To depart as little as possible from the rules for internal routines, the convention for external routines is simple: follow the the semantics of direct reattachment, interpreted as if each formal argument were declared with **exactly** the same type as the corresponding actual.

This also applies to Current if it is one of the actual arguments: in accordance with the semantics of Current, defined by case D4 page 354, with an informal introduction on page 351, what is passed is a reference to the current object if the enclosing class is non-expanded, otherwise the current object itself.

This implies that only cases 1 and 4 of the above table make sense: either the actual argument is of a reference type, in which case the foreign routine will receive a reference, or it is of an expanded type, in which case the foreign routine will receive a copy of the attached object.

For the result of a function, the rule is similar: depending on the type declared for the function's result, the Eiffel side will expect the foreign routine to return a reference or an object.

Clearly, using foreign routines which will handle Eiffel values requires care. You must trust that the routine can manipulate the values it obtains from the Eiffel side, and, if it is a function, produces results which conform to what you expect. This implies that the types of arguments and result must be common to Eiffel and the external language.

For basic types, this property depends on both the foreign language and its implementation.

← The basic types are BOOLEAN, CHARACTER, INTEGER, REAL, DOUBLE and POINTER. See chapter 32.

For other types, no major problem will arise for a foreign routine which, given an object or reference, contents itself with a "store and forward": pass on the value to other routines, possibly keeping a copy in a variable of a suitable type. To do anything more with an Eiffel object, the routine must access its internal structure; it may avoid relying on implementation-dependent properties of object representation by using one of the following two portable mechanisms:

- The features of class *INTERNAL* from the Support Library provide access to the internal properties of objects (such as the various field values) with an implementation-independent interface.

- The Cecil library, described at the end of this chapter, offers access mechanisms for the specific case of the C language.

See "Eiffel: The Libraries" (reference in the bibliography of appendix C) about INTERNAL.

Remember that letting foreign routines operate on Eiffel objects may endanger the consistency of these objects; for example, it is easy to destroy an invariant. The semantic rules defined in this book do not take into account possible erroneous manipulations resulting from external calls. To obtain with certainty the semantics of Eiffel, you must use Eiffel routines only.

24.6 Passing the address of an Eiffel feature

In some cases a foreign routine may need to call Eiffel routines, or to access fields of Eiffel objects.

Foreign access to Eiffel routines may be necessary in particular for the implementation of so-called **call-back** mechanisms as they appear in such areas as user interfaces, graphics and databases. These are techniques enabling an application system to "plant" the address of one or more routines into another routine *r* at initialization time. Later, in various scheduled steps of its own algorithm, *r* will call the planted routines. Because planting is dynamic, the text of *r* does not show what actual routines will be called at the corresponding steps; it only contains "holes" where different applications may plant different routines. Often, *r* is a high-level loop, known as an **event loop**, which will repeatedly execute ritual actions (such as reading user input or updating the screen) provided by the planted routines.

In this description, you will have recognized the notion of **iterator** discussed in the presentation of inheritance and deferred features; indeed, the Eiffel techniques introduced for iterators, relying on deferred routines and dynamic binding, offer simpler, safer and more elegant alternatives to call-back.

← On how to implement a call-back mechanism in Eiffel, see 10.13, page 148.

In some cases, however, you may need to use an existing call-back mechanism implemented in another language, but with individual operations (the planted routines) provided by Eiffel routines. This means that you must be able to pass information about an Eiffel feature to a foreign routine *r*, enabling *r* to call that feature. For a routine, this information is the routine's address; the mechanism also applies to attributes.

The supporting construct is the Address form of Actual argument. An Address, introduced as part of the syntax for Actuals in the discussion of calls, is simply an actual argument of the form

← The syntax for Actuals appeared on page 342.

> *$ some_feature_identifier*

This form of Actual argument is only useful for passing feature addresses to external routines. Internal routines do not need it, since the dynamic binding mechanism provides a better way to tell a supplier what routine it should call at a certain stage of the supplier's execution: you just pass the supplier an entity attached to a certain object; the dynamic type of that object, which may vary from one execution to the next, determines the applicable routine versions.

← On dynamic binding, see 21.9 and 21.10, starting on page 345.

One might expect a constraint prohibiting Actual arguments of the Address form except in calls to external routines. There is no such constraint, however, because it may be useful for an Internal routine *ir1* to pass the address of a routine *r* to another internal routine *ir2*, so that *ir2* may itself pass *r* to an external routine *er*. Were this not permitted, *ir1* would need to call *er* directly, which may not be the desired scheme.

← The hypothetical constraint, an addition to condition 4 of the argument validity rule of page 369, would require the called routine 'df' to be external.

We must prevent *ir2* from performing any operation on its argument *r* other than passing it along to another routine. A type rule achieves this:

> An argument of the Address form is of type *POINTER*.

As a consequence, the declaration for the corresponding formal argument in the receiving routine (whether Internal or External) must be of the form

> *ir2* (*eiffel_routine*: *POINTER*; ...) **is** ...

POINTER, a Kernel Library class, serves only for the purpose discussed here: as type for arguments of the Address form. It has no exported feature; so the body of *ir2*, if Internal, may not apply any feature to *eiffel_routine*.

The validity constraint on actual arguments of the Address form is clause 4 of the argument validity rule, which makes $ *f* valid as actual argument to a call if and only if *f* is the final name of a feature of the enclosing class, and that feature is not a constant attribute (which has no address).

← The argument validity rule appears on page 369.

If the rule is satisfied, the feature will have a version *df* applicable to the current object: this is the version of *f* for the current object's generator (taking into account possible renaming and redefinition). The value passed for attachment to the corresponding formal argument is the address of *df*. This applies to both routines and variable attributes; for an attribute, the call will pass the address of the field corresponding to *df* in the current object.

Clearly, this is meaningful only if the foreign language has a way of dealing with pointers to values and routines.

If *df* is a routine, foreign software components will be able to call that routine. Such calls require one extra argument, appearing at the first position and corresponding to the target of the call. Assume for example a routine

> *some_routine* (*a1*: *A*; *b1*: *B*) **is** ...

Calls to *some_routine* in Eiffel texts may be qualified or unqualified:

> *target*. *some_routine* (*x*, *y*)
>
> *some_routine* (*u*, *v*)

Assume now that a call to an external routine *ext* makes the address of *some_routine* available to a foreign language:

> *ext* (..., $ *some_routine*, ...)

Let *sr* be the formal argument for *some_routine* in the foreign routine corresponding to *ext*. The foreign routine will call *some_routine* with one extra actual argument, appearing at the first position:

> *sr* (*target*, *x*, *y*)
>
> *sr* (*current_object*, *x*, *y*)

WARNING: calls to 'sr', appearing here in Eiffel-like syntax, will in practice be written in a foreign language, which may use different notations for calls and for denoting a routine of address 'sr'.

The extra argument denotes the call's target, which in Eiffel appeared before the dot (as in the case of *target*) or not at all (as with *current_object*). It denotes an object or object reference, passed to the foreign routine as argument to an external call, or obtained through one of the call-in facilities described next.

24.7 The Cecil Library

The just explored Address form of actual argument provides a **call-in** mechanism, enabling foreign software to call Eiffel features, and complementing the call-out facilities studied earlier. It requires the Eiffel side to pass the needed feature addresses as arguments to external calls.

Some developers may wish to write foreign routines which create Eiffel objects and apply features to these objects, without relying on features explicitly passed by the Eiffel side. This last section shows a way to do this from C, using a library of C functions called the C-Eiffel Call-In Library, or Cecil. It is not hard to transpose the Cecil techniques to other foreign languages.

Most developments do not need to use Cecil or its equivalent, and most developers do not need to learn about it. The ideas are of interest to installations with a heavy use of C or some other foreign language, if they want to integrate some Eiffel classes in applications driven by their foreign components. If you are not in this situation, then you most likely should spare yourself the rest of this chapter; but do shed a tear or two for your less fortunate colleagues.

Please send your tax-deductible contributions to the HAVOC fund (Help All Victims Of C!), Box OO, Palma de Majorca.

Call-in mechanisms belong in foreign languages. What this section describes, then, is not part of Eiffel. The NICE Consortium may eventually decide to standardize a call-in facility; Cecil will then be an obvious candidate.

The Cecil library contains macros, functions, types and error codes. All have names beginning with either *eif_* (functions and macros) or *EIF_* (types and error codes); examples are the function *eif_type_id* and the type *EIF_PROC*, explained below. Their declarations appear in a C "header file", *cecil.h*, which you may add to a C program through the C preprocessor directive

Eiffel's emphasis on clarity suggests using 'eiffel_' and 'EIFFEL_' as prefixes, but some of the resulting names would be too long for many C compilers.

```
#include <cecil.h>
```

WARNING: this is C, not Eiffel.

Let us now look at the principal facilities declared in *cecil.h*. First of all, the C side will need to refer to Eiffel types. It will know a type through a "type-id", of type *EIF_TYPE_ID*. To obtain a type-id for a non-generic class of name *CLASSNAME* and record it in a C variable *your_id*, use the function *eif_type_id*, which returns a result of type *EIF_TYPE_ID*:

```
EIF_TYPE_ID your_id;
...
your_id = eif_type_id ("CLASSNAME");
```

WARNING: this is C, not Eiffel.

If the class is generic, replace the last instruction by

```
your_id = eif_generic_id ("CLASSNAME", gen1, gen2, ...);
```

WARNING: this is C, not Eiffel.

where *gen1, gen2, ...* are type-ids corresponding to the desired actual generic parameters. Function *eif_generic_id* has a variable number of arguments; the number of arguments following the first one ("*CLASSNAME*") must match the number of formal generic parameters of the class of name *CLASSNAME*.

The CLASSNAME is the "external" name of the class, which may be different from its Eiffel name as directed by an Ace's Visible *part. See below.*

The result returned by *eif_type_id* or *eif_generic_id* describes a type which is expanded if and only if *CLASSNAME* is declared in Eiffel as **expanded class**. To force a result describing an expanded type, apply *eif_expanded* to the result of either function; the result is another type-id. All these functions return as result the error code *EIF_NO_TYPE* if they cannot compute a type-id (no class with the given name in the universe, more than one class, wrong number of generic parameters).

In the presence of an optimizing compiler which may remove "dead code", you must make sure that the required class is not optimized away. If your implementation supports Lace, the Visible part of the corresponding cluster specification serves this purpose; an External_class_rename subclause will also remove any ambiguities if two or more visible classes have the same name.

→ See appendix D about Lace, in particular D.14, page 529, about External_class_rename.

A C function may access Eiffel objects through references passed to it by the Eiffel side in external calls, or returned by calls to *eif_create* (see below). The corresponding variable must be declared of the Cecil type *EIF_OBJ*.

A value *your_object* of type *EIF_OBJ* is **not** necessarily a C pointer to the corresponding object. To obtain such a pointer (for example to pass it to a C function which manipulates objects directly), use the macro *eif_access*, which takes an *EIF_OBJ* and returns a pointer, of type *char∗*. For example:

Current C ideology suggests that 'eif_access' should return a 'void∗'. But many C compilers only accept 'char∗'.

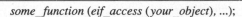

> *some_function (eif_access (your_object), ...);*

WARNING: this is C, not Eiffel. The result is a null pointer if 'your_object' corresponds to a void reference.

The reason for this rule is that an Eiffel implementation supporting garbage collection may move objects around. Then a pointer passed directly to a C function might be obsolete by the time the function tries to access the associated object. Given an *EIF_OBJ*, *eif_access* will retrieve a correct pointer. If the implementation does not move objects, *eif_access* will do little or no work.

What if *your_object* is a variable which does not just allow immediate object processing as above, but retains its value between successive activations of the C side? In the meantime, the Eiffel side might have discarded all references to the corresponding object; but then a garbage collecting implementation must not be allowed to reclaim it! To avoid this, the C side must **adopt** the object, using the function *eif_adopt*. Once C functions do not need to hold the object any more, they may release it through *eif_wean*. Here is the scheme:

> *EIF_OBJ your_object; ...*
> *eif_adopt (your_object);*
>
>   *... Then in the same or another C program unit: ...*
> *some_function (eif_access (your_object), ...);*
> *...*
> *eif_wean (your_object);*

WARNING: this is C, not Eiffel.

As announced above, it is possible to create an object from C, using the function *eif_create* which takes an *EIF_TYPE_ID* argument and returns an *EIF_OBJ*. For example:

> EIF_OBJ your_list;
> ...
> your_list = eif_create (eif_generic_id ("LINKED_LIST",
>   eif_type_id ("INTEGER")));

WARNING: this is C, not Eiffel. A C programmer may prefer to include the initialization of 'your_list' in its declaration.

Assuming class *LINKED_LIST* with one generic parameter, this creates a direct instance of *LINKED_LIST* [*INTEGER*]. Function *eif_create* calls *eif_adopt*; the C side should call *eif_wean* when and if it does not need the object any more.

As you will have noticed, *eif_create* **does not call a creation procedure**. To apply a creation procedure, you will need to include a separate call, using function *eif_proc* as explained below. This departs from Eiffel conventions, which prohibit creating an object without applying a creation procedure if the class has a Creators clause. With Cecil, forgetting to call a creation procedure after *eif_create* may produce an object which violates the class invariant, so you must be particularly vigilant to avoid this error (which is impossible in Eiffel).

← About creation rules in Eiffel and the Creators clause, see chapter 18.

Next, the C side will want to apply Eiffel routines to objects. To do so it needs C pointers to these routines, which it will obtain through one of a set of Cecil functions provided for this purpose. For example, having obtained the type-id *your_list* as shown above, use the following to assign to variable *your_procname* a pointer to a procedure whose Eiffel name in class *LINKED_LIST* is *go*:

> EIF_PROC your_list_go;
> ...
> your_list_go = eif_proc ("go", your_list);

WARNING: this is C, not Eiffel. A C programmer may prefer to include the initialization of 'your_list_go' in its declaration.

Function *eif_proc*, returning a result of type *EIF_PROC*, is one of a group of functions, each corresponding to a different category of Eiffel routines: procedures, functions returning results of basic types, functions returning references to complex objects. (The case of Bit_type is treated below.) Here is the list of these functions, with their types and template arguments:

> EIF_PROC eif_proc (routine_name, type_id)
> EIF_FN_BOOL eif_fn_bool (routine_name, type_id)
> EIF_FN_CHAR eif_fn_char (routine_name, type_id)
> EIF_FN_INT eif_fn_int (routine_name, type_id)
> EIF_FN_REAL eif_fn_real (routine_name, type_id)
> EIF_FN_DOUBLE eif_fn_double (routine_name, type_id)
> EIF_FN_POINTER eif_fn_pointer (routine_name, type_id)
> EIF_FN_REF eif_fn_ref (routine_name, type_id)

The word POINTER in the name EIF_FN_POINTER refers to the Eiffel basic type (used to pass feature addresses to external routines, see 24.6 above), not to C pointers.

In all cases the arguments are a string, representing a routine name, and a type-id (obtained through *eif_type_id* or *eif_generic_ic*):

> char * routine_name; EIF_TYPE_ID type_id;

WARNING: this is C, not Eiffel.

These functions look for a routine of name *routine_name* in the base class of the type corresponding to *type_id*. If no such routine exists, the result is a null pointer. Otherwise it is a pointer to a C function representing the desired routine; you may then call that function on appropriate arguments, not forgetting to add a first argument representing the call's target, as in:

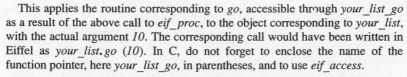

$$(your\_list\_go) \ (eif\_access \ (your\_list), \ 10)$$

WARNING: this is C, not Eiffel. You may use '(your_list_go)' instead of '(your_list_go)'.*

This applies the routine corresponding to *go*, accessible through *your_list_go* as a result of the above call to *eif_proc*, to the object corresponding to *your_list*, with the actual argument *10*. The corresponding call would have been written in Eiffel as *your_list.go (10)*. In C, do not forget to enclose the name of the function pointer, here *your_list_go*, in parentheses, and to use *eif_access*.

There is a major difference between the Eiffel call and its C emulation: Cecil **does not apply dynamic binding**. What you get from *eif_proc* or one of its sisters is a pointer to a function representing the exact Eiffel routine of the given name in the given class. In the presence of polymorphism and redeclaration, the Eiffel call may trigger a different version of *go* depending on the type of the object attached to *your_list* at the time the call is executed. The C form will always call the same version, regardless of the object's type.

Not using dynamic binding is of course potentially dangerous; but then computations which need the benefits of object-oriented technology should be written in Eiffel, not C. Cecil is useful for a C call to an Eiffel routine when you can statically specify, through a routine name and a class name, the exact computation that you require.

The next Cecil facility enables the C side to access fields of complex objects, corresponding to attributes of the generating classes. To obtain a field of an object, use the macro *eif_field*, as in:

> EIF_OBJ *your_object, your_other_object*; int *your_field_copy*;
> ...
> *your_field_copy* = *eif_field (eif_access (your_object),*
>   *"some_integer_attribute", EIF_INTEGER)*;
> *eif_field (eif_access (your_object), "some_complex_attribute",*
>   *EIF_OBJ)* = *your_other_object*;

WARNING: this is C, not Eiffel.

As shown by this example, you may use the result of *eif_field* in two different ways: as an expression, or "r-value" in C terminology; or as a writable entity, or "l-value", which may then be the target of an assignment. Such an assignment will re-attach the corresponding object field. The two instructions illustrate these two cases: the first assigns the result of the call to *your_field_copy*; the second changes the value of the field *some_reference_attribute* in *your_object*.

Function *eif_field* takes three arguments. The first is a value of type *EIF_OBJ*, representing an object; do not forget to protect it by *eif_access*. The second is a string giving the name of the desired attribute. The third is one of the following values, describing the type of the attribute:

EIF_BOOLEAN	EIF_CHARACTER	EIF_INTEGER
EIF_REAL	EIF_DOUBLE	EIF_POINTER
EIF_REFERENCE		

These names are those of macros defined in 'cecil.h'.

The result of *eif_field* is undefined if the object does not have a field with the given name and type.

As with routines, you may have to guard against a compiler unduly optimizing the attribute away, and you may need to use as attribute name (second argument to the above functions) an external name different from the name appearing in the class text. If your implementation supports Lace, the Visible part of the corresponding Ace will take care of these aspects.

→ *See D.14, page 529, about* Visible *parts in Aces.*

There remains the case of functions and attributes of a Bit_type. Its treatment is in line with the techniques just described for other types, but requires a special convention because C has no direct equivalent to the Eiffel notion of Bit_type. A Bit_type is expanded; so for example the possible values for an entity of type *BITS 256* are sequences of 256 bits. In C this is not possible; the values of the corresponding variables will be **pointers** to such bit sequences.

To call an Eiffel function returning a Bit_type result, use this scheme:

← Bit_type *and the corresponding semantics were defined in 12.14, page 209.*

```
EIF_BIT your_bit;
EIF_FN_BIT your_function;
...
your_function = eif_fn_bit (function_name, type_id);
your_bit = (your_function) (eif_access (object), actual_1, actual_2, ...)
```

WARNING: this is C, not Eiffel. A C programmer may prefer to include the initialization of 'your_function' in its declaration.

The last instruction assigns to *your_bit* a reference to the bit sequence returned by the function. *EIF_BIT* describes a pointer type.

Similarly, you may access and modify Bit_type fields as follows:

```
EIF_BIT your_bit1, your_bit2;
...
your_bit1 = eif_bit_field (eif_access (your_object), "some_bit_attribute");
eif_bit_set_field (eif_access (your_object), "some_bit_attribute", your_bit2);
```

WARNING: this is C, not Eiffel.

Here two primitives are needed. Function *eif_bit_field* takes two arguments, an object pointer (returned by *eif_access*) and an attribute name. In contrast with *eif_field*, the result of *eif_bit_field* may only be used as an expression (r-value), not as a writable variable. To change the value of a Bit_type field, use *eif_bit_set_field*, whose last argument is the new value, of type *EIF_BIT*. If the object has no appropriate Bit_type field, *eif_bit_field* returns the value *EIF_NO_BFIELD* and the effect of *eif_bit_set_field* is undefined.

The following primitives are applicable to *your_bit* of type *EIF_BIT*:

```
eif_bit_set (your_bit, position)
eif_bit_clear (your_bit, position)
eif_bit_ith (your_bit, position)
eif_bit_length (your_bit)
eif_bit_clone (your_bit)
```

Here *position* is an integer index which must be in the range of the bit sequence (counted from 1); otherwise the first two calls have undefined results, and *eif_bit_ith* returns *EIF_NO_BIT*. Routines *eif_bit_set* and *eif_bit_clear* set the element of index *position* to 1 and 0, respectively. Function *eif_bit_ith* returns an integer, the value of the element of index *position*. Function *eif_bit_length* returns an integer, the length of the sequence. Function *eif_bit_clone* returns an *EIF_BIT*, a fresh copy of the bit sequence passed as argument.

25

Lexical components

25.1 Overview

The previous chapters have covered the syntax, validity and semantics of software systems.

At the most basic level, the texts of these systems are made of **lexical** components, playing for Eiffel classes the role that words and punctuation play for the sentences of human language. All construct descriptions relied on lexical components such as identifiers, reserved words and special symbols, but their structure has not been formally defined yet. It is time now to cover this somewhat mundane aspect of the language.

This chapter defines the various kinds of lexical element. It also specifies the characters that may be used in Eiffel texts (especially in identifiers), touching on the thorny problem of how to cope with the character sets of keyboards found in various countries.

The lexical structure of Eiffel is simple and predictable. For a first approach to Eiffel, the extracts found in the rest of this book should provide enough models to enable you to write your own class texts without studying this chapter.

25.2 General format

At the lexical level, a class text is made of **tokens, breaks** and **comments**. Tokens are the meaningful components; breaks play a purely lexical role (separating tokens); comments add informal explanations for the benefit of human readers.

The next sections examine breaks, comments and the various categories of tokens.

25.3 Breaks

DEFINITION:
Break
Character,
Break A break is made of a sequence of one or more of the following characters, known as **break characters**:

* Blank (also known as space).
* Tab.
* New Line (also known as Line Feed).

Some platforms do not support the concept of a New Line character, but represent texts as sequences of lines. On such a platform, you may apply the rules of this chapter by considering a text as made of the concatenation of all its lines, with a New Line character between consecutive lines.

25.4 Comments

A class text may contain comments, which have no effect on the semantics of the classes in whose texts they appear, but provide explanations for the benefit of readers of these texts.

Comments may be **expected** or **free**:

* An expected comment is a specimen of the construct Comment, appearing in the syntax as an optional component of some construct. An example is the Header_comment of a Routine.

* Free comments, on the other hand, may appear at almost any position in a class text, and are not covered by the syntax productions.

In both cases the form is the same: a comment is made of one or more line segments, each beginning with two consecutive dash characters -- and extending to the end of the line.

Expected comments appear as part of three constructs: Routine, Assertion_clause and Features.

← *Syntax productions*: *for* Assertion_clause, *page 120*; Routine, *page 112*; Features, *page 60*.

In a Routine, the optional Header_comment, appears after the **is** keyword and serves to express concisely the purpose of the routine, as in the following routine from class *GENERAL_FIGURE* in the Graphics Library:

> *convert_to_resolution* (*res_val*: *REAL*) **is**
>   -- Convert to world coordinates,
>   -- using *res_val* as resolution.
> **do** ... Rest of Routine omitted ...

In an Assertion_clause, you may use a Comment (possibly with a Tag_mark) as an Assertion_clause expressing a property which you have not been able to write formally as an Expression. The first two lines of the class invariant for class *FIXED_QUEUE* of the Data Structure Library show such a case:

```
invariant
    -- If queue is not empty, queue items are in positions
    -- first, first+1, ..., last−1 (mod capacity)
    consistent: empty = (first = last);
    0 <= first;
    0 <= last;
    ... Other clauses omitted ...
```

The third use of expected comments is for introducing each Feature_clause in ← See class LINKED_LIST in 5.4, page 56. a Features part of a class. Since you may use a separate Feature_clause for every group of related features (with the same export status), it is often appropriate to preface such a group by a brief description of its common properties. The discussion of features showed an example, class *LINKED_LIST* from the Data Structure Library, where each Feature_clause is indeed identified by such a header comment.

As for free comments, they may appear before or after any token. They serve to include explanations, for the benefit of a human reader, on some aspect of the neighboring part of the text. A routine of class *BI_LINKABLE* from the Data Structure Library includes such a comment as part of a Conditional instruction:

```
if
    other /= Void       -- Avoid infinite recursion with put_left !
    and then other.left /= Current
then
    ... (Rest omitted) ...
```

where the line portion beginning with -- is a comment.

The following syntax captures the form of both expected and free comments:

Comment	≜	"--" {Simple_string Comment_break ...}
Comment_break	≜	New_line [Blanks_or_tabs] "--"

where New_line represents the end-of-line separator, Simple_string represents any sequence of characters not including a New_line, and Blanks_or_tabs represents any sequence of characters, each of which is a blank or a tab.

This syntactical description means that a comment line coming immediately after the beginning of a comment is part of that comment. For example, the text extract

```
c :=              -- This is comment text
                  -- This is the first comment's continuation
a + b;            -- This is a second comment.

                  -- This is a third comment.
```

contains three comments as indicated (assuming a blank line between the second and the third).

25.5 Text layout

An Eiffel text is a sequence; each of the elements of the sequence is a break, a comment or a token.

You may always insert a break between two sequence elements without affecting the semantics of the text.

A break is not required between two adjacent elements if one is a comment and the other a token or another comment. Between two successive tokens, a break may be required or not depending on the nature of the tokens.

To see the exact rule in this case, we may divide tokens into two categories:

DEFINITION:
Symbol

- A **symbol** is either a special symbol of the language, such as the semicolon ";" and the dot "." of dot notation, or a standard (non-free) operator such as + and ∗, but not including the alphabetic operators (such as **or else** and **not**).

→ The list of special symbols appears below on page 416. The list of standard operators was part of the syntax for Operator, *reproduced page 419 below.*

Word

- A **word** is any token which is not a symbol. Examples of words include identifiers, keywords, free operators and alphabetic operators such as **or else**. Specimens of a word may begin or end with an alphabetic character (letter, digit or underscore).

Then:

It is permitted to write two adjacent tokens without an intervening break if and only if one is a word and the other is a symbol.

Between adjacent words or adjacents symbols a break is required.

For example, a break is needed between a keyword and an identifier (both of which are words); in

if x **then** ...

the breaks both before and after x are required. But the assignment

$c:=a+b$

may be written without any break, although the standard style guidelines suggest using a one-blank break both around the assignment symbol := and around every operator.

→ Appendix A gives the style guidelines.

The reason for this rule is obvious: without intervening breaks, adjacent words (as in *ifxthen*...) or adjacent symbols would be ambiguous.

The syntax permits few cases of adjacent operators; the most common is a prefix operator appearing after an infix operator, as in $3 + -5$.

More generally, the physical layout of components should be so designed as to foster the readability of software texts. For example, indentation (using tab characters) highlights the structure of nested components. Since readability will benefit from consistency, this book introduces some recommended style conventions.

→ Appendix A.

25.6 Token categories

Tokens are the basic meaningful elements of software texts.

As noted in the description of general conventions at the beginning of this   ← See chapter 2.
book, tokens are specimens of **terminal constructs**. For example the token *8940*
is a specimen of the terminal construct Integer. (In contrast, higher-level
syntactical structures, such as class texts or routines, are specimens of non-
terminal constructs such as Class or Routine.) Terminal constructs do not appear
in left-hand sides of the productions of the grammar; instead, their structure is
defined in this chapter.

There are two categories of tokens, fixed and variable:

- Fixed tokens have a single, frozen form. They include reserved words such
  as **class** or *Current*, containing letters only, and special symbols such as :=
  or {, containing non-alphabetic characters. For fixed tokens this book does
  not make the distinction between the form of a token and the underlying
  terminal construct. For example, **class** is the single specimen of a construct
  which could be called Class_keyword but remains implicit; an occurrence
  of the token in the grammar actually denotes the construct.

- Variable tokens are specimens of terminal constructs such as Integer,
  Identifier or Free_operator for which this chapter defines a certain general
  structure within which you can create the tokens that fit the needs of your
  software. For example, the rules for Integer, as given below, specify
  specimens made of one or more decimal digits, possibly preceded by a sign
  + or −; tokens such as *327* and *−8940* satisfy this specification.

The following sections examine reserved words, special symbols, and the
various terminal constructs defining variable tokens: Identifier, Integer, String,
Simple_string, Real, Bit_sequence, Operator, Character.

25.7 Reserved words

The first and simplest tokens are reserved words. Reserved words are sequences   → Appendix G starts on page 553.
of characters made of letters only, belonging to a list given in appendix G.

Reserved words are called that way because you may not choose them as   *→ See below on*
developer-defined identifiers.   *identifiers.*

Reserved words include **keywords** and **predefined names**:

- Keywords, such as **class** or **feature**, serve to introduce and delimit the
  various components of constructs.

- Predefined names come at positions where variable tokens would also be   *← The definition of Result*
  permissible: for example, the predefined entity *Result*, denoting the result of   *as a special kind of local*
  a function, may be used in lieu of a local entity, for example as target of an   *entity appeared in 8.7,*
  assignment, and the basic type *INTEGER* may appear at a position where a   *page 114.*
  type is expected.

SYNTAX

No intervening blanks or other characters are permitted between the letters of   *→ See appendix A, page*
a reserved word. Letter case is not significant for reserved words (so that   *483, about the*
CLASS, *result* or even *rEsULt* are permissible forms of some of the above   *recommended style.*
examples.) There is a recommended style, however, where:

- Keywords appear in lower-case, as with **class**. In a typeset text they should always appear in boldface, as in this book.

- Predefined names start with a capital letter; the rest is in lower case (as with *Result*), except for types since the general convention for all types is to use all upper-case (as with *INTEGER*). When typeset, they appear in italics.

The following general guidelines presided over the choice of reserved words and should help you to learn reserved words quickly and remember them without hesitation:

- Reserved words are simple English words. They are never abbreviations *The exception is* **elseif**. and, with one exception, they are never composite words.

- When a noun is used, it is always in the singular for simplicity and consistency, even if the plural might seem more natural; for example the clause introducing the featur*e*s of a class begins with the keyword **feature**, and types describing bit sequences begin with *BIT*.

- Finally, all names chosen as keywords are common English words.

25.8 Special symbols

A small number of one- and two-character strings, called special symbols, have a special role in the syntax of various constructs. An example is the double exclamation mark used in Creation instructions, as in !! *x*.

Earlier chapters have introduced these symbols in connection with the syntactic form of various constructs. Here is the complete list, with a reminder of their role and, for each of them the page where the corresponding syntax production appears.

DEFINITION:
Special
Symbol

SYMBOL	NAME	USE	SYNTAX SPECIFICATION PAGES
--	double dash	Introduces comments	46, 112, 413
;	semicolon	Separates instructions, declarations, arguments etc. (optional in some cases).	49, 60, 77, 101, 109, 120, 234, 342
,	comma	Separates arguments, entities in a declaration etc.	49, 52, 63, 81, 101, 101, 109, 197, 239, 245, 342, 397
:	colon	Introduces the Type_mark in a declaration, a Tag_mark in an Assertion_clause, and an Index term in an Indexing clause.	49, 109, 120
.	dot	Separates target from feature in feature calls and creation calls. Separates integer from fractional part in real numbers.	285, 342, 421
! !!	Exclamation mark	Creation symbol (two forms since the creation type may be implicit or explicit).	285
= /=	Equal, not-equal signs	Equality and inequality operators.	374
–>	Arrow	Introduces the constraint of a constrained formal generic parameter	52

SYMBOL	NAME	USE	SYNTAX SPECIFICATION PAGES
..	Double dot	Separates the bounds of an interval for a Multi_branch instruction.	239
( )	Parentheses	Group subexpressions in operator expressions, and enclose formal and actual arguments of routines.	109, 245, 342, 376
[ ]	Brackets	Introduce formal and actual generic parameters to classes.	52, 197
{ }	Braces	Specify a Clients part (export restriction) at the beginning of a Creation_clause, Feature_clause or New_export_list.	101
≪ ≫	Angle brackets	Enclose a Manifest_array.	393
:=	Receives	Assignment symbol.	311
?=	May receive	Assignment_attempt symbol.	332
'	single quote	Encloses character constants.	387
"	double quote	Encloses prefix and infix operators and manifest strings.	68, 387
+ −	Signs	Signs of integer and real constants. (Also permitted as prefix and infix operators, but such operators are not listed in this table.)	387
$	Dollar sign	Address operator for passing addresses of Eiffel features to foreign routines.	342
%	Percent sign	Introduces special character codes.	422-423
/	Slash sign	Defines a character by its ASCII code	422, case C3.

Like reserved words, the special symbols must be written as given in the above table, with no intervening blanks or other characters. The style standard is to typeset them in roman.

25.9 Identifiers

So much for fixed tokens, and on to variable tokens.

An important category of variable tokens is identifiers, describing symbolic names which Eiffel texts use to denote various components such as classes, features or entities.

Here are some example identifiers:

> *A*
> *LINKED_LIST*
> *a*
> *an_identifier*
> *feature1*

The construct is defined as follows:

> An Identifier is a sequence of one or more characters, of which the first is a letter and each of the subsequent ones, if any, is a letter, a decimal digit (*0* to *9*) or the underscore character "_"

Letters include elements of the Roman alphabet, a to Z and A to Z.

→ *On potential extensions to the notion of letter, see the Note on non-ASCII letters, 25.16, page 424.*

The definition indicates that the first character of an identifier must be a letter; in particular, an identifier may not begin with an underscore. Also, no intervening blank is permitted within an identifier. The validity constraint is obvious:

VIRW

> An identifier is valid if and only if it is not one of the language's reserved words.

→ *See appendix G, page 553, for the list of reserved words.*

There is no limit to the length of identifiers, and all characters are significant; in other words, to determine whether two identifiers are the same or not, you must take all their characters into account.

Letter case is **not** significant for letters: if you write two identifiers as *a* and *A*, or *lInKeD_liST* and *LINKED_LIST*, they are considered the same. The recommended style includes some standard conventions: class names and other type names in upper-case (as in *LINKED_LIST*); names of routines, variable attributes and local entities in lower-case (as in *item*); names of constant attributes and predefined entities with an initial upper-case letter and the rest in lower case (as in *Avogadro* or *Result*).

→ *See appendix A, page 483, for the detailed style guidelines.*

DEFINITION:
Upper name,
lower name

The form of an identifier written all in upper-case is called the **upper name** of the identifier; the form all in lower-case is called its **lower name**.

25.10 Operators

When it comes to defining a function with one or two arguments, you may wish to use a prefix or infix name. For example, a comparison function in a class *INVESTMENT* might begin with

> **infix** "<=" (*other· INVESTMENT*): *BOOLEAN* **is**
>   -- Is *other* at least as good as current investment?
> ... Rest of function declaration omitted ...

and will then be called under the form *inv1* <= *inv2* rather than through an expression using dot notation, such as *inv1.no_better_than* (*inv2*).

DEFINITION:
Operator

The names that may come in double quotes after **infix** (or **prefix**), and will be used in the corresponding operator expressions, are called **operators**.

There are two kinds of operators: standard and free.

The standard operators, used for prefix and infix features of the classes defining the basic types (*INTEGER* etc.), are part of a predefined list, given in the discussion of expressions. The list also includes the boolean operators, expressed by alphabetical keywords. Here it is again:

Unary	≜	**not** | "+" | "−"
Binary	≜	"+" | "−" | "∗" | "/" |
		"<" | ">" | "<=" | ">=" |
		"//" | "\\\\" | "^" |
		and | **or** | **xor** |
		and then | **or else** | **implies**

← This appeared originally on page 68.

Among the operators listed, the following are keywords and do not properly belong to this discussion: **and, or, xor, and then, or else** *and* **implies**.

A Free_operator is not as free as the name would seem to suggest:

DEFINITION: Free operator

A Free_operator is sequence of one or more characters, whose first character is any one of

@ # | &

and whose subsequent characters, if any, may be any printable characters.

Here the printable characters include letters, digits, underscore, the four characters permitted as first character of a Free_operator and other special characters such as ∗, \ and $. They exclude Blank, New Line, Backspace and other characters with no external representation.

→ A printable character may appear as two or more keyboard keys, for example %% for the percent sign. See 25.15 below.

When used in expressions, the standard operators have various precedence levels, as given in the discussion of expressions; free operators all have the same precedence, higher than that of the standard operators.

← The table of operator precedence is on page 377.

Examples of free operators, used as function names, were given in the discussion of features. A simple one is @, used in infix form as a synonym for *item* for array access: *a @ i* is the *i*-th element of *i*.

← See page 68.

With the exception of @ for arrays, free operators are not used in the Basic Libraries. They are intended for developers in application areas that have a tradition of specialized notations, such as physics and mathematics. The form of a free operator should attempt to suggest its meaning, just as with a well chosen identifier.

The first character of a Free_operator must be one of only four possibilities, not used by any other construct of the language. As a result, any free operator will stand out clearly from its context, and no confusion or ambiguity is possible.

25.11 Strings

DEFINITION: String

A String – a specimen of construct String – is an arbitrary sequence of characters. A Simple_string – a specimen of Simple_string – is a String which consists of at most one line (that is to say, has no embedded new-line character).

Do not confuse String or Simple_string with Manifest_string, seen in the discussion of expressions. A specimen of Manifest_string, a non-terminal construct, is a Simple_string enclosed in double quotes, as in *"SOME STRING"*.

Manifest_string *was studied in 23.18, page 390.*

In the definition of String, a "character" is a legal Eiffel character as defined later in this chapter. This includes in particular:

→ *See 25.15, starting on page 422, for the various forms of characters and the use of the percent sign.*

- Any keyboard key other than %

- Any special character described as *%l* for some appropriate letter *l* (for example *%B* representing the Backspace character).

- A character given by its numerical code under the form *%/code/* (for example *%/35/* for the sharp sign #, which is the character of ASCII code 35).

25.12 Integers

DEFINITION:
Integer

Integer, a variable lexical construct, describes unsigned integer constants in decimal notation, such as the following:

Do not confuse Integer *with* Integer_constant, *seen as part of expressions in 23.14, page 388. A specimen of* Integer_constant, *a non-terminal construct, is an* Integer *optionally preceded by a sign.*

```
0
327
3197865
3_197_865
```

Except for underscores, no intervening characters (such as blanks) are permitted between digits.

Underscores, if any, have no effect on the integer value associated with the integer; so the last two examples above denote the same integer value. Underscores separate three-digit parts of an integer, if so desired for better readability.

You are not required to use underscores, but if you do use them they have to separate groups of exactly three digits, except for the leftmost one which may of course be shorter.

Here is the definition:

An Integer is a sequence of characters, each of which must be either:

- A decimal digit (0 to 9).

- An underscore (_), which may not be the first character.

If any underscore is present, then there must be three digits to the right of every underscore, and there must not be any consecutive group of four digits.

25.13 Real numbers

Real numbers – specimens of construct Real – define the manifest constants for both of the basic types *REAL* and *DOUBLE*.

Examples of real numbers are

```
1.0
0.1
1.
.1
2345.632E−7
2345.632e−7
```

A real number is made of the following elements:

- An optional Integer, giving the integral part. (If this is absent, the integral part is 0.)

- A required "." (dot).

- An optional Integer, which gives the fractional part. (If this is absent, the fractional part is 0.)

- An optional exponent, which is the letter *e* or *E* followed by an optional sign (+ or −) and an Integer. The Integer is required if the *e* or *E* is present. This indicates that the value appearing before the *e* or *E* must be scaled by 10^n, where *n* is the given integer.

← As with Integer, *there is no sign; a* Real *with an optional* Sign *will yield a* Real_constant.

The recommended style is to use E rather than e.

No intervening character (blank or otherwise) is permitted between these elements. The integral and fractional parts may not both be absent. If underscores are used in either the integral part or the fractional part, they must also appear in the other part, unless it has three digits or less.

25.14 Bit sequences

Bit sequences – specimens of construct Bit_sequence – are the manifest constants of Bit_type.

Examples are

```
0B
1B
10010001110101B
10010001110101b
```

As these examples indicate, a Bit_sequence is a sequence of digits 0 or 1, followed by a *b* or *B*, with no other intervening characters.

The recommended style is to use B rather than b.

25.15 Characters

Characters – specimens of construct Character – are used in specimens of various constructs: Character_constant (of which a specimen is a Character in single quotes, as *'A'*); Manifest_string (zero or more characters in double quotes, as in *"ABC DE!#$"*); Identifier.

What exactly is a character? The question is less trivial than it may seem because of the need to take into account the diverse and often incompatible keyboards that exist in various countries. The answer is important for defining the letters that may appear in identifiers and strings, as explained in the next section.

The discussion will assume that the device used to enter software texts is a keyboard, offering its users a number of keys, each defined by a code. The discussion distinguishes between keys, which simply serve to enter certain codes, and characters, which are the units of Eiffel lexical elements.

In the simplest and most common case, of course, you enter a character just by pressing an associated key; but for certain characters you may have to press a succession of two or more keys, and some keys will not yield a character. For example the Manifest_string in

> *String_with_backspace*: INTEGER **is** *"AAA%BZZZ"*

includes a non-printable character, the Backspace (appearing as *%B*). For this character there is in fact a key on usual keyboards, but pressing the Backspace key will not yield a character (it simply erases the previous character you have entered). To make Backspace part of your string, you may represent it by the two-key sequence *%B*, as here. Another possibility, using the ASCII code for this character, is to enter it as *%/8/*.

ASCII (The American Standard for Common Information Interchange) is the character code used by many US keyboards. Various derivatives exist for keyboards used in other countries.

The definition of "character" makes it possible to handle such cases and helps address the portability problems raised by the different in keyboards found in various countries. A character is one of the following.

C1 • Any key associated with a printable character, except for the percent key *%*. (The percent key plays a special role for cases 2 and 3.)

C2 • The sequence *%k*, where *k* is a one-key code taken from the table given below. This is used to represent special characters such as the Backspace, represented as *%B*, or characters which are not available on all keyboards, or have different codes on different keyboards. An example is the opening bracket: when supported by the keyboard, this character may be entered using form C1 as [; it may also, in all cases, be represented as *%(*.

C3 • The sequence *%/code/*, where *code* is an unsigned integer, representing the character of code *code*. For example in ASCII *%/59/* represents the character of code 59, which is the semicolon.

If your platform's documentation offers tables of character codes, make sure you work from a table using decimal values (not octal or hexadecimal).

In form C3, the *code* is expressed, as any integer constant, in decimal form. With both C2 and C3, no blanks must appear between the keys; in other words, *% B* or *% /5 9/* would be illegal.

The table of special character codes for form C2 is the following.

Character	Code	Mnemonic name
@	%A	At-sign
BS	%B	Backspace
^	%C	Circumflex
$	%D	Dollar
FF	%F	Form feed
\	%H	backslasH
~	%L	tiLda
NL(LF)	%N	Newline
'	%Q	[back] Quote
CR	%R	[carriage] Return
#	%S	Sharp
HT	%T	[horizontal] Tab
NUL	%U	nUll character
|	%V	Vertical bar
%	%%	percent
'	%'	single quote
"	%"	double quote
[	%(	opening bracket
]	%)	closing bracket
{	%<	opening brace
}	%>	closing brace

*Upper-case letters in the
last column highlight the
corresponding codes; for
example the L in 'tiLda'
recalls %L.*

The major application of forms C2 and C3 arises for a Manifest_string containing characters that you cannot type directly into the class text. This includes non-printable characters, such as the Backspace in the above *String_with_backspace*, and characters which your current keyboard does not support. As an example of the second case, if you have an American ASCII keyboard but want to define an Manifest_string that an output device supporting French codes will display as *ambiguïté*, you may enter it as the Eiffel string *"ambigu%/139/t%/130/"*.

With two exceptions, a character entered under form C2 or C3 is exactly equivalent to its C1 counterpart when it exists. This means that you may (if you really want to) enter the identifier *ARRAY*, a class name, under the form *%/65/%/82/%/82/%/65/%/89/*, where the numbers given are the ASCII codes for letters *A, R* and *Y*.

The two exceptions are the following:

- In a Character_constant such as *'A'*, the enclosing single quotes must appear as ', and if the character itself is a single quote, it must appear in form C2 (as %') or C3 (as %/39/), as in

     Quote_character: *CHARACTER* **is** *'%''*

- Similarly, in a Manifest_string, the enclosing double quotes must appear as " and any double quote in the string itself must appear in form C2 (as %") or C3.

25.16 A note on non-ASCII letters

An Identifier, as defined earlier in this chapter, contains one or more letters. In this definition, a letter is restricted to the Roman alphabet as used in the English language and included in the American ASCII character set: *a* to *z* and *A* to *Z*.

In non-English speaking countries, however, some keyboards support extended versions of ASCII, which include Roman letters with diacritical marks (such as *à* or *b*), some additional letters (such as the German *β* for double *s*), other alphabets (Hebrew, Cyrillic, Greek), or even non-alphabetic languages.

Developers whose language is not English may wish to define identifiers that include such non-ASCII letters, such as *ambiguïté*. They may also want to write a Manifest_string using such letters in a natural form such as *"virtù"* or *"libertà"* rather than using the C3 form defined in the previous section, which does the job but implies the not extremely readable use of %-codes (*"virt%/151/"*, *"libert%/133/"*).

In principle, it should not be difficult to offer this possibility. One may envision an option of language processing tools enabling developers to specify that certain character codes, outside of the a-z and A-Z intervals, must be acceptable as letters.

To avoid hampering portability, the language definition may not be fickle here: if it *allows* implementations to let developers specify extensions to the letter set, it should *require* them to do so. Otherwise an application developed for an implementation which supports extended letter sets could not be processed by one which does not.

It is indeed not difficult to see how tools could handle extended letter sets. In particular, no insurmountable problem would result from combining classes developed with different variants of the letter set; developers would simply have to write a few "bridge" classes, using forms C2 and C3 introduced in the previous section. The following example illustrates this potential technique. Assume that you are writing a system written in ASCII but need a few classes (perhaps obtained from a foreign country) developed with an extended letter set. If *DOPPELGÄNGER* is one of them and you need its features *télévision* and *ambiguïté*, you would write a bridge class of the form

```
class DOPPELGAENGER inherit
    DOPPELG%/142/nger
    rename
        ambigu%/139/t%/130/ as ambiguite,
        t%/130/l%/130/vision as television
    ...
```

WARNING: syntactically illegal. For purposes of discussion only.

Your other classes, written in ASCII, would then use *DOPPELGÄNGER* (as clients or heirs) under the name *DOPPELGAENGER*, and its needed features under the names *ambiguite* and *television*. The amount of new bridge work needed if your class supplier later delivers a new version of *DOPPELGAENGER* should be moderate (affecting only new features). The bridge class itself uses characters outside of ASCII, even though it is usable by classes written in strict ASCII.

These techniques, and the ability of language processing tools to accept extended letter sets, were given serious consideration at various times in the evolution of Eiffel. Two reasons, however, have so far justified a conservative approach.

The first reason is technical: certain non-ASCII devices have given alphabetical assignments to codes, representing characters in ASCII but used by Eiffel for special symbols. For example the code for the opening bracket [appears on some keyboards and terminals as *è* (*e* with grave accent). In practice only a few characters, which may be called **non-universal**, raise this possibility:

```
# $ @ ~ \ | ' ^ [ ] { }
```

This problem is not unsurmountable. But the second obstacle is more serious. This is simply the lack of a standard for representing non-ASCII characters (and words of non-alphabetical languages). Although current hardware and software systems support a number of such representations, a widely accepted solution is available neither in practice (existing solutions being based on incompatible extensions to ASCII) nor in theory.

At the time of writing, computer manufacturers and international standardization committees are promoting at least two competing "standard" proposals. In the absence of sufficient criteria to decide between the intrinsic merits of these proposals, and of sufficient foresight to bet on one of them, a wait and see attitude was deemed wisest. This is of course regrettable for developers whose language is not English, but results from circumstances beyond the reach of the Eiffel community.

The NICE consortium may wish to reconsider the decision in the future. As shown above, a simple and portable solution is possible provided the hardware codes are known without ambiguity. In the meantime, you will have to restrict your identifiers to non-accented letters of the Roman alphabet, and to use the % codes for any non-ASCII letters occurring in your manifest strings.

Part D

Elements from the Basic Libraries

26

Notes on the Basic Libraries

26.1 Overview

The next few chapters introduce mechanisms which, although important (and in some cases indispensable) to the practice of Eiffel software development, do not belong to the language in the strict sense: instead, they are provided by features of the Basic Libraries.

This chapter provides some background by describing the available libraries, their role and their status.

26.2 Libraries

The libraries listed below are those of ISE's implementation. At the time of writing, other libraries, in part complementary and in part competitive, have begun to appear. This welcome development is a direct realization of the major goal of Eiffel: fostering the growth of an industry of reusable software components.

For details, see "Eiffel: The Libraries". The reference is in appendix C.

A distribution mechanism known as the **Eiffel shelf** is available to make reusable classes from various sources (individual software developers, Eiffel implementors) accessible to Eiffel users worldwide.

For any information about the Eiffel shelf please contact ISE.

The current ISE delivery includes the following libraries:

- Kernel Library: essential components such as *ANY* and other universal classes, *ARRAY* and *STRING*.

→ *Universal classes*: chapter 27. *ARRAY and STRING*: chapter 28.

- Support Library: classes supporting persistence, debugging tools, browsing, access to internal forms of Eiffel structures, fine-grain memory management.

→ *Persistence classes*: chapter 30.

- Data Structure Library: fundamental data structures and algorithms – lists, queues, trees, hash tables, stacks etc.

- Graphics Library: support for graphics, multiple windowing, advanced user interfaces.
- Lexical Library: text scanning.
- Parsing Library: analysis of programs and other structured documents.
- Winpack Library: non-graphical windowing.

The libraries are constantly being enriched, and new libraries are under development.

26.3 Library status

The library interfaces described in the chapters of part D, with the exception of persistence classes in chapter 30, must be provided by any implementation of Eiffel. Only the features described here must be provided, but other features may be present.

Only the class interfaces (flat-short forms, as given in the following chapters) are mandatory. Implementing these interfaces is the responsibility of every Eiffel implementor.

The numerous library extracts given elsewhere in this book (mostly from the Data Structure, Graphics, Lexical and Parsing Libraries) appear for illustration purposes only and are not binding on other implementations.

26.4 New libraries

To facilitate exchange of software and compatibility with existing libraries, authors of new libraries should follow as closely as possible the style guidelines given in this book, especially appendix A.

For any question regarding libraries, standardization proposals or other suggestions, please contact the Library Committee of the NICE Consortium.

← On NICE see the page entitled "About the status of Eiffel" after the preface.

27

Universal features

27.1 Overview

Class *ANY* from the Kernel Library is known as a "universal" class since it is an ancestor of any class that you may ever write.

Universal Class Structure

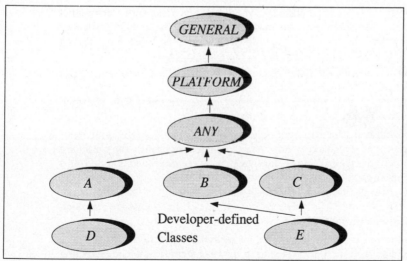

← *The more complete version of this figure, including class NONE, appeared on page 85.*

As you will remember from the discussion of inheritance, the rule is that any class which does not include its own Inheritance clause is considered to have an implicit clause of the form

← *See 6.12, page 85, and subsequent sections.*

> **inherit** *ANY*

Because of this rule, *ANY* serves as both the most general type, to which all types conform, and as the most general set of features, since all developer-defined classes inherit its features.

ANY is in fact empty as delivered, save for an Inheritance clause for *PLATFORM*. Its features, listed below, come from its grandparent *GENERAL* and its parent *PLATFORM*, as shown by the figure on the preceding page. *GENERAL* introduces the features which any class may need in any context, such as procedure *copy* and function *equal*; *PLATFORM*, which has *GENERAL* as its parent, introduces a few platform-dependent features, such as the bit length of integers.

If you wish to make certain non-standard features usable by all of your classes, you may write a new version of *ANY*, normally an heir to *PLATFORM*. The following presentation only considers the default version.

← *See 6.15, page 87, on providing a replacement for ANY.*

27.2 Input and output features

This section and the following ones provide an overview of the facilities offered, beginning with input and output facilities. The full flat-short form of the class is given at the end of this chapter.

Feature *io*, of type *STANDARD_FILES*, gives access to standard input and output facilities. It is appropriate for simple input and output operations. For example, *io.input* is the standard input file and *io.new_line* will print a line feed on the standard output.

→ *STANDARD_FILES and other input-output facilities are covered in chapter 31.*

You may think of *io* as an attribute, whose value is a standard input-output environment, made available to any class that may need it. As noted, however, the standard *ANY* has no variable attributes to avoid imposing a penalty on every run-time object. Feature *io* is in fact implemented as a once function.

Function *out*, returning a *STRING*, yields a simple external representation of any object. For non-void *x* of any type, the string *out* (*x*) is a printable representation of *x*. Because *x* is an argument of the call rather than its target, the function returns a result, an empty string, for void *x*.

Function *out* works for all types: basic types (such as *INTEGER*), reference types, Class_type_expanded. For basic types, it gives the standard representation; for example, *x.out*, for integer *x*, is the representation of *x* as a string of decimal digits. For a non-void reference, or a value of Class_type_expanded, *x.out* is by default the concatenation of the *out* forms of the object attached to *x*. You may redefine *out* in a class, to produce a specific external representation of the instances of the class.

A variant of *out* is *tagged_out* which, for reference types, normally produces a more readable representation where each field is tagged by the corresponding attribute name. This is only intended as a debugging option; as a consequence, the exact format is not guaranteed, and may under certain language processing tools be reduced to that of *out*.

Procedure *print* is a universal output mechanism. The call *print* (*x*) achieves the same as *io.putstring* (*x.out*), printing a string representation of *x* on the standard output.

27.3 Duplication and comparison routines

A group of routines (*copy*, *clone*, *deep_copy*, *equal* and others) provides facilities for copying, duplicating and comparing objects.

The chapter on object duplication and comparison explored the properties of these routines in detail.

← See chapter 19 about object duplication and comparison.

27.4 Object properties

A few features give access to general properties of the current object.

Feature *object_id*, implemented as a function or attribute, yields a *STRING* result which is guaranteed to be a different string for distinct complex objects. The string may be computed from the address of the memory location used to store the object, but this is not part of the feature's specification, which only requires uniqueness of the result for each object. The value of *x.object_id* is only meaningful for *x* of reference type; if *object_id* is used in Unqualified_call form, its value is only meaningful if the target of the current call is non-expanded.

Function *generator* returns a string, the name of the current object's generating class – that is to say, the base class of the type of which the object is a direct instance.

← The notion of generator was defined in 17.2, page 270.

Sometimes you may need to determine at run time whether the type of a certain object conforms to the type of another. The boolean function *conforms_to* provides a way to do this under the form

> *x.conforms_to* (*y*)

The discussion of assignment attempt introduced two complementary techniques for the same goal: using a succession of assignment attempts, or function *dynamic_type* from the Kernel Library class *INTERNAL*. That discussion also explained in detail why such an operation is seldom required, and seldom appropriate, in the Eiffel method of software development.

← See 20.15, page 333.

27.5 Platform-dependent features

Features introduced in class *PLATFORM* give platform-dependent values:

- The integer constants *Character_bits*, *Integer_bits*, *Real_bits*, *Double_bits* and *Pointer_bits* indicate the number of bits used to represent instances of the basic expanded types *CHARACTER*, *INTEGER*, *REAL*, *DOUBLE* and *POINTER*.

- The integer constant *Maximum_character_code*, which may not be less than 128, gives the highest supported character code. Valid character codes are between 1 and this value.

- For any non-void entity *a*, the value of *a.bit_size* is the number of bits used to store *a*.

← See 13.11, page 229, about 'bit_size'.

27.6 Class *ANY*

Here is the flat-short form of class *ANY*.

-- Universal features. All classes inherit from *ANY*,
-- which inherits from *PLATFORM*, itself an heir of *GENERAL*.
-- All features listed, except those marked as introduced
-- in *PLATFORM*, are introduced in *GENERAL*.

class interface *ANY* **exported features** -- Void value

Void: *NONE*
    -- Void reference

exported features -- Equality, clone, copy

is_equal, **frozen** *standard_is_equal*
    (*other*: **like** *Current*): *BOOLEAN*
    -- Is *other* attached to an object field-by-field
    -- identical (on common fields) to current object?
require
    other_not_void: *other* /= *Void*

frozen *equal* (*some*: *ANY*; *other*: **like** *some*): *BOOLEAN*
    -- Are *some* and *other* either both void or attached
    -- to objects field-by-field identical (on fields of *some*)?
    -- Defined in terms of *is_equal*.
ensure
    Result = (*some* = *Void* **and** *other* = *Void*) **or**
            (*some* /= *Void* **and** *other* /= *Void* **and then**
            some.*is_equal* (*other*))

frozen *standard_equal* (*some*: *ANY*; *other*: **like** *some*): *BOOLEAN*
    -- Are *some* and *other* either both void or attached
    -- to objects field-by-field identical (on fields of *some*)?
    -- Defined in terms of *standard_is_equal*.
ensure
    Result = (*some* = *Void* **and** *other* = *Void*) **or**
            (*some* /= *Void* **and** *other* /= *Void* **and then**
            some.*is_equal* (*other*))

copy, **frozen** *standard_copy* (*other*: **like** *Current*)
    -- Copy every field of *other* onto
    -- corresponding field of current object.
require
    other_not_void: *other* /= *Void*;
    other_conforming: *other*.*conforms_to* (*Current*)
ensure
    is_equal (*other*)

---

frozen *clone* (*other*: *ANY*): **like** *other*
     -- Void if *other* is void; otherwise, new object
     -- field-by-field identical to object attached to *other*.
     -- Defined in terms of *copy*.
   ensure
     equal (*Result, other*)

frozen *standard_clone* (*other*: *ANY*): **like** *other*
     -- Void if *other* is void; otherwise, new object
     -- field-by-field identical to object attached to *other*.
     -- Defined in terms of *standard_copy*.
   ensure
     standard_equal (*Result, other*)

deep_equal, **frozen** *standard_deep_equal*
     (*some*: *ANY*; *other*: **like** *some*): *BOOLEAN*
     -- Are *some* and *other* either both void
     -- or attached to recursively isomorphic object structures?

deep_copy, **frozen** *standard_deep_copy* (*other*: **like** *Current*)
     -- Effect equivalent to that of:
     --   *temp* := *deep_clone* (*other*);
     --   *copy* (*temp*)
   require
     other_not_void: *other* /= *Void*
   ensure
     deep_equal (*Current, other*)

deep_clone, **frozen** *standard_deep_clone* (*other*: *ANY*): **like** *other*
     -- Void if *other* is void; otherwise, new object structure
     -- recursively duplicated from the one attached to *other*.
   ensure
     deep_equal (*Result, other*)

exported features -- Simple input and output

io : *STANDARD_FILES*

Lastout: *STRING*
     -- Last string returned by *out* or *tagged_out*

out : *STRING*
     -- Terse printable representation of current object, field by field.
     -- Every call to this function allocates a new result string.

print (*some*: *ANY*)
     -- Write terse external representation of *some*
     -- on standard output. (No effect if void.)

tagged_out : *STRING*
     -- Printable representation of current object including
     -- the same information as for *out* plus, if possible,
     -- the attribute name for each field.

exported features -- Default exception handling

default_rescue
    -- Exception response for routines without a Rescue clause
    -- (Default: do nothing.)

exported features -- Internal object properties

object_id: *STRING*
    -- A value associated with current object;
    -- if this is a complex object, the string is different from
    -- the value for any other complex object in the system.

generator: *STRING*
    -- Name of the current object's generating class,
    -- (base class of the type of which it is a direct instance).
    -- Every call to this function allocates a new result string.

conforms_to (*other*: **like** *Current*): *BOOLEAN*
    -- Is dynamic type of current object a descendant
    -- of dynamic type of *other*?
  require
    other_not_void: *other* /= *Void*

exported features -- Platform-dependent properties (from *PLATFORM*)

Character_bits: *INTEGER*
    -- Number of bits used to represent a character

Integer_bits: *INTEGER*
    -- Number of bits used to represent an integer

Real_bits: *INTEGER*
    -- Number of bits used to represent a real

Double_bits: *INTEGER*
    -- Number of bits used to represent a double-precision real

Pointer_bits: *INTEGER*
    -- Number of bits used to represent a pointer to a feature

Maximum_character_code: *INTEGER*
    -- Maximum supported character code (128 or more)

bit_size: *INTEGER*
    -- Number of bits used to store current object.

invariant properties

Maximum_character_code >= *128*

end interface -- class *ANY*

28

Arrays and strings

28.1 Overview

Arrays and strings are homogeneous sequences of values – characters for strings, values conforming to an arbitrary type for arrays – accessible through contiguous integer indices.

The basic operations on arrays and strings are not special language constructs; instead, two Kernel Library classes, *ARRAY* and *STRING*, describe the corresponding objects and provide features for access and modification. Although for most purposes you may use these two classes as any other library classes, one property sets them apart: the language offers notations for **manifest** values of type *STRING* and *ARRAY* [*T*] (manifest strings of the form *"some text"* and manifest arrays of the form «*element, element, ...*»). This means that language processing tools must know about these classes.

This chapter presents the features of classes *ARRAY* and *STRING* and explains how to manipulate the corresponding objects.

28.2 Representation

The two classes use the same representation technique. Both are non-expanded classes, so that the value of an entity of type *STRING* or *ARRAY* [*T*] for some *T* is a reference to an object. That object is **not**, however, the actual sequence of values (array or string), but a descriptor, which contains information about the sequence and its properties (such as its length and its bounds), and provides access to the sequence itself.

A possible representation is shown below for strings; here the descriptor contains, among other fields, a reference to the sequence of characters, which is a special object. Remember that, in contrast with standard objects, a special object is not a direct instance of a type but simply a sequence of values used only for implementation purposes, and accessible through a descriptor, itself a standard object. For an array the values in the sequence may be of a type other than *CHARACTER*.

← *Special and standard objects were introduced in 17.2, page 270.*

*String
descriptor
and
associated
character
sequence*

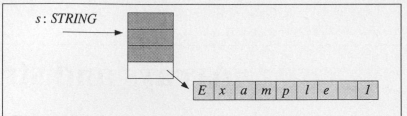

← *A variant of this figure already appeared on page 391. Page 395 shows a similar representation for arrays.*

The representation shown here is an illustration, not necessarily the exact physical form of arrays. In particular:

- An implementation may choose to store no other information in the descriptor than the reference to the special object, any other information (the shaded areas on the figure) being kept in the special object itself.

- Some implementation constraints may require an extra level of indirection.

- At the other extreme, a compiler may even be able to avoid any indirection for a certain array (perhaps because it is never resized). This is permitted as long as the semantic effect of operations on arrays is the one described in this chapter.

What you must remember in practice is that an entity of type *STRING* or *ARRAY* [*T*] does not necessarily give you a direct handle on the actual sequence of values making up a string or array. These representation issues are of little consequence as long as you only access these values through the features of classes *STRING* and *ARRAY*, as given by this chapter in flat-short form. You need to be careful, however, when writing an Assignment or Equality test on such structures, since these are defined as operations on the descriptors rather than the sequences themselves. To obtain operations on the sequences, use the *copy, clone* and *equal* routines for which, as explained below, redefinitions in *STRING* and *ARRAY* yield the expected semantics.

28.3 Resizing

As noted at the beginning of this chapter, each element in a string or array has an associated integer index, and the legal indices form a contiguous interval. In practice, this almost universally means that sequence elements are stored contiguously in memory. Contiguous memory storage is not absolute requirement, but the best means known for the only end that really matters to users of arrays, the guarantee that the time needed to access or replace an element known by its index is constant, and small.

The price to pay for this guarantee is the difficulty of changing the index interval – adding elements before, between or after existing ones. If a high percentage of the operations performed on a data structure are such out-of-bounds additions, then array or string is probably not the appropriate representation; many classes of the Data Structure Library provide more flexible data structures, at some cost in access time, storage occupation, or both.

See "Eiffel: The Libraries" about the Data Structure Library.

To make fast access and replacement possible, then, an Eiffel array or string is a bounded data structure, the bounds being defined at any time by the index interval. But bounded does not mean fixed-size. You may resize an array or string, either explicitly (through procedure *resize*, available in both classes) or implicitly, by assigning a value to an array element outside of the current index interval, using a feature which includes a provision for automatic resizing.

As an example of implicit resizing, *STRING* has a feature *append*, which concatenates a copy of a string at the end of another string, with no length restriction; *append* will automatically resize the target string if the operation causes it to grow beyond its originally assigned capacity. Similarly, *ARRAY* has two features for assigning a value to an element given by its index: one, *put*, requires (as part of its precondition) an index that belongs to the current index interval, but the other, *force*, has no such restriction and will automatically resize the array if needed.

In practice, you should keep the following two considerations in mind when using explicit or implicit resizing:

- Resizing is likely to be much more expensive than the basic array and string operations of accessing or replacing an element within the current index interval. In fact the obvious implementation of resizing to a higher size allocates a fresh array or string and copies the old values, which implies an access and replacement operation on *every* previously allocated element. This means that the ratio of resizing operations to non-resizing ones (basic access and replacement) should normally remain low. For highly dynamic data structures, linked representations supported by classes of the Data Structure Library such as *LINKED_LIST* are usually preferable to arrays.

  The 'resize' procedures keep existing items, and hence cannot be used to make some of the structure's storage space reclaimable. To shrink an array, use 'remake'. For strings, use 'shrink', with the string itself as first argument. See the class specifications below.

- For arrays, the knowledge that a certain array has a fixed *lower* bound may allow compilers to generate faster code for access and replacement operations, especially if that bound is syntactically a constant (rather than a variable attribute or a local routine entity). A good compiler may be able to detect that a certain array will always keep its original lower bound (because it is never resized, or resizing affects its upper bound only). In this case the penalty for changing the lower bound may be higher than just the cost of resizing since it means that even basic access and replacement, although still constant-time, are less efficient than for an array which has a constant lower bound.

28.4 Basic array handling

Class *ARRAY* represents arrays; it is a generic class, with one generic parameter representing the type of the array elements. The arrays it describes are one-dimensional; for multi-dimensional arrays, the Data Structure library offers further classes such as *ARRAY2*, but you may also use *ARRAY* in a nested form, as in *ARRAY [ARRAY [T]]*.

To create an array with bounds *m* and *n* (two integer expressions), that is to say, with an initial index interval consisting of all the values *i* such that $m \leq i$ and $i \leq n$, use the creation procedure *make*, as in

```
up_to_date, delinquent: ARRAY [ACCOUNT];
m, n: INTEGER;
...
m := ...; n := ...;

!! up_to_date.make (1, 300);
!! delinquent.make (m−1, n+1)
```

The current lower and upper bounds are accessible through features *lower* and *upper*, the number of available elements through *count*. An invariant clause states that *count* is *upper* − *lower* + 1.

The two basic operations on an array are accessing and replacing an element known by its index:

- Access uses function *item*. To obtain the i-th element of *up_to_date*, write the expression

  up_to_date.*item* (i).

- Replacement uses procedure *put*. To replace by *a* the i-th value of *delinquent*, write the instruction

  delinquent. *put* (a, i)

Each of these functions has a precondition stating that the index i must have a value between the bounds *lower* and *higher*. (This means in particular that by enabling precondition checking on class *ARRAY* you can get an implementation to check the legality of your array accesses.)   *← On run-time assertion checking see 9.17, page 132.*

In contrast with *put*, procedure *force* has no such precondition. The call

```
delinquent. force (a, i)
```

will put value *a* at index i, even if the value of i is not part of the current index interval. This may cause resizing. To request resizing explicitly, you may also use a call of the form

```
delinquent.resize (1, 2∗n)
```

The semantics of this call is to add to the index interval all the integer values between the arguments given (here *1* and *2∗n*), without losing any previously entered array element. In other words, the call does not necessarily ensure that the new bounds are *1* and *2∗n*, but simply that they accommodate these values and everything in-between. (The bounds may even remain unchanged if the existing index interval already includes the argument values.)

The access function *item* has a synonym with an infix name: **infix** *"@"*. This means that you may express *up_to_date*.*item* (i), if you prefer, as

```
up_to_date @ i
```

Since "@", like any free operator, has the highest possible precedence, you must use parentheses if the index is a non-atomic expression, as in

$$up\_to\_date @ (i - 1)$$

← See the table on page 377 about operator precedence. The definition of free operators is on page 419.

This presence of two equally acceptable names for a single feature is a unique occurrence in the Eiffel libraries – an exception to the style rule which enjoins developers to choose a single name for each feature, and stick to it. The reason for this rare departure from a general guideline is a concession to tradition. Although *item* is the recommended name for the basic access feature for all data structure classes (and is used consistently for this purpose in the Data Structure Library and others), many developers prefer a compact notation for the special and frequent case of array access.

← The style rule was given in the discussion of synonym features: 5.16, page 71. See also appendix A about style guidelines. Remember that redefining a feature through one of its name does not redefine the synonym.

Clearly, you should reserve **infix** *"@"* for a structure that can only be implemented as an array. If there is any possibility of a later change of representation (switching for example to a linked list), you should use the name *item* which will avoid any change to the client code.

28.5 Copying and comparing arrays

Class *ARRAY* redefines *copy* and *is_equal* from *ANY*, so that for arrays these routines will copy or compare not just the array descriptors but the actual sequences of values.

Array Duplication

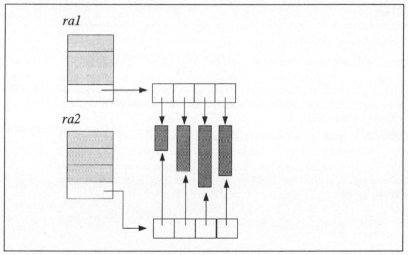

Recall that redefining procedure *copy* also implies a new semantics for function *clone*, and that redefining *is_equal* also implies a new semantics for *equal*, which is called under the form *equal (a, b)* and returns the value of

← See 19.3, page 298, and 19.8, page 303.

$(a = Void$ **and** $b = Void)$ **or**
$(a \neq Void$ **and** $b \neq Void$ **and then** $a.is\_equal (b))$

For example, if the value of *ra1* is an array as illustrated on the top portion of the figure, an instruction of the form

> *ra2.copy (ra1)*

will assign to *ra2* an identical array, as illustrated by the bottom part. This is still a comparatively shallow copy: if the array elements are references (as on the figure), the references are copied but not the objects to which they are attached (represented by the shaded rectangles). *A call to 'copy' requires that its target be non-void.*

Function *clone* also duplicates the array, and duplicates the descriptor as well, returning a result attached to the new descriptor.

In contrast with the semantics of *copy* and *clone*, an Assignment on array entities has the semantics of direct reattachment for entities of reference types, which means that *← See the table of page 317 about the semantics of direct reattachment.*

> *ra2 := ra1*

will attach *ra2* to the array descriptor attached to *ra1*. Any later array operation on *ra2*, for example the call

> *ra2.put (some_value, some_index)*

will have the same effect as the corresponding operation of *ra1*. The same behavior results from actual-formal association in a call

> *r (..., ra2, ...)*

where *ra1* is the corresponding formal argument in *r*.

As with *copy* and *clone*, the version of *equal* for *ARRAY*, using the redefined version of *is_equal*, compares not the descriptors but the actual arrays, recursively applying the appropriate version of *equal* to each successive pair of elements. (In *equal (ra1, ra2)* where *ra1* and *ra2* are of type *ARRAY* [*T*], the comparison applied to element pairs is the version of *equal* for *T*.) *← On the relation between 'equal' and 'is_equal', see 19.7, page 303.*

To copy array descriptors rather than arrays, use the routines *standard_clone*, *standard_copy*, *standard_equal*. To obtain deep operations, which will recursively duplicate or compare not just the array values but (if these values are references) the data structures to which they are attached, use *deep_clone*, *deep_copy, deep_equal*.

28.6 Manifest arrays

You may obtain an array simply by giving its values through a manifest array expression. The expression *← 23.20, page 393, covered manifest arrays.*

> $\ll e_1, e_2, \dots e_n \gg$

denotes an array of *n* elements, the values of expressions $e_1, e_2, \dots e_n$. If every e_i conforms to a type *T*, then the manifest array expression conforms to *ARRAY* [*T*].

28.7 Class *ARRAY*

Here is the flat-short form of class *ARRAY*.

-- One-dimensional arrays

class interface *ARRAY* [*G*] **creation procedures**

  make (*minindex, maxindex*: *INTEGER*)
        -- Allocate array; set index interval to *minindex .. maxindex*
        -- (empty if *minindex > maxindex*).
    ensure
     minindex > maxindex **implies** *count = 0*;
     minindex <= maxindex **implies** *count = maxindex − minindex + 1*

exported features

  all_cleared: *BOOLEAN*
        -- Are all items set to default values?

  clear_all
        -- Reset all items to default values.
    ensure
     all_cleared

  copy (*other*: *ARRAY* [*G*])
        -- Make current array an element-by-element a copy of *other*.
        -- (Redefined from *ANY*)
    require
     other /= *Void*
    ensure
     lower = other.lower; *upper = other.upper*;
     -- For all *i*: *lower .. upper*, *item* (*i*) − *other.item* (*i*)

  count: *INTEGER*
        -- Number of available indices

  empty: *BOOLEAN*
        -- Is array empty?

  force (*v*: *G*; *i*: *INTEGER*)
        -- Assign item *v* to *i*-th entry.
        -- Always applicable: resize the array if *i* falls out of
        -- currently defined bounds; preserve existing elements.
    ensure
     inserted: *item* (*i*) = *v*;
     higher_count: *count* >= **old** *count*

---

is_equal (*other*: *ARRAY* [*G*]): *BOOLEAN*
  -- Is current array element-by-element equal to *other*?
  -- (Redefined from *ANY*)
  ensure
  -- *Result* true if and only if, for all *i*: *other.lower* .. *other.upper*,
  --   *item* (*i*) = *other.item* (*i*)

item, **infix** *"@"* (*i*: *INTEGER*): *G*
  -- Entry at index *i*, if in index interval.
  require
  index_large_enough: *lower* <= *i*;
  index_small_enough: *i* <= *upper*

lower: *INTEGER*
  -- Minimum index

put (*v*: *G*; *i*: *INTEGER*)
  -- Replace *i*-th entry, if in index interval, by *v*.
  require
  index_large_enough: *lower* <= *i*;
  index_small_enough: *i* <= *upper*

remake (*minindex, maxindex*: *INTEGER*)
  -- Reallocate array; set index interval to *minindex* .. *maxindex*
  -- (empty if *minindex* > *maxindex*).
  -- Keep any existing elements in the range *minindex* .. *maxindex*.
  ensure
  minindex > *maxindex* **implies** *count* = *0*;
  minindex <= *maxindex* **implies** *count* = *maxindex* − *minindex* + *1*

resize (*minindex, maxindex*: *INTEGER*)
  -- Rearrange array so that it can accommodate indices down to *minindex*
  -- and up to *maxindex*. Do not lose any existing item.
  ensure
  lower <= *minindex*; *maxindex* <= *upper*

to_external: *NONE*
  -- Address of actual sequence of values,
  -- for passing to foreign (non-Eiffel) routines.

upper: *INTEGER*
  -- Maximum index

wipe_out
  -- Empty the array: discard all items.
  ensure
  wiped_out: *empty*

invariant

  consistent_size: *count* = *upper* − *lower* + *1*;
  non_negative_size: *count* >= *0*;

end interface -- class *ARRAY*

28.8 Strings

Class *STRING* describes character strings.

In principle, a string could be implemented as an object of type *ARRAY* [*CHARACTER*]. Having a special class makes it possible to use a more compact internal representation and to support many specific string operations (such as appending another string or extracting substrings) which are not as interesting for arbitrary arrays.

To create a string, use the creation procedure *make*:

> *text1*, *text2*: STRING; *n*: INTEGER;
>
> ...
>
> !! *text1*.*make* (*n*)

This will dynamically allocate a string *text1* with room for *n* characters. The argument to *make* gives the initial length of the string. This is **not**, however, a hard-wired limit: if further operations result in *text1* growing beyond *n* characters, the string will automatically be resized.

As with arrays, you can also initialize a string by giving its contents: use a Manifest_string of the form

← *See 23.18 and 23.19, starting on page 391, on manifest strings.*

> *example*: STRING **is** *"This string literal contains 42 characters"*

Remember, when using an assignment on strings, that it will be an assignment of string descriptors, not a copy. To obtain a fresh copy of a string, use one of the forms

> *text2*.*copy* (*text1*)
> *text2* := *clone* (*text1*)

relying on the redefined version of *copy* (also used by *clone*), which duplicates the character sequence, not just the string descriptor.

← *See chapter 19 about 'copy', 'clone', 'equal' and 'is_equal'.*

Similarly, a test of the form

> **if** *text1* = *text2* **then** ...

will compare string descriptors, which is not what you will want most of the time; to compare the actual strings, use

> **if** *equal* (*text1*, *text2*) **then** ...

which relies on the redefined version of *is_equal*.

The next section shows the many operations available on strings, such as concatenation, character or substring extraction, comparison. The comparison operations (which have infix names *"<"*, *"<="*, *">="*, *">"*) use lexical ordering, based on numerical character codes (ASCII or an extended version). These functions exist in deferred form in class *COMPARABLE*, a parent of *STRING*.

→ *See 32.2, page 475, about COMPARABLE.*

Function *adapt* is useful if you declare a descendant of *STRING*, say *SPECIFIC_STRING*, and want to initialize an entity *s* of type *SPECIFIC_STRING* by giving its characters explicitly. You may not assign a manifest string such as *"Some Text"* to *s* because of the conformance rules, but you may use

---

> *s* := *adapt* (*"Some Text"*)

---

since the formal argument of *adapt* is of type **like** *Current*; this anchored declaration ensures automatic adaptation to the type of a descendant.

← *See 12.15, page 211, on anchored declaration.*

28.9 Class *STRING*

Here is the flat-short version of class *STRING*.

This class inherits from COMPARABLE and HASHABLE. From the former class it effects "<=" etc.; from the latter, it effects the hash function 'hash_code'.

```
-- Character strings.

class interface STRING creation procedures

   make (n: INTEGER)
        -- Allocate space for at least n characters.
      require
      non_negative_size: n >= 0
      ensure
      capacity = n

exported features

   infix "<=" (other: like Current): BOOLEAN
        -- Is current string less than or equal to other?
      ensure
      Result implies not (Current > other)


   infix "<" (other: STRING): BOOLEAN
        -- Is current string lexicographically lower than other?


   infix ">=" (other: like Current): BOOLEAN
        -- Is current string greater than or equal to other?
      ensure
      Result implies not (Current < other)


   infix ">" (other: like Current): BOOLEAN
        -- Is current string greater than other?
      ensure
      Result implies (not (Current <= other))


   adapt (s: STRING): like Current
        -- Object of a type conforming to the type of s,
        -- initialized with attributes from s
```

append (*s*: *STRING*)
    -- Append a copy of *s* at end of current string.
  require
    argument_not_void: *s* /= *Void*
  ensure
    count = **old** *count* + *s*. *count*

capacity: *INTEGER*
    -- Number of characters guaranteed to fit in space
    -- currently allocated for string

clear
    -- Clear out string.
  ensure
    count = *0*

copy (*other*: *STRING*)
    -- Reinitialize with copy of *other*.
  require
    other /= *Void*
  ensure
    count = *other*. *count*;
    -- For all *i*: *1* .. *count*, *item* (*i*) = *other*. *item* (*i*)

count: *INTEGER*
    -- Actual number of characters making up the string
  ensure
    Result >= *0*

empty: *BOOLEAN*
    -- Is string empty?

extend (*c*: *CHARACTER*)
    -- Add *c* at cnd.
  ensure
    count = **old** *count* + *1*

fill_blank
    -- Fill with blanks.
  ensure
    -- For all *i*: *1* .. *capacity*, *item* (*i*) = *Blank*

hash_code: *INTEGER*
    -- Hash code value of current string

head (*n*: *INTEGER*)
    -- Remove all characters except for the first *n*;
    -- do nothing if *n* >= *count*.
  require
    non_negative_argument: *n* >= *0*
  ensure
    -- *count* = min (*n*, **old** *count*)

index_of (*c*: *CHARACTER*; *i*: *INTEGER*): *INTEGER*
    -- Index of the first occurrence of *c*, starting at
    -- position *i*; 0 if not found.
  require
    index_large_enough: *i* >= *1*;
    index_small_enough: *i* <= *count*
  ensure
    Result = *0* **or** *item* (*Result*) = *c*

is_equal (*other*: *STRING*): *BOOLEAN*
    -- Is current string made of same character sequence as *other*?
    -- (Redefined from *ANY*)

item, **infix** *"@"* (*i*: *INTEGER*): *CHARACTER*
    -- Character at position *i*
  require
    index_large_enough: *i* >= *1*;
    index_small_enough: *i* <= *count*

item_code (*i*: *INTEGER*): *INTEGER*
    -- Numeric code of character at position i
  require
    index_large_enough: *i* >= *1*;
    index_small_enough: *i* <= *count*

left_adjust
    -- Remove leading blanks.
  ensure
    (*count* /= *0*) **implies** (*item* (*1*) /= ' ')

out: *STRING*
    -- Printable representation of current string (redefined from *ANY*)

precede (*c*: *CHARACTER*)
    -- Add *c* at front.
  ensure
    count = **old** *count* + *1*

prepend (*s*: *STRING*)
>   -- Prepend a copy of *s* at front of current string.
> **require**
>   *argument_not_void*: *s* /= *Void*
> **ensure**
>   *count* = **old** *count* + *s*.*count*

put (*c*: *CHARACTER*; *i*: *INTEGER*)
>   -- Replace by *c* character at position *i*.
> **require**
>   *index_large_enough*: *i* >= *1*;
>   *index_small_enough*: *i* <= *count*
> **ensure**
>   *item* (*i*) = *c*

remove (*i*: *INTEGER*)
>   -- Remove *i*-th character.
> **require**
>   *index_large_enough*: *i* >= *1*;
>   *index_small_enough*: *i* <= *count*
> **ensure**
>   *count* = **old** *count* − *1*

remove_all_occurrences (*c*: *CHARACTER*)
>   -- Remove all occurrences of *c*.
> **ensure**
>   -- For all *i*: *1* .. *count*, *item* (*i*) /= *c*
>   -- *count* − **old** *count*   number of occurrences of *c* in initial string

resize (*newsize*: *INTEGER*)
>   -- Reallocate if needed to accommodate at least *newsize* characters.
>   -- Do not lose any characters in the existing string.
> **require**
>   *new_size_non_negative*: *newsize* >= *0*
> **ensure**
>   *count* >= *newsize*;
>   *count* >= **old** *count*

right_adjust
>   -- Remove trailing blanks.
> **ensure**
>   *count* /= *0* **implies** *item* (*count*) /= ' '

shrink (*s*: *STRING*, *n1*: *INTEGER*, *n2*: *INTEGER*)
>   -- Reset from *s*, removing characters outside of interval *n1* .. *n2*
> **require**
>   *argument_not_void*: *s* /= *Void*;
>   *meaningful_origin*: *1* <= *n1*;
>   *meaningful_interval*: *n1* <= *n2*;
>   *meaningful_end*: *n2* <= *s*.*count*
> **ensure**
>   *is_equal* (*s*.*substring* (*n1*, *n2*))

substring (*n1*: *INTEGER*, *n2*: *INTEGER*): *STRING*
    -- Copy of substring of current string containing all characters
    -- at indices between *n1* and *n2*.
  require
    meaningful_origin: *1* <= *n1*;
    meaningful_interval: *n1* <= *n2*;
    meaningful_end: *n2* <= *count*
  ensure
    Result.count = *n2* − *n1* + *1*
    -- For all *i*: *1* .. *n2-n1*, *Result.item* (*i*) = *item* (*n1* + *i* − *1*)

tail (*n*: *INTEGER*)
    -- Remove all characters except for the last *n*;
    -- do nothing if *n* >= *count*.
  require
    non_negative_argument: *n* >= *0*
  ensure
    -- *count* = min (*n*, **old** *count*)

to_c: *NONE*
    -- A value which a C function may cast into a pointer to a
    -- C form of the string. Useful only for interfacing with C software.
    -- Caveat: because C uses null characters as end marker for strings,
    -- a null character occurring in an Eiffel string passed to C will
    -- prevent C functions from accessing any character past the null.

to_integer: *INTEGER*
    -- Integer value of current string, assumed to contain digits only.
    -- When applied to *"123"*, will yield *123*
  require
    -- String contains digits only

to_lower
    -- Convert string to lower case.

to_upper
    -- Convert string to upper case.

invariant

  0 <= *count*;
  count <= *capacity*

end interface -- class *STRING*

29

Exception facilities

29.1 Overview

As explained in the discussion of exceptions, it is sometimes useful to control the details of the exception handling mechanism. Applications include:

← *Chapter 15 discussed exceptions.*

- Finding out the nature of the latest exception (such as assertion violation, running out of memory or platform signal) and any other property, such as the Assertion_tag of a violated assertion clause.

← *"Platform" means hardware plus operating system. See 2.10, page 29.*

- Handling certain kinds of exception in a special way.

- Raising special developer-defined exceptions.

- Prescribing that certain exceptions must be ignored at run-time, or must let execution continue after a call to a specified procedure.

All these facilities for fine-tuning the exception mechanism are available through features of class *EXCEPTIONS* from the Kernel Library, which is the subject of this chapter. To use these facilities in a class *C*, it suffices to ensure that *C* is a descendant of *EXCEPTIONS*.

Since the key concepts were introduced in the general discussion of exceptions, the rest of this chapter will simply give the flat-short form of class *EXCEPTIONS*, after a few comments about platform-dependent signal codes.

← *See the explanations in 15.11, page 258.*

29.2 Platform-dependent signal codes

The exception codes introduced in class *EXCEPTIONS*, such as *No_more_memory* or *Precondition*, cover exceptions which will arise in the same manner on every platform.

Some platform-dependent machine signals, however, will also trigger exceptions. Unix systems, for example, may raise signals such as "change of child process status" or "writing on a pipe with no one to read it".

To enable systems to specify platform-specific exception handling when appropriate, Eiffel implementations may include library classes extending the features of *EXCEPTIONS* with platform-specific exception handling features, in particular exception codes. The recommended names for such classes are of the form *platform_EXCEPTIONS*, for example *UNIX_EXCEPTIONS*, *MS_DOS_ EXCEPTIONS* and so on. Classes which need the specific features should have one of these classes, in addition to *EXCEPTIONS*, as one of their ancestors.

No platform-dependent exception class appears in this book.

A system which uses one of these platform-specific classes will of course require some adaptation to be ported to other platforms. If you do need platform-specific exception handling, you should severely restrict the number of classes that inherit from the appropriate *platform_EXCEPTIONS* class, so as to facilitate any eventual porting effort.

29.3 Class *EXCEPTIONS*

Here is the short form of class *EXCEPTIONS*.

-- Facilities for controlling exception handling.

class interface *EXCEPTIONS* **exported features**

assertion_violation: *BOOLEAN*
    -- Was last exception due to a violated assertion or
    -- non-decreasing variant?

catch (*code*: *INTEGER*)
    -- Make sure that any exception of code *code* will be caught.
    -- This is the default. (See *continue, ignore*.)
  ensure
    status (*code*) = *Caught*

Check_instruction: *INTEGER*
    -- Exception code for violated Check

Class_invariant: *INTEGER*
    -- Exception code for violated class invariant

class_name: *STRING*
    -- Name of the class containing the routine which
    -- was the recipient of oldest exception not leading to a Retry.

continue (*code*: *INTEGER*)
    -- Make sure that any exception of code *code* will cause
    -- execution to resume after a call to *continue_action* (*code*).
    -- This is not the default. (See *catch, ignore*.)
  require
    must_be_a_signal: *is_signal* (*code*)
  ensure
    status (*code*) = *Continued*

---

continue_action (*code*: *INTEGER*)
    -- Action to be executed before resuming normal execution for an
    -- exception of code *code*, resulting from a signal,
    -- on which *contine* has been called.
    -- By default, does nothing; redefine it to get specific behavior.
  require
    must_be_continued: *status* (*code*) = *Continued*

developer_exception_name: *STRING*
    -- Name of last developer-raised exception (see *raise*)

exception: *INTEGER*
    -- Code of last exception that occurred

ignore (*code*: *INTEGER*)
    -- Make sure that any exception of code *code* will be ignored.
    -- This is not the default. (See *catch*, *continue*.)
  ensure
    status (*code*) = *Ignored*

Incorrect_inspect_value: *INTEGER*
    -- Exception code for inspect value which is not one of the
    -- inspect constants, if there is no Else part

is_developer_exception (*code*: *INTEGER*): *INTEGER*
    -- Is *code* the code of a developer-defined exception (see *raise*)?

is_assertion_violation (*code*: *INTEGER*): *INTEGER*
    -- Is *code* the code of an exception resulting from the violation
    -- of an assertion (precondition, postcondition, invariant, check)?

is_signal (*code*: *INTEGER*): *BOOLEAN*
    -- Is *code* the code of an exception due to a hardware
    -- or operating system signal?

Loop_invariant: *INTEGER*
    -- Exception code for violated loop invariant

Loop_variant: *INTEGER*
    -- Exception code for non-decreased loop variant

meaning (*code*): *STRING*
    -- Nature of exception of code *code*, expressed in plain English

message_on_failure
    -- Print an Exception History Table in case of failure.
    -- (This is the default; see *no_message_on_failure*.)

no_message_on_failure
    -- Do not print an Exception History Table in case of failure.
    -- (This is not the default; see *message_on_failure*.)

No_more_memory: *INTEGER*
    -- Exception code for failed memory allocation

original_exception: *INTEGER*
-- Code of oldest exception not leading to a Retry

Postcondition: *INTEGER*
-- Exception code for violated postcondition

Precondition: *INTEGER*
-- Exception code for violated precondition

raise (*code*: *INTEGER*; *name*: *STRING*)
-- Raise a developer exception of code *code* and name *name*.
require
negative_code: *code < 0*

reset_all_default
-- Make sure that all exceptions will lead to their default handling.

reset_default (*code*: *INTEGER*)
-- Make sure that exception of code *code* will lead
-- to its default action.

Routine_failure: *INTEGER*
-- Exception code for failed routine

routine_name: *STRING*
-- Name of routine that was recipient of oldest exception
-- not leading to a Retry

status (*code*: *INTEGER*): *INTEGER*
-- Status currently set for exception of code *code* (default: *Caught*)
ensure
Result = Caught **or** *Result = Continued* **or** *Result = Ignored*

Caught, Continued, Ignored: *INTEGER* **is unique**
-- Possible status for exception codes

tag_name: *STRING*
-- Tag of last violated assertion clause

Void_assigned_to_expanded: *INTEGER*
-- Exception code for assignment of void value to expanded entity

Void_call_target: *INTEGER*
-- Exception code for feature called on void reference

void_call_feature: *STRING*
-- Name of feature that was called on a void reference

end interface -- class *EXCEPTIONS*

30

Persistence and environments

30.1 Overview

When you execute a system which creates objects, you will sometimes find it necessary to keep some of these objects in secondary storage for later retrieval by the same or another session.

Mechanisms permitting this belong to the libraries and supporting environment rather than to the language. The issue is sufficiently important, however, to justify a presentation in this book. The solutions presented below are not the only possible ones, but they have proved useful in practice.

The material presented in this chapter is not part of the specification of Eiffel.

30.2 Classes for persistence

The relevant facilities come from two classes of the Support Library: *STORABLE* and *ENVIRONMENT*.

On the Support Library see "Eiffel: The Libraries" (reference in appendix C).

STORABLE covers the more elementary situations. It suffices when all that is needed is to store away an entire object structure, starting at a certain object attached to x. Then an instruction such as

> $x.store\_by\_name$ *("some_file")*

will produce and write onto the file of name *some_file* an external form of the entire object structure starting at the object attached to x. Later, a system may retrieve the structure by executing

> *retrieve_by_name ("some_file")*

The facilities provided by *ENVIRONMENT* are more elaborate. An instance of this class is a set of objects. If you open an environment, all objects created thereafter belong to that environment, and you may give them keys for individual identification. You can then store an external representation of the environment in a file through a *store* operation, or request that the environment be stored automatically on session termination. The environment can later be retrieved, and its identified objects accessed individually through their keys.

ENVIRONMENT also introduces features for querying the current state of the execution, for example to count the number of instances of a certain type.

This chapter presents classes *STORABLE* and *ENVIRONMENT*.

30.3 Objects and their dependents

Whether you use *STORABLE* or *ENVIRONMENT*, persistence raises an important practical issue: when an object is stored, what happens to the references it contains?

In a class *C* any attribute declared of a reference type, such as

> *attrib*: *SOME_REFERENCE_TYPE*

represents a field which, in any run-time instance of *C*, contains a reference to an instance of *SOME_REFERENCE_TYPE* (or a void reference).

Such references may give an object direct and indirect **dependents**. On the above figure, for example, the object marked OX has one direct dependent, OD; the whole set of its dependents, direct or indirect, includes OX itself, OD, OE1 and OE2.

Direct and indirect dependents

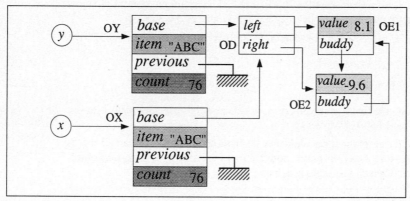

← This is derived from the figure illustrating object copying on page 296.

More generally:

> The **direct dependents** of an object *O*, at some time during the execution of a system, are the objects attached to the reference fields of *O*. The **dependents** of an object are the object itself and (recursively) the dependents of its direct dependents.

Whenever an object is stored by one of the operations described in this chapter, its reference fields would become meaningless for later retrieval unless the operation also stores the dependents of the object, direct or indirect. This imposes a universal rule on the routines of both *STORABLE* and *ENVIRONMENT*:

Persistence Completeness rule

Whenever a routine of class *STORABLE* or *ENVIRONMENT* stores an object into an external file, it stores with it the dependents of that object. Whenever one of the associated retrieval routines retrieves a previously stored object, it also retrieves all its dependents.

In other words, whenever you make a certain object persistent, you implicitly make all of its dependents persistent as well.

The persistence facilities properly handle shared references (references to the same object from several sources) and cyclic dependencies (direct or indirect dependencies from an object to itself).

30.4 Retrieval, typing, and the assignment attempt

How do persistence facilities combine with static type checking?

During the execution of a given system, every object of interest is accessible through one or more entities such as class attributes and routine arguments. Since the language is typed, the type of any such entity is known in the corresponding class texts from the entity's declaration; it indicates the type of the attached objects, or at least an ancestor of this type, which may be viewed as an approximation of it.   *← Typing was discussed in chapter 22.*

These compulsory declarations, combined with the type rules for polymorphic assignment and feature application, make it possible to guarantee that no operation will be attempted on an object unless it is indeed applicable to all objects of the corresponding type.

When objects are stored away in persistent memory, however, they lose their connection with the text of the software system that created them. If the objects are later retrieved during a session of the same or another system, their internal format is no longer guaranteed to match the declared types of the entities attached to them in the new system.

The problem arises when it comes to declaring a type for library features returning objects from persistent storage: attribute *retrieved* in *STORABLE*, a reference to the retrieved structure, and function *item* in class *ENVIRONMENT*, accessing an object of an environment through its key.

These are features of general-purpose library classes and must be applicable to access retrieved objects of any type. The obvious question is then: under what types should these features be declared in classes *STORABLE* and *ENVIRONMENT*?

The only possible answer is the least committing one: because these two classes must be universally applicable, *item* and *retrieved* can only yield a result of type *ANY* – the most general type, to which all types conform.

If we stopped here, no useful operation would be possible on the retrieved objects, since class ANY only provides general-purpose operations applicable to all types − such as copy, clone, equality comparison or output in a default format. But when you store objects of a given type − for example instances of a class *BANK_ACCOUNT* − it is because you expect that at retrieval time you will use them according to this type, applying the corresponding features − such as *deposit, withdraw* or *balance*. The features of *ANY would never suffice*.

← *On ANY see 6.12, page 85, and chapter 27.*

Yet you will still want the benefits of type checking: if for some reason a retrieved object is not an instance of *BANK_ACCOUNT*, you cannot accept it blindly and start applying *BANK_ACCOUNT* features to it, with all the possible consequent damages.

The solution, as you will undoubtedly have guessed, is provided by the **Assignment_attempt** instruction. Assume that *her_account* is an entity of type *ACCOUNT*. Then if *retrieved_object* is an expression of type *ANY*, built from features of *STORABLE* or *ENVIRONMENT* and denoting an object retrieved from persistent storage, the instruction

← Assignment_ attempt *was introduced in chapter 20.*

> *her_account ?= retrieved_object*

makes *her_account* void if *retrieved_object* is void, or attached to an object of a type which does not conform to *her_account*'s declared type, *ACCOUNT*; otherwise, that is to say if the instruction's source *retrieved_object* is attached to an object of the expected type, the instruction also attaches the target *her_account* to the same object.

Here is a more complete form of the example, showing a typical scheme for retrieving persistent objects in a type-safe way.

```
old_accounts: HASH_TABLE [BANK_ACCOUNT, STRING];
her_account: BANK_ACCOUNT;
...
retrieve_by_name ("Old_account_file");
old_accounts ?= retrieved;
if old_accounts = Void then
   -- File Old_account_file doesn't contain what we thought it did!
   ...
else
       -- Deal normally with the hash-table old_accounts:
   her_account := old_accounts.item ("Sarah")
       -- Here item is the search function for hash tables.
   ...
end
```

The use of Assignment_attempt achieves the combination of flexibility and safety required to support persistent objects in a statically typed context.

30.5 Storing and retrieving an entire structure

The features of class *STORABLE* make it possible to store an object structure consisting of an object and all its dependents, and retrieve it later.

There are two storing procedures, called under the form

> *x. store_by_name* ("*file_name*")
> *x. store_by_file* (*file_object*)

The first expects a file specified by its name (a string), and the second expects an instance of the Support Library class *FILE*.

See "Eiffel: The Libraries" about FILE.

In all cases, the base class of the type of *x* must be a descendant of class *STORABLE* for these operations to be applicable to *x*. Only *x* must satisfy this constraint: there is no particular requirement on the types of the dependents of the object attached to *x*.

Alternatively, the client relation could be used: if st is of type STORABLE and has been created, then the forms st. x. store_by_name etc. will work.

Retrieval is provided by two procedures corresponding to the two conventions for referring to files:

> *retrieve_by_name* ("*file_name*")
> *retrieve_by_file* (*file_object*)

In accordance with the methodological advice against functions with side effects, these features are procedures, not functions; they retrieve a structure and make it available through an attribute

See "Object-Oriented Software Construction".

> *retrieved*: **like** *Current*
> -- Last object retrieved by one of the retrieval procedures.

30.6 Class *STORABLE*

The precise specification of *STORABLE*'s exported features, as given by the flat-short form of the class, follows.

> -- Facilities for storing and retrieving object structures
> -- in binary format Classes needing these facilities
> -- should inherit from this class.
>
> **class interface** *STORABLE* **exported features**
>
>   *retrieve_by_file* (*f: FILE*)
>   -- Retrieve an object structure from external
>   -- representation previously stored in file *f*.
>   **require**
>   *good_file*: *f* /= *Void* **and then** *f. exists*

```
retrieve_by_name (filename: STRING)
    -- Retrieve an object structure from external representation
    -- previously stored in file of name filename.
require
    file_name_not_void: filename /= Void


retrieved: like Current
    -- Last object retrieved by one of the retrieval procedures


storable_error: BOOLEAN


store_by_file (f: FILE)
    -- Produce an external representation of the entire
    -- object structure reachable from current object.
    -- Write this representation onto file f.
require
    good_file: f /= Void and then f.exists


store_by_name (filename: STRING)
    -- Produce an external representation of the entire
    -- object structure reachable from current object.
    -- Write this representation onto file of name
    -- filename.
require
    filename_not_void: filename /= Void

end interface -- class STORABLE
```

30.7 Environments

When the aim is simply to store away a snapshot of the current object structure, or part of it, the facilities of *STORABLE* are sufficient. Environments provide a more flexible and selective approach, with a number of concrete advantages:

- The objects belonging to a stored environment may be individually identified by keys. You may then retrieve them selectively through these keys. (In contrast, the procedures of *STORABLE* produce external structures where only one object, the root, is known individually.)

- An environment may be stored not just through an explicit call to a *store* procedure, but also automatically on session termination, if you request it.

- Environments are normal objects and may be manipulated as such. There is no need to inherit from a special class such as *STORABLE*.

- Environments also provide useful information on the objects of a session, independently from applications to persistence. For example it is possible to query an environment about the number of objects it contains, or the number of objects of a certain type.

You may access an environment through an entity of type *ENVIRONMENT*. For example:

```
env: ENVIRONMENT
```

To create an environment, use the single creation procedure of the class, *make*, which takes no argument:

```
!! env.make
```

An environment − instance of class *ENVIRONMENT* − simply represents a set of objects. It is always complete under dependency: in other words, if an object belongs to an environment, all of its dependents, direct or indirect, also belong to the environment.

The various operations on environments, described below, may produce error conditions if the conditions for their application are not met. Class *ENVIRONMENT* contains an integer attribute *error* which every operation sets to the value *No_error* (if all went well) or to one of the error codes described below. The boolean function *ok* has the same result as

```
error = No_error
```

30.8 Opening and closing environments

Once an environment has been created, you may open it. This means that all objects created from then on (until the environment is closed, or another is opened) will belong to this environment; so will all of their dependents, direct or indirect.

Only one environment may be open at a time; opening an environment closes the previously opened one, if any.

To open or close an environment *env*, use

```
env.open
env.close
```

30.9 Recording and accessing objects in an environment

You may identify objects individually in an environment through keys. The keys determine what objects will be stored along with the environment, and make it possible to retrieve stored objects individually.

Because the keys are kept along with the objects when the environment is stored, they must be of a type available to all systems. For this reason, keys are restricted to being character strings.

To associate key *"KEY1"* with the object attached to *x* in an environment *env*, use procedure *put*, as in

```
x: SOME_TYPE;
...
!! x ... (...);
...
env.put (x, "KEY1")
```

The first formal argument of procedure *put* is declared of type *ANY*, so that any type will be acceptable for *x*.

DEFINITION:
Recorded,
In Use After the successful execution of such a call, the object is said to be **recorded** under the given key in the given environment, and the key is said to be **in use** for that environment.

A key may be used for only one object in an environment; if you call *put* with a key that is already in use, the existing object recordings will not be changed and *error* will be set to *Conflict*. To force the new recording (and dissociate the key from any previous object recorded under it), use procedure *force* instead of *put*.

To obtain the object recorded under a certain key, use the function *item*, which returns a result of type *ANY*. As discussed above, you will need an Assignment_attempt to access the objects under their true type, as in

```
x: SOME_TYPE;
...
x ?= env.item ("KEY1");

if x = Void then
    ... The object recorded under "KEY1" is not of the expected type
    ... SOME_TYPE (or the key is not used in the environment)

else
    check x /= Void end;
    ... Here the algorithm may deal with x normally
end
```

To determine whether a key is in use in an environment, call the boolean-valued function *has*, as in

```
key_used := env.has ("KEY1")
```

To change the key under which an object is recorded, use procedure *change_key*, as in

```
env.change_key ("old_key", "new_key")
```

If *"old_key"* was not in use, then *error* will be set to *Not_found*.

30.10 The objects of an environment

The preceding discussion yields the definitions of what objects *belong to* an environment, and which ones among these are *persistent*.

One of the main uses of recording objects is indeed to make them persistent in the following sense:

<table>
<tr>
<td>DEFINITION:
Persistent
Object</td>
<td>The persistent objects of an environment are all the objects recorded under some key in the environment, and their dependents.</td>
</tr>
</table>

As the name indicates, the objects defined as persistent will be kept by the storing procedures seen in the next section. But the persistent objects of an environment are not the only ones that belong to it. More generally:

<table>
<tr>
<td>DEFINITION:
Belonging
to an
Environment</td>
<td>The objects belonging to an environment env are defined as follows.
1 • Any persistent object of env belongs to env.
2 • Any object created while env is open belongs to env.
3 • Any dependent of an object belonging to env belongs to env.
4 • No object belongs to env other than through rules 1, 2 and 3.</td>
</tr>
</table>

30.11 Requesting information about environments

Function *count* of class *ENVIRONMENT* makes it possible to query an environment about the objects that belong to it, making environments useful even without any application to the storage and retrieval of persistent objects. Function *persistent_count* has the same specification as *count* except that it only takes into account an environment's persistent object.

A call to *count* will yield the number of instances of a certain type belonging to an environment. For example,

> *employee_count* := *env. count (some_employee)*

will assign to *employee_count* (assumed to be an integer Writable) the number of objects which belong to *env* and conform to the type of the object attached to *some_employee* (or 0 if *some_employee* is void).

The argument of *count* is an expression (here the entity *some_employee*) whose value is used only for the type of the attached object. So if you want the number of instances of the non-generic class *EMPLOYEE* in *env* you can use the above instruction preceded by

> *some_employee*: *EMPLOYEE*;
> ...
> !! *some_employee*

Recall that **instances** of a reference type include not just direct instances but also instances of any conforming type. So the above will count not just the direct instances of *EMPLOYEE* but also those of any descendants.

As a consequence, you may use *count* to find out about the total number of objects in an environment: just use as argument a direct instance of ANY.

← *See chapter 17 on instances and direct instances.*

Function *count* does not count sub-objects, only "outermost" objects. For example *count* applied to the figure which served to illustrate the notion of sub-object will take only two objects into consideration (O1 and O2).

← *See the figure page 274, belonging to the discussion of complex objects and their sub-objects in 17.7.*

30.12 Storing environments

You may store the persistent objects of an environment into a file, and retrieve the objects of a previously stored environment.

For both storage and retrieval, a file must have been associated with the environment; it will be used as target for storage, and as source for retrieval.

Use procedure *set_file* to associate a file with an environment. For example:

> *env*.*set_file* (*f*)

Here *f* must be attached to an instance of class *FILE* from the Kernel Library. There must be a file associated with *f*, and it must have been opened in the appropriate read or write mode.

→ *Class FILE is described in "Eiffel: The Libraries".*

To store the persistent objects of an environment into the file that has been associated with it, you may use a call of the form:

> *env*.*store*

This is an **explicit** store operation. It is also possible to prescribe an **automatic** store. By executing one or both of the calls

> *env*.*store_on_end*
> *env*.*store_on_failure*

you ensure that session termination (normal termination in the first case, abnormal termination in the second) will automatically result in all the environment's objects being stored in the associated file.

This is a way to guarantee that all the objects of a session, or a selection of these objects (as captured by an environment) will be available for the next session.

In some cases, you may want to use different files for normal and abnormal termination. Only one file may be associated with a given environment at any given time (as the result of the last call to *set_file*). But you may have two environments sharing the same objects. If both *env1* and *env2* are created environments, executing the call

> *env1*.*share* (*env2*)

The effect of env2.share (env1) is identical.

ensures that *env1* and *env2* will contain exactly the same objects under the same keys. The other properties of these environments, such as the associated files, remain separate, so that you may obtain the effect of different normal and abnormal external storage as follows:

```
normal_env, failure_env: ENVIRONMENT;
...
!! normal_env.make; !! failure_env.make;
failure_env.share (normal_env);
normal_env.set_file (normal_file);
failure_env.set_file (failure_file);
normal_env.store_on_end;
failure_env.store_on_failure;
...
normal_env.open;
...
    -- Both environments will contain the same persistent objects.
    -- On normal termination, these objects will be stored in normal_file;
    -- On abnormal termination, they will be stored in failure_file.
```

30.13 Retrieving an environment

To make the persistent objects of a previously stored environment accessible in the same or another session, use procedure *retrieve*. For example:

```
    env.retrieve
```

This will load the recorded objects from the file associated with *env*. If this operation does not succeed, *error* will be set to *Not_retrieved*.

Function *item* is then available to retrieve individual objects from the environment, using the keys under which they were recorded. The method was shown above.

← *See page 462 on how to use 'item' to access retrieved objects.*

30.14 An environment example

The following example shows a typical use of environments. *C1* and *C2* are arbitrary reference types.

A first session creates a number of objects and records some of them under some keys, ensuring that they will persist with the environment.

```
env: ENVIRONMENT;
a: C1;
b: C2;
ext_file: FILE;

    -- Create an environment
!! env.make;

    -- Create a file to be associated with the environment
!! ext_file.make ("SESSION1");
```

```
    ext_file.open_write;

        -- Associate file with environment
    env.set_file (ext_file);

        -- Request that environment be automatically stored
        -- on normal termination.
    env.store_on_end;

        -- Request that environment be automatically stored
        -- on abnormal termination.
    env.store_on_failure;

    ...

        -- Make the objects associated with a and b,
        -- as well as any of their dependents,
        -- persistent in env, with appropriate keys.
    env.put (a, "a_key");
    env.put (b, "b_key");

        -- The following instructions may of course modify
        -- the objects associated with a, b and
        -- their dependents
    ...
    ... The environment may be stored explicitly through
    ...      env.store
    ... If not, it will be stored automatically on session termination.
```

The same session (if an explicit *store* has been executed) or another (executed any time later) may now retrieve the stored objects:

```
    env: ENVIRONMENT;
    a: C1;
    b: C2;
    ext_file: FILE;

    !! env.make;

    !! ext_file.make ("SESSION1");
    ext_file.open_read;
    env.set_file (ext_file);

        -- Load the previously stored environment.
    env.retrieve;

        -- Individual objects may now be accessed through their keys.
        -- Their dependents, if any, have also been loaded.
    a ?= env.item ("a_key");
    b ?= env.item ("b_key")

    ...
```

30.15 Class *ENVIRONMENT*

The precise specification of *ENVIRONMENT*'s exported features, as given by the flat-short form of the class, follows.

---

class interface *ENVIRONMENT* **creation procedures**

make
    -- Create a new environment.

exported features

change_key (*old_key, new_key*: STRING)
    -- Record under *new_key* the object previously
    -- recorded under *old_key*; if no such object, set
    -- *error* to *Not_found*.
  require
    keys_not_void: *old_key* /= *Void* **and** *new_key* /= *Void*
  ensure
    ok **or** (*error* = *Not_found*) **or** (*error* = *conflict*)

close
    -- Make current environment be no longer active; if
    -- it was.
  ensure
    closed: **not** *is_open*

Conflict: *INTEGER* **is unique**

count (*obj*: ANY): INTEGER
    -- Number of objects in the environment whose type conforms
    -- to the type of the object attached to *obj*.
    -- 0 if the value of *obj* is void.

current_keys: ARRAY [STRING]
    -- Array of keys in use, starting from 1

error: INTEGER
    -- Code of last error produced by a routine of the class

force (*obj*: ANY; *key*: STRING)
    -- Record *obj* under *key* in this environment:
    -- Make *obj* and its dependents persistent.
    -- If *key* is already in use, lose the previous association.
  require
    key_not_void: *key* /= *Void*
  ensure
    error = *no_error*

has (*key*: *STRING*): *BOOLEAN*
    -- Is *key* in use?
  require
    key_not_void: *key* /= *Void*

is_open: *BOOLEAN*
    -- Is current environment open?

item (*key*: *STRING*): *ANY*
    -- Object recorded under *key*.
    -- If no such key, void value and *error* set to *Not_found*.
  require
    key_not_void: *key* /= *Void*
  ensure
    (*Result* = *Void*) **implies** (**not** *has* (*key*))

No_error: *INTEGER* **is unique**

no_store_on_end
    -- Disable automatic storage on normal termination.
    -- This is the default.

no_store_on_failure
    -- Disable automatic storage on abnormal termination.
    -- This is the default.

Not_found: *INTEGER* **is unique**

Not_retrieved: *INTEGER* **is unique**

Not_stored: *INTEGER* **is unique**

ok: *BOOLEAN*
    -- Did last retrieve, store, put or remove operation succeed?
  ensure
    Result = (*error* = *no_error*)

open
    -- Close previous environment if any, and make current
    -- environment the active one:
    -- all objects created from now on, until next call to *open* or *close*,
    -- will belong with their dependents to this environment.
  ensure
    open: *is_open*

persistent_count (*t*: *STRING*): *INTEGER*
    -- Number of persistent objects in the environment whose type conforms
    -- to the type of the object attached to *obj*.
    -- 0 if the value of *obj* is void.

put (*obj*: *ANY*; *key*: *STRING*)
    -- Record *obj* under *key* in this environment:
    -- Make *obj* and its dependents persistent.
    -- If *key* is already in use, set *error* to *Conflict*.
  require
    key_not_void: *key* /= *Void*
  ensure
    ok **or** (*error* = *conflict*)

remove (*key*: *STRING*)
    -- Dissociate *key* from object recorded under.
    -- If no such object, set *error* to *Not_found*.
  require
    key_not_void: *key* /= *Void*
  ensure
    ok **or** (*error* = *Not_found*)

retrieve
    -- Load the environment's persistent objects
    -- from the associated external file.
  ensure
    ok **or** (*error* = *Not_retrieved*)

set_file (*f*: *FILE*)
    -- Make *f* the file where environment will be stored
    -- if requested explicitly or implicitly.
  require
    file_created: *f* /= *Void*;

share (*other*: **like** *Current*)
    -- Make Current and *other* share the same persistent objects.

store
    -- Store the environment's persistent objects
    -- into the associated external file.
  ensure
    ok **or** (*error* = *Not_stored*)

store_on_end
    -- Enable automatic storage on normal termination.
    -- This is not the default.

store_on_failure
    -- Enable automatic storage on abnormal termination.
    -- This is not the default.

end interface -- class *ENVIRONMENT*

31

Input and output

31.1 Overview

Class *STANDARD_FILES* from the Kernel Library offers a set of simple but useful input and output facilities.

Another class, *FILE*, provides much more extensive file handling operations, and the original implementation of *STANDARD_FILES* relied on *FILE*. By its very nature, however, *FILE* depends on the operating system, and its original version is closely patterned after Unix file handling mechanisms. For this reason, no further description of *FILE* appears in this book; "Eiffel: The Libraries" presents *FILE* in detail.

See the bibliography of appendix C for the exact reference to "Eiffel: The Libraries".

This chapter explains how to perform simple input and output using the facilities of *ANY* and *STANDARD_FILES*.

31.2 Purpose of the class

If all you need is to print a value using the standard output format, you will not even need *STANDARD_FILES*: procedure *print* from class *ANY*, automatically present in every class, provides this facility. For example:

← *See 27.2, page 432, about 'print' and 'out'.*

```
print ("Today's temperature is");
print (temperature);
print ('%N')
```

← *%N is the new-line character. See 25.15, starting on page 422, particularly the table of special characters on page 423.*

A call *print (x)* outputs on the standard output file the value of *out (x)*, where function *out* yields a printable version of any object. You may redefine this function in a class to yield a specific form of output.

Class *STANDARD_FILES* provides some further output mechanisms, still elementary but more varied, as well as basic input features.

The most common way to use the facilities of *STANDARD_FILES* is through feature *io*, present in class *ANY* and hence in all developer-defined classes (unless you remove it explicitly). Feature *io* is a once function of type *STANDARD_FILES*. Any class may perform simple input and output by calling *STANDARD_FILES* features on *io*, as in the following variant of the above extract:

← *See chapter 27 on ANY*;
27.2 presented 'io'.

> *io.putstring* ("Today's temperature is");
> *io.putstring* (*out* (*temperature*));
> *io.new_line*

Among the features of *STANDARD_FILES* are output procedures such as *putstring, putint* and *putreal*, which apply to the standard output, and input features such as *readint* and *lastint*, used according to the conventions explained in the next section and applying to the standard input.

The class also offers features *input, output* and *error*, all of type *FILE*, giving access to the standard input, standard output and standard error files. These features are implemented as "once" functions; the first call to any of them opens the corresponding files.

Because of the presence of feature *io* in class *ANY*, any class *C* is a direct client of *STANDARD_FILES*. You may prefer to avoid dot notation for calls to input or output features, as in *io.some_feature*, by making *C* an heir to *STANDARD_FILES*; this enables you to write such calls as just *some_feature*. The notational advantage is slim, however, and any attribute of *STANDARD_FILES* will yield an extra field in instances of *C*.

31.3 Input techniques

The input features of *STANDARD_FILES* observe an important style guideline of the Eiffel method: avoiding functions with side effects. This means that to read an input element you must usually execute two calls:

See "Object-Oriented Software Construction" on side effects in functions.

- A procedure call, such as *io.readint* or *io.readdouble*, to advance the input cursor past the element.

- A call to a function or attribute, as in *n := io.lastint* or *n := io.lastdouble*, to return the value of the element read, with a result of the appropriate type (*INTEGER* and *DOUBLE* in the examples).

The most obvious implementation of STANDARD_FILES uses attributes rather than functions for 'lastint' and its acolytes ('lastreal', 'lastdouble', 'laststring', 'lastchar').

Successive calls to a feature such as *io.lastint* or *io.lastdouble* will yield the same value if they are not separated by calls to cursor-advancing procedures.

To use procedures such as *readint* and *readdouble*, you must know in advance the types of the input elements to be read. In some cases, of course, you do not have this information. Other mechanisms are available for reading elements and determining their types on the fly; they are not part of the Kernel Library, however, but are provided by the lexical analysis classes of the Lexical Library.

See "Eiffel: The Libraries" about the Lexical Library.

31.4 Class *STANDARD_FILES*

Here is the flat-short form of *STANDARD_FILES*.

-- Standard input and output.

class interface *STANDARD_FILES* **exported features**

   error: *FILE*
      -- Standard error file

   input: *FILE*
      -- Standard input file

   lastchar: *CHARACTER*
      -- Last character read by *readchar*

   lastdouble: *DOUBLE*
      -- Last character read by *readdouble*

   lastint: *INTEGER*
      -- Last integer read by *readint*

   lastreal: *REAL*
      -- Last real read by *readreal*

   laststring: *STRING*
      -- Last string read by *readstring*

   new_line
      -- Write line feed at end of default output.

   next_line
      -- Move to next input line on standard input.

   output: *FILE*
      -- Standard output file

   putbool (*b*: *BOOLEAN*)
      -- Write *b* at end of default output.

   putchar (*c*: *CHARACTER*)
      -- Write *c* at end of default output.

   putdouble (*d*: *DOUBLE*)
      -- Write *d* at end of default output.

   putint (*i*: *INTEGER*)
      -- Write *i* at end of default output.

---

putreal (*r*: *REAL*)
-- Write *r* at end of default output.

putstring (*s*: *STRING*)
-- Write *s* at end of default output.

readchar
-- Read a new character from standard input.

readdouble
-- Read a new double from standard input.

readint
-- Read a new integer from standard input.

readline
-- Read a line from standard input.

readreal
-- Read a new real from standard input.

readstream (*nb_char*: *INTEGER*)
-- Read a string of at most *nb_char* bound
-- characters from standard input.

readword
-- Read a new word from standard input.

set_error_default
-- Use standard error as default output.

set_output_default
-- Use standard output as default output.

end interface -- class *STANDARD_FILES*

32

Basic classes

32.1 Overview

The term "basic types" covers a few class types describing atomic values: booleans, characters, integers, reals, feature addresses. The corresponding basic classes (*BOOLEAN*, *CHARACTER*, *INTEGER*, *REAL*, *DOUBLE*, *POINTER*) are part of the Kernel Library. Their names are reserved words; this means that language processing tools will know them, and may for efficiency handle the corresponding values and operations in a special way.

This chapter gives the flat-short form of the basic classes. Do not expect any staggering revelation; this is mostly reference material, useful if you need to check the exact form in which a certain operation is available on a certain type of arithmetic, character or boolean value.

INTEGER, *REAL* and *DOUBLE* inherit most of their features in deferred form from two Kernel Library classes: *COMPARABLE*, introducing comparison operations such as "less than" and "greater than or equal", and *NUMERIC*, introducing arithmetic operations such as addition and multiplication. *CHARACTER* is also an heir of *COMPARABLE*. To avoid unnecessary repetition, the presentation begins with *COMPARABLE* and *NUMERIC*, and in later classes includes backward references to these classes rather than reproducing the corresponding feature specifications.

POINTER has no exported feature. Values of this type (written *$ feature_name*) are only useful as arguments to be eventually passed to external routines; so this chapter does not need to discuss *POINTER* any further.

← On arguments of the '$' form and the use of POINTER, see 24.6, page 404.

32.2 Class *COMPARABLE*

Here first is the flat-short form of class *COMPARABLE*, which describes objects belonging to a type equipped which a total order relation. You may use this class as ancestor to classes other than the basic ones described below; for example, a class *TENNIS_PLAYER* could inherit from *COMPARABLE* if it has the appropriate effectings for "<" and other features, describing a total order relation (player ranking) among instances of the class.

COMPARABLE is an heir to PART_COMPARABLE, covering possibly partial order relations.

-- Objects which may be compared for a total order relation

deferred class interface *COMPARABLE* **exported features**

    infix *"<"* (*other*: **like** *Current*): *BOOLEAN*
        -- Is current object less than *other*?
      deferred ·

    infix *"<="* (*other*: **like** *Current*): *BOOLEAN*
        -- Is current object less than or equal to *other*?

    infix *">"* (*other*: **like** *Current*): *BOOLEAN*
        -- Is current object greater than *other*?

    infix *">="* (*other*: **like** *Current*): *BOOLEAN*
        -- Is current object greater than or equal to *other*?

end interface -- class *COMPARABLE*

32.3 Class *NUMERIC*

NUMERIC describes objects amenable to ordinary arithmetic operations. As with *COMPARABLE*, you may use this class as ancestor to many possible classes; for example, a class *SQUARE_MATRIX* could inherit from *NUMERIC* if it has the appropriate feature effectings.

-- Objects amenable to basic arithmetic operations

deferred class interface *NUMERIC* **exported features**

    infix *"+"* (*other*: *NUMERIC*): *NUMERIC*
        -- Sum of current object and *other*
      deferred

    infix *"−"* (*other*: *NUMERIC*): *NUMERIC*
        -- Difference between current object and *other*
      deferred

    infix *"∗"* (*other*: *NUMERIC*): *NUMERIC*
        -- Product of current object by *other*
      deferred

    infix *"/"* (*other*: *NUMERIC*): *NUMERIC*
        -- Division of current object by *other*
      deferred

    prefix *"+"*: *NUMERIC*
        -- Unary addition applied to current object
      deferred

    prefix *"−"*: *NUMERIC*
        -- Unary subtraction applied to current object
      deferred

end interface -- class *NUMERIC*

The formal arguments and results of the routines of class *NUMERIC* are all of type *NUMERIC*. To ensure the validity of arithmetic operations, the class texts for *INTEGER, REAL* and *DOUBLE* (not shown below for brevity) redeclare the arguments and results to be of types *INTEGER, REAL* and *DOUBLE* respectively. *INTEGER* redeclares all the types to *INTEGER*.

In spite of these redeclarations, you may use the traditional forms of mixed-type arithmetic; for example you may add an integer to a real number. Such combinations derive from a purely syntactic convention introduced in the study of expressions: the Arithmetic Expression Balancing rule. The rule explicitly allows an expression such as *3 + 4.5*, and prescribes interpreting it as *3. + 4.5*, all operands being converted to the heavier type, *REAL*.

← *The Balancing rule is in 23.10, page 384. That section also defined the notion of heavier type: REAL is heavier than INTEGER and DOUBLE is heavier than REAL.*

32.4 Non-expanded forms

The five arithmetic basic classes, given below in flat-short form, are expanded. Each inherits from a non-expanded class which has the same interface except for the expansion status. For example, the text of *INTEGER* is just

> **expanded class** *INTEGER* **inherit** *INTEGER_REF* **end**

The four other arithmetic classes are similarly defined in terms of *BOOLEAN_REF, CHARACTER_REF, INTEGER_REF, REAL_REF, DOUBLE_REF*. The non-expanded classes all have a feature *item* yielding the corresponding expanded value: *item* is of type *BOOLEAN* in *BOOLEAN_REF*, *INTEGER* in *INTEGER_REF* and so on.

To change the *item* value of an instance of a _*REF* type, just use assignment, as in

> *x*: *INTEGER_REF*;
> ...
> *x* := *3*

The last instruction, an assignment, results in cloning (case [3] of the semantics of reattachment: expanded source, reference target): it creates a new *INTEGER* object and assigns to *x* a reference to that object. As a result, *x.item* will have value *3*. The instruction would also work for *x* of a reference type such as *NUMERIC* or *ANY* based on an ancestor of *INTEGER_REF*.

← *"Case [3]" refers to the table of reattachment semantics, page 317.*

Why do we need the _*REF* classes? They make it possible to recover basic values which have been kept as objects accessible through references. For example, if *a* is of type *ARRAY [ANY]* or *ARRAY [NUMERIC]*, it is valid to assign a real value to its *i*-th element using the call

> *a. put (3.14592, i)*

According to the semantics of assignment, this will actually assign to element *i* a reference to an object containing the real value. If you want to access element *j*, find out if it is a real number, and if so apply to it a procedure *real_op* which expects a *REAL* argument, you may do so using an Assignment_attempt:

> *rr*: *REAL_REF*;
> ...
> *rr* ?= *a.item* (*j*);
> **if** *rr* /= *Void* **then** *real_op* (*rr.item*) **else** ... **end**

This example satisfies all conformance constraints. It would not be possible with *rr* of type *REAL*, since the constraint on Assignment_attempt requires the target to be of a reference type, and *REAL* is expanded.

← The relevant conformance rule is in 13.5, page 220.

With this scheme, you can write a routine taking as argument an array (or other data structure) which may contain both references and basic values. An example is a formated output routine which will accept calls of the form

← 8.4, page 110, explained how a routine such as 'formated_write' may use as here a Manifest_array argument to deal with a variable number of values.

> *formated_write* (<< *x, 25, −32.1, "A_STRING", 'A'* >>, *format*)

where *x* is of a reference type; the technique sketched above enables the body of *print* to discriminate between various types of arguments.

32.5 Class *BOOLEAN*

Here is the flat-short form of class *BOOLEAN*, covering truth values. Two constants, written as the keywords **true** and **false**, serve to denote these values.

> -- Boolean values
> **expanded class interface** *BOOLEAN* **exported features**
> > **infix** *"and"* (*other*: *BOOLEAN*): *BOOLEAN*
> > -- Boolean conjunction of current boolean and *other*
> >
> > **infix** *"and then"* (*other*: *BOOLEAN*): *BOOLEAN*
> > -- Boolean semi-strict conjunction of current boolean and *other*
> >
> > **infix** *"implies"* (*other*: *BOOLEAN*): *BOOLEAN*
> > -- Boolean semi-strict implication of current boolean and *other*
> >
> > **prefix** *"not"*: *BOOLEAN*
> > -- Negation of current boolean
> >
> > **infix** *"or"* (*other*: *BOOLEAN*): *BOOLEAN*
> > -- Boolean disjunction of current boolean and *other*
> >
> > **infix** *"or else"* (*other*: *BOOLEAN*): *BOOLEAN*
> > -- Boolean semi-strict disjunction of current boolean and *other*
> >
> > **infix** *"xor"* (*other*: *BOOLEAN*): *BOOLEAN*
> > -- Boolean exclusive or of current boolean and *other*
> **end interface** -- class *BOOLEAN*

32.6 Class *CHARACTER*

A character has an associated integer code, whose value is a positive integer no greater than *Maximum_character_code*. The representation of a character uses at most *Character_bits* bits. These two platform-dependent constant attributes are defined in class *PLATFORM*.

← The description of PLATFORM and its features starts with 27.5 on page 433.

> -- Characters
>
> **expanded class interface** *CHARACTER* **exported features**
>
> ... All features from *COMPARABLE* ...
>
> *code*: *INTEGER*
>   -- Associated integer code
>   **ensure**
>   *1 <= Result*; *Result <= Maximum_character_code*
>
> **end interface** -- class *CHARACTER*

32.7 Class *INTEGER*

The representation of an integer uses at most *Integer_bits* bits; this platform-dependent constant attribute is defined in class *PLATFORM*.

← *See 27.5 and the subsequent section, starting on page 433, about the features of class PLATFORM.*

← *See 32.2 and 32.3 above, starting on page 475, about COMPARABLE and NUMERIC.*

> -- Integers
>
> **expanded class interface** *INTEGER* **exported features**
>
> ... All features from *COMPARABLE* and *NUMERIC* ...
>
> **infix** *"^"* (*other*: *INTEGER*): *REAL*
>   -- Result of raising current integer to the power *other*
>
> **infix** *"//"* (*other*: *INTEGER*): *INTEGER*
>   -- Integer division of current integer by *other*
>   **require**
>   *no_null_divisor*: *other* /= 0
>
> **infix** *"\\"* (*other*: *INTEGER*): *INTEGER*
>   -- Remainder of integer division of current integer by *other*
>   **require**
>   *no_null_divisor*: *other* /= 0
>
> **end interface** -- class *INTEGER*

32.8 Class *REAL*

The representation of a single-precision real number uses at most *Real_bits* bits; this platform-dependent constant attribute defined in class *PLATFORM*.

← *See 27.5 and the subsequent section, starting on page 433, about the features of class PLATFORM.*

← *See 32.2 and 32.3 above, starting on page 475, about COMPARABLE and NUMERIC.*

> -- Real numbers in single precision floating-point representation
>
> **expanded class interface** *REAL* **exported features**
>
> ... All features from *COMPARABLE* and *NUMERIC* ...
>
> **infix** *"^"* (*other*: *REAL*): *REAL*
>   -- Result of raising current real to the power *other*
>   **require**
>   *non_negative*: *Current* >= 0.0
>
> **end interface** -- class *REAL*

32.9 Class *DOUBLE*

The representation of a double-precision real number uses at most *Double_bits* bits; this platform-dependent constant attribute defined in class *PLATFORM*.

← See 27.5 and the subsequent section, starting on page 433, about the features of class PLATFORM.

← See 32.2 and 32.3 above, starting on page 475, about COMPARABLE and NUMERIC.

-- Real numbers in double precision floating-point representation
expanded class interface *DOUBLE* **exported features**
... All features from *COMPARABLE* and *NUMERIC* ...

infix *"^"* (*other*: *DOUBLE*): *DOUBLE*
-- Result of raising current double to the power *other*
require
non_negative: *Current* >= 0.0
end interface -- class *DOUBLE*

32.10 Bit operations

As explained in the discussion of types, there is an infinity of possible *BIT* N types, obtained by replacing N with any positive integer. Theoretically you may consider these types as being defined by fictitious classes *BIT_N*, one for every possible N. Here is the flat-short form of a typical one.

← See 12.14, page 209, about Bit_type.

These classes do not actually need to exist in the library, but they provide a convenient fiction.

-- Bit sequences of length N.
-- (This is a template, not a real class interface; to obtain a meaningful
-- class interface, replace N with a positive integer throughout.)
expanded class interface *BIT_N* **exported features**
count : *INTEGER*
-- Number of bits in the sequence (the value of N).

item (*i*: *INTEGER*): *BOOLEAN*
-- True if *i*-th bit is 1, false otherwise
require
1 <= *i*; *i* <= *count*

put (*value*: *BOOLEAN*; *i*: *INTEGER*)
-- Replace *i*-th bit by 1 if *value* is true, 0 otherwise
require
1 <= *i*; *i* <= *count*

infix *"^"* (*s*: *INTEGER*): *BIT_*N
-- Sequence shifted by $\bar{s}$ positions (positive *s* shifts right,
-- negative left; bits falling off the sequence's bounds are lost.)

infix *"#"* (*s*: *INTEGER*): *BIT_*N
-- Sequence rotated by $\bar{s}$ positions (positive right, negative left)

infix *"and"* (*other*: *BIT_*N): *BIT_*N
-- Conjunction with *other*

infix *"implies"* (*other*: *BIT_*N): *BIT_*N
-- Implication of *other*

prefix *"not"*: *BIT_*N
-- Negation

infix *"or"* (*other*: *BIT_*N): *BIT_*N
-- Disjunction with *other*

infix *"xor"* (*other*: *BIT_*N): *BIT_*N
-- Exclusive or with *other*
end interface -- class *BIT_N*

Part E

Appendices

A

Style guidelines

A.1 Overview

To facilitate the exchange of Eiffel software, it is preferable to follow a standardized programming style. This appendix describes a set of guidelines which help in this effort. Clearly, these rules are not part of the language definition.

Many of the rules are rather low-level, dealing with such mundane questions as how to phrase comments, where to put blanks adjacent to parentheses, and whether to use verbs or nouns for routine names. Modest as some of these concerns may seem, they are not to be neglected. Adherence to a uniform style for the more superficial aspects of software texts may indeed be of great benefit to both readers and writers of Eiffel software:

- In the process of getting acquainted with previously written classes, you will feel more comfortable if they follow a commonly agreed style, enabling you to understand the details more accurately, and to move on without delay to the deeper aspects of the classes under review.

- When you write new classes, or modify existing classes, the existence of simple, well-defined guidelines helps you avoid wasting your time hesitating on minor issues.

Far from stifling their creativity, then, the style discipline described in this chapter encourages software developers to apply it to the true challenges of quality software engineering: design of elegant, modular system architectures; selection of appropriate data structures; and use of the best possible algorithms.

A.2 Letter case

Letter case is not significant for entity, feature and type names. The recommended style observes the following conventions.

Any identifier that may be used as a type, or part of a type, should be written all in upper case. This includes:

- Class names, in all possible uses.
- Formal generic parameters, such as *G* in *LIST* [*G*].
- Basic types (*BOOLEAN, CHARACTER, INTEGER, REAL, DOUBLE, POINTER*), *BIT*, *ARRAY* and *STRING*.

Constant attributes should be written with an initial capital letter, with the rest in lower case, as in

> *Area*: *REAL is 43_512.57*;
> *Red, Green, Blue, Yellow*: *INTEGER* **is unique**

The same convention, initial upper-case letter, also applies to *Void*, the entity of type *NONE* representing void references, and to the two predefined entities *Current* and *Result*.

All other features (variable attributes and routines) and local entities should use all-lower-case names.

A.3 Choice of names

Names for features and entities should be clear and informative. Do not use abbreviations, except possibly for formal routine arguments, which are only used in a restricted context.

Complex names should use the underscore character to connect various components, as in

> *put_right*

The use of internal upper-case letters for the same purpose, as in *putAtRight*, contradicts the standard conventions of English and most other languages and is not part of the recommended style.

If two related names have some elements in common, make them differ at the beginning, rather than at the end; for example, use *x_position* and *y_position* rather than *position_x* and *position_y*. This will decrease the probability of confusion.

Clarity does not imply length. Although names may be as long as needed to avoid ambiguity, you should resist the temptation to overqualify. In particular, feature names should not include an identification of the enclosing class. For example, a feature for updating a customer's invoice in a class *INVOICE* should be called *update*, not *update_invoice* or *invoice_update*.

The design of the Basic Eiffel Libraries has gone even further in the direction of simplifying and standardizing feature names. This means in particular that the Data Structure Library makes little use of the specific terminology

Apart from proper names of the form MacName or McName, the only common use of internal upper-case letters seems to be for composite proper names of French origin as spelled in North American English. This convention, however, is unknown in actual French.

traditionally applied by the computer science literature to each individual kind of data structure. For example, you will **not** find features called

- *push, pop, top* for stacks.
- *add, remove, oldest, latest* for queues.
- *enter, entry* for arrays.
- *insert, value, search* for lists and hash tables.

Such names, widely used in textbooks about algorithms and data structures, highlight the differences between the various structures rather than their common properties.

In contrast, the Eiffel libraries are based on a taxonomy of data structures, grouped into well-structured families such as "dispensers", "chains" and "tables". The taxonomy is directly implemented into the library through multiple inheritance from separate hierarchies of deferred classes.

For an in-depth discussion of these issues and other aspects of library design, see "Eiffel: The Libraries" and the chapter entitled "Lessons from the Design of the Eiffel Libraries" in "An Eiffel Collection". The references are in the bibliography of appendix C.

Feature names are in line with this approach; they reflect the deeper common properties rather than the superficial differences. Some of the most important universal names are:

---

make
    (Basic initialization operation; should be creation procedure)

item
    (Basic access operation. **infix** *"@"* is a synonym for arrays only.)

count
    (Number of significant items in a structure.)

put
    (Basic operation to insert or replace an item.)

force
    (Like *put*, but will always succeed when it can.
    For example, it may resize the structure if full.)

remove
    (Basic operation for removing an item.)

wipe_out
    (Basic operation for removing all items.)

empty
    (Test for absence of significant items.
    Should return the same value as *count = 0*.)

full
    (Test for lack of space for more items.)

to_external
    (Function providing a pointer to actual data structure, for example
    the sequence of values making up an array or string, useful for transmission
    to external routines. May have language-specific variants such as *to_c*
    or *to_fortran*. All such functions should have a result of type
    NONE to preclude any feature application on the Eiffel side.)

> *from_external*
> (Inverse of *to_external*: procedure to reinitialize a data
> structure such as a string from an external form. May have
> language-specific variants such as *from_c*.)

Although such names as *item, put* and *remove* for stacks (replacing the traditional *top, push* and *pop*) may be a shock to some users accustomed to the more traditional terminology, this unifying move was felt inevitable if client users are to master easily a large number of powerful reusable classes describing many data structures variants.

The inevitable differences in signatures and specifications should not be compounded by differences in names which (in a typed language where incorrect calls will be detected automatically) only stand in the way of understanding.

If you are familiar with these conventions, you will easily recognize the purpose of the major routines when you explore a class that follows them, and you will be able to find out quickly whether the class suits your needs.

Thanks to their systematic presence in the Basic Libraries, these names have acquired a status which is next in importance to that of the language keywords. Make sure you use them whenever they are applicable.

A.4 Grammatical categories for feature names

Since procedures are commands to perform actions, their names should be drawn from **verbs** in the imperative mode: *put, write, remove* etc.

In contrast, functions and attributes (which are indistinguishable by clients, except through the presence or absence of arguments) describe access to information. A function or attribute of a type other than *BOOLEAN* should usually use a **noun**, possibly qualified by an adjective, as in *item* or *last_transaction*. Sometimes the noun may be implicit; then only the adjective or adjectives remain, as in *last_read*, which really stands for *last_item_read*.

The names of boolean functions or attributes should be of either of two forms:

• The name may suggest a question, usually with the prefix *is_*, as in *is_leaf* for a boolean feature used to determine whether a node is a leaf.

• Adjectives are also appropriate in some cases, as in *opened* for a boolean feature used to determine whether a file is open.

"opened" rather than "open" because the later might be confused with a verb, indicating a command to open the file.

Of the two possible names for a boolean feature, the one chosen should suggest the property which is **false** in the default case. This is because the default initialization rules will initialize a boolean attribute to false, so that there will be no need for the creation procedure to include a specific initialization. For example, if files are to remain closed until some call explicitly opens them, use an attribute *opened* rather than *closed*. Then the creation procedure of the class does not need to do anything special for this attribute.

Using a verb such as *get* for a function is usually inappropriate. Functions should not "do" something, but return information in a non-destructive way.

See "Object-Oriented Software Construction" about side effects in functions.

For example, a sequential read operation which advances the input cursor may be implemented as the combination of a procedure *get*, changing the state, and an attribute or function *last_item*, returning the last element read. A call to *get* updates the value of *last_item*, but calling *last_item* several times in a row repeatedly yields the same result.

← The input routines from the Kernel Library class STANDARD_FILES, discussed in chapter 31, follow these rules: a procedure such as 'readint' will read an element, and an attribute such as 'lastint' will give access to the last value read.

A.5 Grouping features

Classes introducing many features should group them into logical categories. The syntax encourages this by allowing a class to have more than one Feature_clause, each beginning with a Header_comment. (A Header_comment has the same form as a free comment, but appears as an official although optional component of some construct in the syntax. The constructs which take header comments are Feature_clause, Creation_clause and Routine. The next section will examine header comments of routines.)

← Syntax productions: Feature_clause, page 60; Creation_clause, page 285; Routine, page 112.

The presentation of features sketched a class text organized in this way: the Data Structure Library class *LINKED_LIST*, with feature groups introduced by

← See 5.4, page 56.

```
-- Number of elements
    Special elements
-- Cursor movement
-- Chaining
-- Representation
```

Such header comments should be short, simple phrases characterizing a set of logically related features.

In some cases it may be more convenient to read a class text in alphabetical order of feature names. Part D of this book indeed used this convention for most of its presentations of library classes in flat-short form. In the class texts themselves, however, grouping by feature categories is usually better; then a good language processing tool (for example through options of the **short** and **flat**commands) will be able to produce alphabetical output from a class organized by category – the reverse being of course impossible.

*← See 7.14, page 103, about **short**, and 7.15, page 106, about **flat**.*

A.6 Header comments

Every routine should begin with a Header_comment. Here is an example:

```
distance_to_origin: REAL is
        -- Distance to point (0, 0)
    local
        origin: POINT
    do
        !! origin.set_to_origin;
        Result := distance (origin)
    end -- distance_to_origin
```

Header comments should be informative, clear, and concise. In general, brevity is one of the essential qualities of comments in programs; over-long comments tend to obscure the program text rather than help the reader. The following principles should help achieving brevity.

Avoid repeating information which is obvious from the immediately adjacent program text. For example, the header comment for a routine beginning with

> *tangent_to* (*c*: *CIRCLE*; *p*: *POINT*): *LINE*

should not be

> -- Tangent to circle *c* through point *p*

but just

> -- Tangent to *c* through *p*

as it is clear from the function header that *c* is a circle and *p* is a point.

For the same reason, the header comment should not usually include restrictions on using the routine (such as "Call only on non-void argument") since such restrictions are the business of the Precondition clause, which will give a more complete and more precise view.

Avoid noise words and phrases. An example is "Return the..." in explaining the purpose of functions. In the above cases, writing "Return the distance to point (0, 0)" or "Return the tangent to..." does not bring any useful information as the reader knows a function must return something. Another example of a noise phrase is "This routine computes...", or "This routine performs...". Instead of

> -- This routine updates the display according to the user's last input

write

> -- Update display according to last user input.

Every header comment should begin with an upper-case letter.

Do not use abbreviations in header comments. The purpose of a comment is to explain; a reader may not know the meaning of an abbreviation.

Header comments should have the following syntactical form, which parallel rules given above for routine names:

- The header comment for a procedure should be a sentence in the imperative, as in the last example. The sentence should end with a period.
- The header comment for a non-boolean function should be a nominal phrase, such as "Tangent..." above. A final period is not necessary in this case, unless the comment contains more than one sentence.
- The header comment for a boolean function should be a question, ending with a question mark, as in "Is current node a leaf?".

Header comments should be consistent. If a function of a class has the comment "Length of string", a routine of the same class should not say "Update width of string" if it acts on the same attribute.

In general, comments should be of a level of abstraction higher than the code that they document. In the case of header comments, the comment should concentrate on the "what" of the routine rather than the "how" of the algorithm used.

Finally, remember that much of the important semantic information about the effect of a routine may be captured more precisely and concisely through the Precondition and Postcondition clause than through natural language explanations.

A.7 Other comments

Although this does not appear in the syntax, a class should also begin with a comment. The class comment should be brief and come before the beginning of the class text proper. For a class describing a set of objects, the comment should characterize these objects in the plural, as in

```
    -- Binary search trees, pointer representation
```

Other parts of class texts may also include free comments, used to explain potentially unclear components. They should be indented to the right of the normal text so as not to interfere with the understanding of the software text proper.

Classes and routines should have ending comments repeating their names. These comments are in fact optional parts of the syntax.

← See 4.11, page 53 for comments ending classes and 8.2, page 107 for comments ending routines.

It is not necessary to label the end of a control structure by a closing comment (such as in "**end** -- *if*"). The nesting depth of control structures should remain small in well-written Eiffel texts, not requiring any supplementary help for matching the beginning and end of each structure.

A.8 Eiffel names in comments

In the examples above in the rest of this book, the name of a feature or other entity appearing in a comment is shown in italics to avoid any confusion with common words. For example a header comment could be of the form:

```
    -- Record element under key
```

where *element* and *key* are formal arguments of the enclosing routine.

The corresponding convention in actual software texts (where font variation is not a possibility) is to enclose such an Eiffel name in single quotes (one opening quote ', one closing quote '). So the actual form of the above comment in its class text should be:

> -- Record 'element' under 'key'

Language processing tools which produce typesettable forms of classes should recognize this convention and use italics for Eiffel names quoted in comments. (As seen below, italics is the recommended convention in typeset output.)

A.9 Layout

The recommended layout of Eiffel software texts results from the general form of the syntax, which is essentially an "operator grammar", meaning that any text is a succession of alternating "operators" and "operands". An operator is a fixed language symbol, such as a keyword (**do** etc.) or a separator (semicolon, comma etc.); an operand is a user-chosen symbol (identifier or constant).

As a consequence, the text should follow a "comb-like" structure where every syntactical component either fits on a line together with a preceding operator, or is indented just by itself on one or more lines, as in a comb whose branches normally begin and end with operators:

Comb-like layout

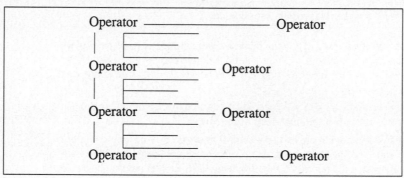

For an example, depending on the size of its components *a*, *b* and *c*, the same Conditional may be written, among other possibilities, as

> **if** *c* **then** *a* **else** *b* **end**

or

> **if**
>   *c*
> **then**
>   *a*
> **else**
>   *b*
> **end**

or

```
if c then
    a
else b end
```

The same principle applies to classes and routines. The following extract from the *ARRAY* class of the Kernel Library illustrates the standard indentation conventions for the different clauses. Ellipses (...) indicate omitted features.

```
-- One-dimensional arrays
indexing
    names: array;
    access: index;
    representation: array;
    size: fixed, resizable
class ARRAY [T] creation
    make

inherit
    INDEXABLE [T, INTEGER];

    INDIRECT [T];

    BASIC_ROUT

feature
    set (minindex, maxindex: INTEGER) is
            -- If minindex <= maxindex, allocate array with bounds
            -- lower and upper; otherwise create empty array.
        do
            upper := -1;
                -- lower initialized to 0 by default, so invariant holds
            if minindex <= maxindex then
                lower := minindex; upper := maxindex;
                actual_lower := lower; actual_upper := upper;
                allocate (maxindex - minindex + 1)
            end
        ensure
            empty_if_impossible: minindex < maxindex implies count = 0;
            consistent_size: minindex <= maxindex implies
                (lower = minindex and upper = maxindex and
                count = upper - lower + 1)
        end; -- set

    lower: INTEGER;
            -- Minimum current legal index

    upper: INTEGER;
            -- Maximum current legal index
```

```eiffel
    item (i: INTEGER): T is
            -- Entry of index i, if within bounds
        require
            index_large_enough: lower <= i;
            index_small_enough: i <= upper
        do
            Result := ext_item (area, i − lower )
        end; -- item

    force (v: T; i: INTEGER) is
            -- Replace i-th entry by v.
            -- Always applicable: resize if i not in current bounds.
        local
            extra_block_size: INTEGER
        do
            extra_block_size :=
                max (Block_threshold, Extra_percentage ∗ count // Hundred);
            if i < actual_lower then
                resize (i − extra_block_size, upper);
                lower := i
            elseif i > actual_upper then
                resize (lower, i + extra_block_size);
                upper := i
            else
                lower := min (i, lower);
                upper := max (i, upper)
            end;
            put (v, i);
        ensure
            inserted: item (i) = v;
            higher_count: count >= old count
        end; -- force
    ...

feature {NONE} -- Representation details

    actual_upper: INTEGER;
            -- Actual upper bound
    ...

feature -- Obsolete features

    enter_force (i: INTEGER, v: T) is
            obsolete "Use 'force (value, index)' "
        do
            force (v, i)
        ensure
            inserted: item (i) = v;
        end; -- enter_force
    ...
```

```
invariant
    consistent_size: count = upper − lower + 1;
    non_negative_size: count >= 0
end -- class ARRAY [T]
```

Note in particular the indentation used for routine header comments.

The indentation step is the "tab" character. Blank characters should never be used for indentation.

Closely related to layout is the question of optional semicolons. For most repetition constructs which use the semicolon as separator, semicolons are optional (except between two adjacent specimens if the second one begins with an opening parenthesis). The recommended style is to include the semicolon between adjacent specimens, but not before the very first one or after the very last one. (Such extra semicolons would have no effect but would not be illegal.) The Invariant clause of the class text shown above provides a typical example: no semicolon after **invariant** or before **end**, but a semicolon between the two assertion clauses.

← Semicolons are optional between feature clauses (page 60), parent clauses (page 77), declarations of local entities (page 114), assertion clauses (page 121) and instructions (page 234).

A.10 Lexical conventions

Lexical conventions follow the practice of ordinary text, both in language components and in comments. In particular:

- There should be a blank before an opening parenthesis, and after a closing parenthesis, but none after an opening parenthesis or before a closing one. The same rule applies to square brackets.
- A comma should always be followed by a blank, never preceded by one.

In a comment, a period should be followed by a blank, never preceded by one.

As an exception to non-software textual practice, the dot (period, full stop) used for qualified feature calls is neither preceded nor followed by a blank, as in *this_window.display*. As this example indicates, it is preferable, for typeset texts, to use a very small bullet (appearing in this book and in the output of the **short** command when it is meant for typesetting), more visible than a dot.

Three further conventions govern the use of blanks:

- An Assignment or Assignment_attempt symbol (:= or ?=) should be preceded and followed by one blank.

These are single symbols: it would be invalid to insert a blank before the = character.

- Arithmetic operators should also have a blank to the left and one to the right. When typesetting an Eiffel text with asterisks in expressions, make sure they appear properly as ∗; by default, typesetting systems will often print an asterisk as * (appearing too high above the line).
- In a Creation instruction which does not explicitly list a Type, the two successive exclamation marks should appear without an intervening blank, as !!.

← As mentioned on page 285, however, a form with intervening blanks would be valid.

A.11 Fonts

When Eiffel texts are typeset, as in this book, the following font conventions should be observed.

Keywords should appear in boldface:

> **class**

Type, class, feature and entity names (including predefined types and entities) should appear in italics:

> *INTEGER*
> *ARRAY*
> *put*
> *x*
> *Result*

Ending comments of routines and classes should appear in italics, except for the word "class" in roman:

> **end**; -- *restart*
> **end** -- class *FINANCIAL_MARKET*

Other comments, especially header comments of routines, should appear in roman font, except for names of features or arguments which should appear in italics:

> -- Change lending rate to highest of *rate1* and *rate2*.

As mentioned above, these names should appear in single quotes in the corresponding source texts.

A.12 Guidelines for indexing classes

The Indexing clause which optionally begins a class text may be used to record information about the class, for use by class browsing and retrieval tools. Such tools are important in the Eiffel approach to software construction, based on the reuse of industrial quality software modules.

The very idea of an Indexing clause assumes a degree of standardization of indexing conventions. This section introduces some important guidelines.

It is important first to put the overall purpose of the Indexing clause in perspective. The general principle of documenting Eiffel software is that as much of the documentation as possible should be within the class texts themselves. Documentation and browsing tools should use these texts as their primary source of information. *See "Eiffel: The Environment" about documentation and browsing tools.*

Some properties of class designs, however, are of a higher level of abstraction than what is usually expressed in the class text proper. They include indexing categories, descriptions of design and implementation decisions, references to algorithms or data structures as published in the literature etc. The Indexing clause is meant for such information. It should record it in a standardized format for use by documentation, archival and retrieval tools. Such tools should enable users to retrieve archived classes using query languages that express queries based on *<index, value>* pairs.

The following guidelines were used in the Basic Eiffel Libraries and are recommended for other software as well.

- Keep the Indexing clauses short (2 to 10 entries is typical).
- Avoid repeating information which is in the rest of the class text.
- Use a set of standardized indices for properties that apply to many structures (such as choice of representation).

→ *Such standardized indices are suggested below.*

- For values, define a set of standardized possibilities for the common cases.
- Include positive information only. For example, a *representation* index is used to describe the choice of representation (linked, array, ...). A deferred class does not have a representation. For such a class the clause should not contain the entry *representation*: *none* but simply no entry with the index *representation*. A reasonable query language will make it possible to use a query pair of the form *<representation, NONE>*.

Here are a few of the standard *index* terms and typical values.

An entry of index *names* records alternative names for a structure. Although a class has only one official name, the abstraction it implements may be commonly known under other names. For example, a "list" is also called a "sequence".

An entry of index *access* records the mode of access of the data structures. The standard values include the following; more than one value may be listed.

- *fixed* (only one element is accessible at any given time, as in a stack or queue).
- *fifo* (first-in-first-out policy).
- *lifo* (last-in-first-out).
- *index* (access by an integer index).
- *key* (access by a non-integer key)
- *cursor* (access through a client-controlled cursor, as with the list classes).
- *membership* (availability of a membership test).
- *min, max* (availability of operations to access the minimum or the maximum).

An entry of index *size* indicates a size limitation. Among common values:

- *fixed* means the size of the structure is fixed at creation time and cannot be changed later (there are few such cases in the library).
- *resizable* means that an initial size is chosen but the structure may be resized (possibly at some cost) if it outgrows that size. For extendible structures without size restrictions this entry should not be present.

An entry of index *representation* indicates a choice of representation. Value *array* indicates representation by contiguous, direct-access memory areas. Value *linked* indicates a linked structure.

An entry of index *contents* is appropriate for container data structures, used to keep objects. It indicates the nature of the contents. Possible values include *generic* (for generic classes), *integer_c, real_c, boolean_c, character_c* (for classes representing containers of objects of basic types).

← *The notion of container data structure was presented in 10.17, page 156, and 12.7, page 200.*

For example, the *ARRAY_LIST* class describes lists implemented by one or more arrays, chained to each other. The clause in this case is:

> **indexing**
>   *names*: *block_list*;
>   *representation*: *array, linked*; -- In this case it is both!
>   *access*: *fixed, cursor*;
>   *size*: *resizable*;
>   *contents*: *generic*

B

On language design and evolution

After an evening at the theater, we may have enjoyed the show or hated it, but meeting the playwright for a few more explanations at no extra charge – our last chance of understanding what he *really* meant – is not most people's idea of how to finish off the evening nicely.

Undaunted by the dangers, however, I have included in this appendix a few comments on the process of language design, which will perhaps help put the rest of this book in a broader perspective. The only other aims of this informal and unpretentious discussion are to encourage further thinking, and to direct the reader's attention to the seldom discussed topic of language evolution – what happens after the initial design.

The classic article on language design is C.A.R. Hoare's "Hints on Programming Language Design", reprinted in [Hoare's] "Essays in Computing Science", ed. C.B Jones, Prentice-Hall International, 1989, pp. 193-214.

B.1 Simplicity, complexity

In bel canto competitions, it is said that an unbeatable strategy is available to a judge who wants to crush the hopes of any given contestant. Just mumble: "Pretty voice, uh... too bad it's slightly out of tune." Then no other panel member will stand up for the poor soul – who would let others think that his ear is not as good as theirs?

A similar technique applies to the discussion of a programming language: just pronounce the word "PL/I" about someone else's design. Then everyone starts imagining a jungle of hopelessly intricate language constructs, and no one will stand up for the language: who would let others think that he likes *complexity*?

The abuse thrown at the not-too-young PL/I is not wholly unfair but rather facile. One can see much worse horror stories in more recent languages that initially were reasonably small but then started to develop carcinomatous cells in all directions.

Such unjustified complexity has triggered a reverse reaction: the "small is beautiful" school, according to which anything that cannot be defined in less than ten pages is dangerously complex and, as a result, useless.

I believe the truth is in-between. Complexity is of course unacceptable; as has often been noted, a programming language is the software developer's primary tool, and every engineer should master his essential tools entirely. The experience of teaching Eiffel has in this respect been deeply rewarding: the almost universal observation is that people learn Eiffel in two to five days. (Becoming a master of Eiffel software development, including all the methods of object-oriented design, techniques for producing industrial-quality reusable components, and the proper use of assertions, exceptions and other aspects of Design by Contract, may of course take longer.)

But languages should not be too simple, and valuable extensions should not be resisted. A sad example is Pascal, which could have had a much more significant industrial role if a few reasonable extensions (such as variable-length array access and an elementary module facility), on which most users would have readily agreed, had been included in the standard in the late nineteen-seventies or early eighties. They were not, and Pascal faded from the industrial scene; one may think that software engineering would be more of a profession and less of a slogan if events had unfolded otherwise.

Simplicity, in any case, is difficult to define objectively. One criterion is the space it takes to describe the language. But then what description do we use as reference? If you consider that this books talks about Eiffel in 594 pages, then Eiffel is complex. But such a measure is of course unfair: most of these pages are devoted to comments and explanations, and it is possible to talk just about pure Lisp (or for that matter just about love, another seemingly simple concept) over many more pages. Then if you consider that the syntax diagrams occupy only four pages, Eiffel is very simple. From yet another viewpoint, the language properties which enable a beginner to start writing useful software, may be defined in the 20 pages of chapter 1; that is pretty short too. I suspect a mathematical specification of the language's syntax, validity and semantics, in an appropriate formalism, would occupy about 50 pages.

In practice, two properties, easier to assess than an imprecisely defined notion of simplicity, seem more useful: uniqueness and consistency. These goals have been constant concerns in the design and evolution of Eiffel.

B.2 Uniqueness

The Principle of Uniqueness is easy to express: the language design should provide one good way to express every operation of interest; it should avoid providing two.

You will find this idea throughout Eiffel. It explains, for example, why the language, almost alone among general-purpose languages, supports only one form of loop. Why offer five or six variants (test at the beginning, the end or the middle, direct or reverse condition, "for" loop offering automatic transition to the next element etc.) while a single, general one will be easy to learn and remember, and everything else may be programmed from it?

The loop example deserves further attention. A well-written Eiffel application will have few loops: a loop is an iteration mechanism on a data structure (such as a file or list); it should be written as a general-purpose routine in a reusable class, and then adapted to specific contexts through the techniques illustrated in

← See 10.13, page 148, for a discussion of iteration and an introduction to the Iteration Library.

the discussion of iterators. (Such pre-programmed iteration mechanisms are indeed available in the Iteration Library.) Then having to write $i := i + 1$ manually for the equivalent of a For loop is not a problem.

This observation, which would not necessarily transpose to another language, illustrates an important aspect of the Eiffel method, which makes almost all "X considered harmful" observations, for arbitrary X, obsolete.

The mechanism for marking constructs as harmful is paradoxical: as soon as you recognize some pattern X as useful, this immediately makes it harmful, by suggesting that you should not from then on reproduce X-like patterns in your software texts, but instead hide X in a reusable software component and then reuse that component directly.

A few words of context for the younger generation: after E.W. Dijkstra's 1968 indictment of the goto instruction, many more programming language features over the years were the target of "X considered harmful" articles.

Loops are harmful, then, not because they pose a danger by themselves (as may be argued of goto instructions), but because their very usefulness as a common pattern of data structure traversal suggests packaging them in reusable components describing higher-level, more abstract forms of these patterns. The only danger here would be long-term – not taking advantage of potential reuse.

B.3 Consistency

Consistency means having a goal: never departing from a small number of powerful ideas, taking them to their full realization, and not bothering with anything that does not fit with the overall picture. Transposed to human affairs this may lead to fanaticism, but for language design no other way exists: unless you apply this principle you will never obtain an elegant, teachable and convincing result.

Note the importance for the selected ideas to possess both of the properties mentioned: each idea should be *powerful*, and there should be a *small number* of them. Eiffel may be defined by less than twenty key concepts, and they are certainly powerful. Here, as an illustration, are a few of them:

- Software architectures should be based on elements communicating through clearly defined contracts, expressed through formal preconditions, postconditions and invariants.

- Classes (abstract data types) should serve as both modules and types, and the modular and typing systems should entirely be based on classes. (Two immediate consequences are that no routine may be defined except in relation to a class defining its target type, and that Eiffel systems do not have a main program.)

- Classes should be parameterizable by types to support the construction of reusable software components.

- Inheritance is both a module extension facility and a subtyping mechanism.

- The only way to perform an actual computation is to call a (dynamically bound) feature on an object.

- Whenever possible, software systems should avoid explicit discrimination between a fixed list of cases, and instead rely on automatic selection at run time through dynamic binding.

- Client uses of classes should only rely on the official interface.

- A strong distinction should be maintained between commands (procedures) and queries (functions and attributes).
- A contract violation should lead to either organized failure or an attempt to use another strategy.
- It should be possible for a purely static tool to determine the type consistency of every operation by mere examination of the software text, before any execution ("static typing").

Eiffel is nothing else than these ideas and their companions taken to their full consequences.

Why is consistency so important? One obvious reason is that it determines your ability to teach the language: someone who understands the twenty or so basic ideas will have no trouble mastering the details.

Another major justification of the consistency principle is that with more than a few basic ideas the language design becomes simply unmanageable. Language constructs have a way of interacting with each other which can drive the most careful designers crazy. This is why the idea of orthogonality, popularized by Algol 68, does not live up to its promises: apparently unrelated aspects will produce strange combinations, which the language specification must cover explicitly.

As an extreme example, look at the last line of chapter 10. Who would ever ← *Page 166.*
have imagined that the possibility of declaring a feature obsolete – so as to support the smooth evolution of reusable software components in an industrial environment where older versions may still be needed for some time – would conflict with a totally unrelated idea, joining deferred features – the ability to merge some existing abstractions, given by operations (features) inherited from parent classes in a form that specifies their properties but does not provide an implementation? No two mechanisms seem at first sight more "orthogonal" with each other.

Yet they raise a specific question: the Join rule must give all the properties of the feature that results from joining deferred features, in terms of the properties of the inherited versions; but then one of these features may be obsolete. Not the most fascinating use of language facilities; but there is no reason to disallow it. (This would require an explicit constraint anyway, and simplicity would not be the winner.) But then does this make the joined version obsolete? The language specification must give an answer. (The answer is no.)

Such cases should suffice to indicate how crucial it is to eliminate anything that is not essential. Many extensions, which might seem reasonable at first, would raise endless questions because of their possible interactions with others.

B.4 A case study: creation instructions

Eiffel's Creation instructions provide an interesting test case of the preceding ideas.

A Creation instruction, in its most general form, appears as

> [1]
>
> ! *Creation_type* ! *target.procedure* (*arguments*)

meaning: create a new object of type *Creation_type*, initialize it with *procedure* using the given *arguments*, and attach entity *target* to it.

Several parts may be absent: if there is no creation procedure for *Creation_type*, omit the period and everything that follows; if *Creation_type* is the type declared for *target*, omit *Creation_type*; and of course *procedure* may be a procedure without arguments.

The flexibility of this notation makes it appropriate for diverse cases of object creation. Yet in one situation you must express your goals under a form that may appear less than ideal. Assume that a routine *r* needs to call a routine *s*, passing to *s* a newly created object of type *T*. This has to be written as

> [2]
>
> *r* ... **is**
>   **local**
>   *new*: *T*
>   **do**
>   ...
>   !! *new* ... ;
>   *s* (..., *new*, ...);
>   ... (Rest of routine omitted)

The routine requires a local entity, *new*, used only for naming the newly created object, and a creation instruction. This is somewhat unpleasant, especially if *s* is not a procedure (as assumed in the example) but a function, called as part of an expression.

How could we address the problem? One way seems to be the introduction of "creation expressions" as well as creation instructions. Such an expression, with a syntax similar to that of creation instructions, would return a reference to a newly created object; so it could be used as actual argument to a routine call, without any use of intermediate entities and assignments as above.

Such a convention, natural as it may seem, immediately raises conceptual difficulties far beyond what seems justified by the desire to avoid the minor inconvenience of [2]. If we have creation expressions, we may write the Creation instruction [1], in the general case, as

> [3]
>
> *target* := ... Creation expression for *Creation_type*, *procedure*
>   and *arguments* ...

But then we have two equally good ways, [1] and [3], to do the same thing. This runs contrary to the Uniqueness Principle. Since [3] appears more general, we should then make it the only creation technique. This immediately produces an unpleasant consequence: in a Creation expression, we must specify the *Creation_type* in all cases; yet it appears that in practice perhaps 80% of

Creation instructions do not name the *Creation_type*, being of the form

> *target*: *T*;
> ...
> !! *target* ...

where the declared type *T* of *target* serves as creation type and remains implicit. Are we going to complicate the vast majority of Creation instructions for the notational convenience of a few infrequent cases such as [2]?

One might of course suggest a form of [3] in which the creation type may be omitted, being then taken from the type of the target (the left-hand side) of the assignment, *target*. But using the target of an assignment to determine the type of the source would be a radical departure from a universal rule, which states that it must be possible to determine the type of an expression solely from the expression itself and the properties of its components. The type of *a* + *b*, and in fact all other properties of that expression (particularly its semantics) only depends on properties of *a*, *b* and the function **infix** "+". Any context in which the expression is used, such as the following three instructions

> *x* := *a* + *b*
>
> *print* (*a* + *b*)
>
> *y* ?= *a* + *b*

does not influence these properties except through its impact on the three components of the expression. Properties of *x*, *y* and *print* are irrelevant.

Should we renounce this general principle, so consistently beneficial – for understanding existing software, for learning the language, for writing compilers – just for the sake of calls requiring newly created objects? Clearly no.

Should we then renounce the Principle of Uniqueness in this case, and accept both [1] and some form of creation expression in the style of [3]? I believe not. The problem is not serious enough to justify adding one level of complexity to the language. Others may think differently, and they may eventually convince the Language Committee of the NICE consortium. Until then, however, the responsibility of the original language designers is to preserve the minimality of the language design. (Of course, the possibility is always there that someone will come up with the perfect solution to the issue of creation expressions, avoiding all the above pitfalls.)

This example also highlights the comments made above on what makes Eiffel special for language design: the emphasis on reuse and libraries. The scheme described above is typical of a pattern which, if deemed useful, may be encapsulated in a class and then reused by clients or descendants. If a class frequently needs direct instances of *T* built according to the pattern defined by [2], the proper solution is to write a function which will produce such instances according to the appropriate specification:

On such general rules of language design, see R.D. Tennent, "Principles of Programming Languages", Prentice-Hall International, 1981.

```
[4]
    new_T (...): T is
        -- Freshly created direct instance of T
    do
        ...
        !! Result ... ;
    end -- new_T
```

This makes it possible to write the call of [2] in the simplest possible form:

```
[4]
    s (..., new_T (...), ...);
```

This example illustrates some important aspects of language design and of the Eiffel method:

- An apparently innocuous extension may trigger endless conflicts and uncertainties.

- When in doubt, always abstain. If today you decide against a language extension, you can always change your mind tomorrow. But the reverse does not work: once the construct is there, you are stuck with it *in saecula saeculorum*. Many people have tried to remove obsolete facilities from publicly available programming languages; they have invariably failed.

- Mastering the theoretical issues of language design is not enough; one also needs an understanding of what developers need in practice, of what is common and what is rare. This is a slippery road, of course: what is common today may be rare tomorrow, what is essential for you may be marginal for me. Yet – as with the design of an interactive system – it is difficult to proceed without an idea of "the user" and his needs.

- A major task of a class designer is to foresee the use of the class by clients and descendants, and to provide all needed facilities in a form that is easy to use.

- What seems to be a language problem can often be solved by judicious use of reusable software components.

B.5 The language and the libraries

The last comment should remind us that in a method supporting reusability, it is often possible and desirable to provide a new feature through a library facility rather than through a language change.

We encountered an example above: the use of Iteration Library features instead of special loop constructs. More elementary facilities such as the *out* function (which produces a printable image of any value or object) or the *copy* procedure (which copies any object), although initially envisioned as language mechanisms, were in fact made available as normal features in a standard library class, *ANY*, inherited by every class.

← *See chapter 27 about ANY.*

A cynic might question the benefit of extending the libraries to keep the language simple. Indeed, tough problems of consistency and simplicity do arise for libraries. There is an important difference, however: one of level. The library as well as any user application are defined with respect to the basis provided by the language. Because everything else relies on it, this basis must be kept simple at all costs. Complexity should be avoided in libraries too, of course, but the consequences are less grave.

On library design see "Eiffel: The Libraries" and the article "Tools for the new culture..." in "An Eiffel Collection". References in appendix C.

Mathematical theories provide the appropriate comparison. Adding a language construct is like adding an axiom, certainly not a decision to be taken lightly. Adding a library class or routine is simply like adding another theorem, inferred from the current axioms.

B.6 Tolerance and discipline

A somewhat disciplinarian attitude is not infrequent in the software community. One commonly hears such phrases as "preventing the programmers from doing their dirty tricks". It is as if language designers were invested with a moral duty, and languages were a rampart against the threat of the developers' natural uncleanliness.

I disagree with this view. (This will seem surprising to those who have heard Eiffel being categorized, I believe quite wrongly, as a language of the restrictive school.) Programming language designers are not in the chastity belt business. Their role, to repeat a comment which I first heard many years ago from C.H.A. Koster, is not to prevent developers from writing bad software (a hopeless endeavor anyway), but to enable them to write good software; and perhaps to make the task pleasurable as well.

This must be applied together with the Principle of Uniqueness stated above. If you exclude a certain facility, be it the goto or function pointers, it is not to save humanity from some abomination (although you may also be doing that) but because you are providing elsewhere a better way to achieve the goals which the excluded constructs purported to address. Loops and conditionals are better than gotos, and dynamic binding under the control of static typing is better than function pointers.

In other words, if, as stated in the preface to this book, a design is defined as much by what it leaves out as by what it includes, one cannot justify the exclusions without knowing the inclusions.

Nowhere are these ideas more present than in Eiffel. The language's goal is to support an elegant and powerful method for analysis, design, implementation and reuse, and to help competent developers produce high-quality software. The method is precisely defined, and the language does not attempt to promote any other way of developing software; but it also does not attempt to prevent its users from applying their creativity.

The details of the inheritance mechanism provide a clear example of these principles. The relation between inheritance and information hiding is a somewhat controversial topic; Eiffel takes the view, argued in detail in the chapter on type checking in this book, that descendants should be entirely free to define the export status of inherited features, without being constrained by their ancestors' choice. Although I hope this discussion (and your own practical experience) will have convinced you, you should note that nothing really forces everyone to agree: a project leader may take a more restrictive approach and, for

← See the discussion of property P1 in 22.6, page 360.

example, prohibit the hiding of a feature exported by a parent. It is not difficult to write a tool that will check adherence to this rule. Had the language specification taken the restrictive stand, it would have been impossible for a project leader to enforce the inverse policy.

In summary: language designers should not exclude "bad" constructs out of a desire to punish or restrict the users of the language; that is not their job. The exclusions are justified only by the inclusions: the designer should focus on the constructs that he deems essential, and his responsibility is then to remove everything else, lest he produce a monster of complexity.

B.7 On syntax

One of the most amusing characteristics of the software development community, from a language designer's viewpoint, is the discrepancy between professed beliefs and real opinions on the subject of programming language syntax.

The official consensus is that syntax, especially "concrete" syntax (governing the textual appearance of software texts) does not matter. All that counts is structure and semantics.

Believe this and be prepared for a few surprises. You replace a parenthesis by a square bracket in the syntax of some construct, and the next day a million people march on Parliament to demand hanging for the traitors.

Of the pretense (syntax is irrelevant) and the actual reaction (syntax matters), the one to be believed is the latter. Syntax is important. Not that haggling over parentheses is very productive, of course, but unsatisfactory syntax usually reflects deeper problems, often semantic ones: form betrays contents.

Once a certain notation makes its way into the language, it will be used thousands of times by thousands of people: by readers to discover and understand software texts; by writers to express their ideas. If its esthetically wrong, it cannot be successful.

There is no recipe for esthetic success, but here again consistency is key. To take just one example, Eiffel follows Ada in making sure that any construct that requires an instruction (such as the body of a Loop, the body of a Routine or a branch of a Conditional) actually takes a sequence of instructions, or Compound. This is one of the simple and universal conventions which make the language easy to remember.

For syntax, some pragmatism does not hurt. A modern version of the struggle between big-endians and little-endians provides a good example. The programming language world is unevenly divided between partisans of the semicolon (or equivalent) as terminator and the Algol camp of semicolon-as-delimiter. Although the accepted wisdom nowadays is heavily in favor of the first approach, I belong to the second school. But in practice what matters is not anyone's taste but convenience for software developers: adding or forgetting a semicolon should not result in any unpleasant consequences.

In the syntax of Eiffel, the semicolon is theoretically a delimiter (between instructions, declarations, Index_terms clauses, Parent parts); but the syntax was so designed as to make the semicolon syntactically redundant, useful only to improve readability; so in most contexts it is optional.

This tolerance is made possible by two syntactical properties: an empty construct is always legal; and the use of proper construct terminators (often **end**) ensures that no new component of a text may be mistaken for the continuation of the previous construct. For example in

$$x := y$$
$$a := b$$

The recommended style suggests including a semicolon after 'y'.

no construct may involve two adjacent identifiers, so that a after y must begin a new instruction, even without a semicolon.

B.8 From the initial design to the asymptote

Although the programming literature contains a few references on language design, less attention has been devoted to the subject of evolution after initial design. Yet successful languages live and change; none of the major languages in use today still adheres to the letter of its original definition. How do the design principles governing the childhood of a language carry over to adolescence and adulthood?

Software developers are inordinately opinionated people, especially on the subject of languages. Inevitably, they will come up with requests for change and extensions. Add to this tremendous and constant source of ideas the contribution of co-workers, users, course participants, colleagues in panels at conferences, and you get a constant influx of new ideas.

In the current state of Eiffel there is another, totally new element, exciting and at the same time somewhat frightening: the net. Electronic mail and forums such as the *comp.lang.eiffel* Usenet news group, entirely devoted to the discussion of Eiffel-related issues, mean that thousands of people can learn in a few hours about the latest announcements, ideas, proposals, opinions and suggestions – and react to them. For Eiffel this has been a tremendous benefit. The number of people who have sent public or private comments is incomparably greater than what it would have been just a few years ago. Even Ada, probably the language most widely and thoroughly debated before its final design, was born before network access became available on a grand scale, and did not benefit from the unique combination of breadth, depth and timeliness made possible by the technology available today.

It is striking to see how many of these ideas are in fact excellent; but this does not mean that they should all be included!

First they may raise subtle or major incompatibilities with other language features; but even if this is not the case they will make the language more complex. The designers must weigh the evidence: is the purported benefit really worth the increase in complexity? In nine out of ten cases the answer is no. Again this usually is no reflection on the quality of the idea. But the designers' primary responsibility is to keep in mind the elegance of the overall picture.

What can one do in such a context? The best tactics is to say "no", explain that you are on your way to Vladivostok, and emerge some time later to see if there is still anyone around. This is the basic policy: do not change anything unless you cannot find any more arguments for the status quo.

But saying "no" most of the time is not an excuse for not listening. Almost any single criticism or suggestion contains something useful for the language designers. This includes comments by novices as well as expert users. Most of the time, however, you must go beyond what the comment says. Usually, what you get is presented as a solution; you must see through it and discover the *problem* that it obscures. The users and critics understand many things that the designers do not; the users, in particular, are the ones who have to live with the language day in and day out. But design is the job of the designers; you cannot expect users to do it for you. (Sometimes, of course, they will: someone comes up with just the right suggestion. This happened several times in the transition between Eiffel 2.3 and Eiffel 3. Then you can be really grateful.)

So there are deep and shallow comments but almost no useless ones. Sometimes the solution simply resides in better documentation. Often it lies in a tool, not in any language change. Even more often, as discussed above, the problem should be handled by library facilities: after all, this is the aim of Eiffel as a language – not to solve all problems, but to provide the basic mechanisms for solving highly diverse problems.

Once in a while, however, none of this will work. You realize that some facility is missing, or inadequately addressed.

When this happens – and only as a last resort – the tough conservative temporarily softens his stance. There are two cases, which are really different: an extension, or a change.

B.9 Extensions

Extensions are the language designer's secret vice – the dieter's chocolate mousse on the evening of his birthday. After much remonstrance and lobbying you finally realize what many users of the language had known for a long time: that some useful type of computation is harder to express than it should be. You know it is extension season.

There is one and only one kind of acceptable language extension: the one that dawns on you with the sudden self-evidence of morning mist. It must provide a complete solution to a real problem, but usually that is not enough: almost all good extensions solve *several* potential problems at once, through a simple addition. It must be simple, elegant, explainable to any competent user of the language in a minute or two. (If it takes three, forget it.) It must fit perfectly within the spirit and letter of the rest of the language. It must not have any dark sides or raise any unanswerable questions. And because software engineering is engineering, and unimplemented ideas are worth little more than the whiteboard marker with serves to sketch them, you must see the implementation technique. The implementors' group in the corner of the room is grumbling, of course – how good would a nongrumbling implementor be? – but you and they see that they can do it.

When this happens, then there is only one thing to do: go home and forget about it all until the next morning. For in most cases it will be a false alarm. If it still looks good after a whole night, then the current month may not altogether have been lost.

B.10 Changes

What happens if you realize that some existing language feature, which may be used by thousands of applications out in the field, could have been designed better?

The most common answer is that one should forget about it. This is also the path of least resistance: listening to the Devil of Eternal Compatibility with the Horrors of the Past, whose constant advice is to preserve at all costs the tranquillity of current users. The long-term price, however, is languages that forever keep remnants from another age. For a glimpse of the consequences, it suffices to look at the most recent versions of Fortran, which (although meant for the most powerful parallel computers of tomorrow) still reflect the idiosyncrasies of the IBM 701's 1951 architecture, or at recent "object-oriented" extensions of C, faithfully reproducing all the flaws of their parent, compounded by extra levels of complexity.

The other policy is harder to sustain, but it is also safer for the long term: if something can indeed be done better, and the difference matters, then change the construct. Such cases should of course be rare and far between – otherwise one can doubt the very soundness of the original design. They should meet two key conditions:

1 • There must be wide agreement that the new solution is significantly better than the original one. It must not entail any negative consequence other than its incompatibility.

2 • The implementors must provide an automatic conversion mechanism for existing software. The conversion must be complete and safe.

If these conditions are met, then I believe one should cut one's losses and go ahead with the change. To act otherwise is to act arrogantly (pretending that something is perfect when it is not), or to sacrifice long-term quality for short-term tranquillity.

All the issues discussed above arose in the transition from Eiffel 1.7 (the level used in the book *Object-Oriented Software Construction*) to Eiffel 2.1, and then again from 2.3 (which was essentially the same as 2.1) to Eiffel 3, as described in the present book. It will be for the reader to judge whether the changes and extensions described in appendix E were justified, and whether they followed the principles discussed here.

More striking than the changes has been the stability of Eiffel: the language's key properties, especially its semantics, are essentially identical to what was described in the very first publication.

In all likelihood, nothing fundamental will change in the foreseeable future. (At the time of writing, the only extension being considered is simple support for parallel computation; some thought has also gone into making the assertion sublanguage more powerful.) Valuable ideas for extensions or modifications are bound to come forward. I hope the above observations have shed some light on how to handle the process.

C

An Eiffel bibliography

The documents listed below describe various aspects of Eiffel: method, language, diverse user applications, implementation, supporting tools. The order is not chronological. A code beginning with TR- indicates a technical report available from Interactive Software Engineering. Works without an author indication are by the author of the present book.

Not included are the proceedings of the **International Eiffel User Conferences** (ten sessions as of this writing, in Paris, Sydney, San Diego, New Orleans, Ottawa, Santa Barbara, Dortmund). These collections of articles about actual user experiences with Eiffel were distributed to conference participants but have not been republished as yet.

1 • *Object-Oriented Software Construction*, a book published by Prentice-Hall. 534+xviii pages. Explains the Eiffel approach to the design and implementation of high-quality software. — *TR-EI-10/OO. ISBN: 0-13-629049-3*

2 • *Eiffel: The Language*, a book published by Prentice-Hall. Provides a complete description of the language. — *This book.*

3 • *Eiffel: An Introduction*. Presents a brief overview of the language and ISE's environment. (The material is close to chapter 1 of this book.) — *TR-EI-3/GI. Version 2.3, October 1990.*

4 • *Eiffel: The Libraries*. Describes the Eiffel Libraries of reusable software components. Revised version will be published by Prentice-Hall. — *TR-EI-7/LI. Version 2.3, October 1990.*

5 • *Eiffel: The Environment*. Shows how to use Eiffel in practice through the tools of ISE's environment (compiling, debugging, browsing). Revised version will be published by Prentice-Hall. — *TR-EI-5/UM. Version 2.3, October 1990.*

6 • *An Eiffel Collection*. A collection of articles, many of them previously published in journals or conferences, about various Eiffel-related topics. Contains some of the articles in the present list, as indicated below. — *TR-EI-20/EC. Version 2.3, October 1990.*

7 • *Introduction to the Theory of Programming Languages*, a book published by Prentice-Hall. 448+xvi pages. Although not devoted to Eiffel, this book on the fundamentals of programming language theory (abstract syntax, denotational and axiomatic semantics, complementarity of methods) may help understand many of the ideas behind Eiffel software development, in particular assertions and typing.   *TR-EI-27/TL. ISBN: 0-13-498510-9*

8 • *Design by Contract*. Reviews the Eiffel approach to software reliability, emphasizing assertions, disciplined exceptions and controlled inheritance. Chapter 1 of *Advances in Object-Oriented Software Engineering*, eds. Dino Mandrioli and Bertrand Meyer, Prentice-Hall, 1992.   *TR-EI-14/CO. Version 4, 1991. (Original version, 1987.) Appears in "An Eiffel Collection".*

9 • *From Structured Programming to Object-Oriented Design: The Road to Eiffel*. Appeared in *Structured Programming*, Volume 10, Number 1, pages 19-39, January 1989. A free-form discussion of the thinking that led to the design of Eiffel.   *Appears in "An Eiffel Collection."*

10 • *Conversation with Editorial Board Member B.M.* Appeared in *Journal of Object-Oriented Programming*, Volume 2, Number 2, pages 41-42, May-June 1989. An interview where the author explains some of the background that led to Eiffel, and his views of the evolution of object-oriented technology.   *Appears in "An Eiffel Collection."*

11 • *The New Culture of Software Development: Reflections on the Practice of Object-Oriented Design*. Appeared in *TOOLS 1* (Technology of Object-Oriented Languages and Systems, Paris, November 1989), SOL, Paris, pages 13-23, November 1989. Revised version in *Journal of Object-Oriented Programming*, Volume 3, Number 4, pages 76-81, November-December 1990; also as chapter 2 of *Advances...* (see number 8 above). Discusses object-oriented programming as a new "component" culture, a radical departure from the traditional "project" culture. Addresses the managerial consequences of an organization's move to object-oriented technology and software reuse.   *Appears in "An Eiffel Collection."*

12 • *Sequential and Concurrent Object-Oriented Programming*. Appeared in *TOOLS 2* (Technology of Object-Oriented Languages and Systems, Paris, 23-26 June 1990), Angkor/SOL, Paris, pages 17-28, June 1990. Justifies and describes a concurrency mechanism for Eiffel, meant to cover parallel, coroutine, real-time, distributed and process control applications.   *Appears in "An Eiffel Collection."*

13 • *Tools for the New Culture: Lessons from the Design of the Eiffel Libraries*. Appeared in *Communications of the ACM*, Volume 33, No. 9, pages 69-88, September 1990. Discusses the design and implementation of the Eiffel libraries, and general principles for developing good libraries of reusable software components.   *Appears in "An Eiffel Collection."*

14 • *A Development in Eiffel: Design and Implementation of a Network Simulator*, by Cyrille Gindre and Frédérique Sada. Appeared in *Journal of Object-Oriented Programming*, Volume 2, Number 2, pages 27-33, May-June 1989. A report on the experience of developing an industrial product with Eiffel at Thomson-CSF. Includes discussion of design issues and measures of productivity and reusability.   *Appears in "An Eiffel Collection."*

15 • *My Life with Eiffel*, by Koichiro Yoshida; column in *Software Design* magazine, Tokyo, appearing in every issue (monthly) since November 1989. In Japanese.

16 • *Reusability*: *The Case for Object-Oriented Design*; appeared in *IEEE Software*, March 1987. Analyzes the object-oriented approach to software reusability, emphasizing the Eiffel approach through examples.

TR-EI-6/RE. Version 1.2, September 1986. Appears in "An Eiffel Collection"

17 • *Genericity versus Inheritance*, Proceedings of ACM OOPSLA Conference, Portland, Sept. 1986, SIGPLAN Notices, 21, 10, pp. 391-405; revised version appeared in *Journal of Pascal, Ada and Modula-2*, 1987. Compares the object-oriented notion of inheritance with the genericity mechanism of Ada. Explains how the two concepts were reconciled by the design of Eiffel.

TR-EI-8/GI. Version 2, 1987.

18 • *Eiffel*: *Applying the Principles of Object-Oriented Design*. Appeared in *Computer Language*, pages 81-87, May 1988. A short introduction to Eiffel and ISE's environment.

19 • *Bidding Farewell to Globals*. Appeared in *Journal of Object-Oriented Programming* (Eiffel column), Volume 1, Number 4, pages 73-76, August-September 1988. An explanation of why global variables, which hamper software quality, do not exist in Eiffel, and a presentation of Eiffel techniques for sharing information between modules.

Appears in "An Eiffel Collection."

20 • *Harnessing Multiple Inheritance*. Appeared in *Journal of Object-Oriented Programming* (Eiffel column), Volume 1, Number 5, pages 48-51, November-December 1988.

Appears in "An Eiffel Collection."

21 • *You can write, but can you type?*. Appeared in *Journal of Object-Oriented Programming* (Eiffel column), Volume 1, Number 6, pages 58-67, March-April 1989. An introductory discussion of what typing means in the object-oriented context.

Appears in "An Eiffel Collection."

22 • *Static Typing for Eiffel*. A detailed technical discussion of some of the more intricate aspects of static typing for object-oriented programming, explaining the design choices made in Eiffel.

TR-EI-18/ST. July 1989 (original: Jan. 1989). Appears in "An Eiffel Collection"

23 • *Writing Correct Software*. Appeared in *Dr. Dobb's Journal*, pages 48-63, February 1990. An explanation of how assertion and exception techniques can aid class correctness.

24 • *Pure Object-Oriented Programming with Eiffel*. Appeared in *Programmer's Update*, pages 59-69, February 1990. An interview where the author explains some of the key Eiffel ideas.

Appears in "An Eiffel Collection."

25 • *Object-Oriented Analysis*: *Case Studies*, by Jean-Marc Nerson, Tutorial Notes for TOOLS 2 (Technology of Object-Oriented Languages and Systems, Paris, 23-26 June 1990). Describes an object-oriented system analysis method. The notation is Eiffel-based.

TR-EI-25/AN. Version 1, June 1990.

26 • *Objective Reality*, by Alan Winston. Appeared in *Unix World*, pages 72-75, April 1990. Taken from an article on applications of object-oriented programming, this extract gives the view of a company developing telecommunication applications in Eiffel.

Appears in "An Eiffel Collection."

27 • *The Eiffel Environment*. Appeared in *Unix Review*, Volume 6, Number 8, pages 44-55, August 1988. Describes the tools supporting software development in ISE's implementation, as they existed in 1988.

Appears in "An Eiffel Collection."

28 • *ArchiText User's Manual*. Introduces the general-purpose ArchiText language-customizable editor, developed in Eiffel; a specialized version of this editor exists for Eiffel itself.

TR-EI-33/AT. July 1991

29 • *Eiffel Types*. A unified view of the type system (version 2.2).

TR-EI-19/ET. July 1989 (original: March 1989).

30 • *Eiffel: A Language and Environment for Software Engineering*. Appeared in *Journal of Systems and Software*, 1988. Offers a detailed introduction to the language and ISE's environment as they existed in 1988.

TR-EI-2/BR. Version 2.2, January 1987.

31 • *Eiffel: Programming for Reusability and Extendibility*. Appeared in *ACM SIGPLAN Notices*, Volume 22, Number 2, pages 85-94, February 1987. The first published introduction to Eiffel.

"An invitation to Eiffel" is an updated version.

32 • *Eiffel: Object-Oriented Design for Software Engineering* by Bertrand Meyer, Jean-Marc Nerson and Masanobu Matsuo. Appeared in Proceedings of ESEC 87 (First European Software Engineering Conference), Strasbourg, 8-11 September 1987, Springer-Verlag, LNCS, Berlin-New York, 1987. An overview of the principles of Eiffel, describing the then current state of ISE's implementation.

33 • *Extending Eiffel Toward O-O Analysis and Design* by Jean-Marc Nerson. Describes an approach to software systems analysis and design, with the associated BON graphical formalism (Better Object Notation); covers case studies.

TR-EI-28/AD. Version 1, December 1990

34 • *Release 2.2 Overview*. Surveys the enhancements and extensions introduced in release 2.2 of Eiffel (August 1989).

TR-EI-16/22. August 1989

35 • *Release 2.3 Overview*. Surveys the enhancements and extensions introduced in release 2.3 of Eiffel (October 1990).

TR-EI-23/23. October 1990

D

Specifying systems in Lace

D.1 Overview

As you start producing clusters of classes, you will expect the supporting environment to provide language processing tools – compilers, interpreters, documenters, browsers – to process these classes and assemble them into systems.

These tools will need a specification of where to find the classes and what to do with them. Such a specification is called an **Assembly of Classes in Eiffel**, or Ace for short. This appendix presents a notation, the **Language for Assembling Classes in Eiffel**, or Lace, for writing Aces.

Lace is not part of Eiffel, and Eiffel environments are not required to support Lace (although, as explained below, they are encouraged to do so if appropriate). As a consequence, you may consider this appendix as supplementary material. But since the goals of Lace are important for the practice of Eiffel software development, you may wish, even on first reading, to get familiar with the essential ideas by perusing just this section and the next.

One word of encouragement if you feel that after reading 512 pages about Eiffel you should not have to learn yet another language: even in an environment that supports Lace, it is not necessary to study Lace details the way you would learn a design or programming language; the tools should provide you, whenever you need a new Ace, with a template having all the default fields, which you will simply customize for your application. Furthermore, the format of Lace is very much Eiffel-like, so that you will find yourself treading familiar ground.

→ *If you are familiar with Lace basics and simply need a reminder on some details, you may find it profitable to use the complete example which starts on page 516 and illustrates the major possibilities. The complete Lace grammar starts on page 533.*

D.2 A simple example

Typical elements of an Ace include information about directories and files containing the text of the system's clusters and classes, compilation options (assertion monitoring, debugging etc.) for the classes involved, name of the root class (used to start off execution), location of non-Eiffel elements such as external libraries, target file for the compilation's output.

To help you get quickly a idea of the basic concepts of Lace, here is a simple but typical Ace.

Although simple, this example includes the Lace facilities that suffice for many practical Eiffel systems.

---

system *browser* **root**

   EB (*browsing*)

default

   assertions (**ensure**); *trace* (**no**);
   collect (**yes**); *debug* (**no**);

cluster

   "$INSTALLATION/library/support";

   "$INSTALLATION/library/parsing";

   browsing: *"~/current/browser"*
     default
      assertion (**all**)
     option
      debug (**yes**): *LAYOUT, FUNCTIONS*;
     end -- *browsing*

end -- system *browser*

This describes a system called *browser*. The root of this system is a class called *EB*. The text of *EB* is to be found in cluster *browsing* (described a few lines below in the Ace); this mention of the root class's cluster, in parentheses, is optional if the entire system has only one class of the name given, here *EB*.

Default compilation options for the classes of this system are: for assertions, check postconditions (**ensure** clauses), which also implies checking preconditions; do not trace execution; enable garbage collection (*collect*); do not execute **debug** instructions.

These options are system-wide defaults; individual clusters may override them through their own **default** clauses, as does cluster *browsing*. Individual classes may also override the system and cluster defaults through the **option** clause.

The Clusters part, beginning with the **cluster** Lace keyword (reminiscent of the **feature** keyword introducing a Features part in Eiffel), defines the universe by listing the clusters where the supporting environment's tools may look for needed classes. Here clusters are given as directories, using the Unix file conventions.

← *The notion of universe was discussed in 3.6, starting page 38.*

The specification of the first two clusters only gives directory names, each written as a Manifest_string. By default, the cluster consists of all classes to be found in the files having names ending with **.e** in this directory. Each one of these files may contain one or more classes. The **.e** name convention is the default; we shall see below how to include files with other names, or to exclude some **.e** files.

A Manifest_string is a string in double quotes.

On some operating systems, a name ending with **.e** *may not be permitted. The default convention may be different in such a case.*

The first two clusters are elements of the Basic Libraries (support and parsing). Their names use Unix-like conventions for environment variables (such as *$INSTALLATION*) to facilitate using the same Ace on different machines. Clearly, such conventions are operating-system-dependent.

The last cluster also has a directory name (this is always required), preceded here by a Cluster_name, *browsing*, and a colon. You will need to include such a Cluster_name whenever other elements of the Ace refer to the cluster: here, for example, the Root clause refers to cluster *browsing* through its Cluster_name, to indicate that this is where the root class *EB* is.

For this cluster, the default assertion monitoring option, overriding the default specified at the system level, is **all** (monitor everything). Furthermore, the *debug* option is enabled for two classes of the cluster, *LAYOUT* and *FUNCTIONS*.

This example is typical of Aces used to assemble and compile systems without any advanced options.

D.3 On the role of Lace

Before showing the remaining details of Lace, it is important to ponder briefly over the connection of this description to the rest of this book.

Lace support, it was mentioned above, is not a required element of an Eiffel implementation. Why then talk about Lace at all as part of a specification of the Eiffel language? There are two reasons, one pedagogical and one practical.

The pedagogical reason is that since some Lace-like mechanisms, at least elementary ones, will be necessary anyway to execute your software, you would not get a full picture of Eiffel software development without some understanding of possible assembly mechanisms.

Together with the short Lace overview given in chapter 3, the preceding two sections are probably sufficient to get a general idea of the purpose of Lace, but the rest of this appendix will give more details for those readers who are seriously interested. As mentioned already, these details are not essential on first reading, hence the SHORTCUT sign which signals the rest of this appendix as non-crucial material.

The practical reason for paying attention to Lace involves **portability**, and should be of particular concern to authors of Eiffel implementations.

True, because of the variety of possible implementation platforms (hardware, operating systems, user interfaces) and of possible implementation techniques such as interpretation, compilation to machine code, compilation to an intermediate assembly-like code such as C etc., one may not guarantee total portability or enforce a fully general Lace standard. For one thing, an implementation could altogether bypass text-based descriptions such as those of Lace, in favor of interactive input of compilation and assembly options (with a modern graphical or "point and click" user interface); then it would have no need for a description *language* in the textual sense of this word, even though it will still provide the Lace semantics – specification of compilation options, class text location etc. – in some other way.

Even if system descriptions use a textual form, an individual implementation may have non-portable characteristics, stemming for example from the peculiarities of the file and directory system of the underlying platform, or from specific optimization options provided by the implementor.

Along with such non-portable aspects, however, certain facilities will be needed in every implementation. For example, it is necessary to let developers specify whether or not to monitor the assertions of any given class at run time. Then everyone will benefit if all implementations using text-based system descriptions rely on a common set of notations and conventions. This does not guarantee full portability, but avoids unjustified sources of non-portability.

The design of Lace is a result of these considerations. It suggests a default notation for the standard components of system descriptions, while leaving individual implementors the freedom to add platform-dependent or implementation-specific facilities.

D.4 A complete example

For ease of reference (especially meant for those readers who already know the basics of Lace but are coming back to this presentation for a quick and informal reminder on the form of some clauses), here is a complete Ace using most of the available possibilities. The various components are explained in subsequent sections.

Because it illustrates all the major Lace facilities, this Ace is more complex than most usual ones, which tend to use the basic facilities illustrated by the simple example on page 514.

```
system browser root

    EB (browsing)

default

    assertions (ensure); trace (no);
    collect (yes); debug (no);

cluster

    "$INSTALLATION/library/support";

    basics: "$INSTALLATION/library/structures"

    parsing: "$INSTALLATION/library/parsing"

   browsing: "not/current/browser"
    use
     ".lace"
    include
     "commands";
     "states"
    exclude
     "g.t.e"
```

adapt
  graphics:
    rename *CURSOR* **as** *GRAPHICS_CURSOR,*
        WINDOW **as** *GRAPHICAL_WINDOW*;
  basics:
    rename *CURSOR* **as** *LIST_CURSOR*;
  parsing:
    ignore
default
  debug (*"level2"*);
  debug (*"io_check"*)
option
  assertion (**all**): *CONSTANTS, FULL_TEXT*;
  trace: *FUNCTIONS, QUIT, RENAMED*;
  debug (**yes**): *LAYOUT, FUNCTIONS*;
  debug (*"format"*): *FULL_TEXT, OUTPUT*;
  debug (*"numerical_accuracy"*): *OUTPUT*;

visible

  CONSTANTS **as** *BROWSING_CONSTANTS*;

  LAYOUT
    rename
      choice_menu **as** *"choice.menu"*, *set_reverse* **as** *"set.reverse"*
    end;

  EB
    creation
      initialize
    export
      execute, set_target, initialize
    rename
      set_target **as** *"set.target"*
    end
  end -- *browsing*

external

  Object: *"object_name.o"*, *"../basics.o"*, *"-ltermcap"*, *"otherlib.a"*;
  C: *"previous.h"*, *"/usr/$MACHINE/src/screen.c"*;
  Make: *"../Clib/makefile"*

generate

  executable: *"$INSTALLATION/bin"*;
  C (**yes**): *"$INSTALLATION/src/browser/package/eb.c"*;
  Object (**no**): *"$INSTALLATION/bin/browser"*

end -- system *browser*

D.5 Basic conventions

Let us now proceed to the details of Lace.

You should not have been too surprised by the syntax, which is Eiffel-like. The syntax descriptions below use the conventions applied to Eiffel throughout the rest of this book.

← *The notation for describing syntax was introduced starting on page 23.*

Comments, as in Eiffel, begin with two consecutive dashes -- and extend to the end of the line.

The grammar of Lace also uses some of the same basic components as Eiffel:

← Identifier: *25.9, page 417.* Manifest_string: *23.19, page 391.* Integer_constant: *23.14, page 388.*

> Identifier, such as *A_CLASS_NAME*
> Manifest_string, such as *"A STRING$"*
> Integer_constant, such as *−4562*

As in Eiffel, letter case is not significant for identifiers; the recommended standard is to use upper case for class names and lower case for everything else. Letter case is also not significant for strings except when they refer to outside elements such as file names, directory names or linker options; such strings will be passed verbatim to outside tools (such as the operating system or linker), which may or may not treat letter case as significant.

Lace has the following keywords, which may not be used as identifiers:

Lace Keywords

> **adapt**, **all**, **as**, **check**, **cluster**, **creation**, **default**, **end**, **ensure**, **exclude**, **export**, **external**, **generate**, **ignore**, **include**, **invariant**, **keep**, **loop**, **no**, **option**, **require**, **rename**, **root**, **system**, **use**, **visible**, **yes**.

An important convention applied throughout the Lace syntax is that an Identifier is syntactically legal wherever a Manifest_string is, and conversely. For this purpose, the grammar productions given below do not refer directly to these two constructs, but use the construct Name, defined as

SYNTAX

> Name   ≜   Identifier | Manifest_string

As a consequence, if your system contains a class called *CLUSTER*, which is not a valid Lace identifier since it conflicts with one of the keywords in the above list, you may still refer to it in the Ace by using the Manifest_string *"CLUSTER"*. Similarly, although you may give a simple file name such as *my_file* as an identifier, one which does not conform to Lace identifier conventions, such as *"-/directory/my_file"*, will have to be expressed as a string.

For clarity, all the examples of this presentation use strings for file and directory names.

VDCN

A consistency condition applies to names used in an Ace: the Cluster_name must be different for each cluster. It is valid, however, to use the same identifier in two or more of the roles of Cluster_name, System_name, Class_name.

D.6 Ace structure

The structure of an Ace is given by the following grammar.

Ace	≜	System
		Root
		[Defaults]
		[Clusters]
		[Externals]
		[Generation]
		end ["--" system System_name]
System	≜	system System_name
System_name	≜	Name
Root	≜	root
		Class_name
		[Cluster_mark]
		[Creation_procedure]
Class_name	≜	Name
Cluster_mark	≜	"(" Cluster_name ")"
Cluster_name	≜	Name
Creation_procedure	≜	":" Name

All clauses were present in the long example above; the earlier, shorter example had all clauses except Externals and Generation.

The long example was on page 516, and the short example on page 514.

The Defaults clause gives general options which apply to all classes in the system, except where overridden by cluster defaults or options specified for individual classes. It may also indicate options that apply to the system as a whole; for example, the option

> *collect* (**yes**)

requests garbage collection to be turned on; this only makes sense for the whole system. The precise form of options is explained below.

→ *See D.11, starting page 524, about options.*

The Clusters part lists individual clusters and the associated options.

The Externals clause gives information about any non-Eiffel software element needed to assemble the system.

The Generation clause indicates where to store the output of system assembly and compilation (executable module, object code, code in another target language). By default the output will be produced in the directory where the compilation command is executed.

The order of these clauses should be easy to remember: first you give the system a name (System) and express where it starts its execution (Root); then you specify the options that apply across the board, except where specifically overridden (Defaults); you list the Clusters that make up the system's universe; you indicate what else is needed, beyond Eiffel clusters, to assemble the system (Externals); finally, you indicate where the outcome of the assembly and compilation process must be generated (Generation).

The next sections study the various clauses of an Ace.

D.7 Basics of Cluster clauses

In an Ace containing a Clusters part, the keyword **cluster** will be followed by zero or more Cluster_clause, each specifying the location in the file system of one of the clusters of the universe, and the properties applying to the classes of that cluster.

Let us examine the possibilities by writing a Cluster_clause through successive additions showing most of the available possibilities.

In its simplest form, a Cluster_clause is simply a Directory_name, expressed as a Manifest_string, as in:

On some operating systems, directories may be called differently (for example "folders") or replaced by some other mechanism.

> *"$INSTALLATION/library/browsing"*

If you must refer to the cluster in other clauses of the Ace, you will need to give it a Cluster_name. (This will be the name for Lace, and is distinct from the cluster's name for the operating system, which appears as the Directory_name.) The Cluster_name will precede the Directory_name, separated by a colon. If you want to call the above cluster *browsing*, you will declare it as

> *browsing: "$INSTALLATION/library/browsing"*

An optional Cluster_properties part may then appear, specifying further properties of the cluster. It may contain the following paragraphs, all optional, in the order given: Use, Include, Exclude, Name_adaptation, Defaults, Options and Visible. If present, the Cluster_properties part is terminated by an **end** (and, as with an Eiffel routine, a suggested comment repeating the cluster name).

Here is the syntax of the Clusters and Cluster_properties parts:

Clusters	≙	**cluster** {Cluster_clause ";" ...}
Cluster_clause	≙	[Cluster_tag]
		Directory_name
		[Cluster_properties]
Cluster_tag	≙	Cluster_name ":"
Directory_name	≙	Name
Cluster_properties		[Use]
		[Include]
		[Exclude]
		[Name_adaptation]
		[Defaults]
		[Options]
		[Visible]
		end ["--" **cluster** Cluster_name]

The following sections explore the various Cluster_properties paragraphs. If, in the meantime, you fear that you might forget the order of paragraphs in a Cluster_properties part, remember the following simple principle: the order is the natural one from the point of view of a language processing **tool** that must process the cluster. For example, a compiler which uses a Cluster_properties specification to compile the classes a cluster, and has already obtained any default specifications associated with the cluster (through the Use paragraph), will take the following actions:

- Find any files to take into account besides the default (Include).
- Discard any unneeded files (Exclude).
- To prepare for compiling the class texts, find out if any class name appearing there actually refers to a class having another name (Name_adaptation).
- Find out the cluster-level compilation options (Defaults). and start compilation of the cluster's various classes.
- When compiling a given class, find out if a specific option applies to it (Options).
- Having compiled classes, decide which ones of their properties, if any, must be made available to other systems (Visible).

As mentioned earlier, developers should produce an Ace by completing a pre-filled template, rather than from scratch. The template will have the paragraphs in the right order.

D.8 Storing properties with a cluster

The Cluster_properties part may begin with a Use paragraph, as in

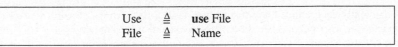

browsing: "~/*current*/*browser*"
   use
     "*.lace*"
   end -- *browsing*

to indicate that the cluster's directory contains a "Use file" (here of name *.lace*) containing the specification of some of the cluster's properties. The content of a Use file must itself be a Cluster_properties conforming to the Lace syntax. This makes it possible to specify cluster properties (for example compilation options) in a file that remains stored with the cluster itself.

In the above example, the Cluster_properties part for cluster *browsing* in the Ace has no further paragraphs beside Use, so all the cluster properties for *browsing* will be taken from the Use file. In the examples that follow, however, the Ace will contain other paragraphs for *browsing*, such as Include, Exclude or Options. In such a case the properties specified in the Ace are added to those of the Use file, and they take precedence in case of conflict.

It is a general Lace principle that whenever two comparable properties may apply (here a property specified in a Use file, and a property specified in the Ace after the Use paragraph) the one appearing last is added to the first or, in case of conflict, overrides it.

Here is the syntax of the optional Use paragraph of a Cluster_properties part:

Use	≙	**use** File
File	≙	Name

To keep things simple, the Cluster_properties part contained in a Use file may not itself contain a Use paragraph.

VDUC

D.9 Excluding and including source files

The next two optional Cluster_properties paragraphs, Include and Exclude, serve to request the explicit inclusion or exclusion of specific source files. Two important applications are overriding the default naming convention for files containing class texts, and selecting non-standard versions of a library class.

By default, when you list a cluster as part of a system, this includes all the class texts contained in files having names of a certain standard form in the cluster's directory; normally this standard form is *xxx.e* for any string *xxx*, although certain platforms may have different conventions (for example if periods are not legal characters in file names). The rest of this presentation assumes the *xxx.e* convention.

A *xxx.e* file may contain one or more classes, written consecutively. It is often a good idea to have just one class per file, with the *xxx* part of the file name being the lower-case version of the Class_name; for example file *cursor.e* would contain the source text for class *CURSOR*. In some cases, however, you may wish to group the texts of a few small and closely related classes in a single file.

The *xxx.e* convention or its equivalent is only the default. You may wish to remove from consideration a file with a name of this form (because you do not want to include the corresponding classes in your system, or simply because the file contains non-Eiffel text); conversely, you may wish to add to the cluster some classes residing in files having non-conforming names. The **exclude** and **include** clauses achieve this.

Here is a typical use, which excludes file *g.t.e* and includes two files with non-standard names:

```
browsing: "-/current/browser"
  use
    ".lace"
  include
    "commands";
    "states"
  exclude
    "g.t.e"
  end -- browsing
```

You may also apply the Exclude facility when you wish a class from a certain cluster to override a class from another cluster. If you exclude a file containing a class of name *C*, and another cluster contains a class with the same name, this class will override the original *C*. This is useful in particular if you wish to replace a library class by your own version. Assume for example you want to use your own version of *ANY*, the universal class serving as ancestor to all developer-defined classes. You may achieve this by storing the new version in one of your clusters and excluding the default one (assumed to be in file *any.e* in cluster *default*):

← About ANY see 6.12, page 85, and chapter 27.

Normally, the substitute version of ANY should still inherit from PLATFORM, making it a descendant of GENERAL; but it may add new features, which will be inherited by all classes of the system.

> *default*: *"/usr/local/Eiffel/library/kernel"*
> **exclude**
>   *"any.e"*
> **end** -- *default*

Here is the syntax of the Include and Exclude optional paragraphs of a Cluster_properties part:

Include	≜	**include** File_list
Exclude	≜	**exclude** File_list
File_list	≜	{File ";" ...}

D.10 Adapting class names

The next Cluster_properties paragraph, Name_adaptation, takes care of class renaming. Typically, this facility is not needed except for large developments, or those combining classes from various sources, so that you may safely skip this section on second reading.

If this is your **first** *reading you are already on the long route. (See "shortcut" on page 515.)*

A Name_adaptation paragraph makes it possible for the classes of a cluster to refer to classes of some other clusters under a locally adapted name, or to ignore them altogether. Here is our *browsing* cluster extended with such a paragraph:

> *browsing*: *"~/current/browser"*
> **use**
>   *".lace"*
> **include**
>   *"commands"*;
>   *"states"*
> **exclude**
>   *"g.t.e"*
> **adapt**
>   *graphics:*
>   **rename** *CURSOR* **as** *GRAPHICS_CURSOR,*
>   *WINDOW* **as** *GRAPHICAL_WINDOW*;
>   *basics:*
>   **rename** *CURSOR* **as** *LIST_CURSOR*;
>   *parsing:*
>   **ignore**
> **end** -- *browsing*

The major application of this facility is to resolve class name clashes. Although it is not permitted to have two classes with the same name in a given cluster, such clashes may happen in a universe, as defined by the entire Clusters list of an Ace. The class renaming mechanism, directly patterned after the Eiffel facilities for feature renaming in inheritance, makes it possible for the classes of a cluster such as *browsing* to refer to a class name which appears in more than one cluster; in this example, both the *graphics* and *basics* clusters have a class called *CURSOR*, and renaming enables *browsing* to use both.

Classes of *graphics* will use the names *GRAPHICS_CURSOR* and *LIST_CURSOR* rather than *CURSOR*. Class *WINDOW* from *graphics* is similarly renamed. The Name_adaptation paragraph of a Cluster_properties part for a certain cluster may only rename classes from other clusters, not from the cluster itself (here *browsing*).

← *See the end of chapter 3, starting with 3.7 on page 39, for a more complete discussion of the need for class renaming. Feature renaming for inheritance was described in 6.9, starting on page 81.*

A name clash could also occur between a class of the current cluster and some other cluster in the universe. For example, *browsing* could have a class of name *CONSTRUCT*, conflicting with the name of a class in cluster *parsing*, also part of the universe. You may apply renaming in this case too; if, however, the classes of *browsing* do not refer to the classes of the offending cluster at all, it suffices to use a Cluster_ignore subclause, which, as illustrated above, simply consists of the keyword **ignore**.

A system will be said to have a name clash if, taking into account every Cluster_rename_clause and Cluster_ignore, a class reachable from the root refers to a class name used by more than one class in the system. A system that has such a name clash is invalid. Note that it is not invalid for the entire universe to have identically named classes; only clashes in classes reachable from the root matter.

A class B is "reachable" from a class A if A refers to B directly or indirectly. See below.

The Name_adaptation paragraph, if present, has the following form:

Name_adaptation	≜	**adapt** Cluster_adaptation_list
Cluster_adaptation_list	≜	{Cluster_adaptation ";" ...}
Cluster_adaptation	≜	Cluster_ignore |
		Cluster_rename_clause
Cluster_ignore	≜	Cluster_name ":" **ignore**
Cluster_rename_clause	≜	Cluster_name ":"
		rename Class_rename_list
Class_rename_list	≜	{Class_rename_pair "," ...}
Class_rename_pair	≜	Class_name **as** Class_name

D.11 Specifying options

Option values govern actions of the tools that will process the Ace; for example they may affect compilation, interpretation or linking.

An option specification may appear in any of the following three Ace components, all optional:

- The Ace-level Defaults clause.
- The Defaults paragraph of a Cluster_properties part.
- The Options paragraph of a Cluster_properties part.

In the last two cases, the Cluster_properties may be in the Ace itself or in the Use file for one of its clusters.

If two or more conflicting values are given for an option, the last overrides any preceding ones. This means that values in the Options paragraph override cluster-level Defaults values, which override Ace-level Defaults values, and that a value in any of these components overrides any preceding value in the same component.

Here is a specimen of an Ace-level Defaults clause already shown above:

> **default**
>
>   *assertions* (**ensure**); *trace* (**no**);
>   *collect* (**yes**); *debug* (**no**);

This example enables options as indicated. It is also acceptable as a cluster-level Defaults, except for the presence of *collect* (enabling garbage collection), which may only be given at the Ace-level since garbage collection applies to an entire system.

To get an example of cluster-level Defaults and Options, let us extend our *browsing* Cluster_clause example:

> *browsing*: *"~/current/browser"*
>   **use**
>   *".lace"*
>   **include**
>   *"commands"*;
>   *"states"*
>   **exclude**
>   *"g.t.e"*
>   **adapt**
>   *graphics:*
>   **rename** *CURSOR* **as** *GRAPHICS_CURSOR,*
>   *WINDOW* **as** *GRAPHICAL_WINDOW*;
>   *basics:*
>   **rename** *CURSOR* **as** *LIST_CURSOR*;
>   *parsing:*
>   **ignore**
>   **default**
>   *debug* (*"level2"*);
>   *debug* (*"io_check"*)
>   **option**
>   *assertion* (**all**): *CONSTANTS, FULL_TEXT*;
>   *trace*: *FUNCTIONS, QUIT, RENAMED*;
>   *debug* (**yes**): *LAYOUT, FUNCTIONS*;
>   *debug* (*"format"*): *FULL_TEXT, OUTPUT*;
>   *debug* (*"numerical_accuracy"*): *OUTPUT*
>   **end** -- *browsing*

The Defaults paragraph overrides any Ace-level default for the *debug* option by enabling execution of Debug instructions in routines of classes of the cluster, for the Debug_key *level2* and the Debug_key *io_check*.

← *See 14.8, starting on page 244, about* Debug *instructions and* Debug_key.

The Options paragraph in turn overrides all preceding Defaults. The syntactic structure of is the same as for a Defaults paragraph, except that here every Option_tag (and optional Option_value in parentheses) may be followed by a Target_list, beginning with a colon, which lists one or more Name; these must be the names of classes in the cluster. In that case the option given overrides the default only for the classes given.

If there is no Target_list, the option applies to all classes in the cluster.

Here is the syntax of Options and Defaults paragraphs:

Defaults	≜	**default** {Option_clause ";" ...}
Options	≜	**option** {Option_clause ";" ...}
Option_clause	≜	Option_tag [Option_mark] [Target_list]
Target_list	≜	":" {Class_name "," ...}$^+$
Option_tag	≜	Class_tag | System_tag
System_tag	≜	*collect* | Free_tag
Class_tag	≜	*assertion* | *debug* | *optimize* | *trace* | Free_tag
Free_tag	≜	Name
Option_mark	≜	"(" Option_value ")"
Option_value	≜	Standard_value | Class_value
Standard_value	≜	**yes** | **no** | **all** | Free_value
Class_value	≜	**require** | **ensure** | **invariant** | **loop** | **check** | Free_value
Free_value	≜	File_name | Directory_name | Name

A Target_list may only appear in an Options paragraph, not in a Defaults paragraph. A System_tag may only appear in an Ace-level Defaults clause.

The syntax permits only one Option_value, not a list of values, after an Option_tag. You may obtain the effect of multiple values by repeating the same Option_tag with different values, as was done in the example with the lines

> *debug ("format"): FULL_TEXT, OUTPUT;*
> *debug ("numerical_accuracy"): OUTPUT;*

which imply enabling the debug option for class *OUTPUT* both for the Debug_key *format* and for the Debug_key *numerical_accuracy*. In case of conflict, as usual, the last value given overrides any preceding ones.

This syntax shows that for an Option_tag as well as an Option_value you may use not just predefined forms (such as *assertion* for an Option_tag and **no** for an Option_value) but also Free forms, each of which is defined just as a Name (Identifier or Manifest_string). This means that along with general-purpose options which are presumably of interest to all implementations of Eiffel (level of assertion monitoring, garbage collection etc.), individual implementors may add their own specific options.

The predefined possibilities for Option_tag (*collect, assertion* etc.) are not Lace keywords, and so may be used as identifiers in an Ace. The predefined possibilities for Standard_value, however, are keywords; they appear in boldface (**yes, require** etc.). Remember that you can always use a Manifest_string (such as "*YES*" or "*DEFAULTS*") to write a Lace name, for example the name of a class in the system, which conflicts with a keyword.

← *The lexical conventions appeared in D.5, page 518.*

When the predefined forms are supported, they should satisfy the constraints and produce the effects summarized in the following table.

Option	Governs	Possible values	Default	Scope
assertion	Level of assertion monitoring and execution of Check instructions.	**no, require, ensure, invariant, loop, check, all.** Monitoring at each level in this list also applies to the subsequent levels (**ensure** implies precondition checking etc.). Value **invariant** means class invariant; **loop** means monitoring of loop invariants and of loop variant decrease; **check** adds execution of **check** instructions; **all** means the same as **check.**	**require**	
collect	Garbage collection	**no, yes.**	**no**	No class list (applies to entire system)
debug	Execution of Debug instructions	**no, yes, all** or a Name representing a Debug_key. Value **yes** means the same as **all.**	**no**	
optimize	Optimization of generated code	**no, yes, all**, or a Name representing a specific optimization level offered by the compiler. In the Defaults or Options clause for a given cluster, **yes** governs class-level optimization and **all** means the same as **yes**. In the Ace-level Defaults clause, **yes** governs systemwide optimization, and **all** means the same as **yes** plus class-level optimization.	**no**	
trace	Generation of run-time tracing information for every call to, and return from, routines of classes to which the option applies.	**no, yes** or **all**. Value **yes** means the same as **all.**	**no**	

D.12 Specifying external elements

To assemble a system you may need "external" elements, written in another language or available in object form from earlier compilations. The Externals clause serves to list these elements.

Here is an example Externals clause:

> **external**
>
> *Object*: *"object_name.o", "../basics.o", "-ltermcap", "otherlib.a"*;
> *C*: *"previous.h", "/usr/$MACHINE/src/screen.c"*;
> *Make*: *"../Clib/makefile"*

Such a clause contains one or more Language_contribution, each being relative to a certain Language. Every Language is given by an Identifier, such as:

- *Object*: object code, produced by a compiler for some language, to be linked with the result of system compilation or included for interpretation.
- *Ada*: Ada language elements.
- *Pascal*: Pascal language elements.
- *Fortran*: Fortran language elements.
- *C*: C language elements.
- *Make*: Descriptions of dependencies needed to recompile non-Eiffel software elements.

Remember that letter case is not significant, so that "FORTRAN" and "make" would also be permitted.

Make is a Unix tool, with equivalents on many other operating systems, which works from a dependency list, or Makefile, to recompile or reconstruct software. Make and makefiles are normally not needed for Eiffel classes, but may be needed for external non-Eiffel software.

The exact list of supported Language possibilities depends on the implementation.

In each Language_contribution, the Language is followed by a semicolon and a list of File names containing the corresponding elements.

The syntax of the Externals clause is the following.

SYNTAX

Externals	≜	**external** {Language_contribution ";" ...}
Language_contribution	≜	Language ":" File_list
Language	≜	*Eiffel* | *Ada* | *Pascal* | *Fortran* | *C* | *Object* | *Make* | Name

The predefined language names (*Eiffel, Ada* etc.) are not Lace keywords, and so may be used as identifiers in an Ace.

D.13 Generation

The Generation clause indicates what output, if any, should be generated by the assembly process, and where that output should be stored.

A specimen of the clause is:

> **generate**
>
> *Executable*: *"$INSTALLATION/bin"*;
> *C* (**yes**): *"$INSTALLATION/src/browser/package"*;
> *Object* (**no**): *"$INSTALLATION/bin/M_68040/eb"*

This Generation clause requests generation of both an executable module and a C package containing the translation of the original Eiffel. Clearly, although any Eiffel environment which is not solely meant for analysis or design will support *executable* generation, the availability of any other target language is implementation-dependent.

ISE's Eiffel compiler generates executable code as well as C packages (including a copy of the run-time system, a Make file and all other elements needed to compile and run the result). The C package generation mechanism provides support for cross-development.

The generate Target, coming after the colon, is either a Directory, as in the first example, or a File, as in the second. If it is a directory, the output will be stored in a file of that directory; the name of that file will normally be the System_name, here *browser*. The tools may also use both the System_name and the name of the root's chosen creation procedure to make up the name of the executable output file.

The Language name (*Executable, C* or Object in the example) may be followed by a Generate_option_value, **yes** or **no**, in parentheses. The absence of this component, as in the first two cases of the example, is equivalent to (**yes**). The last line requests that no *Object* package be generated. The Ace's author may re-enable *Object* generation simply by replacing **no** by **yes**.

Here is the syntax of the Generation clause:

Generation	≜	**generate** {Language_generation ";" ...}
Language_generation	≜	Language [Generate_option] ":" Target
Generate_option	≜	"(" Generate_option_value ")"
Generate_option_value	≜	**yes** | **no**
Target	≜	Directory | File

D.14 Visible features

As you generate output from a system, you may want to make some of the system's classes available to external software elements that will create instances of these classes (through creation procedures) and apply features to those instances (through exported features).

Using the Visible paragraph of a Cluster_properties part, you may indicate which classes of the cluster must be externally visible; this will apply by default to all the creation procedures and exported features of these classes, but you may also request external visibility for some of them only. Furthermore, you may make some of them externally available under names which are different from their original names in the class text, for example if they are to be called from a language whose identifier conventions differ from those of Eiffel.

Some external software may also need to refer to the class name itself; this is the case with *eif_proc* and similar functions from the Cecil library, which obtain a routine pointer. If the Eiffel name of the class is not appropriate for this purpose (in particular when it would cause ambiguity), you may define a different external class name.

← *See 24.7, page 406, about Cecil; 'eif_proc' and similar functions are defined on page 408.*

Here is the *browsing* cluster extended with a Visible paragraph:

```
browsing: "not/current/browser"
  use
    ".lace"
  include
    "commands";
    "states"
  exclude
    "g.t.e"
  adapt
    graphics:
      rename CURSOR as GRAPHICS_CURSOR,
        WINDOW as GRAPHICAL_WINDOW;
    basics:
      rename CURSOR as LIST_CURSOR;
    parsing:
      ignore
  default
    debug ("level2");
    debug ("io_check")
  option
    assertion (all): CONSTANTS, FULL_TEXT;
    trace: FUNCTIONS, QUIT, RENAMED;
    debug (yes): LAYOUT, FUNCTIONS;
    debug ("format"): FULL_TEXT, OUTPUT;
    debug ("numerical_accuracy"): OUTPUT;

  visible

    CONSTANTS as BROWSING_CONSTANTS;

    LAYOUT
      rename
        choice_menu as "choice.menu", set_reverse as "set.reverse"
      end;

    EB
      creation
        initialize
      export
        execute, set_target, initialize
      rename
        set_target as "set.target"
      end
  end -- browsing
```

Here you are requesting external visibility for three classes of the cluster: *CONSTANTS, LAYOUT* and *EB*.

For *CONSTANTS*, you have defined a different external class name, *BROWSING_CONSTANTS*, for use by external software such as Cecil functions.   ← *See 24.7, page 406, about Cecil.*

For *CONSTANTS* and *LAYOUT*, external software can create objects using all the creation procedures of these classes (if any), and call all exported features on these objects. Two features of *LAYOUT* are available to external software (for creation or call) under names different from their Eiffel names, making them callable from a language which prohibits underscores _ in identifiers.

For *EB*, feature *set_target* is also externally renamed. In addition, you have only requested external availability for specific features of *EB*: among creation procedures, you only need *initialize* to be externally available for object creation; and among exported features, you only need *execute, set_target* (under its external name *set.target*) and *initialize* to be externally available for calls.

External software may never use a feature for creating objects unless the class text declares it as a creation procedure, and may never use a feature for calls unless the class text declares it as exported. The Export_restriction subclause (beginning with **export**) and the Creation_restriction subclause (beginning with **creation**) are not permitted to extend external availability beyond what is implied by the Eiffel class text. (For one thing, a secret feature is not required to preserve the invariant, so calling it from external software elements could put an object into an inconsistent state, which is the first step towards Armageddon.)

← An "exported" feature is one that is generally available to all clients (exported without restriction). A "secret" feature, which is a special case of non-exported feature, is one which is available to no client except NONE. See page 100.

It is not incorrect for an implementation to make all exported features of all classes externally available. With such an implementation, you will usually not need any Visible paragraph. You may still, however, use an Ace (perhaps written for another implementation) that has a Visible paragraph: the semantics of such a paragraph is to specify that certain features should be externally visible; it does not preclude an implementation from providing *more* externally visible features – the implementation just does more than it has to.

Even an implementation which by default makes all compiled features externally visible may in fact need to support the Visible paragraph. The reason is that a compiler may include a global system optimizer, which will detect routines that are not reachable from the creation procedure of the system's root class, and eliminate such routines from the generated code. The optimizer might also decide to inline all calls to certain routines, and then remove the object code for these routines. In such cases you will need to use a Visible paragraph to guarantee that the routines remain available for use by external software.

The syntax of the optional Visible paragraph is the following:

SYNTAX

Visible	≜	**visible** {Class_visibility ";" ...}
Class_visibility	≜	Class_name [Visibility_adaptation]
Visibility_adaptation	≜	[External_class_rename]
		[Creation_restriction]
		[Export_restriction]
		[External_feature_rename]
		end
External_feature_rename	≜	**as** Name
Creation_restriction	≜	**creation** {Feature_name "," ...}
Export_restriction	≜	**export** {Feature_name "," ...}
External_feature_rename	≜	**rename** External_rename_list
External_rename_list	≜	{External_rename_pair "," ...}
External_rename_pair	≜	Feature_name **as** Name

D.15 Lace Grammar

For ease of reference, you will find below the complete grammar of Lace, repeating the individual descriptions given earlier in this appendix.

Ace	≙	System
		Root
		[Defaults]
		[Clusters]
		[Externals]
		[Generation]
		end ["--" **system** System_name]
System	≙	**system** System_name
System_name	≙	Name
Root	≙	**root**
		Class_name
		[Cluster_mark]
		[Creation_procedure]
Class_name	≙	Name
Cluster_mark	≙	"(" Cluster_name ")"
Cluster_name	≙	Name
Creation_procedure	≙	":" Name

Name	≙	Identifier	Manifest_string

Clusters	≙	**cluster** {Cluster_clause ";" ...}
Cluster_clause	≙	[Cluster_tag]
		Directory_name
		[Cluster_properties]
Cluster_tag	≙	Cluster_name ":"
Directory_name	≙	Name
Cluster_properties		[Use]
		[Include]
		[Exclude]
		[Name_adaptation]
		[Defaults]
		[Options]
		[Visible]
		end ["--" **cluster** Cluster_name]

Use	≙	**use** File
File	≙	Name

Include	≜	**include** File_list
Exclude	≜	**exclude** File_list
File_list	≜	{File ";" ...}

Name_adaptation	≜	**adapt** Cluster_adaptation_list
Cluster_adaptation_list	≜	{Cluster_adaptation ";" ...}
Cluster_adaptation	≜	Cluster_ignore |
		Cluster_rename_clause
Cluster_ignore	≜	Cluster_name ":" **ignore**
Cluster_rename_clause	≜	Cluster_name ":"
		rename Class_rename_list
Class_rename_list	≜	{Class_rename_pair "," ...}
Class_rename_pair	≜	Class_name **as** Class_name

Defaults	≜	**default** {Option_clause ";" ...}
Options	≜	**option** {Option_clause ";" ...}
Option_clause	≜	Option_tag [Option_mark] [Target_list]
Target_list	≜	":" {Class_name "," ...}⁺
Option_tag	≜	Class_tag | System_tag
System_tag	≜	*collect* | Free_tag
Class_tag	≜	*assertion* | *debug* | *optimize* | *trace* |
		Free_tag
Free_tag	≜	Name
Option_mark	≜	"(" Option_value ")"
Option_value	≜	Standard_value | Class_value
Standard_value	≜	**yes** | **no** | **all** | Free_value
Class_value	≜	**require** | **ensure** |
		invariant | **loop** | **check** |
		Free_value
Free_value	≜	File_name | Directory_name | Name

Externals	≜	**external**
		{Language_contribution ";" ...}
Language_contribution	≜	Language ":" File_list
Language	≜	*Eiffel* | *Ada* | *Pascal* |
		Fortran | *C* | *Object* | *Make* |
		Name

Generation	≜	**generate** {Language_generation ";" ...}
Language_generation	≜	Language [Generate_option] ":" Target
Generate_option	≜	"(" Generate_option_value ")"
Generate_option_value	≜	**yes** | **no**
Target	≜	Directory | File

Visible	≜	**visible** {Class_visibility ";" ...}
Class_visibility	≜	Class_name [Visibility_adaptation]
Visibility_adaptation	≜	[External_class_rename]
		[Creation_restriction]
		[Export_restriction]
		[External_feature_rename]
		end
External_feature_rename	≜	**as** Name
Creation_restriction	≜	**creation** {Feature_name "," ...}
Export_restriction	≜	**export** {Feature_name "," ...}
External_feature_rename	≜	**rename** External_rename_list
External_rename_list	≜	{External_rename_pair "," ...}
External_rename_pair	≜	Feature_name **as** Name

E

Old-new dictionary

E.1 Overview

The Eiffel language, as defined in this book, has undergone some changes from earlier versions. This appendix and the next highlight the areas where the new version, **Eiffel 3**, differs from previous ones, the last of which was 2.3.

→ *Appendix F is in the new-to-old direction.*

These changes do not affect any of the fundamental concepts and conventions of the language but provide a number of improvements resulting from the feedback of hundreds of developers using Eiffel worldwide, from numerous discussions with authors of other implementations, and from the designers' own further thinking

The translation from old to new is sufficiently simple and systematic to be performed by an automatic tool. So, with one exception, developers should not have to do any manual conversion. (The exception is the need to rename any identifier which conflicts with one of the ten new reserved words.)

ISE's Eiffel 3 compiler includes an old-to-new converter.

The list of new reserved words appears below in E.19, page 546.

The differences are of three kinds:

- Changes to the concrete syntax, improving the consistency of the language and the clarity of software texts.

- Adjustment or clarification of the semantics of a few constructs, taking care of cases which proved confusing, such as the combination of repeated inheritance and redeclaration.

- A few new constructs, easing the developers' task in some frequent situations.

In all cases, the constant concern was to keep Eiffel a simple language, easy to learn, to use and to remember, without yielding to the temptation of "featurism", but also without sacrificing the expressive power required of a universal language used to produce quality systems in all application areas of computers. In other words, borrowed from a famous quotation: making Eiffel as simple as possible, but no simpler.

If you are new to Eiffel you do not need this appendix. You should find it useful, however, if you belong to either one of the following two categories:

→ *Appendix B presents a view of language evolution.*

- You have not yet had access to an actual Eiffel environment, but are one of those people whose main previous introduction to Eiffel was the book *Object-Oriented Software Construction* (OOSC), which described an even earlier version of Eiffel than 2.3.

- You know Eiffel but have only had access so far to Eiffel tools supporting Eiffel 2.3 (or earlier).

In the first case, you should begin with the next section, which summarizes improvements made between the publication of OOSC and 2.3.

→ *See section E.2*

In the second case, you may safely skip the next section, which will not teach you anything, and move directly to the description of the new facilities in E.3 and the subsequent sections.

E.2 Older post-OOSC extensions

Prior to the introduction of Eiffel 3, the following mechanisms were added between the original publication of the book *Object-Oriented Software Construction* in 1988 and the release of Eiffel 2.3:

- Constrained genericity, enabling a generic class to place certain requirements, expressed through inheritance, on possible actual generic parameters. (OOSC in fact mentioned this, but only through an exercise.)

← *12.8, page 202.*

- The Indexing clause for recording important information on a class, to be used by archival, browsing and query tools.

← *4.7, page 49.*

- The Assignment_attempt ?=, for type-safe assignments going against the inheritance hierarchy.

← *20.13, page 330, and subsequent sections.*

- Infix and prefix operators, for more flexible call syntax.

← *5.13, page 67.*

- Expanded types, supporting composite objects and avoiding unnecessary dynamic allocation.

← *12.10, page 204, and subsequent sections.*

- The Obsolete clause (in classes and routines) for smooth library evolution.

← *4.10, page 52 (classes); 5.17, page 73 (routines).*

- Unique values for integer codes not explicitly assigned by class authors.

← *16.6, page 264.*

- The Multi_branch instruction for discriminating between a set of cases without using dynamic binding.

← *14.5, page 236*

- The boolean operator for implication (**implies**), which previously had to be expressed using the operator **or else**.

← *23.4, page 375.*

- Support for double-precision reals (type *DOUBLE*).

- Basic expanded classes from the Kernel Library, defining *BOOLEAN, CHARACTER, INTEGER, REAL* and *DOUBLE*.

← *12.13, page 209, and chapter 32.*

- The join mechanism for merging one or more inherited deferred routines with compatible signatures and specifications. (In 2.3 this required a now obsolete keyword, **define**, and an effecting of the resulting features.)

← *10.13, page 150. Eiffel 3 requires neither effecting nor a keyword.*

- More flexibility in the interface with other languages, in particular through the introduction of the *$* symbol (@ in 2.3).

← *Chapter 24, especially 24.6, page 404.*

E.3 Feature adaptation

Any Feature_adaptation subclause (in the Parent clause of an Inheritance part) indicating changes in inherited features, must now be terminated with an **end**, as in the following example (involving repeated inheritance from B):

```
class C inherit
    B
        rename
            f as g, u as v
        redefine
            g, x
        end;

    B
        rename
            f as h
        select
            h
        end
    ...
```

As before, the various Parent subclauses must be separated by a semicolon. Previously, there was no **end**; this meant that an extra semicolon, for example between a Rename and a Redefine subclauses, could make the construct ambiguous, resulting in minor but annoying syntactical errors. Such an extra semicolon will now be harmless. The use of **end** is also more consistent with the conventions used elsewhere in the language (routine declarations, instructions).

E.4 Specifying export status

There is no more **export** clause at the beginning of a class; this clause was used to specify the export regime of every feature of the class. Instead, there may be more than one Feature_clause; each defines the export regime of the features it introduces. If a Feature_clause just begins with the **feature** keyword with no further qualification, all the features it introduces are publicly available. To obtain the effect of a secret feature, begin the Feature_clause with

```
feature {NONE}
```

To obtain the effect of a feature available selectively to specified classes, begin the Feature_clause with

```
feature {A, B, C, ...}
```

As a consequence, there is no more need for the **repeat** subclause (which was part of an **export** clause and served to repeat a parent's export specification). By default, inherited features keep the original export status they had in the parent, unless they are redefined. The status of a redefined feature is determined by the qualification of the Feature_clause in which the redefinition occurs. To change the status of an inherited feature which is not redefined, use an **export** subclause in the Feature_adaptation clause at the point of inheritance, as in

```
class D inherit
    C
        rename
            remove as new_remove, count as new_count, put as new_put;
            ...
        redefine
            ...
        export
            {NONE} all;
            {A, B} new_remove, new_count;
            {ANY} new_put
        select
            ...
        end;
    ...
```

Here all features inherited from *C* and not redefined are secret, except for *remove* and *count*, available to *A* and *B* under their new names *new_remove* and *new_count*, and *put* which is available to all clients under its new name *new_put*. As illustrated by this example, the **export** specifications, as all other subclauses of the Feature_adaptation clause, refer to features under their final names in the current class, that is to say, to the names obtained after the application of the Rename subclause.

E.5 Adapting preconditions and postconditions

Another important language improvement affects the rule on adaptation of preconditions and postconditions for redefined routines is now a language mechanism, rather than a purely methodological guideline. In pre-version 3, a Precondition or Postcondition always appeared in full, even for a redefined routine for which the assertions had not changed. If they did change, you were only supposed to replace an original precondition with a weaker one, or an original postcondition with a stronger one; but the language did not support these rules directly.

It now does. In a redefined routine, an absent Precondition means "keep the original's precondition", and similarly for an absent postcondition. To change these assertions, you may use the respective forms

```
require else new_precondition_clause

ensure then new_postcondition_clause
```

Calling *original_precondition* and *original_postcondition* the inherited routine's assertions, this yields as new precondition and postcondition the assertions

> *new_precondition_clause* **or else** *original_precondition*
>
> *new_postcondition_clause* **and then** *original_postcondition*

← **or else** *and* **and then** *are the versions of the "or" and "and" operators which do not evaluate their second argument unless they have to. See 23.9, page 381.*

which by their very construction satisfy the weakening-strengthening rule.

E.6 Removing ambiguities in repeated inheritance

Separate paths of repeated inheritance may cause a feature to be redefined in different ways. The 2.3 language specification left the resolution of dynamic binding conflicts in such a case implementation. It turned out, however, that developers need finer control. The Select clause addresses the problem.

Assume B and C both inherit a feature f from A, and at least one of them redefines f. D is an heir of both B and C, so it is a repeated descendant of A.

← *This will be clearer if you follow on the figure on page 178.*

If D inherited both versions of f under the same name, the rules of repeated inheritance would imply sharing; this would cause ambiguity and is prohibited. If the final names in D are different, causing replication, an ambiguity remains for the run-time interpretation of a call $a.f$ where a, of type A, is dynamically attached to an instance of D.

← *The Repeated Inheritance Consistency constraint appears on page 191; read first the discussion in 11.6, page 177.*

A Select clause must indicate which version to trigger in such a case. The scheme is straightforward:

```
class D inherit
    B
        rename
            f as bf, ...
        redefine
            ...
        select
            bf
                -- This select the B version for dynamic binding from A.
        end;
    C
        rename
            f as cf
        ...
        end
    ...
```

E.7 Renaming, redefining, joining and undefining

In pre-version 3, it was possible to duplicate an inherited feature by renaming it and keeping the old one under a different name; dynamic binding would then apply to entities of the parent type will trigger the redefined version. The scheme was:

```
class C export ... inherit
    B
        rename
            f as inherited_f
        redefine
            f
    ...
```

WARNING: *not valid in Eiffel 3.*

This possibility has been removed since some details of the resulting mechanism proved difficult to explain. (The table on "combining redefinition and renaming, present in both *Object-Oriented Software Construction* and earlier versions of the present book, is not necessary any more.) It was in fact unnecessary since repeated inheritance also achieves feature duplication in a more uniform way. To obtain the effect of the above, you may write:

```
class C inherit
    B
        redefine
            f
        select
            f
        end;

    B
        rename
            f as inherited_f
        end;
    ...
```

The Select subclause ensures that dynamic binding (on an entity of type B attached at run-time to an object of type C) will use the redefined version.

Complementing Redefine, a new clause, Undefine, makes it possible to de-effect a feature inherited in effective form, turning it into a deferred feature. A related constraint is the impossibility of redefining an effective feature into a deferred one: in such a case you must use undefinition. ← *Undefinition: 10.16, page 155. Redeclaration rule: page 163.*

Two or more deferred features inherited under the same name will yield a single deferred feature. This is known as the join mechanism and is useful to merge abstractions. An essentially equivalent mechanism existed in pre-version 3 but required the inheriting class to effect the features and to mark them using the keyword **define** (not a reserved word in Eiffel 3). These restrictions do not apply any more. ← *10.17, page 156.*

By combining the previous two possibilities, you may merge a set of effective features inherited from parents, one of these features imposing its implementation on the others. ← *Merging effective features: 10.18, page 158.*

E.8 Synonyms

You may now define two or more features with the same name, as in

> $f1, f2 (...)$ **is** ...

← See 5.16, page 71.

This is equivalent to duplicate declarations; the features declared together are not otherwise connected. Redefining or renaming one in a proper descendant has no effect on the others.

E.9 Frozen features

If you want to preserve not just the specification of a feature (through its assertions) but also its exact implementation in descendants, you may declare it as **frozen**. This prevents any redefinition in descendants.

Syntactically, the keyword **frozen** comes just before the feature before the feature name in the declaration. This may be used in conjunction with the previous facility, synonyms, as in

← See 5.9, page 63.

> **frozen** $f1, f2 (...)$ **is** ...

which prevents $f1$ from being redefined, but does not restrict $f2$. This enables clients to choose between a version guaranteed to remain identically implemented even with dynamic binding, and one that may be adapted to local contexts.

Many of the basic features of the universal class *ANY* follow this pattern: for example, *copy* and *is_equal* are in fact defined as

← See chapters 19 and 27 about 'copy' and 'is_equal'. 'equal', usually convenient to use than 'is_equal', will automatically follow redefinitions of 'is_equal'.

> *copy*, **frozen** *standard_copy* (*other*: **like** *Current*) **is** ...
>
> *is_equal*, **frozen** *standard_is_equal* (*other*: **like** *Current*):
>   *BOOLEAN* **is** ...

providing clients with a fixed, universal implementation of these basic operations under the standard names, while allowing them to use custom-redefined versions for local variants (under the control of the assertion redefinition rules), which is the desired effect in normal cases.

E.10 Anchoring to a formal argument

In an anchored declaration (**like** *anchor*) the *anchor* may now be not just *Current* or an attribute of the enclosing class, but also, in a routine text, a formal argument of that routine.

← See 12.15, page 211, about anchored declaration and 13.8, page 224, about the corresponding typing constraints.

This technique is used in the routines just discussed. Two further examples from *ANY*:

> *equal* (*some*: *ANY*; *other*: **like** *some*): *BOOLEAN* **is** ...
>
> *clone* (*other*: *ANY*): **like** *other* **is** ...

In a call to *equal*, the type of the second actual argument must conform to the type of the first. In *y* := *clone* (*x*), the type of *x* must conform to the type of *y*.

E.11 Creation syntax

The syntax for Creation instructions has changed. Instead of using a special procedure *Create*, you may designate any procedure of a class as being a "creation procedure" by listing it in the Creators part at the beginning of the class.

The most general notation for the Creation instruction is

> ! *DESCENDANT* ! *entity.creation_procedure* (*argument1*, ...)

This creates an instance of *DESCENDANT*, using *creation_procedure* with the actual arguments given, and attaches it to *entity*. Class *DESCENDANT* must conform to the type of *entity*, and must list *creation_procedure* in its Creators part.

By omitting some of the components in the above form, you get some useful special cases:

> ```
>         -- If DESCENDANT has no creation procedure
>         -- (default initializations only):
> ! DESCENDANT ! entity;
>
>         -- If DESCENDANT is in fact the type of entity:
> !! entity.creation_procedure (argument1, ...);
>
>         -- Simple case (combination of above two).
>         -- Valid only if the class has no creation procedure
>         -- (default initializations only):
> !! entity
> ```

This new syntax offers several advantages:

- There can be more than one creation procedure in a class, corresponding to various forms of initializations. For example, we may want to initialize a point by giving either its polar coordinates or its cartesian coordinates, through two creation procedures *set_polar* and *set_cartesian*.

- The creation procedures are normal procedures which, if exported, can also be used by clients with normal dot notation. For example *set_polar* and *set_cartesian* may be used to reset the coordinates of an already created point.

- The creation procedures may be inherited like any other procedure. Previously, *Create* could not be inherited except through a combination of renaming and redefinition. Every class remains free to choose its own creation procedures, which may include none, any or all of its parents' creation procedures.

- Dot notation now always has the same semantics, whereas it previously had special semantics for *Create*. Creation uses a different syntax.

E.12 Uniform semantics for dot notation

Creation was not the only case in which the dot notation in $x.f$ had special semantics. For all "normal" f, the notation $x.f$ described the application of feature f to the object attached to f, and required x to be non-void, triggering an exception otherwise. For a few special language-defined features, however (*Create*, *Clone*, *Forget*, *Void* and *Equal*), the convention was different: the operation really applied to the reference value of x, and was legal even if x was void (not attached to any object).

These cases have been removed to ensure full consistency: dot notation always has the semantics of an operation applicable to an object (and requires x to be non-void).

Clone, Forget, Void and *Equal* are no longer reserved words of the language; instead, the operations use features of the universal class *ANY*, of which all Eiffel classes are descendants. The names of these features (*clone, Void* and *equal*) are normal identifiers, and the features may be renamed in proper descendants of *ANY*.

- For cloning, the instruction $y.Clone\ (x)$ is now written as the assignment $y := clone\ (x)$.

- The forget instruction $x.Forget$ is written as the assignment $x := Void$. Feature *Void* of class *ANY* returns a reference of type *NONE*, the class which has no instances.

- The test for a void reference, previously written $x.Void$, is now $x = Void$.

- The field-by-field object equality test, instead of $x.Equal\ (y)$, is now $equal\ (x, y)$.

The previous special cases of dot notation being now handled by the Creation instruction or by routines of class *ANY*, it is never correct to apply a feature to a void reference. The result of such an erroneous event is to produce an exception.

Because routines of class *ANY* such as *clone* and *equal* are normal routines, you may adapt them in descendants – for example to provide a form of equality testing adapted to a specific class rather than the field-by-field comparison of the default *equal*. In some cases, however, a client may want to request the default operation, regardless of any possible redefinition. For this purpose, as noted above, *ANY* introduces frozen synonyms for these routines: *standard_copy*, *standard_equal* and so on.

Actually 'clone' and 'equal' are also frozen, but are defined in terms of 'copy' and 'is_equal', which are not frozen, and so they will follow any redefinition of these routines. See chapter 27 for details.

E.13 Manifest arrays and variable-length argument lists

In the same way that a *STRING* object may be given in manifest form (such as   ← *See 23.20, page 393.*
"*some string value*"), rather than by successive calls to fill its character
positions, you may now obtain a pre-allocated and pre-filled array through the
notation

$$\ll val_1, val_2, \ldots val_n \gg$$

which avoids the need to declare an array, allocate it, and use *put* operations to
fill in the values. The array indices start at one.

One benefit of this notation is the ability to declare a routine such as

formated_write (*values*: *ARRAY* [*T*]; *format*: *STRING*) **is** ...

and to call it with a variable number of values corresponding to the first
argument, as in

formated_write ($\ll a, b, c, a, d \gg$, *my_format*)
-- *a, b, c, d* must all conform to *T*.

You may use this possibility in any case where you need the effect of a
variable number of arguments. The routine will have access to these arguments
as elements of an array, with all the array operations available to ascertain the
number of arguments and access them directly or sequentially.

E.14 Default rescue

It is often convenient to define a default exception response for those routines
which do not have a specific Rescue clauses. In pre-version 3, this was done by
having a Rescue clause at the class level. The rescue clause was not passed on to
descendants because of potential conflicts in the case of multiple inheritance.

As simpler and more flexible convention is now used. The universal class   ← *See 15.5, page 251.*
ANY has a procedure *default_rescue*, which does nothing. Any class may
redefine this procedure to perform specific exception handling actions. Any
routine with no Rescue clause is considered to have a Rescue clause of the form

rescue
   def_resc

where *def_resc* is the local version of *default_rescue*, possibly redefined (and
possibly renamed). Classes inherit this routine like any other one, multiple
inheritance conflicts being handled in the standard way through renaming and
Select.

E.15 Expanded classes and basic types

As a notational facility, it is now possible to declare a class as

> **expanded class** *E* ... The rest as before ...

The only difference between such a declaration and one not beginning with **expanded** is that any type based on *E* will be expanded. This means that declaring *exp*: E (with generic parameters if any) makes *exp* expanded.

It is still possible, for any non-expanded class *N* satisfying the appropriate constraints, to declare *exp* as **expanded** *N*. If this is always desired for all entities whose type is based on a certain *C*, however, the above class declaration avoids the need for writing **expanded** for every such entity (and the risk of forgetting it).

The "expanded" status of a class has no influence on its role in the inheritance hierarchy: expanded classes may inherit from non-expanded ones and conversely.

The usual limitations on **conformance** continue to apply, however: the only cases of conformance of a reference type *R* to an expanded type *X* (conditioning the validity of such reattachments as the assignment *exp* := *ref* for entities and expressions of these types) are those in which *R* is the base type of *X* or conversely − in other words, the associated objects are guaranteed to be of exactly the same format, so that the assignment is a simple copy. In this case no conformance will be possible as soon as inheritance is involved.

← The precise rules appear in the definition of indirect conformance on page 219.

One of the consequences of the introduction of expanded classes is that the basic types *BOOLEAN, CHARACTER, INTEGER, REAL* and *DOUBLE* are now defined directly as classes, just as any other Class_type; there is no need for a special convention defining *INTEGER* as an abbreviation for **expanded** *INT* (for a non-expanded class *INT*) and so on.

← Chapter 32 introduces the features of the basic classes.

E.16 Semantics of expanded types

In what is probably the only non-trivial modification of an existing semantic property, the effect of an assignment

> *ref* := *exp*

where the type of *ref* is a reference type and the type of *exp* is expanded, is to create a new object identical to the value of *exp* (a clone) and attach *ref* to it.

Previously, no cloning occurred; *ref* would just become attached to the value of *exp*, a sub-object or some other object. This introduced a possibility for objects to contain references to sub-objects of other objects. This possibility, of dubious benefit, appears to have been used rarely if ever; it did, however, considerably complicate the run-time model and the implementation.

E.17 Infix and prefix operators

Infix and prefix operators may now use any sequence of characters of certain special characters, letters and digits. The first character must be one of the four characters @ # | &. Operators such as @ or |–f> are thus possible.

← See 25.10, page 418.

For compatibility with tradition, boolean operators still use alphabetic keywords (such as **and** and **or else**). They are the only ones, however; integer operators use non-alphabetic symbols:

Old Form	New Form
div	//
mod	\\

In a related change, the address symbol (a reserved special character, not a freely usable operator name), used to pass to feature addresses to external routines, previously @, is now written $. A feature address is of type *POINTER*, a new basic type with no applicable features.

← 24.6, page 404.

E.18 Place of obsolete clause

For consistency, the Obsolete clause of an obsolete routine now appears after the **is** keyword rather than before.

A class may also have an obsolete clause, indicating that usage of the class as a whole is discouraged – presumably because you have written a better version replacement which is not fully compatible or, more simply, because you prefer a different name for the class. The Obsolete clause in this case comes just before the Class_header (that is to say, before **class**, **deferred class** or **expanded class**, but after the Indexing clause if any).

← See 4.10, page 52 about obsolete classes and 5.17, page 73, about obsolete routines.

E.19 New reserved words

The following names were not reserved words in pre-3 Eiffel and hence could be used as identifiers. They are now reserved words; if you have used any of them to name a feature or entity, you must choose another name.

elseif *replaces* **elsif**; **alias** *replaces* **name**. **separate** *is not used in this book, but will be part of Eiffel's concurrency mechanism.*

> **alias**
> **all**
> **creation**
> **elseif**
> **frozen**
> *NONE*
> *POINTER*
> **select**
> **separate**
> **strip**

In the reverse direction, a number of reserved words of pre-3 Eiffel have lost their reserved status. Since their list is mainly of interest to developers currently using an older compiler, it appears in the next chapter. That list is in fact longer than the above one, making the number of reserved words shorter in Eiffel 3.

→ See F.6, page 551, for the list of words no longer reserved.

E.20 Other lexical changes

To improve readability of manifest number constants (integers, reals), it is now possible to use underscores delimiting groups of three digits in both the integral and (for a real constant) decimal parts. The commas do not affect the value. For example, 62_525_300.751_6 denotes the same value as 62525300.7516.

You are not required to use underscores, but if you do include one you must be consistent: the number may contain no group of four consecutive digits, every underscore in the integral part must be followed by exactly three digits, and every underscore in the decimal part must be preceded by exactly three digits.

The representation of special characters uses the percent sign % rather than the backslash \ as marker.

On the representation of special characters, see 25.15, starting on page 422.

F

New-old dictionary

F.1 Overview

The previous appendix highlighted the improvements that have been brought to Eiffel 3 as compared to earlier versions. This appendix includes some of the same information, but reversed.

You should find it useful if you are an Eiffel developer and use this book as your language reference, but temporarily have access to compiler or other tools that have not yet been brought up to the new conventions.

This is dated material; soon, it is hoped, no one will need it any more.

As noted in the previous appendix, you may expect your tool supplier to provide an automatic converter at the time the new version of the tools come out – so that you will not have to translate back manually to the new form.

F.2 Notations not previously supported

The following notations have no equivalent in previous versions.

Official Notation (Eiffel 3)	Old Notation
require else, **ensure then**	Write full assertions
select	Not supported
Free operators	Not supported
Manifest syntax for arrays, as in $\ll u,\ v,\ w,\ x,\ y,\ z\gg$	Not supported
Strip expressions, as in **strip** (a, b, c)	Not supported

Older versions had a more restricted notion of creation procedure. A special instruction of the form $a.Create$ was used instead; it could refer to a procedure called *Create* in the class.

Official Notation (Eiffel 3)	Old Notation
$!!\ a$	$a.Create$
$!!\ a.proc\ (x, ...)$	$a.Create\ (x, ...)$
	(Only one creation procedure; must be called *Create*. No **creation** clause.)
$!\ CONFORMING\ !\ a\ ...$	With entity d declared of type *CONFORMING*:
	$d.Create\ ...;\ a := d$
$a\ !\ CONFORMING\ !\ f\ (x, ...)$	With entity d declared of type *CONFORMING*:
	$d.Create\ (x, ...);\ a := d$
	(Only one creation procedure; must be called *Create*. No **creation** clause.)

F.3 Specifying export status

Instead of multiple Features clauses, each declaring a specific export status for the feature it introduces, a class in pre-version 3 Eiffel would specify the export status of its features in an Export clause at the head of the class.

Official Notation (Eiffel 3)	Old Notation
feature ... (no qualification)	Include names of the corresponding features in the **export** clause of the class.
feature {*NONE*} or **feature** { }	Use **feature** without qualification; do not include the names of the corresponding features in the **export** clause of the class.

feature {$A, B, ...$}	Use **feature** without qualification; include features in **export** clause with selective export specification, as in
	    export
	        f {$A, B, ...$}, g {$A, B, ...$}, ...

F.4 Join and external subclauses

The next two entries of this dictionary apply to the join mechanism and to External clauses.

Official Construct (Eiffel 3)	Old Notation
joined deferred features	**define** (There must be an effective feature implementing the joined features.)
External clause as routine body	Use an External subclause as part of the body of an Eiffel routine

F.5 Place of obsolete clause

The Obsolete clause for an obsolete routine is before the **is** keyword in pre-3 Eiffel, after that keyword in Eiffel 3.

F.6 Words no longer reserved

The previous chapter listed the few reserved words which were not reserved in pre-3 Eiffel. To ease the transition to Eiffel 3, you should avoid using them as identifiers.

In the reverse direction, the following names, not reserved in Eiffel 3, are reserved in pre-3 Eiffel and may not be used as identifiers.

← See E.19, page 546 for the list of new reserved words.

elsif has been replaced by **elseif. name** *has been replaced by* **alias, div** *by* **//** *,* **mod** *by* **\\. repeat** *is no longer needed thanks to the default rules on export and inheritance.*

> *Clone*
> *Create*
> **define**
> **div**
> **elsif**
> *Equal*
> *Forget*
> **mod**
> **name**
> *Nochange*
> **repeat**

G

Reserved words, special symbols, operator precedence

G.1 Overview

This chapter gives the reserved words, the reserved special (non-alphabetic) symbols, and the precedence of operators appearing in expressions.

G.2 Reserved words

The following are the reserved words of the language, in alphabetical order. They may not be used as names of classes, features or entities. Keywords appear in boldface, other reserved words (basic types, predefined entities) in italics.

Every reserved word has an entry in the index, with a reference to the page of the corresponding syntax productions, if any.

separate is not used in this book, but is reserved for Eiffel's future concurrency mechanism.

alias	all	and	as	*BIT*	*BOOLEAN*
CHARACTER	check	class	creation	*Current*	debug
deferred	do	*DOUBLE*	else	elseif	end
ensure	expanded	export	external	false	feature
from	frozen	if	implies	indexing	infix
inherit	inspect	*INTEGER*	invariant	is	like
local	loop	*NONE*	not	obsolete	old
once	or	*POINTER*	prefix	*REAL*	redefine
rename	require	rescue	*Result*	retry	select
separate	*STRING*	strip	then	true	undefine
unique	until	variant	when	xor	

G.3 Special symbols

The following table, already given in the presentation of the lexical structure, is ← *See page 416.* repeated here for ease of reference. It shows all the special symbols of the language, together with the page of the syntax productions where they appear.

SYMBOL	NAME	USE	SYNTAX SPECIFICATION PAGES
--	double dash	Introduces comments	46, 112, 413
;	semicolon	Separates instructions, declarations, arguments etc. (optional in some cases).	49, 60, 77, 101, 109, 120, 234, 342
,	comma	Separates arguments, entities in a declaration etc.	49, 52, 63, 81, 101, 101, 109, 197, 239, 245, 342, 397
:	colon	Introduces the Type_mark in a declaration, a Tag_mark in an Assertion_clause, and an Index term in an Indexing clause.	49, 109, 120
.	dot	Separates target from feature in feature calls and creation calls. Separates integer from fractional part in real numbers.	285, 342, 421
! !!	Exclamation mark	Creation symbol (two forms since the creation type may be implicit or explicit).	285
= /=	Equal, not-equal signs	Equality and inequality operators.	374
–>	Arrow	Introduces the constraint of a constrained formal generic parameter	52
..	Double dot	Separates the bounds of an interval for a Multi_branch instruction.	239
( )	Parentheses	Group subexpressions in operator expressions, and enclose formal and actual arguments of routines.	109, 245, 342, 376
[ ]	Brackets	Introduce formal and actual generic parameters to classes.	52, 197
{ }	Braces	Specify a Clients part (export restriction) at the beginning of a Creation_clause, Feature_clause or New_export_list.	101
≪ ≫	Angle brackets	Enclose a Manifest_array.	393
:=	Receives	Assignment symbol.	311
?=	May receive	Assignment_attempt symbol.	332
'	single quote	Encloses character constants.	387
"	double quote	Encloses prefix and infix operators and manifest strings.	68, 387
+ –	Signs	Signs of integer and real constants. (Also permitted as prefix and infix operators, but such operators are not listed in this table.)	387
$	Dollar sign	Address operator for passing addresses of Eiffel features to foreign routines.	342
%	Percent sign	Introduces special character codes.	422-423
/	Slash sign	Defines a character by its ASCII code	422, case C3.

G.4 Operators and their precedence

The following table repeats the precedence of operators. For more details, see the discussion of expressions.

← *On operator expressions and their precedence, see 23.5, page 376. The table appeared first on page 377.*

Level	Symbols
12	. (Dot notation for Unqualified_call expressions)
11	**old** (in postconditions) **strip** **not** unary + unary − All free unary operators
10	All free binary operators
9	⌃ (power)
8	* / // (integer division) \\ (integer remainder)
7	binary + binary −
6	= /= (not equal) < > <= >=
5	**and and then**
4	**or or else xor**
3	**implies**
2	<< >> (for manifest arrays).
1	; (semicolon as separator between an Assertion_clause and the next)

H

Syntax summary

H.1 Overview

This appendix repeats the syntax specifications of the preceding chapters, in the order in which they were introduced.

→ *Appendix I gives the same information in alphabetical construct order.*

For each construct, the number at right indicates the page on which the syntactical specification originally appears in the text.

H.2 Syntax

Class_declaration	≜	[Indexing]	16
		Class_header	
		[Formal_generics]	
		[Obsolete]	
		[Inheritance]	
		[Creators]	
		[Features]	
		[Invariant]	
		end ["--" **class** Class_name]	

Indexing	≜	**indexing** Index_list	49
Index_list	≜	{Index_clause ";" ...}	
Index_clause	≜	[Index] Index_terms	
Index	≜	Identifier ":"	
Index_terms	≜	{Index_value "," ...}⁺	
Index_value	≜	Identifier | Manifest_constant	

Class_header	≜	[Header_mark] **class** Class_name	*50*
Header_mark	≜	**deferred** | **expanded**	
Class_name	≜	Identifier	

Formal_generics	≜	"[" Formal_generic_list "]"	*52*
Formal_generic_list	≜	{Formal_generic ","...}	
Formal_generic	≜	Formal_generic_name [Constraint]	
Formal_generic_name	≜	Identifier	
Constraint	≜	"–>" Class_type	

Obsolete	≜	**obsolete** Message	*52*
Message	≜	Manifest_string	

Features	≜	**feature** {Feature_clause **feature** ...}⁺	*60*
Feature_clause	≜	[Clients]	
		[Header_comment]	
		Feature_declaration_list	
Feature_declaration_list	≜	{Feature_declaration ";" ...}	
Header_comment	≜	Comment	

Feature_declaration	≜	New_feature_list Declaration_body	*63*
Declaration_body	≜	[Formal_arguments]	
		[Type_mark]	
		[Constant_or_routine]	
Constant_or_routine	≜	**is** Feature_value	
Feature_value	≜	Manifest_constant | Unique | Routine	

New_feature_list	≜	{New_feature "," ...}⁺	*63*
New_feature	≜	[**frozen**] Feature_name	

Feature_name	≜	Identifier | Prefix | Infix	*68*
Prefix	≜	**prefix** ’”’ Prefix_operator ’”’	
Infix	≜	**infix** ’”’ Infix_operator ’”’	
Prefix_operator	≜	Unary | Free_operator	
Infix_operator	≜	Binary | Free_operator	

Unary	≜	**not** | "+" | "–"
Binary	≜	"+" | "–" | "*" | "/" |
		"<" | ">" | "<=" | ">=" |
		"//" | "\\" | "^" |
		and | **or** | **xor** |
		and then | **or else** | **implies**

68

Inheritance	≜	**inherit** Parent_list
Parent_list	≜	{Parent ";" ...}
Parent	≜	Class_type [Feature_adaptation]
Feature_adaptation	≜	[Rename]
		[New_exports]
		[Undefine]
		[Redefine]
		[Select]
		end

77

Rename	≜	**rename** Rename_list
Rename_list	≜	{Rename_pair "," ...}
Rename_pair	≜	Feature_name **as** Feature_name

81

Clients	≜	"{" Class_list "}"
Class_list	≜	{Class_name "," ...}

101

New_exports	≜	**export** New_export_list
New_export_list	≜	{New_export_item ";" ...}
New_export_item	≜	Clients Feature_set
Feature_set	≜	Feature_list | **all**
Feature_list	≜	{Feature_name "," ...}

101

Formal_arguments	≜	"(" Entity_declaration_list ")"
Entity_declaration_list	≜	{Entity_declaration_group ";" ...}
Entity_declaration_group	≜	Identifier_list Type_mark
Identifier_list	≜	{Identifier "," ...}$^+$
Type_mark	≜	":" Type

109

Routine	≙	[Obsolete] [Header_comment] [Precondition] [Local_declarations] Routine_body [Postcondition] [Rescue] **end** ["--" Feature_name]	*112*

Routine_body	≙	Effective | Deferred	*113*
Effective	≙	Internal | External	
Internal	≙	Routine_mark Compound	
Routine_mark	≙	**do** | **once**	
Deferred	≙	**deferred**	

Local_declarations	≙	**local** Entity_declaration_list	*114*

Instruction	≙	Creation | Call | Assignment | Assignment_attempt | Conditional | Multi_branch | Loop | Debug | Check | Retry	*116*

Precondition	≙	**require** [**else**] Assertion	*120*
Postcondition	≙	**ensure** [**then**] Assertion	
Invariant	≙	**invariant** Assertion	
Assertion	≙	{Assertion_clause ";" ...}	
Assertion_clause	≙	[Tag_mark] Unlabeled_assertion_clause	
Unlabeled_assertion_clause	≙	Boolean_expression | Comment	
Tag_mark	≙	Tag ":"	
Tag	≙	Identifier	

Old	≙	**old** Expression	*124*

Check	≙	**check** Assertion **end**	*129*

Variant	≙	**variant** [Tag_mark] Expression	*130*

Redefine	≜	**redefine** Feature_list

159

Undefine	≜	**undefine** Feature_list

160

Select	≜	**select** Feature_list

192

Type	≜	Class_type |
		Class_type_expanded |
		Formal_generic_name |
		Anchored |
		Bit_type
Class_type	≜	Class_name [Actual_generics]
Actual_generics	≜	"[" Type_list "]"
Type_list	≜	{Type "," ...}
Class_type_expanded	≜	**expanded** Class_type
Bit_type	≜	*BIT* Constant
Anchored	≜	**like** Anchor
Anchor	≜	Identifier | *Current*

197

Compound	≜	{Instruction ";" ...}

234

Conditional	≜	**if** Then_part_list [Else_part] **end**
Then_part_list	≜	{Then_part **elseif** ...}$^+$
Then_part	≜	Boolean_expression **then** Compound
Else_part	≜	**else** Compound

235

Multi_branch	≜	**inspect** Expression
		[When_part_list] [Else_part] **end**
When_part_list	≜	**when** {When_part **when** ...}$^+$
When_part	≜	Choices **then** Compound
Choices	≜	{Choice "," ...}
Choice	≜	Constant | Interval
Interval	≜	Integer_interval | Character_interval
Integer_interval	≜	Integer_constant " **..** " Integer_constant
Character_interval	≜	Character_constant
		" **..** " Character_constant

239

Loop	≜	Initialization [Invariant] [Variant] Loop_body **end**	*243*

Initialization	≜	**from** Compound	*243*
Loop_body	≜	Exit **loop** Compound	
Exit	≜	**until** Boolean_expression	

Debug	≜	**debug** [Debug_keys] Compound **end**	*245*
Debug_keys	≜	"(" Debug_key_list ")"	
Debug_key_list	≜	{Debug_key "," ...}	
Debug_key	≜	Manifest_string	

Rescue	≜	**rescue** Compound	*256*
Retry	≜	**retry**	

Unique	≜	**unique**	*265*

Entity	≜	Writable | Read_only	*276*
Writable	≜	Attribute | Local	
Attribute	≜	Identifier	
Local	≜	Identifier | *Result*	
Read_only	≜	Formal | *Current*	
Formal	≜	Identifier	

Creators	≜	**creation** {Creation_clause **creation** ...}$^+$	*285*
Creation_clause	≜	[Clients] [Header_comment] Feature_list	

Creation	≜	"!" [Type] "!" Writable [Creation_call]	*285*
Creation_call	≜	"**.**" Unqualified_call	

Assignment	≜	Writable ":=" Expression	*311*

Assignment_attempt	≜	Writable "?=" Expression	*332*

Call	≙	[Parenthesized_qualifier] Call_chain	*342*
Parenthesized_qualifier	≙	Parenthesized "."	
Call_chain	≙	{Unqualified_call "." ...}⁺	
Unqualified_call	≙	Entity [Actuals]	

Actuals	≙	"(" Actual_list ")"	*342*
Actual_list	≙	{Actual "," ...}	
Actual	≙	Expression | Address	
Address	≙	"$" Identifier	

Expression	≙	Call | Operator_expression | Equality | Manifest_constant | Manifest_array | Old | Strip	*373*
Boolean_expression	≙	Expression	

Equality	≙	Expression Comparison Expression	*374*
Comparison	≙	"=" | "/="	

Operator_expression	≙	Parenthesized | Unary_expression | Binary_expression	*376*
Parenthesized	≙	"(" Expression ")"	
Unary_expression	≙	Prefix_operator Expression	
Binary_expression	≙	Expression Infix_operator Expression	

Constant	=	Manifest_constant | Constant_attribute	*386*
Constant_attribute	=	Entity	

Manifest_constant	≙	Boolean_constant | Character_constant | Integer_constant | Real_constant | Manifest_string | Bit_constant	*387*
Sign	≙	"+" | "−"	
Integer_constant	≙	[Sign] Integer	
Character_constant	≙	"'" Character "'"	
Boolean_constant	≙	**true** | **false**	
Real_constant	≙	[Sign] Real	
Manifest_string	≙	'"' Simple_string '"'	
Bit_constant	≙	Bit_sequence	

Manifest_array	≜	"<<" Expression_list ">>"	*393*
Expression_list	≜	{Expression "," ...}	

Strip	≜	**strip** "(" Attribute_list ")"	*397*
Attribute_list	≜	{Identifier "," ...}	

External	≜	**external** Language_name [External_name]	*402*
Language_name	≜	Manifest_string	
External_name	≜	**alias** Manifest_string	

Comment	≜	"--" {Simple_string Comment_break ...}	*413*
Comment_break	≜	New_line [Blanks_or_tabs] "--"	

I

Syntax in alphabetical order

I.1 Overview

This appendix gives the full syntax of Eiffel. For ease of reference, the constructs are given in alphabetical order.

For each construct, the number at right indicates the page on which the syntactical specification appears in the text.

← *Appendix H gives the same information in the order in which the constructs were introduced in this book.*

I.2 Syntax

Actual	≜	Expression │ Address	*342*
Actual_generics	≜	"[" Type_list "]"	*197*
Actual_list	≜	{Actual "," ...}	*342*
Actuals	≜	"(" Actual_list ")"	*342*
Address	≜	"$" Identifier	*342*
Anchor	≜	Identifier │ *Current*	*197*
Anchored	≜	**like** Anchor	*197*
Assertion	≜	{Assertion_clause ";" ...}	*120*
Assertion_clause	≜	[Tag_mark] Unlabeled_assertion_clause	*120*
Assignment	≜	Writable ":=" Expression	*311*
Assignment_attempt	≜	Writable "?=" Expression	*332*
Attribute	≜	Identifier	*276*
Attribute_list	≜	{Identifier "," ...}	*397*
Binary	≜	"+" │ "−" │ "∗" │ "/" │ "<" │ ">" │ "<=" │ ">=" │ "//" │ "\\" │ "^" │ **and** │ **or** │ **xor** │ **and then** │ **or else** │ **implies**	*68*

Binary_expression	≜	Expression Infix_operator Expression	*376*
Bit_constant	≜	Bit_sequence	*387*
Bit_type	≜	*BIT* Constant	*197*
Boolean_constant	≜	**true** | **false**	*387*
Boolean_expression	≜	Expression	*373*
Call	≜	[Parenthesized_qualifier] Call_chain	*342*
Call_chain	≜	{Unqualified_call "." ...}$^+$	*342*
Character_constant	≜	"'" Character "'"	*387*
Character_interval	≜	Character_constant	*239*
		".." Character_constant	
Check	≜	**check** Assertion **end**	*129*
Choice	≜	Constant | Interval	*239*
Choices	≜	{Choice "," ...}	*239*
Class_declaration	≜	[Indexing]	*46*
		Class_header	
		[Formal_generics]	
		[Obsolete]	
		[Inheritance]	
		[Creators]	
		[Features]	
		[Invariant]	
		end ["--" **class** Class_name]	
Class_header	≜	[Header_mark] **class** Class_name	*50*
Class_list	≜	{Class_name "," ...}	*101*
Class_name	≜	Identifier	*50*
Class_type	≜	Class_name [Actual_generics]	*197*
Class_type_expanded	≜	**expanded** Class_type	*197*
Clients	≜	"{" Class_list "}"	*101*
Comment	≜	"--" {Simple_string Comment_break ...}	*413*
Comment_break	≜	New_line [Blanks_or_tabs] "--"	*413*
Comparison	≜	"=" | "/="	*374*
Compound	≜	{Instruction ";" ...}	*234*
Conditional	≜	**if** Then_part_list [Else_part] **end**	*235*
Constant	=	Manifest_constant | Constant_attribute	*386*
Constant_attribute	=	Entity	*386*
Constant_or_routine	≜	**is** Feature_value	*63*
Constraint	≜	"->" Class_type	*52*
Creation	≜	"!" [Type] "!" Writable [Creation_call]	*285*
Creation_call	≜	"." Unqualified_call	*285*
Creation_clause	≜	[Clients] [Header_comment]	*285*
		Feature_list	
Creators	≜	**creation**	*285*
		{Creation_clause **creation** ...}$^+$	
Debug	≜	**debug** [Debug_keys] Compound **end**	*245*
Debug_key	≜	Manifest_string	*245*
Debug_key_list	≜	{Debug_key "," ...}	*245*
Debug_keys	≜	"(" Debug_key_list ")"	*245*

Declaration_body	≜	[Formal_arguments]	*63*
		[Type_mark]	
		[Constant_or_routine]	
Deferred	≜	**deferred**	*113*
Effective	≜	Internal | External	*113*
Else_part	≜	**else** Compound	*235*
Entity	≜	Writable | Read_only	*276*
Entity_declaration_group	≜	Identifier_list Type_mark	*109*
Entity_declaration_list	≜	{Entity_declaration_group ";" ...}	*109*
Equality	≜	Expression Comparison Expression	*374*
Exit	≜	**until** Boolean_expression	*243*
Expression	≜	Call | Operator_expression | Equality |	*373*
		Manifest_constant | Manifest_array |	
		Old | Strip	
Expression_list	≜	{Expression "," ...}	*393*
External	≜	**external** Language_name	*402*
		[External_name]	
External_name	≜	**alias** Manifest_string	*402*
Feature_adaptation	≜	[Rename]	*77*
		[New_exports]	
		[Undefine]	
		[Redefine]	
		[Select]	
		end	
Feature_clause	≜	[Clients]	*60*
		[Header_comment]	
		Feature_declaration_list	
Feature_declaration	≜	New_feature_list Declaration_body	*63*
Feature_declaration_list	≜	{Feature_declaration ";" ...}	*60*
Feature_list	≜	{Feature_name "," ...}	*101*
Feature_name	≜	Identifier | Prefix | Infix	*68*
Feature_set	≜	Feature_list | **all**	*101*
Feature_value	≜	Manifest_constant | Unique | Routine	*63*
Features	≜	**feature** {Feature_clause **feature** ...}⁺	*60*
Formal	≜	Identifier	*276*
Formal_arguments	≜	"(" Entity_declaration_list ")"	*109*
Formal_generic	≜	Formal_generic_name [Constraint]	*52*
Formal_generic_list	≜	{Formal_generic ","...}	*52*
Formal_generic_name	≜	Identifier	*52*
Formal_generics	≜	"[" Formal_generic_list "]"	*52*
Header_comment	≜	Comment	*60*
Header_mark	≜	**deferred** | **expanded**	*50*
Identifier_list	≜	{Identifier "," ...}⁺	*109*
Index	≜	Identifier ":"	*49*
Index_clause	≜	[Index] Index_terms	*49*
Index_list	≜	{Index_clause ";" ...}	*49*
Index_terms	≜	{Index_value "," ...}⁺	*49*
Index_value	≜	Identifier | Manifest_constant	*49*

Indexing	≜	**indexing** Index_list	49
Infix	≜	**infix** ’"’ Infix_operator ’"’	68
Infix_operator	≜	Binary | Free_operator	68
Inheritance	≜	**inherit** Parent_list	77
Initialization	≜	**from** Compound	243
Instruction	≜	Creation |	116
		Call |	
		Assignment |	
		Assignment_attempt |	
		Conditional | Multi_branch | Loop |	
		Debug | Check | Retry	
Integer_constant	≜	[Sign] Integer	387
Integer_interval	≜	Integer_constant " .. " Integer_constant	239
Internal	≜	Routine_mark Compound	113
Interval	≜	Integer_interval | Character_interval	239
Invariant	≜	**invariant** Assertion	120
Language_name	≜	Manifest_string	402
Local	≜	Identifier | *Result*	276
Local_declarations	≜	**local** Entity_declaration_list	114
Loop	≜	Initialization	243
		[Invariant]	
		[Variant]	
		Loop_body	
		end	
Loop_body	≜	Exit **loop** Compound	243
Manifest_array	≜	"<<" Expression_list ">>"	393
Manifest_constant	≜	Boolean_constant |	387
		Character_constant |	
		Integer_constant | Real_constant |	
		Manifest_string | Bit_constant	
Manifest_string	≜	’"’ Simple_string ’"’	387
Message	≜	Manifest_string	52
Multi_branch	≜	**inspect** Expression	239
		[When_part_list] [Else_part] **end**	
New_export_item	≜	Clients Feature_set	101
New_export_list	≜	{New_export_item ";" ...}	101
New_exports	≜	**export** New_export_list	101
New_feature	≜	**[frozen]** Feature_name	63
New_feature_list	≜	{New_feature "," ...}⁺	63
Obsolete	≜	**obsolete** Message	52
Old	≜	**old** Expression	124
Operator_expression	≜	Parenthesized |	376
		Unary_expression | Binary_expression	
Parent	≜	Class_type [Feature_adaptation]	77
Parent_list	≜	{Parent ";" ...}	77
Parenthesized	≜	"(" Expression ")"	376
Parenthesized_qualifier	≜	Parenthesized "."	342
Postcondition	≜	**ensure [then]** Assertion	120

J

Syntax diagrams

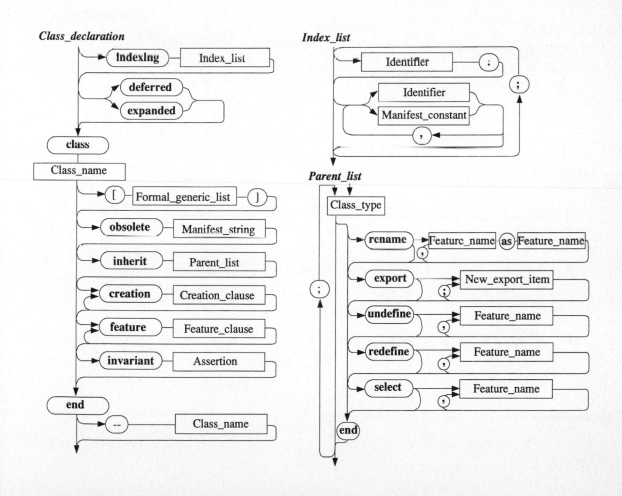

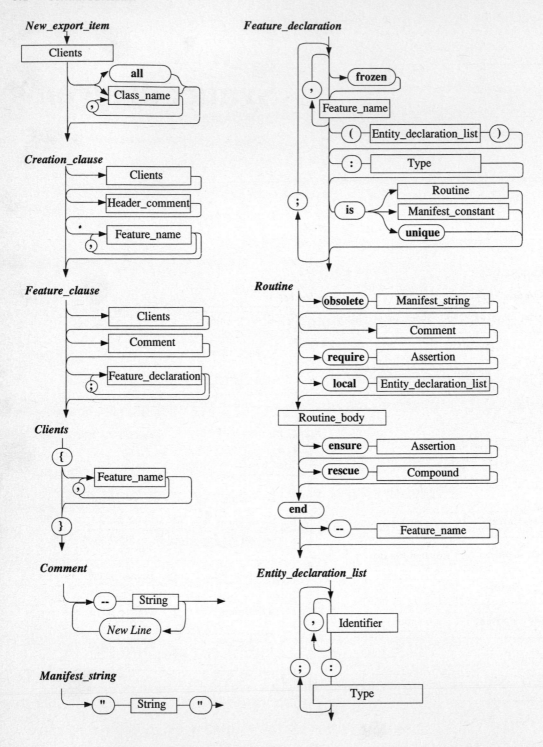

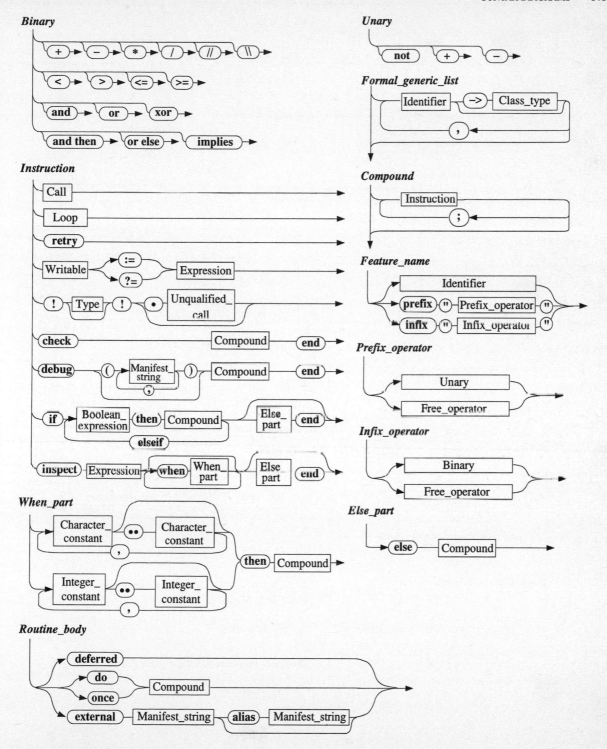

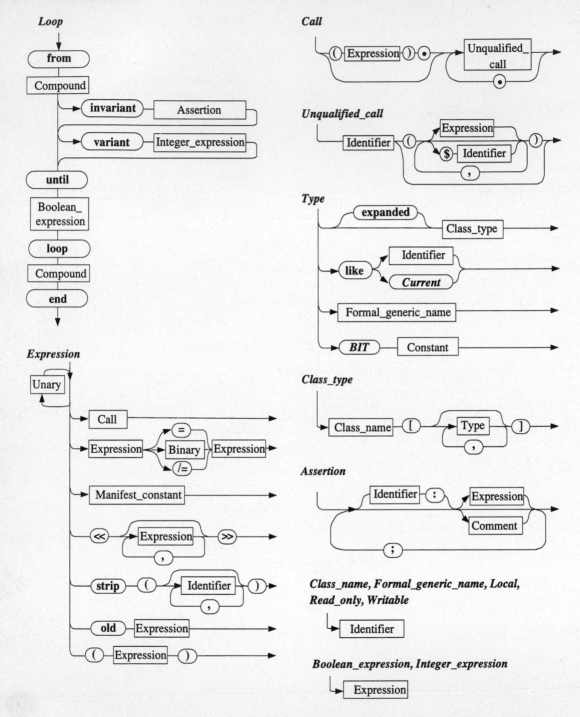

Loop

Call

Unqualified_call

Type

Class_type

Assertion

*Class_name, Formal_generic_name, Local,
Read_only, Writable*

Boolean_expression, Integer_expression

Expression

Index

Page numbers in boldface indicate a place of definition. Page numbers in smaller font, such as 21, indicate pages of the informal "Invitation to Eiffel" (chapter 1), which is not part of the language reference.

For every construct name, an entry indicates the corresponding syntax production, for example page 120 for Assertion. Such construct names appear in roman with an upper-case first letter. This explains the presence of dual entries: the entry for "assertion" refers to the discussion of the assertion concept; the entry for "Assertion", which follows it, refers to the syntactic definition of the construct. As in the text, keywords appear in boldface, for example **debug**.

All keywords, such as **class**, and other reserved words, such as *Result*, have an entry referring to the corresponding syntax productions. The classes from the Basic Libraries discussed in part D and their features appear with their names in italics, for example *ANY* and *clone*. Four-character constraint codes appear in the entry "validity codes".

VALIDITY road sign **xx**

value **270**-271

variable, see entity, variable attribute

variable-length argument list 110-111, 478, 544

variable attribute 61, 261-262

variant 130

variant 129-131

Variant **130**

versions of a feature 189-191

    potential **189**

visible feature (Lace) 529-531

visible (Lace keyword) 531, 534

void **270**

Void (class *ANY*) 88, 271, 345, 434, 543

Void_assigned_to_expanded (class *EXCEPTIONS*) 454

void_call_feature (class *EXCEPTIONS*) 452

void_call_target (class *EXCEPTIONS*) 452

when 239

When_part **239**

When_part_list **239**

window 15, 70, 111, 172, 173, 174, 196, 197, 198, 212, 233, 248, 249, 262

    resizing 248, 249

Winpack Library 430

wipe_out (class *ARRAY*) 444

word 414

    see also keyword, reserved word

Writable **276**

xor 68, 376, 419

    infix, class *BIT_N* 480

    infix, class *BOOLEAN* 478

yes (Lace keyword) 526, 529, 533-534

Put Eiffel to Work for You!

Eiffel is not just a superb language and method. ISE's Eiffel 3 environment implements everything described in this book, plus:

- A snappy graphical environment supporting interactive browsing and debugging.
  - Very fast recompilation, combining the best of compiled and interpreted environments.
  - Advanced graphical and GUI libraries and tools based on industry standards.
  - High-level CASE tools for analysis and design.
  - Persistence facilities for storing, retrieving and exchanging object structures.
  - A full set of libraries covering data structures, fundamental algorithms, lexical analysis, relational database access and more.
    - And of course support for the full Eiffel language.

To discover how Eiffel can dramatically improve the quality of your software development, as it has done for hundreds of companies worldwide, fill in the coupon below and return it to:

Interactive Software Engineering Inc.
270 Storke Road, Suite 7 Goleta CA 93117 USA
Phone: 805-685-1006   Fax: 805-685-6869

Alternatively, you may contact your International Eiffel Distributor (see list on back) or send an Email message to: info@eiffel.com

❑ Please send me information on ISE's Eiffel 3 implementation.

❑ I am particularly interested in the following platform(s):

_____

_____

❑ I'd like to know the address of a distributor/reseller in my area.

❑ I teach courses on _____ .
To see how Eiffel can boost my teaching, I'd like to receive details on the Eiffel University Partnership.

❑ I'd like information about the Eiffel User's Group.

❑ I'd like to receive an Eiffel poster.

Name: _____

Address: _____

_____

_____

Telephone: _____

Fax: _____

Email: _____

Distributors Worldwide

ARGENTINA

Cybertech
Systems Integration
for CIM Technology
Suarez 1281,
Third Floor, Apt. A
CP-1288 Buenos Aires
Argentina
Phone: +54 1 28 1950
Fax: +54 1 322 1071 or
+54 1 963 0070
Contact: Daniel Fernandez Blanco

AUSTRALIA

Class Technology Pty Ltd
6 Pounds Road
Hornsby NSW 2077
Australia
Phone: +61 2 477 6188
Fax: +61 2 476 4378
Email:class@peg.pegasus.oz.au
Contact: David Braunstein

Ease Pty Ltd
4 Edinburgh Avenue
Carlingford NSW 2118
Australia
Phone: +61 2 683 6930
Fax: +61 2 630 8717
Email:
buckdale@extro.ucc.su.oz.au
Contact: Richard Buckdale

**Forefront Computing
Services P/L**
115 Seaford Road
Seaford, Victoria 3198
Australia
Phone: +61 3 785 1122
Fax: +61 3 770 0961
Contact: Howard Small

CANADA

Jay-Kell Technologies Inc.
48 Lakeshore Road, Suite #1
Pointe Claire, Quebec
Canada H9S 4H4
Phone: +514-630-1005
Fax: +514-630-1456
Contact: Walter Keirstead

COLUMBIA

Compucom Ltda.
Cra 8a-A No. 99-51 of 203
World Trade Center Tone
A.A. 29774, Bogota, Columbia,
South America
Phone: 57-1 218 33 39
Fax: 57-1 218 32 59
Contact: Nelson Reyes

ENGLAND

Applied Logic Distribution
9 Princeton Court
55 Felsham Road
London SW151AZ
England
Phone: +44 81 780 2324
Fax: +44 81 780 1941
Contact: Caroline Brown

FRANCE

**Société Des Outils Du
Logiciel (SOL)**
104 rue Castagnary
75015 Paris
France
Phone: +33 1 45 32 58 80
Fax: +33 1 45 32 58 81
Email: eiffel@eiffel.fr
Contact: Francois Dupont

GERMANY

SIG
Zu den Bettern 4
6333 Braunfels-Altenkirchen
Germany
Phone: +49 64 72 20 96
Fax: +49 64 72 72 13
Email: fm@sigbr.sigcomp.sub.org
Contact: Frieder Monninger

ITALY

Etnoteam
Via Adelaide Bono Cairoli 34
20127 Milano
Italy
Phone: +39 2 261621
Fax: +39 2 26110755
Contact: Marco Galbiati

Unirel
Centro Comerciale Osmanoro
Via Volturno, 12
50019 Sesto Fiorentino (FI)
Italy
Phone: +39 55 373043
Fax: +39 55 318525
Contact: Sandro Saccenti

INDIA

**Sritech Information
Technology (SIT)**
744/51 2nd Floor
10 Main Road, 4th Block
Jayanagar, Bangalore
India 560011
Phone: +91-812-640661
Fax: +91-812-643608
Contact: Partha Sarathy

JAPAN

**Software Research
Associates**
1-1-1 Hirakswo-Cho
Chiyoda-ku Tokyo 102, Japan
Phone: +81-3-3234-2623
Fax: +81-3-3234-4338
Email: kaizu@sra.co.jp
Contact: Tatsuo Kaizu

JAPAN

**Information and
Mathematical Science
Laboratory, Inc.**
2-43-1, Ikebukuro, toshima-ku
Tokyo 171, Japan
Phone: +81 3 3590 5211
Fax: +81 3 3590 5353
Email: fushimi@idas.imslab.co.jp
Contact: Satoshi Fushimi

MEXICO

Cromasoft S.A. de C.V.
Mazatlan 101, Col. Condesa
06140 Mexico, D.F.
Phone: +52 5 286 82 13
Fax: +52 5 553 1201
Contact: Antonio Sollano

NEW ZEALAND

Objective Methods
PO Box 17356
77 Chamberlain Road
Karori, Wellington, New Zealand
Phone: +64 4 476 9499
Fax: +64 4 476 9237 or
+64 4 476 8772
Email:
des.kenny@bbs.actrix.gen.nz
Contact: Des Kenny

SPAIN

Seinca
C/Jorge Juan, 19 - #4
28001 Madrid
Spain
Phone: +34 1 577 99 95
Fax: +34 1 577 49 81
Contact: Roman Lopez-Cortijo

SWEDEN

Enea Data
Box 232
Nytorpsvagen 5
S-183 23 Taby
Sweden
Phone: +46 8 792 25 00
Fax: +46 8 768 43 88
Email: kim@enea.se
Contact: Kim Walden

EUROPE
(Countries not listed)

**Société Des Outils Du
Logiciel (SOL)**
104 rue Castagnary
75015 Paris
France
Phone: +33 1 45 32 58 80
Fax: +33 1 45 32 58 81
Email: eiffel@eiffel.fr
Contact: Francois Dupont

To follow Eiffel and its evolution: *Eiffel Outlook* magazine, the independent source for the International Eiffel Community. For information and subscription rates contact: Eiffel Outlook, 3300 Bees Cave Road, Suite 650, Austin, TX 78746, USA. Phone: +1 512-328-6406, Fax: +1 512-328-0466. **Note:** Eiffel Outlook is not affiliated with Interactive Software Engineering.